Dec. 10, 1970

68-29460

ISRAEL
AND THE ARAB WORLD

ISRAEL
AND THE ARAB WORLD

AHARON COHEN

FUNK & WAGNALLS · NEW YORK

CONTENTS

MAPS

FOREWORD TO THE
ENGLISH-LANGUAGE EDITION

Israel and the Arab World is an English translation of a book of the same title, which was written in Hebrew and published in July 1964, in Israel, by Sifriat Poalim. The last chapter of the book, however, has been almost entirely rewritten, with the purpose of covering events since then and bringing the picture up to date.

The author is particularly gratified that, with the publication of this English edition, his book will reach that broad public he had in mind even when writing the work in Hebrew: Intellectual circles in the countries of the Middle East, where the problem of the relationship between the Arab world and Israel demands the attention of every thinking person; people all over the world who are concerned with the problems of international politics in general and of the Middle East in particular; and Jews everywhere who are close to, and concerned with, the problems relating to the Jewish people, the Zionist movement, and Israeli affairs both local and international.

Details that would have been of no particular interest to the English reader, as well as some episodes whose omission does not detract from the essence of the book, have been left out of this version. Similarly, most of the references to Hebrew sources have been omitted; these include the many footnotes concerning background material drawn from the author's other works on the history and problems of the Arab world and the changes that have taken place there in recent generations. An entire chapter of bibliography (containing almost 500 references in Hebrew and some in Arabic and other languages) has also been omitted, while occasional explanations that were not required for the Hebrew reader have been inserted. The book was translated from the Hebrew by Aubrey Hodes, Naomi Handelman, and Miriam Shimeoni, to whom the author wishes to express his thanks.

Though every effort has been made to adapt this version to the requirements of the English-reading public, it must nevertheless be borne in mind that the book was conceived in Hebrew, in an Israeli and Middle Eastern setting.

The introduction to the Hebrew edition noted that this work should be regarded as "a link in a chain of efforts forged over the years, by Jews, Arabs, and well-wishers from other nations, to achieve peace between two related peoples whose fate and future are inextricably and inevitably bound together. This hoped-for peace has not yet come about, but we are confident that the conditions for its emergence are ripening within the context of historic development. Whether the road to peace is to be a short or a long one depends primarily on the two peoples concerned."

Recent years have seen a tragic deterioration of the situation and that is why it is so vital that the leadership of both peoples should ponder the lessons of this history. To this we feel the need to add that people from other nations who cherish peace and progress can also do a great deal to help achieve these goals, to the extent that instead of coming out in total and undiscriminating support of one side against the other, they will exert their influence in favor of mutual reconciliation and a just and honorable solution to the problems at hand.

I should like to express my gratitude to Jacob Sonntag, editor of the London *Jewish Quarterly*, who facilitated the publication of the English version of this book. It is thanks to his devotion to the idea of an English edition that the book gained the favorable attention of the English publisher and his colleague in America; and his consistent efforts ensured that all those concerned were able to remove the minor obstacles that might have stood in the way of publishing an English version.

I owe profound thanks to two friends, Y. Abbady and D. Leon, who have devoted untiring efforts to the preparation of the English edition. Yitzhak Abbady, of Jerusalem, was a veteran writer and publicist, whose sympathetic approach to Jewish-Arab cooperation was founded on a deep knowledge of the subject and a spiritual affinity with the national movements both of his fellow Jews and of the Arabs. He was a close observer of political processes under the Mandatory Government during his many years of service (1920–1944) as the chief Hebrew translator for the British mandatory regime; his many articles and research reports provide ample evidence of his experience. From the moment that he read the Hebrew version, he insisted on the need to make it available to the English-speaking public, and it has been my privilege to be able to have recourse to his most valuable advice. To our deep sorrow, he died on 22 December, 1969 at the age of 72.

Dan Leon, a native of England and a member of *Hashomer Hatzair* in that country, has been in Israel since 1951 and is an active member of *Mapam*. Believing that, because of its singular approach, this book could make an unusually significant contribution to the problems with which it deals, he has taken infinite pains in editing the English edition, despite problems which might have daunted anyone less able and devoted. His uncommon sensitivity toward both politics and toward language made it possible for him to advise me at all stages of the work on how best to present the material to readers of English all over the world in a form and spirit preserving as much as possible of the original character of the book.

Last, but not least, I thank my wife and lifelong partner Rivka, without whose constant encouragement and help it is doubtful that I would have been able to complete the work involved in the preparation of this edition.

I know that, not only for myself, but also in the name of all those connected with me in this labor of love, it would be appropriate to note in conclusion that if this book can make some contribution, however modest, toward strengthening Jewish-Arab understanding and paving the way to peace, it will be ample reward for our efforts.

Kibbutz Shaar Haamakim, Israel   A. C.

PREFACE

Aharon Cohen's book *Israel and the Arab World*, which I have read in manuscript, is an extremely important scientific work. Like every scientific book, it is as objective as possible and puts before the reader tested and confirmed facts which, even if they were assembled together with a certain conception in mind, are undeniably true and enable the reader to learn what actually happened and to draw his conclusions.

Only one who lived through these events as a witness could have written this book. Aharon Cohen grew with his experience, and in effect continued faithfully what the late H. M. Kalvarisky and others had begun. A book like this can only be written with an inner fervour and a love of the cause. History is written not in order to recall the past nor for the future, but essentially for the present, so that the members of the present generation might learn its lessons.

Because of objective conditions, it is natural that in a book like this the facts as they were, and as they appeared from the Jewish and Arab sides, cannot possibly be equally reflected. No matter how great the effort to expose all sides of the picture, it is impossible to reflect Jewish and Arab views equally. This is not the fault of the author but, as I noted, the result of objective historical conditions. To present the developments on the Arab side with the same authority and the same command as the happenings on the Jewish side, the author would have to be an Arab, as deeply acquainted with Arab life as the author of this book is acquainted with Jewish life. Let us hope that perhaps one day such an Arab author will take up the task and will fill in what, in this respect, may be missing in this book.

MARTIN BUBER

INTRODUCTION

The Arab-Israeli dispute in our times is a national and political tragedy that has gravely impaired the wholesome development of both peoples and become an explosive force on the international scene. If we wish to find a way to settle this dispute, the first step must be to expose its roots and trace its development.

The real problem is not to seek a compromise based on the partial surrender of vital interests or just aspirations. There is no paramount need for any such concessions; both peoples' genuine interests and aims can be satisfied without fear of perennial or lasting conflicts. The problem is to see to it that practical interests tally with national aspirations; to create conditions that will enable both peoples to cooperate in joint efforts to exploit potentialities; and to foster those forces that will further the material and spiritual progress of both parties. This is a formidable political, educational, and cultural task.

No basic change in the present situation can take place as long as each party sees only its side of the argument and ignores the other side.

By far the most deplorable aspect of the great Jewish national revival in Palestine was the failure of the Jewish repatriates to understand this and their short-sightedness in relations with the Arabs, from the time of the Bilu settlers in the 1880s to the present day. If we lack the intellectual and moral courage to admit this shortcoming, we shall not be able to correct the mistakes arising from it. In other words, there can be no hope of breaking out of the vicious circle without a degree of self-criticism on the Jewish side. After all, the permanence of such an historic undertaking as the renaissance of the Jewish people in its homeland cannot be judged by the yardstick of fifteen or thirty years. Both the prospects and the dangers must be seen in their broad historical perspectives.

Only actions can bring about real changes and pave the way for the solution of problems. But these must be preceded by thinking, and realistic thinking can be based only on a knowledge of all the facts.

The application of a scientific analytical approach naturally entails eschewing all bias and overcoming psychological barriers that could prevent an objective investigation and make it impossible for the analyst to draw the correct conclusions. A faithful historical survey can be made only if the writer places himself "on the ramparts of the besieged city, gazing at

xiii

the attackers and the besieged at one and the same time," in the words of one historian.

The reader, whatever his personal approach to the issues discussed in this book, may legitimately expect the author to lay before him a correct and undistorted presentation of the facts. In other words, no attempt should be made to fit the facts into some preconceived political pattern, and the entire sweep of events should be unfolded as it occurred. Historical events have a logic of their own and social forces do not develop at random—but facts are sacred to the historian, and my purpose is to present them and to interpret them in their natural order.

The main sources of the material in this book were public and private archives (including the writer's own archives), official records, journals, memoirs and political papers, periodicals, and newspapers. A considerable volume of important material on Jewish-Arab relations, published in the Hebrew, Arabic, and foreign press, awaits collection and analysis. Public and private archives also contain a wealth of unpublished documents that have not yet been subjected to scientific scrutiny. I hope that this book is a beginning, which will be taken up and continued by others.

For my survey I made use of the sources available. I am well aware that no absolute historical accuracy is possible so long as some archives are still barred to researchers, both in the Arab world and, to some degree, in Israel.

Powerful official information services can easily suppress correct data as to the cause-and-effect relationship in certain developments, and this does not make the honest historian's task any easier. In writing this book, I have tried to let the facts speak for themselves in the belief that they will confirm my basic approach to the issues under discussion.

All the facts contained in this book derive from reliable sources and have been carefully checked. I have not included events on which authentic material was not available (even though we know this material exists). In many cases I have drawn the reader's attention to studies based on documents from various archives that are accessible to all. In noting the names of Arab figures, I have sometimes seen fit to avoid mentioning the names of some people who were allies in the past and might be so again one day.

While the chapters on the contacts between the two peoples since the end of the nineteenth century are the result of my independent research, the first chapter, which treats the contacts in the distant past, is essentially a summary of the findings of several scholars. This chapter, and some of the material in Chapter 2, should give the relations between the two peoples a historical perspective and establish the background to what follows.

Perhaps many of the generation that grew up in British Mandate days, when Jewish-Arab relations were poisoned, will be unable to free themselves entirely from the impact of the lamentable ideological and psychological heritage of those colonial days. But in Israel and the Arab lands a new generation is growing up under different historical conditions. This generation will be able to see the region's problems through new eyes. It is a good sign that the Jewish public is taking increased interest in the Arab world. An increasing number of scholars is undertaking research in Arab studies; more Israeli university students are taking degrees in Oriental affairs; and a number of high schools have introduced courses in the Arabic language and literature. The growing interest in the Arab world on the part of the mass of the people—soldiers, teachers, youth instructors, and wide sections of the general public—is also significant evidence of this trend.

It is no coincidence that radio programs in Arab countries now include Hebrew broadcasts, and that they too have begun to study Israeli affairs and the history of the Zionist movement. These studies of our problems are justified by the patriotic dictate "know your enemy." In the long run, however, objective truth and reality will prove stronger than prejudice. This has begun to happen in Israel. The scores of Arab students at the Hebrew University in Jerusalem and other institutions of higher learning in Tel Aviv and Haifa who are studying the past of the Jewish people at first hand may be expected to help bring about rapprochement between the two peoples.

Since Israel's establishment, there has appeared an entire library of memoirs and studies that depict the political history of Palestine in our time as predestined and decreed by fate.

Most of this growing body of literature glosses over and suppresses, perhaps unwittingly, the historical truth on major political facts. Despite the changed political circumstances in the years following Israel's establishment, the educational as well as the political importance of a correct historical evaluation of this period cannot be overestimated. It was perhaps inevitable that the history of the decisive years in Israel's history should have been presented with controversial overtones. But this does not release us now from the duty of examining these facts without bias and against the backdrop of their times, without trying to adapt them to the picture that some people might rather want to paint today.

Many refer to Israel's establishment as a "miracle." The struggle for the state is usually presented in a subjective manner, without regard for the objective factors involved. Subjective efforts were undoubtedly important, yet the history of the pre-state period demands a more rational explanation of the objective background. The valor of the Israeli soldiers will not be dimmed if we analyze the reasons for the Arabs' military weakness or note the international circumstances surrounding Israel's rebirth.

Although I was not "neutral" in the historical struggle I am surveying, I have tried as far as possible to eschew any bias, for it is this that so often leads to chauvinism. I write about the Arab people as I would wish an Arab to write of the Jewish people. It follows that, to take one example, the passages on the consequences of the 1948 and 1967 wars for the Arabs of Palestine were not written in a spirit of gloating, but out of the desire to explore the historical truth. As a man and as a writer, I share in the sorrow of the victims of this tragedy.

It is important to distinguish between erring leaders and simple people who become the prey of the leaders' foolish and disastrous policies. This general historical truth has a poignant relevance in the Middle East and in the history of Jewish-Arab relations in our times.

CHAPTER ONE

INITIAL ENCOUNTERS IN THE DISTANT PAST

The first reported contact between Israelites and Arabs in Palestine and its environs is noted in Biblical and other sources dealing with the period from 1,500 to 500 B.C. This period, which was a sort of prehistory of Jewish-Arab relations, saw the birth of the myth about the common Semitic ancestry of the Hebrew and Arab tribes. It witnessed the beginning of the tradition of the two peoples' common patriarchs and the cousinly ties between the offspring of Isaac (the children of Israel) and the children of Ishmael, the son of Abraham. Guillaume[1] believes that considerable trade relations existed between the land of Israel and the Arabs as far back as the time of Solomon (tenth century B.C.). He points out that various books of the Bible, particularly Job and Proverbs, contain many Arabic words that testify to this close and constant link.

The first important encounter between Jews and Arabs took place in the Arabian peninsula before the emergence of Islam. There was a considerable Jewish population in the peninsula hundreds of years before the Prophet Muhammad appeared on the scene. Rome's domination and destruction of Judea in the first and second centuries A.D. brought large numbers of Jews to the northern area of the Arabian peninsula. They took with them their experience as successful peasants in the fertile land of Judea. The Jewish settlements in Wadi el-Kura (the Valley of the Villages) and the desert oases near the Gulf of Eilat, all of which were fortified and prosperous, were focal points for the wandering and nomadic Arab tribes, who settled near the Jews and under their protection. Many sources indicate that these Arabs were familiar with Jewish traditions, customs, and views on religious and social matters. Before the coming of Muhammad several Arab tribes even accepted the Jewish doctrine of "the chosen people" and other basic elements of Judaism.

A striking example of Jewish participation in the creation of early Arabic poetry is the distinguished Jewish poet Shmuel Ben Adiya, better known by his Arabic name, Al-Samawal. He was born c A.D. 500, and came from Taima, north of Medina.

Various scholars have pointed out the references in Arab sources to the friendly relations between Jews and Arabs in the pre-Islamic period. Proof of the Jews' spiritual influence in the southern Arabian peninsula is provided by the proselytization of the Kings of Himyar (present-day Yemen) during the second half of the fifth century A.D. The last of these kings, Youssuf dhu Nauwas, fell in battle in 525, or about a century before the beginning of the Hijrah Moslem calendar (which starts in A.D. 622).

Meanwhile, in the northern peninsula, the Hanafis emerged during the sixth and early seventh centuries. This movement was centered in the Hejaz, among the Arab tribes settled permanently in the vicinity of Mecca, At-Taif, and other places. The Hanafis abandoned idol worship, abstained from eating carrion and the flesh of cattle slaughtered during the idolatrous ritual sacrifices, firmly opposed the barbaric practice of burying girl children after their birth, dressed in sackcloth as a sign of grace, abstained from wine, and followed other religious customs. Some of them studied the holy books of the Jews and the Christians, and this greatly influenced the evolution of their monotheistic faith.

This religious movement in the Arabian peninsula before Muhammad also resulted from the close contacts of the Arabs with the Jews of Arabia. Some scholars believe that Muhammad used Jews to spread the ideas of Islam. The influence of Jewish socio-religious views on the Arabs of that time undoubtedly played an important role in the national climate that gave rise to Islam, and helped the Arabs to make their dramatic entry onto the stage of world history.

Many scholars have noted Islam's great debt to Judaism. Since the publication of Abraham Geiger's book *What Did Muhammad Take From Judaism?*2 other scholars have shown that the roots of Islam and its early development were in effect the Arabian version of the Israelite religion. No scholar could fail to observe the wealth of Biblical tales, Talmudic legends and Midrashic fables embodied in the Koran and its extensive commentaries.

The fundamental principles of the Moslem faith and many of its most important commandments and customs have their origin in Jewish tradition. The Moslem attitude to the Koran was influenced by the Jewish attitude to the Old Testament. Both religions follow the practice of reading passages from the sacred works during the respective Sabbath prayers and on festivals. The doctrine of "the chosen people," and the unity and qualities of the Creator (who is eternal, all-powerful, the only Deity, jealous and vengeful, merciful and graceful, good and all-knowing, loving and forgiving, etc.), the belief in angels, the refusal to recognize saints as intermediaries between man and God, the belief in a day of judgment, in the eternity of the soul, in the end of the world (at which time people would be sent to heaven or to hell) the belief in man's responsibility in the next world for his life in this one, the faith in the efficacy of prayer, repentance, charity and fasting, the similarity between the mosque and the synagogue as a place of worship and assembly (neither contains statues or images, in accordance with the absolute ban on statues and the making of graven images, common to both religions), the pilgrimage (*hajj*), fasting, purification and such customs as male circumcision, abstention from pork and other kinds of forbidden meat, the laws governing ritual slaughter and such rules of moral conduct as the concern for the poor, honoring one's parents, and so on—all these show distinct parallels between Islam and Judaism.

In his interesting essay, "The Mutual Influence of Hebrew and Arabic Culture" (in Hebrew), P. Birnbaum pointed out that in the process of introducing into Islam concepts and views borrowed from Judaism, Muhammad transferred to the Arabic language talmudical words, both Hebrew and Aramaic. Many of these words presented formidable problems to the commentators of the Koran, who had no knowledge of Hebrew, and frequently erred if they did not consult their Jewish neighbors. There was also a considerable body of research on the Koran by Jews who became converted to Islam; this was the principal source of the numerous additions and clarifications from the Talmud and the Midrash in Arabic exegesis and folklore.

Most scholars agree that Muhammad did not originally intend to found Islam as a new religion, but believed the Jews and Christians would welcome it with open arms. He claimed that he was, in effect, preaching the religion of Abraham and Moses, which had been debased over the centuries. Muhammad regarded himself as bearer of the mission to reform that religion and so spread it among the nations. It was only at a later stage, when he realized that the religion thus reformed proved unacceptable, that Muhammad began presenting Islam as a new religion.

The Jews of Arabia, who maintained close ties with their fellow Jews in Palestine and Babylon, remained faithful to the Torah and followed traditions accepted by Jews everywhere. They opposed Muhammad's attempts to convert them to Islam. When Muhammad's hopes of winning them over to his new movement were dashed, he turned against them with all his might. He accused them of forging their own sacred scriptures and eliminating all references in the Old Testament to his future appearance as the emissary of God and "the last of all prophets." He also attacked the Jews as a stiff-necked people, who never hearkened even to their own prophets.

In the fifth year of the Hijrah (626), Muhammad attacked the Jewish tribes of Yathrib (Medina) and destroyed them outright. Many of these Jews were killed, some of them were deported to the north, and others sought refuge in Islam. Hence the first steps taken by Islam brought ruin and destruction to the Jews of Arabia.

However in 628, when the Jews of Khaibar, Fadak, and Taima were subjugated, they were permitted to remain in their homes and maintain their religion and customs on the condition that they hand half their crops to the

Moslem state, which had proclaimed all the country's land the property of the state. As we know, Islam finally united the entire Arab world under its banner. After Muhammad's death, the young Arab state began to surge northward, rapidly increasing the boundaries of its rule. Now, a new era opened for the Jews of Arabia. This was to be one of the most relaxed and fruitful periods in Jewish history.

A Breathing Space

Wherever Byzantine rule was replaced by Arab rule, the Jews breathed more freely. The new Moslem authorities allowed the Jews greater freedom and gave them more security. Under Moslem rule the Jews had wider economic and cultural opportunities than under the Byzantines.

The Jews benefited from the basic distinction the Moslems drew between idolators, who were given a choice between conversion to Islam or death, and Ahl-ul-Kitab ("The People of the Book," members of other religions that also had sacred writings). As far as this latter category was concerned, the Moslem rulers contented themselves with imposing their political authority and placing their non-Moslem subjects in the situation of Ahl-ul-Dhimmah (trustee peoples, who had to pay the state an annual per capita tax, called jiziah). However, these trustees' lives, property, religion, customs, and laws were protected by Islam, which pledged itself to look after them. The tax was paid by all males over the age of eighteen, while women and children were exempt.

While in the Christian lands the Jews were invariably the only "heretics," in the Moslem lands they were in the company of other religious groups (the Christians, and later also the Parsis). Compared with these groups, the Jews enjoyed a superior position. The Moslem rulers considered them less dangerous and more loyal than their Christian subjects. As the Jews were also closer to the Arabs in spirit, language, and tradition, they were not considered as alien as the Christians, and were consequently given privileges not granted to the Christians.

Caliph Omar Ibn Al Khattab (634–644), the second Caliph after the death of Muhammad, and the real founder of the Arab Empire, allowed the Jews to return to Jerusalem, after occupying the Holy City from Byzantium. Despite the opposition of the Christian leaders, a Jewish community was re-established in the Old City of Jerusalem, after Jews had been banned from it for nearly 500 years. The Jewish community, which had remained in Palestine after the prolonged evil rule of Byzantium, now breathed more easily under Arab rule. When the rulers of the House of Umayya decided to proclaim the Old City and Mount Moriah sacred to Islam, and Abd el-Malik built the Dome of the Rock and later the Aksa Mosque, the right of the

Jews to pray at the Wailing Wall was retained. Later the Jews were permitted to purchase the Mount of Olives. The crosses of the Christian churches on this site had been removed. (Some of these churches had been destroyed during the Persian conquest in A.D. 614, and not rebuilt.) The Jews began to use the Mount of Olives as a center of assembly and religious celebrations.

The Cave of The Patriachs in Hebron was restored to the Jews, who erected a synagogue next to this holy spot where Abraham was thought to be buried. In addition to the rural Jewish population, which had remained attached to the land, important Jewish communities soon developed in Tiberias, Jerusalem, Caesarea, Tyre, and Ramle; the latter town was founded during the reign of Caliph Sulaiman (715–717), and became the leading administrative and commercial center of Palestine.

When the Arabs occupied Alexandria, they specifically emphasized in their agreement with the Greek inhabitants of the city that the local Jewish population was there by right and not on sufferance.

A Unifying Political Framework

The Arab conquests and the expansion of their empire from India, Central Asia and the Caucasus to the Pyrenees united most of the Jewish people (at least 80 to 90 percent) within a single political framework. The establishment of the Arab Caliphate broke down the barriers between the Jews of the Byzantine lands in western Asia and North Africa and those of the large and prosperous community which had developed since the destruction of the Temple by the Romans, in Babylon (present-day Iraq), within the framework of the Persian Sasanid Empire (226–641).

At the time of the Arab conquest of Mesopotamia the Jews of Babylon were the largest (two thirds) and most powerful group in Jewry. These Jews had suffered persecution and oppression from time to time even under the relatively tolerant Persian regime. The Persian culture and religion did not have any special inclination to expand, and displayed little talent for assimilating their non-Persian minorities. Despite the intermittent persecution of the Jews and the other religious and cultural minorities, the situation of the Jews in Sasanid Persia was infinitely better than in the Christian lands. The Persian Jews engaged in almost all spheres of the economy, lived their own community life and left their imprint on the areas in which they lived; this helped them to preserve their culture and traditions.

For the second time in Jewish history the land called Babylon became a focal point for masses of Jews and a principal, if temporary, center of the Jewish people's spiritual life in the Diaspora. As in the days of Ezra and Nehemiah, in the fifth century B.C., forms of Jewish communal life evolved.

Treasures of religious writings and cultural traditions—which accumulated in houses of study, synagogues and academies over a period of nearly three centuries—were crystallized into the Babylonian Talmud, destined to become a religious guide of tremendous importance to the entire Jewish world for generations afterwards. The Jews had their own autonomous institutions, headed by a *Resh Galuta* (literally, "head of the Exile"), who was recognized by the Persian authorities as the representative of the Jewish community. This post descended from father to son, and, according to tradition, could be traced back to King David.

However, during the reign of the Sasanids, this large and important Jewish community was cut off from the other Jewish communities living in the Christian lands of western Asia, including the Jewish community of Palestine (which had recovered to a certain extent after the abolition of Hadrian's harsh decrees in the middle of the second century), and the Jews of North Africa and some European lands. When the Arabs conquered the Sasanids and took control of Persia, this large and powerful Jewish community was able to take its rightful place at the head of the Jewish people. Apart from the Jews living in the Moslem countries, there were only small sections living within the reduced boundaries of Byzantium, Italy, Gaul (France), the Rhineland (Germany of today), and several places in what is today Hungary and the Balkans.

Increased Autonomy

From the reign of the fourth Caliph, Ali (656–661), when the city of Kufa became the capital of the Caliphate for some time, Jewish autonomy in Mesopotamia took on greater importance, eventually embracing the entire Jewish population of the Caliphate. During the period of Arab rule, the *Resh Galuta's* tasks increased in scope. He was empowered to nominate in the Jewish communities heads of religious academies and local judges who pronounced judgments according to Jewish law. He was accepted by all the Jews of the Arab Empire as their spokesman and political leader. Further, the Caliph himself recognized the *Resh Galuta* as "the prince of the Jewish people," who was empowered to levy taxes on the members of his community (property taxes, poll taxes on people and cattle, taxes for the ritual slaughter of cattle, building taxes, etc.) in order to meet their special religious and communal needs.

In the same way that the Nestorian Catholicos was responsible to the Caliph for all the Christians in the Caliphate, and was considered a high government official paid from the state treasury, so the *Resh Galuta* was held to be responsible for all the Jews of the Caliphate. He was a member of the state council and was paid a salary by the treasury. His bureau maintained ties with Jewish communities everywhere in the Caliphate, and he served them as a spiritual guide.

The *Resh Galuta* symbolized the Jewish people's communal and administrative autonomy in the Caliphate. Great prestige and standing was also enjoyed by the *Gaonim*, the heads of the Sura and Pumbedita religious academies in Mesopotamia, which were recognized as the highest Jewish religious authorities.

Some scholars believe the *Gaonim* date back to the end of the sixth century, or before the birth of Islam. In any event, they do not appear to have enjoyed any special status or privileges before the reign of Caliph Ali. After this time, the *Gaonim* became the supreme Jewish spiritual authorities in the Moslem Empire, and their status remained intact even when the Caliphate disintegrated into various Arab kingdoms over the years. During the tenth and eleventh centuries, the title *Gaonim* was given to the heads of religious academies in Palestine, and in the twelfth and thirteenth centuries to the heads of colleges in Baghdad, Damascus, and Egypt also.

In the early days of Islam, and even during the Umayad period (661–750), when Damascus was the political center of the Arab empire, the large Jewish community in Mesopotamia played no significant role in public life. But when the Arab regime began entrenching itself, and particularly when the Abbasid dynasty (750 and later) transferred the capital of the Caliphate to Baghdad (762), the Jews of Mesopotamia, headed by the *Resh Galuta* and the *Gaonim*, once more played a vital role in uniting and leading the Jewish people.

This administrative and spiritual autonomy of the Jews in the Arab Caliphate gave the *Resh Galuta* and the *Gaonim* an increasingly powerful influence over secular as well as civil affairs. They appointed the *dayanim*, or religious judges, who, together with the local Jewish notables, formed the powerful Jewish courts. The Jewish community, which was responsible for the taxes paid to the Treasury in its name, gave its leaders widespread powers in all its affairs. Apart from collecting the poll tax paid to the Caliph, and the specific Jewish taxes referred to above, the communal leaders levied taxes for services rendered to the community: the execution of marriages or divorces, the confirmation of bills of sale or contracts, and similar services. Any person who tried to hide a transaction of this kind from the eyes of the *dayanim* was deemed to have committed an offence punishable by a fine, flogging, boycott, and even excommunication. The community's spiritual leaders (the *dayanim* and other members of the court) created a nucleus organization, whose members received their salaries from the *dayan's* bureau and duly served it in various ways. The members of this "religious civil service" included a cantor (and sometimes a *paitan*, or writer of prayers and liturgical poems), a court scribe, messengers, and tax collectors. The authority to levy and collect taxes, which was given to the *Resh Galuta* during the golden age of the Caliphate (and later to the presidents of the Jewish community in Spain), vested in them very considerable powers.

The struggle between the secular and the spiritual leaders of the Jewish community, e.g., between the *Resh Galuta* and *Gaonim* of Mesopotamia, or the presidents and the religious scholars of Spain, was not always devoid of pressures by groups of wealthy Jews—tax collection contractors, men of property, traders—who were obviously concerned about the safeguarding of their own economic interests and equally indifferent to those of the farmers, artisans, and petty traders, both Jews and non-Jews. When the central regime was weak, the masses of Jews often suffered considerably from the corrupt practices of a handful of wealthy and influential Jews, as in the massacre of the Granada Jews in December 1066.

The rulers of the Arab Caliphate (like the Persian rulers before them) had their own good reasons for allowing their Jewish subjects such internal autonomy. The Jewish community was an excellent instrument for tax collection. The community structure gave the Jews a sort of collective responsibility. An individual Jew could leave his home or his country in an attempt to evade paying taxes; he could even sell all his property and smuggle his money out of the country; but the entire Jewish community could not flee overnight. Knowing that their leaders were, in effect, hostages, the Jews fulfilled their duty towards the regime more willingly under this particular system.

Nevertheless, these considerations of Arab rulers enhanced rather than reduced the general prestige of the Jews and their community. It enabled them to adhere to their religious traditions and social principles, to keep alive their cultural and historical legacy, to place their internal affairs in the hands of their own spiritual and social leaders, and to maintain nuclei of independent Jewish leadership, even in the Diaspora.

New Horizons

When the Caliphate reached its zenith, in the middle of the eighth century, new horizons opened up before the Jewish community. In the same way that the Jews had accompanied the Greeks, they now accompanied the Arabs. Wherever the Arabs established their rule, flourishing Jewish settlements sprang up. During the Umayad dynasty, the Jewish community in Palestine came to life once more. Important communities were founded in al-Fustat (Cairo), Kairouan (Tunisia), and Fez (Morocco), and the Jewish community of Spain began to grow in size and importance. Although there are no reliable figures, historians believe that, numerically, the Jewish population grew rapidly during this period.

The evolution of the mighty Arab empire, which had a central political regime, a single official language, one calendar (based on the *hijrah*), and an almost uniform code of law, opened new fields for Jewish initiative. True, the Jews were hindered economically by the enforced payment of the poll tax; this was a heavy burden on all non-Moslems, and it continued to hamper even Moslem converts. (The Umayads did not do this, because they feared a loss of revenue from the poll tax.) The Jews took less advantage of the opportunity of conversion than other religious groups. The per capita tax levied on Jewish farmers—in addition to the *kharaj*, or land tax, which they paid, as did everyone working state land—was one of the most decisive factors in the general transformation of the Jewish people's economic structure. In an attempt to evade these laws, many Jews abandoned farming and turned to crafts and commerce, in which they displayed considerable aptitude. They soon came to play an important role in the Caliphate's economic prosperity. The Arab empire's geographical location gave it the role of a natural intermediary between the Far East and Europe, North Africa and central Africa (Sudan, the Sahara, and West Africa). Baghdad, Damascus, Cairo, Tripoli, Kairouan and Fez, and the ports of Basra, Aden, Alexandria, Beirut, Antioch, Tangier, and Cadiz, were prosperous international trade centers and one of the Caliphate's main sources of wealth.

The Jews played a major part in these world-wide trade activities. According to ninth century Arab and Latin Catholic sources, and documents found in the famous Cairo Geniza,* it appears that these Jewish traders operated trade routes running from the Mediterranean ports to what is today the northern Suez Canal; from there the goods were taken by camel back to the Red Sea and then shipped to the Persian Gulf, India, and China. Some of these Jews traded with Rome and Constantinople. They had trade routes extending from the south of France to Antioch, and then by land to Aleppo and the Euphrates, down which the goods traveled to Mesopotamia and the Persian Gulf. They also conducted trade along all the land routes of the Caliphate and the countries which maintained close ties with the Arabs, including Palestine, North Africa, Syria, Southern Iraq, Persia, India, and China. Through Central Europe, the Caspian Sea, and the Volga river they came into contact with the Khazars, the Bulgarians, the Slavs, and the Scandinavians. S. D. Goitein, who has studied the Cairo Geniza, found references to over seventy kinds of goods that Jewish traders brought from the East to the West, and over one hundred articles which were transported in the opposite direction.

* The Cairo Scrolls (Old Fustat), most of which were discovered in 1896–1897, were found in the loft of an ancient synagogue. Thanks to the clear, dry climate (similar to that of the Judaean desert where the Qumran Scrolls were preserved and discovered), these scrolls were preserved in an excellent state, and some 200,000 pages have reached various research institutions in Europe. The earliest document dates back to 750 C.E.

Apart from being fluent in Arabic, the Jews of the Arab empire also spoke Persian and Greek, and the Iberian, Slavic, and Frankish languages. Their own Hebrew language was regularly used in commercial correspondence with other Jews and thus became the *lingua franca* of international commerce at that time. As the Jewish traders were neutral in the bitter dispute between the Moslem and Christian worlds, they were able to reach places which were inaccessible to members of the other two religions. In the most outlying Jewish community the visiting trader felt at home and among people he trusted, particularly if he carried a recommendation from the religious leader in his home community to the head of the community he was visiting. In addition, the close ties of family and kinship between these distant Jewish communities—the fruit of their long persecution and flight from oppression—offered the Jewish traders no small advantage.

They were also helped by the uniform nature of Jewish law throughout the Diaspora. This enabled a trader from Baghdad or Ispahan to sign a contract with another Jewish trader in Bordeaux or Genoa. In the event of a dispute, they would bring their case before Jewish *dayanim*, who would judge it according to prescribed Jewish law.

A class of prominent Jews gradually emerged in the centers of Arab culture. These Jews were financiers, important traders (particularly in foreign currency), scientists, scholars, and civil servants up to the rank of cabinet ministers.

However, at the end of the era of military conquests, the ruling Moslem class abandoned its warlike pursuits and devoted itself to commerce and trade, which had previously been dominated almost entirely by "non-believers." When this happened, an atmosphere of commercial competition and jealousy began to make itself felt and this soon affected the situation of the leading Jews in the Caliphate. Discriminatory laws and persecution were felt from time to time.

During the Umayad dynasty period (661–750) there were virtually no signs of intolerance towards the Jews, apart from the reign of Omar II (717–720) and Hisham (724–743), whose attitude was not typical of that shown by the Umayad Caliphs. However, in the midst of the flowering of Arab culture, under Caliph Haroun Al Rashid (786–809), his legal adviser, Abu Youssuf, suggested giving the Jews a special status, making them wear distinctive garments, forbidding them to ride horses, and banning the construction of new centers of religious study (a ban of this nature had been imposed by the Byzantine rulers, but was later annulled by the Arabs). During the reign of Caliph Al-Ma'moun (813–833), who was an ardent supporter of Arab learning, the Jews were dismissed from their government posts. Under Caliph Al Mutawakkil (847–861), the Jews were ordered to wear a distinctive yellow badge, "so that they can be recognized at once." This badge of shame later became a badge of discrimination worn by Jews in many Christian lands, especially under the Nazi regime.

However, such discriminatory laws could not last. The special talents of the Jews and their unique status in international trade as well as in the Caliphate's internal struggles, made it impossible for the Arab state to dispense with their services for long. The Jews returned to their positions in the Arab empire's contacts with other countries, and were once again actively associated with all measures designed to enhance the Caliphate's prestige. During the golden age of the Abbasid dynasty in Baghdad, when the Moslem empire attained great material and spiritual wealth, it gradually lost its initial military power. Various internal processes contributed to disintegration. Countries and provinces that had formed part of the Caliphate from the beginning seceded from it and established separate states (the Idrissi and Aglabi dynasties in the Maghreb, the Fatimid Caliphate in Egypt, Palestine, and Syria, the Caliphate of Cordoba, the Samanid and Ghaznawid dynasties and the Sultanate of Mosul in the East). All these created new political borders within the former united empire, with corresponding effects on the unity of Jewry.

But these Jewish communities remained culturally united for a long time, indeed for as long as the Arab world itself was so united. The kinship between the Hebrew and Arabic languages brought about the direct impact of Arab science, literature, and philosophy upon Jewish thought, and the Jews soon began to engage in intensive theological, philosophical, and medical research. The Arabs repaid the debt they owed the Jews, who had helped so much to prepare the conditions which gave rise to Islam and brought the Arabs onto the world stage. The close ties between the nations' languages and spiritual traditions, and the fact that in the course of time Arab culture became a sort of continuation of Hellenism, to which many Jews had earlier been attracted, led to a cultural symbiosis between the two peoples.

The Influence of the Arabic Language and Arab Civilization on Hebrew Culture

Within a relatively short time, Arabic, which was the dominant language of the new empire, replaced the spoken Aramaic, which the Jews living in the Caliphate had used as a *lingua franca*. This adaptation was made easier by an affinity of spirit between Hebrew and Arabic. Arabic became a major element in the cultural development of most Jews over generations, and most of the great works of medieval Jewish thought were written in it.

The term "Middle Ages" was coined by certain historians for whom the centuries between the decline of the brilliant classical cultures of Greece and Rome and the new golden age of the Renaissance were nothing but a transition period of little or no importance. This has been one of the characteristic errors of historians motivated by an exclusively European orientation. In any event, it should be stressed that in the history of the Jewish people— as in the history of the Arabs and other Oriental peoples—the several hundred years that are lumped together under the heading of "the Middle Ages" were by no means a period of decline and decay, but one of unusually productive creativity, and one of the most glorious periods in Jewish history.

Scholars have pointed out that during the first centuries of the emergent Arab culture the Jews wrote their poems—even secular verse—in their national tongue, Hebrew, whereas their commentaries on the Bible and the Talmud and philosophical problems were written in Arabic. For their poetical work, Jewish writers found sufficient literary resources in the Hebrew sacred books and ancient prayers; but the Hebrew vocabulary was an inadequate vehicle for the writing of books of science. Moshe Ibn Ezra, who lived from the late eleventh to the early twelfth century, dwelt on this problem in his book *The Rules of Poetry*:

Because we have lived in the Diaspora for so long, he wrote, the Hebrew language has been forgotten and lost. The study of Hebrew has ceased, or virtually ceased. . . . All that is left to us of the Hebrew tongue is the twenty-four sacred books, which contain only the words needed for the matters they discuss. From these holy books our people has taken the fundamentals with which to compile prayers, liturgical poems and elegies, laments and other types of rhetorical speech.

Professor Birnbaum adds:

When the *Gaonim* wanted to explain the laws of Judaism in a precise manner, they were compelled to use Arabic, which they found extremely accurate and suited to this purpose. The same held true when they interpreted the Talmud, whose Aramaic language was no longer spoken by the Jewish people. And when they replied to questions of religion and Jewish life, they were again forced to have recourse to Arabic, as this was the easiest language to use. However, poetry does not require a completely clear and precise language, and hence the poets were not afraid to write in Hebrew.

Birnbaum also quotes Shlomo Yehuda Rapaport, in his preface to *The Prepared Notebook* by Rabbi Shlomo Farchon:[3]

Although most of the *Gaonim* used only Arabic, they did not cease using fluent and beautiful Hebrew in their poems and prayers . . . for they found our sacred tongue suitable only for the biblical subjects. . . . But the great clumsiness with which they express their innermost ideas [in Hebrew] is apparent to any perceptive reader.

Important achievements in semantics were registered as early as the beginning of the Arab Caliphate (seventh to eighth centuries), when Arabic became the language of the state and of the dominant religion. The Caliphs and their intimates encouraged great research efforts in both literary and colloquial Arabic, the compilation of Bedouin folklore and pre-Islamic Arabic poetry, the recording of *Hadith* and so on. In course of time, Arabic continued to develop, reaching a delicacy, richness, and flexibility far exceeding those of any other language before it.

At first this very development of Arabic had a stultifying effect on the evolution of Hebrew. In his foreword to *The Duties of the Heart* (which was written in Arabic by Bahya ben Yosef ibn Pakuda in the eleventh century), the translator, Yehuda Ibn Tibbon, explained that during the tenth and eleventh centuries, Jewish intellectual circles thought Arabic should become the language of their spiritual and creative expression, because it was so much richer than Hebrew: "Arabic is an extensive language which meets every purpose and serves the need of every speaker and author; its rhetoric is direct and lucid, with an immediate application to every matter, more than is possible in Hebrew, because all the Hebrew we can use is found in the Holy Bible and is inadequate for our needs."

Only the first book of Rabbi Saadya Gaon,* *Agron*, published at the beginning of the tenth century, was written in Hebrew; all his other books were written in Arabic. This was true even of the founders of Hebrew grammar and philology (Yehuda Hayyuj, Yonah Ibn Janah, and others), who lived and worked in the second half of the tenth century and the first half of the eleventh. Their great works on Hebrew language and grammar were written in Arabic.

Nevertheless, this was nothing but a phase. The achievements of the Arabic language became a model for Jewish scholars, which inspired them to improve the Hebrew language and increase its linguistic standing. In fact, when Arabic reached the zenith of its development, it became a sort of rival that evoked the envy of Hebrew scholars.

One of the greatest Jewish authors, Yehuda al-Harizi (twelfth to thirteenth centuries), in his introduction to *Tachkemoni*, commented on the role played by Arabic in encouraging original Hebrew creation. He admitted that he did not like to see "Hagar giving birth to beautiful children, while Sarah remained barren." Hence, he decided to take up the cause of the language in which the Bible was written, in order to prove that it could be used, not only for writing on lofty religious subjects, but also for ordinary, everyday

---

* Born in a small village in the Fayum of Egypt (892), lived for some years in Palestine, from 928 was head of the Sura *yeshiva*, died in about 942. The first of the Jewish thinkers to lay the foundations of Jewish religious philosophy in the Arabic language. Translated the Bible into Arabic with his own commentary. Argued against the Karaites and against Jewish heretics, especially their spokesman Hiwi Habalky. Defended the Jewish faith at a time of fierce struggles in Islamic philosophy. Left a rich legacy of commentaries on the Bible and the Talmud, on religious philosophy etc.

matters; not only to preach about morals, but also to make jokes and gladden the heart of an audience.

The rapid rise of Arabic had a stimulating effect on Jewish authors as well. While taking part in the great body of creation in Arabic, they also recorded great achievements in their independent national writings in Hebrew. The most important Jewish works written during that period, which were invariably first penned in Arabic, were later translated into Hebrew.

This Jewish–Arab cultural cooperation attained its peak during the period of Moslem rule in Spain.

The Golden Age in Spain

At the end of the sixth century, the Visigoth rulers of Spain embraced Christianity. Throughout the seventh century, the Jewish community in Spain suffered from a wave of persecution which almost wiped it out. The hostile policy towards the Jews, enforced by the Byzantines in the eastern Mediterranean, now spread to the West.

In the early stages of Islam in the East, the Spanish Jews were considered the allies of this new force, which began threatening Spain in the middle of the seventh century, after reaching the eastern border of what is now Tunisia. At the Council of Toledo in 653, the King of Spain declared that "the sect of Jews, who crucified the Lord, must be shown the true way or smitten with a vengeful staff." In the ensuing persecution some of the Spanish Jews fled to North Africa. Others became forced converts, or even remained faithful to their religion and ancient traditions, paying for this with their lives. For each of these groups of Spanish Jews the Arab conquest (711–716) was a liberation that offered them immediate relief.

After the Arab conquest, masses of Christians embraced Islam. The first to do so were the Christian slaves, who thus escaped from their Christian masters. Then these masters themselves became converted, so that, as "true believers," they could regain their property and wealth. Despite this mass conversion, the Arabs treated the Christians with considerable suspicion. This distrust was increased by the fact that the Christian kings outside Spain and the ruling Christian class within Spain refused for a long period to reconcile themselves to the Moslem conquest. Their resistance continued for many years. On the other hand, the Jews were treated with trust and confidence, and were given economic, political and cultural opportunities the like of which they had never enjoyed since coming to Spain.

The Arabs brought with them the technological achievements they had acquired from other conquered nations, and the Moorish conquest brought prosperity to the stagnant Spanish economy. Crops such as rice, sugar, and perfumes were introduced, and wool and silk were produced. The Jews were allowed to return to agriculture, from which they had been banned by the Visigoths. Mining of silver, gold, iron, lead, sulphur, and precious stones began to be developed. Industry and commerce prospered through the manufacture of silken textiles, paper, glass vessels, ivory, arms, and jewelry, skin, glass, and brass. Both internal and foreign trade rose to new heights. The Jews soon occupied an important place in industry, commerce, and finance, complementing the Arabs, who were not skilled in these pursuits. They also played an important role in Spain's political life. There were Jewish ministers, financial and political advisers, diplomats and generals. The freedom and internal national autonomy that the Jews now won after long persecutions and humiliation stimulated in them new and substantial creative forces. The Jews played an active part in the evolution of Arab culture without neglecting their own. They studied Arabic language and literature, and learned new forms of poetry, philological systems, scientific values, and philosophy, with the help of which they developed their own national culture. The renaissance of Hebrew poetry coincided with the revival of research in the Hebrew language. Hebrew prose and Jewish scientific and philosophical writing reached unprecedented heights.

The liberal regime of "enlightened absolutism" that then ruled Spain was the fruit of the many different elements that together made up the Caliphate of Cordoba (Arabs, Moslemized Christians, Berbers, Slavic serfs, Christians, Jews) and a principal factor in the cooperation between these various elements. This regime was based on cultural tolerance, a large measure of equality, and full cooperation between members of all the religions. This climate gave rise to great spiritual figures. The Jews made an important contribution to the country's economic prosperity, and enjoyed their full share of its fruits.

This golden age of Spanish Jewry lasted for about 200 years. During this period, the Jews played an active role in Arab culture and economic, political, literary, and scholarly endeavor, while enriching their own spiritual legacy. Hebrew poetry flowered anew, the Hebrew language was studied, and philosophy, religious studies, and public affairs all enjoyed a new lease of life.

It is impossible to recall all the great Jewish figures of that time. But reference to a few of them will present some idea of their scope and quality.

The beginning of the Golden Age of Jewish-Arab cooperation in Spain is symbolized by the remarkable personality of Hasdai Ibn Shaprut (910–970), the court physician and political adviser to Caliph Abd-ur-Rahman (912–961) and his son and heir Al Hakam (961–976). During this period, Spain enjoyed a respite from the lengthy wars which had plagued it for so long. The country attained relative political stability and economic and cultural prosperity. Ibn Shaprut's proficiency in the Romance languages (Latin, Italian,

French, and Spanish) and his outstanding diplomatic and financial abilities earned him high posts at the Caliph's court and in the country as a whole.

He also helped establish new centers for the study of the Bible and the Talmud, with the intention of liberating Spanish Jewry from the spiritual hegemony of the large Jewish community in Mesopotamia, under the Abbasid Caliphate. (As the rulers of Spain belonged to the rival Umaya dynasty, they took a favorable view of this trend.) Under Ibn Shaprut's sponsorship and with his generous material assistance, the large Andalusian *yeshivot* (Talmudic academies) flourished and attracted the best brains of Mesopotamia and North Africa. In the same way that Caliph Al-Hakam, a confirmed bibliophile, sent emissaries far and wide so that they could make copies of important manuscripts for his large library near the University of Cordoba, Ibn Shaprut acquired accurate copies of the Talmud from the famous Mesopotamian *yeshivot* of Sura and Pumbedita, and placed them in the new Spanish academies. Just as the Caliph's palace was crowded with philosophers, scientists and poets, so the Jewish Minister's house was a meeting place for Jewish intellectuals.

Ibn Shaprut's secretary, Menahem ben Saruk (910–970), compiled a Biblical dictionary in Hebrew and Aramaic, which was widely read outside the Arabic-speaking lands (particularly in France and Italy). Ibn Shaprut was the patron of the gifted poet and Hebrew scholar Dunash Halevy ben Labrat, a pupil of Rabbi Saadya Gaon. Dunash introduced a basic change into Hebrew poetry when he followed the strict rhythmic patterns of Arabic verse and added to the hitherto purely religious and liturgical themes secular essays on nature, recreation, friendship, and other human experiences. The development of Hebrew poetry, and the new stimulus given to the study of Scripture, led to intensive study of Hebrew semantics and generally enriched the Hebrew language.

There were a number of outstanding Hebrew scholars at that time. Foremost among them was "the chief grammarian," Yehuda Hayyuj, who was born in Fez in the middle of the tenth century and died at the end of the same century. Hayyuj broke entirely new ground in Hebrew-language studies. He laid down the rule, taken from the laws of Arabic grammar, that every Hebrew root consisted of three letters. According to Moshe Ibn Ezra, Hayyuj was "the first to write an entire and comprehensive book on Hebrew grammar" and he made a valuable contribution to Semitic philology in general.

He was followed by his great pupil Yona Ibn-Janah (born in Cordoba in 990, died in the middle of the eleventh century), who is acknowledged as the founder of Hebrew grammar and the first competent lexicographer. He was one of the foremost philologists in medieval Europe. His book *Kitab-ut-Tankih* (or "The Book of Texture"), on Hebrew grammar and semantics, is considered "the richest and most beautiful fruit of Hebrew-language study" (Zinnberg).

These two grammarians were only the greatest in a galaxy of Jewish scholars and philologists of the time. Their researches added wealth to Hebrew culture and considerably influenced its historical development.

Shortly after Ibn Shaprut's death, another Jewish Minister attained fame in the court of Granada. Shmuel Halevy ben Yosef Ibn Nagrela, better known as Shmuel Hanagid was born in Cordoba in 993 and died in Granada in 1056. He was educated at the Cordoba *yeshiva*, after which he studied mathematics, philosophy, and foreign languages (he was fluent in seven languages). He became an authority on Arabic language and literature. This brought him to the high post of Political Adviser to the ruler of Granada. Shmuel Hanagid also frequently led his master's armies against Granada's enemies.

For over thirty years this Jewish statesman also acted as the leader of the Granada Jewish community. The considerable setbacks he encountered did not prevent him from studying the Talmud, and Hebrew literature and poetry. The title *Nagid* (or "Prince") was given him by the Jews of Granada in recognition of his important work on behalf of Jewish culture and his material support of scholars and sages in Spain, North Africa, Sicily, Palestine, and Mesopotamia. He also had copies made of the Talmud from the Babylonian academies, which he placed at the disposal of impoverished scholars.* For a certain time he even directed his own *yeshiva*, at which he lectured on the basic elements of the Talmud and its method (these lectures formed the groundwork for his important book, *Preface to the Talmud*). His Hebrew writings included a Biblical dictionary used by scholars and grammarians for many years after his death. His volume of poetry also opened up new vistas for Hebrew verse.

A contemporary of Shmuel Hanagid's was the famous poet and philosopher Shlomo ibn Gabirol (*c.* 1021–1056), one of the most original thinkers of his time. His book *The Source of Life* (known by the contemporary world as "Fons Vitae," the title of its Latin translation) written in Arabic, was translated into Hebrew in the middle of the twelfth century, and was also studied at the universities of Christian Europe during the Middle Ages.

The flowering of Jewish studies in Spain increased the prestige of the Spanish Jewish scholars among the other Jewish communities. During the eleventh century a scholar from Fez, Morocco, attained great fame: Isaac Alfasi (1013–1103), whose monumental work *The Abridged Talmud* (from which he omitted the proceedings of the *amoraim* or talmudical sages, and in effect laid down the *Halakha* or religious law), was the first of a number of major works by the great Spanish Jewish thinkers.

* His special attitude to the Holy Land was shown in the yearly supply of olive oil sent from his groves to the synagogues of Jerusalem.

During the Christian reconquest of Spain there was considerable dissension in the Moslem regime between the Andalusian noblemen and the Murabitin, also called Almoravides, of North Africa, who rushed to the help of Moslems against the Christian kings. The Christian regime began to entrench itself once more. Again a special role was reserved for the Jews. Their age-old ties with the non-Moslem world, and the neutral position they occupied between the two rival non-Jewish religions, enabled them to mediate between Christians and Moslems. They came to occupy leading positions in the courts of the new rulers. They became court physicians, financial and economic advisers, scribes and diplomats, scientists, philosophers, poets, and linguists. Many of these Jews also devoted time to Jewish studies and the development of Hebrew poetry, philosophy, and philology.

The Jewish community of Granada, which by the last quarter of the eleventh century had recovered from the massacre of December 1066—the first of the onslaughts on Jews in Moslem Andalusia—produced Moshe Ibn Ezra (c. 1055–1139). This brilliant student of Arabic language and literature attracted the attention of many young Jewish poets and intellectuals. When Granada was conquered by the Almoravides in 1090, and the Jews were forced to flee, Ibn Ezra took refuge in the Christian province of Navarra. The transition from the civilized Moslem south to the dark and provincial Christtian north, his poverty-stricken life in exile, and the plight of his family—which was scattered all over Spain—left an indelible imprint on his life and poetry.

Both his poems and philosophical writings are on a highly pessimistic note, even though later in his life he attained a state of stoic resignation. He published many important books: a collection of rhymed couplets called *The Giant Book*, the sublime poem "Tarshish," a book of dialogues and debates especially on rules of poetry, *Kitab-ul-Muhadara Wal-Mudhakara*. His philosophical work, *Kitab-ul-Hadiqa fi Ma'ani-l-Majaz w-al-Haqiqa*, and his religious poetry and liturgical prayers are among the finest works produced in the Golden Age of Spanish Jewry.*

One of the most illustrious Jewish figures of that time was the poet Rabbi Yehuda Halevi (c. 1086–1142). He was a physician by profession, and a poet by temperament. Side by side with his religious poetry, he gave powerful expression to the Jewish people's longings for its ancient homeland. In the time of the Crusades, when clashes between Islam and Christianity increased so sharply, he sensed the danger to the Diaspora Jewish communities in this

---

* On the basis of various authorities, P. Birnbaum points out that a comparison of the commentaries of Avraham Ibn Ezra with those of certain Jewish thinkers who wrote in Arabic (Yefet Ben Ali Hakarai, Jonah Ibn Janah, Rabbi Saadia Ga'on) leads one to the conclusion that almost all Ibn-Ezra's writings are in fact summaries of Arabic books which he used.

battle between giants, and called upon the Jews to return to "the nest of the dove." Eventually he left Spain and set out for the Land of Israel. His well-known philosophical work, *The Book of the Kuzari* (written in Arabic *c.* 1140), contains an imaginary dialogue between the King of the Khazars and a Jewish sage. It deals with the relation between faith and philosophy, the religion of Israel and the spiritual and moral greatness of the Jewish people. Another towering figure was Avraham ibn Ezra (1090–1164), poet, philosopher, writer on mathematics, astronomy and philology, and one of the greatest Biblical commentators of all time.

Up to the age of fifty he lived in Spain, visiting North African centers and contacting the sages there. Later, he traveled in Italy and France where Arabic was not known, bringing with him the brilliant Arabic works of Jewish scholars. His writings had a marked effect on the development of a Hebrew prose style suitable for scientific writings.

From the community of Tudela in Aragon came the famous traveler and explorer, Benjamin of Tudela. The record of his travels in Southern Europe, Asia, and North Africa is valuable not only for the study of Jewish life in the Middle Ages, but for the light it sheds on general conditions at that time.

In this brief survey of the great figures who thrived in the atmosphere of Jewish-Arab cooperation, a unique place is occupied by Rabbi Moshe ben-Maimon (Maimonides or "Rambam," 1135–1204), a master physician, a profound philosopher and one of the greatest Biblical and Talmudic authorities of all time. His scientific writings, the peak of Jewish learning and scholarship, have influenced generations of scholars.

Although Maimonides lived outside Spain during most of his life (particularly in Fez and Cairo), he is definitely a product of the Spanish (Arab) school. He was born into a family which had produced generations of sages, religious judges, and scholars. Possessed of a remarkable mind and a phenomenal memory, Maimonides was an unrivalled methodical codifier. His numerous works include the encyclopedic *Commentary on the Mishna*, *The Guide to the Perplexed*, *The Strong Hand*, and such epistles as "Letter to (the Jews of) Yemen." These volumes, written in both Arabic and Hebrew, laid the foundations for Jewish thought during the centuries which followed.

This cursory list would not be complete without reference to Yehuda ben-Shlomo Al-Harizi (1165–1225). Although he was not the first to use Arabic poetic forms in Hebrew, it was Al-Harizi who introduced the *maqama**

---

* *Maqama*—adventure tales in verse that are linked together by the narrator, who comes into contact with all strata of society. Even more important than their content is their humorous form—the play on words and punning—and their skilful use of language: verses which can be read in both directions (from the beginning to the end and vice-versa) without losing their verse-form and when read backwards make sense—though contrary to the original.

into Hebrew literature. The Arabic poet Al-Hariri had excelled in this form, and Al-Harizi followed in his footsteps, and also translated into Hebrew some of Al-Hariri's verse. His collection of fifty such *maqamas*, Tahkemoni, is one of the great poetic anthologies of the Spanish Golden Age.

Al-Harizi translated Rambam's monumental commentary on the Mishna from Arabic into Hebrew. To this day his poetry is one of the most important sources of research into medieval Hebrew poetry. His tours of Jewish communities in North Africa, Egypt, Palestine, Syria, and Mesopotamia, produced fascinating poetical accounts of life and love in such countries.

Within the compass of this particular study it has been impossible to do more than list a few of the leading creative figures of the Golden Age of Jewish-Arab cooperation. For a more comprehensive study the interested reader should turn to the vast specialized bibliography of which one of the latest important works is Israel Zinnberg's *The History of Jewish Literature*.*

The focal points of the great Jewish cultural renaissance in Spain were the courts of the feudal rulers. The first of these courts to welcome Jewish scholars were the Caliphate of Cordoba and those of subsidiary, or successor, Emirates. Competition between the princes during the period of decline spurred the development of artistic creation and scientific research. The intellectuals accredited to these courts were relatively free from the cramping supervision of theologians and the clergy. The overall technical and economic development stimulated the evolution of medical science, mathematics, astronomy, geography, and a freer and more tolerant type of philosophy, which strove for man's liberation from superstitions and prejudices originating in a purely religious view of the world. The pupils of Ibn Bajjah and Ibn Rushd (otherwise known as Averroës) extolled science and developed a system of thought based on reason and knowledge, rather than dogmatic faith. The Jewish philosophers feared for their people's cultural heritage, the basis of their independent existence in the Diaspora. Hence, they struggled against the influence of the more secular and materialistic Arab philosophy. At the same time, they drew on neo-Platonic and Arab thinking when they interpreted the logical foundation of Maimonides' commentaries on the Mishna.

Several of these Jewish thinkers attempted, in a cautious and guarded fashion, to discuss a possible compromise between religion and science,

* A monumental Yiddish work in eight volumes, written in Russia from 1915–1927 and published in Vilna ("Tamar" publications) in 1933, in New York (M. S. Sklarski publications) in 1943, and in a Hebrew translation in Israel. Vol. I is devoted entirely to the Spanish era.

after arriving at conclusions which seemed to contradict certain fundamental elements of religious belief (such as Maimonides' rejection of the concept of life after death). However, the struggle between the Jewish philosophy, based on orthodox beliefs, and the rational philosophies of the influential school of Arab thinkers in Spain did not upset the prevailing relations of mutual tolerance and respect. Ibn Rushd, the man who developed the materialistic basis of Aristotelian philosophy, and a great opponent of Moslem dogmatism (writing that "a man can reach the highest degree of awareness, not through mystical enthusiasm, but through developing his philosophic and scientific consciousness"), found a spiritual refuge in the Jewish community. His commentary on Aristotle, which was suppressed by the Al-Muwahideen rulers, was translated into Hebrew, and from Hebrew into Latin. This work played an important role in developing materialistic thought in Renaissance Europe.

There is no need to paint an overly idealistic picture of the golden age. Even this glorious chapter in the history of Jewish life in the Diaspora was by no means free of the limitations and humiliations of a people in exile. Nevertheless, the situation of the Jews in medieval Spain cannot be compared to their position in the Roman and Byzantine empires before them or to their life under Christian rule, after the expulsion from Spain. *If Islam had not sprung out of close contact with Jewish ideas, and had not maintained friendly relations with Jews at its inception, it would have developed very differently. Without the influence of Islam and the creative symbiosis between Arab and Jewish culture, the Jewish people's development and culture would also have taken a different course.*

From the end of the thirteenth century and onward, with the decline of Arab culture and the approach of the sterile cultural desert of the Ottoman Empire, evidences of Arab cultural creativity and Jewish-Arab cooperation became few and far between. For several centuries the Arabs virtually vanished from world history. The focal point in Jewish life now moved to Europe, and the Jews of the Oriental lands were far from the main stream of Jewish existence.

However, the encounter between the two peoples, who were at one time the most decisive factors in the Middle East and whose cooperation proved so fruitful and gave so much to human culture as a whole, was destined to be renewed. Each of these peoples, in its own way and under the influence of the specific historical conditions that affected it, aspired to regain its national independence and restore its ancient glory. Unfortunately, this third encounter took place during an era in which nationalism often degenerated into chauvinism, and foreign rule into "divide-and-rule" policies. These and other regrettable historical factors left an indelible mark on the fate of the Jewish-Arab encounter in modern time.

References

1. Alfred Guillaume, *The Influence of Judaism on Islam* (Oxford, 1928), p. 132.
2. Abraham Geiger, *Was hat Mohammed aus dem Judenthum aufgenommen?* (Bonn 1833; Leipzig, 1902).
3. Rabbi Shlomo Farchon, *The Prepared Notebook* (Pressburg, 1843), p. 14.

CHAPTER TWO

MEETING ANEW IN PALESTINE

After the great Jewish war against the Romans (A.D. 66–73) and the destruction of the Second Temple, there still remained in Palestine a sizeable Jewish community attached to the land and maintaining its own religious and internal life. These Jews' longing for freedom once more gave rise to rebellious forces, who eventually kindled the revolt led by Bar Kochba (132–135). In the three and a half years of bitter fighting there was much destruction and the country's Jewish population dwindled. Only in Galilee did a fairly large Jewish community remain; Jews were completely banned from the Jerusalem area.

However, at the end of the second century, some of the devastated towns and villages were rebuilt, the study of the Law increased, and the community's leaders attained great influence once again. This revival coincided with the grave economic crisis in the lands of the Roman Empire during the third century, when the links between the various provinces weakened, the sea routes were filled with pirates, commerce declined, and trade and manufacturing shrunk in the wake of restricted local and international economic activity. The agricultural population suffered from the corruption and exploitation of the Roman legions and their agents, and the towns were totally impoverished. After Christianity became the official religion of the Roman Empire and began the persecution of the Jews of Palestine, many Jews left the Holy Land for other countries. When the Roman Empire split in 395, Palestine, and indeed the entire eastern part of the Empire, came under the rule of Byzantium and its capital city of Constantinople. Palestine remained a Byzantine province until the Arab conquest in the fourth decade of the seventh century.

After the Moslem conquest, Palestine formed part of the large Arab Caliphate, first under the Umayads (661–750), whose capital was Damascus, and then under the Abbasids (750–945), who reigned in Baghdad. When the Baghdad dynasty disintegrated, Palestine began passing from one regime to another. In 886 it fell under the Bani Tulun dynasty in Egypt, which had proclaimed its independence from Baghdad, and which ruled for twenty years. At the beginning of the tenth century, after the Carmathians had been defeated in Syria, the Abbasids conquered Palestine once more (905–906). Thirty years later (935), when the powerful Governor Muhammad ibn Tunj became ruler of Egypt, he seized Palestine and most of Syria (including Damascus).

With the establishment of the Fatimid dynasty, which captured Egypt in 969 and founded Cairo as its capital, Palestine became a province of this Caliphate. In 1071, most of the Holy Land was conquered by the Turkish Seldjuks, who established a large empire in western Asia and maintained it for the next fifty years. In 1096, Jerusalem returned to the Fatimids for several years, until it was taken by the Crusaders in July 1099. The Crusaders controlled most of Palestine and even certain areas of southern Transjordan (the hills of Moab and Eilat).

The Crusader conquest virtually wiped out what was left of the Jewish population in Palestine, especially in the towns. The Jews who had helped the Arabs to defend Jerusalem and other places against the invading Crusaders were killed or taken prisoner. Those who could escape fled for their lives. However, the Saracens, led by Salah-ud-Din (Saladin) defeated the Crusaders in two decisive battles: at Hittin on July 4, 1187 and in Jerusalem on October 2 of the same year. This ushered in another period of relative ease and freedom for the small number of Jews who remained in Palestine. When the Ayoubi regime was overthrown by the Mamelukes (1253–1516), Palestine became part of the Mameluke kingdom. In 1517, the Ottoman Turks defeated the Mamelukes and ruled the country for 400 years, until the British defeated them in 1917, in the first World War.

Since the Moslem Arab armies occupied Palestine in the seventh century (634–638), the country had undergone a process of Arabization, and many of the inhabitants became Moslems; the same trend was prevalent in other lands taken over by the Arab Caliphate. These processes, which took place over many generations, turned most of the former inhabitants of Palestine— Christians, Jews, and Samaritans—into Arabs by language and Moslems by religion. At the same time, the Arab conquerors themselves were assimilated gradually into the local population. The constant streams of Arab tribes coming into Palestine from the desert and Arabic-speaking Moslem immigrants arriving from other parts of the Caliphate were also absorbed into the local population in the course of time—forming, in time, the predominantly Moslem Palestinian Arab community. It was this community that the Turks found when they conquered Palestine in 1517. The Arab character of Palestine's population was preserved during the four centuries of Ottoman rule.

The Jewish community remaining in the Holy Land after the fall of Judea in 70 C.E. was also subject to the pressure of these changing historical processes which dominated the centuries. There was always a Jewish community in Palestine, albeit a numerically small one, in every generation and under every regime. While under the Romans the Jews still formed a sizeable minority of the country's population, the persecutions they suffered in the Byzantine era severely reduced their numbers. There are no reliable

figures for the Jewish population during the Arab conquest, after which
the Jews of Palestine came under the same pressures of Arabization and
the adoption of Islam as the rest of the indigenous population. The Jewish
traveler Benjamin of Tudela (in Aragon) found, in 1170, 1,500 Jewish families
in the whole of Palestine. In 1520, shortly after the Turkish conquest, there
were about 5,000 Jews. The Israeli historian R. Mahler estimates that at the
beginning of the nineteenth century, the entire Jewish community numbered
"5,000 at the least, 7,000 at the most."

This small community maintained its identity because of the constant
arrival of individuals who came to Palestine mainly for religious reasons:
the desire to pray at the Wailing Wall and other Jewish holy shrines, and
the desire to be buried in the soil of the Holy Land. But fully as important
as the continued existence of a Jewish community in Palestine throughout
the ages was the Jewish people's link with, and attachment to, the Land of
Israel. This never faltered over generations of exile.

The Jews' desire to return to their ancient homeland and to rebuild their
lives as a nation in Palestine dates back to the beginning of their exile. The
Jews of the Diaspora never ceased dreaming of the return to Zion. The bitter
history of the Jewish people, and its tormented wanderings in exile during
centuries of persecution, kept this burning desire alive. The Jews' link with
Palestine was expressed in a wide range of religious and social customs and in
their general way of life. The Jews never ceased mourning the destruction of
the Temple on the Ninth of Ab. Every Jewish home contained one brick
left unpainted—in memory of the destruction of the Temple. At every
wedding ceremony a glass was broken, to remind the assembly that the
Temple was still in ruins. Daily prayers were redolent with the longing for
the return to Jerusalem. During the rainy season in Europe, the Jews prayed
for dew, since it was spring in Palestine.

Jewish Immigration to the Holy Land

The attachment to Palestine was also expressed by the constant trickle of
immigration to the Holy Land. This virtually never stopped, even during
periods when it was extremely dangerous and when only a few daring
individuals ventured to make the arduous journey.

In 1211, after the Moslem defeat of the Crusaders, about 300 rabbis
and scholars from France and England settled in Jerusalem and Acre. Many
of them built houses, and several synagogues were also established. They were
received in Jerusalem by Sultan Al-Adil, Saladin's brother, who welcomed
the Jewish immigrants and granted them special rights.

In 1267, Nahmanides (Ramban) the greatest religious authority of the age,
migrated from Spain to Palestine and settled in Jerusalem, where he gathered

round him other devout Jews. In the thirteenth century, several groups of Jews arrived from Germany. After the expulsion from Spain in 1492, many of the Jews who had taken refuge in Turkey attempted to reach Palestine. Some of them settled in Safed, and made this town a center of intellectual life and Cabbalistic thought during the sixteenth and early seventeenth centuries, with an influence extending far beyond the borders of Palestine. During Safed's golden age, the city was the home of several illustrious scholars, including Shlomo Alkabez (1505–1584), the commentator and writer of liturgical verse; Rabbi Moshe Cordovero; and his pupil and successor as head of the Cabbala Academy, the great mystic known as "Ha-Ari" or Rabbi Yitshak Luria (1534–1572). His principal teachings were recorded in *The Tree of Life* by his chief disciple, Haim Vital (1542–1620). Other influential figures include the great codifier of Jewish law, Rabbi Yosef Karo (1488–1575), the author of the *Shulhan Aruch* (the Jewish Code of Conduct); his pupils Rabbi Moshe Galanty, Rabbi Avraham Halevy Bruchim, and others. The first Hebrew printing press in modern Palestine was established at Safed, 1577 to 1587.

During the second half of the sixteenth century, Don Yosef Nasi and Donna Gracia Mendes (Spanish Marranos who had considerable influence in Constantinople) attempted to rebuild the ruined city of Tiberias and to develop the surrounding countryside. For some time this attempt, which was sponsored by the Sultan of Turkey, aroused hopes among the Jews. But before very long it petered out and ended in disillusionment.

The real history of the modern rebirth of a Jewish community in Palestine dates from the beginning of the eighteenth century. In 1700, Rabbi Yehuda Hasid arrived from Shedlitz in Poland, bringing with him about a thousand Jews from Poland and Russia. This group established the Ashkenazi congregation in Jerusalem, centering round the "synagogue of Rabbi Yehuda Hasid"; after this community's expulsion in 1720, the ruined synagogue was called "The Ruin of Rabbi Yehuda Hasid."

In 1740, the Jewish community in Tiberias was re-established by Rabbi Haim Abulafia. He came from Izmir in Turkey at the invitation of Sheikh Dahir al-Omar, who controlled Upper Galilee for about fifty years. In the middle of the eighteenth century the few remaining Jewish farm settlements in Galilee (Kefar Yassif, Shfar'am, Peki'in) were repopulated.

In 1777 300 "Hasidim" arrived from Poland and White Russia. These pupils of the Baal Shem Tov, the founder of the Hasidic movement, were headed by Rabbi Mendel of Vitebsk, and settled in Safed and Tiberias. They were followed (1810–1812) by the members of the *Hazon Zion* (Vision of Zion) movement, which had been formed in Shklov by the disciples of the *Vilna Gaon*, Rabbi Eliahu, the greatest anti-Hasidic scholar of the eighteenth century. These settlers revived the Ashkenazi congregation in Jerusalem.

The Jewish community in Haifa was founded by immigrants from Morocco and Algeria (1817); the Sephardic Jewish community of Jaffa was founded by Yeshayahu Ajiman of Constantinople in 1820, when he acquired buildings for an immigrants' house and a synagogue. The so-called *Habad* (Ashkenazi) community (which took its name from the initial letters of the Hebrew words for *wisdom, understanding, knowledge*) settled in Hebron in 1823. These settlers and those who followed in their wake founded the various *Kolelim*, organizations of Jews of the same geographical origin in the Diaspora. There were *Kolelim* of Jews from Holland and Germany (1837), Wolhy (south-east Russia) (1841), Warsaw and Poland (1850), Austria-Galicia (1854), Hungary (1862), and finally, one overall general committee of *Kolelim* of Ashkenazi rabbis (1866). Thus the old *yishuv* continued to maintain its organization until the arrival, at the beginning of the present century, of considerable numbers of settlers inspired by political Zionism, which was mainly secular in outlook. This heralded the emergence of the Jewish national movement in its modern form.

Growth of Jewish Community in Nineteenth Century

In the middle of the nineteenth century, the Jewish community of Palestine began growing at a much greater pace: from 10,500 people in 1856, to 20,000–25,000 in 1880. Nearly all these Jews lived in special areas in the holy cities, about half of them in Jerusalem and the other half in Safed, Tiberias and Hebron. Most of the community's income came from the *Halukkah* funds collected in the Diaspora, and similar charities.*

In 1856, Dr. Ludwig August Frankl of Vienna visited Jerusalem on behalf of Lippet Herz, a wealthy woman of the Laemmel family, who had donated 50,000 florins in memory of her father, Simon von Laemmel. (The first school in Jerusalem was founded in his memory in the same year.) Dr. Frankl found 6,000 Jews in the Holy City—one third of the total population of the town. Only about 240 of these Jews earned their living as laborers and craftsmen, or as members of the free professions; the remainder were supported by the meagre *Halukkah*-dole.

The 1860s saw the first signs of a movement among the pious Jewish inhabitants of the Old City of Jerusalem to leave their cramped intramural quarters and unproductive existence. Prayers, study of sacred writings and support from *Halukkah* funds did not satisfy some rebels, who dreamed of a

---

* "Halukkah" meant financial support given since the end of the eighteenth century to the members of the Jewish "Ashkenazi" community living in the four holy cities, Jerusalem, Safed, Tiberias and Hebron, thanks to which this community survived until the creation of the new "Yishuv" (the Jewish population in Palestine). The funds were collected by emissaries sent from Palestine overseas for this end.

new productive life of manual work and creation. In 1860, twenty houses were completed in the first housing estate outside the walls, following a plan made by Sir Moses Montefiore* several years earlier. In 1862, the first Jews plucked up courage to leave the Old City and take up residence in these houses. They had to be protected by Arab watchmen from thieves and robbers. In 1873, the first tenants took up residence in the *Nachlat Shiv'a* quarter in Jerusalem, which had been founded in 1869. In the same year, the construction of the *Mea She'arim* quarter began.

In 1869, new kinds of settlers arrived in Palestine. These were no longer Jews who sought first and foremost eternal rest in the sacred soil, but Jews who had grown to maturity in the atmosphere of the Hungarian people's liberation struggle. The emancipation of Hungarian Jews led to an anti-Semitic outbreak; at the same time, the Hungarian government's attempt to impose on Hungarian Jews the authority of the Reform congregations—an assimilationist minority—resulted in a split Hungarian Jewry. A group of Orthodox youth consequently emigrated to Palestine and began exploring the possibilities for a creative life in the Holy Land. In 1878, this group, together with a number of Jews who had been born in the Old City of Jerusalem, was among the founders of the first Jewish agricultural village or colony Petah Tikva. The only agricultural settlement which preceded Petah Tikva was the agricultural school of Mikveh Israel, founded by Charles Netter in 1870 on behalf of Alliance Israelite Universelle.

The Messianic Movements

The Jewish longing for Palestine and for the return to Zion found expression in various Messianic movements throughout the centuries of the Diaspora.

The first of these is generally thought to be the movement founded by Abu 'Issa, who hailed from Ispahan, in Persia. At the end of the seventh century (or, perhaps the middle of the eighth), Abu 'Issa organized and led a group of Babylonian and Persian Jewish warriors determined to march on Palestine in revolt against the Caliph. Eventually the Jewish army was defeated by the Caliph.

The waves of religious enthusiasm in the wake of the Crusades and the clashes between Moslems and Christians also produced "Messiahs" or Messianic heralds among the Jews. During the first half of the twelfth century David Alroy of Kurdistan, placed himself at the head of a company

* A Jewish financier, philanthropist, and initiator of social services in Britain (1784–1885). Was among the first to fight for equality of rights for the Jews in various countries. In 1838 was elected Chairman of the Board of Deputies of British Jews. Held leading positions in the British judicial system. Was an observant Jew, who displayed special love for Palestine, which he visited several times between 1827 and 1875.

of Jews from the Persian mountains that rebelled against the ruler of Persia and was about to conquer Jerusalem. At the request of the Caliph of Baghdad, the supreme Jewish religious leaders exerted pressure on the Jewish rebels to return home. When this failed, they bribed Alroy's son-in-law to murder him.

Shortly afterward, a self-proclaimed Messiah appeared in Yemen; his career is described at length in Maimonides' *Iggeret Teiman* (*Epistle to the Jews of Yemen*). This Messiah was caught and executed shortly after proclaiming his mission. (According to one version of the story, still circulated, he was saved from torture and asked to be beheaded, asserting that he would return again and live once more, this serving as final proof of his Messianic nature.)

The Messianic images and references in the Bible, the Talmud and the Midrashim were reinforced by the development of the Cabbala and proliferated among the Jewish people. Every Messianic movement that arose after the end of the thirteenth century was influenced by the Cabbala.

After the expulsion from Spain in 1492, the Messianic idea continued to be cherished among Jews. In 1502, the "prophet" Rabbi Asher Lamlein appeared in the area of Venice. He proclaimed fasts and announced to the Jews of Italy and Germany that the Messiah's coming was imminent. A large number of Jews declared their support and undertook many acts of charity and repentance. They ceased to work for a livelihood, on the assumption that the final redemption was at hand. Eventually Asher Lamlein was killed, and many of his disillusioned followers abandoned Judaism.

During the first quarter of the sixteenth century, when new scientific discoveries had broadened men's horizons, shaken the foundations of outmoded beliefs and ideas, and served as a stimulus to reformation movements in the West, the Messiah-diplomat David Hareubeni appeared on the scene. He first attracted attention in Italy in 1524, when he appeared wearing the exotic clothes of a "Minister from the Land of the Orient." He spoke a strange Hebrew, which the Italian Jews found difficult to understand, and presented himself as the Minister of War of his brother Joseph, King of the tribe of Reuben, ruler of a Jewish kingdom comprised of the tribes of Reuben and Gad, and the half-tribe of Menashe in the Arabian peninsula. (His tales contained motifs drawn from the legends about the lost Ten Tribes, the Sambatyon River, and other traditional Jewish folklore.)

When Hareubeni succeeded in obtaining an audience with Pope Clemence VII, he explained that he had been sent on a mission to persuade the Christian European nations to attack the Turks, who were oppressing his brother's kingdom. He proposed that the Christian countries, acting in concert with the Reubeni kingdom, should retrieve Palestine from the Turks, who had taken it in 1517, and return it to the Jews.

The Pope's recommendation opened the doors of the court of Portugal to Hareuebeni, and King Juan III received him with great pomp. The fact that the Inquisition was postponed in Portugal because of his visit increased Hareubeni's prestige. Many Portuguese Marranos joined his camp and began to regard him as the Messiah, or at least as a harbinger of their approaching redemption. One of them, a young Marrano named Diego Piras, better known by his Hebrew name of Shlomo Molcho, attained fame for his powerful sermons on esoteric lore and wisdom, and became Hareubeni's assistant. When Hareubeni's hopes were finally shattered on his return to Italy in 1530, he and Molcho decided to travel to Regensburg in Germany to meet Emperor Charles V. The Jewish dignitary closest to the Emperor, Rabbi Yoselman of Rosheim, cautioned them against this step. But they did not heed his counsel. The Emperor ordered them to be arrested. Molcho was sentenced to be burned at the stake, after he had rejected the Emperor's offer to spare him if he would become converted to Christianity. David Hareubeni died in a Spanish prison several years later. His activities, which ceased in 1532, set off waves of disillusionment among European Jews, and prompted many of them to change their religion.

During the second half of the seventeenth century, Messianic hopes suffered a further setback. In 1648 to 1649 the Russian Cossacks, led by the infamous Chmelnicki, massacred many Jews in southern Russia. Many Jews from Poland and the Ukraine were captured by the Cossacks' allies, the Tartars, and sold as slaves in the marketplaces of Salonika, Constantinople, Izmir and other Turkish towns; many of these slaves were ransomed by the Turkish Jews. The Thirty Years' War in central Europe, which ended in 1648, also inflicted ravages on the Jews.

Now a new self-proclaimed Messiah appeared in the person of Shabtai Zvi. This Jew from Izmir was a flamboyant personality who dealt in mystic lore. He traveled to the Holy Land, and then undertook a mission to one of the wealthiest Jews in Egypt. Visiting Gaza in 1665, he met Nathan of Gaza, an energetic and devoted man who later became his aide. This Ashkenazi Jew (Zvi was a Sephardi) was influenced by the mystical ideas originating in Safed. Soon a tremendous and unprecedented Messianic movement began to spread through the whole of the Jewish world. Many Jews in Europe, eastern Asia, Yemen, and North Africa believed that the Messiah was about to appear.

However, Shabtai Zvi was arrested by the Turkish authorities as a rebel against the Ottoman Empire. He was imprisoned in his native city. Eventually he saved his life by becoming converted to Islam. The false Messiah who had aroused such waves of enthusiasm among masses of Jewry became Muhammad Kapiji. The shock of his conversion gave birth to an extreme movement, which considered conversion another form of spiritual redemption. The Dönmeh, an offshoot of Shabtai's group, followed their leader to the end and converted to Islam. The Shabtai Zvi affair had repercussions in the Jewish world for many decades after the false Messiah's conversion.

From Messianic Movements to a Modern National Liberation Movement

In the more distant past the Jews' longings for redemption were of a religious and mystical character, taking the form of waiting for the Messiah, who would be sent by the Almighty in order to redeem the Jewish people from its exile and return it to Zion.

In the nineteenth century, however, a fundamental change occurred in these aspirations: the modern national liberation movement was born. As noted above, even at this stage there is a remarkable resemblance between the development of national movements among the Jewish people and the Arab people. In both cases the origin was a social and cultural awakening and enlightenment movement that soon evolved into a national liberation movement with political aspirations. Among both Jews and Arabs, the movements developed from comparatively small nuclei that had to struggle for a considerable time under adverse political conditions. In both cases, the national liberation movements encountered initial disillusionments and defeats until they gained strength and support among their own people and elsewhere and began making progress towards their cherished goals.

At the same time that emerging internal and international conditions were making it possible for a national movement in the Arab world to develop, a major change took place in the life of the Jewish people, which made possible the realization of aspirations that the Jews had cherished for some two thousand years.

The Jewish people and the Rise of Capitalism

The development of capitalism and the creation of a world market had a dual influence on Jewish life. First, in the pre-capitalist period, the Jews solved the problem of an unfavorable situation in any one country by moving to another (e.g., migration from Rome to Germany, France, and Spain; from western Europe to the Slav lands of eastern Europe; from Spain to the Moslem countries and Holland; from eastern Europe to western Europe and the New World). However, with the spread of the capitalist system, the wheel of the Jewish Diaspora came full circle and the problem took on an international character.

Secondly, the development of communications and the resultant closer contact between various countries created the conditions for more intensive contact among the Jewish communities scattered all over the world. This emphasized the common fate of the homeless Jewish people. At the same time, the potential political props backing up the age-old craving for renewed Jewish independence in the Land of Israel took on new importance. Now the positive aspect of the Diaspora attained expression: the Jews shared not only in the misfortunes of the declining areas, but also in the new possibilities being created in the emerging and progressing regions.

At the end of the eighteenth and the beginning of the nineteenth century strong motives were produced for the migration of masses of Jews from their countries of residence. At the same time, Jews in certain lands enjoyed growing political and economic power. This made it possible in the course of time to direct a growing proportion of these migrants to Palestine and to enable them to strike roots there as a national group. The persecution and oppression of Jews in eastern Europe was paralleled by growing Jewish economic and political strength in those countries. Concurrently, the Jewish masses, particularly the intelligentsia, were greatly influenced by the important political events that took place from the end of the eighteenth century onwards, such as the French Revolution, the Napoleonic Wars, and the emergence of national movements in Europe. Under the influence of the enlightenment movements in Europe,* a similar movement developed among the European Jews in the late eighteenth century. In the nineteenth century, this spread to the eastern European Jewish communities as well.

This Haskalah ("Enlightenment") movement aimed at fostering education among the masses and abolishing the barrier between the Jewish people and other nations, so that civic rights could be won for the Jews. It also represented a revolt against anti-Jewish discrimination and against the persecution of this helpless minority. The Haskalah was also a challenge to conservative and reactionary elements within the Jewish communities, which had consolidated themselves behind the protective walls of the ghetto and wished to prevent new ideas and the light of secular culture, education, and freedom penetrating to the masses. The Haskalah movement brought about a revival of secular Hebrew literature and a flowering of Jewish thought.

The Haskalah Movement and "Hibbat Zion"

The second half of the nineteenth century saw the rise of other national movements and the renaissance of a number of large and small nations in the wake of the rise of European capitalism and the gradual disintegration of the Ottoman Empire. The Jewish Haskalah movement, too, began to take on the

* A movement in European countries during the rise of capitalism that strove for "the rule of reason" in political and judicial affairs, science, and literature, and fought against prejudice and superstition, rejecting absolute rule and the authority of the Church in the sphere of secular life.

nature of a national movement, deriving its main driving force from the deep-rooted springs of Jewish history: the dream of redemption from exile, the revival of the nation's life in its historic homeland, a return to the land and to nature, the revival of Hebrew culture, and similar goals. Among the masses of the Jewish people, the vision of national redemption was inseparably linked with longings for a society based on justice and moral values, such as had been conceived and foreseen by the ancient Hebrew prophets.

These aspirations, which for many generations had borne a religious, mystic character, took on a secular nature as a result of the *Haskalah* movement and its political and economic ideas.

These ideas first attained clear and vigorous expression in the writings of the socialist thinker and organizer Moses Hess (1812–1875). His book, *Rome and Jerusalem* (1862), came out strongly against the concept of Jewish assimilationism, which was favored by part of the Jewish intelligentsia. Hess called for the reconstruction of Jewish life in the only place in the world where this was possible: the ancient homeland of Palestine.

At the beginning of the 1870s, a vehement struggle of ideas was being waged among the large Jewish communities of eastern Europe. This struggle took place on two fronts: on the one hand against medieval ideas and in favor of enlightenment and knowledge, and on the other hand, against the spiritual slavery and intellectual sterility of assimilation, and in favor of a modern national life, liberated from religious domination. In the 1870s this struggle was led by the author and essayist Peretz Smolenskin (1840–1845), whose Hebrew monthly *Hashahar* ("The Dawn"), which appeared between 1868 and 1886, gathered around it the best forces in the revived Hebrew literature and exerted a powerful influence on those of the Jewish youth who had first received a traditional education and were then swept up by the *Haskalah* movement. These circles became the principal supporters of the *Hibbat Zion* (Love of Zion) movement.

Hibbat Zion was consistently propagated by the Hebrew periodicals that were intended largely for the Jewish community in Czarist Russia, which at that time also included Poland, Lithuania, and Bessarabia (although some of the periodicals were in fact published outside Russia). The most important of these were *Hamaggid* ("The Messenger"), a weekly published in Lyck (eastern Prussia) between 1856 and 1890, the full title of which was *Hamaggid, a chronicle of events, which will inform the children of Jacob of happenings in all parts of the world among all the inhabitants of the earth, and which will entertain and instruct every son of Israel—for his edification and the sake of the beautiful Hebrew tongue*; *Hacarmel* ("Mount Carmel"), published in Vilna from 1860 to 1871 as a weekly, and then appearing as a monthly until 1890, with appendices in Russian and German (*a periodical letter to the sons of Israel in the holy tongue, with appendices in the Russian and German languages*); and *Hammeylitz* ("The

D

Preacher"), which appeared as a weekly for forty-three years (1860–1904) with occasional intervals, first in Odessa and then in St. Petersburg. After the Kattowitz conference (1885) *Hammeylitz* became the principal advocate of the *Hibbat Zion* movement.

Hatzfirah ("The Clarion") was first published in 1862, but after twenty-five issues it was banned by the authorities and did not resume publication until 1873. For the next thirteen years, it appeared as a weekly, and then as a daily paper. It was published in Warsaw until World War I, after which it appeared in a new format in Palestine. In 1896, the influential monthly *Hashiloah* began appearing in Berlin. From there it was transferred to Odessa, where it appeared until World War I. From 1923 to 1927, *Hashiloah* was published in Palestine. The first Hebrew newspaper in Palestine was *Halevanon* ("The Lebanon"), which commenced publication in Jerusalem in 1863, the editors being Yehiel Brill, Michael Hacohen, and Yoel Moshe Solomon. *Havatzelet* ("Rose of Sharon"), edited by Israel Beck (who founded Jerusalem's first Hebrew printing press in 1841), Michael Hacohen, and Israel Dov Frumkin, was published in 1870. This newspaper appeared for forty-one years.*

The First Aliyah

As we have noted, the "old Yishuv"—the Jewish community that existed in Palestine at the end of the 1880s—was formed of individuals or small groups whose *Aliyah* (literally, "ascent") to *Eretz Israel* was prompted by purely religious motives. Only at the end of the nineteenth century did a new wave of immigration begin, motivated, not by the desire to pray at the holy places and be buried in the land of their forefathers, but by the desire to establish a creative, productive Jewish community rooted in the soil and capable of renewing its national life. These settlers came from eastern Europe. Their arrival opened a new chapter in the history of the Jewish people.

In 1881, the assassination of Czar Alexander II set off a wave of bloody pogroms against the Russian Jews. In response to the rise of the Socialist movement, and with the intention of diverting the masses' attention from the actions of the corrupt Czarist regime, reactionary Russian circles launched a campaign of agitation against the Jews. These events greatly stimulated the rise of nationalist feelings among the masses of Jews and strengthened the *Hibbat Zion* movement. Peretz Smolenskin, the leading *Haskalah* figure, M. L. Lilienblum (1843–1910), and other public figures placed themselves at the head of the movement, which gave rise to the *Bilu* society. The *Bilu*

---

* It is interesting to note that there is a surprising similarity between the Hebrew press and the Arabic press in terms of the times of their beginnings and in their stages of development.

took its name from the Hebrew initials of the Biblical phrase, "House of Jacob, let us arise and go." The movement had a total membership of 525 in Russia.

The arrival of the initial *Bilu* group, comprised of fourteen men and one woman, in 1882 opened the *first Aliyah* (wave of immigration), which brought approximately 25,000 Jewish settlers to Palestine in the next twenty-two years; these included *Hibbat Zion* pioneers and other groups of settlers from Russia and Rumania. Most of these settlers took up agriculture, and founded the first *moshavot* (villages based on farming). However, not all the settlers were able to stand up to the conditions of the new life, and to overcome the many obstacles encountered on their way to the attainment of their dream. Those who had the strength to stand firm, with the encouragement of the *Lovers of Zion* in the Diaspora and the considerable help given by Baron Edmond de Rothschild (who had been persuaded by *Hibbat Zion* emissaries to aid Jewish settlement in Palestine from as early as 1883),* laid the foundation of the new Jewish settlements in Palestine.

The first wave of immigrants (1882–1884) laid the foundations of the earliest *moshavot*: Rishon Lezion, Zikhron Ya'akov, Rosh Pina (1882), Nes Ziona, 'Ekron, Yesod Hama'ala, Gedera (1883–1884); Petah Tikva was founded in 1878, but faced a crisis soon afterwards, and recovered only when it absorbed new immigrants in 1883. To these first *moshavot* were soon added a number of other settlements, founded mainly by the second wave of immigrants in the 1890s: Rehovot and Mishmar Hayarden (1890), Hadera, Shfeya, Bat-Shlomo, 'Ain Zeitim (1891), Hartuv (1895), Metulla and Be'er Tuvia (1896). The Sejera farm was founded in 1899, and 1901 to 1904 saw the founding of the first *moshavot* in Lower Galilee: the *moshava* of Sejera, Kfar Tabor, Menahemiya, Yavniel, and Bet Gan. The first railway line between Jaffa and Jerusalem, in 1892 improved communications between the two main towns and stimulated the country's economy and social life, which began stirring once more after generations of stagnation.

Baron de Rothschild's officials found ways and means of ensuring the Turkish government's goodwill. However, Baron de Rothschild's support of the growing *Yishuv* in Palestine also carried weighty political significance at that time. The Turkish Empire, which was in the throes of a severe economic crisis and at the mercy of its debtors, could not ignore the House of Rothschild's influence in international finance, and was forced to behave with

---

* According to a conservative estimate, Baron de Rothschild invested £1,600,000 in settlement projects in Palestine from 1883 to 1899 as against the £87,000 invested by *Hovevei Zion* from all countries. Even if we add the capital of the settlers themselves, these sums would not equal the investments of the Baron. Even after the settlement projects were taken over in 1900 by the ICA (later on the PICA), Baron de Rothschild continued to give them generous support (see note on p. 62, Chapter Three).

due consideration toward the settlements that he had placed under his patronage.*

As a result of the first *Aliyah*, the *Yishuv* grew to approximately 50,000 people; of these, about 28,000 lived in Jerusalem, 3,000 in Jaffa, 6,000 in the twenty agricultural settlements, and the remainder in Tiberias, Safed, Haifa, and other places. The area of land acquired by the Jewish settlers approached 400,000 *dunams* (a *dunam* is one-quarter of an acre), including 90,000 in Transjordan. Side by side with the old *Yishuv*, whose horizons, founded on the *Halukkah* system seemed so narrow and limited, a new dynamic *Yishuv* was growing up, created out of a desire for a revival of Jewish life and based on a healthy economic outlook, national culture, a new pattern of social life and democratic political conceptions linked to the idea of national independence.

An expression of the wellsprings of the new *Yishuv* was given by the first conference of Palestinian Jews, held at the initiative of M. M. Ussishkin in Zikhron Ya'akov in 1903. The sixty-seven delegates elected an executive board, which decided to establish its headquarters in Jaffa.

Revival of the Hebrew Language

The hope of Jewish redemption and the revival of the ancient, little-used Hebrew language were always closely linked. In addition to the *Hovevei Zion* (Lovers of Zion) movement, various branches of a society named *Lovers of an Ancient Tongue* were also founded at the end of the nineteenth century. They produced a group of determined people who began to take action in order to revive the language of the Bible and stimulate its use in everyday life.† One of the leaders of this movement, Eliezer Ben-Yehuda (Perlman) (1858–1922), came to Palestine in 1882. He settled in Jerusalem and devoted his entire life to the practical implementation of this vision, at first in his own home and then among his immediate circle. His activities, which were later conducted with the help of idealistic teachers and other cultural organizers, encountered strong opposition from the old *Yishuv*, which considered the everyday use of Hebrew a desecration of the sacred tongue. Gradually the foundation of the present Hebrew cultural renaissance was laid.‡

* As Kalvarisky (see Chapter Three) remarked: "The Baron's officials, who enjoyed much prestige in Palestine, often protected the farmers against the tyranny of the Turkish officials. In some instances the Baron's officials were able to oust regional governors from their posts, when they began oppressing the Jews too much." Naturally incidents like these made a considerable impression on the Jewish farmers' Arab neighbors.

† The *Arabia-l-Fatat* (Young Arab) Society, among the first Arab national associations, which in the course of time was to play an important role in the Arab national movement, also had its beginnings in the *An-Natikin Biddad* (Arabic-language-speaking) association.

‡ Ben-Yehuda compiled the first modern Hebrew dictionary (seventeen volumes).

The protracted struggle for the revival of the Hebrew language and literature became one of the chief bones of contention between the old *Yishuv* and the new settlers.

The first Hebrew school in which the Hebrew-in-Hebrew method of teaching was employed was founded by Ben-Yehuda in Jerusalem in 1903. In addition to its use in Bible study, Hebrew was taught as a modern language. At the end of the 1880s, the schools in the *moshavot* also began teaching Hebrew, despite the opposition of Baron de Rothschild's officials to its replacing French. Most of the teachers came from the ranks of the settlers and had not received any specialized training. In 1892, the first conference of Hebrew teachers took place, at which a curriculum was established and Hebrew terms approved for use in various subjects.

During all these years the old *Yishuv* continued its campaign against the revival of Hebrew. In 1894, these circles informed the Turkish authorities that Ben-Yehuda had called for a rebellion, after the journal *Hatsvi* had published an article of his on the occasion of Hanukkah (the Feast of Lights) in which he praised the Maccabeans' heroism and proposed reviving the festival's national content. *Hatsvi* was closed by the authorities, and Ben-Yehuda was arrested. He was found guilty of incitement to revolution, and sentenced to a year's imprisonment. The branding of Ben-Yehuda as a rebel against the Ottoman Empire did considerable political harm to Jewish activities in Palestine. The affair aroused the *Lovers of Zion*, and even Baron de Rothschild intervened on Ben-Yehuda's behalf. Two months after his arrest his appeal was heard, and he was released.

Professor A. S. Yahuda (see Chapter Three, page 65) thinks that the orthodox Jews persecuted Ben-Yehuda because of his opposition to the *Halukkah* rather than because of his support of colloquial Hebrew. The *Sephardi* (Oriental) Jews needed the Hebrew language, which was alive not only among their rabbis but also among educated circles as the common tongue of Jews from Aleppo and Salonika, Morocco, and Bukhara, etc.

In 1903, the Association of Hebrew Teachers was founded, with the aim of promoting Hebrew education in Palestine. By this time the children of the new *Yishuv* were being taught in Hebrew. As for the adults, few of them made an effort to speak Hebrew. Most of them continued speaking the languages with which they were familiar: Yiddish, Ladino, or Arabic. The intelligentsia spoke Russian or French.

The importance of Hebrew in the Jewish renaissance can be ascertained from Arthur Ruppin's reminiscences of his first visit to Israel in 1907 (*Passages in My Life*, II). When visiting a Hebrew kindergarten in Jerusalem, he noted that the parents of the children spoke thirteen languages among them. It was clear to Ruppin that a united Jewish nation needed a common language. This could not be one of the European tongues, as there would be intense and prolonged competition among the advocates of French, Russian, German, and English. "I came to the conclusion," Ruppin wrote, "that it was absolutely essential to introduce Hebrew into the schools."

From Hibbat Zion to Political Zionism

The *Hibbat Zion* movement continued to develop. Leo Pinsker (1823–1891) exerted great influence on the movement's ideological evolution through his pamphlet, *Auto-Emancipation* (first published in German in 1882, and later in Hebrew and Russian). This work was the strongest expression of the change in thinking on the part of the Russian Jewish intelligentsia, following the rising tide of anti-Semitism and pogroms. Instead of considering assimilation a solution to the Jewish national problem, these circles came to feel that the only positive solution was the Jewish people's national revival and the consolidation of its life in its own country. Pinsker placed the emphasis on the nation's independent efforts and "auto-emancipation," as against the emancipation which had been, or would be, granted to the Jews living outside Palestine. He also made clear the distinction between "national emancipation" and the "civil emancipation" that was being demanded by various Jews at the time.

During the last decade of the nineteenth century, the *Hibbat Zion* movement in eastern Europe established contact with the thinkers in western and central Europe who had taken up the concept of a national renaissance. It was from these circles that Theodor Herzl (1860–1904) came. He proposed the establishment of a Jewish state that would solve the Jewish problem and eradicate the nation's economic and spiritual problems.

However, Herzl was not only a visionary of Jewish national renewal. As a far-reaching social reformer, he saw in the return of the Jews to manual work, and in particular to the land—a condition of national redemption. His anti-clerical stand and his aspirations for social equality, gave him an image of a humanist who was not satisfied only with the return of the Jews to their Homeland but saw Zionism as a moral and spiritual entity.

In Herzl's opinion, the origin of the Jews' problems lay not in external hatred but in their own way of life, in the nation's dispersion and in its economic structure, which compelled it to compete with the inhabitants of the countries in which it lived. The larger the number of Jews in any given country, the greater the competition and the accompanying hatred and suffering. But when Jews leave the lands in which they suffer and move on to other countries, they merely take the Jewish problem with them. Herzl held that political reforms and social changes are unable to eradicate the Jewish problem, because it is inherent in the Jewish way of life. Assimilation can solve the problem of a small number of individuals, but the whole nation cannot and does not want to assimilate. The Jewish question, he concluded, is not a religious or social one, but a *national* one. It would therefore be essential to find a national solution to the problem of the Jewish masses who did not want to assimilate or could not do so. Only the re-establishment of the Jewish people in its own country, he felt, would make it equal to other nations and end the Jews' wanderings over the face of the earth.

Herzl's lucid analysis and daring conclusions, and his concrete proposals for their implementation (particularly in his book, *The Jewish State* published in 1896), aroused powerful reactions in both western and eastern Europe, and prepared the ground for the First World Zionist Congress, which met in Basle in August 1897, under Herzl's chairmanship. The Basle congress was attended by delegates representing the entire Diaspora. The congress formulated the program of the World Zionist Organization in the following terms:

"The aim of Zionism is to create for the Jewish people a home in Palestine secured by public law.*

"In order to attain this object the Congress adopts the following means:

"1. The systematic promotion of the settlement of Palestine with Jewish agriculturists, artisans, and craftsmen.

"2 The organization and federation of all Jewry by means of local and general institutions in conformity with the local laws.

"3. The strengthening of Jewish sentiment and national consciousness.

"4. Preparatory steps for the procuring of such Government assents as are necessary for achieving the object of Zionism."

The World Zionist Organization was charged with carrying out the great task of renewing Jewish national life in Palestine. This organization soon began to respond to the throbbing pulse of the Diaspora, even though for the first few years after the First Congress its practical work in Palestine was limited and experimental.

"Spiritual Center" or "Territorial Concentration"?

The organized Zionist movement that was founded at the beginning of the twentieth century lacked a broad base. Within Zionism, the influence of "spiritual Zionism" was at that time considerable. This school of thought, founded by Ahad Ha'am (1856–1927), held that the entire Jewish migration

---

* There was considerable discussion before agreement was reached on the original German text, "*öffentlich-rechlich gesicherte Heimstätte.*" A number of delegates insisted upon the term "*völkerrechtlich*" ("according to international law") to signify the distinction between the new political Zionism and the previous colonization activity, but as that was thought to impinge upon the independence of the Ottoman Empire, a compromise was reached in the term "*öffentlich-rechtlich*" ("according to public law"), which was meant to convey that the Jewish Home should be guaranteed by the constitution of the Ottoman Empire.

of about a million people from greater Russia (in which lived about six million Jews) fell below the rate of natural increase of the Russian Jews over a period of thirty years. Hence, they concluded, the Jewish emigration movement (directed at that time towards North America) would be unable to change the specific nature of the large Russian Jewish community and would not solve the Jewish problem. For this reason, the main purpose of the Zionist enterprise appeared to them to be the establishment of an exemplary "spiritual center" for the mass of Jews, the great majority of whom would continue to live in the Diaspora.

This view also seemed justified by formidable difficulties facing the realization of the Zionist idea during its initial stages in Palestine: the obstacles facing urban Jews who became farmers, and the problems of renewing an independent national Jewish existence, after so many centuries of decadent Diaspora life. For the intelligentsia and middle class, who constituted the overwhelming majority of the Zionist movement at that time, the concept of a "spiritual center" was a convenient remedy for their failure to carry out the idea of personal self-realization, which was inherent in Zionism from the very beginning.

The dynamics of urban Jewish life, the process of Jewish emigration in general and of territorial concentration in Palestine in particular, and the normalization of the Jewish people's national and social life—this was the subject matter of the pioneering theoretical work undertaken by Ber Borochov (1881–1917), the outstanding theoretician of the Jewish national movement's socialist wing. Borochov's was a Marxist analysis of the Jewish problem opposing the ideas advanced by the *Bund*—a Jewish socialist group which negated Zionism. Borochov rejected the concept of "social and national autonomy on an individual basis," which the *Bund* favored, and unequivocally supported national independence on a territorial basis. The Russian revolutionaries, under the influence of their comrades among the assimilated Jewish intelligentsia and of slogans from the bourgeois revolution, refused to recognize the existence of a Jewish nation; Borochov set out to prove that this was an anti-historical and anti-Marxist view and that territorial concentration in Palestine was the only answer to the Jewish dilemma. He and his followers argued that Palestine's capacity to absorb (as testified by the distant past, although it was currently thinly populated), its conditions of production, its geographical situation, its historical and spiritual links with world Jewry, as well as the fairly successful beginning of the settlement work—all these and other historical factors made Eretz Israel (Palestine) the most suitable country for the task of Zionist realization.

Borochov's teachings served as the basis of the Poalei Zion movement, which became a major factor in the Zionist movement's labor and socialist wing.

The Second Aliyah

From 1904 on, a new type of Jewish settler began to arrive in Palestine. This was the period of the second *Aliyah* (1904–1914), which brought approximately 40,000 Jews to the country before World War I. Most of these young Zionist immigrants were imbued with the ideals of labor and of national and social Jewish renaissance.

In April 1908, the Palestine Bureau was opened in Jaffa, under the directorship of Arthur Ruppin (1876–1943), and the Zionist movement's practical settlement work began. Ruppin embarked upon his activities virtually without funds or legal power, in a country controlled by the authoritarian Turkish government. After completing an initial tour of inspection in Palestine in 1907, Ruppin recommended that the World Zionist Organization set up a Settlement Company, whose function would be to acquire land in town and country for parcellation and allocation to individuals, as a means of enabling private capital to take part in the country's development.

The company's capital was to have been £50,000. However, only one-tenth of this sum was actually raised. This £5,000, and another £10,000 collected by the Jewish National Fund from contributions made for planting trees in Palestine, was all that could be made available to Ruppin in 1908 to finance Jewish settlement in Palestine.

The Zionist movement's financial instruments—the Jewish Colonial Trust and the Jewish National Fund, which were founded in 1902—were not under the control of the Palestine Bureau. The Jewish National Fund had raised not more than £75,000, £30,000 of which was invested in purchasing land and lending money to various institutions. The Fund's board of directors originally decided to keep most of the income in reserve, and not to spend it until a larger sum of money accumulated. As for the Jewish Colonial Trust, in 1908 it had a paid-up capital of £225,000, of which £36,000 was invested in the Anglo-Palestine Bank in Jaffa and another £15,000 in the Anglo-Levantine Banking Company. The Trust's board of directors opposed risking this money in direct investments in Palestine, and gave all too few money grants-in-aid to settlement projects.

When World War I broke out in 1914, the population of the *Yishuv* was 85,000. The area of land acquired by the Jews of Palestine was 420,000 *dunams* (of which 16,000 belonged to the Jewish National Fund). The new Jewish colonies, including those supported by Baron de Rothschild, numbered no more than forty-four altogether, and they had only 12,000 inhabitants. Jewish industrial production did not total even £500,000 annually. However, even these modest beginnings hinted at the vitality and effectiveness of the Zionist idea: a new type of Jewish village was emerging and the first cells of a Jewish working class in the Land of Israel were being formed; Hebrew was a living language again; living blood was beginning to flow through the veins of the Jewish national liberation movement.

Striving for Official Status

Under the Ottoman regime, Jewish immigration and settlement were without any legal foundation. Herzl's efforts to secure such a basis by a charter* from the Turkish Sultan proved unsuccessful, as did his no less strenuous efforts to obtain the German Kaiser's patronage for Jewish settlement work in Palestine.

In 1903, the British government offered Dr. Herzl a 5,000-square-mile tract of land in the British colony of Uganda, in East Africa. Herzl was facing great difficulties in Palestine and was eager to find a territory to which Jews who were forced to emigrate could do so without delay. He proposed to the Sixth Zionist Congress that the Uganda offer be accepted as a temporary solution ("a night shelter"), without surrendering the ultimate goal of Palestine. A vehement struggle ensued in the Zionist camp over the Uganda proposal. The "Zionists of Zion" faction was formed, under the leadership of Menahem Ussishkin (1863–1941). This group opposed the Uganda plan even as a provisional arrangement. A committee sent to Africa to examine the details of the British proposal reached negative conclusions about its feasibility, and it was finally rejected by the Seventh Congress in 1907.

Some of the delegates at that congress, led by Israel Zangwill, left the Zionist Organization and founded the Territorial Movement, which aimed at finding other territories as a place of refuge for Jewish emigrants. As late as the 1920s, this organization was still trying to find territories other than Palestine, with the support of wealthy Jews and even some European governments. But all these efforts proved fruitless.

Despite the small dimensions of Jewish immigration to and settlement in Palestine, the Turkish authorities viewed with disfavor the increase in the number of foreign nationals, who were exempt from Turkish law by virtue of the "Capitulations." The foreign consuls frequently used the presence of these foreign nationals in order to intervene in Turkey's domestic affairs. The Jewish settlers, most of whom came from Russia, were in no hurry to cut off their ties with the land of their birth and surrender the protection of their consuls by adapting Turkish nationality, with all that this implied.

Jewish Representations to the Sultan

The political terms that the Zionist leaders wished to obtain from the Turkish Sultan on the eve of his deposition were extremely modest: the immigration

---

* A government document (an official basic declaration) permitting a company to settle a specific district.

within twenty-five years of 50,000 families from Russia, Rumania, and Galicia, to the provinces of Damascus and Beirut (which included Samaria, Galilee, and most of Transjordan), and the *Sandjak* (district) of Jerusalem, excluding Jerusalem itself and other holy places in the *Sandjak*; the allocation of "the Sultan's lands" (state domains) for the settlement of these immigrants, according to the decision of a committee comprised of an equal representation of Turkish officials and Jewish spokesmen; municipal or local self-government for settlers, who would become nationalized Turkish subjects; and exemption from taxes during the twenty-five years duration of the immigration.

However, the Sultan's deposition by the "Young Turks," who were soon to become unfriendly to Zionist aspirations, defeated even that modest program.

The "Young Turks" in Power

The Young Turks, who deposed the Sultan and announced their intention of turning Turkey into a constitutional, secular State instead of an authoritarian Moslem theocracy, at first took a fairly favorable attitude toward the arrival of Jewish settlers. The leaders of the "Union and Progress" Party, which formed the new Turkish government, even issued unofficial invitations to Jews to settle in Turkey, which needed their presence and skills. At first, the new regime adopted a sympathetic approach to the Zionist movement in the hope that it would organize Jewish immigration to Turkey, to the benefit of both sides.

However, the more determined the new leaders became to preserve the Ottoman Empire and the centralized government, and to adopt a policy of "Turkifying" the non-Turkish peoples, the more suspicious they became of Zionist aspirations in Palestine. The Young Turks wanted to integrate the Jewish settlers all over the widespread Ottoman Empire, particularly in places where they hoped they would weaken the growing nationalist demands made by various groups that had been suppressed by the sultans. If the Jews had been scattered all over the Empire they could strengthen the Turkish rulers; but Jewish concentration in Palestine would only add another people to the list of those who were demanding autonomy from Constantinople—a demand that, to the Young Turks, was another nail in the coffin of the Empire.

CHAPTER THREE

JEWS AND ARABS UNDER THE
OTTOMAN REGIME

When the first *Aliyah* came to Palestine, the country formed part of the Turkish Empire. According to the administrative arrangement laid down in 1862 ("on the French model"), the entire Ottoman Empire was divided into *vilayets,* or major provinces. The *vilayets* were in turn divided into *sandjaks,* or districts, and these into *kadhas,* or subdistricts. Each of these administrative units was headed by an official of appropriate rank. But all these officials were subject to the authority of the "Supreme Porte," or central government in Constantinople.

From an administrative standpoint, Palestine was divided into the following regions:

In the north of the country—the *sandjaks* of Acre (including Haifa, Nazareth, Tiberias, and Safed) and Nablus (Shechem, including Jenin and Tulkarm), which were part of the Beirut *vilayet.*

In the south—the Jerusalem *sandjak* consisted of Jerusalem, Jaffa, Gaza, Hebron, Beersheba, and el-Hafir. Because of this *sandjak's* special status (due to the presence of holy places in the Jerusalem area, which attracted thousands of pilgrims and foreign tourists), it was placed directly under the supervision of the central government in Constantinople. It, together with other districts of significant political importance, was given a special status by the Sublime Porte, which selected competent senior officials as its governors. Transjordan was divided into two *sandjaks:* the Hauran in the north and Amman in the south. Both of them were subject to the Damascus *vilayet.*

The Arab population (within the borders of what became mandated British territory including Trans-Jordan after World War I) numbered about half a million at the end of the nineteenth century. As noted earlier, the Jewish population had been doubled by the first *Aliyah* (1882–1903) and reached 40,000.

Abd-ul-Hamid's Rule

The rule of Sultan Abd-ul-Hamid (1886–1908) gave the inhabitants of Palestine little feeling that an orderly administration was at work. Like all the millions of Arabs in the Turkish Empire, the Arab population of Palestine

44

lacked not only national or political autonomy, but also the most elementary cultural and national rights, such as Arabic-language schools, and recognition of Arabic as an official language. Most of the Jews living in Palestine were still citizens of the countries from which they had come, and enjoyed the benefit of the "capitulations,"* as did other foreign nationals, such as the Christian missionaries and the German Templars.† Because of this special status and their protection by foreign consulates, the Jews enjoyed internal cultural autonomy (schools run by the community with a Hebrew curriculum, Hebrew periodicals, etc.), and even a certain degree of municipal and communal autonomy. The *Hacham Bashi*, or Chief Rabbi of the Sephardic and Oriental communities—who were considered by Constantinople to be loyal subjects—was given a status equal to that of the other non-Moslem religious leaders. His residence was guarded by a Turkish soldier in full uniform. When Eliezer Ben-Yehuda saw the status accorded the *Hacham Bashi*, he gained a glimpse of "the glitter of Jewish authority, of Jewish rule."

Effects of the First Aliyah

The Jewish community of Palestine at the start of the first *Aliyah* was purely

* An agreement between the subjugated (dependent) countries of the East and the capitalist states, guaranteeing unilateral civil and political privileges to the citizens of the latter (the right of their subjects resident in countries of the Ottoman Empire to trial by the consuls of their own countries and not by the Turkish courts, even in cases of disputes between an Ottoman subject and a subject of a foreign power; exemption from certain taxes; the right to special services, even exterritorial postal service, etc.). The capitulations were originally granted by Ottoman Turkey on the sultan's own initiative, first to Genoa and Venice, then to France (1575), to England (1580), and to Holland (1612). When the Turkish empire was at the height of its power, the capitulations discriminated against foreigners. However, as the Empire grew weaker, this situation changed: foreigners ostracized in the past now enjoyed privileges that the sultan was forced to grant. According to a treaty in 1740 between Sultan Mahmud I and King Louis XV, France was granted not only special immunity for its diplomatic personnel and traders in Turkey but also special privileges for French sailors, artisans, and missionaries in the countries under Ottoman rule. Subsequently, similar rights were obtained by other European countries also. The capitulations were no longer voluntarily granted, but were forced upon the Ottomans by the rulers of more powerful countries. They remained in force until after World War I, when they were gradually rescinded.

† The Templars ("Sons of the Temple"): Members of a Christian sect founded in 1854 in southern Germany. Their first settlers arrived in Palestine in 1868, and set up their quarters in Jerusalem, Jaffa, and Haifa, and in the agricultural settlements of Sarona, Wilhelmina, and Bethlehem (Galilee). By the end of the nineteenth century, the German community in Palestine numbered 1,500 persons: some of them had established exemplary farms, others were among the most skilled in technical trades in the country, still others were doctors, engineers, hotel owners, etc. They were so well organized that the community later served as a prop in the efforts of Kaiser Wilhelm of Germany to establish a foothold in the Middle East.

urban. Half of the community was Sephardic, or Oriental, and the other half
Ashkenazi, or European.

As Kalvarisky* noted in one of his writings:

Among the Ashkenazis it was considered almost shameful not to receive money
from the Halukkah. Among the Sephardic community it was only Hahams, or sages,
who received Halukkah funds. It is easy to understand that the Ashkenazi communities,
who did not speak the language of the country, were not familiar with its life, and
were as far removed from the manners and customs of the East as Lithuania, Poland
and Hungary were from the Middle East, had hardly any contact with the Arab
inhabitants of Palestine. The Jews lived in special neighborhoods and ghettos and spoke
the languages to which they were accustomed. Nothing led them to establish any
relationship with the indigenous population. In their eyes the Arabs were the Ishmae-
lites who brought fruit and vegetables, fish and other products to the market; but
what could they have in common with these people? From their standpoint, the Jews
and Arabs lived in completely different worlds. The Sephardim, on the other hand,
invariably spoke Arabic, and in the course of their work or commerce had business
connection with the Arabs and sometimes went into partnership with them. The
relations between the Sephardic Jews and the Arabs were good, and many Jews and
Arabs became firm friends. The Arabs invited the Jews to their homes on Moslem
feast days, and vice versa.

The new Jewish settlers, particularly those who turned to farming,
found the reality of Palestine—a difficult climate, disease and malaria, poor,
dry and impoverished soil, an almost complete absence of roads and communications, a cruel and arbitrary regime—harsh and uncompromising.
But one of the chief surprises awaiting the *Lovers of Zion* who immigrated to
Palestine was the fact that it was populated. They had been under the impression that it was empty and uninhabited, and that if there were any local
residents, they were so primitive that they could be ignored. However, on
arrival they found Arabs, some of whom were shrewd, intelligent townsmen
who controlled most of the country's commerce and trade, but the majority
of whom were farmers whose standard of living was low and whose methods
of cultivation were indeed primitive, but who were spread out over the whole
of the country.

Moshe Smilansky, in one of his historical essays,† wrote:

* Haim Margalit-Kalvarisky (1868–1947): Born in Russia. Completed his studies in
agronomy in France, and settled in Palestine in 1895. From 1899 to 1923, was head of the
executive of "the Baron's colonies" in Galilee. After World War I, was a member of the
National Council of Palestine Jews. A member of the Zionist Executive. Devoted many
years to seeking ways toward understanding and agreement between the Jews and the
Arabs, and was in the forefront of various organizations and associations created for this
purpose. From 1939 until his death, was head of the "League for Jewish-Arab rapprochement and cooperation" (see Chapter Seven).

† Moshe Smilansky (1874–1953): a native of the Ukraine. Came to Palestine in 1891;
became an agricultural worker and one of the founding settlers of Hadera, and later a

From the very first day, the indigenous population took a suspicious attitude towards the new settlers. At all times and in every country the old established population is suspicious of new arrivals, especially if the native population has a relatively primitive way of life and feels itself weak and powerless to resist the new immigrants, who, they fear, will disinherit them. Further, the local population felt contempt for the members of the "infidel" people, whom God had exiled from their native lands because of their sins. A community of "children of death"—this is how the Arabs regarded the miserable, poor and pitiful Jews who lived in the four holy cities: Jerusalem, Hebron, Tiberias, and Safed.

The new settlers reached Palestine on the crest of a wave of enthusiastic idealism, which inspired them with a powerful longing to feel the physical presence of the land. They adapted themselves to the climate, the soil, the lack of water, the poor communications, and to the Turkish regime. But they did not find a common language with the Arab inhabitants. Their contact with their Arab neighbors was barred by differences in language and ways of life. Many of the clashes between members of the two communities, particularly during the early years after the colonies were established, took place because of ignorance of the Arabs' language, customs and manners. For instance, D. Shub, one of the founders of Yesod Hama'ala, relates in his memoirs a tragic incident in the settlement in 1900. Sheikh Maghribi, who had come down from Safed to stay at the village of At-Tallil, near the *moshava*, came to the Jewish colony with several of his men in order to see the rose garden planted by Baron de Rothschild's gardeners. When the sheikh and his party stepped on the beds and damaged some bushes, the Jewish gardener shouted at them, hurling at them Arabic curses whose precise meaning he did not understand. The insulted sheikh beat the gardener with his stick, but one of the Jewish workers who arrived on the scene hit the sheikh and seriously injured him. The sheikh's companions summoned the villagers of At-Tallil, who rushed to the scene and attacked the Jews. The people of the *moshava* barricaded themselves in a large building and sent an urgent message to the authorities in Safed asking for help. It was only after the intervention of the sheikh from a nearby village that the incensed fellaheen agreed not to massacre the handful of Jewish settlers. The injured sheikh died of his wounds. The gardener was forced to leave the *moshava*. Only with the help of one of Baron de Rothschild's officials in Galilee an end was put to the feud between the settlers of Yesod Hama'ala and their Arab neighbors;

farmer in Rehovot. At the time of the second Aliyah, was close to labor circles and a regular contributor to *Hapoel Hatzair*; at a later stage, was active in farmers' circles and, for a time, head of the National Farmers' Association. A talented writer (among his finest works are his stories of Arab life, under the pseudonym Hawadja Mussa). Had wide contacts with the Arab public and was one of the leading participants in endeavors to achieve understanding and cooperation between the Jews and Arabs.

Palestine in the period of Turkish Rule (from the Peel Report)

this resolution was symbolized by the dead sheikh's son being appointed the watchman of the *moshava*.

The attack in 1892 on Rehovot by the Arabs of Zarnuka was caused by a similar misunderstanding. The leading sheikh of the village came to the Rehovot council to lodge a complaint. There he met a young man "who was not familiar with the custom of the country, namely, that even an opponent must be received in a hospitable fashion, and reprimanded the sheikh." (Moshe Smilansky, *Rehovot*). The humiliated sheikh, who harbored a grudge against the colony, summoned his fellow-villagers of Zarnuka to redeem his violated honor.

Each wave of immigration gradually acquired an understanding of the Arab way of life and learned Arabic in the course of time. This led to better relations with their Arab neighbors. But then a new wave of immigration would arrive, bringing settlers wholly unfamiliar with Arab customs and conduct, who had to acquire this experience all over again.

The First Twenty Years

In a country without adequate security, as Palestine was in those days, ambushes and attacks on passers-by or robberies of isolated houses were everyday occurrences. All the country's inhabitants, regardless of creed, suffered from this plague. There were frequent land and grazing disputes between the Jewish colonies and their Arab neighbors. These often led to attacks on the new settlers working in the fields, or raids directed against the whole settlement. But, according to the official *Chronicles of the Hagana*, "the Arab practice of avoiding bloodshed, added to their fear of involving their families and villages in a quarrel with the Turkish government and the foreign consuls, led to relatively few cases of murder being committed against members of the first *Aliyah*. It is doubtful whether the total number of casualties among the new Jewish settlers during this period was more than about ten." On the other hand, Smilansky stresses that there are positive phenomena on record: Arabs who assisted Jewish neighbors against robbers and marauders, respected Arab notables who declared openly that the Koran hints at the persecuted Jews' return to their country and that the believers should help them implement this wish of Allah's.

Until the beginning of the twentieth century, no one gave any thought to the political aspect of the Jewish-Arab question. True, in 1891 the new wave of immigration that came in the wake of intensified pogroms (e.g., the expulsion of the Moscow Jews in the winter of 1891), and reports that the vineyards of Palestine had been an economic success, led to more Jews buying land, and prompted Arab notables in Jerusalem to present the Turkish authorities with a petition signed by 500 people. This document claimed that

E

"the Jews are taking all the land away from the Moslems, starting to control all the commerce and bringing arms to Palestine." This petition—the first organized Arab action against Jewish immigration and settlement—was apparently one of the reasons that Jewish immigration was banned in the summer of that year, and that land purchases by Jews were forbidden by Constantinople.

Since the Lebanese Christians had obtained autonomy in 1864, the Turkish rulers feared every non-Turkish minority in the Ottoman Empire. They had enough on their hands with the Greeks, Armenians, Serbs, and Bulgarians—not to mention the Arab problem, which was also becoming more trouble-some—without creating an additional problem with the Jews.

When Ahad Ha'am (1856–1927) visited Palestine in 1891, he seemed to have discerned the embryo Arab national movement and sensed the great danger this would pose to the Jewish enterprise. In his famous article, "Truth from the Land of Israel," published in June 1891, Ahad Ha'am, one of the great spiritual leaders of the "Lovers of Zion", wrote *inter alia*:

Outside Palestine we are accustomed to believing that the Arabs are all wild beasts of the desert, a people akin to jackasses who do not understand what is going on around them. But this is a great mistake. Like all Semites, the Arab has a sharp mind and is full of cunning. The cities of Syria and Palestine are full of Arab merchants who know how to exploit the masses and trick all comers, exactly as is done in Europe. The Arabs, the townsfolk in particular, see and understand our actions and our desire for the country. But they pretend not to notice this, because they do not think our present actions pose any threat to their future, and hence they try to exploit us as well, to derive some benefit from the new arrivals while this is possible. At the same time, in their heart of hearts they laugh at us. The peasants are glad when a Jewish colony is founded, because they are given a good wage for their work and grow richer year by year, as has been shown by experience; and the large landowners are also pleased, because we pay them a high price, of which they had previously never dreamed, for rocky and sandy ground. But should a time come when the life of our Jewish brethren in Palestine develops so far that they push out the inhabitants of the country on a small or on a large scale, then the latter would not lightly yield their places.

These prescient words stated the gravity of the problem, without drawing any concrete conclusion.

In view of the economic benefits the Palestinian Arabs derived from Jewish immigration and settlement, and the possibilities such immigration promised for the country's technical and cultural progress, Jewish public opinion was that the Arabs would consider immigration to be profitable to them, and would not place any obstacles in its path. This view was also at the root of Herzl's thinking on the subject. In his book *Altneuland*—a futuristic description of the Jewish state-to-be, published in 1902—there is no national or communal discrimination; the entire population, both Jewish and Arab, lives in peace and friendship. The Arabs take part in the life of the Jewish state and its institutions. All is harmony and brotherhood in Herzl's vision.

This idyllic view of the situation prevailed for about twenty years. The number of Jews in the country was relatively small, and they had few political aspirations for the immediate future. A sizeable part of the Jewish community still viewed the country from a religious and mystic, rather than a secular and political, standpoint. The question of the relations between Jews and Arabs as two peoples (nations) did not occupy the minds of the Zionist or Palestinian Jewish leaders. The main focus of their political interest was the Turkish government, not the Arab inhabitants.

But at the beginning of the twentieth century, this situation underwent a basic change. On the one hand, the Arab national movement, which had revived in the last quarter of the nineteenth century, was growing by leaps and bounds, and it was beginning to influence the mood of the Palestinian Arabs as well. On the Jewish side, a new Jewish *Aliyah*—the second—was starting to arrive, bringing with it more crystalized and far-reaching social and national aspirations than those of the first *Aliyah*.

The Arab National Movement

The first overt expression of the Arab population's wish to throw off the yoke of Turkish rule in western Asia and attain political conditions that would enable them to make unhampered national progress came in 1875, when a secret Arab society was formed in Beirut; branches were later established in Damascus, Tripoli, and Sidon. Egypt, which had been only nominally part of the Turkish Empire since the 1860s, underwent considerable national ferment at the end of the 1870s. This reached its peak with a rebellion, led by Ahmed Arabi Pasha, in 1882. Its suppression marks the beginning of the British rule in Egypt.

As the crisis in the Ottoman Empire deepened (e.g., the bankruptcy of the Sultan's Treasury in 1875), and political influences penetrated from Europe, the emerging Turkish bourgeoisie and intelligentsia—officials, army officers, teachers, journalists, etc.—began conceiving the salvation of the Empire in the creation of a constitutional bourgeois state, rather than a theocratic, autocratic kingdom. They felt the need to base the new Turkey on secular nationalism, on the western European pattern. In the spring of 1876 the so-called "New Ottomans," headed by Midhat Pasha, staged a *coup d'etat*, overthrew Sultan Abd-ul-Aziz (1861–1876), and adapted a constitution that set up a Chamber of Deputies (with a four-year term, and one deputy for every 50,000 adult males), and a Senate, whose members were nominated for life. The constitution guaranteed freedom of the press, immunity for members of Parliament, public sessions of the Parliament and the courts, compulsory education in all government primary schools (whose language of instruction was Turkish) and other democratic measures. But the forces which led to the Proclamation of the Constitution were too weak to overcome the *ancien régime*. Shortly after ascending the throne, the new Sultan, Abd-ul-Hamid (1876–1908, the thirty-fourth Sultan of the House of Ottoman), enacted amendments to the constitution that in effect rendered it valueless. Exploiting the state of emergency that prevailed after the Russo-Turkish War (1877–1878), Abd-ul-Hamid dissolved Parliament and set up a cruel regime based on oppression and persecution. The New Ottoman movement was suppressed, and its leaders fled to Europe.

Abd-ul-Hamid's tyranny was able to crush the tender buds of the Arab national movement in the Levant, but this movement was not entirely stifled. It began to recover from the blows leveled against it, producing Arab thinkers and men of action, several of whom fled to Egypt under pressure from the Turkish police and censorship. In Cairo they laid the foundation of the most important Arab newspapers and periodicals, whose influence was felt beyond Egypt's boundaries.

The writer Abd-ul-Rahman Al-Kawakibi, a Moslem from Aleppo (1849–1903), traveled the length and breadth of the Arab world publishing articles exposing the Turkish reign of oppression and calling for the revival of Arab culture. In 1904, Syrian emigrées living in Paris founded the League for the Arab Homeland, which launched a campaign for the liberation of the Arab lands from the Ottoman domination.

It goes without saying that the Arabs of Palestine were not indifferent to this national awakening. Although the movement's nerve centers were in Beirut and Damascus, many Palestinian Arabs played an active role in it. Among the seven Moslem students who founded the secret Arab organization *Arabia Al-Fatat* in Paris, in 1911, were the Palestinians 'Auni Abd-ul-Hadi and Rafik At-Tamini, later a prominent figure on the Palestinian scene. The leader of the League for the Arab Homeland was a Christian Arab from Palestine named Najib Azuri, the deputy Turkish pasha in Jerusalem. His book *The Revival of the Arab Nation in Turkish Asia*, published in Paris in 1905, played an important role in the early days of the Arab national movement. Two years later, in April 1907, along with French authors and journalists he founded the monthly *L'Indépendence Arabe*, which published information about the Arab lands and stimulated interest in their liberation.

It must be remembered that for almost all Europeans—apart from the statesmen of the great powers and some merchants, missionaries and scholars —the entire Arab East was unknown territory at that time. The Jewish immigrants who arrived from Europe (particularly from eastern Europe, which was more backward culturally at that period), speaking no Arabic and unfamiliar with the Arab world, were almost wholly ignorant of even the most obvious aspects of life in the Orient, and completely unaware of the slow rise of the Arab national movement. Even people who had spent scores of years in the country did not always comprehend what this movement's growth portended.

The Beginning of Anti-Jewish Activities

The first Palestinians to take action against the new Jewish settlers were Christian Arabs. The Moslems were so fanatical at that time that they would not allow their children to study foreign languages. All instruction in the colleges, even in mathematics, philosophy, and philology, was given in Arabic. The Christian Arabs, on the other hand, were free of this limitation, and because of their fluency in both Arabic and French (the most widely used European tongue at that time), they were appointed to important posts in the government as well as in foreign consulates. They played a considerable role in foreign affairs and in contact with the foreign consuls and the heads of the European Christian communities. These Christian Arabs were influenced by Christian European anti-Semitism disseminated in the press and literature, and through the priests and nuns of various missionary groups. The Palestinian Christians in turn passed these anti-Semitic feelings on to the Moslem Arabs, who made up the great majority of Palestine's population, and to whom anti-Semitism was completely foreign. Anti-Jewish sentiments also had an economic background. Most of the Christian Arabs were merchants and members of the free professions, and they looked askance not only at the new Jewish settlers but even at those Jews who had been living in the country for generations, considering them competitors endowed with superior ability and connections. Nevertheless, it took a long time before the heads of the Jewish *Yishuv* and the Zionist movement understood the true significance of the anti-Jewish propaganda circulated by the Christian Arabs.

Ahdut, the paper of the Jewish Labor group, Poalei Zion, wrote in August 1910: "The Christian priests and teachers from Nazareth, the world headquarters of Christianity and anti-Semitism, are stirring the people up to rise against the Jews, to take away their land, to loot their property and threaten their lives." Because they were more urbanized and better educated (having studied in the local mission schools or even abroad), the Christian Arabs played a more important role than the Moslems in developing the Arab press and literature. They provided the yeast which kept the Arab national movement in ferment in all the principal centers, including Palestine. "The moment freedom was granted and the newspapers were able to write whatever they pleased," David Ben-Gurion observed in *Ahdut* of August 1910,

"The Christian press began to come out with strong propaganda against the Jews. The Arab Christian propaganda was particularly vehement against the Jewish *Yishuv* in Palestine." Recalling Najib Azuri's book, published several years before the July 1908 uprising, Ben-Gurion added: "This was the act of one man, whose book was aimed at foreign governments. But today there are already many papers in Palestine, Syria and Egypt which fight us, and Najib Azuri's pupils no longer turn to foreign governments, but address their propaganda to the Arab people and the Turkish government."

Agrarian Relations in Palestine and Jewish Settlement

The immigration of the Jews at the end of the nineteenth century came at a time when agrarian relations in the Turkish empire were seriously disturbed. The background to this crisis was the empire's internal corruption, the backward feudal conditions in the villages, and the heavy burden of taxes imposed on the villages after the Capitulations had ruined commerce and small industry, and foreign powers had made heavy political and economic inroads. This trend increased after the sultan was forced to declare his empire bankrupt in 1875 and the entire Ottoman economy was subjugated to foreign debtors.

During the second half of the nineteenth century, land-ownership arrangements were subjected to further shocks. The policy of oppression drove many farmers off the land. Much arable land was allowed to lie idle, or was worked by nomadic Bedouin tribes. The government, which had lost a sizeable part of its revenue to foreign debtors (especially the revenue from tobacco, salt, silk, and timber), increased taxation on the remaining sources of income. In the 1860s, a law was passed that confiscated any *miri** (or state-owned) land that had not been worked for three successive years. This law resulted in many farmers losing the rights to their land, which was then sold by the government. Several wealthy individuals bought up large areas of land at ridiculously low prices. The land of the Jezreel valley, containing more than twenty villages with over 4,000 inhabitants, was purchased by the Christian banker Sursuk of Beirut, in 1872. He paid £6,000 to the Turkish government, and £12,000 to the politician in Constantinople who arranged the transaction.† Urban property owners acquired the title deeds to extensive tracts of land in various parts of Palestine.[1] A new class of landowners emerged, symbolizing the capitalist penetration into the agrarian relations.

These new landowners leased the land to the fellaheen. With their primi-

---

* From the Arabic word *Amiri*: Pertaining to the government, i.e., state lands, the holder of which is entitled only to use of the land for payment of a tithe.

† In 1921, the Zionist institutions purchased 62,633 *dunams* of land in the Valley of Jezreel from the Sursuk family at a cost of £282,388.

tive methods of agriculture and the arid, backward conditions that prevailed in the country as a whole, these tenants had only a small income. From this they had to pay their debts to the landowners, who often lent them work animals as well, advanced seeds and food until harvest-time, and sometimes even advanced money for a family celebration or the purchase of equipment. It can readily be imagined that the tenants were not anxious to pay the landowners the excessive sums demanded of them and tried to evade their debts. The landowners, who had invariably paid insignificant sums for their land, were ready to sell it to anyone for a reasonable price. It is a fact that in the 1880s and 1890s large areas of land in Palestine (for example, land in the Jezreel, Zevulun, and Hefer Valleys) were put up for sale without any buyers showing an interest.

There were other reasons for the gradual concentration of land in the hands of the strong and the wealthy and financial circles. In accordance with the Ottoman Land Law of 1858, the government began registering the land handed out to the fellaheen listed in the official records from the time of Muhammad Ali and giving them *tabu* (title deed) documents.* The fellaheen, who feared that the registration of their ownership would bring new taxes or demands in its wake, sought outside patronage. In his book *The Oriental Lands* Hirschberg noted cases of fellaheen who ostensibly "sold" their land to various so-called "patrons," paying about 5 percent of its value for this cover. These "patrons" frequently exploited the trusting peasants. In the Hebrew periodical *Hashiloah* of 1907, one of the Jews in Galilee wrote: "The Bedouins living in Safed asked their urban patrons to give their names as the owners of their land, in turn for a certain payment. These people agreed to their request and became legal owners of the land. Later they bequeathed the property to their children, who leased it back to the children of the original owners who had been robbed of their land."

Land registers were not properly kept in those days, and legislation on land matters dragged on for years and cost far more money than the ordinary fellah could afford.

So it came about that large areas of land passed into the hands of landowners. The fellaheen were poor, their equipment inadequate and their productivity low. Their primitive methods of cultivation yielded small crops, and they were unable to obtain credit at reasonable rates of interest in order to pay back the many people who were sucking their blood. The commercial banks were interested only in the large property owners, who could give guarantees which the fellaheen could not provide.

In addition to the customary tithe (one-tenth) of the crop that went to

* *Tabu*: The Turkish name for the government offices in Syria and Palestine at which land estate records were kept and land purchases and transfers, mortgages, etc., recorded (popularly, "taboo").

the government, the fellah had to pay a tax on land and buildings (*werko*), a tax on his beasts of burden, and another on roads (*darbiyeh*). Non-Moslems had to pay a tax in lieu of army service (*Badal 'Askariyah*). In many places the fellah also had to contribute towards the upkeep of the *madafa* (guest house) in the village, and to pay sums of money to placate various local rulers and patrons. All these demands impoverished the fellaheen and placed them at the mercy of large landowners, who were able to obtain credit from the urban banks at regular rates of interest. This money was then lent out to the fellaheen at rates of 5 percent a month, or even higher. This extortion forced the fellaheen into a vicious circle of debt from which they could never escape, and eventually they were obliged to hand their land over to their "patrons" and lease it from them as tenants, in return for a fixed payment or a share of the crop.

Land Disputes and Problems of Tenure

The men who guided Jewish settlement policy in Palestine paid no attention to the social problems that had already arisen in the 1880s and 1890s, and that became more prominent as Jewish settlement expanded and Arab national feelings developed. When the Biluim came to the country, signs of this Arab awakening were already evident. This was noted by Israel Belkind, one of the Bilu pioneers and a veteran Hebrew teacher: "In Elul of 1882 the influence of the Arabi Pasha revolt was felt in Palestine. Many of the panic-stricken Europeans fled to Jaffa and other towns, afraid a rebellion against the Europeans might break out in Palestine as well, and the Arabs were indeed restless and in ferment. Arabi Pasha was considered a national hero."

Belkind added that when he was walking from Mikveh Israel to Jaffa one day he met a Bedouin who was watering his horse. He could not understand the Bedouin's dialect, but he caught the words "Arabi Basha" and realized, when the Bedouin put his hand across his throat with an expressive gesture, that he was telling him all the Europeans would be killed.

The land disputes that accompanied Jewish settlement in Palestine from the earliest days sprang partly from the faulty land system in force under the Turkish regime and partly from mistakes made by the Jewish settlers themselves. Some Jews were conscious of these mistakes from the beginning and warned of their consequences.

A typical example was Mikveh Israel, the first agricultural enterprise of the first *Aliyah*. When the Turkish authorities gave Charles Netter a piece of land in 1870 in order to set up an agricultural school, they took the land from the fellaheen of Yazur. This led to clashes between the villagers of Yazur and the farmers of Mikveh Israel. Netter was supported by the French consul and the Turkish officials, who naturally gained the upper hand. But Yehiel Michel Pines, a member of the *Hovevei Zion* who came to Palestine with the first *Aliyah*, when he helped to found Petah Tikva and Gedera, wrote strongly in the Hebrew press against Netter's methods and attitude towards the Arab fellaheen: "The land which the Turkish government gave him [Netter] was given largely because of bribes. A quarter of the sums Netter spent to get this land would have sufficed to buy it permanently from its owners, without being dependent on any special arrangement and without provoking our neighbours, who will never forget that we took their land."

In a letter written in April 1886, Elazar Rokah, secretary to Avraham Moyal, who handled the *Hovevei Zion's* affairs in Palestine, said about the relations between the Jewish settlers of Petah Tikva and their Arab neighbors:

The Arabs and fellaheen ask the opinion of the oldest and wisest man in the village about everything. The same is not true of our brethren in Petah Tikva. There everyone does as he pleases. For example, we have urged our brother colonists several times to avoid unnecessary quarrelling with the fellaheen. Even if one of the settlers does have a dispute with a fellah, he should go with him to the head of the *moshava*, who should judge between them and settle all their differences. But as none of our brethren is able to speak in the language of the country and to talk to the inhabitants in a way they will understand, each of them does as he sees fit. If he finds a sheep or cow grazing in his fields, he will at once take possession of it, and if the Arab will not surrender it, the settler will beat him black and blue. The end will be that the fellaheen will grow tired of these incidents and will hit back.

An example of a land dispute that had a distinct effect on the relations between the Jewish settlers and their Arab neighbors for years afterwards is that of the *moshava* Gedera, founded by the Biluim. Avraham Moyal, who was born in Palestine and knew the ways of the country, wrote to Dr. Pinsker in this connection.

None of the *moshavot* founded in the Holy Land by our brethren to this day have encountered as many obstacles as Gedera.... The land bought in Gedera was the heart and soul of the Arab village of Katra. This land was taken from the fellaheen through various stratagems. M. Pollibiere, a Frenchman, lent them money with interest, and the debts grew so high that they were forced to give him the land for a song, although they could not support themselves for even a single year without this land. As long as M. Pollibiere was the owner of the land the fellaheen did not realize the full extent of their disaster, as he leased the land back to them. But now, when the fellaheen saw that our brethren intended working the land themselves, and that they could no longer lease it, no matter how much rent they offered to pay, they fought for their lives, for how would they earn their bread? Hence it is hardly surprising that the fellaheen of Katra placed obstacles in the way of the *moshava's* growth, in the hope that the Jewish settlers would lose patience and go elsewhere.

In Rehovot, the Satria tribe, which had been living there for forty years, was driven off its land. The small tribe (composed of "about forty warriors") launched two attacks on the new *moshava*, which repulsed them. The tribe had no choice but to reconcile itself to the situation, and some of its members even found work in the farms of the Jewish settlers. This incident is reflected in the story "Sheikh Abd-ul-Kadier," by the Rehovot author Moshe Smilansky. This story, written about fifty years ago, was the first attempt in Hebrew literature to describe the emotional reaction of Arabs to Jewish settlement.

This problem was even more acutely felt in Galilee. Here the fellaheen's economic conditions were even worse than in Judea and in Samarian areas, which had better land and more water and were closer to the market. On the other hand, the Jewish colonies in Galilee were poorer, basing themselves mainly on dry farming and grain crops. Thus they could offer neither employment nor a market for the fellaheen who may have previously worked the same lands. If the disputes with Arab tenants in Galilee became more intense over the years, this was due in no small measure to the errors committed by Baron de Rothschild's officials, who, in the words of *The Chronicles of the Hagana*, "relied upon the Baron's money, exploited the authorities and made use of force, money, and the government's soldiers" (Chronicles of the Hagana).

One of the most striking examples of this was in Metulla, where there were over one hundred Druze families, who had been living there for ninety years and who worked rented land. The ownership of this land changed hands several times. The owner at that time was unable to obtain the share of the crop due to him (government troops had literally waged war on the Druze villagers in order to levy the tithes they owed the sultan), and he also failed to evict them. At this point he suggested to the Baron's officials that they buy the land. One of these officials, Yehoshua Ossowitsky, bought the land and began negotiating the evacuation of the Druze tenants. These negotiations continued for four years without any results. In 1896, when the Druze revolted in Syria and the Druze leaders were sent to Constantinople, Ossowitsky considered the time ripe to find a "solution" to the problem. The veteran settler Yizhak Epstein relates:

One day, the Baron's official came to Metulla with a sack full of gold coins in his cart. As if by coincidence, he was accompanied by soldiers who had come to arrest those Druze villagers who had evaded military service. The soldiers were ready to arrest any fellaheen who refused to sign the deeds of sale. Naturally all of them signed the deeds, and several days later more than 600 people left the village of their birth. . . . For a week, about sixty Jewish farmers gathered there, the most active members of the moshavot, and settled in the homes of the Druze. . . . As long as the government was persecuting the Druze and their leaders were forced to flee, things were quiet in Metulla. But a year later the Turkish authorities let the Druze leaders go free and granted the sect a general amnesty. Only a few months later the Druze of Metulla filed a suit against the Baron's officials, for taking unauthorized control of their houses and vineyards.[2]

Metulla suffered from Druze attacks for many years and its settlers paid a heavy toll, in money and blood for the short-sighted policies of the Baron's officials.

In 1900, the Jewish Colonization Association acquired extensive areas of land in lower Galilee at Sejera (Ilania), Yamma (Yavniel), Mesha (Kfar Tabor), Beth Gan, Milhamiya, and other localities. This land, purchased from effendis and traders in Beirut, was worked by subtenants. Neither Ossowitsky, who handled the transaction for Baron de Rothschild, nor the wealthy sellers, were interested in the fate of these tenants. As the buyer had paid the full price asked for the land, he claimed the right to evict the tenants without compensation. A bitter dispute broke out between the villagers and Ossowitsky's officials. The *Wali* (governor) of Beirut took Ossowitsky's side, while the district office in Tiberias supported the tenants. Shots were fired at Ossowitsky, and he retaliated by bringing troops to arrest many of the Arab villagers. Kalvarisky intervened. He cabled Paris and asked to be given authority to settle the dispute, arranging for the tenants to be given compensation. Order was restored, and the colonies of Yavniel, Kfar Tabor, and Milhamiya were established in a peaceful manner. Several years later Kalvarisky wrote in his memoirs:

> That was the first time I came into contact with Arab nationalism. The *wali* of Beirut, Rashid Bey, was a Turk who did not care whether the Tiberias district was populated by Arabs or Jews. He ordered the tenants to be evicted. But the *kaimmakam* (district officer) of Tiberias, the Arab Druze Amin Arslan, fought not only against the evil of evicting the tenants without compensation, but also—as he admitted to me— against the change in the national character of the district. He was already under the influence of Najib Nassar who lived in Tiberias and was hostile to Zionist settlement.

How to Attain "Bon Voisinage"

The Zionist leaders and the Jewish settlers did not agree on the way to approach the indigenous Arab population: "the new settlers and the younger people favoured strong-arm methods and were against compromise, while the veterans and older settlers argued in favour of concessions and mutual understanding" (*Chronicles of the Hagana*). These two approaches to the everyday relations between the new settlers and their Arab neighbors were the subject of a debate that went on for many years.

The Jewish settlers followed the customs of their countries of origin. These laid down, for example, that the owner of the land enjoyed grazing rights. Only after some time did the Jews learn, as Belkind wrote, that

> ... the Arabs do not allot special grazing areas to their cattle and sheep, which graze on every open site without paying any attention to the boundaries of the village.

One village sends its sheep to graze in its neighbour's fields. . . . As all the fields of Rishon Lezion were planted, the farmers of the colony used to send their cattle to graze in the fields of their Arab neighbors. The latter never even thought of protesting against this as long as the animals did not actually enter sown fields. But in the early days, when we were unfamiliar with farming customs in Palestine, we would not allow the Arabs to graze their flocks in our fields under any conditions. The clashes with the Arabs were the result of our ignorance, and many of them could have been prevented had we known the language of the country and its customs, as we know them today.

This was the background to the frequent clashes during the initial years of the first colonies. The Arabs were taken aback by the Jewish settlers. Loubman-Haviv, a founder of Rishon Lezion, wrote that the Jews took control as if they were the masters of the country, so much so that they forbade anyone to graze his flocks on the boundaries of their land, even on grass, which is the gift of God and free to everyone, as has been the custom from time immemorial. This violation of an age-old and almost sacred custom led to many violent clashes, followed by lengthy vendettas and blood feuds.

Even after the settlers got to know the local customs about pasture rights, not all of them accepted them. As the authority on settlement affairs, Y. M. Pines, put it, "If the people of the country permit flocks to graze on other farmers' fallow fields, then the settlers in the colonies should do likewise. In this way they would avoid coming to blows with their neighbours, and the borders of the colonies would be secured more effectively than if they were defended by force."[3]

However, from the memoirs of the early settlers and other sources, it would appear that Pines's approach was not always followed by newer and younger settlers. The importance of neighborly relations and of preparing newcomers for their first encounters with the Arab environment—problems that later came to occupy the leaders of the Jewish community in Palestine—were not fully understood in the period under review. The colonies' attitude toward the Arabs was noted by Ahad Ha'am in *The Truth from Eretz Yisrael*, published in 1891:

We could certainly learn from our past and present history how careful we have to be not to bring down upon us the wrath of the country through reprehensible acts, how cautious we have to be in our behavior toward a non-Jewish people among whom we are coming to live once more, to treat these people with love and respect and—it goes without saying—with justice and respect for the law. And what are our brethren in Palestine doing? The exact opposite! They were slaves in the land of their exile and suddenly they find themselves in the midst of unlimited freedom, a wild kind of freedom which can only be found in a country like Turkey. This sudden change has produced in them a tendency to despotism, which always happens when "a slave becomes a king." They treat the Arabs with hostility and cruelty, trespassing on their territory unjustly, beating them shamefully without any valid reason and then boasting about it. No one is calling a halt to this contemptible and dangerous trend. Our brethren were right when they said that the Arabs only respect those who display courage and bravery; but this only applies when the Arab feels his adversary is in the right, not when he has good reason to believe that his acts are oppressive and unjust. When this is the case, the Arab may keep silent and exercise restraint for a long period, but in his heart he will cherish animosity and harbor vengeance.

Indeed, the correct balance between a courageous stand and scrupulous attention to honesty and the rights of other people is far from easy even under less complex conditions. It was natural that the encounter between two worlds as different as that of the Jewish immigrants from Europe and that of the fellaheen and Bedouin in Palestine at the end of the nineteenth century should cause complicated problems. These should be seen in the context of their time, not judged by the totally changed standards of seventy years later. Ahad Ha'am's warnings would be better appreciated in the light of the following complaint, by a farmer of Rishon against one of Baron de Rothschild's officials:*

Do you remember how afraid the Arabs were of us in the early years? They shuddered when they saw us. None of them dared utter a curse in front of us. The Arab knew that he must honor the Jew or be punished. Today one cannot even beat an Arab, because he would complain to Bloch [one of the Baron's officials], and Bloch will summon the man who beat him and will fine him in the presence of the Arab.

[Hissin, *The Hand of Destiny*, published in Russian.]

This is a good illustration of the fact that there were always many different approaches among the Jews to the problems of Jewish-Arab relations, stretching back to the very beginnings of modern Jewish settlement in Palestine.

The Second Aliyah *and Jewish Labor Problems*

In 1904, the members of the second *Aliyah* began to arrive. These people belonging mostly to the Poalei Zion and *Hapoel Hatzair* movements,† were determined to become workers and laborers. The second *Aliyah* introduced a basic change of values in the Jewish population, which had reached a crisis in the wake of which many Jews left Palestine. The Zionist organization set up at the First Zionist Congress, held at Basle in 1897, had not yet begun its

---

*The Baron's officials did not insist that the Jewish farmers work their own field and saw nothing wrong in hiring Arab fellaheen to do the work in the settlements and Arab watchmen to guard the *moshavot*.

† The *Hapoel Hatzair* (Young Worker) Party (its original name was "The Union of Young Hebrew Workers in Palestine" to distinguish it as distinct from the workers who had come over with the first *Aliyah*): Founded in 1905; *Poale Zion*: founded in 1906 as a branch of the World Union of Poalei Zion (whose full title was "The Jewish Social-Democratic Workers' Party, Poalei Zion").

practical operations in Palestine. The first *moshavot* were struggling for their very existence with help of Baron de Rothschild and the ICA.* The Baron's officials committed grave economic and administrative errors. Some of these were the virtually inevitable result of resettlement activities in a backward and neglected land; others sprang from the bureaucratic nature of these officials and their alienation from the national and social aspirations of the new settlers. But the most serious harm the officials did to Jewish settlement in Palestine was to corrupt the farmers and to deprive them of their former idealism. The farmers stopped doing actual agricultural work. The vineyards, which were the main support of the economy at that time, were worked by Arab laborers, with the Jews serving only as experts and supervisors. Many of the Jewish settlers and their children became "idlers who lived on a monthly allowance. The only efforts they made were to find favor in the eyes of the Baron's officials," as the *Chronicles of the Hagana* stated.

This situation had a devastating effect on the morale of the *Yishuv*. It also planted the seeds of a far-reaching danger to national relations among the peoples living in Palestine, since the relations between the Jewish settlers and the Arabs who worked their fields often began to look like those of master and servant, characterized by contempt, hatred, and fear. The first *Aliyah's* dream of establishing a new Jewish society in Palestine, with a healthy economy, a national culture, and an independent political structure, seemed about to end in the creation of a class of "Jewish planters," exploiting cheap Arab labor.

The men and women of the second *Aliyah* took a firm stand against these dangers. They considered the main principle underlying the Jewish people's return to its homeland to be the labor of Jewish farmers and manual workers. The ethical and ideological principle of Jewish labor was also an economic necessity for the new immigrants, who brought nothing with them to Palestine except their vision and will to work. The demand that Jewish workers should be employed on Jewish farms—the only ones that could employ them at that time—expressed the desire to eliminate the danger of quasi-colonial exploitation of Arab by Jew. The young Jewish agriculture had to create reasonable living conditions for the immigrant Jewish workers, who lacked the economic base of the Arab fellah, with his village and family farm, primitive as it might be. The comparatively well-established farmers of the colonies, who had become accustomed to the cheap and unorganized

* ICA: Jewish Colonization Association, the Jewish settlement company founded in 1891 by Baron Hirsch for the settlement of east European Jews in Argentina and other countries. From January 1900 onward, it took over the management of the *moshavot* in Palestine, which were supported by the Palestine Jewish Colonization Association (the Palestinian division of the ICA), according to instructions from Baron Rothschild. When the *moshavot* of Baron Rothschild were transferred to ICA, the organization received £600,000 for their rehabilitation and consolidation (see note on p. 35, Chapter Two).

labor of the Arab peasants, with their less sophisticated demands, were reluctant to accede to the demands of the more organized Jewish workers. When the farmers rejected these demands, and even tried to boycott Jewish workers, the latter started a campaign for "the conquest of labor" and "pure Jewish labor." Strikes were organized by Jewish workers in places where only Arabs were employed. This sounded a new note, which paralleled the increasing nationalist overtones in the Arabs' attitude towards the Jews of Palestine.

The Turkish rulers soon exploited these first indications of nationalist antagonism between Jews and Arabs. According to Smilansky, "A whispering campaign hinted to the Arabs that the Jews who came to Palestine were not only looking for employment and a livelihood, but also had nationalist motives: to establish a Hebrew kingdom and drive the Moslem Arabs out of the country. This is what Turkish secret agents whispered, for reasons of their own."

The Ottoman government was trying to block the growing Arab movement for separation from Turkey, or at least for greater cultural and administrative autonomy for the Arab provinces of the Empire. From this standpoint, it is interesting to note that on March 2, 1908 (the day of Purim), after a clash between Jewish and Arab workers in Jaffa in which some of the Arabs were injured, the Turkish authorities searched the Jewish workers' hostel with unusual cruelty and brutality.

During this period, almost every new Jewish settlement had difficulties with its Arab neighbors. Arab propaganda against Jewish settlement in Palestine had left its mark. The attitude of some of the Jews toward the local Arabs also left much to be desired.* Nevertheless, there were bright spots in the relations between the two peoples. Though there were many land disputes during this period, anyone studying the records will also find many examples of Arabs inviting Jews to settle in their vicinity and promising them every possible assistance and friendship.

In the summer of 1903, for example (shortly before Dr. Herzl's mission visited El-Arish), a delegation of Bedouin sheiks from the Negev called on Dr. Isaac Levi, director of the ICA colonies in Judea, in his Jaffa office. They proposed that land be allocated to Jewish settlers in the Beersheba area,

---

* For example, a letter from Z. D. Levontin, one of the founders of Rishon Lezion, and at that time manager of the Anglo-Palestine Bank in Jaffa, to David Wolfsohn, president of the World Zionist Organization, written in 1908, complains as follows about young fellows from the Poalei Zion organization: "They always walk about armed with large sticks. Some of them also carry knives and most of them treat the Arabs with contempt and quarrel with them maliciously. . . . Articles in the Hebrew press have been responsible for much of this, particularly *Hapoel Hatzair's* demand to oust Arabs from their work on Jewish farms. All these articles are copied and read by the [Turkish] officials and the educated Christian Arabs, if not by the masses."

so that an alliance of Jews and Bedouins could be formed in the Negev, where the nomadic Bedouin were in constant conflict about taxes with the Turkish authorities. "Let as many Jews as possible come," said the delegation's spokesman, Sheikh Salim Abu-Rabi'a. "The Bedouins will give them as much land as they need. The Jews have wisdom and influence in high places, and the Bedouin have courage. I, Salim Abu-Rabi'a, can summon ten thousand armed warriors. If the Jews and the Bedouin form an alliance, no force will be able to withstand them."

Dr. Y. Thon, who was Ruppin's deputy at the Palestine Office, observed:

Arabs often expressed the wish that Jews should buy land in their area and settle near them. I remember vividly taking part in a delegation which included Hissin, Dizengoff, Eisenberg, Ruppin and Vilkansky. Gaza was a city filled with religious fanaticism and opposition to all non-Moslems, whether these were Christians or Jews. All the same, when we strolled through the streets many groups of people accompanied us, not in hostility, but in order to encourage us and to extend a cordial and friendly invitation to come to Gaza and its environs and establish settlements there. They promised us every assistance, in a spirit of brotherhood and neighborliness.

H. M. Kalvarisky, who was administrator of the ICA settlements in Galilee at that time, wrote: "The Arab officials aided our settlement project before World War I, in the face of all the Turkish administration's regulations against Jewish settlement. The Arabs felt instinctively that Jewish immigration not only did not harm them, but in fact benefited them."

On the Eve of The Young Turks' Revolt

The political nature of Jewish-Arab relations took on added significance with the proclamation of the constitution in the Ottoman Empire.

Following the shock of the Russo-Japanese War and the first abortive Russian revolution, there was an awakening of the Asian peoples in 1905 to 1906. The increased strength of the Young Turks movement kindled new hope in the hearts of Arab nationalists. Many of the Arab intelligentsia, students, army officers, clerks, merchants, and religious figures were sympathetic to the underground movement, and some of them even played an active and important role in the Unity and Progress committees, in the hope that a change of regime in the Ottoman Empire would accelerate the realization of Arab autonomy and cultural freedom.

Years later, Kalvarisky recalled (in a lecture delivered in 1930) what he and others had argued at that time:

If only we had been wise enough to enter into negotiations with the Arab intelligentsia! But unfortunately we always repeat the same mistakes. . . . We set up an office in Constantinople in order to negotiate with the Turks. But we have not done anything to come closer to the Arabs. . . . The fact is that we have not really understood the problem. In the Diaspora we knew how to intercede with the non-Jews and now that we have returned home and have to conduct an independent national policy, we have remained interceders. We have always known how to influence this minister or that important official. But to foresee the way things will turn out, to create mutual ties between two peoples who are in the same boat—of this we are not capable.

In short, for too long a time the Zionist movement was not aware of the Arab national movement and ignored its importance, which grew as the country developed and changed. The roots of this lack of awareness were already present in Herzl's rhetorical catch word on "a people without a land returning to a land without a people."

Did not Herzl know at the outset of his activities that there were Arabs living in Palestine, and did he not realize that this posed a problem for the Jews returning to their homeland? That Herzl knew this problem existed (even if he was not familiar with Ahad Ha'am's article "Truth From the Land of Israel," published in 1891), is testified to by A. S. Yahuda (1877–1951), a native of Jerusalem, who was a student at Frankfurt-on-Main in 1895 and one of the founders of the Hebrew-Speaking Society in Germany. Later, as Professor Yahuda, he became a world-famous Orientalist who lectured at the universities of Madrid, Heidelberg, Frankfurt, Zurich, and Oxford, and at many American universities. Yahuda attended the First Zionist Congress, held in Basle in 1897, as a delegate from Heidelberg. As a Palestinian who was familiar with conditions in that country, he told Herzl how essential it was to find ways of reaching an understanding with the Arabs. He even offered his services in this connection.

Recalling this period many years later, on the occasion of the publication (in the New York Hebrew periodical *Hadoar*, 1944, No. 29) of Yahuda's 1897 correspondence with the poet Shaul Tshernichovsky on the subject of Arab poetry, Yahuda noted:

Despite the deep and lofty impression the Congress made on me and the spiritual elevation I felt all the time I was in Basle, I could not overcome the doubts which seized me for various reasons. Some of them evaporated later on: but others proved justified, particularly on the Arab question. I could not persuade Herzl and his advisers to take this seriously, though the time was ripe to prepare the ground for the future.*

According to the Hebrew records of the First Zionist Congress, Professor Yahuda said:

* An article about Yahuda's meeting with Herzl in 1896 and their conversation regarding the Arab question at the Basel Congress in 1897 was published by Professor Yahuda in *Zionews*, the publication of the New Zionist Organization (New York, July–August, 1943).

F

I met Herzl in London in July 1896, after his first public address on the idea of a Jewish State. . . . As a delegate to the Congress, I was asked to represent the Hebrew-Speaking Society, which I had founded among the university students. I was the youngest delegate to the Congress. My main purpose in attending the Congress was to continue my conversation with Herzl about the Arabs of Palestine. I tried to prove to Herzl that the Arabs of Palestine should be won over to our cause, so that they should realize the benefits which would accrue to them and to the country as a whole from the idea of the Return to Zion. I urged him to establish friendly relations with the Arab notables and to create ties of mutual understanding. But Herzl's intimate advisers scoffed at my views. Time has shown that I was right. We neglected the task of informing our neighbours about our aims, leaving the field open to the seeds of hatred, sown by troublemakers and agitators.

Martin Buber related (in the Hebrew anthology *At the Crossroads*): "When Max Nordau, Herzl's right-hand man, learned for the first time full details about the presence of Arabs in Palestine, he was greatly concerned. He came to see Herzl and called out: 'I did not know about this. We are doing an injustice!'"

The Arab problem continued to be virtually ignored even when the Arab national movement spread through the lands of the Ottoman Empire, including Palestine. The Sublime Porte, Constantinople, the Turkish pashas in Jerusalem, Beirut or Damascus, the Turkish governors in various Palestinian towns—these seemed to be the really important forces; and everybody understood the importance of the European powers, through which the Sultan himself could be influenced. The same did not apply to the voices that spoke about the Arabs as a *political force*, whose sympathy and goodwill it was important to acquire.

Twenty-five years after the immigration of the Bilu pioneers, Dr. Yitshak Epstein,* who came to know the leaders of the Arab national movement during his student years in Switzerland and to understand their deepest aspirations, raised the question of Jewish-Arab relations in public. Since Arab nationalist sentiment could not be openly expressed in Palestine, where stringent measures were taken against anyone suspected of revolutionary ideas and "Arab separatism," Epstein outlined his views for the first time at a meeting of the *Ivria* group during the Seventh Zionist Congress, held in Basle in 1905. Later his views were published as an article, "A Hidden Question," in the Hebrew Journal *Hashiloah* (1907). Epstein wrote:

* Yitshak Epstein (1862–1943): Born in Russia. Came to Palestine in 1886. Lived for many years in Galilee, first as a farm worker and later as a teacher. From 1902 to 1908, he studied at the University of Lausanne; subsequently, he was appointed headmaster of the Alliance school at Salonika (1908–1915). Was among the founders of the modern Hebrew school in Palestine and the Diaspora. A writer and fine scholar and one of the great linguists of modern Hebrew. After World War I, was appointed inspector of schools of the Zionist Executive in Palestine.

Among the grave questions linked with the concept of our people's renaissance on its own soil there is one question *which is more weighty than all the others put together*. This is the question of our relations with the Arabs. Our own national aspirations depend upon the correct solution of this question. It has not been eliminated. It has simply been forgotten by the Zionists and is hardly referred to at all in its true form in Zionist literature.

The regrettable fact that our attention could be diverted from such a fundamental question, and that after thirty years of settlement activity it is being talked about as if it is a new topic—all this proves that our movement is unreasonable, that we still treat things superficially rather than exploring them deeply in order to discover what is truly important.

At a time when we feel the love of our homeland, love for every corner of the land of our forefathers, we forget that the people now living in this land also has a heart and a soul. Like all men, the Arab is bound to his homeland by strong ties. The less developed a people is, the stronger the bond between it and its native country, and the harder it is for individual members of that people to leave their villages and their farms.

I am not suggesting for a moment that we should humble ourselves and give in to the local inhabitants. If we are courageous and daring, they will respect us and we shall be able to live securely among them in our villages. But we shall commit a grave sin against our people and our future if we throw away so lightly our principal weapons: righteousness and sincerity. As long as we cling steadfastly to these, we need fear nobody. But if we abandon them, we shall lose all our strength and our courage will fail.

Epstein showed that he already understood one of the most important aspects of the problem:

This people [the Arabs of Palestine] forms only a small part of a great nation, which holds all the territory surrounding our country: Syria, Iraq, Arabia and Egypt. ... We should not trust the ashes which cover the embers: one spark may rekindle the fire and bring about a conflagration which will not be extinguished.

He opposed any tendency on the part of some Jews to be "like all other peoples." Instead, Epstein declared:

We can learn much from the Germans: science, work, persistence. But we should not learn the laws of morality from them. They received the doctrine of justice from us, and they will have to learn it from us for a long time to come.

Noting the ferment in the Turkish Empire and the demand for the national autonomy of the non-Turkish peoples, including the Arabs, Epstein wrote:

The Jewish people—the first of all the nations to teach justice and law, absolute equality, and human brotherhood—respects not only the individual rights of every man, but also the national rights of every people and tribe. The Jewish people, which wants to revive itself, is a brother in thought and deed to all peoples who are awakening to new life. The Jewish people takes a loving and sympathetic attitude towards these peoples' aspirations and wants to develop its national consciousness through contact with them.

Calling upon the Jews "to avoid a narrow, limited nationalism, which sees no farther than itself," Epstein urged "an alliance with the Arabs and a pact with them which will benefit both sides and the whole of mankind." At a time when official Zionist diplomacy was seeking to obtain the Charter from the Turkish rulers of Palestine, Epstein called for an agreement "written not on paper or on parchment, but on the heart and brain of an entire people." He described his vision of a Jewish-Arab alliance as "a tremendous undertaking unparalleled in the history of human progress and development, because it would result in the resuscitation of two ancient peoples, equipped with great talents and potentialities, who complement one another."

Epstein's plea evoked a reply from Ze'ev Smilansky, one of the leaders of the second *Aliyah*, and father of the modern Hebrew writer Yizhar Smilansky (S. Yizhar). He published a series of articles in *Ha'olam*, the central organ of the World Zionist Organization, under the pen name of Vofsi.* Whereas Epstein had expressed highly unorthodox views, Smilansky voiced the general mood of the Zionist movement and the heads of the new *Yishuv*. He charged that Epstein's opinions were not "based on reality," but that "he was a victim of his own fantasies." In his reply to Epstein's criticism of errors made when the Jewish *moshavot* were founded (e.g., the case of Metulla, noted above), Smilansky said that Epstein had "gone too far and had made a mountain out of a molehill. . . . He is attracted to the miserable Arabs. . . . Epstein is trying to find a compromise between the Jews and the Arabs, in such a way that the wolf would be satisfied while the sheep would remain whole."

Criticizing the attitude towards Arab tenants and sharecroppers, and demanding a radical change of approach, Epstein had written: "We do not have to buy the land offered by the official owners in every case. . . . Unless we want to deceive ourselves deliberately, we have to admit that we have thrown people out of their miserable lodgings and taken away their sustenance." In support of this statement, Epstein gave several examples drawn from the history of Jewish settlement in upper Galilee. Vofsi countered this by saying: "When other nations come to settle in a new land they set about it with their swords, even if they have no historical claims going back to the days of their forefathers. . . . Even when these settlers argue that their main

* *Ha'olam*, issues of August 28 to September 25, 1908. The editorial board of this weekly noted, in the wake of the first article, that "in view of the changes taking place in Turkish regime, this question will be one of the most pressing issues for practical Zionism in the coming years. Although we do not agree with all the ideas expressed in the article, and although it is of a highly political nature—we have given it space in our columns for the above reason."

purpose is to spread knowledge and education, it is obvious that they are motivated primarily by economic considerations and benefits. . . . But we are told by Epstein that we are not entitled to redeem the land of our forefathers with money, even if we do this and in a fair and peaceful manner. . . . Do we have nothing to worry about except the fate of the Palestinian Arabs?" Vofsi criticized Epstein for "being concerned about the Arabs," and accused him of having "a Diaspora way of thinking" and of tending to discuss matters on the basis of "what the non-Jews say," whereas, in Vofsi's opinion, "the main thing we should take into account should be what is good and effective for ourselves."

In his article, Epstein had called for efforts to win the Arabs' confidence and goodwill: "Our purpose is not to Judaize the Arabs, but to prepare them for a fuller life, to develop them and change the narrowness of their outlook, so that in the course of time they can become faithful allies of ours, true friends and brothers."

Vofsi opposed this view on principle: "How will we be able to compete with the Arabs, if they have the best or even the middling good lands, which will produce cheaper crops since the fellaheen content themselves with so little and will be guided by our agricultural instructors? . . . Everyone will think us mad if we take upon ourselves the task of handing out money in order to foster a rival who will lose no time in putting us out of business."

Epstein declared: "Let us build them up and build ourselves at the same time! . . . Let us prepare the people of Palestine and train them on our farms. Let us be the light of science in the country, and let us pave the way for justice and law. Let us fight the prejudices of the different and hostile nationalities. We shall become the angels of peace, who compromise between religious sects out to exterminate each other. And we can do all these things by virtue of the sincerity and purity of our aspirations and opinions—we alone and nobody else." Vofsi, on the other hand, summed up his reservations about Epstein's views by saying: "Not only is it difficult to follow his methods, but it is also impossible to implement them."

Here we already have in embryo the essence of the debate that was to characterize discussions within the Zionist movement over the years.

Epstein's article was published at the end of 1907. The reply to his proposals was published in the spring of 1908, before the Young Turks' revolt in July of that year. The political storm accompanying the revolt produced far-reaching political changes in Turkey, which changed the nature of the situation and of the discussion.

The Young Turks' Revolt

In 1906, the Young Turks transferred their European headquarters to

Salonika and strengthened their contacts with the intelligentsia and the army. These measures bore fruit in the summer of 1908. Faced with the threat by the armed forces that they would launch an uprising and march on the capital, Sultan Abd-ul-Hamid surrendered to the Young Turks' demands on July 23 and announced that the 1876 Constitution would be revived. In April 1909 the Sultan tried to turn the clock back, with the help of the supporters of the *ancien régime* and the standing army in the capital. He dismissed the government and dissolved Parliament. But the Young Turks defeated him and formed a new Parliament, which ousted the Sultan.

The new currents of reform and greater secularization in the Ottoman Empire weakened the link between the Turks and the Arabs. Until that time, their religious cooperation as Sunni Moslems had proved stronger than any differences between them on the score of national aspirations, language, or cultural tradition. The revival of the Turkish Constitution and the formation of the new Parliament brought the Arab national movement out of the underground and into the open, giving it broader horizons. The beginning of September 1908 saw the formation of the Arab society *Al-Akha' al-'Arabi al-'Uthmani* (Ottoman Arab Brotherhood), founded by the Arab colony in Constantinople. This society, whose membership was made up of both Moslems and Christians, embarked on a political campaign, including the publication of an Arabic newspaper.

When the new Turkish Parliament was inaugurated in November 1908, the Arabs comprised a quarter of its membership: 60 out of 245.* Jewish attempts to ensure at least one seat for a representative of the *Yishuv* in Palestine failed completely. In the north of the country, which formed part of the Beirut *vilayet*, the Jews were only a small fraction of the population. In the Jerusalem *sandjak* (which sent three members to Parliament) the Jews carried more weight and had a greater chance of electing a representative—but most of these Jews were foreign citizens. Only 6,277 of the 50,000 Jews living in Jerusalem had the right to vote; and the 11,227 voters in Jaffa, Petah Tikva, Ramle, and Beit Dagon included only 306 Jews who were Turkish subjects.

Nevertheless, the Jews did not give up. They chose as their candidate Dr. Isaac Levi,† who was known to be an ardent Zionist. When, directly after

* According to Antonius (in his book, *The Arab Awakening*), the population of the Turkish Empire—excluding Egypt—in 1908 totalled twenty-two million, of whom 7,500,000 were Turks "in racial terms," 10,500,000 Arabs, and four million Greeks, Albanians, Kurds, etc. The ratio between Turks and Arabs was therefore 2 to 5 in favor of the Arabs, whereas the ratio between their representatives in the assembly was 5 to 2 to the advantage of the Turks. Out of a senate of forty persons appointed by the sultan only three were Arabs.

† Dr. Isaac Levi (1866–1950): Born in Constantinople. Won a government scholarship for studies in agriculture in Germany. Worked as government inspector for agriculture

the Young Turks' revolt, a branch of the Unity and Progress Party was formed in Jerusalem, with both Arab and Jewish members, Dr. Levi and Eliezer Ben-Yehuda refused to declare that they were not Zionists, and as a result they were not elected to the committee. On the other hand, several Jewish members stated that they were not Zionists; these included Albert Antebi (the Jerusalem representative of the Alliance Israelite Universelle), David Yellin (then a teacher in a *Hilfsverein* school, founded by German Jews), Aharon Eisenberg (a leading settler from Rehovot), and Malkiel Many (a Jerusalem lawyer who was a native of Hebron). All these leaders agreed to serve on the committee. Levi's stand was supported by Ruppin, who, like Dr. Levi, felt that a nationally-conscious Jew ought not to conceal his views, although he should stress that the new Turkish Constitution promised the Jews what the Zionists had always demanded.

The Zionist Executive and such other public bodies as the so-called "Odessa Committee" and the German Jewish Aid Society understood the political significance of the elections and allocated funds for the election campaign. This enabled a group of Jews and Arabs to publish a newspaper in Arabic, as a supplement to the *Hashkafa*, edited by Ben-Yehuda. (When the election campaign ended, the paper ceased publication.) Dr. Levi contacted the Moslem politician Hussain Al-Hussaini (who was elected Mayor of Jerusalem in 1910), and they issued a joint call to the voters, requesting their support. At that time, the elections were held in two stages: the voters chose an electoral college, which then chose the members of the Parliament. In the second stage, each representative could vote for three members. Of the 175 members of the electoral college, 140 were Moslems, 30 Christians, and 4 Jews. Dr. Levi withdrew his candidature, and Al-Hussaini was not elected. To represent the Jerusalem *sandjak*, three members of influential families were chosen: Ruhi Al-Khalidi (formerly Turkish Consul in Bordeaux), Said Al-Hussaini (a former mayor of Jerusalem) and Said Hafez, of Gaza. However, as noted earlier, they constituted only three of the sixty Arab members of Parliament.

The problem of Jewish-Arab relations now took on a new, decisive importance. It was no longer possible to ignore it. The Arab members of Parliament launched a campaign in the Turkish press in Constantinople and in Parliament itself. Only a short time after the July 1908 uprising and

in Macedonia, then in Anatolia, Beirut, and Damascus. When the Baron's *moshavot* were transferred to ICA's management, he was asked to manage the *moshavot* in Judaea and the Rishon Lezion wine cellars. Made contact with Arab circles. It was due to his efforts that the bitter dispute between the settlers of Metulla and the local druzes was settled. (He went to Jabal Ad-druze to hold talks with the Al-Atrash family, who had the predominant influence there.) Levi was obliged to resign from the ICA management because of his support for the farmers against the ICA administration.) From 1904 onward, he was manager of the Jerusalem branch of the Anglo-Palestine Bank.

the proclamation of the Constitution, Arab periodicals, published by Christian Arabs, began to appear in Palestine. The first of these was the weekly *Al-Carmel*, founded in Haifa in 1908 by Najib Nassar, a Greek Orthodox Arab; this appeared with occasional interruptions until 1942. The daily newspaper *Falastin*, founded in Jaffa in 1911 by Issa Al-Issa and his family, who were also Greek Orthodox, appeared in Jaffa until 1948, and afterwards, under Jordanian rule in the Old City of Jerusalem. In 1912, *Al Muntada* (The Club) was founded in Jerusalem. These papers formed focal points of anti-Jewish propaganda, which was picked up, in turn, by the Damascus and the Beirut press. Even if the new rulers of Turkey showed sympathy for the Jewish enterprise in Palestine, they could not ignore Arab public opinion, which carried more weight in the wake of the political changes in the Otto-man Empire. As Kalvarisky noted:

The Arabs considered Zionism an enemy which could oust them from an area they considered purely Arab in character. Before the new Constitution was pro-claimed, the Arab officials would occasionally help us to found *moshavot*, turning a blind eye to the various laws forbidding Jews to settle in the country and build it. After the Constitution was promulgated, there appeared on the scene new officials, who had studied and graduated in Constantinople and were fanatical nationalists. Such were Shukry Al-'Asali [the Kaim makam in Nazareth, who opposed the purchase of Merhavia in 1910], At-Tamimi, Muhammad Al-Inglizi and others who began placing obstacles in our path systematically. Members of Parliament from Jerusalem spoke against us and our work in official debates.

Zionist Mission in Constantinople

In his book *The Growth of the Zionist Movement* (Vol. III, Chapter 10), Yitshak Gruenbaum wrote that the July 1908 coup "came as a great surprise to the Zionist movement and its leaders." Naturally the Zionist leadership had been aware of the Young Turks' existence, and Max Nordau had even had contacts with some of this group's leaders. But "the relations with the Sultan and his entourage and the attempts to win favor at the Yildiz Kiosk prevented Herzl and his aides from establishing any contact with the revolu-tionary forces." The Zionist leaders "did not take this factor into account. Indeed, it is not unlikely that while they were endeavoring to prove to the Sultan and his advisers that the Zionist program could rehabilitate and strengthen the Empire, they hinted to him that the rise of the Zionist force could help Constantinople internally as well. The policy of maintaining complete loyalty towards the ruling sultan and averting any suspicion that Zionism might seek to gain the support of his external and internal enemies was a cardinal tenet of Zionist policy."

When the revolution broke out, and the Sultan did not even try to defend his regime. Gruenbaum writes:

This was astonishing to the Zionist spokesmen. . . . Wolfsohn [the President of the Zionist Organization since Herzl's death], and apparently Nordau as well, did not believe the Young Turks' victory would be a lasting one. They considered the Sultan's submission a stratagem meant to lull the revolutionaries' vigilance, to split their ranks and demoralize them. They were certain the Sultan would prove stronger in the long run. Hence they decided to act with great caution, and to wait and see how matters turned out.

About a month after Sultan Abd-ul-Hamid's surrender and his reproclamation of the 1876 Constitution, Dr. Victor Jacobson arrived in Constantinople. Dr. Jacobson (1869–1934) was one of the leading Russian Zionists, and had been a member of the Zionist Executive since 1899.* His task was mainly a political one: to act as a political representative of the president of the Zionist Organization in the Turkish capital. With the help of a small fund for publications (£2,000 a year, 80 percent of which came from the Zionist Organization and the rest from the German Jews' Aid Society), he financed two Jewish weeklies: the French-language *Aurore* (Dawn) and the Hebrew-language *Hamevaser* (The Messenger). He also reached an agreement with the Constantinople paper *El Tiempo* about encouraging Zionism, and supported the paper *Le Jeune Turc* (The Young Turk), which was acquired by the Zionist Executive in May 1912. This paper gathered around it a group of Turkish writers and politicians and won a relatively large readership, becoming an important factor in shaping Turkish public opinion. *Le Jeune Turc* was often quoted by the foreign press, which needed non-Turkish sources on Turkish affairs. Jacobson and his aides also made efforts to bring the Turkish Jews closer to the Zionist movement and to enlist their assistance in its political struggle.

There was then good reason for believing that favorable conditions had been created for Zionist political efforts in Turkey. Even so cautious an observer as Ahad Ha'am grew enthusiastic, writing:

The revolution in Turkey paves the way forward to an extent which would have been quite unthinkable only a short time ago. If all the indications are correct, the gates of Palestine are destined soon to be opened before us without hindrance. The conditions of Jewish settlement and labor will change for the better in every respect. Those who buy land and build houses will no longer encounter such grave obstacles; the tax system will also be easier; and, in general, all the external handicaps which until now have made large-scale colonization in Palestine almost impossible will soon be more or less eliminated. Further, it is being rumored that the new leaders of Turkey

* Victor Jacobson: The manager of the Anglo-Palestine Bank in Beirut. Shortly before the Young Turks' revolt he was appointed the representative of the Anglo-Levantine Banking Company, which had formerly belonged to the Spanish-Jewish banker Metrani and then became part of a merger between him and the Zionist Bank in London. The Anglo-Levantine Banking Company's operations were modest: the entire capital was only £20,000. But it gave Dr. Jacobson the status of a bank manager.

are pleased by the Jewish settlement and are ready to give the new arrivals a warm reception.

Apparently the Young Turks' attitude toward Jews and Zionism was quite positive; every now and then one of the new Turkish leaders expressed the view that the gates of Turkey should be opened to the persecuted Jews, as had been done after the expulsion from Spain in 1492. "While they did not speak publicly about Palestine, they plainly referred to the immigration of Jews to this part of the Ottoman Empire, and to the Zionist Organization's being given permission to start settlement work" (Gruenbaum). Several of the Young Turk leaders had been educated in the Alliance School in Salonika and were close to the Jews. Further, many Jews gave both material and moral support to the Unity and Progress Committee, and there were members of Parliament and Jewish senators who belonged to it. Some of the Turkish Jewish leaders who belonged to the Young Turks' circles declared themselves to be Zionists and expressed their willingness to help implement the ideas of Zionism. They firmly believed that this approach concurred with their Turkish patriotism, that it showed a desire to work for the renaissance and strengthening of the Ottoman Empire, which Abd-ul-Hamid's regime had brought to the brink of chaos. It was true, that, as Gruenbaum wrote, "if the aim of the Zionist movement [were] to establish a Jewish state in Palestine and to tear it away from the Ottoman Empire, as they say it is, then there [would be] no hope for Zionism in Turkey, which does not permit separatist national movements. The revolution was carried out in order to unify the Empire, to put an end to its disintegration, to the trend towards the drift of non-Turkish nations and their territories away from Constantinople." But they believed "that the Jews who would immigrate to Turkey in general, and Palestine in particular, would play a valuable role. With their capital, education and energy they would develop this country, enrich it and strengthen it, and in cooperating with the Turks they would form a unifying force in the Empire" (Gruenbaum).

Dr. Jacobson and Vladimir Jabotinsky (1880–1940), who had also arrived in Constantinople shortly after the July revolt, as the correspondents of the liberal Moscow paper *Ruskyeh Viyedomosti* undertook an intensive information campaign in Constantinople. Now that the local Zionist leaders no longer had reason to fear the Hamidi regime, they founded a Zionist committee and assisted this campaign.

Jacobson and Jabotinsky pleaded that Zionism did not aim to separate Palestine from the Ottoman Empire. On the contrary, the Zionists knew full well that the existence of a Jewish center in Palestine could not be guaranteed unless it was located within the boundaries of, and under the protection of, a large and strong Ottoman Empire. During the tyranny of Sultan Abd-ul-Hamid, they added, the Zionists had been forced to demand a special status and even international guarantees, for fear that one day the tyrant might order the destruction of everything the Jews had built in Palestine. But in a Turkey that was free and that had a restored constitution, there was no need for external assurances or a special status: the constitution and the freedom prevailing in the country were adequate guarantees.

This view was succinctly expressed by Max Nordau at the Ninth Zionist Congress, which met in Hamburg in December 1909:

> In a Turkey that was under autocratic rule we were compelled to demand a certain freedom, which, in the general atmosphere of non-freedom, was tantamount to enjoying special rights. We needed official guarantees, in the form of a charter. In a constitutional state, in which all citizens enjoy freedom under the law, we do not need special rights. The general law is enough.

This position was officially announced by the President of the Zionist Organization, David Wolfsohn, at the Tenth Zionist Congress. He declared that the conditions of constitutional and legal freedom in the new Turkey were sufficient for Zionist work in Palestine to be carried on, if Jews were given the right to immigrate. Wolfsohn added that the Zionist movement no longer posed the conditions pertaining under Abd-ul-Hamid's tyrannical rule.

The Young Turks' constitutional program, and their economic and cultural policy, naturally ensured the Jews special place in their plans. The Turkish traditions and record of assistance to the Jews over the centuries, as well as the status of the Jewish community in Turkey under the *ancien régime*, reinforced this trend. It is true that there was only a small number of Jews in Turkey— not more than half a million in the entire Ottoman Empire, and that if they were to fulfill the role the Young Turks had in mind for them, their numbers would have to be increased. Hence the new leaders of Turkey reiterated their unofficial invitations to Jews to settle in their country. This was the reason for their favorable attitude toward the Zionist organization, which, they hoped, would sponsor the immigration of Jews for the joint benefit of Turkey and the Jewish community.

There was no inclination on the part of the Young Turks to exclude Palestine from the rest of Turkey. At the same time, they refused to agree that Palestine should be the only and final objective for the Jews settling in Turkey. They wanted Jews to come to Macedonia, the Izmir (Smyrna) area, and other parts of the country with only a small Turkish population. In Palestine there were scarcely any Turks; on the other hand, Constantinople feared that Jewish immigration might arouse the resentment of the Arabs. As Gruenbaum noted, "The Zionist representatives in Constantinople tried as hard as they could to explain to the Unity and Progress leaders that their fears were unfounded and that the Jews would bring the hoped-for benefits to Turkey. If Palestine were opened to them, they might settle in other places as well. But if they were invited to Turkey while Palestine was closed to them, they would not come at all."[4]

According to Gruenbaum, "at that time Jabotinsky was the only one who really understood the problem deeply." He wrote an article in the Russian Zionist weekly *Razsvet* arguing that "we must increase the power and strength of the Jews in Palestine by mass immigration, so that the Arabs will not remain the only people living in this country and the neighbouring lands—in Asia to the north and Africa to the south. A large and culturally advanced Jewish population could serve as a sort of watershed, separating vast bodies of water on both sides."

Even at this early date, Jabotinsky's approach already embodied the kernel of the Revisionist political concepts, which relied, not on finding ways to attain understanding and cooperation with the Arabs, but on competition with them and on a contest against them vis-a-vis the Turks, then the British, etc.). Jabotinsky's idea was not in itself new. It had been suggested earlier by Nordau, who said in his address to the Ninth Zionist Congress on July 27, 1905:

A movement containing a large part of the Arab people could easily take a direction which would harm Palestine. Then the land of our forefathers would once more be at the center of world political interest, as it has so often been in the course of history.
The Turkish government might consider itself compelled to preserve its rule over Palestine and Syria by force, even against its own subjects. If this happens, the European governments will face a grave dilemma. . . . In this state of affairs Turkey might recognize that it is important for her that Palestine and Syria should be inhabited by a strong and well-organized people, with all its appreciation of the rights of those formerly living in the land, would not only oppose any attack on the Sultan's authority but would defend it with all its might. Europe will also benefit greatly if the Jewish people, after conquering Palestine peacefully but energetically, would protect it from an enforced change in its regime; this would do away with the need for the intervention of the powers, the dangers of which are fully understood in diplomatic quarters. But in order that the Jewish people will be able to play the role hinted at here, it will have to inspire Turkey and Europe with confidence in its will and ability.

Nordau's remarks at the Zionist Congress were echoed by similar statements and articles. In 1905, for example, Ussishkin wrote an essay entitled "Our Program," in which he demanded that "the whole of Palestine, or at least most of it, shall belong to the Jewish people", and said that Arab labor on the Jewish farms was "a gnawing cancer."

The Arab national movement was of course familiar with this school of thought. In 1909, various politicians and journalists received the French translation of the book *Palestine—the Jewish Land*, written in German in 1908 by Jacobus Kann, a financier from the Hague and a member of the

World Zionist Executive. At the end of his book he summed up his approach by saying that an autonomous Jewish government should be formed in Palestine ("whose natural limits are Mount Lebanon in the north, the Hejaz railroad through Ma'an in Transjordan in the east, the Ma'an-Akaba line south to the Sinai Peninsula in the south, and the Mediterranean Sea to the west"). This Jewish government should be protected by the Turkish Sultan. All the land in the country, apa   from that registered as private property, should be leased for a minimum of one hundred years to a body representing the Jewish people. The Turkish government should transfer all its authority, including the right to collect taxes, to the Jewish authorities, who would be headed by a Jewish governor, protected directly by the Sultan. Immigrants settling in Palestine would be obliged to adopt Turkish nationality. A Jewish army would be formed. ("In Russia alone there are more than 50,000 Jewish soldiers." As far as officers and instructors were concerned, "the Turkish government will be ready to place them at our disposal.") For, "even if we organize a strong police force on a high level, this will not be enough. If we want peace, we shall have to prepare for war. If we want order and quiet to reign in the country, we must be ready to suppress riots and disturbances."

This book aroused considerable resentment among the leadership of the Zionist movement. The heads of the Zionist mission in Constantinople feared that it would upset the trust and confidence they had won for themselves and would make it impossible to continue the Zionist information campaign. Jabotinsky sent David Wolfsohn a cable in his own name and in the names of his comrades. They demanded that the President of the World Zionist Organization declare immediately that Kann's book did not express the views of the Zionist Executive. So that Wolfsohn's official disassociation would carry sufficient weight, Jacobus Kann should resign. In his letter to Wolfsohn, Jabotinsky stressed that "no revolutionary party among the peoples of Turkey has made such far-reaching political demands to date."

This demand by Jabotinsky and his colleagues, and the formalistic stand taken by Wolfsohn, led to a prolonged crisis in the leadership of the Zionist movement. But this crisis remained an internal matter—whereas Kann's book had an adverse effect on the Zionist movement's external struggles.

Attempts to Contact Arab Representatives

More than anyone else at that period, Dr. Victor Jacobson concentrated on the question of Jewish-Arab relations in Zionist policy. Soon after arriving in Constantinople, he realized how important the Arab factor was in the political arena. He saw in the Arabs' opposition to the aspirations of the Zionist movement a grave obstacle, which could foil the current political efforts in Constantinople.

The four Jews elected to the Turkish Parliament in the fall of 1908 (representing Constantinople, Izmir, Salonika, and Baghdad) were not Zionists, and they could hardly be expected to defend Jewish immigration to Palestine if the Arab members of Parliament came out against it. (Jacobson wrote to Wolfsohn that one of these Jewish members, Sasson of Baghdad, "speaks like an Arab nationalist.") At that time, even Jacobson did not have a constructive and positive idea that could have formed the basis of Jewish-Arab negotiations. He thought it necessary to enter into discussions with the Arab delegates from Palestine, "in order to influence them and prevent them acting against Zionism in the Parliament." On the other hand, Dr. Jacobson regarded the Jewish-Arab dispute as a bargaining point. He thought this could perhaps be used in the talks with Turkish politicians, who took a suspicious view of the Arabs' national awakening and were aware of the fact that mass Jewish settlement could counter separatist Arab tendencies in Syria (an idea already expressed publicly by Nordau, in his speech to the Seventh Zionist Congress in Basle, 1905).

At the beginning of December 1908, shortly before the opening of the first session of the Turkish Parliament, Dr. Jacobson visited two Arab members from Jerusalem, Said Al-Hussaini and Ruhi Al-Khalidi. As Jacobson wrote to Wolfsohn afterward, the conversation was friendly but produced no results. However, in a later letter (dated March 5, 1909) Jacobson informed the president of the Zionist Organization that in further talks Ruhi Al-Khalidi had stressed the mutual interests of the Jews and the Arabs, their common Semitic origin, and their opposition to the Turks.[5]

However, Zionist policy continued to concentrate on the Turkish rulers, even after it was obvious that the Arab national movement was a growing force. About eighteen months after the Young Turks' revolt, Max Nordau explained this policy to the Ninth Zionist Congress, held in Hamburg in December 1909:

> The land of our hopes, our aspirations and our labors, the holy land of our fathers, lies within the borders of the Ottoman Empire. Its coasts and borders are guarded by Turkish soldiers. The keys to the house which we Zionists want to make our national home are in the hands of the Turkish government. Hence it is natural that all our efforts are directed towards Turkey.

This declared policy aggravated Arab opposition to Jewish immigration and to the acquisition of land in Palestine. When the land at Fula (the site of Merhavia) was bought in 1910, the leading Constantinople papers carried a cable sent by the heads of the Arab communities in Nazareth, noting the danger that Jewish immigration posed to the political and economic status of the local Arab population. The cable claimed that "the Zionists plan to drive us off our land and these purposes of theirs are matters of life and death to us."

Le Jeune Turc published an answer to these charges. But the Arab spokesmen raised the issue with the Unity and Progress committee, and demanded that the Minister of the Interior, Tal'at Bey, should not facilitate the entry of Jews into Palestine and that Jews should not be allowed to buy Arab land. Following this discussion, the local authorities in Palestine were ordered to see that the erstwhile restrictions on Jewish immigration and land purchases— limitations that the Zionist representatives in Constantinople were trying to remove—should be scrupulously observed. As the above-mentioned cable from Nazareth was signed by one Moslem and six Christians (representing the various communities in the town), P. A. Alsberg writes:

> Dr. Jacobson drew the Turkish politicians' attention to the fact that behind the Christian Arabs stood Russia, which wanted to use them to increase its influence in Palestine. Dr. Jacobson knew very well that the Turks were more afraid of increased Russian influence than of further Jewish settlement and his remarks made an impression on his listeners. As usual, the Turkish government promised both sides that it would take note of their demands and the situation remained unchanged.*

Like the affair of the lands in lower Galilee in 1900, the case of the Fula lands in 1910 became a focal point of the relations among the Jews, Arabs, and Turks. One of the most active individuals on the Arab side was an official named Shukry Al-Asali,† who adhered to the Arab national movement and was *Kaimmakam* of Nazareth in 1910 to 1911. He did all he could to prevent the land's being transferred to the Jews, and, when he failed in this, he refused to register the transfer in the Land Registry, although he was ordered to do so by the Turkish *wali* of Beirut. This cost Al-Asali his post, but his dismissal won him added prestige in Arab nationalist circles. Later, Al-Asali, one of the chief opponents of Jewish settlement, was elected to Parliament as deputy for the Damascus district. During World War I, he was one of the twenty-two heads of the Arab national movement who were hanged in the spring of 1916 in Damascus and Beirut by the Turkish Commander-in-Chief, Jamal Pasha, on charges of planning an uprising.

In the spring of 1911, several Arab members of the Turkish Parliament used a budget debate as an opportunity for a violent attack on Zionism. The speakers—the aforesaid Shukry Al-Asali, Ruhi Al-Khalidi, and Said Al-Hussaini, all deputies for Jerusalem—noted that the Jewish *Yishuv* had a strong internal organization and that the colonies enjoyed self-government

---

* From: "The Arab Question in the Policy of the Zionist Executive before World War I," an interesting research project at the Hebrew University under the guidance of Professor B. Dinur. It is based mainly on documents in the Central Zionist Archives in Jerusalem (the files of the Central Zionist Office in Cologne 1905–1911, in Berlin 1911–1920, and in the Palestine Office in Jaffa 1908–1918). Part of the work (in Hebrew) was published in the fourth issue of *Shivat Zion*, a research forum for Zionist questions.

† A member of the secret Arab organization *Al-Qahtaniah*, set up in 1909.

without a single government official. They pointed out that the Jews had
formed organizations that gave their members training in order to accustom
them to military activities. The Jews had their own schools, a national
anthem, and a blue-and-white flag bearing the emblem of Zion, which they
carried openly at processions. They even had their own stamps, bearing the
portraits of their leaders. (The Parliament was shown Jewish National Fund
stamps bearing images of Herzl and Nordau.) All these, in the opinion of the
Arab members of Parliament, proved that the Zionist movement had a
political purpose. As further proof of their charges, they produced Ussishkin's
brochure *Our Program* and the book by Jacobus Kann. Ruhi Al-Khalidi drew
a distinction between "Jews" and "Zionists." He had nothing against the
first, whereas most of the Zionists were Russian subjects, who preserved their
foreign citizenship and thus endangered the Arab population of Palestine
and the Ottoman Empire.

The debate in the Turkish Parliament had repercussions among the Arabs
of Palestine. On March 31 of that year, Dr. Ruppin wrote from Jaffa to Dr.
Jacobson saying that, on the initiative of Nashashibi of Jaffa, more than 150
Arab notables had sent a cable to the Turkish Parliament protesting land
purchases by Jews. None of the Jewish members of Parliament spoke in
defense of Jewish aspirations in Palestine. After Dr. Jacobson had taken the
initiative, one of the Bulgarian members, Dmitri Vlachov, answered the
Arab arguments.* Vlachov used the figures supplied by Jacobson in order to
rebut the Arab attack. The data he used contained figures on the improved
situation of the indigenous population of Palestine, thanks to Jewish immigration: the increased wages paid to Arab workers in the Jewish agricultural
areas, compared with other areas; figures that refuted the claim that fellaheen

* Dmitri Vlachov was one of the two principal leaders of the International Workers'
Union in Macedonia, which had headquarters at Salonika and other branches elsewhere
in Macedonia, Constantinople, and Anatolia. It was composed, on a federative basis, of
four national divisions, the largest of which was that of Jewish workers (which had a
paper of its own in the language spoken by the Sephardic Jews; it was called *Solidaridada
uvradeira*). This Jewish division was led by Abraham Ben-Aruia, one of the two top
leaders of the general workers' union, an assimilated Jew who called himself a "Sephardic
Bundist." The second in size was the Bulgarian division, led by Vlachov. The other two
divisions, composed of Greek and Turkish workers, also issued a paper, each in its own
language. Vlachov, who formed a friendship with Y. Ben-Zvi, was a keen supporter of
Zionism. In elections to the Turkish Parliament, the Zionists cast their vote for the
Bulgarian, Vlachov, rather than for Ben-Aruia, the assimilated Jew (who was not
elected).

When Salonika was separated from Turkey after the Balkan War, its place in the
Turkish delegation to the Socialist International was taken by the Poalei Zion union on
the grounds that in Salonika and, particularly in its labor movement, the Jews were
predominant.

Interesting information regarding this transfer of Salonika's place to Poalei Zion in
1912, may be found in Berl Locker's article in *Hapoel Hatzair*, Nos. 41–42, July 18, 1950.

were being displaced from their land by Jewish settlers; and proof that the percentage of Jews in Palestine was lower than the Arabs had claimed and did not endanger the Arabs' political status.*

The debate in Parliament ended without a vote being taken. But it underlined the difficulties in the Zionist movement's political struggle. *Ahdut*, the organ of the Poalei Zion movement, called upon the Jewish members of Parliament to act like the Bulgarians, Greeks, and Armenians. If they would not do this, the paper declared, "we shall know, and the entire world will know, that the half a million Jews living in the Ottoman Empire are like scattered sheep without a shepherd, who have no spokesmen in the Turkish Parliament."

Poalei Zion and Zionist Policy

One of the most important Jewish political groups at that time was the Zionist labor party, Poalei Zion. Its members were generally influenced by the Russian Zionist leaders' belief that the sultan's overthrow had created a new and hopeful situation. They had faith in the Young Turks and in the emerging liberal trends, which they thought would lead to the creation of an Ottoman Empire based on the brotherhood of peoples. Within this framework, there would be a place for the Jews as an autonomous nation in Palestine. Yet, despite the Zionist mission in Constantinople, despite Zionist periodicals and the contacts with influential politicians, little concrete political progress was made.

In the summer of 1910, a call for a reappraisal of the situation was heard in the paper *Ahdut*:

The Ottoman Empire embraces various peoples and tribes that are very different in race, language, culture, socio-economic structure, and national interests. Under the Sultan's authoritarian rule all of them were equally suppressed. Now that the revolution has taken power out of the hands of one ruler and given it to the people, a new period of national development has begun in the lives of the various peoples. . . . Political liberation and economic development also bring in their wake a national awareness and renaissance. This national consciousness is spreading among broad sections of the population. The peoples are showing a growing desire for self-determination. Hence, as long as the national question will not attain a proper solution, competition will be severe and wars will break out between the various peoples of the Empire.[6]

We need not go into the reasoning behind this enthusiastic evaluation of the Young Turks' revolt and the claim that it had transferred the rule to the

* According to *The Levant Herald*, Constantinople, of May 17, 1911. D. Vlachov's notes on this session of the Turkish Parliament are preserved in the Central Zionist Archives in Jerusalem.

hands of the people. In any event, the July 1908 revolt clearly influenced the Arab national movement in its clash with the Jewish national movement.

In view of this development, what policy should the Zionist Organization have followed? How could a bridge of understanding have been built between the two peoples, so that the growth of a mutually destructive national dispute could have been averted? Not even the socialists within the Zionist movement had a basic answer to this question. Often confusing national interests with class interests, they were inclined to give priority to temporary political advantages, losing sight of long-term national and social plans and perspectives. The above-mentioned *Ahdut* article raised the question: What was the source of the Jewish-Arab antagonism, expressed in the on-slaughts against various Jewish *moshavot* and in the attacks by the Arab press? The answer—somewhat oversimplified—was, the article continued:

This hatred originates in the Arab laborers working in the Jewish *moshavot*. Like all other workers, the Arab laborer resents and hates anyone who exploits him. But as in addition to the class distinction there is also a national difference between the Arab workers and the Jewish employers, this hatred takes on a national character. In fact, the national factor sometimes overcomes the class element and the Arab laborers begin entertaining a vehement hatred for the Jews.

The matter of Jewish labor was certainly basic to an understanding of the problem at the time. The dismissal of several thousand Arab workers by Jewish farmers aggravated the situation. This was well understood by Arthur Ruppin, who considered the demand of labor-Zionist circles for "exclusively Jewish labor," an *economic* factor creating Jewish-Arab tension. Ruppin argued that the positive aspect of the "Jewish labor" campaign—i.e., that of providing work for Jewish laborers—should be stressed, but that it should not be construed as a tendency to boycott Arab workers. Trying to influence the Jewish workers to reach a *modus vivendi* with their Arab counterparts, Ruppin went so far as to advise against insisting on the "Jewish labor" slogan. He also thought it important that the Jewish workers should speak Arabic and learn to understand their Arab neighbors and their way of life.[7]

In the autumn of 1910, the Poalei Zion Council met in Jaffa. The political discussion was opened by David Ben-Gurion. Outlining the party's policy, he stated:

We cannot limit our social activity to the workers in Palestine, nor are we entitled to do so. For apart from the common interests we have in Palestine, there are national and political matters concerning us both as workers and as Jews which bind us to the Jewish workers in the other parts of Turkey and to the workers of the other peoples in the Ottoman Empire. For example, there is the question of the workers in Parliament, the freedom to form unions and to strike, laws defending work, and so on. We cannot attain anything in these spheres by ourselves. The Jewish workers in Palestine will not carry weight in this respect or exert political influence. And for this reason we must unite with all the Ottoman workers, and first and foremost with the Jewish workers.

Ben-Gurion also noted the wish of the new Turkish regime to throw off the yoke of European domination and subjugation, symbolized by the capitulations. He called upon the Jewish community to display a positive attitude toward this Turkish desire, through refraining from applying to foreign consuls, and relying upon their own efforts. He did not touch on the political aspects of the Jewish-Arab problem.

Before Palestinian delegates Y. Ben-Zvi and Rachel Yanait returned home from the Second Convention of Poalei Zion (Cracow, September 1909), the organization provided them with money for a journey through the Balkan countries of Serbia, Bulgaria, and European Turkey. There they made personal contact with the socialist leaders who, in January 1910, were to found (at their convention in Belgrade) the Balkan Social-Democratic Federation, in conjunction with Rumanian and Greek socialists. Ben-Zvi and Yanait also met with the two Armenian Socialist deputies in the Turkish Parliament.

The Third Convention of Poalei Zion (Vienna, July–August 1911), passed a resolution that the party's Palestinian members "would work together with the Jewish socialist groups in the other parts of Turkey for the unification of the socialist Ottoman proletariat in a single national federation."

At the Tenth Zionist Congress (Basle, August 1911), one of the Poalei Zion delegates, S. Kaplansky, raised the question of relations with the Arabs and the need to explain to the latter the benefits the Zionist enterprise could bring them. The labor-Zionists undoubtedly conducted important political activities, both in Palestine and in contacts with Socialist leaders in the Balkans and elsewhere. But the basic political problem of Jewish-Arab relations was becoming graver.

The Dilemma Facing Zionist Policy

Under Abd-ul-Hamid's regime, Zionist policy was based on the principle of absolute loyalty to the Turkish Sultan and avoidance of the slightest suspicion of a connection with his internal or external enemies. During this period, no section of the Zionist movement—not even its socialist wing—demanded that contact be established with the opposition elements in Turkey that rallied to the Young Turks. The Zionist leaders even refrained from bringing Turkish Jews into the picture, for fear that this would create an impression of disloyalty to the sultan. For their part, the Jews of Turkey were careful not to give even a hint of their sympathy for Zionism, even when Herzl and other Zionist leaders visited Constantinople.

When the Young Turks overthrew the sultan and raised the banner of a Turkish renaissance that would give all its people autonomy within the framework of the Ottoman Empire, Zionist policy placed its hopes in the development of a constitutional commonwealth of nations, within which the Jewish people could attain its own center and a degree of national and political autonomy in Palestine.

This confronted Zionist policy with at least two mutually contradictory tasks:

(a) While Zionism favored a Turkish renaissance, the great powers, apart from Germany, wanted to see Turkey weaken and eventually disintegrate. The Zionist leaders wanted these powers, to help them. Russia (the center of the largest Zionist groups) and Great Britain supported the movements formed by the suppressed people in the Ottoman Empire. Russia supported the Armenians, while Britain and France backed the Arabs. They also upheld the claims of the new states that had liberated themselves from the Turkish yoke with Russian and British help. At this time, British political circles took a suspicious view of the Zionist movement, regarding it as one of the forces aiding Germany's Eastern policy—the strengthening of Turkey as a bridge to the entire Middle East.

(b) If Turkey became a constitutional Monarchy of different nationalities, this would inevitably lead to the Arabs' gaining autonomy in their own countries, and would hence reinforce the Arab national movement. The small, weak, Jewish community in Palestine, and the Zionist movement—still in its infancy and not so strong as it was to become later—faced a grave dilemma: whether to try to convince the new rulers of Turkey that a large Jewish immigration would provide a counterweight to Arab nationalism (a step that would naturally make it impossible to cooperate with the growing Arab national movement), or to dare to seek an alliance with the Arab national movement (with all that this implied for relations with the Turkish rulers).

The Zionist movement and leadership were unable to resolve this dilemma. Writing from Jaffa on July 15, 1911, to David Wolfsohn, the President of the Zionist Actions Committee in Cologne, Arthur Ruppin gave an illuminating evaluation of the situation. The Arab leaders resented the Turks, he noted, but were too weak to express clearly what they really wanted—Arab autonomy. In this situation, Jewish settlement was an excellent theme for propaganda among the masses, who were receptive to this type of agitation. On the other hand, the Turkish government, which probably considered Jewish settlement a sort of barrier against the Arab danger, did not dare to come out openly against the Arabs; in order to reassure them, it even gave them minor concessions at the expense of the Jews. If there were no other factors involved, the Turkish government would almost certainly be ready to take a tolerant attitude toward Jewish settlement, and perhaps even to encourage it quietly. Ruppin did not agree with those of the Jewish community who insisted that "the Jews must go either with the Arabs or the Turks." He felt that under the circumstances no such dogmatic position could be laid down. "It is necessary to manoeuver with great tact," he wrote, "in order to reassure both the Government and the Arabs at the same time. We believe the present agitation will die down, because the Arabs will realize that they gain nothing for themselves by agitating against the Jews."

The Intricacies of Turkish Policies

Dr. Jacobson never stopped hoping that he would be able to sign an agreement with the Turkish rulers. At the same time, he worked for closer ties with the Arab members of the Turkish Parliament and with other Arab politicians in Constantinople, with a view to interesting them in cooperation with the Jewish community. In 1911, he and his aides met the heads of Arab clubs and organizations. Abd-ul-Karim Al Khalil, president of *Al-Muntada Al-Adabi* (a cultural-nationalist Arab organization that brought together several groups in the Arab national movement); Saif-ud-Din Al-Khatib, an activist in the Arab national movement in Constantinople, and As'ad Daghir, a Christian Arab who was foreign editor of *Al Ahram* in the 1930s; Riad As-Sulh, one of the leaders of the national movement in Syria under the Turkish regime, and several times Prime Minister of Lebanon after it attained independence; Faris Al-Khoury, Prime Minister of Syria after World War II, and Syrian delegate to the United Nations on a number of occasions, and others. These meetings were not intended to determine any specific policies, but to explore possibilities of cooperation. According to the evidence presented by Asher Saphir* to the Peel Commission in February 1937, the political program discussed at these meetings was based on the understanding that "when the Arabs would implement their plan for 'decentralization' of autonomy of the Arab provinces, they would agree to give the Jews Palestine as a 'centralized' area among the autonomous countries, provided they [the Jews] assist the economic development of all the Arab provinces."

Arab nationalist circles were already disappointed by the Young Turks'

---

* Asher Saphir (1893–1942): A native of Palestine, descended from a family that had been living in the country for over two centuries. During his studies at the University of Constantinople (and later at the School of Political Studies in Paris) in the years preceding World War I, he was accepted into the Arab society *Al-Muntada al-Adabi*. He became friendly with many leading personalities in the Arab national movement who later became leading statesmen in the Arab countries. During the above-mentioned period, Saphir was one of Dr. Jacobson's assistants in Constantinople. He presented evidence to the Enquiry Commission under the chairmanship of Lord Peel (in February 1937), which was published as a leaflet entitled "Unity or Partition", with an introduction by Professor David Yellin (Jerusalem, July 1937), p. 13.

policies. As early as 1909, the Arab-Ottoman Brotherhood Society had been closed down by the authorities; and at the end of 1910, Constantinople took a clear turn towards centralization in the government and Ottomanization of all peoples living in the Ottoman Empire.

During the Moroccan crisis in the summer of 1911, Italy invaded Tripolitania, then a Turkish province, and declared it an Italian colony. At the time of the war in Tripolitania (1911–1912), the Zionist movement sought a way to express its support for the Turks, who were on the defensive. One proposal was to raise a regiment to help the Turkish campaign. But the Turkish Jews did not volunteer, and the Turkish government would not accept Jewish volunteers from other countries. Then it was proposed that a sanitary squad should be recruited to help the Turks. (An envoy was, in fact, sent to Tripoli on an exploratory mission.) But this would have cost more money than was available. All the Zionist Actions Committee could do was to seek support for Turkey by arousing European and American public opinion.

Turkey's debacle in Libya encouraged the Balkan peoples. In the summer of 1912, Bulgaria, Serbia, Montenegro, and Greece signed a joint security pact openly aimed against Turkey. In the face of this new war threat, the Turkish government signed a peace treaty with Italy at Lausanne, on October 15, 1917, acknowledging its defeat in Libya. That same month, war broke out in the Balkans. The Balkan-Pact countries soon defeated the Turkish Army, and the Greek forces entered Salonica. In December, an armistice was declared, and, at the initiative of the great powers, a round-table conference was called in London. Under the London Treaty, signed in May 1913, Turkey lost its remaining European territories, apart from the Constantinople area and a narrow strip of land west of the Bosphorus. Because of the quarrels of the Balkan countries over these former Turkish possessions, Constantinople was able to defeat Bulgaria and recover Eastern Thrace (including Adrianople) in July 1913.

During all these vicissitudes, the Zionist leadership remained loyal to the Turkish regime. Before the London round-table conference, Max Nordau and his friends (the "political" wing of the Zionist movement) urged a policy based on the assumption that Turkey's fate was sealed and that Zionist demands on Palestine should now be pressed. The Zionist Executive opposed this on the ground that the movement should not join those calling for the dismemberment of the Ottoman Empire; on the contrary, Constantinople should be shown that the Zionist movement and the Jewish people as a whole were its faithful friends. The Executive wished to present the Zionist aspirations to the Turkish authorities as proposals which could confer great benefits on Turkey, without trying to impose the Zionist movement's will on the Turkish rulers through enlisting the help of those who sought to dismember the Ottoman Empire.

These external developments influenced political developments within the Ottoman Empire. The Union and Progress cabinet fell in July 1912 and was replaced by the Liberals. Later the Young Turks took over, after a military coup. On January 23, 1913, while the cabinet was meeting, a group of officers headed by Enver Pasha stormed the Sublime Porte Building. War Minister Nazim Pasha was killed in the ensuing struggle, and the Sultan was informed that his government had resigned. A Young Turk leader, Mahmoud Shevket, was charged with forming a new government.

But these high-level changes could no longer save the Ottoman Empire. The new Young Turk government was forced to sign the London Treaty in May 1913. They tried to balance this and other international setbacks by so-called "successes" at home. The persecution of legal Arab nationalist organizations in Syria and Iraq was stepped up. The central demands of these organizations were: decentralization of the Ottoman Empire; regional national governments with real authority; Arabic as an official language in Arab areas, etc. The stringent measures against them, and the growing political tension, prompted Arab nationalist circles to hold their first national conference in Paris (June 18–23, 1913). This conference—held outside the borders of Turkey with the support of foreign elements who hoped to inherit the near-moribund Ottoman Empire—was a portent of things to come.

The complexities of Turkish policy posed several delicate questions for the Zionist leaders. When elections to the Turkish Parliament were held in the spring of 1912, it appeared that the Union and Progress Party (the Young Turks), which favored Ottomanization, would gain a majority and once again form a government. Hence any support given to the Liberals would be wasted. At the same time, it was known that those Arab circles which wanted decentralization and cultural autonomy leaned towards the Liberals. It followed that supporting the Young Turks meant angering the Arabs. Since in any case there was little chance of a Jew being elected deputy for the Jerusalem *sandjak*, Dr. Jacobson thought at first that the Jews should refrain from taking part in the elections. But at a later stage, a semi-official proposal was made through a Jew who had been a member of the first Turkish Parliament, and belonged to the Young Turk leadership: If Jewish leaders would persuade the Jews of Syria, and particularly of Damascus and Beirut, to vote for the Union and Progress list, in return, the Young Turks would agree that one of their Jerusalem *sandjak's* deputies would be a Jew and the others would be acceptable to the Jewish community. Faced with this tempting proposal, Dr. Jacobson changed his mind and supported it.

A special meeting was held in the Palestine Office at the end of January 1912, to discuss ways and means of implementing the proposal. But when it came to selecting the candidates, the Young Turks did not keep their promises. The Jews voted only for their candidate, David Yellin—who was not elected—and for Ahmad Arif of Jaffa, who was not considered hostile by the Jews. The three members elected in the Jerusalem *sandjak* were all Young Turks: 'Uthman An-Nashashibi and Ruhi Al-Khalidi(Jerusalem), and Ahmad Arif (Jaffa).

Founding a Jewish Arabic Paper

Ever since the Arab national movement had emerged on the Middle East scene, the Jewish community of Palestine had discussed the possibility of publishing an Arabic newspaper. However, there were differences of opinion on how to do this. In 1907, Ish 'Ivri (the pen name of Joseph Klausner) expressed concern over attempts to teach Jewish adults Arabic.[8] He was prepared to agree that Jews be taught the "market-place Arabic' 'needed for everyday contact with the Arabs, but was opposed to teaching "the language of Arab literature."

Three years later, when the Arabic press was conducting anti-Jewish propaganda, the question of a Jewish-Arabic newspaper again was raised—this time by Kadish L. Silman. He noted the danger presented by the growth of the Arabic press and Arab literature, but nevertheless concluded that "an Arabic-language Jewish paper would be not only superfluous but harmful."[9]

However, Jewish authorities were now concerned by the attacks on Jews in the Arabic press, and were seeking ways to answer them. According to documents in the Central Zionist Archives, as early as February 1910, the Zionist Actions Committee approved a budget of 2,000 francs per annum, "for the purpose of influencing the Arab press." The Palestine Office in Jaffa paid 750 francs for twenty-five subscriptions to daily papers, 100 francs for five subscriptions to weeklies, 500 francs for commercial advertisements, and 500 francs for reading the Arab newspapers and writing replies to points raised. On September 24, 1911, Ruppin wrote to Professor Warburg, asking for another 5,000 francs per annum to meet the cost of a press office in Jaffa, part of the duties of which would be to see that the Hebrew press did not carry items that would arouse bitterness among the Arabs.

In 1912 to 1913 the Hebrew press conducted an interesting debate on the best way of reacting to the anti-Jewish propaganda in Arab papers like *Falastin* and *Al Carmel*. Several influential Jews suggested founding an Arabic-language daily paper, with Arab writers among the contributors. In their opinion, the proposed paper would be able to reply to Arab press charges and explain the benefits the Jews were bringing to Palestine. The more intellectual members of the Sephardi Jewish community, who were fluent in both classical and colloquial Arabic and had close personal ties with the Arab public, understood the importance of this newspaper. The Russian-born leaders of the first and second *Aliyah*, however, had little understanding of the need for such a paper. For the most part, this latter group dismissed the problem as unimportant, thus betraying their lack of knowledge and understanding of what was at stake though there were exceptions.

The young Rabbi Y. M. Toledano (later the chief Rabbi of Tel Aviv and Israel's Minister of Religious Affairs in 1958) argued that "founding a Jewish-Arabic newspaper would not only be useful but is in fact almost a duty." (*Haherut*, August 28, 1912). In his opinion, this paper should take up the cudgels against those Christian Arab writers who stirred up hatred against the Jews. Hebrew writers were urged by Toledano to search for Arab weaknesses and to denounce them as the Arabs had condemned the Jews' shortcomings—which Toledano was prepared to recognize.

Dr. Nissim Malloul added another reason for publishing an Arabic-language paper: "A Jewish-Arab paper would be the best means of winning over our brethren in Syria, Egypt, Tunis, Algeria, and Morocco to our cause and to the benefit that can be obtained from the Zionist movement."[10]

Other voices were raised against the program. A. Ludwifol (1865–1921), a Zionist journalist who had been a delegate to the earliest Zionist congresses, felt that some of the young Sephardic Jews "preached assimilation with the Arabs and wanted to accept their language and culture, at the expense of Hebrew language and culture." Others questioned the political wisdom of publishing a political Jewish organ in Arabic, and suggested that it would be better to find subscribers to an existing Arab paper, such as *Al Ahram*.

The difference between the views of those Jewish intellectuals who spoke Arabic and those who did not was well expressed by David Yellin, who wrote, "I know that there are many among us who make light of this matter and think it can be ignored. This comes about simply because they do not know Arabic and are not familiar with the actual words of those who oppose us, except through rumors or occasional translations."[11]

Among the few European settlers who favored the idea of the Arabic-language paper in principle was one of the heads of Poalei Zion who wrote under the pen name of Avner. This was Yitshak Ben-Zvi, later to be the second President of the state of Israel. In October 1912, he published an article in *Ahdut* under the title "Founding an Arabic Paper." He argued that the proposed paper would achieve several objectives such as "gradual influence on some of the progressive Arab intelligentsia, who have not yet been harmed by the anti-Semitic venom of the Christian sects and the new anti-Semites, and step-by-step education of the Arab masses in the spirit most suited to us: the spirit of democracy and international peace."

An Arabic-language paper called *Saut-ul-Uthmaniah* (the Voice of Ottomania), edited by Dr. Shimon Moyal,* began appearing in Jaffa at the end of January 1914; however, shortly after World War I broke out, it closed down. Dr. Moyal and his wife had invested much effort in the paper, and lost a great deal of money when it failed. *Saut-ul-Uthmaniah* was conceived as the Arabic organ of the Jewish community and sought Arab sympathy for Jewish aspirations.

In 1913, a secret society called *Hamagen* (The Shield) was formed by Dr. Shimon Moyal, advocate David Moyal, Avraham Elmaleh, Joseph Chelouche, Jacob Chelouche, and Nissim Malloul. It aimed at fostering understanding and brotherhood between Jews and Arabs, and countering Arab attacks on the Jewish population. The society established contact with the leaders of the Arab national movement. When the homes of prominent Arab leaders were searched by order of the Commander-in-Chief of Jamal Pasha, the members of *Hamagen* faced a similar danger. Nissim Malloul managed to burn "incriminating" correspondence, but after various documents were found on Arab nationalist enthusiasts, Malloul was arrested and deported to Damascus.

Attempts at Jewish-Arab Negotiations, 1913

The Arab Congress in Paris, in June 1913, was an overt anti-Turkish demonstration. Its object was to bring Arab nationalist demands to world attention. Arab nationalist leaders attached much importance to Jewish influence on the world press and in the European political arena. When they extended their anti-Turkish campaign, they also saw fit to modify their tactics on Jewish-Arab relations. While previously, in 1911 to 1912, they had tried to prevent a rapprochement between Turkish rulers and Zionist leaders, and had represented the Zionist movement as a separatist group which wanted to cut off Palestine from the Ottoman Empire, they now sought to cooperate with the Jews in the hope of forming a common front against the Turks.

On the eve of the Arab Congress in Paris, Salim Najar, a Syrian Arab who had been active with the Young Turks but now lived in Cairo and worked for Syrian independence, approached Sami Hochberg,† the managing

* Shimon Moyal (1866–1955): Born in Jaffa. Until the age of 16, he attended *heder* and *yeshivot* (religious schools); he later attended Zaki Cohen's boarding school at Beirut, where he learned Arabic and French. For some time, he read Islamic studies and Arabic literature at Al-Azhar in Cairo, and he obtained his M.D. at the (French) Jesuit university in Beirut. He settled in Cairo, practicing medicine and publishing articles in Arabic and French calling for progress and brotherhood in the Arab world and for brotherhood between Jews and Arabs. After the Turkish revolution and the granting of the constitution (1908), he returned to Jaffa, where he resumed his medical practice and his literary and public activities.

† Sami (Samuel) Hochberg: Born in the Jewish farming village of Dombroveni in Bessarabia in 1869. Came to Palestine in 1889; worked as laborer and watchman in the vineyards of Rishon Lezion, later was one of the founders of Nes Ziona. Became a

editor of *Le Jeune Turc* and one of Dr. Jacobson's assistants in Constantinople and proposed setting up an Arab-Jewish alliance. In his letter to Hochberg, Najar wrote that in view of the Turkish government's attitude towards the Arab demands, the Arabs were considering an appeal to the London conference, that was discussing Turkey's relations with the Balkan countries. Najar added that the Arabs wanted to make their problem an international one. "Please emphasize to Dr. Jacobson once more," he wrote, "that the return of the committee [Union and Progress] to power will not be for long and you will have to work with us. Would it not be best to start now? The time has come to foresee the shape of things to come. If you decide sincerely on a pact between us, kindly inform us who is the authorized Zionist representative here [in Cairo] so that we can make contact with him."

Jacobson had long sought a connection with the Arab movement, and had contemplated sending an envoy to the Syrian nationalist circles in Cairo, which was then under British rule and had become the focal point of anti-Turkish Arab agitation. He grasped this opportunity eagerly and sent Hochberg to Cairo. Jacobson told the Zionist Executive in Berlin that Hochberg could not undertake an official mission but was eminently suitable for the task of making contact with persons in Syrian circles, many of whom he knew well. He spoke French and Arabic and had excellent contacts with both the Arabs and the Young Turks, so that he could obtain a balanced picture of the situation.

Hochberg's original report to Dr. Jacobson on his mission to Cairo and Beirut in May 1913 (written in French) has been preserved in the Central Zionist Archives. It contains a wealth of information on the Arab national movement ("which is based on the equal rights and duties of all communities, large and small alike"). He noted that there was no discrimination against Jews living in Arab areas, that they were accepted into public posts, were allowed to study Hebrew ("and will soon be given the right to employ Hebrew in the courts"). The report gives interesting details of Jewish participation in the various nationalist gatherings held in greater Syria (which then included Palestine, Lebanon, and Transjordan) and pointed to the important possibilities open to the Jews if they took an increased interest in the movement. As far as immigration to Palestine was concerned, he wrote:

teacher in Rehovot and for some time head of the village council. Was appointed teacher of Arabic at Mikveh Israel, and later principal of the Alliance school at Tiberias; director of the Alliance institutions in Persia and for some time in Istanbul, where he became involved in political discussions. Was one of the editors of *Hamevaser* (*The Messenger*) in 1910 to 1911, and was active in the leading circles of the Young Turks. When they came to power, was appointed editor of their paper *Le Jeune Turc*. Died in Instanbul (poisoned, it is believed) in March 1917. The *Chronicles of the Hagana* refers to him as "well versed in all matters of Palestine and the East."

The Arab committees have not yet had an opportunity to determine their stand on this question, as on other matters which have not yet been studied. There are various opinions on the subject. Some people are in favour of Jewish immigration and are even enthusiastic about it. Some are ready to accept Jewish immigration unreservedly, some accept it with reservations and some are opposed to immigration.

Most surprising of all, Hochberg wrote, and contrary to what Zionist circles had always believed, the Christian Arabs were enthusiastic supporters of Zionism. The Christian Arab members of the Cairo and Beirut committees explained their position to Hochberg in the following manner: Not only did they want Jews to come to Palestine and Syria, but they hoped that this influx of settlers would be large and quick, because it matched their own political and economic interests as Christian Arabs. The Arab Christians were a minority and so were the Jews. If both these minorities increased in numbers, they could form a bloc that would counterbalance the overwhelming numerical superiority of the Moslems, which the Christians feared. The intellectual superiority of the Jews and Christians could balance the Moslems' numerical supremacy. The Christian Arabs wanted to see the Jews become a majority in the country and attain complete autonomy so that they could restrain the uniform, compact mass of Moslems in Mesopotamia, Syria, Egypt, the Hejaz, and Yemen. From an economic standpoint, the Arab Christians knew full well that the Jewish immigrants would bring with them valuable skills that would help develop these areas. The Christians were first and foremost men of trade and commerce and, as such, they realized that capital, modern industrial plants, and up-to-date production methods would create a climate of prosperity, not only for those who introduced them to the Middle East, but also for the indigenous population.

As far as the Moslems were concerned, added Hochberg, they saw only the economic side of the question, even though their approach was not as unequivocal as that of the Christians. The most intelligent and outstanding Moslems took a positive view of Jewish immigration; some offered no reservations, others added such provisions as the allotment of a viable quota of land for the fellaheen—which could not be sold—or the introduction of a quota system of immigration (as enforced in the United States of America). Some Moslems suggested that every Jewish immigrant entering the country should prove that he had sufficient means to maintain himself, so that he would not become a public charge.

Among the twenty leaders with whom Hochberg conferred, two were opposed to Jewish immigration to Palestine on principle. Apart from the argument that the Zionists wanted to rob the fellaheen of their land, they claimed that the Jews were Europeanized, their behavior and *mores* not those of the East. True, the Jews were brothers in race to the Arabs, and Hebrew was a Semitic language. But the Jews had adopted a European way of life and were not coming to Palestine in order to assimilate into Arab patterns, but in order to preserve their own nationality and language. Introducing a new element, a new nationality, into the unified Arab bloc of peoples—whose strength lay in a common language, tradition, and way of life—would weaken Arab unity, they argued. Some Arabs who took a positive attitude toward the Zionist movement believed there was no need to make these views known until the situation had become clearer. These circles were afraid that their opponents, headed by the Unionists (who favoured communal integration), would criticize them "for selling the country to the Jews."

"In any event," Hochberg summed up, "it is clear that most of the members of the Cairo and Beirut committees take a positive view of Zionism and would like to come to an agreement with the Zionists with a view to cooperation." Hochberg explained to the Arab leaders that in his opinion the Zionists would not enter into an agreement with the Arabs so long as the latter had not accepted the Zionist claims as part of their own program. "It is natural and logical that the Zionists would refuse to contribute to the creation of a force that might oppose them later on."

According to Hochberg's report, neither the Cairo committee (which mainly represented the decentralists' party, banned within the Turkish Empire), nor the Beirut committee (which represented the legal wing of the Arab national movement in the Turkish territories), nor both of them together, were authorized to formulate a definite policy towards Zionism. This could only be done by an all-Arab organization, such as was to be established by the Paris Congress.

Nevertheless, Hochberg reached a preliminary verbal summing-up of the situation with the Cairo committee. His report summarized the measures agreed upon:

(a) The committee was basically in favor of Jewish immigration to Syria and Palestine and in favor of an agreement with the Zionists. It would work for closer relations between the Arab and Jewish worlds, and would endeavor, through person-to-person communication and articles in the Arab press, to eliminate those misunderstandings among the Arabs on the question of Jewish immigration that had been, and were still, an obstacle to a rapprochement between the two peoples.

(b) *Le Jeune Turc* would support the Arab movement within the framework of the unity and territorial integrity of the Ottoman Empire. The paper would do all in its power to see that the European press, and particularly the German press, with which it was in contact, should adopt a similar position.

Hochberg added that this summing-up was only the first step. The joint measures that had been agreed upon were meant to explain to the Arab public the purport and object of Zionism. This had hitherto not been presented in a way that could prepare the ground for a full accord in the future. The agreement was rounded off by a resolution adopted by the Cairo committee, and noted in the minutes. The president of the committee, Rafik Bey Al-Azm, made a statement—which was approved by the committee and published in *Le Jeune Turc* and the Arab press—declaring:

> The party has decided to protect Jewish national rights and not to adopt any law or resolution limiting them or placing them beyond the pale. As Ottoman citizens, the Jews should enjoy the same rights as all citizens of the Ottoman Empire; as foreigners, they should enjoy the same rights enjoyed by other foreigners. Any limitation imposed by the government on the Jews because of their nationality would violate the Constitution and the liberal principles of the party.
>
> It is known, that there is a stream of Jewish immigration to Syria and Palestine. To our regret, our party has not been able, because of lack of time, to study this question thoroughly. But I am certain that when this question is raised, it will be solved by joint agreement on the part of both interested parties, the Jewish and the Arab populations. We fully understand the valuable assistance that the capital, the diligence, and the intelligence of the Jews can provide to the accelerated development of our areas, and hence we must not err by not accepting them. Certainly there might be a need for regulating immigration, both Jewish and other, as is done in all civilized countries. But there is a difference between reasonable, fair regulations and extraordinary measures, such as were introduced by the old Turkish regime and have been maintained by the new regime.

Salim Najar (of whom more hereafter) was charged with writing a series of articles, in the spirit of Al-Azm's remarks, for publication in the Egyptian, Syrian, and Palestinian press, over the signatures of various members of the Cairo committee.

Ahmad Mukhtar Baihum, an influential member of the Beirut committee, took part in the negotiations and the resulting verbal agreement. The members of the Beirut committee were also kept informed of developments; Hochberg was asked to meet with them, and ultimately formed a relationship with them similar to the one he had established with the Cairo committee. The Beirut committee approved the Cairo agreement with the Zionist movement. Rizk-Allah Arkash, one of the leading members of the Beirut committee, also made a statement in favor of guaranteeing Jewish national interests in the same way that the interests of other nationals living in Arab districts were protected. The importance of the Jewish immigrants' cultural standards was stressed once again, but special reference was also made to the capital they would bring with them and the modern methods of production and labor they would introduce. Arkash stated:

> It would be a sin toward the homeland, to block immigration of this type. Those who oppose it are no more nor less than people with an axe to grind; either they hope in this way to obtain bribes from Jewish companies engaged in immigration activities, or they are usurers who fear that the arrival of the Jews will enrich the fellaheen and

improve their lot—something that would make it impossible for them to continue exploiting the fellaheen, robbing them of their land, and turning them into slaves. The educated and honest people want to encourage this immigration. The government should appreciate this, and should annul Abd-ul-Hamid's restrictions on this immigration, which is useful and nonaggressive.

Hochberg summed up the concrete results of his mission as follows:

1. Increased understanding of the nature of the Arab movement and its attitude toward Zionism;

2. the formation of initial contact with the movement's members, for the purpose of the agreement;

3. clarification of those points that would make an agreement possible;

4. an initial agreement on enlightening the public;

5. declarations in favor of the Zionist movement by several important Arab leaders.

Jacobson's emissary also held talks with the Beirut Turkish *wali*, to whom he presented important recommendations from Constantinople. The *wali* assured Hochberg that he took a favorable view of Jewish immigration, which he considered useful and nonaggressive. He added that he would categorically oppose the limitations on Jewish immigration when he wrote to the Sublime Porte in Constantinople.

Hochberg stated:

I am certain that the Turkish government's lifting the restrictions will not bring about any authoritative complaints by the Arab committees. This is one of the results —perhaps the most important result—of my journey.

The Arab movement is more important than Constantinople believes. When it improves its organization, it will be a strong and powerful force, which it will be impossible to ignore. It should not be thought that there is no bridge between their movement and Zionism. We must influence their initial steps, and not give our opponents time to influence them in the opposite direction. To do this we should: (1) be in constant contact with the leaders of the Arab movement; (2) follow all stages of this movement's development and be in a position that will enable us to use the Arab press in Syria and Palestine. One of the conclusions: we should follow the work of the Arab Congress, scheduled to meet in Paris in the second half of July 1913. This congress will accept important resolutions, and we should know about them. We should also try to influence the congress to adopt a positive resolution on Jewish immigration to Palestine.

On the strength of the reception he had enjoyed in Cairo and Beirut, and the contacts he had established with the delegates to the Paris Congress, Hochberg expressed himself ready to undertake this mission and to act as an observer, on behalf of the Zionist movement, to this congress. He was granted the authority to do so.

In a series of letters sent to Dr. Jacobson from Paris, Hochberg informed him of the composition of the delegates to the congress, its aims, the trends that emerged during the discussions, its resolutions, and the results of his own talks with the leaders of the various delegations and the congress leaders.

The keynote address on the question of immigration was delivered by Sheikh Ahmad Tabbara, who noted that "Syria could support a population four times if present population." Tabbara attributed the emigration of so many Syrians from the country to Turkish mismanagement. As far as new immigrants were concerned, he pointed out that "on this subject there are schools of thought for and against." Hochberg reported that "Tabbara chose the positive alternative, because it is more correct. The country needs controlled immigration."

This address was meant to introduce the resolution in favor of immigration, which could raise the general standard of the country. However, the debate touched on another problem as well: the immigration of Turks to Syria, with the active encouragement of Constantinople. Some speakers favored such immigration, but most of the congress opposed it vehemently. Khairalla, a member of the Arab committee in Paris and the editor of Le Temps, remarked that only settlers who came with means could be effective. And Ahmad Mukhtar Baihum, of the Beirut committee, declared simply: "The entry of Jews—yes! but the entry of Turks—no!" Eventually, the president of the congress announced that the resolution on immigration would not be passed at that session but postponed. Under these conditions, no specific resolution on Jewish immigration was presented. Hochberg summed up in one of his letters the results of his efforts:

1. The most influential members of the congress presidium favored Jewish immigration. Several of them had expressed this in one way or other;

2. no resolution opposing Jewish immigration had been adopted;

3. no statements hostile to Jewish immigration were made at the Congress.

Hochberg was not, however, overlooking the anticipated difficulties in obtaining passage of a favorable resolution. He demanded increased activity by the Zionist movement in Arab circles in Paris, Syria, and Egypt. He also quoted the president of the congress, Abd-ul-Hamid Zahrawi, as saying: "What makes a bad impression on the Arabs is that the Jews [in the Arab areas of the Ottoman Empire] stand aloof as far as the Arab movement is concerned."

Despite the fact that no decisive resolution in favor of Jewish immigration to Palestine had been adopted, the leaders of the Arab movement wished to express their affirmative point of view. Their statement resulted in what Hochberg termed "a new and extremely successful formula, according exactly with the mentality and thinking of the congress members." The new formula stated that "all the Jews in the world are in the nature of Syrian émigrés, like the Syrian Christian émigrés and others in America, Paris, and other places. Both the Jews and the other émigrés long for the homeland."

This formula was included in Zahrawi's declaration, handed to Hochberg in the latter's capacity as manager of *Le Jeune Turc*. These remarks were prepared for publication in question-and-answer form, at the end of the congress:

QUESTION: In all the congress resolutions there is no reference to Jewish matters. Do you not think that the Jewish world could consider this omission on your part a sign of ill will toward it?

ANSWER BY ZAHRAWI: The Jewish world would not be right if it thought that. All of us [the Arabs], both Moslems and Christians, have the best of feelings toward the Jews. When we spoke in our resolutions about the rights and obligations of the Syrians, this covered the Jews as well. Because they are our brothers in race *and we regard them as Syrians who were forced to leave the country at one time but whose hearts always beat together with ours,** we are certain that our Jewish brothers the world over will know how to help us so that our common interests may succeed and our common country will develop both materially and morally. Your paper and the Arab press recently published correct declarations by Rafik Bey Al-Azm, Sheikh Ahmad Tabbara, and Rizk-Allah Effendi Arkash, and I can promise you that most of the Arabs who think logically agree with these statements of ours.

During the Paris Congress, Hochberg maintained contact with the leaders of the Arab national movement, who considered that his extensive contacts qualified him to act as mediator between them and the Turkish rulers. In one of his letters Hochberg rejected the argument that an Arab-Turkish dispute would serve Jewish interests. On the contrary, he insisted, these interests would be better served if the Arabs and Turks came to an understanding, especially if this was attained with Zionist help.

It appears from his letters that Hochberg played an important role in Arab-Turkish contacts at that time. Abd-ul-Karim Al-Khalil, the president of the Arab Committee in Constantinople, informed Abd-ul-Hamid Zahrawi, president of the Arab Congress in Paris, that Hochberg's report to the Turkish Minister of the Interior, Tala'at Bey, had "made a great contribution to the Arab cause." Hochberg also acted as a mediator between the heads of the Arab Congress and the leaders of the Union and Progress group, the rulers of Turkey at the time of the Paris Congress. Fearing that the Arabs might turn European public opinion against them during the London conference on the Balkans, Constantinople came to an agreement on basic changes in the Arab areas of the Empire, in line with the resolutions of the Paris Congress.

On the basis of his talks with the Arab leaders, Hochberg advised Dr. Jacobson "to follow in the footsteps of 'Union and Progress' and reach an official agreement with the Arabs." Writing the day after the congress closed, Hochberg noted: "I have spoken to Zahrawi and Abd-ul-Karim about this, and they think it should be done."

* My emphasis—A.C.

H

"Events are moving quickly," Hochberg added, urging Jacobson and Sokolov, or another member of the Zionist Executive, to come to Paris without delay and begin negotiations. The Arab representatives asked him to prepare a draft agreement that could form a basis for the negotiations.

It appears from Hochberg's letters that in the ranks of the Zionist movement there was a fear that agreement at that time might be premature and might arouse Turkish suspicions, harming the interests of both the Arabs and the Jews. But, in the opinion of the Arab leaders, the time had come for a preliminary *internal* agreement that would lead to a definitive agreement with the Zionist leaders in Constantinople. Hochberg waited for instructions, but these did not arrive.*

Dr. Jacobson himself later came to Paris to explore the possibility of an agreement with the Arabs. However, he did not bring with him any concrete proposals. "In effect, the Zionist Executive did not know what to offer them" [i.e., the Arabs], Dr. Alsberg observed when commenting on Jacobson's Paris visit.

Richard Lichtheim, who was political secretary to the Zionist Executive at that time, has given us an enlightening picture of Jacobson's negotiations with the Arabs. Writing to the Zionist central office in Berlin, Lichtheim reported:

> Dr. Jacobson met Abd-ul-Hamid and Zahrawi, the president of the Paris Congress. Their discussion was a repeat performance of all the affectionate signs of a rapprochement. Dr. Jacobson declared that we had to be given the opportunity of buying land. At last Zahrawi asked: "Which lands do you want to buy?" Dr. Jacobson promised to bring concrete proposals to their next meeting.

It is not difficult to appreciate what impression the president of the Paris Congress gained from this conversation, after waiting in vain for the chief political representative of the Zionist movement in Constantinople to propose a draft agreement. Indeed Jewish leaders who worked for a Jewish-Arab agreement in later years were frequently reminded of these negotiations in 1913.

New Orientation of Zionist Policy

After the Tenth Zionist Congress in 1911, when the new Executive was chosen and Professor Warburg (1859–1938) was elected president, the

* The original documents that throw a light on this affair may be found in the files of the Central Zionist Archives in Jerusalem, and were first published in the original (Dr. Jacobson's letters in German, Hochberg's report and letters in French) as appendices to Dr. Alsberg's essay in *Shivat Zion*, Vol. IV, pp. 180–206. Certain aspects of these talks were described by Kalvarisky, whose words were recorded by the author of this book at the time.

political department was placed in the hands of Nahum Sokolov (1860–1936) and Dr. Jacobson. Richard Lichtheim was appointed political secretary.*

Since arriving in Constantinople in 1908, Dr. Jacobson had been trying to reach an agreement with the rulers of Turkey. When he realized how much weight the Arab national movement carried, he began seeking contact with its leaders and examining the chances of reaching an agreement with them. Jacobson's approach derived from his belief that the Young Turks' revolt could save the Ottoman Empire from decay and disintegration. The new rulers of Turkey might also meet Zionist aspirations, if this would not provoke the Arabs. Although power was in the hands of the Turks, a Jewish-Arab agreement based on loyalty to the Ottoman Empire could eliminate the principal obstacle to a Zionist agreement with the Turkish government. During the years he spent in Constantinople, Dr. Jacobson came somewhat closer to the Oriental scene. He established direct and indirect ties with the spokesmen of the Arab national movement and probably pondered the problem of Jewish-Arab relations more deeply than any other Zionist leader at that period (apart from Dr. Ruppin, who was in charge of the Palestine Office in Jaffa).

Unlike Jacobson, Sokolov was far removed from the Oriental political scene. His political activity was stimulated by Italy's defeat of Turkey in Libya and subsequent Turkish defeats in the Balkans. Everything seemed now to indicate that the "Sick Man" was in his death agony, but no one knew what would replace the waning Turkish regime. Colonialism was still in full bloom, the great powers ruled with an iron hand, and the campaign for liberation of colonial peoples—including those in the Middle East—was supported only by the left wing of the socialist movement. (The right wing of the Social Democrats had already abandoned this position at the Sixth Congress of the International, held at Amsterdam in August 1904.)

Like the other Zionist statesmen of that period, Sokolov was concerned with the European powers. In March 1913, he had an interview with two senior officials of the British Foreign Office, to whom he explained the benefits that would accrue to Britain if it supported the Zionist movement. Sokolov also raised the possibility of a German orientation in Zionist policy, as German influence in Turkey appeared stronger after the Balkan war. He was one of the main advocates of contact with the European powers, in view of Turkey's decline. Sokolov proposed cautious direct contacts in the

---

* Richard Lichtheim: Born in Berlin in 1885. As a student, joined the Zionist movement and soon held important positions in its ranks. Visited Palestine in 1910. For some time was editor of *Die Welt*, organ of the World Zionist Organization. From 1913 to 1917, worked with Jacobson in Constantinople. Later became a supporter of the Revisionist trend in Zionism advocated by Jabotinsky for a time. Died in Jerusalem 1964.

western European capitals as well as through the embassies in Constantinople.

With a caution that is perfectly understandable, the Zionist Executive evolved a policy of "conducting as broad an information campaign as possible," with the express purpose of winning world statesmen and public opinion over to the Zionist idea without offending Turkish rulers. In 1912 to 1913, Zionist policy was directed particularly toward Britain, which many Zionists had long considered the power that would one day rule Palestine, and toward the United States, which had the largest and most powerful Jewish community of any western country. Considerable thought was also given to Germany and Austria, whose influence in the Ottoman Empire was rising steadily; to Italy, which defended the rights of the Vatican and the Catholic Church in Palestine; and to France which, like Britain, was trying to establish footholds in the Levant. In any event, the capitals of the Arab world were not included in these political and informational efforts of Zionist leaders.

A study of Sokolov's and Lichtheim's correspondence and the record of the Zionist Actions Committee's proceedings shows that "after the Balkan wars, which made all the statesmen in Europe realize that the Young Turks could not muster enough strength to prevent the total collapse of their Empire, those responsible for Zionist policy thought England would eventually decide Palestine's fate. Hence an attempt was made to give Zionist policy a pro-British orientation. This gave the Arab question a new significance in Zionist policy: England, which had to take into account the Moslem population living in the British Empire, supported the Arab national movement so that it would be able to use it in the future, and was unable to negotiate with the Zionist movement because this would have angered the Moslem population. Hence one of the steps in the new Zionist orientation towards Britain should have been to seek a compromise agreement with the Arabs as well" (Alsberg).

Richard Lichtheim, the third member of the triumvirate formulating Zionist policy at that time, was even farther removed than Sokolov from Oriental affairs. When he was appointed to his post in 1911 (at the age of twenty-six), he was already imbued with contempt for the alien peoples of the Orient, while his attitude toward the Western powers was one of awe. It is no coincidence that he later joined Jabotinsky and the "Revisionist" trend in Zionism.

Lichtheim's attitude towards Jewish-Arab cooperation (as well as the Arab national movement *per se*) is fully expressed in his letters and reports from Constantinople to the Zionist Actions Committee. On October 9, 1913, he wrote:

It appears that in several Arab circles the "Ottoman" direction is losing ground to a nationalist direction, which is stronger and more vigorous. The Arabs are disappointed, because the most important government posts in Syria are given to Turks. In the large hotels here in Constantinople more and more Arab leaders are in evidence: large landowners, sheiks, journalists and so on. The Pera Palace Hotel is the headquarters of the rich effendis, who seek peace as a rule. In the Tokatlian Hotel the younger and more nationalistic circles hold round-the-clock consultations. There is talk of putting out a Turkish newspaper that would serve Arab interests. They also want to give the Arabs systematic education and to train them as an Arab political movement. These circles propose going hand in hand with the Jews. Apparently these circles genuinely seek practical cooperation with the Jews. True, I take a very sceptical view of this whole theory about Jewish-Arab brotherhood. But this situation and this undoubtedly temporary inspiration could be exploited for our benefit, if we maintain constant vigilance, support the Arab press and in this way make it impossible for the [Turkish] government to reject our request, on the pretext that it does not want to anger the Arabs.

In his memoirs, Lichtheim refers to his friendly relations with Najib Shukeir, the editor of the new Turkish-language paper, *Fiyem* (Mission), set up by the Arab movement. A Druze from Lebanon, Lichtheim termed him "one of the first men to fight for an Arab national movement," and added, "I could rely on him and his word." After a meeting between Jacobson and Shukeir, Lichtheim reported to Berlin that "Shukeir also favors closer ties with us." Lichtheim informs us in his memoirs that "over the years Shukeir became more and more enthusiastic about the idea of Arab-Jewish understanding." The Druze editor played a role in Weizmann's negotiations with Emir Faisal (see Chapter Four), and in 1919 he accompanied Faisal to the Paris Peace Conference, "where he did us good and useful service as a mediator between Faisal and the Zionist delegation." An interesting sidelight on his Arab friend appears in a letter written by Lichtheim on April 28, 1914, to his colleagues in Berlin: "People like Najib really seem convinced that it would be foolish of the Arabs to lose the Jews' friendship."

Summing up his term of office in Constantinople on the eve of World War I, Lichtheim did not conceal several truths that Zionist statesmen were not fond of recalling in later years:

All my reports repeat the same refrain, namely, that the leaders of the Arab national movement—the effendis and also the intellectuals—cannot be won over to our cause by the assurance that the fellaheen's living standard will be raised. The only thing that sometimes seems as if it might afford a basis for mutual understanding is the idea of a large-scale peace treaty between the Jews and the Arab national movement. However, we would be taking too much risk if we followed this line, as long as Palestine belongs to the Turks. . . . The activities I suggested were, for some reason, nothing more than proposals made without any other alternative being available, so that the aggressive Arab press campaign against Zionism could be restrained and silenced, and also so that the Arab leaders, and in particular the members of Parliament, could be influenced towards moderation as much as possible.

Jewish-Arab Negotiations in 1914

Hochberg's mission to Cairo and Beirut during April and May 1913, and his subsequent visit to Paris at the time of the Arab Congress in June of the same year, did not lead to a Jewish-Arab agreement. But the trips were not entirely unproductive. As A. Saphir testified to the Peel Commission in 1937: "When the Arab leaders returned to Constantinople from Paris in July 1913, several of them met the late Dr. Jacobson, who represented the Zionist organization, in order to work out a concrete program that would give tangible expression to their statement about cooperation."

Anti-Zionist propaganda had died down in the Arab press. Following the discussions in Paris about Jewish immigration to Palestine, the Zionist spokesmen in Constantinople renewed their negotiations with the Turkish authorities concerning the annulment of the so-called "red card,"* and in September 1913, the Turkish Cabinet decided to abolish it and to do away with the three-month limitation on Jews entering the country. Lichtheim reported to Berlin on October 3 that according to the *Hacham Bashi* (Chief Rabbi)† the Minister of the Interior, Tala'at Bey, had ordered the "red card" to be abolished and the First Secretary of the Prime Minister had approved this report. There was also some discussion about ways of making it easier for Jews to buy land. The Arab silence on these matters, which was inter-

---

* After a general ban on immigration of Jews to Palestine had already been imposed in 1887 and 1897, a special ordinance was enacted at the beginning of 1901, which intensified these bans. Any Jew who wished to travel to Palestine—whether he was a foreign subject and resident abroad, or a Turkish subject or resident in Turkey—was obliged to place his travel documents in the keeping of the port authorities and was issued a special document permitting him to stay in the country for three months. This document came to be known as the "red card" because of its color. Under the law, the holder of the "red card" was obliged to present it to the authorities upon demand and was to leave the country within three months. In this way, the authorities were able to maintain a special control over the entry of Jews into Palestine and their departure from the country. Special records were kept for this purpose in the port towns. While this law was in fact not carried out, since the foreign consuls protected their subjects against expulsion from Palestine (on the basis of the above-mentioned "capitulation"), the ordinance did cause a reduction in immigration of Jews to Palestine in the period before World War I.

† *Hacham Bashi*: The title of the Chief Rabbi of Turkish Jewry. Like the heads of the other religions in the empire (the Sheik-el-Islam, the Greek Orthodox Patriarch, the Armenian Patriarch, etc.), the Chief Rabbi enjoyed privileged status and was regarded as the spokesman for the Jews of the Ottoman Empire. He was invited to official receptions given by the Sultan and had access to the *vizirs*. This tradition, dating back to the times of the Sultan's absolute rule, was kept up after the 1908 coup d'etat. At that time, Rabbi Nahum was the *Hacham Bashi* (after the first World War, he became the Chief Rabbi of Egyptian Jewry). He was not a Zionist but, like most of the Sephardic Jews, he had nationalist tendencies. He was regarded as an expert in the Arabic language and in Islamic affairs.

preted as implicit consent, was of major importance for the Zionist policy-makers in Constantinople.*

When A. Saphir traveled to Paris in November 1913, he took with him a letter of recommendation from the Arab leaders in Constantinople to the members of the Arab committee in Paris—Shukri Ghanim and N. Mutran (both Christians), Auni Abd-ul-Hadi, of Nablus, Jamil Mardam, of Damascus (who became Prime Minister of Syria after World War II), Muhammad Al-Muhamazani and Abd-ul-Ghani Al-'Uraysi (both of Beirut), and others. The Arab leaders in Turkey urged their compatriots in Paris, and Saphir, to continue their efforts to reach an agreement. When Jacobson's talks with the Arab representatives in Paris produced no practical results, a new wave of anti-Zionist propaganda appeared in the Palestinian Arab press. In the summer of 1914, the Arabs stepped up their campaign against Jewish immigration, and eventually the Turkish authorities in Palestine reimposed limitations on the legal length of stay of Jewish visitors. This time the Jaffa paper *Falastin* set the tone for the anti-Zionist propaganda. (The chief rabbi complained to the Turkish government about the articles in *Falastin* and the paper was closed down for a while and the editor found guilty.)

In April 1914, elections to the Turkish Parliament were held for the third time. Jacobson and Lichtheim concluded it would be best not to nominate a Jewish candidate, so as not to aggravate relations with the Arabs (and as, in any event, there was no chance of a Jewish deputy's being elected). Dr. Ruppin shared this view, with the result that the Zionist Executive voted no funds for the election campaign. The nine Jewish electors (out of a total of 152 chosen for the Jerusalem *sandjak*) voted for Said Al-Hussaini, who had made frequent anti-Zionist statements in Parliament and the press but had asserted that "all [his] declarations and speeches were nothing but propaganda aimed at Arab public opinion, and they would only make it easier for [him] to help the Jews, as no one would suspect [him] of taking bribes from them." The deputies chosen to represent the Jerusalem *sandjak* were Ragheib Nashash-ibi (133 votes), Faidi Al-Alami (100) and Said Al-Hussaini (86). The mood among the Arab public in Palestine is reflected to a certain degree by the fact that the largest number of votes went to Nashashibi, who had once declared, "The Ottoman government should adopt the methods used by Rumania. I am not opposed to the Ottoman Jews, but to those Jews who are foreign citizens and have come to fight us with their foreign nationality as a weapon. . . . If I am elected, I shall devote all my strength, day and night, to averting the danger and harm we can expect from the Zionists and Zionism."[12]

Indeed, at the beginning of 1914, the relations between the Arabs and the

* An evaluation of the political significance of the Arab leaders' silence may be found in Dr. Jacobson's letter to Kalvarisky (at the end of 1913), the summary of which was recorded at the time by the writer of this book.

Young Turks once again worsened. Arab leaders became aware that the Turkish rulers were not implementing the agreement reached at the Paris Congress. On the other hand, Jewish leaders noted that the Arab press was resuming its anti-Zionist campaign, and they feared further attacks by the Arab members of the new Parliament, which was due to open shortly. Hence, it was felt by both sides that negotiations should again be attempted. The apprehension about Turkish reaction to any such Jewish-Arab talks was dispelled after the *wali* of Beirut told Kalvarisky that he was favorably disposed toward them.

It should be noted that several versions of the *wali's* remarks are on record. Dr. Alsberg writes that "the *wali* of Beirut expressed to Haim Margalith-Kalvarisky, the ICA representative in Rosh Pina, the wish that the representatives of the (Jewish) Yishuv should enter into negotiations with the Arab representatives." The official "Chronicles of the Hagana" (Vol. I, p. 190) relates that "at the beginning of 1914 negotiations began between the Jewish and Arab representatives in Constantinople and Damascus on the conditions of an agreement between the two movements (Jewish and Arab). The Turkish Government knew about these negotiations, and assisted them." Five lines later it is noted that "at the first meeting (between the Jewish and Arab representatives) it was decided to summon a sort of clandestine conference of Jewish and Arab nationalist leaders." Two lines afterwards the Hagana history states once more that "the *wali* of Beirut took it upon himself to act as chairman and as the mediator between the two sides."

The contradictions between these reports are obvious. If the *wali* of Beirut knew about the Jewish-Arab talks and was actively assisting them, there would have been no need for a *clandestine* conference, at which he could not have been the chairman or the principal mediator. Even Alsberg's more cautious version of events is not consistent with the relations of all three sides in this Jewish-Arab-Turkish triangle.

The incident is clarified by Kalvarisky's own report. According to Kalvarisky, who played an important role in the negotiations, it was not the *wali* who "expressed the wish" for Jewish-Arab talks, but he himself. Several years earlier Kalvarisky had tried to bring about Jewish-Arab negotiations (and had been told that "this could spoil relations with the Turkish authorities"). When he put this idea to the *wali* of Beirut (explaining that the Jews and Arabs should discuss "an agreement which would prevent difficulties over land and tenants"), the latter replied: "Why not? Do so!"*

The participants in the talks, which took place during April and May of 1914 in Constantinople, were Jacobson, Lichtheim, and Hochberg on the Jewish side, and, on the Arab side, the members of Parliament Hussaini and

---

* According to notes taken by the writer during a visit, with Kalvarisky, to Arab leaders in Syria and Lebanon during September, 1942 (see Chapter Seven).

Nashashibi (Jerusalem), Faris Al-Khoury (Damascus) and other members from Nablus, Beirut, and Tripoli. The Arabs were also represented by Mukhtar Baihum, of the Arab committee in Beirut, and Najib Shukeir, editor of the Turkish-language Arab nationalist organ *Fiyem*. Lichtheim has noted in his memoirs that Faris Al-Khoury, who later became one of the most vehement opponents of the Jewish enterprise in Palestine, held, in 1914, that a certain number of Jewish immigrants would be a good thing for the country. He even proclaimed himself a friend of the Jews, adding, however, that in the future the Jews would undoubtedly wish to oust the Arabs from Palestine.

He was not the only one who thought so. When Jacobson proposed a toast to the Arab members of Parliament from Palestine ("whom we consider our representatives as well, because they handle the affairs of Palestine") and referred to the great economic benefits the Jews were conferring on the country, "it could be concluded that the Arabs replies, and from the wishes they expressed, that they considered the Jews a potentially dangerous force and feared lest they push the Arabs out."

As Lichtheim wrote from Constantinople to Dr. Jacobson in Berlin on June 7, 1914: "The Arabs will never agree that we are needed if the Palestinian Arab cause is to make headway. They feel that all the economic or sanitary benefits we shall bring to the country with us cannot be measured against the fact that any progress on our part automatically ousts them."

Summing up his mission in Constantinople during the period of 1913 to 1917 (in his book *She'ar Yishuv*, Chapter 12), Lichtheim claimed that certain passages of his reports showed that "even then we already understood the Arab question and did not neglect it, as some people later contended." Lichtheim believed that "we could have won the Arabs' hearts [for a mutual understanding] only by giving very large sums of money to their national movement, so that they could organize." But he himself was compelled to admit that this approach could hardly bring about Jewish-Arab understanding, saying that "the only argument which makes any impact at all is the political one." In his letter of May 28, 1914, he remarked; "The argument that Dr. Jacobson advanced in a most effective manner made a great impression: namely, that the Palestinian Arabs should not look at this question only from a Palestinian viewpoint. There are perhaps 15 million Arabs in Turkey; but only 600,000 of them live in Palestine. If the Arabs wish to advance their nation as a whole, they should not ignore the valuable assistance they can obtain from the Jewish side. These words seemed to have an impact." What Jacobson implied was that if the Arabs would agree to the Jews' immigrating to Palestine, buying land there, and settling in the country, the Jews would help them to obtain economic aid and to carry out the large public works the Arabs needed so badly. Zionist representatives demanded the cessation of anti-Zionist attacks in the Arab press and the Turkish Parliament. They also wanted a halt to the Palestinian-Arab petitions against Jewish immigration and land acquisition. The Arabs, on the other hand, demanded that the Jews extend to them political and economic assistance and that guarantees be given that the fellaheen would not be ousted from lands acquired by the Jews.*

Questions that were specifically political were not touched on during the 1914 negotiations. The two sides' lack of boldness and mutual trust apparently kept the discussion within the limits of the concrete matters noted above, well inside the framework of the Ottoman Empire. It appears from Lichtheim's letters that he felt that the Arab leaders were convinced that a large Arab Kingdom was destined to arise and that Arab national interests made an agreement with the Jews imperative, so that economic, organizational, and scientific aid could be obtained through them. As Lichtheim observed in a letter to Dr. Jacobson in Berlin, on June 7, 1914: "A peace pact is possible only on the basis of future Arab policies, and this is naturally very dangerous."

At the beginning of May 1914, Jacobson informed Ruppin of the Arab demands as reflected in his conversations with them. Ruppin asked Jacobson to emphasize that the Jewish bodies did not buy any land from the fellaheen, and that most of the purchases were of large estates, most of which had been only sparsely cultivated. Ruppin also suggested raising the possibility that if Jewish settlement increased in scope, a parallel settlement program would be carried out for Palestinian Arab fellaheen or tenants not too far away—for example, in the Homs-Aleppo region in Northern Syria. (At that time there was no political frontier between Palestine and Syria.) In the Homs area, large plots of land could be acquired on good terms, Ruppin noted, and this land was better than that bought by the Jewish settlers in Palestine.†

In the spring of 1914, the rift between the Arab leaders and the Turkish rulers widened. Both sides began preparing for a crucial political struggle in the international arena. Arab leaders feared that Constantinople would use the Zionist movement as a counter to the Arab movement. The fact that several of the limitations on Jewish immigration and land purchase were lifted

---

* This problem had for long been a cause of concern to the leaders of Zionist activity in Palestine. The prevailing conception was that by an intensification of agriculture, it would be possible simultaneously to promote new Jewish settlement in Palestine and to improve the situation of the Arab fellah by modernizing his farm. This would be financed by compensation that he would receive for part of the land that he had previously cultivated more primitively. From a letter from Ruppin to Jacobson (May 12, 1914), it is evident that Jacobson had put forward a proposal that out of the new land areas to be purchased by the Jews, a certain proportion should be allocated to the Arab fellaheen, to be paid for in instalments.

† Ruppin's letter to Jacobson, Jaffa, May 12, 1914.

in the second half of 1913 was considered proof of this theory. In view of the prospect of a full-scale war, some Arab circles began putting out feelers concerning their chances of joining the Western Powers against Turkey, in return for a promise by the Western Powers to meet Arab aspirations once Turkey had been defeated. In April 1914, Emir Abdullah, the son of Hussain, Sherif of Mecca, visited Cairo on his way back to the Hejaz from Constantinople. In Cairo, he held a secret meeting with the British representative to ascertain whether Britain would help the rulers of the Hejaz to throw off the Turkish yoke.

At the end of March 1914, Henry Morgenthau, then the United States Ambassador to Constantinople, visited Cairo. Morgenthau, who was a Jew, had shown considerable interest in Palestine and maintained contact with the Zionist representatives in Constantinople. During his talk with the Egyptian Khedive, Abbas Hilmi, Morgenthau told him about the Zionist negotiations that were about to be concluded successfully with the rulers of Turkey. Egypt was then a major center of the Arab national movement in the Ottoman Empire. William Yale, who headed American intelligence in Cairo during World War I, claimed later that Morgenthau conceived the idea of splitting Palestine off from the Turkish Empire shortly after hostilities began and annexing it to Egypt, perhaps with a view to Cairo allowing a Jewish center (or state?) to be formed there under its protection.[13] This plan could have been in line with the British idea of redrawing the frontier between Egypt (which was shifted north of Wadi-l-Arish, to the Rafah-Eilat line, in 1906) and placing it north of Gaza, so that Turkey (with its growing German influence) should be removed from the Suez Canal.

Whether or not Morgenthau wanted to urge Abbas Hilmi to come to an agreement with the Zionist movement, the result of this development was that the Arabs evinced a wish to negotiate and instructed their representatives in Constantinople and Syria to meet the Zionist spokesmen, with a view to forming a common front in the general political arena.

Arab circles in Jerusalem approached Dr. Yitshak Levy in this connection. Levy was acceptable to them as a representative of the new Jewish *Yishuv* and was a well known Zionist. He wrote to Dr. Ruppin about this on May 13, 1914, and Ruppin replied on behalf of the Palestine Office that the Zionist Executive favored holding unofficial meetings, with a view to the preliminary study of the questions at issue.*

At the same time, Kalvarisky relates in his reminiscences, the Turkish *wali* of Beirut, Sami Bakr Bey, who was favorably inclined toward the work of the Jews in Palestine, paid him a visit. The *wali* was accompanied by several important Arab figures, including Nassif Bey Al-Khalidi. During luncheon, when the conversation turned to the relation between Jews and

* According to the files of the Zionist Archives, Alsberg, p. 177, footnote 61.

Arabs, Kalvarisky raised the possibility of an agreement between the two peoples. The Arabs expressed themselves sympathetic to such a possibility. At the close of the meeting, the *wali* himself took Kalvarisky aside and told him the idea was an excellent one, adding that the authorities would definitely support it.

At about the same time, Kalvarisky continues, the Zionist Control Commission came to the country. He talked to several of its members, and noted that "Mr. [Nahum] Sokolov showed great interest in this question, without paying any attention to the fact that all those around him tried to prove to him that the Arab question does not exist in reality and that the Arabs were a bunch of illiterates and sycophants, who were ready to sell everything for a mess of pottage."* At Sokolov's request, Kalvarisky accompanied him to Beirut and Damascus and introduced him to several of the Arab nationalist leaders—the engineer Nassif Bey Al-Khalidi, of Beirut; Dr. Abd-ul-Rahman Shahbandar (later one of the men behind the 1925 to 1927 revolt in Syria); Muhammad Kurd Ali (a writer and historian, who became the president of the Arab Academy in Damascus); and the members of Parliament Shukry Al-Asali and Muhammad Al-Inglizi (both of whom were hanged by Jamal Pasha during World War I, on charges of maintaining contact with the leaders of the Arab revolt in Hejaz). In these talks, Sokolov discovered to his surprise that the Arab leaders wanted an agreement with the Jews and were interested in holding a joint conference as soon as possible. It was agreed that ten representatives from each side would meet on July I of that year at Brumana, near Beirut. To enable the proposed conference to make binding decisions, the Arabs demanded that a leader of high caliber, like Sokolov or Jacobson, should take part. The Zionist Executive, on the other hand, was not eager to send its higher ranking representatives, and it agreed that Dr. Ruppin should attend only on condition that he be an observer, but not an official member of the delegation. The Palestine Office invited the following Jews to join the delegation: Meir Dizengoff, Dr. Luria and Dr. Haim Hissin (Jaffa), Aharon Eisenberg (Rehovot), Menashe Meyerowitz (Rishon Lezion), David Yellin and Dr. Yitshak Levy (Jerusalem) Shabtai Levi and Rosenheck (Haifa), and Kalvarisky. The Zionist Executive's approach to the forthcoming discussion is summed up in Sokolov's letter to Dr. Yehiel Tschlenov: "The gentlemen can meet. Our representatives are earnest and quiet people, who will only conduct a noncommittal conversation. I have spoken to Dr. Ruppin about this as well. There will be no commitments and no agreements. This is only an initial attempt at a personal encounter."†

Why did the Zionist Executive hesitate?

---

* Kalvarisky's notes from 1913. The Zionist Archives, File 11B, L4/276.

† Details on this affair are based on Kalvarisky's account; for Sokolov's letter in the original (German), see *Shivat Zion*, Vol. IV, p. 209 (Appendix).

Dr. Alsberg, who made an exhaustive study of the Central Zionist Archives on this question, reached the following conclusion:

There were two reasons for these hesitations on the part of the Zionist Executive. On the one hand, it thought open negotiations with the Arabs on political problems might anger the Turks [although as we have seen, the *wali* of Beirut had expressed his favourable attitude to the negotiations]. On the other hand, the Zionist Executive had no concrete proposals to make that could appease the Arabs. Hence they thought it preferable not to hold a high-level conference rather than to hold it and see it end in a failure.

In short, the Zionist Executive had to make a clear-cut decision. "The Arabs are waiting for us to submit our proposals," Lichtheim wrote to Jacobson in Berlin on June 19, 1914. "They are ready for talks in Cairo and Syria." But the Zionist Executive did not have the necessary resolution and daring. On July 3, Lichtheim informed Jacobson: "Matters have progressed so far that we must do something. . . . We must arrange a meeting with them, because if we do not do so the press will start provoking us once more with even greater force."

At the beginning of June 1914, the Zionist Council met for a discussion on political affairs, among other things. According to Gruenbaum's account, Jacobson confirmed that the so-called "red card" had been annulled, and that the restrictions imposed on Jewish foreign nationals who wished to buy land had been lifted, although no express order had yet been given permitting these Jews to buy land in Palestine. Naturalization had also been made easier for non-Ottoman subjects: no longer did the applicant require five years' prior residence and permission from the consul of his country of origin. However, Turkish officials observed that the Jews were in no hurry to apply for naturalization *en masse*, as they had anticipated. The government's attitude to the Jews was positive, as a rule, but it did not want to arouse the Arabs by granting concessions to Jews who settled in the country.

Jacobson added:

Among the Arabs, there are circles who see the benefit inherent in Jewish immigration, but complain of the separatism of the new settlers, their special suburbs and schools, and the slogan of "Jewish labor," aimed against the employment of Arabs by Jews. The Arabs outside Palestine are ready to discuss the question from an all-Arab standpoint and assume that the Jews could help them. But they impose a condition: that the Arabs of Palestine agree to the results of any negotiations. Their demands are: a) The Jews living in Palestine should become Ottoman subjects; b) they should settle not only in Palestine, but in other Arab countries as well; c) they must cooperate in public life—in other words, first and foremost, they must accept Arab children into Jewish schools. This is difficult for several reasons and it has given rise to the idea of introducing comparable courses for Arab children, at our expense. There is also cause for discussing the joint exploitation of concessions held by the Arabs, such as the Hulah Reclamation concession. Jacobson proposed this to Rothschild, and negotiations were in progress.

Following this report, a lively debate ensued on various political matters, including "the Arab question." A. Podlishevsky stated that his proposal that medical and social care should be provided for the Arabs had not been implemented. He also criticized the ousting of Arab workers by Jewish employers. S. Kaplansky noted that when land was bought from the large landowners, the Arab sharecroppers were evicted; he demanded that they be given land elsewhere out of Palestine (as noted, a similar proposal had been made by Dr. Ruppin). The Arab fellaheen can benefit from selling the surplus land to the Jews, thus saving them from userers robbing them of their lands. "They should not be prevented from working for Jews, and Arabic should be introduced as a compulsory discipline in Jewish schools." L. Motzkin, who had just returned from a visit to Palestine, called for greater efforts to establish contact with the Arabs, hinting at the forthcoming conference and arguing that the Palestine Office did not undertake effective work in this sphere.

The report on this debate indicates that the July 1 conference with the Arabs was not discussed and no resolution about it was adopted. Replying to the debate, Jacobson did refer to "difficulties on the part of the Arabs, whose influence and opposition to Zionism are growing." The general reference to "a political line that was approved, without an explicit resolution being passed," included a passage about "taking the Arab factor into account and seeking way of agreement and compromise with it." However, it appears that this amounted to nothing more than giving the executive a free hand—a position it did not exploit.

At the end of June, when the date of the Brumana meeting was approaching, it was decided to postpone it for several weeks. M. Medzini noted that "several responsible Jewish politicians announced that there was no need for Jews to hold meetings with Arabs, as the government was on our side." When Nassif al-Khalidi, one of the Arabs who had met Sokolov, heard that the meeting had been cancelled, he told one of the Jewish leaders, "Be very careful, gentlemen of the Zionist movement. Governments come and governments go, but a people always remains."[14]

World War I broke out, and the meeting agreed upon by both sides never took place. Later on, official circles explained the crucial delay by saying, for example, that "the Jews were against inviting Nassar, the editor of *Al-Carmel*, to the conference."[15] Kalvarisky stated that this meeting did not take place "for various reasons, the main one being that the Jews did not realize how important it was and took a frivolous view of the Arab national movement, and even denied its existence."[16]

References

1. L. Oliphant, *The Land of Gilead* (New York, 1881).
2. Article in *Hashiloah* magazine, 1907, Vol. XVII, pp. 197–198.
3. *Chronicles of the Hagana*, Vol. 1, p. 73 (Hebrew).
4. The Zionist Movement in Its Development, part III, p. 137 (Hebrew).
5. The files of the Central Zionist Archives, File D1B2.
6. David Ben-Gurion: "Clarifying our Political Situation," *Ahdut* (Unity) No. 3 (1910).
7. Files of the Palestine Office in Jaffa in the collection of the Central Zionist Archives, Jerusalem: Dr. Ruppin's letter to the Workers' Council of Petah Tikva of September 5, 1911 (Copy Register No. 25), and his letter to Merhavia of June 5, 1911 (Copy Register No. 21).
8. *Hashiloah*, Vol. 17, pp. 574–576.
9. *Ibid*, Vol. 22, No. 5, May 1910.
10. *Haherut*, June 18, 1913.
11. *Haor*, 27 Shevat (February) 1912.
12. A. Elmaleh's, *Palestine and Syria at the Time of the World War* (Jerusalem, 1927), Vol. I, p. 175 (Hebrew).
13. *World Politics*, Vol. I, p. 397, 1947–1949.
14. M. Medzini, *Ten Years of Palestine Policy.* (Jerusalem, Hasepher Publishers. 1928), p. 80 (Hebrew).
15. *Chronicles of the Hagana*, Vol. I, p. 190.
16. *At the Parting of Our Ways* (Jerusalem, March 1939), p. 32 (Hebrew).

CHAPTER FOUR

DURING WORLD WAR I

World War I broke out in August 1914. Three months later, Turkey entered the war on the side of Germany. Even the most tentative attempts to reach an Arab-Jewish *modus vivendi* ceased. Jewish-Arab relations now entered an entirely new phase, and by the time the war had ended, the whole political background had undergone a radical change.

For both the Jews and the Arabs of Palestine, the war brought years of severe trial and great hardship. The Jewish community, which depended largely on aid from abroad, suffered from the disruption of its contact with other countries. The farms producing citrus, wine, almonds, and other export commodities were badly hit. This caused unemployment and affected the entire credit system, with the result that the banks closed down. The price of imported foodstuffs soared, and the Turkish currency dropped in value. During the last two years of the war, there was famine in Palestine.

Syria and Palestine had to supply the manpower for the Fourth Turkish Army stationed there. A special war tax was levied, on the basis of estimates determined by government committees. During the first six months of the war, the Jewish *moshavot* in Judea alone paid 200,000 francs in war tax, in addition to the usual taxes. All through the war, the authorities continued to confiscate vehicles, food, and other items needed by the army, promising to pay for them after the war. Grain, sheep, oxen, mules, and other livestock were confiscated in Arab villages. From the Jews, the Turks took carts, beasts of burden, barbed wire, and pipe-lines. Many peoples were pressed into forced labor groups working on the roads, building railroads, and cutting down trees for use as fuel. Male Ottoman citizens aged twenty-one to forty-five (and later eighteen to fifty) were recruited into the ill-equipped and undernourished Turkish Army. Those over the age of twenty-four could avoid military service on payment of a ransom of 1,000 gold francs a year (about £40 sterling). Whoever could afford to do so mortgaged his property or took a loan at exorbitant rates of interest to pay this sum and avoid being drafted. Smilansky (see Chapter Three), tells us in his *Annals of the Yishuv*:

The Jews who were attached to units made up mostly of Arabs suffered a harsh fate. In the Turkish regiments the situation was slightly better. The new Ottoman citizens were usually not sent to combat units, but put to work as laborers. Their conditions were infinitely worse than those of the soldiers on active duty. . . . Their "camps" had no tents, and the "soldiers" were exposed to blazing heat in summer and to rain and cold in winter, without any protection whatsoever. The food and clothing they were given were far below army standards. These units—hungry, near naked and barefoot—wandered from place to place, driven by the blows of their oppressors. Hundreds of them died, and their corpses filled the cemeteries and the fields and the desert.

Small wonder that so many people fled from the army, and that, once having fled, they lived in constant dread of being caught. Many of them made ends meet by theft and robbery. People engaged in civilian work that helped the war effort were exempt from military duty however, if they produced a certificate to this effect. For many building contractors these certificates became a source of profit.

In the spring of 1915, the country was plagued by locusts and the entire year's crop was devastated. In the summer of 1916, the grain harvest was reduced by a long and severe heat wave. Food prices rocketed sky-high, and many families faced starvation. Infectious diseases spread by the Turkish troops also caused havoc among the civilian population. During the last three years of the war, 350,000 people—or 10 percent of the population—died of starvation in Syria (which then included Lebanon and Palestine). The war caused terrible suffering to both Jew and Arab in Palestine. Famine was rife, particularly in the towns. At the beginning of 1917, 300 Jerusalem Jews were dying of starvation each month, and at the end of the war, there were 4,000 registered orphans in need of help.

The small Jewish community of Palestine dwindled still further. On December 17, 1914, the Turkish census inspectors in Jaffa collected all non-Ottoman Jews and deported them on an Italian ship bound for Alexandria—the Turkish Government having annulled the capitulations on October 1, 1914. The deportation of these 700 people led to a mass exodus of Jews from all over the country. Within one month, about 7,000 had left Palestine, and by the end of 1915, the number of emigrants totalled 11,277. Apart from those Jews who died as a result of the famine, many died in one or another of the epidemics that prevailed at various times during the war. At the outbreak of the war, there were 85,000 Jews in Palestine; at the end of hostilities there were no more than 56,000.

There is no necessity to detail the atrocities committed by Jamal Pasha, the commander of the Fourth Turkish Army Corps, who was virtually the supreme ruler of Syria and Palestine, and by his adjutant Baha ud-Din, by Hassan Bey, the Military Governor of Jaffa, and by other Turkish officers, whose names alone are enough to evoke horror. At his first meeting with the heads of the Jewish community and the rabbis, Jamal Pasha spoke in no uncertain terms about "the separatist tendencies of the Jews in Palestine." Later, he rounded up thirty-two representatives of the *Yishuv* and kept them

I

in custody in Jerusalem for several days in order to "talk to them," as he put it. He levelled every possible accusation at them: the Jews maintained their own autonomous institutions; most of them were still foreign nationals; they did not have recourse to the Turkish courts; they had their own flag, stamps, and other political symbols; they drove the Arabs off their lands and from their jobs; they did not respect the dignity of the Turkish authorities (because there were no pictures of Turkish leaders in Jewish offices); they did not learn Turkish; and their children were brought up in a Jewish nationalist and anti-Turkish spirit. All these things, Jamal Pasha declared, showed that the Jews wished to remove Palestine from the Turkish Empire and to set it up as their own state. For this reason, he said, he had decided to send some of the leaders of the *Yishuv* to Constantinople, where they would face a court-martial. This decree was not implemented (and in the long run, fifteen of the thirty-two were deported no farther than Tiberias for eleven days). But a wave of bans and restrictions swept over the *Yishuv*: the Anglo-Palestine Bank was not allowed to issue its own bank notes; letters could no longer be written in Hebrew or Yiddish (because this made things more difficult for the censor); all Hebrew-language schools had to teach Turkish as well; the Jewish courts were banned, as were all the Jewish companies not registered under Ottoman law. The Turkish authorities arrested Jewish leaders and threatened to execute anyone found with a Jewish National Fund stamp. Among the Jewish leaders ordered to leave the country were Yitshak Ben-Zvi, David Ben-Gurion, Professor Boris Schatz, Dr. Arthur Ruppin, Dr. Isaac Levi, and many others.

Within the country itself, collective deportations were the order of the day. These included the expulsion of all the 9,000 Jews living in Tel Aviv and Jaffa in April 1917, when the British launched their offensive in the south of the country. This order applied to all Jews, whether Turkish citizens or not, and to all non-Moslem Ottoman subjects. The Arabs were allowed to leave for villages in the immediate vicinity of Tel Aviv, and some of them later returned to Jaffa. The Jews, on the other hand were ordered to leave the boundaries of the Jerusalem *sandjak*, where a state of war had been declared. It was only after considerable diplomatic activity and entreaties, both in Constantinople and abroad, that the Jewish farmers were not deported. The Palestine Office was transferred from Jaffa to Jerusalem, and placed under the direction of Dr. Thon. Most of the Jews exiled from Tel Aviv and Jaffa went to Galilee. Although the relief committee set up in Petah Tikva and the hospitable Jewish *moshavot* in Galilee averted starvation, fifty of the refugees died from infectious diseases and malnutrition.

In January 1915, Jamal Pasha's army marched on the Suez Canal. He soon returned crestfallen, after losing part of his troops in the desert. During his absence, Baha ud-Din ruled Palestine. He continued to pour out his wrath on the *Yishuv* but also made an attempt to win over certain circles which were opposed to the Zionist settlement endeavors, such as the various orthodox *Kolelim*.

In January 1915, according to the annals of the *Yishuv*, Baha ud-Din ordered the Jerusalem Hebrew daily, the *Herut*, to publish the following official statement:

> The Jews are our allies. Together with us they are sons of the fatherland, and they enjoy equal rights. May they always be our comrades in the homeland, with the help of God. . . . But . . . the government is opposed to the activities of the dangerous element that is trying to set up a Jewish government, in the name of Zionism, in the Palestinian part of the Ottoman Empire. Since this could harm the members of the Jewish race, the government has ordered that the stamps, the Zionist flag, and the Anglo-Palestine bank notes and paper money be destroyed, and all the secret Zionist societies and bodies be disbanded. We are friends of all the Jews in the Homeland who are with us in one alliance. It is only Zionism and the Zionists, that corrupt element of confusion and revolutions, that we will always suppress.

It is outside the scope of our subject to dwell at length on the reaction of the small and weak Jewish community, or to explain how the Jews, who managed to enlist external political support and maintain a strong internal organization, were able to escape the terrible fate which was to overcome, for example, the Armenians. However, the Jewish fate was harsh enough— starvation, deportation, anti-Zionist decrees and dire threats by the authorities against the Jews.

When the Turkish government abolished the capitulations, the over-whelming majority of the Palestinian Jewish community lost the protection of the foreign consuls, to which they had been accustomed for decades. True, at the ceremony held in Jerusalem to mark the abolition, advocate Ammon spoke in Turkish, and the Arab poet Sheik Ali Rimawi spoke in Arabic, while Yitshak Ben-Zvi spoke in Hebrew. But, as A. Elmaleh has noted, "we mourned the destruction of this strong protective fortress, which alone has saved the entire *Yishuv* from being destroyed." Everything the Jewish community had done in Palestine had been achieved by virtue of "the six strong ropes placed around Turkey's neck" (i.e., the special privileges enjoyed by the subjects of six foreign powers).

Several groups of Arab nationalists tried to exploit the situation created by the abolition. They began agitating against "the foreign Jews" and circulating rumors to the effect that the Turkish authorities would soon turn on the Jews and take away their lives and property. This agitation grew even more intense when Turkey joined the war officially (on October 29, 1914) and tried to give it the character of a *jihad* (or holy war). In sermons preached in mosques, and in special manifestos, the Moslems were urged "to fulfil their duty to defend Islam and defeat the heretics"—a propagandistic device that created a favorable climate for attacks on "the foreign heretics" living in Palestine itself. The Turkish rulers, who themselves considered the Jewish community a potential danger and saw in the war emergency a good opportunity to eliminate it, were afraid of Arab disturbances and did not allow the anti-Jewish agitation to go too far. It was enough to poison the relations between the two peoples.

The Arabs suffered no less than the Jews from the stringent military regime imposed by the Turks, who were anxious to suppress any incipient nationalist ferment. "The fellaheen and the urban Arabs suffered more from Turkish headquarters in Jaffa than the Jews. For every small offense they were dragged off to the police station, beaten, trampled on, and insulted incessantly. Several Arabs who were accused of espionage were hanged."[1]

At the end of 1915, the Turkish Army launched an unsuccessful attack on the Suez Canal front, suffering heavy casualties. The same fate befell another attack launched in August 1916. Jamal Pasha blamed his defeat partly on the need to maintain large forces in Palestine against a possible uprising. When he returned to Jerusalem he began persecuting anyone suspected of disloyalty to the Ottoman regime. During 1915 and 1916, many Arabs from Syria, Lebanon, and Palestine were exiled, and many Arab nationalist leaders were sentenced to death. In May 1916, Jamal Pasha ordered twenty-two Arab leaders hanged in public in Beirut and Damascus for "taking part in activities designed to detach Syria, Palestine, and Iraq from the Ottoman Sultanate and form an independent state."[2]

The state of emergency that prevailed in Palestine, the economic distress, and the shortage of food overshadowed the political problem of relations between the Jews and Arabs, whose fate hung on the outcome of the fighting.

Since the Brumana meeting in 1914, day-to-day Jewish-Arab relations had vacillated between light and shade, resulting from the troubled situation brought about by the war. In Jaffa, the government committee that levied war taxes was made up entirely of Moslem and Christian Arabs, without a single Jew, and it taxed Jews disproportionately. But in other parts of the country the two peoples maintained better relations. As Kalvarisky wrote:

During the war, at a time when the masses of Arabs and Jews were suffering and dying for lack of food, they stretched out their hands to one another. In several places the Jews opened soup kitchens for poor people, without distinction as to creed, and in other localities schools were set up for Arab children. Hearts came closer together, and educated people from both sides began thinking about working together and even about a political pact between the two peoples.*

* Further information of great interest concerning Jewish-Arab relations during the first World War may be found in the extracts from the memoirs of H. M. Kalvarisky, published in She'ifotenu (Our Aspirations), the organ of Brit-Shalom (Peace Union), Vols. II and III.

A sizable number of Jews was saved from starvation thanks to the supplies Kalvarisky obtained from some of his Arab friends (at a time when wheat was worth its weight in gold). In 1916, all the Jewish colonies in Galilee were saved because of 6,000 bushels of wheat supplied by the Arabs in Hauran. When Kalvarisky was short of golden napoleons for the new Jewish settlements established during the war (at Mahanayim, Ayelet Hashahar, Kfar Gil'adi, and Tel Hai), he was helped by his Arab neighbors. An eyewitness related years later, "I was present one day when a neighboring Arab handed Kalvarisky a large sum of money in gold. When Kalvarisky wanted to sign bills of payment, the lender said to him: 'Mr. Kalvarisky, give the money back to me when you have it. I do not need bills.' "

However, all attempts to attain a political *modus vivendi* between the Arab and Jewish national movements ceased during this period.

An Attempt at Rapprochement

An interesting development during this period was a Jewish-Arab gathering held in Jerusalem in December 1915, with the object of encouraging the Jews to become better Ottoman citizens and bringing the two peoples closer to one another. The Hebrew Teachers Training College, where the meeting took place, was packed. The praesidium was composed of leading Jews and Arabs from Jerusalem. Among those present were Jewish leaders from various circles, as well as visitors from Jaffa and the colonies. The chairman, E. Ben-Yehuda, dwelt on world events and the havoc caused by the war and called for joint action for the benefit of both peoples. Ben-Yehuda welcomed the audience on behalf of the Mayor of Jerusalem, Hussain al-Hussaini, who was unable to attend the meeting but announced that he fully shared its aims and hoped it would lead to concrete results. Ben-Yehuda was followed by Sheik Abd-ul-Kadir al-Muzaffar, who opened by regretting that he could not speak in Hebrew. He discussed ways of bringing Jews and Arabs closer together and creating greater unity. Everyone present stressed the great importance of the gathering—the first joint public meeting since modern Jewish settlement in Palestine.

In this initial meeting, the Arabs spoke openly. Some of their words were pleasant for the Jews to listen to, and some less pleasant. This meeting was to have been followed by a series of gatherings in Jerusalem and other towns. But when one of the Jerusalem Moslem notables visited Jaffa to arrange a similar meeting, he was summoned to the Turkish commander, Hassan Bey, "who threatened him with deportation if he dared to do anything like that in Jaffa. The Arab notable was forced to return to Jerusalem without doing anything." The Turkish commander in Jerusalem, Zaki Bey, who encouraged a *rapprochement* between Jews and Arabs, was dismissed, and the

search for common ground between the two people came to a speedy end.
(A. Elmaleh)

Arab Policies During the War Years

After the outbreak of war, Arab leaders began to respond to British and
French propaganda, which endeavored to arouse their national sentiments
and stir up a rebellion against their Turkish oppressors and coreligionists. The
refusal of the Hashemite Sharif Hussain, the religious leader of the ruling
circle in Hedjaz, to sign the appeal of the Sultan Caliph for a *jihad* (Holy War)
was only the first stage in the deterioration of Arab-Turkish relations during
the war. The negotiations between Hussain and the British Commissioner in
Egypt, Sir Henry MacMahon (in late 1915), led to the Arab revolt against the
Turks, which started in Hejaz in June 1916 and had an immediate effect on
the central diplomatic and military constellation in the whole of western Asia.

Arab leaders were not aware of the secret Sykes-Picot agreement of May
16, 1916, which divided Syria, Palestine, and Iraq between England and
France after the defeat of Turkey; nor were they aware of the conflicting
promises made by the British to the Arabs and the Jews. But the Arabs
decided to stake everything on an Allied victory, in the hope that the British
and French promises to them would be implemented after the war. The
MacMahon pledge, one of the most obscure episodes in the diplomatic history
of the first World War, was the subject of a violent exchange between the
Arab leaders and the British government in the 1930s.

The Zionist Movement During World War I

Jewish leaders in Palestine and Zionist leaders abroad pursued two main
objectives during the war years. First, they wanted to keep the Jewish
community of Palestine—the *Yishuv*—intact in the face of the economic,
political, and physical threats to its existence. Here an important role was
played by the Zionist representatives in Constantinople and the members of
Zionist bodies in neutral countries, all of whom worked ceaselessly to enlist
the support of world Jewry and other influential political groups. Second,
the Zionist movement sought to ensure the support of the great powers for
its aspirations and its plans for Palestine after the war.

When war broke out in August 1914, the Zionist movement faced a
difficult situation. Although there were large Jewish communities in the
Allied lands (e.g., in Russia and the Western countries), there were also masses
of Jews on the other side—in Germany and Austro-Hungary, etc. Turkey
was, of course, a part of the camp aligned against the Allies. This prompted
the Zionist movement to adopt a neutral position, refraining from identifying

itself with either of the warring camps. The twenty-five man Zionist Actions Committee, which met in Copenhagen on December 3-8, 1914, appointed five members of the Zionist Executive and determined that its chairmen, Professor Warburg and Dr. Hantke would remain in Berlin (where the central Zionist office had been since 1911), Dr. Jacobson would return to his post in Constantinople, and Dr. Tschlenov and Nahum Sokolov would set up headquarters in London. It was also decided to open an intermediary office in neutral Copenhagen headed by Leo Motzkin. Justice Louis Brandeis, and Shmaryahu Levin, were placed in charge of Zionist affairs in the United States. This meant, in effect, that the Zionist movement maintained its formal headquarters in the capital of Germany, Turkey's most important ally. At the same time, it kept a close watch on Zionist interests in Turkey itself through the mission in Constantinople, while underlining its official neutrality through its bureaus in London and Copenhagen and its work in the United States (which was then neutral, not entering the war until April 1917).

In the light of subsequent events, there can be no doubt that the Zionist leaders followed a wise policy. Were the Zionist movement to have immediately adopted a clear-cut stand against Turkey and Germany—as demanded by various circles, including Jabotinsky and his followers—it is hard to imagine what might have become of the Jewish position in Palestine.

For a long time, the outcome of the war continued to be in doubt, and the Zionist movement maintained its declared neutrality. Yet beneath this neutral facade, two opposing political viewpoints struggled for domination. One placed its faith in an Allied victory, while the other claimed that the Central European powers and Turkey would eventually win the war. The longer the war lasted and the clearer it became that the Allies were going to win, the more active became the first school of thought. Its advocates tried to obtain from Britain and the Allies what Herzl had tried in vain to get from the Sultan of Turkey and what those Zionist leaders who succeeded him had tried to obtain from the Young Turks: the right to free Jewish immigration and settlement in Palestine.

The chief spokesman of this latter group was Dr. Chaim Weizmann (1874-1952). He held that neutrality was no longer compatible with Zionist interests in the new international circumstances and urged that instead of relying on "the Berlin-Baghdad axis, which ran through Constantinople," the Zionist movement should act through "the London-Baghdad axis, via Jerusalem." In 1915 to 1916, forceful representations had already been made to the British Cabinet and to the British public. With the help of several leading public figures, Weizmann found his way to several Cabinet ministers, including Lloyd George, who became Prime Minister during the latter part of the war; Arthur James Balfour, who was Foreign Secretary under Lloyd

George; and Herbert Samuel, a British Jew who was Home Secretary in World War I. Weizmann's diplomatic efforts helped to consolidate support for Zionism in influential government circles and in British public opinion. Eventually, the goal that Weizmann and his colleagues had set themselves was attained.

The Balfour Declaration: Origins and Significance

On November 2, 1917, the British Foreign Secretary, Mr. Arthur James Balfour, addressed to Lord Rothschild, head of the Jewish community in Britain, the following statement, which had been approved by Lloyd George's Cabinet.

Foreign Office,
November 2nd, 1917

Dear Lord Rothschild,

I have much pleasure in conveying to you, on behalf of His Majesty's Government, the following declaration of sympathy with Jewish Zionist aspirations which has been submitted to, and approved by, the Cabinet.

"His Majesty's government view with favour the establishment in Palestine of a national home for the Jewish people, and will use their best endeavours to facilitate the achievement of this object, it being clearly understood that nothing shall be done which may prejudice the civil and religious rights of existing non-Jewish communities in Palestine, or the rights and political status enjoyed by Jews in any other country."

I shall be grateful if you would bring this declaration to the knowledge of the Zionist Federation.

Yours faithfully,
Arthur James Balfour

There has been much speculation about the real background of the Balfour Declaration. When the full story of the behind-the-scenes negotiations emerged in the course of time, it was shown conclusively that the Declaration sprang not so much from pangs of conscience about the Jewish people's bitter fate but from very specific interests of the British Empire. While it is true that the study and love of the Bible had led some British circles to believe that the chosen people would one day go back to its ancient homeland, it is also true that since the Ottoman Empire had begun to show the first signs of disintegration, in the 1780s, Britain, France, and other European powers had been pondering the chances of dismembering Turkey's territorial possessions. During the whole of the nineteenth century, such designs remained wishful thinking—mainly because the powers could not agree on how to distribute the spoils.

Anglo-French rivalry, which had prevailed since the days of the French Revolution and Napoleon, aggravated the Middle East question and made it a factor in world politics. In both England and France there had for some time existed various groups urging the revival of a Jewish state in Palestine, as a lever for "national aspirations" on the eastern shore of the Mediterranean. One of the most remarkable of these was that of Napoleon Bonaparte and his followers, who called for a Jewish state under the protection of Paris, as announced by Napoleon shortly before his invasion of Egypt and Palestine (1798–1799).

The concept of a Jewish return to the land of Israel had indeed attained literary and philosophical expression ever since the seventeenth century. But British political circles began to see it as a matter of practical politics primarily during Muhammad Ali's war against Turkey in 1840. Muhammad Ali was presented with an ultimatum by the great-power conference in London and was ordered to evacuate Cilicia, Syria, and the Holy Places without delay. It was then that the British Foreign Secretary, Lord Palmerston, began considering a plan for removing Palestine from the sphere of influence of both the Turks and Muhammad Ali. Certain British circles broached the idea of a new Jewish political center in Palestine; one such proposal was made by Earl Ashley (later Lord Shaftesbury), in a memorandum of September 1840 to Lord Palmerston that set forth specific recommendations for a Jewish return to Palestine.

Articles in *The Times* during August of 1840 maintained that the establishment of a Jewish state in Palestine, under the protection of the powers, would preserve peace more effectively than any Turkish or Egyptian dominion of the Holy Land. Some newspapers compared Britain's role to that of King Cyrus, who allowed the Jews to return to Jerusalem from Babylon; others hinted that it would primarily serve British interests.

This school of thought was fortified when the Suez Canal was opened in 1869. The discussion on ensuring short and safe means of communication between London and the British territories in the Far East had touched on the future of Palestine and the Jewish people. George Eliot's novel *Daniel Deronda* (1876) helped to spread the idea of a Jewish national renaissance. During the Russo-Turkish war of 1877 to 1878, the formation of a Jewish state in Palestine was often discussed. One of the most enthusiastic supporters of this idea was Laurence Oliphant (1829–1888), a well-known journalist and diplomat, who worked out a detailed plan for Jewish settlement in Palestine. When he visited the East in 1879, Oliphant tried unsuccessfully to enlist official Turkish support for the project. His emotional appeal, supported by biblical quotations, did not overlook the political considerations involved. In 1880 Oliphant wrote:

> The political events in the East took a turn which made Palestine, and in particular the provinces of Transjordan, the axis around which all other matters revolve whether they like it or not. Because of their geographical location between the Holy Places in

Jerusalem and near the Russian border on the Asian side, between the Mediterranean and the Red Sea, between Syria and Egypt, they have a great strategic and political value. And apparently the day is not far off when it will be realized that the most important British political interests are endangered, because we missed an opportunity of taking care of things which could happen in the near future.

It was therefore understandable that the *Hovevei Zion* movement and the early Jewish sotlers tin Palestine in the 1880s should have received the attention of British statesmen, writers, and strategists. Lord Cromer, the all-powerful "British agent" to Egypt who was governing in the 1890s, held that the desert frontier between Egypt and Turkey should be defended by Britain's taking over some or all of Palestine. This view prompted British interest in the Zionist movement and attempts to cooperate with Zionism. The first step in this direction was the British government's 1902 proposal for settling the El-Arish area, in the northern Sinai peninsula. When the El-Arish negotiations failed to produce any concrete results, Joseph Chamberlain, then Cabinet Minister, suggested Jewish settlement in Uganda. The proposal was for a Jewish colony in an area of 40,000–90,000 square miles, which would be guaranteed considerable internal autonomy under an executive headed by a Jewish official. The territory would be under the protection of the British government. The Uganda plan was rejected by the Zionist Congress, but the Zionist movement continued to be viewed by His Majesty's Government as a factor in its Middle East policies which would be brought into account as necessary.

Addressing the Jewish Historical Society in London on May 25, 1925, Lloyd George, who had been Prime Minister of Britain at the time the Balfour Declaration was granted, noted Britain's appreciation of Dr. Weizmann's important scientific assistance to its war effort. His words are recorded in the London *Jewish Chronicle* of May 29, 1925:

I felt a deep sense of gratitude, and so did all the Allies, to the brilliant scientific genius of Dr. Weizmann. When we talked to him and asked him "What can we do for you in the way of any honor?" he replied: "All I care for is an opportunity to do something for my people." It was worth anything to us in honor, or in coin of the realm, but all he asked for was to be allowed to present his case for the restoration of his people to the Ancient country that they had made famous throughout the world. Acetone converted me to Zionism. So the case was put before us, and when the War Cabinet began to consider the case for the Declaration, it was unanimously in favor.

In addition to the appreciation of Dr. Weizmann's help as scientist to the war effort and the sentimental attachment to the idea of the People of the Book returning to the land of the Bible, Britain could not overlook her own political interests. It had become clear during the second year of the World War that unless the United States of America came into the war, the Allies could not win. Attempts were made to enlist the influence of American

Italians; but these efforts failed to persuade Washington. When the idea of using the influence of American Jews was first raised (on a secret mission undertaken on behalf of the French government by the Jewish Professor Victor Basch), it appeared that American Jewry could indeed exert considerable influence, but that—like the Jews in most neutral countries—American Jews, too, leaned to the Central Powers because Czarist Russia, which persecuted its Jews, was on the side of the Allies. All the experts agreed that a declaration that would appeal to Jewish interests would help influence the prospects of bringing the United States closer to the Allies. Talks concerning some such statement continued quietly for some time until 1917. In March of that year, French Prime Minister Ribot informed Nahum Sokolov that the French government was favorably inclined toward the Zionist plan, and that he was authorized to inform the Zionist organizations in Russia and America to this effect.

The political intentions behind the Balfour Declaration were plainly set forth in a memorandum of March 3, 1916 from the British Legation in Petrograd to Russian Foreign Minister Sazunov. This memorandum quoted a cable from the British Foreign Secretary, Sir Edward Grey, who requested the Legation to inform the Russian government that the British government took a favorable view of Jewish settlement in Palestine and wished to discuss it with its Allies. The memorandum went on:

> Although many Jews adopt an indifferent attitude towards the Zionist idea, most of the Jewish people in all countries would appreciate the proposal for an agreement on Palestine which would fully gratify the aspirations of the Jews. If this standpoint is correct, then it is clear that by using the Zionist idea important political results can be obtained. *Inter alia* the Jews in the East, the United States and other countries, a great part of whom are now hostile to the Allies, will change their attitude.

Shortly after the issue of the Balfour Declaration, it was decided at a meeting held at the British Foreign Office that Dr. Tschlenov, Sokolov, and Jabotinsky should be dispatched to Russia, and Aharon Aaronson sent to the United States "in order to foster the mutual interests of the Allied Powers and Zionism, and in particular to explain the connection between the aims of Zionism and those of the Allied Powers and to attract Jewish public opinion in Russia and the United States to the side of the Allies." The delegation did not go to Russia because of internal disorders in that country. In the end, Aaronson went to New York as an intermediary between London and New York.

The year 1917 was a grave one for the Allied forces. The Russian Revolution weakened the struggle against Germany in the east. Revolutionary Russia refused to fight and, as a result, the Germans and Austrians were about to transfer ninety divisions from the Russian to the western front before the American troops reached France. The British government thought it important to secure Russian-Jewish support for the continuation of the war. In coordination with the British government, the Russian government in a telegram to its Consul-General in Salonika, instructed its representatives abroad to inform the Jews that "the provisional government is favorably inclined towards the creation of a political Jewish center in the Holy Land".[3] The monthly *Palestine* wrote in October 1917 that "the Russian government has expressed its sympathy with the Zionist aim and declared that it would accept the Jewish claim on Palestine, if this will be the wish of the Jewish people."

British planes dropped leaflets containing the text of the Balfour Declaration over German and Austrian territory. The manner in which the Allies exploited the Declaration was clear from a (British) Yiddish-language pamphlet circulated to Jewish troops in the Central European armies after the British occupation of Jerusalem. The pamphlet said:

Jerusalem has fallen! The hour of Jewish redemption has arrived! Every day more of the Holy Land is falling into the hands of the great democratic powers but not only for them, but for the Jewish people. Palestine must be the national home of the Jewish people once more. For 1,800 sad years the Jews have sought Zion and longed for it. Who stood in the way? Turkey. The gates of the Land of Israel were barred to the wandering Jew, as Jericho was barricaded before Joshua. These gates have now been opened by the Allied victory. The Allies are giving the Land of Israel to the people of Israel. Every loyal Jewish heart is now filled with joy for this great victory. Will you join them and help to build a Jewish homeland in Palestine? Or do you wish to extend the exile and Jewish suffering by helping Turkey and Germany prevent the Jews from entering their ancient homeland? Stop fighting the Allies, who are fighting for you, for all the Jews, for the freedom of all the small nations. Remember! An Allied victory means the Jewish people's return to Zion—its hope for generations past! Every day you remain in the Turkish and German ranks you are delaying the redemption. Change sides now! Jerusalem has fallen to the Allies. But the Allies will establish the Jewish people in Jerusalem. Come, all of you, to help us build Zion!*

The German government must have had some misgivings about these moves, for it saw fit to publish a statement in January 1918 welcoming "the Imperial Ottoman government's intention of aiding the fruitful settlement of the Jews in Palestine by granting permission for free immigration and settlement within the limits of the country's absorptive capacity, for local self-government within the framework of the law of the land, and for the free development of their [Jewish] cultural independence."[4]

At that stage in the war, the Allied powers were forced at least to pay lip-service to President Wilson's famous Fourteen Points. One of these points— the right of all peoples to self-determination—could have endangered the

---

* The proclamation in Yiddish, by courtesy of the Weizmann Archives, Rehovot.

Turkish inheritance, which Britain and France had agreed in the Sykes-Picot agreement of 16.5.1916 to divide between them (following the revolution, Russia had withdrawn from its previous agreement to this division). The declaration of support for a Jewish national home was considered one of the bulwarks against this danger, which threatened British and French interests on the eastern shore of the Mediterranean.

As the war moved to its conclusion, Britain made use of Zionism to modify its agreement with France in its own interest. According to the original agreement for carving up the Turkish Empire, the French sphere of influence was to include Syria, Lebanon, and the northern part of Palestine, up to a line joining Acre and the Sea of Galilee. Sokolov's diplomatic representations in France and Italy played an important role in preparing the ground for a new Franco-British pact, the Deauville agreement between Lloyd George and Clemenceau, reached on September 15, 1919. This agreement placed the southernmost French boundary at the line between Rosh Hanikra and the northern Hulah Valley. After protracted negotiations, the French agreed in December 1920 to add to the British borders the narrow strip of land between the Sea of Galilee and Metulla, which Jewish farmers had been working and had defended, not without loss of life (e.g., at Tel Hai in the spring of 1920).

From the Jewish standpoint, the fact that the Balfour Declaration was linked with Britain's imperial interests did not minimize the importance of this recognition that the Jews were entitled to the same rights as any other people. The Declaration which was confirmed by fifty-two governments, paved the way for the League of Nations, the supreme international forum in the political world in which Palestine was situated, to recognize these rights, and the British Mandate over Palestine was finally approved on July 24, 1922. This changed the Balfour Declaration from a purely British commitment to an international act that served as the legal basis of Jewish claims on Palestine for several decades to come. For the first time the Jewish national liberation movement had received moral and legal recognition; and for the first time there was an international guarantee that recognized the historical link between the Jewish people and the land of Israel.

The Jewish Attitude to the Balfour Declaration

Not all sections of the Jewish people received the Balfour Declaration with equal enthusiasm. The socialist wing of the Zionist movement split over the question of the pact with Britain. At its meeting in Kiev, December 3 to 10, 1917, the central committee of the Poalei Zion party referred to the Declaration as "one of the attempts of world imperialism to exploit liberation movements for its own ends." At the world conference of the Poalei Zion movement, held in Vienna in 1920, the left wing decided to secede from the

Zionist Congress because of its opposition to the plans for a British Mandate.

There were sceptics among non-socialists too: Ahad Ha'am wrote to Nahum Sokolov on July 11, 1917, "For myself, I would have refrained from suggesting to them [i.e., the British] a formulation [about Palestine], so as to see what they would write of their own accord. Then we would understand better what we can hope for from them."

At that time, the Zionist movement as a whole lacked the necessary political acumen and experience that might have advised caution in the face of what could be seen as an exaggerated enthusiasm engendered by the Balfour Declaration in Palestine and the Diaspora. Few people could grasp the political motives behind the declaration; and few discerned in the ambiguity of its wording the seeds of future British disavowals, which would revolve around the significant distinction between "Palestine as a national home" and "a national home in Palestine." The masses of Jews were not familiar with the recondite nuances of British diplomacy and colonial politics. They could not know that simultaneously with solemn promises to the Jews, qualified only by the condition that "nothing shall be done which may prejudice the civil and religious rights of existing non-Jewish communities in Palestine," the same "non-Jewish communities" had been given apparently contradictory pledges about "the freedom of the indigenous population, from both an economic and political standpoint" (the wording used by D. G. Hogarth, head of the British bureau in Cairo, in his letter to Sharif Hussain in Mecca).

Nevertheless, when we take into account the standing of the Zionist movement in those days, and the actual alternatives it faced, there can be no doubt that the Balfour Declaration was an important historical and international event. It was a turning point in the annals of the Jewish national liberation movement and in Jewish history. It constituted recognition of the Jewish people as a living historical entity for the first time since it had been exiled from Palestine by the Romans in 70 C.E. The League of Nations gave this status further recognition a few years later. A new chapter in Jewish history began.

The British Occupation of Palestine

After their abortive attacks on the Suez Canal in January 1915 and August 1916, the Turks launched no further frontal onslaughts in this sector. When the British had concentrated sufficient forces in Egypt, plans for an attack on Palestine were set in motion. In January 1917, the Sinai Peninsula was occupied, and the British troops advanced to Rafah, thanks to the railroad and the water pipeline installed near El-Arish. In March of that year, the British began moving northward. Beersheba was occupied on October 31 and Gaza on November 7. On November 15, the British troops entered Jaffa. Another column marched on and occupied Jerusalem, which the Turks evacuated on December 9; two days later, General Allenby entered the city. In February 1918, Jericho was occupied, ending this stage of the British offensive. Allenby controlled the entire south of the country, while the Turks still held the north.

On September 19, 1918, the British resumed their attack and pressed northward. Haifa, Acre, Tiberias, and Samakh fell in a few days. British troops pursuing the fleeing Turkish Army joined forces with Emir Faisal's Arab forces, which were moving northwest of the Jordan river. At the end of September, they occupied the important railway junction, Dera'a. On September 30, they entered Damascus. Beirut fell on October 6, and Aleppo on October 26. After losing further battles to the British in Iraq as well, the Turks signed a treaty of surrender on October 30. This sealed the fate of the 500-year-old Ottoman Empire. On November 11, 1918, an armistice was signed and World War I came to an end.

Jewish Troops in Action

In March 1915, Jewish refugees who had been expelled (or fled) from Palestine by Jamal Pasha formed the Zion Mule Corps. This 600-man unit was commanded by a British officer, Lieut-Colonel Patterson, whose leading Jewish officer was Captain Joseph Trumpeldor (1880–1920) a Russian who had fought with distinction against Japan. The Zion Mule Corps took part in the abortive Gallipoli expedition, after which it returned to Alexandria. The corps was disbanded in May 1916.

Shortly after Turkey entered the war, Vladimir Jabotinsky began calling for a Jewish Legion. He argued that Zionism could hope for nothing more from Turkey. The latter was destined to lose the war and the Zionist movement should therefore seek an ally in the new political constellation. If a Jewish legion fought on the Allied side and took part in the occupation of Palestine, this would focus world attention on the Zionist movement and would stand the Jewish people in good stead at the peace talks after the war.

For a long time the Zionist leadership was unsympathetic to this proposal, partly because it feared a Turkish reprisal against the Jewish community. It was also felt that the Zionist movement should continue to adhere to its policy of strict neutrality between the opposing blocs. A stormy debate ensued in Zionist circles. Jabotinsky and his supporters were for a considerable period unable to secure British agreement to the formation of a Jewish legion. One of the principal British opponents of Jabotinsky's proposal was Sir Mark Sykes (1879–1918), who warned that the Arabs would create difficulties. The British government reversed its stand only as the end of the war came nearer. In July 1917, the Kerensky government in Russia permitted the British government to recruit Russian subjects living in Britain, most of whom were Jews. By that time, too, the United States had come into the war and the Zionist leaders began to change their mind about the proposed Jewish legion. Another factor was the military situation in Europe, which made it impossible to transfer troops to the Palestine front. The Allied commanders hoped to strike at Turkey—the weakest link in the Central Powers' alliance—by attacking Palestine, in the hope that this would affect the entire progress of the war.

Three units of Jewish volunteers were set up during the last year of the war. One was the 38th Battalion Royal Fusiliers, formed around the veterans of the Zion Mule Corps and commanded by Colonel Patterson. The second was the 39th Battalion of the King's Rifles, composed of Jewish volunteers from the United States. The third unit was recruited in Palestine after the British occupation. Among the volunteers were Ben-Gurion, B. Katznelson, Y. Ben-Zvi, M. Sharett, L. Eshkol, and others, who afterwards played a leading role in Palestine and Israel.

A lively debate took place in Palestine over the formation of these units. The Provisional Committee of Palestine Jews, formed in Tel Aviv after the return of the Jewish refugees, opposed volunteering for the British Army on the grounds that this might harm Jews who were still under the Ottoman rule. The Hapoel Hatzair Labor Party opposed it because of its very special concern for the guarding of Jewish settlements and the pressing need to repair war damages.

Some people, including A. D. Gordon, warned against "the hypnosis inherent in the idea of militarism, war, conquest by the sword" and also expressed their fear that "even those veterans most loyal to the concept of labor will not return to it after army service."

Some circles disassociated themselves completely from Jabotinsky's "legion ideology." Jabotinsky is recorded as saying that "the Zionists told the British [in the course of the negotiations over the Balfour Declaration] that support for their aspirations would assure the Empire of an important strategic outpost, under conditions that would improve as Zionism was implemented. This would also ensure the sympathy of socialist elements in the world who are opposed in principle to imperialist conquests." Jabotinsky saw fit to add another reason, in line with his political thinking: "In the Middle East, nationalism will spread among indigenous populations; only the stable support of a nation that is foreign in culture and social forms from the other peoples in the region can serve as a prop for the British forces in this region."[5]

A. D. Gordon succinctly expressed the mood of those circles that opposed Jabotinsky's ideology:

In the political sense the country belongs to the conqueror, and in the national sense, to the Arabs. True, we have a historical right to the country. But in practice the country will not be ours even if the broadest autonomy is given. It will only be ours, in the national sense, if there is in it a living, working, and productive *Yishuv*. In the political sense, our hope of standing on our own feet is certainly even farther removed today than it was under the Turkish regime. Whom are we now going to fight? The Turks, with whom we no longer have any dealings; the Germans, with whom we have never had any dealings; or the Bolsheviks in Russia, whom we have no desire to fight, or whose victory we would like to see? What are we going to fight for? For capitalism, for the enslavement of other peoples, even if such subjugation is civilized and not barbarian!"

When Weizmann came to Palestine with the members of the Zionist Commission* in April 1918, the opposition to the Jewish units died down and in June of that year the plan was officially approved. The total number of volunteers eventually reached 5,500. (The number of Jewish soldiers who took part in World War I in the different armies was estimated at about 700,000.) A number of these volunteers eventually saw active service under Allenby, who commanded an army of 60,000 men, which fought on the Palestinian front in an attack on the Turkish troops in September 1918.

After the Armistice, the Jewish units dwindled in number, and only about 260 of the volunteers from abroad remained. Their situation reflected the struggle, among the British authorities, between supporters and opponents of the Jewish battalions. General Bols, chief of the G.H.Q., was among the veteran opponents of the idea of the battalions.

The remnants of the Jewish units were concentrated in Haifa (40th Battalion) and commanded by Colonel Margolin. Its British N.C.O.s were replaced by Jews and—under the name of "the First of Judea"—the unit took on a Jewish character. Under Arab pressure, it was transferred from Haifa to the Sinai border. This step was one of the reasons for an atmosphere of depression pervading the unit at this time.

Eliahu Golomb (1893–1945), one of the leading volunteers in the battalion (and later an outstanding figure in the Hagana) noted that the move from Haifa was the result of Arab protests against clashes between Jewish soldiers and the Arab population. These incidents—which were few and far between—were provoked by a small part of the battalion that Golomb called "irresponsible elements," and were condemned by the more idealistic members of the battalion.

* A committee representing the Zionist Organization, which arrived in Palestine in April 1918 and, with the approval of the British authorities in London, acted as the supreme Jewish representation in Palestine from that time until September 1921 (when its powers were transferred to the Zionist Executive). The committee of delegates was first under the chairmanship of Dr. C. Weizmann, then under that of Dr. Eder, and, from the autumn of 1919 onward, under that of M. M. Ussishkin.

K

When the war ended, the Zionist leadership devoted some thought to the question of the future of the Jewish units. At the Zionist conference in London in the summer of 1919, two schools of thought emerged. Y. Sprinzak, Yitshak Vilkansky, and Dr. Arthur Ruppin favored placing the emphasis on productive labor rather than on military forces, and called for a policy of peace with the Arabs. Dr. Y. Thon, Israel Shohat, and Berl Katznelson (the last two acting as spokesmen for the legions) defended the need to enlist volunteers from abroad. In March 1920 an official order was given to disband the battalion. When it was finally disbanded on July 31, it did not number more than 400 men.

Jewish-Arab Contacts During War Years

Kalvarisky was one of the few Jewish leaders who remained in Palestine during the war. He frequently conferred with Jamal Pasha in an attempt to mitigate the harsh anti-Jewish decrees and to convince him of the uselessness, in terms of Turkish interests, of destroying the Jewish *Yishuv*.

In the fall of 1917, the *Nili* group's pro-British espionage was uncovered. Turkish authorities suspected the *Hashomer* movement of similar hostile actions. Jamal Pasha was incensed, and the Jewish community was in great danger. Kalvarisky went to Damascus to see the pasha (even though he knew that a warrant of arrest was ready against him). He told Jamal, "We will not allow you to treat us the way you treated the Armenians." To this the pasha replied, "Kalvarisky, I will hang you in your own village!" It appeared that Jamal Pasha was suspicious of Kalvarisky's correspondence with Arab leaders. Kalvarisky did not deny these contacts, but suggested that Jamal should examine the correspondence. He would see, Kalvarisky said, that he had always been loyal to the Turkish government. Eventually, Kalvarisky was able to convince the pasha that the *Hashomer* group and the Jewish farmers were innocent of espionage, and those who had already been arrested were set free.

Even during these difficult years, Kalvarisky never ceased his efforts to find a way of attaining a Jewish-Arab understanding. In his papers* he relates:

During the war and as it drew to a close, well known Arab leaders Mahmoud Baihum and the Sulhs (both father and son), proposed that we should make joint representations to Jamal Pasha junior, who was a personal friend of mine and did not hate the Arabs as much as Jamal Pasha senior.† They thought we should ask him to move the Turkish government to proclaim a dualist [Turkish-Arab] regime in

* Some of Kalvarisky's papers were handed in to the Central Zionist Archives in Jerusalem and others are preserved by the writer of this book.
† The reference is to Jamal Pasha, the commander-in-chief of the Fourth Army Corps, whose headquarters was transferred to Damascus after the fall of Jerusalem.

the region, on the pattern of Austro-Hungary. In return they promised us an autonomous Jewish Palestine—rather like Croatia in Hungary or Galicia in Austria. This did not come about because Turkey's fate had already been sealed by the Allied powers and it could no longer be saved by any political administrative concessions to the peoples living within the tottering Ottoman Empire.

A. Saphir has also testified to the continuous contacts between Jewish and Arab leaders through the war years. When he returned to the Middle East with the French Army in 1917,* he found that, like the other leaders with whom talks had been held before the war, "they were filled with the same wish that when the time came for a final political settlement in the Middle East the negotiations that had been interrupted by the war should be resumed, because this would be in the interests of both the Arabs and the Jews."

A New Era Opens

In December 1917, when southern Palestine as far as the Jerusalem-Jaffa line was British-occupied territory, the Zionist representatives in London asked that a commission be allowed to go to Palestine, so that the work of reconstruction might begin. At a meeting with Foreign Secretary Balfour on December 4, 1917, Dr. Weizmann remarked that "the Jewish people is waiting to know what Palestine's fate is going to be, or—in clearer language —how the British government is going to interpret the Declaration." When Weizmann stated that there was enough room in Palestine for a large Jewish population without prejudice to the Arabs' rights, Balfour observed that "the Arab problem is not a serious obstacle. In any event, it is desirable to reach an agreement with Faisal." To this Weizmann replied that he believed in an agreement along these lines.

At the beginning of 1918, the British government decided that a Zionist commission should go to Palestine to study the situation and draw up a plan of action in the spirit of the Balfour Declaration. As Weizmann noted in his memoirs, the commission was to have represented the Jews living in all the principal Allied countries. But the United States nominated no representatives to the commission—because it was not at war with Turkey—and the delegates from Russia could not join because of political vicissitudes in that country at the end of the war. As a result, the commission was comprised of— apart from Dr. Weizmann—the representatives of British Jewry (Joseph Cowen, Dr. M. D. Eder, Leon Simon, and Israel Sieff); Italian Jewry

---

* Upon the outbreak of the first World War, A. Saphir volunteered for the French Army. Until 1917, he fought in the trenches, was wounded twice, and awarded the Victoria Cross. Later, in view of his familiarity with Near East affairs, he was sent as a political officer attached to the Command of the French Expeditionary Force at Salonika and the Near East (see Chapter Three).

(Commandante Levi Bianchini), and French Jewry (Professor Sylvain Levy, an anti-Zionist who was forced onto the commission against his will; Weizmann noted, in fact, that Biancini and Levy appeared to be more concerned with Italian and French than with Zionist interests). Captain James de Rothschild was the adjutant, and the liaison officer with the British army authorities was Major Ormsby-Gore.*

The very composition of the commission epitomized the major policy differences among the great powers over Palestine. As Weizmann wrote later in his autobiography, *Trial and Error*:

> In the light of subsequent developments it is easy to understand the deep interest displayed by the Italians in Zionist activities in Palestine even in those early days. Already the Jewish national home was viewed with a certain jealousy and suspicion as tending to strengthen British influence in "Mare Nostro"; and every effort was made to offset this by encouraging Italian participation in Palestine's economic development. It was repeatedly suggested to us that we might make use of Italian firms, Italian workers, Italian supplies for the execution of our preliminary work.

The commission was scheduled to leave London on March 8. Sir Mark Sykes, who organized it and made the arrangements for its journey under difficult wartime conditions, thought its prestige would be increased if King George received Dr. Weizmann, the chairman. An audience was arranged. But when Weizmann arrived at the Foreign Office at the appointed hour, he found Sykes disturbed. He told Weizmann that a sheaf of worrying cables had just been received from Cairo. "The Arabs are starting to ask embarrassing questions," he said. Sykes was so concerned that he wanted to cancel Weizmann's audience with the King. It was only due to Balfour's personal intervention that the audience took place as planned.

The question of possible Arab opposition in Palestine and of future Jewish-Arab relations arose at the second meeting of the commission, held at the beginning of March 1918. The only person at the meeting who could say anything concrete on the subject was Aharon Aaronson,† who had been coopted as Weizmann's adviser. Like those of many Western experts, Aaronson's views sprang from an inability to appreciate the dynamics of the Arab world and its sources; this gave rise in turn to a lack of belief in the Arab national movement's validity and in Arab public opinion

---

* Born in 1876. A member of Parliament, during the war he was an officer at the Intelligence Division of the General Headquarters in Cairo. From 1936 to 1938, he was Colonial Secretary. Died in February 1964 as Lord Harlech.

† Born in 1876 in Bacau, Roumania. Came to Palestine in 1882 with his parents who were among the founders of *Zichron Ya'akov*. Studied agronomy in France and won fame for his research into the flora of Palestine and its surroundings. Was among the founders of *Nili* (1916). In 1917, acted as adviser to the British Expeditionary Force Headquarters in Cairo.

in general. His views on the question could be summed up quite simply: the Arab masses were completely indifferent to political affairs, and the nucleus of the opposition to Jewish aspirations in Palestine was the effendis, who were afraid of losing their influence in Arab society because of the modernization that Zionism would introduce. At the same time, their anti-Zionist propaganda also served to raise the price of the land they would eventually sell to the Jews.

Aaronson regarded the changes that had recurred in the Arab national movement during the war as so mixed up that it was difficult to know the proper Arab leaders with whom to negotiate. On the other hand, Weizmann stressed the need for an information campaign in Arab circles. He wanted to allay Arab fears that the Zionist movement planned to oust the Palestinian Arabs from their lands and to push them out of the country, and to convince them that Zionism considered Palestine a land common to both peoples. To avoid clashes with the effendis from the moment the commission arrived in the country, Weizmann proposed that no private land should be bought until the end of the war, and that emphasis should be placed on the purchase of government land or uncultivated land in outlying districts.[6]

Several days after arriving in Cairo, the members of the commission met the British High Commissioner in Egypt, Sir Reginald Wingate, who, according to Weizmann, "had considerable experience in the Arab world and knew their mentality." Ormsby-Gore presented the members of the commission. Wingate expressed his gratification at the opportunity to meet the delegation. He added that he was sympathetic to the Zionist idea, and had been impressed by the Jewish colonies he had seen when visiting Palestine, stating that "they rebut the argument that Jews cannot be good farmers." The High Commissioner, on the basis of reports from his political officers in the region, acquainted the commission with the mood of Arab public opinion on the Zionist movement. "The Arabs are nervous and suspicious of Zionist trends. They also fear that after the war a Jewish government will be set up in Palestine, and that the Jews will rob the Arabs and expel them from Palestine." He advised the commission to meet Arab spokesmen, so that their fears might be dispelled and, if possible, to bring about unity and cooperation between the Jews and the Arabs. "An Armenian-Arab-Jewish agreement would be extremely important," Wingate declared. This was no easy task; but he did not think the obstacles were insurmountable. The trouble was that various agents were trying to convince the Arabs that it would be a mistake to trust Britain and that Syria should be given back to the Turks. Wingate's advice was to direct their information efforts toward small segments of the public and to establish contact with influential leaders, particularly religious figures.

Dr. Weizmann, speaking on behalf of the delegation, said that it was fully aware of the difficulties the High Commissioner had noted and was ready to meet influential Arab representatives to allay their fears—if such representatives could be found. There was no intention of uprooting the Arabs living in Palestine or of forming a Jewish government in the near future. In their negotiations with the British government, Zionist spokesmen stressed their wish to see Palestine placed under British rule after the war. A Jewish campaign to this end was bound to carry weight at the peace conference. Dr. Weizmann stressed the complete harmony between British and Jewish interests in Palestine. It followed that any campaign against Jewish interests meant a campaign against those of Great Britain. The High Commissioner expressed his agreement with these views.

After the formal meeting with the commission, Wingate, Weizmann and Ormsby-Gore held a private conversation.[7]

On March 27, five days after the Cairo meeting, several members of the commission met with three Arab notables: Dr. Faris Nimr, Said Shukeir, and Sulaiman Bey Nassif.* This meeting was arranged by Ormsby-Gore. The Arabs were all known to belong to the Syrian Party, and all three of them had spent the war years in Cairo because of the Turkish authorities' hostility to their movement. The most outstanding Arab spokesman at this meeting was Dr. Faris Nimr. He had been active in the first Arab national organization, secretly formed in Beirut in 1875. In 1882, he was the founder and owner of the well-known Cairo daily *Al Mukattam*. At the meeting with the commission, Dr. Nimr said he had been assured by Ormsby-Gore that the Zionist aspirations and intentions were not opposed to those of the Arabs. He said that as far as he personally was concerned, he was happy to meet Dr. Weizmann and the members of the commission and hoped they would be able to work together in harmony and understanding.

Dr. Weizmann also expressed his satisfaction over the meeting with the Arab leaders. He had received information about Ormsby-Gore's talk with Dr. Nimr. One of the commission's most important tasks he recognized was to prevent land speculation in Palestine. He said that he had urged Balfour to reach a decision on this matter and to inform the authorities in Palestine and Egypt accordingly. The Zionists earnestly wanted to live on friendly terms with the Arabs, Weizmann declared. The Jews did not claim a monopoly on the leadership of the country, and he wanted to make it plain that the Zionists did not wish to establish a Jewish state in Palestine directly after the war. The Zionists hoped that when the war was over Palestine would be under British rule and that Britain would adopt a fair and just approach to all the groups comprising the country's population. He hoped the Arabs would realize that everything the Zionists planned to do would benefit the country

* Nassif was later to become an Arab member of Sir Herbert Samuel's Advisory Council.

as a whole and make it more prosperous. As far as the Holy Places were concerned, the Jews wanted nothing more than that their own Holy Places be protected.

Sulaiman Bey Nassif and Shukeir expressed their gratification with these statements by Dr. Weizmann. Sulaiman Nassif said that there was room for another million people in Palestine, without prejudice to the status of its present inhabitants. Ormsby-Gore pointed out that the British government had not demanded that Palestine be placed under British rule; this would be decided by the peace conference. Aharon Aaronson raised the question of the Arabs in the Jewish colonies, stating that their economic situation had improved immensely and their numbers had increased. No specific political problems concerning Palestine's political future or Jewish immigration were discussed at the meeting.[8]

The impressions of the Arab participants at this meeting were described by George Antonius:

> Dr. Weizmann, with his great gift of persuasion, scored a temporary success in interviews he had with several Arab personalities, and in this he was ably and zealously seconded by Major the Hon. W. Ormsby-Gore, who was accompanying the commission as political officer delegated by the foreign office. They gave their hearers such a comforting account of Zionist aims and dispositions as dispelled their fears and brought them to a state of acquiescence in the idea of Zionist-Arab cooperation. Meetings were arranged and held between Zionist and Arab leaders. Dr. Faris Nimr, the proprietor of an influential newspaper in Cairo,* was so far impressed with Dr. Weizmann's and Major Ormsby-Gore's assurances that he made use of the weighty columns of his journal to dispel Arab fears about their political future and advocate an understanding between the two races.[9]

In short, Dr. Weizmann encountered an atmosphere of goodwill toward the Jewish enterprise in Palestine on the part of these Arab leaders.

When King Hussain was informed of the Balfour Declaration, he asked the British to clarify its significance and consequences. During the first week of January 1918, Commander D. Hogarth of the (British) Arab Bureau in Cairo arrived in Jeddah. As Antonius noted, the statement Hogarth brought with him completely reassured Hussain (and hence ensured the continuation of the Arab revolt against the Turks during the final stages of the Palestinian offensive). Hogarth made his announcement orally, but Hussain wrote it down in Arabic: "Jewish settlement in Palestine should only be allowed in so far as would be consistent with the political and economic freedom of the Arab population." On the basis of Hogarth's oral statement, Hussain declared his readiness to exert all his influence towards the promotion of the objectives thus enunciated. Later, he sent messages to his representatives in Cairo and to the troops taking part in the Arab revolt, informing them that the British

* Dr. Nimr was George Antonius' father-in-law.

government had assured him that the Jewish settlement in Palestine would not conflict with Arab independence in this country. He ordered his sons to reassure the people who had been alarmed by the Balfour Declaration and a special emissary went on this matter to his son Faisal, whose troops were then near Akaba. On March 23, 1918, Hussain's official organ, *Al Qiblah*, published an appeal to the Arab population in Palestine in which he urged that their sacred writings and traditions commanded them to be hospitable to their guests and to treat them with tolerance. They should accept the Jews as brothers and cooperate with them for the common good. According to Antonius, this article was written by King Hussain himself. It indicates not only that he was free from religious prejudices and fanaticism but also that he reflected the attitude of many Arabs toward the Jews at the end of the war.

The Zionist Leadership and the Arab National Movement

When the members of the Zionist commission arrived in Egypt in March 1918, they soon discovered that Balfour's appeasing remark that "the Arab problem is not a serious obstacle" was incompatible with the realities of the situation. British circles in Egypt as well as in Britain itself considered the Arab revolt and the Arab national movement of major importance. This they said in unmistakable terms. None of the Zionist leaders, however, was acquainted with developments in the Arab national movement during the war years. Arab leaders who had favored decentralization and cultural autonomy for the Arab areas within the framework of the Ottoman Empire had seen the ground cut from under their feet. The leading Arab nationalists in 1918 belong to such secret Arab societies as *Al Qahtaniah*, *Al'Arabiah al-Fatah*, and *Al'Ahd*, which had been founded after the Young Turks' honeymoon with Arab nationalism had come to an end. Many active Arab nationalists had supported the Arab revolt against the Turks and some had even joined Faisal's army. Their relations with the decentralist groups were invariably tense.*

Dr. Weizmann immediately noted the special problems confronting him in his efforts to improve Jewish-Arab relations. These problems derived first from the absence of any political ties between the Jews and Arabs of Palestine, and second from the internal situation of the Arab national movement. The Arab leaders in Egypt or Hejaz took a broad view of Arab-Jewish relations. They could perceive their wider applications and were ready to help the Jews obtain what they wanted in Palestine in return for Jewish help in achieving the large Arab federation toward which they were striving.

* The reader of Arabic will find details concerning internal relations within the Arab movement in the period under review in Amin Said's book, *Ath-Thaurah al-Arabiah al-Kubrah*, (*The Great Arab Uprising*), Book II.

On the other hand, Palestine Arab leaders were concerned about Jewish-Arab relations only within the confines of Palestine itself and felt that they were being asked to give up something without receiving anything in return.

Weizmann tried to eliminate the first problem when he arrived in Palestine with the Zionist commission. His opportunity came at a reception given on April 27, 1918 by the Governor of Jerusalem, Sir Ronald Storrs. As he tells us in his memoirs, this reception was attended by a number of prominent Arab leaders, including Mussa Kazim al Hussaini, the Mayor of Jerusalem; D. Salameh, the Deputy Mayor, who was a member of the Greek Orthodox Church; Arif Pasha Daoudi, formerly a high official of the Turkish government; Ismail al-Hussaini, Director of Education; and representatives of the Latin, Greek Orthodox, and Armenian churches.

In his speech, Dr. Weizmann tried to dispel the Arab leaders' fears and to find a way of reaching a mutual understanding. Turning to the heads of the various communities, he declared:

I am not foreign to this country, even though I was born a little to the north; none of my brothers who are scattered over the whole world is foreign to this country. By summoning up tremendous strength, through wars and revolutions our forefathers heroically defended their everlasting right to this holy place, and only after they were defeated by dreadful and bloody events, more terrible than what has taken place in our times in Belgium and Armenia, only then was Palestine taken out of their hands. But our forefathers did not surrender their right to it. In the place of a material Palestine, they created for themselves a spiritual and moral Palestine, which stood like a firm rock against all the destructive forces in the world. Hence we are not *coming* to Palestine now, but *returning* to our borders. We are returning in order to link the tradition of our brilliant past with the future, in order to create once more a great Jewish center that might perhaps be a source of new life for a tormented and suffering world. If this center is to be real and solid, it will have to be built on real foundations, to put down roots in the soil, to suck from the soil of Palestine. In order to do this we intend to create here the conditions for the material and moral development of all sons of our people who decide to come here of their own free will. We are certain that this will prove possible, and that it can be done, not at the expense of the large communities that have already taken root in the country, but, on the contrary, for their benefit.

There is enough land and enough room in Palestine to settle several times the number of people it now holds. A number of your leaders have also told me this. All the fears expressed by the Arabs, openly or in secret, lest they be ousted from the land on which they now live, are nothing but the fruit of a gross error about our approach and our aspirations, or the result of phantoms created by our common enemies. Both spiritually and materially speaking, it is better for us to live in peace, and only if this is the case will the country develop in a proper manner.

Our *halutzim* [pioneers] have proved that even under the oppressive regime of the Turkish government they could turn an empty desert into flourishing settlements.

Hence what could not a hard working and intelligent community do under more suitable conditions, under a strong and honest government? It will be able to turn Palestine into a land of milk and honey once more, and all the country's inhabitants will benefit from this change to an equal degree. This is what we seek with all our heart, and I ask you, by all you hold sacred, to beware of incorrect and vain interpretations.

It is with a heartfelt sympathy and strong interest that we watch the war of freedom now being waged by the ancient Arab people. We see the scattered Arab force uniting under the benevolent eye of the Allied governments and those who love peace; and through the fog created by the war, new and tremendous political possibilities await us. Once again, we are witnessing the formation of a strong and united Arab body, which is taking on new life and is about to resuscitate the glorious tradition of Arab science and literature, which are so close to our heart. This closeness attained brilliant expression during the Spanish period of Jewish-Arab development in particular, when the greatest Jewish writers wrote and thought in Arabic as freely as in Hebrew. . . .

We Jews seek the possibility of free national development in Palestine. And if justice and righteousness is to be done, our appeal cannot be rejected. We want to till our soil, which has been abandoned for so long, using the latest economic methods and on a basis of justice. We strive to avoid the mistakes from which the enlightened European countries are only now starting to liberate themselves. . . .

In all these endeavors, whether agricultural or spiritual, we shall not harm our neighbors in Palestine. On the contrary, we shall help them to make their lives fuller and richer. And do not underestimate the value of this assistance. True, we are only a small number of people here at present; but the eyes of our fellow Jews who are scattered over the four corners of the earth are fixed on us and on our work here.[10]

At that time Jewish-Arab relations had not reached the height of tension that they attained later on. Nevertheless, the clouds gathering on the horizon could scarcely be ignored. Weizmann's unsuccessful attempts to meet several Arab notables (including the Mufti of Jerusalem, Sheik Kamal al-Hussaini) showed that these Arab leaders were deeply suspicious of Jewish intentions and that their suspicions led to strong opposition. At the meeting of the Zionist commission on April 13, 1918, Weizmann expressed his surprise and concern at the extremist Arab propaganda. He had anticipated some resistance on the part of the Arabs, especially as they had a mistaken view of the Zionist movement's objectives, but he had hoped to counter that resistance with appropriate information. But Arab opposition now appeared to be much more serious than he had envisaged, and he found among Palestinian Arabs a substantial following of Arab nationalists. He noticed among them "a stand that made any negotiations impossible."

Unlike the Arab leaders whom the Zionist commission had met in Cairo, the Palestinian Arab leaders whom Weizmann met took an extreme and uncompromising position, which aggravated his fear of the utter impossibility of reaching a *modus vivendi* with them. Zionist representatives derived little comfort from Ormsby-Gore's analysis of the Arab national movement's social and cultural background and the reasons for its sudden growth—an analysis leading him to conclude that Arab nationalism was not aimed at Zionism as such, but against all foreign powers in general, and Great Britain in particular.[11]

It should be remembered that this was the spring of 1918, the war was still going on, and most of Palestine (north of the Yarkon-Jericho line) was being held by the Turks. When the war came to an end and the struggle over future political settlements began, the situation became far more tense.

Zionist policy was now confronted with the consequences of its past mistakes, against which some of the more far-sighted Jewish leaders had long since warned. It was no easy matter to repair at this late hour what had been neglected for so many years. It became an urgent need to give flesh and blood to the conception of political cooperation with the Arabs, in order to prevent the menace of a serious obstacle rising to block the path of Zionist policy.

On Balfour's advice, Weizmann approached Emir Faisal ibn Hussain (1883–1933). His standing in the Arab revolt and the Arab national movement (for whom he later became chief spokesman at the peace conference), and his close ties with Britain, eminently qualified him to exercise his authority in the matter of Jewish-Arab cooperation. At the beginning of June 1918, while the war was still being fought and the Turks still controlled the north of Palestine, Dr. Weizmann and Major Ormsby-Gore proceeded to Faisal's headquarters in Transjordan, just north of Akaba, for a discussion on the future relations between the two peoples. As Weizmann noted in his memoirs, all authorities agreed that because of his personal qualities and his status as commander-in-chief of the Arab forces who had rebelled against Turkey, Faisal was "the only representative Arab whose influence was of more than local importance."

At their meeting, Weizmann expressed the wish of the Jews to do everything within their power to allay the Arabs' misgivings and suspicions. He stressed the fact that there was considerable room in the country if intensive development were undertaken and that the Arabs' lot would be improved by the Jewish effort.

Weizmann later wrote:

> With all this I found the Emir in full agreement, as Lawrence later confirmed to me by letter. The reader will find ample evidence that the Emir was in earnest when he said that he was eager to see the Jews and Arabs working in harmony during the peace conference which was to come, and that in his view the destiny of the two peoples was linked with the Middle East and must depend on the good will of the great powers.[12]

Weizmann's meeting with Faisal was a source of encouragement to the second general assembly of the Jews of the liberated part of Palestine, which took place in the summer of 1918.* Replying to Ormsby-Gore's greetings on the first day of the conference, Weizmann stated: "I have seen Emir Faisal, the chief Arab military commander, and after the audience I had with him I am authorized to say that a *modus vivendi* can be found in the solution of the extremely complex Arab political problem, because we want to live on the very best terms with the Arabs."

When the general meeting came to consider resolutions submitted to it, the chairman announced that Dr. Weizmann had presented to a specially appointed committee a report of the details of the political situation and of everything the Zionist commission had done to reach a settlement in Palestine. After hearing Weizmann's report, the committee adopted the following resolution:

We heard with satisfaction that, with the help of government officials in Palestine, the Zionist commission has been able to establish friendly relations with the leaders of the great Arab nation [loud applause]. We have learned that the Zionist commission has largely succeeded in allaying suspicions and dispelling the erroneous view hitherto held by Arab leaders on the precise aims and aspirations of the Zionist movement. The commission proved to the Arab leaders that the mutual interests of the Jewish and Arab peoples demand common work and mutual assistance and that the future success and happiness of each of these peoples depend on that work. [Prolonged and stormy applause].

An exchange of cables between Dr. Eder and Faisal on the occasion of the first anniversary of the Balfour Declaration (November 2, 1918) throws light on the relations between the Zionist commission and the Emir at that time. Eder's cable, sent to Faisal in Damascus on October 25, noted that it had not been possible to celebrate the Declaration the previous year, whereas this year, "when Allenby's victorious forces are in Jerusalem—with a place of honor accorded to a Jewish brigade—and your courageous armies are in Damascus, this festive day can be celebrated in a fitting manner, and it would be a source of joy for us if you could share this unique occasion with us."

Faisal's reply cable was sent on November 4:

Doctor EDER,
        JERUSALEM.
        I received with pleasure and thanks your wire of invitation. I am extremely sorry to offer you and the venerable my excuse of not having the honour to be present at your great meeting owing to my departure to Aleppo. I beg you to allow me to say that I am considering a such meeting as an important factor to approach each other the two nations tied by old friendly links. Will you kindly consider this wire also as a proof to our mutual friendship and please accept my best greetings and respects.
                                        FAISAL, DAMASCUS.[13]

* The first preparatory assembly was convened on December 13, 1917.

The June meeting between Weizmann and Faisal, and further talks between the two men and other Zionist leaders, which took place in Europe in December 1918, led to the Weizmann-Faisal agreement of January 3, 1919. The preamble to this agreement referred to "recognition of the racial kinship and ancient bonds existing between the Arabs and the Jewish people," and expressed the realization that "the surest means of working out the consummation of their national aspiration is through the closest possible collaboration in the development of the Arab state and Palestine." This implied Faisal's agreement to Palestine's not being part of the large Arab state whose establishment the Arabs were demanding at the time, in accordance with the 1915 agreement between the British representative McMahon and Sharif Hussain of Mecca.

Clause 2 of the agreement laid down that "immediately following the completion of the deliberations of the peace conference, the definitive boundaries between the Arab state and Palestine shall be determined by a commission to be agreed upon by the parties concerned." Clause 3 stated that "in the establishment of the constitution and administration of Palestine all such measures will be adopted as will afford the fullest guarantees for carrying into effect the British government's declaration of November 2, 1917" (i.e., the Balfour Declaration). Clause 4 promised that all necessary measures would be taken to encourage and stimulate Jewish immigration to Palestine on a large scale and to settle the Jewish immigrants on the soil as quickly as possible. The land was to be worked intensively by Jewish settlers. At the same time, the Arab fellaheen and tenant farmers would be protected and their rights maintained, and they would be helped to progress economically. Clause 5 contained a guarantee of freedom of religion in Palestine and equality between members of the different religions. No religious criteria would be applied to civic or political rights. Clause 6 guaranteed that the Moslem holy places would be under Moslem supervision.

Clause 7 declared that a committee of experts, which the Zionist Organization intended to send to Palestine in order to study the country's economic possibilities with a view to making recommendations about development programs, would be placed at the disposal of the Arab state for similar purposes. "The Zionist Organization will use its best efforts to assist the Arab state in providing the means for developing the natural resources and economic possibilities thereof." Clause 8 noted that both sides agreed "to act in complete accord and harmony in all matters covered by this agreement at the peace congress." Clause 9 stated that any differences of opinion that might arise between the sides would be submitted to the arbitration of the British government.*

* The agreement was published in 1924 by L. H. Miller, legal counsellor to the American delegation at the peace conference.

Next to the body of the agreement Faisal added this reservation in Arabic, in his own handwriting: "If the Arabs are established as I have asked in my manifesto of January 4 addressed to the British Secretary of State for Foreign Affairs, I will carry out what is written in this agreement. If changes are made, I cannot be answerable for failing to carry out this agreement."

Because of this reservation, many Arab politicians later doubted the authenticity of the agreement and even denied its very existence. The Arab writer 'Issa as-Sifri, for example, tried to prove through an analysis of the document's semantics and calligraphy that there was no agreement between Weizmann and Faisal and that the entire report on the document was a forgery perpetrated by T. E. Lawrence.[14] George Antonius, who published the agreement as an appendix in his book *The Arab Awakening*, attributed Faisal's signing it to his political inexperience and described the Emir as the victim of a Zionist-British plot.[15] The boldest attempt to rebut the Weizmann-Faisal agreement, however, was made by the Arab lawyer Auni Abd-ul-Hadi. In his evidence on behalf of the Higher Arab Committee to the Anglo-American Commission of Enquiry on March 12, 1946, he asserted:[16]

I myself was a private secretary to King Faisal in 1919. I was with Emir Faisal at the time in London. In November 1918 King Faisal was Emir Faisal. He came to France and then went to England. He was at once given to understand that the French government would not guarantee for him a seat at the peace conference of Versailles because the Allies did not recognize formally the government of Hejaz. He proceeded to London. There he was faced with the Sykes-Picot agreement for the first time. He saw that agreement in London. Faisal was in a very difficult position. France was kicking him and England was facing him with the Sykes-Picot agreement. He was facing at the time the loss of the whole Arab world. The Foreign Office suggested, through the late Colonel Lawrence and other friends of the Emir Faisal, that they should arrange a meeting between him and Dr. Weizmann. They gave him to understand that if he showed a measure of leniency to Dr. Weizmann he could save Syria. They explained to him that the whole question was that certain persecuted Jews wanted to go back to Palestine and that that would not affect the Arab government at all. In fact, it was suggested to him that the Jews had always lived in Arab countries, and that now the question was to allow them a certain measure of immigration. They showed him an agreement written in England; and he knew not one word of English at the time. Colonel Lawrence explained to him certain parts of it and made him understand that the terms of that agreement would not in the least affect the rights of the Arabs. But despite all these explanations, Emir Faisal was careful enough and made a reservation in Arabic that if the memorandum he had sent to the peace conference, dated January 4, 1919, was accepted by the peace conference, then he would accept the agreement. The fact that Colonel Lawrence explained the agreement the way he wanted can be adduced from the fact that he himself made a translation of the reservation of Emir Faisal in a few words, which he wrote under the Arabic version. To suggest that Emir Faisal had accepted this agreement as it was written is absolutely untrue. He did not, in fact, understand its terms. At any rate, Emir Faisal was not representing all the Arabs at the time.

When Arab-Jewish tension later increased, Faisal refrained from any reference to the agreement. As the Arab demands had not been met, and as he had made his agreement conditional on their fulfilment, he considered himself released from any undertaking connected with the agreement.

But apart from the Weizmann-Faisal agreement, there are other documents confirming that in those days there was genuine striving for Jewish-Arab cooperation. The claim that "Faisal did not understand" is refuted by a declaration made on February 13, 1919, by the Syrian delegation to the peace conference. One of the members of the delegation was Jamil Mardam, (graduate of the University of Paris and Geneva) a leader of the Syrian-Arab national movement and the secretary of the 1913 Arab congress in Paris. While the Syrian delegation did not favor separating Palestine from Syria, it was ready to ensure Palestine a special status within the Syrian framework, so that the national aspirations of the Jews could be realized:

Can we be permitted to say a word about Palestine, even though this is a painful topic for us? There can be no controverting the fact that Palestine is the southern part of our country. The Zionists demand it for themselves. We have suffered too much persecution, akin to the persecution they have suffered, not to open the gates of Palestine wide open to them. All of them who are suffering in reactionary countries will be welcomed. Let them settle in Palestine, but in an autonomous Palestine linked with Syria only through a federation. Will not a Palestine that enjoys complete internal autonomy constitute sufficient guarantee for them? If they become a majority there, they will be the ones that rule. And if they are a minority, they will be represented in the government in proportion to their numbers. Is it necessary, in order to strengthen them, to split up Syria, to take away its hinterland and its historic safeguard against any invasion (which always took this route), and to establish a state in the center of a country, which, as a result, will always be hostile to it?[17]

Emir Faisal addressed the supreme council of the Allies, in Paris, in the spirit of his agreement with Dr. Weizmann. Faisal's faithfulness to the agreement was also expressed in his letter to Professor (later Justice) Felix Frankfurter. This followed an interview with Faisal published by the French paper Le Matin on March 1. Faisal's statements in this interview were in total contradiction to the spirit of his talks with Weizmann and the agreement between the two men. According to the Matin correspondent, Faisal made the following statement:

The unhappy Jews will find an asylum in Palestine. But they must behave there like good citizens. Our humane heart will only be happy about this. But it is necessary that the rule over them be in the hands of a Christian or Moslem government, appointed by the League of Nations. And if they will want to set up a state and to demand the right to rule in this country, I must express serious doubts. It is to be feared that there will be clashes between them and the other races.

According to Medzini, when the Palestinian Jewish emissaries called on Faisal at about the same time, he gave them a warm welcome and spoke to them as to brothers. However, he also recalled Zangwill's proposal that camels should be hired to transport the Arabs from Palestine to Iraq and Arabia. Faisal drew a middle course between confidence and fear, between friendship and opposition.

After the *Matin* interview, Faisal's secretary denied that the Emir had made the statements attributed to him. Several American Zionist leaders called on him in order to clarify his statements. After this meeting with the Zionist l aders, Faisal sent Frankfurter the following letter:

> Delegation Hedjazienne
> Paris
> March 3, 1919

Dear Mr. Frankfurter,

I want to take this opportunity of my first contact with American Zionists to tell you what I have often been able to say to Dr. Weizmann in Arabia and Europe.

We feel that the Arabs and Jews are cousins in race, having suffered similar oppressions at the hands of powers stronger than themselves, and by a happy coincidence have been able to take the first step towards the attainment of their national ideals together.

We Arabs, especially the educated among us, look with the deepest sympathy on the Zionist movement. Our deputation here in Paris is fully acquainted with the proposals submitted yesterday by the Zionist Organization to the Peace Conference, and we regard them as moderate and proper. We will do our best, in so far as we are concerned, to help them through: we will wish the Jews a most hearty welcome home.

With the chiefs of your movement, especially with Dr. Weizmann, we have had and continue to have the closest relations. He has been a great helper of our cause, and I hope the Arabs may soon be in a position to make the Jews some return for their kindness. We are working together for a reformed and revived Near East, and our two movements complete one another. The Jewish movement is national and not imperialist. Our movement is national and not imperialist, and there is room in Syria for us both. Indeed I think that neither can be a real success without the other.

People less informed and less responsible than our leaders and yours, ignoring the need for cooperation of the Arabs and Zionists, have been trying to exploit the local difficulties that must necessarily arise in Palestine in the early stages of our movements. Some of them have, I am afraid, misrepresented your aims to the Arab peasantry, and our aims to the Jewish peasantry, with the result that the interested parties have been able to make capital out of what they call our differences.

I wish to give you my firm conviction that these differences are not on questions of principle, but on matters of detail, such as must inevitably occur in every contact with neighboring peoples, and as are easily adjusted by mutual goodwill. Indeed, nearly all of them will disappear with fuller knowledge.

I look forward, and my people with me look forward, to a future in which we will help you and you will help us, so that the countries in which we are mutually interested may once again take their places in the community of civilised peoples of the world.

Believe me,

Yours sincerely,

FAISAL

Frankfurter replied:

March 5, 1919

Royal Highness:

Allow me, on behalf of the Zionist Organization, to acknowledge your recent letter with deep appreciation.

Those of us who come from the United States have already been gratified by the friendly relations and the active cooperation maintained between you and the Zionist leaders, particularly Dr. Weizmann. We knew it could not be otherwise; we knew that the aspirations of the Arab and the Jewish peoples were parallel, that each aspired to reestablish its nationality in its own homeland, each making its own distinctive contribution to civilization, each seeking its own peaceful mode of life.

The Zionist leaders and the Jewish people for whom they speak have watched with satisfaction the spiritual vigour of the Arab movement. Themselves seeking justice, they are anxious that the just aims of the Arab people be confirmed and safeguarded by the Peace Conference.

We knew from your acts and your past utterances that the Zionist movement— in other words the national aims of the Jewish people—had your support and the support of the Arab people for whom you speak. These aims are now before the Peace Conference as definite proposals by the Zionist Organization. We are happy indeed that you consider these proposals "moderate and proper", and that we have in you a staunch supporter for their realization. For both the Arab and the Jewish peoples there are difficulties ahead—difficulties that challenge the united statesmanship of Arab and Jewish leaders. For it is no easy task to rebuild two great civilizations that have been suffering oppression and misrule for centuries. We each have our difficulties we shall work out as friends, friends who are animated by similar purposes, seeking a free and full development for the two neighbouring peoples. The Arabs and Jews are neighbours in territory; we cannot but live side by side as friends.

Very respectfully,

FELIX FRANKFURTER[18]

In pinning all their hopes on Faisal, the Zionist policymakers believed that he might help them to come to some arrangement with the leaders of the Palestine Arabs. The Zionist Central Archives contain no document that could enlighten us as to any direct political efforts by Jewish bodies toward cooperation with the Palestinian Arabs. The most solidly established members of the Jewish community—people who either had contacts with the Arab community or could establish such contacts—were not brought into play for this purpose, while the Zionist commission and the people it recruited

L

to help had no contacts with the Arabs and were invariably far removed from the Arab spiritual world and approach. Meanwhile, the Arabs of Palestine began to display growing opposition to the expanding Jewish enterprise there—an opposition that coincided with the development of relations between the Zionist commission and Faisal.

At the meeting of the commission of April 13, 1918, Weizmann had already referred with concern to mass meetings organized by the Arab national movement in Palestine, at which various slogans against Jewish national aspirations were raised. When Sir Ronald Storrs referred to the Balfour Declaration in a speech at his reception for the Zionist commission in April 1918, there were cries of opposition from the assembled Arab notables, and the Mufti of Jerusalem, Sheik Kamal al-Hussaini (the older brother of Haj Amin al-Hussaini, who succeeded him), left the reception in protest. Other official British spokesmen who tried to explain the British Palestine policy to Arab audiences encountered similar reactions.

An eyewitness account of "a grand Arab reception in Jerusalem," in April 1918, refers to a large gathering attended by Governor Sir Ronald Storrs and many Arab representatives and British officials. The stage was decorated with a map captioned "This is Palestine." Palestinian songs were sung, and among the slogans decorating the hall was one asking, "Will they remove us from our beloved country, in order to put others in our place?" The Arabs were enjoined not to sell land to the Jews. Sir Ronald, who expressed thanks on behalf of the Palestine government, called out: "Long live the Arab nation!" and "Long live all the inhabitants of Palestine!"[19]

In spite of growing tension, there were still various possibilities for the future development of Jewish-Arab relations. The die had not yet been finally cast. The same Mufti of Jerusalem who had left the Governor's reception in protest, because the Balfour Declaration was mentioned, attended the laying of the cornerstone of the Hebrew University in July 1918 and even participated in the ceremony by placing one of the twelve stones representing the twelve tribes of Israel, in position.

Arab nationalist propaganda, which was relatively moderate and restrained as long as the war lasted, became far sharper in tone with the signing of the armistice in November 1918. Relations between Jews and Arabs became more tense. In a letter to the Military Governor of Jaffa, the Zionist commission said it was making great efforts to explain Jewish intentions to the Arabs and to allay any suspicions, not only toward the Jewish community, but also toward the British authorities. Yet "our expressions of goodwill were not sufficiently appreciated," the letter said, adding, "The Jews are disciplined and obey their own institutions." (apart from "a few irresponsible individuals"), but "the situation among the Moslem and Christian leaders is very different."[20]

At the beginning of 1919, in the days of the Weizmann-Faisal agreement and other Jewish-Arab contacts, the Arabs of Palestine began displaying growing opposition to the Balfour Declaration policy. The Central Zionist Archives tell the story in press cuttings, with reports from all over the country, particularly the large towns—reports of propaganda meetings, gatherings in private homes attended by officers serving in Feisal's army, agitation in cafés, the allocation of money for arms purchases, complaints to the authorities against alleged pro-Jewish discrimination, memoranda and cables sent to Syria, and threats against Jewish homes.

On January 28, 1919, a rally of Arab notables and delegations from all over the country was held in Jerusalem. The slogans proclaimed at this rally included: "Palestine is part of Syria, and the Arabs of Palestine are part of the Arab nation!" "Complete independence for the Arab countries!" "No Jewish immigration to Palestine!" and others on similar themes. It was suggested that a delegation be sent to the peace conference, which was then meeting in Paris, "in order to draw its attention to the dangers facing the Moslems and Christians of Palestine because of Zionist aspirations." Most of the participants in the rally were Moslems, and its chairman was a Moslem, Arif ad-Daoudi. The deputy chairman was a Christian, Youssuf al-'Issa, the publisher of the daily newspaper *Falastin*.

During the course of the conference, a reception was held at the Grand Hotel. Sir Ronald Storrs attended with several of his assistants. Storrs, who spoke Arabic, greeted the assembly, adding: "I am happy to see here united all the most notable people in Palestine. Let us hope that the results of your work will be good, and that you will attain your objective. Let us hope that your wish will be granted and that Palestine will belong to the Palestinians."

On February 4, 1919, a manifesto was issued under the heading "The First warning: Palestine calls out to the nations of the whole world, and especially to the Arabs." In florid phrases, and with many historical inaccuracies, the manifesto addressed "the nations of the world, the League of Nations, and the Arabs who have shed their blood like water on the altar of independence." It declared:

The Jewish leaders and orators, women and men, old and young are turning days into nights in order to swallow up Palestine. . . . They seek to erase all memory of Islam and Christianity in Palestine, to rob Moslems and Christians of their tombstones and their remains in the Holy Land. . . . We have given the Jews convincing proof—historical, linguistic, and archaeological—that they have no right to this country, from which they were exiled by the Babylonians thousands of years ago.

Our country was conquered by our forefathers over 1,300 years ago, and they settled in it and have spilled rivers of blood defending it during all these centuries. . . . The children of Israel, who do not have sufficient room in any of the countries, have met opposition wherever they have gone. They have not seen eye to eye with any nation and have been like venomous adders, bringing disaster and subversion to the world. Now they want to drive us out of our land, to place their government over it and to swallow it alive. . . . Know that Palestine is our country, the pearl of our [Arabian] peninsula, and they shall not gain it until the Jordan and the Yarmuk turn into blood.[21]

Other documents preserved in the Zionist Central Archives contain thirty-five slogans, some printed and some handwritten, circulated at about the same time as the above poster. Some of these slogans were: "Zionism is a disaster for Palestine!" "The Zionist danger is real, not imaginary!" "Selling land to the Zionists is treason!" "Palestine is the fortress of Syria!" "The al Aksa, the third holiest in Islam, is located in Palestine!" "Palestine will be Zionist when England will become German!" "The Zionists' strength is money, the Arabs' strength is unity!"

At the end of 1918 and the beginning of 1919, Arab terrorist groups began operating in various parts of Palestine. These groups—al-Feda'iah (suicidal fighters or commandoes) and al-Kaf as-Sauda' (the Black Hand)—were founded by fanatical Arabs who opposed British rule, proclaimed war on the Jews, and wanted a free and independent Palestine. One of the founders of the Black Hand was Wadi'al Bustani, an adviser to the British military governor in Jaffa (and directed by him, according to a version popular in those days).

In February 1919, several weeks after the Weizmann-Faisal agreement, the first national meeting of the Moslem-Christian Association took place in Jaffa. This association (Al Jam'iah al-Islamiya al-Massihiya) set up branches in various parts of Palestine. The most important resolutions passed at the conference expressed opposition to the Balfour Declaration and to Zionist activities in Palestine. On March 16, a group of leading Bedouin sheiks held a conference in the south of the country, and later another Bedouin meeting took place at Kastina. These gatherings gave vent to super-patriotic Arab nationalism, and speakers confidently predicted that before long Jews and Englishmen would be expelled and the Arabs would take over the country.

From April 1919 on, there was increasing activity among the Arabs of Palestine. Propagandist speakers toured villages, ceaselessly preaching Arab nationalism in private homes and even in cafés. Their main aim was to prepare Arab public opinion for the King-Crane commission and to stir the Arabs up against the Jews as well as the British. To do this, they stressed the success of the people of Egypt in forcing the British to accept their demands (a general uprising had broken out in Egypt in March 1919), and other Moslem anti-British revolts in India and elsewhere, promising that "the Arabs will be the world's strongest power." The Palestinian Arabs were urged "to defend the country against foreigners with all their force, including force of arms."

The nationalistic mood of the Palestinian Arabs at this time is reflected in a letter on May 8, 1918, from Alex Aaronson to his brother Aharon and Felix Frankfurter:

The Arabs prefer the Turks to the English, as the former are Moslems. They never dreamed that Damascus, the pearl of the East, would be handed over to them.They insult British officers and form ties with the Young Turks in Constantinople, encouraged as they are by events in India and Egypt. . . . The Arabs of Palestine consider their attitude toward the Jews a touchstone of Britain's strength and decisiveness. There is a propaganda campaign against selling land to Jews, for making Palestine a part of Syria, opposing Jewish immigration and so on, climaxing in open agitation for the murder of Jews. . . . The local Christians are encouraged by an incessant flow of French gold, lent by an anti-Jewish movement. The idea is to strengthen France's claims against the British. The Christians, who only a few years ago were humiliated and despised by the Moslems, are now uniting with them against the Jews. . . .

The British are looking on as neutral observers. Every British governor or deputy governor has an Arab adviser. These advisers influence the British against the Jews and persecute Jews applying to the authorities. The administration is in the hands of the Arabs against the Jews. The British are losing their strength and their prestige. The Arabs are dictating to them. . . . Arab agitators are received with respect by the British governors. Is this the way to preserve British strength and self-respect? Only unequivocal and firm action can save Britain's standing in its relations with the Moslems. But they [the British] are following a suicidal policy unprecedented in their colonial record.[22]

The stand of the British military and civil authorities in Palestine during this period undoubtedly played no small role in the deterioration of Jewish-Arab relations. To understand motives and causes it must be remembered that the land was then "occupied enemy territory," where continuance of the *status quo* and avoidance of any political or social change were compulsory under international law. The *status quo* was naturally incompatible with the Jewish national aspirations, the realization of which was envisaged by the Balfour Declaration. Moreover, the postwar period was marked by a bitter conflict between the British and French over influence in the Middle East and the division of the Turkish Empire. Mark Sykes, the architect of the Sykes-Picot agreement, observed pertinently: "There is no Allied pact east of Brindisi". In this struggle over political influence in western Asia, the Arab national movement allied itself with British colonial designs and often acted as a political tool of Britain. It followed that at grass-roots level this alliance with Britain was directed not only against the French but also against the Jews. Again, the political struggle of the Jews for their rights, and their frequent clashes with British colonial officials, often brought the latter closer to the Arabs. Perhaps the Arabs, who had been accustomed to the Turkish regime, felt more at home under British colonialism than did the European-born Jews who had come to Palestine imbued with a burning national and social vision.

At that time, the Arabs were frankly voicing their disillusion at the failure of the Allies to keep their promises. There was considerable ferment in the large Arab cities and much opposition to the Sykes-Picot agreement, which had been reached behind the backs of the peoples concerned. Revolts and uprisings in some of the neighboring countries stirred up the Arabs of Palestine as well. The mere fact of the Jewish leaders having managed to cultivate friendly relations with the statesmen of the Allied powers, with whom the Arabs had fought side by side, was sufficient to exacerbate Jewish-Arab relations.

On the other hand, senior British officials in Palestine attempted to win the rebellious Arabs over to their side by directing their anger toward the Jews. Weizmann, who made such great efforts to attain an understanding between the Jewish *Yishuv* and the British administration, remarked in his book *Trial and Error*:

I was placed between the hammer and the anvil—between the slow-moving, unimaginative, conservative, and often unfriendly British administration, military or civil, and the impatient, dynamic Jewish people, who saw in the Balfour Declaration the great promise of the return to them of their own country, and contrasted it resentfully with the administrative realities in Palestine. There were, of course, notable and noble exceptions in those early days, like Wyndham Deedes and Gilbert Clayton and the Commander in Chief himself. But they were not the men in daily contact with the population; they were immersed in the conduct of the war, and had to leave the details of administration to men of lower rank in the military hierarchy; and these were, almost without exception, devoid of understanding, or vision, or even of kindness.

The governor of Jaffa—and thus of Tel Aviv—was at this time a Colonel Hubbard. Under him he had, if not the largest, then certainly the most active, Jewish community in Palestine. But in all his actions and utterances, trivial as most of them were, he went out of his way to discourage the Jews and encourage the Arabs, insofar as it was possible for him to do so. A typical instance, taken from a note made at the time, was his reception of a small committee of Jewish agricultural engineers, surveyors, and so on, who had occasion to visit Nablus (under official government auspices) to inspect some *jiftlik** (state) land in the neighborhood. Colonel Hubbard told them—jokingly, perhaps, but if so it was a bad joke—that if they did not leave immediately they ran the risk of being half killed by the excited populace. He added a contemptuous reference to President Wilson, "who meddles too much with Palestine," and concluded by saying that if the committee wished to travel through the *jiftlik* it would have to take a regiment of soldiers along. In conversation with friends he was wont to say that if "trouble" should occur in Jaffa, he would take no responsibility for it, and would not interfere, or allow troops under his command to interfere.

Then there was Colonel Ronald Storrs, in Jerusalem. He was much more subtle in his approach. He was everyone's friend; but, try as he might, he failed to gain the confidence of his Jewish community. The chief administrator, General Money, had

* *Jiftlik*: Turkish for real estate owned by the Sultan's government.

on his staff several advisers and officials who, from the first moment, felt it to be their duty to impress upon the Jewish communities under their charge that, whatever the politicians in London might have been fools enough to say or do, *here* we were in a quite different world: "*Nous allons changer tout cela.*"

The growth of anti-colonial and later anti-Western feelings among Arab nationalist circles gradually reduced the influence of Faisal and his supporters, who favored cooperation with the Western powers and also stressed the value of the Jews' diplomatic connections, and financial and scientific potential. On the other hand, the influence of those demanding a strong anti-colonial policy was growing, and with it the negation of an Arab-Jewish agreement, which was part of the political orientation of Faisal and his supporters.

The Palestinian Arab leaders demanded that Faisal, in his representations to the peace conference, urge the inclusion of Palestine in the projected large Arab state, or at least in greater Syria. The first Arab political paper founded in Palestine after World War I was, characteristically, entitled *Suryia al Junubiya* (southern Syria). One of the plans mooted at this time called for a Syrian federation and an autonomous Palestine as part of it.

The year 1919 witnessed far-reaching changes, not only in the Arab world but indeed in the Middle East as a whole. The British government reconciled itself to the French presence in Syria; British statesmen advised Faisal to meet French Prime Minister Clemenceau and to try to reach an agreement with him. At this meeting, which took place in April, Clemenceau told Faisal that France expected to have a mandate over Syria. This meant that Britain had more or less left Faisal in the lurch and, in effect, denied him any further political support over Syria. That was the true purport of Lloyd George's agreement with Clemenceau on the division of the Levant between Britain and France (September 15*). At the same time, Britain had abandoned its former interest in an understanding between Faisal and the Zionist leadership —the two pro-British factors that the British had hoped to use against French claims in the region. In the middle of 1919, these political *volte faces* were already in evidence.

At the beginning of May 1919, it was learned that the King-Crane commission was due to visit the Middle East. King and Crane were two American statesmen appointed by the United States delegation to the peace conference "to ascertain the wishes of the inhabitants of the former Turkish Empire."

---

* Much interesting and illuminating information on British policy and relations with France over this issue may be found in *Documents on British Foreign Policy, 1919–1939*, First Series (1952), Vol. IV, Chapter 2: "His Majesty's Government's Policy on Syria and Palestine Before the First Conference in London (May 30, 1919–February 11, 1920), pp. 241–634, and in the Appendix: two documents concerning British policy toward Syria and Palestine, June 1919, pp. 1275–1278.

The Northern border.

············   According to Sykes–Picot treaty. May 1916
– – – – – –   According to Zionist Federation memorandum. February 1919
–·–·–·–·–   According to Deauville agreement. September 1919
– – – – –   Final boundary according to boundaries agreement. December 1920

Originally Britain, France, and Italy were to take part in the commission's work, but they later refused to do so.

When the Zionist commission learned this, it tried to meet with Faisal, who had returned to Damascus at the beginning of May. A letter written by the Zionist commission in Tel Aviv on May 20, 1919, to the Zionist executive committee in London refers to a cable sent by Faisal to the commission, in response to a cable welcoming him on his arrival in Syria. Faisal cabled on May 9: "Many thanks for your greetings on my return and the good wishes expressed in your cable. I shall consider it a great pleasure to see a delegation of your commission in Damascus at the earliest opportunity."

A letter written on May 11 to Dr. Eder by the chief political officer in the region, General Clayton, confirmed that arrangements would be made for the commission's representatives to visit Damascus. Dr. Eder was asked to suggest a suitable date. This was fixed at May 17, and Faisal was informed accordingly. On May 15, Clayton wrote to the spokesman of the Zionist commission, Harry Friedenwald, that "the Commander-in-Chief does not consider it desirable that any conference should take place at present between Faisal, the Zionist commission and Palestinian notables." The reason given was that "any such conference would trench on the sphere of the peace commission, which is shortly arriving." (the reference is to the King-Crane commission).

The Zionist commission informed Faisal of the reasons for the postponement of the meeting. At the same time, the commission made another approach to the British authorities. In a cable sent on May 20, Friedenwald drew General Clayton's attention to the fact that the intention had been to meet with Faisal only, not with other Arab notables as well. But the meeting was not allowed to take place even at a later date. Friedenwald's letter of June 23 to Faisal, in which he noted that the Zionist commission had informed the King-Crane Commission of the mutual understanding and cooperation it enjoyed with Faisal, announced that no change had taken place in the British decision on the postponement of the scheduled meeting. Writing on July 7, Faisal stated, "We received your letter through the British liaison officer in Damascus. Thank you for the sentiments expressed in it and your good wishes. We are awaiting your arrival and shall be happy to meet you. Faithfully, Faisal."[23]

In the light of these documents, an initiative taken by the Arab side at this juncture takes on a special significance. When the Syrian Congress was meeting in Damascus, two special emissaries—the lawyer Mu'in al-Madi of Haifa and Riad as-Sulh of Beirut—called on Kalvarisky, in the name of Faisal and his council, and invited him to Damascus. Kalvarisky met several members of Faisal's council: Ihsan al-Jabri, Emir Adel Arslan, Rafik Tamimi, and Hashim al-Atassi. They asked him to explain how the Zionists thought Palestine should be governed, and asked him to put this down in writing.

"This demand," wrote Kalvarisky, "embarrassed me, as I had no authority to speak in the name of the Zionists. I told my hosts this, but they continued to press me, saying that this would not bind either side unless it was agreed to by the authoritative bodies." Kalvarisky agreed to the Arab request and drew up the draft of a basic constitution; this was submitted to Faisal and the president of the Syrian Congress. The draft stated:

1. Palestine is the homeland of all its inhabitants: Jews, Moslems, and Christians—all of whom are citizens with equal rights.

2. As the Jewish people, whose origins are eastern and Semitic, needs a territory in order to develop its national culture, Palestine, its birthplace—which constitutes a small island in the broad sea of countries and peoples with eastern and Semitic origins, stretching from the Taurus mountains to Gibraltar and the entire length of North Africa—forms *the Jewish national home*.

3. *Freedom of religion:* No religion shall be dominant in Palestine.

4. *Government:* Every man can take part in the government of the country, without distinction as to race or creed. When officials are appointed, the only consideration will be the candidates' abilities. For the general good it is necessary that every official shall know both languages of the country, Hebrew and Arabic (and, it is hardly necessary to add, English, which is the language of the Mandatory Government). However, as at present it is difficult to find among either the Jews or the Arabs people who know both languages, five, ten, or fifteen years will be allowed for studying the other language, and after this period all government officials will have to know both languages.

5. *Schools:* In the government schools, particularly the secondary schools, the study of both languages, Hebrew and Arabic, will be compulsory. Each language complements the other. Apart from the spiritual and moral advantages (increased mutual understanding, greater contact between the two basic elements of the population, the evolution of a Hebrew-Arabic literature that will recall to us the golden age of the Arab Caliphs, etc.), this will also have economic advantages. All government service will be open to those who know both languages (and English, which is the language of the Mandatory power). In commercial, industrial and financial circles those candidates who are fluent in both languages will naturally be given preference. As far as the private schools are concerned, we have advised our Jewish brethren to make the study of Arabic compulsory there as well, and I hope that our Arab friends will understand the advantages of this system and will do the same with regard to the study of Hebrew in Arabic schools.

6. *Annulment of any exclusive separatism whether Jewish, Moslem, or Christian*: Until now the Jews of Palestine have existed as a religious community with its own charitable and social welfare institutions. The same has applied to the Moslem and Christian communities. With the foundation of the Jewish national home in Palestine, the Jewish community was given tasks in the political sphere. The state must take care of everyone, without distinction as to religion. There are no longer any Jewish,

Moslem, or Christian paupers. Every community will have the same right to public treatment. We shall open schools, orphanages, and hospitals for all. We shall set up agricultural and industrial banks for everybody, and shall extend aid to the fellaheen.

7. *Freedom of immigration*: As the flow of Jewish capital and labor to such a poor and thinly populated country as Palestine can benefit all its inhabitants, complete freedom will be given to Jewish immigration.[24]

The Arab leaders favored the draft proposal, and Faisal even congratulated Kalvarisky on his successful wording. However, as the Palestinian delegates to the Pan-Syrian Congress were directly concerned, in this matter, Faisal and his advisers thought it necessary that Kalvarisky hold special consultations with the Palestinian delegation. This meeting took place the same day in the Victoria Hotel. It was attended by all the Palestinian *Istiklal* leaders from Palestine, as well as by many Syrians. The discussion lasted for several hours, and it closed with a resolution accepting the draft as a foundation for a basic Palestinian constitution and asking Kalvarisky to obtain the approval of the Jewish bodies.

Kalvarisky first brought the draft proposal to the provisional committee—a body chosen by the assembly of Palestine Jews—held on December 31, 1917, immediately after the British capture of Jerusalem.

What was the provisional committee's attitude toward this important matter?

M. Medzini writes:

When the question of our relations with the Arabs first came up for discussion in the provisional committee in the summer of 1919, most of its members evinced absolute ignorance of the subject. . . . When Kalvarisky proposed a program of common activities, based on the assumption that "Palestine is the homeland of all its inhabitants: the Jews, Moslems, and Christians are citizens of equal status," even the heads of the most progressive section of the *Yishuv* and the leaders of the workers called it "a ridiculous and dangerous plan." This will be recorded as an unforgivable sin on the part of most of the members of the provisional committee, and in particular its left wing. Several months after the end of the war, when the waves of Arab awakening strengthened, the provisional committee refused even to appoint a subcommittee that would determine the Jewish attitude to the question of relations with the Arabs. Its chairman, Dr. Thon, did, it is true, stress in his speeches that without mutual understanding with the Arabs and mutual confidence we could not build our national home. When the provisional committee reverted to this subject in the spring of 1920, and decided to appoint a committee and issue an appeal to the Arabs, it was too late.

In its defense, it should be noted that the provisional committee was an impotent body virtually incapable of taking concrete action on any matter of public concern. M. Medzini notes in his *Ten Years of Palestine Policy* that at the hands of the committee "hardly a single question found a practical solution." Instead, there were "flowery rhetoric, superficial slogans, and plans that had no relationship to the facts of life." "On every question, tens of speeches were delivered, but when it came to action, the strength of the Yishuv ebbed away." Characteristic of the ineffectiveness of the provisional committee was the fact that out of taxes of £.P.1465* imposed on the urban and rural councils, the committee actually collected only £.P.529.

There was tension between the provisional committee and the Zionist commission, which held differing views on various issues, including the formulation of Jewish national representations. The provisional committee was far removed from day-to-day Middle Eastern political affairs and moved in an abstract world of dreams and visions. The leaders of the Zionist Organization were then busy drafting the Jewish political proposals for submission to the Versailles peace conference. The provisional committee decided to formulate its own proposals. A special subcommittee was appointed, which included Dr. Thon, Jabotinsky, Vilkansky, and Berligne. It drew up "A Draft Plan for Provisional Rule in Palestine," which called, in effect, for making Palestine a Jewish state at once, under British protection ("the Zionist flag will become the official flag of Palestine, together with the flag of the protective government"). Dr. Weizmann and the other Zionist leaders, who were more familiar with political realities, rejected most of the clauses in the program. One member of the provisional committee asked Weizmann, "Why did you not demand a Jewish state?" Weizmann replied categorically, "We did not demand a Jewish state, because we wouldn't have received it."

Nevertheless, the provisional committee persisted. In its memorandum of October 1919, it said, according to Medzini: "We want the Zionist leaders to prove to those who direct world affairs that there is only one political question here in Palestine, namely the establishment of a Jewish state. There is an Arab political question in each of the big Arab countries, and there it should be resolved. But it cannot be decided in Palestine, where the sole object is to solve the political problem of the Jewish people."

Kalvarisky also approached the Zionist commission. Medzini asks, somewhat rhetorically, "Can it be said that the Zionist commission's policies were more successful? Did the commission, and with it the entire Zionist movement, rise to the call of that great hour?"

Medzini's conclusions are clear cut. After analyzing the relevant documents, he concludes:

The gravest political failure of the *Yishuv* was its failure to create an atmosphere of mutual understanding between Jews and Arabs. It can be said that the relations with the Arabs should have been the main political issue facing the *Yishuv*—an issue on which it could have displayed its political maturity. The sad fact is, however, that the *Yishuv* showed the same lack of understanding and appreciation of this question immediately after the war that it displayed before and during the war. There were

* £.P.: Palestinian pounds.

then at least one or two people who realized the great importance of the Arab question and sought ways of solving it, as is clear from Kalvarisky's efforts and attempts. But the *Yishuv* as a whole was deep in economic preoccupations and internal quarrels, and paid no attention to this.

What was the ultimate fate of Kalvarisky's draft proposal, that which awaited approval by the leaders of the *Yishuv*?

Kalvarisky himself noted afterwards, "To our great regret, the draft was not approved, and for the same reason that foiled the first attempt in 1914: contempt for the Arab national movement and the Arab people, which were dismissed as unimportant, and an exaggerated appraisal of our own strength and the help of Europe and America."[25]

Kalvarisky, who was one of the few people actively involved in the Jewish settlement enterprise and at the same time in close touch with the Arab world, was not even informed of such important developments as the correspondence between the Zionist commission and Emir Faisal. When analyzing the Zionist leaders' short-sightedness on the Arab problem, he appears to gloss over the deepest reason; namely, the obstructive British policy, which the Zionist leadership was not strong enough to overcome and which it did not even try to circumvent. For a short time, there was some hope for a possible settlement with Faisal that might ultimately "solve the Arab problem." When it appeared that the British administration was placing obstacles in the way of these contacts (e.g., in preventing the Zionist commission from meeting Faisal), Zionist leaders found themselves unable to disobey these authorities on whom they were relying to implement the Balfour Declaration and to protect the small and weak Jewish community of Palestine.

The meeting with Faisal never took place, and no reply at all was given to Kalvarisky's proposals. Meanwhile, the Syrian Congress passed several resolutions, including one which demanded "complete political independence for Syria, without any protection or patronage, within the following limits: the Taurus mountains in the north, the Tigris and Khabour rivers in the east, al-Jouf and Akaba in the south, and the Mediterranean Sea in the west." In July of the same year, the Syrian Congress submitted to the King-Crane commission a memorandum that expressed "opposition to the Zionist wish to found a Jewish republic in the southern part of Syria, known by the name of Palestine." Faisal spoke in a similar vein when he addressed the King-Crane commission on July 3. He considered Palestine an integral part of Syria and was opposed to separating them. Several months earlier, he had, it is true, been ready to accept the Zionist program in the form in which it had been presented. But the Zionist aspirations, as they had been revealed during this period, had instilled fear in the hearts of the local Arab population, and he was now convinced that the Palestinian Arabs were firm in their resolve to oppose Zionism, whatever form this took.[26]

The King-Crane commission, which arrived in June 1919, toured Syria and Palestine, met the spokesmen of various groups, and presented its report to the American delegation to the peace conference on August 28, 1919. An interesting account of the Arab statements will be found in the memorandum by A. Elmaleh[27] who was sent to Syria and Lebanon on behalf of the Zionist commission to organize the appearance of Syrian and Lebanese Jews before the commission and to follow Arab reaction to the investigation of the commission. Kalvarisky recapitulated the Arab statements in a secret document submitted to the Jewish bodies on June 27, 1919.[28] The commission attached particular importance to its meetings with various Arab representatives in Damascus, which at that time was the focal point of Arab political activities in the Middle East. It was in Damascus that the commission heard Faisal and the members of his council, a delegation of Moslem leaders (led by the Mufti of Syria), and spokesmen of the Greek Orthodox, Greek Catholic, Druze, and Jewish communities, as well as delegations representing fellaheen, Bedouin, and the Damascus municipality. In Palestine itself, the commission visited Jerusalem, Jaffa, Hebron, Gaza, Nazareth, Nablus, and other towns.

At that time there were two main schools of thought among Palestinian Arabs. One, centering around the Moslem-Christian Association, was completely opposed to the Zionist movement and demanded that the gates of Palestine be closed to Jewish immigration. The second, consisting of diverse Moslem and Christian elements in the towns and villages—several of which had benefited from the Jewish settlement in their vicinity—took a relatively positive view of Jewish immigration and the Zionist plans. The questions posed by the King-Crane commission included several along the lines of "Would you accept a Zionist government?" The reply to this was invariably, "Never!" This type of interrogation naturally did not do much to foster improved Jewish-Arab relations.

Justice Gad Frumkin's autobiography contains an absorbing account of Jewish-Arab relations in 1919.[29] Frumkin writes:

> The time was ripe for a reconciliation between the Jews and the Moslem Arabs, who considered themselves close to the Jews in religion and race. During the Ottoman Empire these Arab circles, like the Turkish officials, had looked down upon the Jews and considered them inferior. But in most cases the personal relations between the Moslems and the Jews were good and even friendly. Now, when the Moslems saw that the new regime was inclined toward the Jews, they were ready to follow it. . . . The heads of the Arab families which had stayed in the country were eager to "settle down," to find honorable positions and work for themselves and their associates, and—in the absence of political agitators—the time was ripe for cooperation between the Jews and the Arabs, and particularly the Moslems.

Frumkin pays special attention to the interplay of relations among the

Jews, the Moslem Arabs, and the Christian Arabs. He observes:

The Christian Arabs knew full well that they were numerically weak, and that if a Moslem-Jewish alliance came into being they would be an insignificant minority. On the other hand, they knew that most of the Arab intelligentsia were members of the church, and they were confident that they would dominate any Moslem-Christian alliance. Their main objective was plain: to offset any Jewish-Moslem rapprochement, to form a Moslem-Christian bloc, which they would dominate, and in this way to become the spokesmen of the Palestinian Arabs before the British authorities, who were also Christians.

This was the background to the speedy formation of the Moslem-Christian Society, on the advice of the British governor in Jaffa. This society's first branch was established in Jaffa, and later other branches were formed in other parts of the country. The society launched an overt and covert campaign against the Jews and their interests.

How did the Jews react to this development? Frumkin tells us:

Dr. Eder, who directed the Zionist commission's political section, considered the main task of his department to be straightening out relations between the Zionist commission and the British government, and Arab affairs were handled almost incidentally. ...As far as the Zionist commission was concerned, there was no Arab problem at all, particularly when Menahem Ussishkin arrived in Palestine in the fall of 1919 to head the commission. He considered the Arabs insignificant numerically speaking, and his attitude to them was akin to that of some Gentiles to the Jews. He used to say: there is a Jewish problem everywhere, and what is being done about it? Here there is an Arab problem. And what should we do about it? In other words, he implied that the "Arab problem" should be solved by dismissing it or ignoring it.

At Kalvarisky's initiative, a central political committee was formed in Jerusalem with the approval of the Zionist commission. The members of the committee were Yosef Meyouhas, Gad Frumkin (secretary), Yehoshua Hankin, and Yitshak Levy, and the representatives of the *moshavot* (Aharon Eisenberg and Menashe Meirowitz), Tel Aviv-Jaffa (Meir Dizengoff), and Haifa (Shabtai Levy). Kalvarisky acted as chairman. The representatives of the various areas were asked to form regional committees. Dr. Thon was the liaison man between the committee and the Zionist commission's political section, headed by Dr. Eder.

On the strength of the minutes of the committee's sessions, Frumkin notes "differences in outlook between those members of the committee who were involved in the daily life of the country, on the one hand, and the heads of the Zionist commission, on the other hand. There was a lack of coordination between these two bodies. Although the committee was formed with the approval of, and partly financed by, the Zionist commission, they did not find a common language; Dr. Thon, as mediator, was in a difficult situation, because each side complained that the other acted without consultation."

Several members of the central political committee felt that it should not bear the official stamp of the Zionist commission, so that it would be able to act with greater freedom. Dr. Thon, however, wanted the committee to be a department of the Zionist commission (like the education department, which was then being formed), with Kalvarisky, its chairman, an official of the commission.

The committee discussed definitive proposals on relations with the Arab population. Eisenberg proposed setting up a loan fund, which would lend money to Arabs, and also proposed that the Hadassah medical organization extend medical help to Arabs in the Lydda-Ramle area. The members of the committee were active in Arab circles during the King-Crane commission's visit. There were exchanges on the possibility of forming a Jewish-Arab association ("parallel to the Moslem-Christian Association and with the aim of taking its place"). As a Supreme Court Justice, Frumkin was debarred from active participation in such political work and he eventually withdrew from the committee. But, he adds, "I knew that Kalvarisky, Eisenberg, and Dizengoff argued constantly all these years that the Zionist commission was not handling these affairs properly".

Within the Jerusalem Jewish community, some young people also thought it important to foster better relations with the Arabs. Frumkin recorded that "for the first time Jews and Arabs have been meeting one another as equals and working together in various government offices." In order "to give this idea of closer relations a concrete form," several Jerusalem residents formed a society that "established contact with Arabs of similar social standing." The discussion centered around proposals for "friendly contacts, mutual assistance, and information on developments in the country." It was decided to establish a joint club. "But this program was not carried out, because of lack of funds."

The initiative of this group led to at least one educational project, subsidized by the ICA—evening courses, that taught Hebrew to the Arabs, Arabic to the Jews, and English to both of them. The Hebrew teacher was Yitshak Abbady, who was a translator in the courts, and who had among his pupils several prominent Arab figures. The Arabic teacher was the well known poet and author Khalil Sakakini. These courses continued for over a year.

Frumkin observes:

All these were pointless efforts that did not produce any real results, because of the obstructive campaign of the Moslem-Christian Association, and the open and hidden support given to it by several senior British officials, and above all because the Zionist commission had no definite program for winning over to our side all those Arabs who opposed the Association. The Zionist commission seemed almost indifferent to this. As a result, opposition to the Jews of Palestine increased, and the situation worsened, until the disturbances of April 1920.

The Break With Faisal

The single link connecting Jewish and Arab policies was also severed in the course of time. Many years afterward *The Chronicles of the Hagana* noted:

The joint Jewish and Arab demand for British protection, for which there was some sympathy on both sides of the Atlantic, had helped Britain to withstand France's firm demands. But the moment Britain's international status in Palestine became established, British agents in the East began interfering with every attempt at a Jewish-Arab rapprochement. This sealed the fate of any policy that sought a Jewish-Arab agreement.[30]

The story of Faisal's relations with the Jewish leadership would not be complete without a passing reference to two further developments in 1919 and 1920.

At the end of September 1919, Faisal arrived in London, and on October 3, the *Jewish Chronicle* published an interview with him. Faisal repeated his opposition to the dismemberment of Palestine from Syria and warned against the dangers of Jewish-Arab clashes in Palestine because of extremist Jewish plans to take over the country and set up a Jewish state.

In those days, Zionist leaders still attached much importance to Faisal, and a meeting with him was held in the Carlton Hotel on October 15. It was attended by Sir Herbert Samuel, Harry Sacher, B. W. Cohen, and Said Pasha, Faisal's adjutant. Samuel asked whether the statements made in the interview had been correctly translated. Faisal explained that the *Jewish Chronicle* correspondent had told him that the Zionists wanted to found a Jewish state in Palestine at once and had asked him whether he agreed to this. Faisal told the correspondent that he had never approved any such plan and that Dr. Weizmann had never raised it. To this the correspondent replied, "Dr. Weizmann is a politician. But what the Zionists really want is to establish a Jewish state in Palestine outright." Faisal replied that he could not agree that a small minority of Jews should rule a country most of whose inhabitants were Arabs.

At this point, Samuel interrupted Faisal and said that the Zionists had never demanded the immediate formation of a Jewish state, as this would lead to disturbances in Palestine.

Faisal, who asked that his remarks be treated as having been made off the record, added that he had not changed his attitude to Zionism. He believed that he and Dr. Weizmann had reached a full agreement, and he agreed with the Zionist proposals to the peace conference. He had stated this not only in his letter to Frankfurter but also in a previous exchange with Weizmann. He had not read the interview in the *Jewish Chronicle*. However, if he was given a translation of it, he said, he would read it carefully.[31]

At the beginning of November, Samuel said that there had been a mis-

M

understanding between Faisal and the *Jewish Chronicle* correspondent. The *Chronicle* denied this at once. But Faisal stood firm and repeated his version of the interview in a letter to Samuel in December 1919.

In April 1920, the Council of the Allied Powers, meeting at San Remo, ratified the British Mandate for Palestine and the French Mandate for Syria. On July 1 of that year, the military administration of Palestine was replaced by a civil administration, with Sir Herbert Samuel as High Commissioner and Commander-in-Chief. The Syrians forcibly opposed the entry of French troops, and when Damascus was occupied by France on July 26 Faisal fled the country.

On August 6, 1920, Faisal passed through Haifa and met Dr. Eder, then chairman of the Zionist commission. There are two records of this conversation: the record of Eder's interview with the High Commissioner on August 9, at which Eder reported on his talk with Faisal of August 6, and Eder's letter to Weizmann, dated August 9.[32] As revealed in these documents, the tenor and tone of the conversation was quite different from the exchanges of the days when Faisal was a major political factor. Faisal, who had not yet lost all hope of taking power in Syria, asked the Zionist Executive for assistance, adding that the Jewish press and other influential newspapers had not supported him adequately. Eder replied that, in his opinion, Faisal's policies had failed "because he had been a Zionist in Europe and an extreme anti-Zionist in Damascus." The Jews supported a united Arab nation outside the borders of Palestine, with a representative body with whom Jews could negotiate. Zionist policy had to reckon with actual political realities, and now that Faisal had clashed with the French, Zionist policy could not come to odds with France on his account. The Jewish *Yishuv* in Palestine was under the British Mandate, and it had no military strength. The only action on behalf of Faisal that the Zionist Executive might approve, Eder said, was unofficial intervention by Weizmann and Sokolov in London and Paris, and by Brandeis in Washington. As to the press, the Jewish press was free, and Jews writing for non-Jewish papers were not under the influence of the Zionist movement. Eder urged that Faisal recognize the Zionist interests in Palestine, accept the French Mandate over Syria, stop his campaign for a greater Syria (including Palestine), and use his influence to restrain anti-Zionist propaganda among the Palestinian Arabs.

This unproductive meeting proved to be the end of the Zionist leadership's contacts with Faisal. Even after he became King of Iraq, Faisal took no stand on Palestine and Zionism. The Zionist leaders, for their part, took no further political initiative towards a Jewish-Arab settlement and made no further efforts to that end.

In September 1933, Faisal died suddenly in a Swiss hotel. His coffin passed through Haifa en route to Baghdad. During the stopover in Haifa, representatives of various Jewish organizations paid their respects to the late Arab ruler. Among these were members of the Jewish Agency, the Jewish community of Palestine, the Jews of Haifa (the flag over that city's central office was at half-mast), Rabbis Marcus, Kaniel, and Kalvarisky, etc. The Jewish Agency, the national council, and the Tel Aviv municipality sent cables of condolence to the Prime Minister of Iraq and Emir Abdullah, who later replied. *Mir'at Al-Shark* noted "with gratitude and appreciation" the attitude of the Jewish public and its official bodies to the late King." Other Arab newspapers carried similar comments.

We can sum up this period of transition from Turkish to British rule by noting the two opposing trends among both Jews and Arabs. The eventual pattern of relations between the two peoples was not a foregone conclusion. The fluid political situation at the end of World War I offered various possibilities. Weizmann's basic idea was that a single large Arab state would arise, based on the Damascus-Baghdad-Riad axis, and that in return for their overall help toward the rise of such an Arab state, the Jews would be allowed to establish their national home in Palestine. This concept, which lay at the basis of the Weizmann-Faisal agreement, was undermined by British and French policies. Instead of carrying out the promises made to the Arabs during the war, London and Paris divided the Arab lands between them and imposed their colonial rule on all of them. These new political boundaries became established facts in 1920. The Arab domains were split up and placed under foreign control, direct or indirect. On the other hand, the Jews failed to appreciate the strength of the ties between the Arab community living in Palestine and the large Arab national movement outside its borders. The Jewish community for the most part adopted an increasingly contemptuous attitude toward the Arab element and came to believe that the British were their allies while the Arabs were their "natural" enemies.

Years later, when surveying the Zionist commission's attitude toward the proposals he had submitted to Faisal in Damascus, Kalvarisky found a parallel between the approach then preponderant in the Jewish institutions and the approach of the Palestine Arab leadership. The Jews then, and the Arabs later he said, believed that *ad-daula ma'ana*: "the government is on our side." And if the government was on their side, what need was there for an agreement or an understanding with the other side?[33]

Time would show to what extent this approach was justified.

References

1. *The Chronicles of the Hagana*, Vol. I, pp. 323–4.
2. George Antonius, *The Arab Awakening* (London: Hamish Hamilton, 1945), p. 189.

3. Zionist Archives, London files, No. 1731.

4. *The Chronicles of the Hagana*, Vol. I, Part 2, p. 473.

5. *Ibid.*, Vol. I, Part 2, p. 471.

6. Central Zionist Archives, Jerusalem, File L3/285.

7. *Ibid.*, File Z4/2847 (Archives of the Zionist Office in London).

8. *Ibid.*, File L4/276.

9. Antonius, *loc. cit.*, pp. 269–270.

10. C. Weizmann, *Collected Works* (Hebrew) (Mitzpeh publications, 1936–1937), Vol. I, pp. 97–100.

11. Central Zionist Archives, File L3/285.

12. C. Weizmann, *Trial and Error* (Hamish Hamilton, 1949), p. 293.

13. Zionist Archives, File L3/27.

14. Issa As-Sifri, *Arab Palestine Between the Mandate and Zionism* (Arabic), (Jaffa, 1937), Chapter 5, pp. 13–19.

15. Antonius, *loc. cit.*, pp. 283–284.

16. Minutes of the Anglo-American Commission of Enquiry on Palestine.

17. *Zionism: A Treasury of Political Documents*, Document No. 249 (Hebrew).

18. Committee on Constitutional Development in Palestine. Report, Vol. I, Jerusalem, June 1941. Appendix B. (Confidential.) Central Zionist Archives, No. 11127.

19. Zionist Archives, File L4/276, 11 b.

20. *Ibid.*

21. *Ibid.*, File L4/276 1 b.

22. *Ibid.*, File L4/276 11 b.

23. Zionist Archives, File Nos Z4/2847 and L4/245.

24. H. M. Kalvarisky: "Plans and Speeches," *At the Parting of Our Ways* (1939), pp. 25–26 (Hebrew).

25. *Ibid.*, p. 33.

26. *Documents on British Foreign Policy*, *loc. cit.*, Colonel French's report of July 10, 1919, pp. 311–315.

27. Zionist Archives, London, File B.1329/1.

28. *Ibid.*

29. Gad Frumkin, *The Way of a Judge in Jerusalem*, pp. 218–221 (Hebrew).

30. *The Chronicles of the Hagana*, Vol. I, Part 2, p. 542.

31. Zionist Archives, File L3/27–29.

32. *Ibid.*, Files L3/222 and L3/289.

33. Kalvarisky's lecture at the gathering of "Kedmah Mizracha" at Mikveh Israel on May 18, 1937; published in the anthology *At the Parting of our Ways*, pp. 30–37 (Hebrew).

CHAPTER FIVE

THE BRITISH MANDATORY PERIOD

It is not our intention to trace in detail the history of the Arab community or of the Jewish colonization effort in Palestine following the first World War; nor will space permit more than a bare summary of the extremely complex Jewish-Arab-British relationships during the period. The interested reader can study Palestinian political history of that time as viewed by Jews, Arabs, and Britishers. We are concerned here with summarizing the developments that yield the answers to two fundamental questions: First, was the accentuation of the Jewish-Arab dispute inevitable, and were the vital interests and legitimate national aspirations of the two peoples irreconcilable? Second, who is principally responsible for the deterioration of Arab-Jewish relations into the tragic conflict that is still with us today?

The answers to these questions may determine the future relations between the two peoples and the prospect of reviving that collaboration through which both peoples produced such splendid achievements in the past, to the benefit of themselves and of all mankind.

British Influence Decisive

The history of Arab-Jewish relations before the British Mandate and in its early stages warrants the assumption that if the Jews and Arabs had been left to themselves, they would have been able to reach mutual understanding, and the Jewish national renaissance in Palestine might have integrated peaceably with the Arab national movement in the Middle East.

Considerable evidence is available—and has been referred to throughout this work—showing that the return of the Jews to Palestine was viewed initially with favor by many members of the Arab community, including some of the most important Arab leaders of the time. Unfortunately, on this occasion the Jews and Arabs did not confront each other alone; the determining influence on developments in Palestine throughout the thirty years of the British Mandate (1918–1948) was British. A careful study of developments in Palestine during this period leads to the conclusion that the policy of both Jewish and Arab leaders was largely the effect, rather than the cause, of basic British policy and orientation.

"British" in this content does not refer to the British "man in the street," nor to the British people in general. The British Mandatory administrative machinery included a goodly proportion of honest, well-intentioned, peace-loving British officials who personally believed in fraternity among nations. Indeed, several of them evinced sympathetic understanding for the aspirations of Jews and Arabs in Palestine and genuinely thought they could be reconciled. British policy, however, was not determined by these people. It was decided in accordance with British imperial needs and contingencies, which were all too frequently founded on the "divide and rule" method in opposition to the legitimate national interests and aspirations of the peoples concerned.

Contradictory Promises, Disappointments, and Disillusion

During World War I, far-reaching promises were given by Britain to both Jews and Arabs. For both peoples, the breach of these promises aroused a deep and bitter disappointment, which could have been directed either against the Mandatory power or against each other. At this stage, Arabs and Jews met as two modern nationalist movements, and the question was whether they would cooperate or clash as they followed their separate destinies.

From the perspective of the decades that have passed, and in the light of an objective analysis of the facts and of the conditions that shaped them, it is clear that none of the leaders of either national movement was capable of providing the right answer to that fateful question. In the historical conditions pertaining during this period, socio-political forces capable of setting a different course of development had not yet ripened to the extent that they had any decisive influence in determining the main lines of policy. Within the Zionist movement, sharp criticism was voiced from time to time against the leadership for failing to appreciate the potential force of the Arab national movement and the obstacles that would stand in the way of the realization of Zionist aspirations in the absence of cooperation between Jews and Arabs. Had the two national movements been prepared to see "the shape of things to come," a way would have been found to an alliance between them. However, it should not be forgotten in retrospect that even the Zionist movement and its political leadership approached the problem of Jewish-Arab relations with a deeper understanding, they were too weak to lend a helping hand to the Arab national movement in face of the consistent and devastating "divide and rule" policy adopted by the British government.

In the first few years after World War I, the Jewish population in Palestine was insignificant in size and feeble in organization. Those Jews living on *Halukka* funds, and the ultra-orthodox *Agudat Yisrael* and *Neturei Karta* factions, seceded from the organized Jewish community; the Jewish role in the economy and government of the country was quite small. At that time the Mandatory authorities (backed by British influence in the League of Nations) had the power to stunt the growth of the Jewish community, to crush it, or to abandon it to the mercy of dark Arab reactionary and religious fanaticism. Zionist leaders often found themselves under compulsion to withdraw from Arab-Jewish negotiations on the very eve of a successful outcome. In his testimony before the Anglo-American Enquiry Commission in March 1946, Moshe Shertok (later Sharett), then head of the political department of the Jewish Agency for Palestine, stated that "Arab leaders were inclined to agree to a very large Jewish immigration, but demanded conditions that we could not then accept. It was not our task to destroy the British Mandatory regime, and at that time we ourselves were not too eager to see its speedy destruction."

This lack of strength during a certain period—the inability to do without British Mandatory rule in Palestine—continued to form the major obstacle in the way of a policy of *rapprochement* and cooperation between Jews and Arabs. And what about the Arab side?

The young Arab nationalist movement, in its endeavor to awaken and inspire the masses, was not sufficiently far-sighted to link hands with the Jews in the realization of long-standing national aspirations in their historic homeland. The Arabs should have been concerned to help the Jews free themselves from dependence on Britain, to win them over as useful allies and collaborators in the liberation of the Arabs themselves. As the British carried on their own dubious policy in Palestine, the Arab camp resounded with the increasingly violent voices of leaders hoodwinked into attacking the Jews and their national movement, and determined to fight them— sometimes encouraged by, sometimes even in opposition to, the Mandatory government.

Both peoples were to pay a high price for their weakness at the end of World War I, a turning point in the history of the Middle East and its peoples.

Sources of Arab Antagonism to the Jews

The growing opposition among the Arabs to constructive Jewish settlement in Palestine drew its sustenance from a number of sources. The members of the propertied class among Arab leaders opposed Jewish immigration because it consisted mainly of workers and young pioneers whose relatively high standard of living and tradition of progressive thought and communal life seemed to shatter the semi-feudal structure of most of Arab Palestine— thus undermining the foundations of their supremacy. Arab intellectuals, old as well as young, whose development took place on a background of the economic prosperity engendered by Jewish immigration and settlement nonetheless adopted an antagonistic attitude to the Jews. These members of the professional classes (generally upper- or middle-class in origin—lawyers, doctors, journalists, civil servants, teachers, and students) feared and resented the superior education and organizational ability, and the better economic and social conditions, of the Jews. They were particularly angry at their co-operation—limited as it was—with the hated British rule.

Arab workers, the great majority of whom came from a rural society, found themselves at a double disadvantage in their contact with Jewish employers. For the same work, the Jewish employer paid the Arab less than he paid organized or even unorganized Jewish labor; and on the other hand, the Jewish worker regarded employment in his sector as his exclusive patrimony, to the exclusion of the Arab worker. However eloquent the explanation of the moral, nationalist, and socialist motives that impelled the Jewish labor movement to take this stand* it could not remove the sting from the fact that the Jewish Labor Federation made no effort to organize the Arab workers, even those who worked in the Jewish sector. Jewish labor developed no sort of trade union association or solidarity with the Arab workers in order to improve their working conditions. The Arab fellaheen, who constituted the majority of the Arab population in Palestine, were directly affected by the benefits derived from Jewish immigration and the resultant speed-up in the development of Palestine: The demand for agricultural produce rose, as did its price; there was increased income from the transportation of building materials (sand, shells, gravel, lime, etc.), from the supply of fertilizers to expanding orchard acreage, and from employment —permanent, seasonal or casual—in the Jewish economic sector; as government revenue increased with immigration (immigrant taxes, customs revenues, etc.), the burden of taxation on the Arab villages was lightened; and the income flowing to Arab villages from sale of some of their lands to Jews, and the living example of the more advanced and prosperous Jewish villages had their beneficial effect on the Arab rural areas near Jewish settlement. However, the masses of Arab fellaheen failed to develop a specific and independent political consciousness of their own and continued to be dominated by conservative sheikhs, nationalist agitators, and religious fanatics— by all those who feared the modernization, secularism, and social freedom

* The desire to earn a living by physical work, as one of the basic aspirations of the Zionist labor movement; the fact that the Arab economic sector and the governmental labor market were largely closed to Jewish labor, leaving them only the labor market in the Jewish economy now being built up; the desire to prevent the Arab worker, with his lower standard of living and non-union tradition, from becoming a barrier to the greater demands of the better organized Jewish worker, with his higher living standards; the fear of the socio-political consequences resulting from possible exploitation of Jewish labor by Jewish employers in the absence of parallel relations between Arab employers and Jewish workers.

which accompanied Jewish immigration to Palestine. It was not difficult, therefore, to represent the Jewish carriers of modernism and emancipation as enemies of the sacred and conservative Arab tradition. This added fuel to the fires of political Arab nationalism.

It was thus from a variety of sources and from different social strata that the opposition of the Arab community to the Jewish community and its work in Palestine arose. Moreover, the suspicion of all things European— deeply engraved in the Oriental mind—and hatred of any foreign rule added to the hostility. Paradoxically, so did the impact of the Zionist movement itself: The accelerated development of Palestine, the economic effect of Jewish immigration and settlement, progressive and democratic organizational forms, the Jewish educational and cultural achievements—all these set an example for Palestinian Arabs and stimulated their advancement. From the point of view of living standards, educational level, etc., the Palestinian Arabs became one of the most highly developed communities in the Middle East, and it was because of this that the oppression of the colonial regime and the absence of self-government were felt so strongly.

The Jewish community and the Zionist movement disregarded the Palestinian Arabs' fear of their growing importance in the country and therefore saw no need to dispel it by effective proof that it was possible to build a life of mutual respect and understanding together. They also underrated the natural nationalist aspirations and political rights of the Arab community, its political strength and ties with the Arab nationalist movement as a whole. Official Jewish policy regarded the British government, rather than the Arabs, as the second party to political negotiations. This complex of attitudes increased estrangement and suspicion and created ideal conditions for the British policy of "divide and rule."

British Policy in Palestine

In a speech to his constituency on his return from a visit to Palestine at the beginning of 1922, Ramsay MacDonald, the British Labor Party leader and later Prime Minister reported:

In Palestine I learned that, during the war, our government authorized the previous High Commissioner to advise the Arabs that we would establish an Arab state, on condition that they support us in the war. . . . At the same time we promised to give Palestine to the Jews as their national home and to facilitate Jewish immigration in every way until finally the Jews are a majority in Palestine. And at the same time we made an agreement with a third party, namely France, according to which England and France were to have divided Syria, Palestine, and Iraq between them. Thus we assumed three obligations, each one of which contradicts the others.[1]

It was for reasons other than these contradictory promises, however, that the Balfour Declaration itself was received with little enthusiasm by British diplomatic personnel in the East, by the colonial office, and by the British administration in Palestine following its conquest. The colonial office plan for ensuring British hegemony in the Arab East included the establishment of a chain of independent Arab states and principalities. In return for Britain's recognition of their "independence," they were to promise "alliances" that would ensure Britain's *de facto* control.

In British officialdom, there were some who feared that to carry out this commitment would be likely to arouse anger against Britain in the Arab world; others feared that the development of a European Jewish community with a special political status would have an undesirable effect on the "exotic" Eastern nature of the area, on the preservation of which their political plans were founded.

On the other hand within British government circles a more far-sighted approach was also evident.

There was no place in these plans for a Jewish national home as envisaged by the Balfour Declaration. Competent spokesmen of His Majesty's Government made no secret of their emotional and political approach to the problem: While they saluted the idea of the return of the people of the Bible to the land of the Bible, they were not unmindful of the more concrete political benefit to British imperial interests. Such benefit, it was often declared, was bound to accrue when a (not too large) Jewish community became dependent for its survival on British protection, and thereby provided a moral pretext for continuous, perhaps perpetual, British control.

Since the major interests of the Jews were immigration, settlement, and the development of their national life in Palestine, there evolved between the leadership of the Zionist movement and the Mandatory government a certain community of interests that for a time became the basis of cooperation between the Jews and the British.

This cooperation could continue for only a limited period, however. Before very long, a clash ensued between the Zionist purpose and the basic British political interests, especially in relation to two questions of prime importance—(1) the pace of Jewish development in Palestine; and (2) Arab-Jewish relations.

Although a certain community of interests prevailed between the Jews and the British in the early stages of the Mandate, the conflict over the rate of Palestine's progress began almost immediately. Not only did British policy itself incorporate a wide range of varying attitudes and objectives in regard to Jewish aspirations in Palestine (all the way from limited support to unlimited hostility), but even Zionist sympathizers found it hard to keep up with the rapid pace demanded by the needs of the Zionist movement as it pushed ahead the upbuilding of Palestine.

From the time of conquest by the British Army until Sir Herbert Samuel became High Commissioner (July 1, 1920), Palestine was under military rule. General Allenby, a conservative English army man who was in supreme command of the country at the time, could see in Zionism little more than "fancy and theory," as he later confirmed. Until May 1920—two and a half years after its publication—no report of the Balfour Declaration was allowed to appear in Palestine. Most British Army officers treated Jewish aspirations with disparagement and enmity even after August 1919, when the Foreign Minister, Lord Balfour, reminded Palestinian authorities that the Allies had undertaken to help in the establishment of a Jewish national home in Palestine.* Even the administration of Sir Herbert Samuel† (July 1920–June 1925), whose very appointment was apparently meant to emphasize the British government's determination to carry out its aim of assisting the Jewish national home, bore the marks of duality in policy: while it permitted the growth of the Jewish community, the expansion of its land holdings, and a special, perhaps somewhat privileged, political status, it gave a limited interpretation to the British promises embodied in the Balfour Declaration and to the Mandate itself.

While Sir Herbert Samuel was in office, the Jewish community in Palestine doubled in size (from 55,000 in 1919 to 108,000 in 1925), and the number of Jewish agricultural settlements rose from only forty-four in 1918 to one hundred. Recognition was accorded to the representative bodies of the Jewish community (the Elected Assembly, the National Council—*Vaad Leumi*—and the local council), and Hebrew was recognized as one of the three official languages of the country. Pinchas Rutenberg was granted a concession (1921) to found the Palestine Electric Company. Public security in the country was improved, and a network of courts (rural, district, and supreme) was set up. Farm machinery and animals were exempted from customs duty,

---

* The period of military occupation was, by international law, one of transition and *status quo*; any special Zionist activity not authorized under the Turkish regime was, of course, forbidden (e.g., the singing of *Hatikva*, the blue-white flag, and even Jewish National Fund stamps). New regulations prohibiting the entry of Jews to Palestine were added to the old Turkish ones. Land purchase by Jews was in effect impossible (land-registry offices were established only in April 1920). The number of Jews in government service and in the police force was practically nil. Hebrew was not recognized as an official language. The report of a committee of the World Union of Poalei Zion, which toured Palestine from January to May 1919, stated, "The Jewish community appeared confused and shocked; for a long time they could not understand or appreciate what was happening. The earlier terrible trials of war, and the subsequent enthusiasm after the Declaration, intoxicated the people; they were so blinded by the glory of the future that they could not see the present threat."

† An Anglo-Jewish statesman, born in 1870. As Home Secretary in the Asquith Cabinet he declared, as early as 1915, his active support of the Zionist program in a memorandum to the Prime Minister on the future of Palestine.

as was equipment for educational and charitable institutions. The Hebrew University in Jerusalem was opened on April 1, 1925, in the presence of Lord Balfour and a galaxy of representatives of other governments and foreign academic personalities.

Yet, during the same period, British officials who had publicly declared their opposition to the Balfour Declaration were appointed to important posts in Palestine. By 1920, restrictions had already been placed upon Jewish immigration; in 1921, the High Commissioner announced a temporary suspension and, later, statutory limitations in the "interests of the present population" and the "absorptive capacity" of the country. The British government, which was pledged to foster the establishment of a Jewish national home, took upon itself to supply the needs of the Arab population of Palestine, but expected the Jews to defray the costs of Jewish public services. In October 1921, Sir Herbert Samuel attempted to set up an "advisory council" to serve as the nucleus of a representative body of sorts ("limited self-government") for Palestine residents. Appointments to the council included ten high government officials and ten members of the public: four Moslems, three Christians and three Jews, with the High Commissioner as chairman. Arab leaders refused to participate in the council both in 1921 and in 1923, when an expanded legislative council was proposed; they demanded the establishment of parliamentary government and the abolition of the Mandatory regime—as did the Arabs of Syria, Lebanon, Iraq, and Egypt at that time.

The objectives of British policy as regards the scope and pace of Jewish development in Palestine were explained by Winston Churchill, who frequently described himself as an "old Zionist." In a speech in the spring of 1921, when he visited Palestine in his capacity as Colonial Secretary, he said, "The present form of Palestinian government [colonial rule] will continue for many years. We shall gradually develop representative institutions leading to complete self-government. All of us alive today, and our children and grandchildren as well, shall have gone the way of all flesh before this is realized in full."*

In a memorandum of the Colonial Office dated June 3, 1922 (later published as a white paper), the Zionist Organization was asked to agree to the following: (a) that the Mandatory regulations regarding the Jewish national home should not apply to 77 percent of the Palestine Mandatory area—the area east of the Jordan (in the final instance, this amounted to 90,000 square kilometers out of a total of 117,000 included in the Palestine Mandate); (b) that the intention should not be for all of Palestine to be the Jewish national home, but that a Jewish national home be founded within Palestine; (c) that

* History belied Churchill's fond hope: After only twenty-six years, a long time before it was his grandchildren's turn to go the way of all flesh, he himself was privileged to see with his own eyes how "the thing is realized in full."

the Zionist Organization participate in the economic development of Palestine but not be permitted to take part in any way in its administration; (d) that the number of Jewish immigrants (in the years following the war 25,000 had immigrated, mostly from eastern Europe) not exceed the economic absorptive capacity of the country, and that "politically undesirable persons" not be permitted to immigrate;* (e) that some self-government be initiated and gradually developed—the first step to be the establishment of a legislative council presided over by the High Commissioner and consisting of twelve elected and ten appointed members.

The demands of the Colonial Office were transmitted to the Zionist Executive at the time that the League of Nations was about to deal with the Palestine Mandate. As we have noted, the Zionist movement, as well as Palestinian Jewry in general, was too weak to oppose the British government, which both controlled Palestine and had great influence in the League of Nations. After studying the memorandum, the Zionist leadership decided to "take note of the statement of British policy in Palestine transmitted to it by the Colonial Office on June 3, 1922, and to promise His Majesty's Government that the Zionist Organization would direct its activity in accordance with the policy laid down in that statement."

On July 24, 1922, the League of Nations Council approved the granting of the Palestine Mandate to the British government. On August 10 of the same year, the Palestine Order-in-Council of 1922 was issued as the country's basic constitution and in September, the League of Nations Council agreed to the British government's proposal that Mandatory provisions dealing with the Jewish national home and the holy places should not apply to Transjordan.

The White Paper of 1922 was only the first of a series of impediments to the progress of the Jewish endeavor in Palestine. The dynamic development of this venture, stimulated by Jewish difficulties in the Diaspora, was abruptly to terminate any community of interests. Instead, there developed a rapidly growing contradiction between the interests of the Zionist movement and those of the British administration. As the needs of the Jewish people impelled them to destroy the arbitrary limitations fixed by the British, the relations between the Jews and the British in Palestine were characterized by an unceasingly intensified struggle—sometimes quiet and hidden, sometimes open and stormy—between the necessary progress of the Jews (and of the country as a whole) and British interests, which dictated its slowing down,

* Following the convention of the Poalei Zion World Union in Vienna in 1920, the Left Poalei Zion called for unrestricted immigration to Palestine and for the up-building of the country in cooperation with Arab workers, without acknowledging British authority in the country. Because of this, their members were not permitted to immigrate to Palestine and were persecuted by the British authorities.

for fear of the effect on neighboring Arab countries. This essential contra-diction led inevitably to the breakdown of Jewish-British cooperation and pointed to the pressing need for reorientation of Zionist policy.

The most fundamental contradiction, however, arose from the clash between the long-term political interests of the Jews and those of the British: Whereas the Jews, returning to their ancient homeland in the East, had a vital interest in winning the sympathy and support of Arabs in Palestine and neighboring countries, the British administration took no positive steps to encourage such relations of goodwill. Indeed, they pressed policies that were bound to widen the gulf between the Jews and Arabs and prevent the Jewish renaissance movement from integrating peaceably into the liberation move-ment of the East as a whole. This British policy left its seal on Arab-Jewish relations during the whole period under discussion.

Evolution of Arab-Jewish Relations

In earlier chapters, we have reviewed the attempts to reach some *modus vivendi* that were made by the leaders of the Jewish and Arab national movements up until the proposal submitted in June 1919 by H. M. Kal-varisky to Faisal's council in Syria, which accepted it as a basis for a Pales-tinian constitution. That the proposal was approved by Arab leaders as a basis for an agreement on Palestine between the two people was confirmed by one of the heads of the Palestinian Arab delegation to the 1939 round table talks. In the June 1941 report on the constitutional development of Palestine (see note 18 to Chapter 4) it was stated that in a private conversation between that Arab leader and a member of the Jewish delegation to the commission, the Arab leader said that "at the beginning of the British administration of Palestine, the Arabs were prepared to agree [though he himself had always objected] to Jewish immigration and settlement in Palestine, if the Kalvarisky plan had been accepted by the Zionist Organiza-tion as a basis for agreement." (see page 154).

On June 28, 1919, the Versailles peace treaty ratified the Mandatory regimes for countries which had been detached from the Ottoman Empire, thus rejecting the Arab demand, presented by Faisal, that—with the exception of Palestine—they be granted immediate political independence in all areas of eastern Asia settled by them. Faisal and his council agreed that a special status should be granted to Palestine to permit the implementation of the Balfour Declaration policy, while developing close cooperation between Jews and Arabs. The Kingdom of Hejaz refused to concur in the Versailles treaty. Consequently, it took part neither in the League of Nations nor in the peace conference that later determined the conditions of peace with the Turks (Treaty of Sèvres, 1920). Faisal's Damascus government, which refused to recognize the French Mandate on Syria, decided to resist the curtailment of its powers by the French Mandatory authority. Faisal hoped to be assisted by the British, some of whose agents secretly encouraged him to oppose France. When the French and English came to an agreement, however, Faisal was exiled from Damascus. Syria bowed to French rule, and Palestine became British Mandated territory—in all but name, an integral part of the British colonial empire. Before long, the British Mandatory authorities began whittling away—gradually but methodically—their international commitments to the Jewish national home.

This was done primarily by fanning the flame of Arab opposition to the Jews, so that the British would be in the position of having to put down this resistance by force in order to "keep Palestine at sword's point for the benefit of the Jews," in the words of Sir Ronald Storrs, the governor of Jerusalem at that time.

How the Job Was Done

There is considerable evidence in support of our thesis that the British officials, military and civil, took an active part in crystallizing Arab opposition to the Jewish endeavor in Palestine. Sir Louis Bols, the third and last chief administrator of O.E.T.A. (Palestine), and his aides Chief of Staff Colonel Waters-Taylor, and Colonel Hubbard, then governor of Jaffa and Tel Aviv, encouraged the Arab community to offer resistance to Jewish immigration and to the Jewish national home. It was later learned from well-informed Arab circles that British officers and officials played a far from insignificant role in early efforts that led to the foundation of the Moslem-Christian Association, the first postwar Arab organization in Palestine (see Chapter Four). Immediately after its first national congress in February 1919, the Association embarked upon political activity against Jewish aspirations in Palestine and the Balfour Declaration. Its members, with government permission, organized the first Arab demonstration in Jerusalem on February 27, 1920, the day the all-Syria convention opened in Damascus; they also organized the March 8 demonstration, in which thousands of people • took part, the day after Faisal was proclaimed King in the Syrian capital. At the head of this violently anti-Jewish demonstration marched Musa Kazim al-Hussaini, Mayor of Jerusalem. This association was to become the backbone of Palestinian Arab conferences,* at which resolutions time after time

---

* The all-Syrian congresses held in Damascus from June to July 1919, and from February to March 1920, in which Palestinian delegates also took part, are usually termed the first and second congresses; the third took place in Haifa in December 1920, the fourth in Jerusalem from June to July 1921, the fifth in Nablus in August 1922, the sixth in Jaffa in 1923, and the seventh in Jerusalem in 1928.

insisted on the stoppage of Jewish immigration to Palestine; prohibition of the sale of Arab lands to Jews; the granting of self-government and immediate independence to an Arab-Palestinian state in which the Jews were to remain an eternal minority, at the mercy of the Arab majority, whose leaders publicly negated the possibility of any Jewish national rights in the land of their forefathers.

A description of the British Palestine policy in that period appears in a letter written by an officer of the Jewish battalion, as quoted in a book by Colonel Patterson, the commander of the 38th battalion Royal Fusiliers in the British Army:

> Palestine became the arena for an overtly anti-Semitic policy;* the most elementary equality of rights is denied to the Jewish population; the Holy City [Jerusalem] in which the Jews are the overwhelming majority, was handed over to an extremely anti-Semitic municipality; acts of violence against Jews are permitted, and entire districts are closed to them by threats of force in full view of the authorities; high officials, guilty of acts which any court would consider incitement to violence against the Jews, go unpunished and even retain their official positions. The Hebrew language is ridiculed in official circles. Anti-Semitism and hostility to Zionism have become the fashion among officials who imitate their superiors; any direct attempt at Jewish-Arab agreement is put to nought by the penalization of Arab notables who show any inclination in favour of the Jews.†

In cooperation with Arab groups hostile to Jews, the British administration in 1924 dismissed Hassan Shukri (1876–1940), who had been Mayor of Haifa since 1916. The Mayor, who had been honored and respected by Jews and Arabs alike, was penalized for having addressed a greeting to the High Commissioner, Sir Herbert Samuel, upon his arrival in Palestine. At the next elections (1927), however, he was reelected by a majority of Arab and Jewish votes and retained the mayorality until his death (January 29, 1940).

The atmosphere created in the country by the British military chiefs at a time when Arab-Jewish relations were on the verge of a definitive turn— either toward mutual understanding and cooperation or toward mutual hostility and political antagonism—is shown by a characteristic order issued to the British forces in March 1920, in which it was stated, among other things, that: "Since the government has been charged with administering in

---

* More properly, an "anti-Jewish" policy, for after all, the Arabs are also "Semites."

† In the 1940s, the author and his friends often heard Arabs of the Bet Shean, Nablus, Jaffa, and Jerusalem areas describe how British officials were courteous and helpful to Arab notables who opposed the Jews, and were discourteous, or worse, toward those Arabs who strove for peace and cooperation. Arabs who nevertheless remained friendly to Jews had to hide this not only from Arab extremists but also from British officials. The British would often inform anti-Jewish Arab notables of the "treason" of pro-Jewish Arabs, who were more than once penalized for this.

Palestine a policy unpopular with the majority of the population, disturbances between Jews and Arabs are likely to break out. . . ."

In striking contrast to the political atmosphere in London, which justified the political hopes of the Jews, British officials in Palestine encouraged the resistance of Arab leaders to Jewish aspirations, primarily on the grounds that the political future of the country had not yet been definitely decided and everything was in a state of flux. Anti-Jewish demonstrations were held in Jaffa and Jerusalem (at the end of February 1920), by permission of the government, in spite of Jewish warnings that they were bound to lead to violence.

In the first days of March 1920, the Tel Hai incident took place. In the background was the political confusion and disagreement between Britain and France as to the implementation of the Sykes-Picot agreement, but on the stage itself sufficient blood was shed to recall the culmination of a Shakespearean tragedy. Under the Clemenceau-Lloyd George agreement of September 15, 1919, the British withdrew from the area north of the Ras-an-Nakura/Merom line; the French, now in control of Upper Galilee, showed little understanding of the problems of the heterogeneous population of that area (Moslems, Christians, Mutawali-Shiites and Sunnites, peasants, and Bedouin tribes) and the complex internal relationships that had developed under Turkish rule. When it transpired that Syria was to be put under French Mandate, the Arabs launched a fierce struggle against the French. The resultant isolation of the Jewish settlements of northern Galilee (Metulla, Hamra, Kfar Giladi, and Tel Hai) made them targets of Bedouin bands. The local Arab leaders protested that they were not fighting the Jews and that the attacks on Jewish settlements were the work of irresponsible bands. The position of the Jewish settlements deteriorated when the control of the anti-French struggle in the area passed from the local Arab leaders to Damascenes, who combined violent anti-Zionist propaganda with their political campaign against the French. On the other hand, the French authorities refused to ensure the safety of the Galilee Jewish settlements within their territory. Although the Jews declared their neutrality in the war between the Arabs and the French, and tried their best to maintain it, the French persisted in setting up bases in Metulla and Kfar-Giladi, to the detriment of Arab-Jewish relations. Reinforcements in men and supplies were rushed to these Jewish settlements by the Jewish community of Palestine, but in the reigning chaos the defenders of these few isolated and sparsely populated settlements had no chance against attackers whose superiority in numbers and arms was considerable and who enjoyed unrestricted movement and supplies. All the Jewish settlements together had only about one hundred defenders, with very limited equipment, ammunition, and supplies.

On March 1, 1920, a numerically overwhelming Arab force attacked Tel

N

Hai. Joseph Trumpeldor* and his comrades (Dvora Drachler, Benjamin Toker, Benjamin Munter, Sarah Chijik, and Zeev Scharf) after an heroic stand against impossible odds were killed, and five others wounded—two of them badly. The rest retreated to neighboring Kfar Giladi. This point was attacked on March 3 by a large force of well-armed Bedouins, and the defenders were forced to abandon it as well (Hamra had been evacuated as early as January). Carrying their arms and ammunition, they went up the mountains on the west to the Mutawalli Arab village of Taibe, where they were hospitably received by the local leader, Kamal al-As'ad. His people treated them warmly and with kindness, fed them, let them rest, and even provided them with pack animals and escorts for their journey south to Ayelet Hashahar, within British territory.

In October 1920, after the French had subdued the stormy region and restored relative security, the Jewish settlers returned to rebuild the ruins of Kfar Giladi, Tel Hai, and Metulla. Under the terms of the San Remo agreement (December 23, 1920), the area passed to British control, and its Jewish settlements were included in the boundaries of Mandatory Palestine.

At the beginning of April, bloody riots broke out in Jerusalem, following anti-Jewish propaganda carried on with the encouragement of several senior British officials. An Arab crowd gathered for the *Nabi Musa* celebrations was incited to vengeance against the Jews. For three days, British and Indian sentries stood guard at the approaches to the old city, to prevent any Jewish defenders from coming to the assistance of the harried Jews within the walls. At that time, only 400 men remained of the disbanded Jewish battalions; they were stationed in Sarafand and not allowed to go to the aid of the attacked. The organizers and members of the Jewish defense force were imprisoned; twenty of them were sentenced to hard labor, nineteen to prison terms of three years, and one—Z. Jabotinsky—to a term of fifteen years. (The sentences, however, were later quashed). On the other hand, the Arab leaders arrested for incitement to riot were released on bail. To add insult to injury, the Zionist Executive offices and Dr. Weizmann's home were searched. While overt incitement against the Jews was permitted in Arab newspapers, a strict censorship was imposed on the Hebrew press, which was forbidden even to reproduce the scurrilous Arab press reports and refute them.

The chief administrator, General Bols, thereupon forwarded to G.H.Q. in Cairo a long memorandum antagonistic to the Jews. One of its recom-

---

* Joseph Trumpeldor (1880–1920): A Russian Jew who distinguished himself as an army officer in the Russo-Japanese War of 1905, where he lost an arm. Founded the *Hechalutz* (Pioneer) Movement in Russia after World War I and came to Palestine. Worked in the early collectives and after his death in the defence of Tel Hai became a symbol of the synthesis of Jewish labor and self-defense.

mendations stressed the need for drawing "logical conclusions" from the anti-Jewish outbreaks (organized under the aegis of his indifferent officials, and even with the encouragement of some of the more important ones!). Bols' main suggestion was the abolition of the Zionist commission, symbol of the special status accorded to the Palestinian Jewish community in conformity with the solemn promises of the British government. General Bols' undisguised hostility was further reflected in his reply to a telegram that the Arab Mayor of Jaffa sent expressing thanks to the general "for the admirable things he did in this country with devotion and friendship." In his reply, the British Governor-General said: "I will never forget the past six months during which you demonstrated your fairness and friendship." Yet those six months of "fairness and friendship" of the Arab groups for whom the Mayor of Jaffa was spokesman were months of demonstrations and attacks against the Jews in their national home.

Further evidence of the dubious role played by the British administration of Palestine in those early days can be found in the memoirs of Colonel Meinertzhagen, who held important positions in the British administration at the time. In 1917, he was Intelligence Officer at General Allenby's headquarters, where he remained until after the conquest of Jerusalem; in 1918, he was transferred to the War Office in London and joined the British delegation to the peace conference in Paris in 1919; in the autumn of the same year, he returned to the Allenby headquarters as Chief Political Officer for Palestine and Syria. Because of the criticism he leveled against the local British command and administration for carrying out policies opposed to the Balfour Declaration, he was removed from this position in 1920 and employed in an advisory military capacity in the Middle East department of the colonial office, then reconstituted. From that vantage point he continued to follow the events of our region.*

Meinertzhagen states unequivocally that the heads of the Palestine British administration, both civil and military, "all worked against Zionism in the hopes of choking it while it was still young," and that "everyone here works against Zionism, some openly and others secretly" (diary entry, June 2, 1920). He mentions General Bols and his Chief-of-Staff, Colonel Waters-Taylor, as the principal culprits. When Meinertzhagen gave orders to have Haj Amin al-Hussaini—Mufti of Jerusalem, later president of the Supreme Moslem Council—followed, he soon learned that "Mr. Waters-Taylor recommended arranging anti-Jewish riots in Jerusalem so that the administration should be impressed by the unpopularity of Zionist policy."

In a personal and confidential letter to Lord Curzon (diary entry, April 16, 1920), Meinertzhagen says:

* His memoirs, which illustrate many aspects of British policy, appeared as *Middle East Diary 1917–1956* (London, 1959).

On April 2, [Governor of Jerusalem] Storrs summoned the Moslem leaders of Jerusalem and warned them to refrain from mixing politics with religious ceremonies. The Moslems said that this was impossible and suggested that Storrs address Jerusalem Moslems. Storrs replied: "They won't listen to me, for they think I am a friend of the Jews, while the contrary is the case."

Waters-Taylor saw Haj Amin on the Wednesday before Easter and told him that during the holiday he would have a unique opportunity to prove to the world that the Palestinian Arabs would not stand for Jewish rule; that Zionism was uncongenial not only to the Palestine administration but also to Whitehall; and that if sufficiently large demonstrations were to take place in Jerusalem at Easter, both General Allenby and General Bols would recommend renouncing the Jewish National Home. Waters-Taylor explained that freedom could be achieved only by violence. On the day of the riots, Waters-Taylor retired to Jericho. Two days after the riots, he summoned the mayor of Jerusalem, Musa Kazim Pasha, and said: "I gave you an excellent chance. Jerusalem was without military protection for five hours. I hoped you would take advantage of the opportunity, but you failed!" This conversation was confirmed by two sources.

The perfidious British policy did not change materially even after Sir Herbert Samuel, known to be in favor of the Balfour Declaration, was appointed High Commissioner (July 1920) to replace the chief (military) administrator. High positions in the civil administration were still being awarded to officials who showed open antipathy to all that the Jews were doing in the country; some of them were known to have been specifically opposed to the Balfour Declaration, and there were those who even took an active part in encouraging the Arabs to resist the officially declared policy.

The neighboring countries were in ferment: There was an anti-British rebellion in Iraq at the beginning of July 1920, a struggle between the nationalist movement led by Faisal's government and the French forces in Syria, and a growing tumult in Egypt following the Milner Report. These naturally had repercussions among Palestinian Arabs, whose growing opposition to British rule was now directed against the Jews in Palestine.

The unrestricted hate propaganda against the Jews led to bloody anti-Jewish riots, which broke out in Jaffa on May 1, 1921,* and in the course of a week spread to Petah Tikva, Kfar Saba, 'Ain Hai, Hadera, and Rehovot. In Jaffa, forty-three Jews, including the writer Y. H. Brenner, were killed, and one hundred and thirty-four wounded. Fourteen Arabs were killed and fifty wounded. In Petah Tikva, four Jews were killed and about twenty wounded. By the time British troops finally intervened (in the Hadera area, a plane machine-gunned and bombed an Arab mob indulging in excesses), dozens of Arabs had been killed and many wounded. The country calmed

---

* Rumors of organized fighting between Arabs and Jews spread in the wake of quarrels and street fighting between two opposed wings of the Jewish labor movement, *Achdut Haavoda* and one of the earliest communist groups.

down in five or six days, but Samuel's political advisers and aides presented him with a picture of what was happening in Palestine that indicated the presence of a general movement of revolt similar to those in Iraq and Egypt. Army commanders insisted that they lacked the necessary forces to control an outbreak, thereby implying that what was needed was "to calm the winds by political means." This was the origin of the announcements cutting off immigration, and the other restrictive measures that found their definitive expression in the white paper of 1922 (see page 190). Jewish feelings that the Arabs were standing in their way were encouraged, and the Arabs were taught that their enemies were the Jews. A more sober view by both Arabs and Jews of the political realities of the situation might have led them to reach the conclusion that the meddlesome British Mandatory administration was the common enemy of both Arabs and Jews.

The Zionist Executive, whom nobody could possibly accuse of anti-British bias, stated in its report to the twelfth Zionist Congress (summer of 1921):

In early spring of 1918, the Arab leaders in Palestine and Egypt were eager to come to an agreement with Zionists on the basis of mutual concessions. The Jews answered with the greatest willingness and friendship. The Arab position grew more and more equivocal, and antagonism to Zionism and the Jewish demands grew within the British military administration. There are clear indications that in certain cases direct advice was given to Arab leaders to refrain from making any concessions to the Jews.

Sir Herbert Samuel had good intentions toward both the Jews and the Arabs. A true liberal (and not only by virtue of party membership), he had hoped, in accepting the position of High Commissioner for Palestine, to serve historical Jewish interests, to provide a liberal regime of justice and progress for the Arabs of Palestine, and to achieve a *rapprochement* of the two peoples that would lead to cooperation for their own benefit and for the glory of the British Empire. It was Samuel's bad luck to be cast into a center of imperial intrigue—into a world of conspiracy, in which he had to work with unsympathetic aides who undermined his noble objectives.

A classic example of this was the elevation of Haj Amin al-Hussaini* to

---

* A member of the Hussaini family, descended (according to tradition) from Hussain, the son of Caliph Ali and Muhammad's daughter Fatma. The family, of Yemenite origin, came to the Jerusalem area either in the thirteenth or in the sixteenth century. A widely-connected and wealthy family, it rose to importance in Turkish days, when one of its members was appointed Mufti of Jerusalem. Amin Hussaini was born in 1893, and educated in a government school in Jerusalem. At the age of nineteen, he was sent to Cairo and studied at Al-Azhar University. On the death of his father, Sheik Tahir, who was Mufti of Jerusalem, Amin's elder brother, Sheik Kamal, was appointed his successor and supported his brothers in Cairo out of his meager salary (five Turkish pounds a month). After his pilgrimage to the holy places in Hejaz, he was designated *Haj Amin*. When war broke out in 1914, he was sent to an officers' training school in Constantinople

leadership of the Palestinian Arabs by his appointment as Mufti of Jerusalem in April 1921, and President of the Supreme Moslem Council in 1922. The anti-Jewish objectives of Haj Amin were never in doubt. Nonetheless, when, on the death of the Jerusalem Mufti, Sheik Kamal Hussauni, a successor had to be chosen, the authorities selected Haj Amin. Candidates for the position of Mufti were elected by representatives chosen by the few privileged to vote in Turkish parliamentary elections. Haj Amin received only nine votes, whereas his opponents received twelve, seventeen, and eighteen votes respectively. Since, according to regulations, the government could appoint the Mufti from among the three highest pluralities, one of Haj Amin's rivals was induced to resign, thus making Haj Amin's election certain. After his appointment to the presidency of the Supreme Moslem Council—a position that conferred upon him the title of *Ra'is al-'Ulama* (Principal Religious Authority)—Haj Amin found himself in control of great channels of influence and power: Administration of the *Waqf's* budget and personnel, the appointment of judges to the Sher'ia courts, etc. With the support of friends on the Supreme Moslem Council and later on the Arab Executive Committee,* he forged himself a triple position of power as religious head, national leader, and senior government official (the post of Mufti was, in effect, a government office). Haj Amin was the moving spirit behind the anti-Jewish movement in the country and guided the bloody attacks made on the Jewish community in 1929, 1936, and later. Nevertheless, he continued to be *persona grata* with the British authorities, and even benefited indirectly from their support of his program. In 1931, the Pan-Islam Committee, which he headed, was permitted to meet in Jerusalem; and later (1934) he was called upon to arbitrate between Yemen and Saudi Arabia,

---

and subsequently served as a Turkish officer in Izmir (Smyrna). He returned to Jerusalem immediately after the British occupation and soon became politically active in Arab affairs. He was successively appointed clerk in the office of the Arab adviser to the governor of Jerusalem, controller of smuggling traffic at Kalkilia, and also an officer in the security department in Damascus. He was dismissed from the last-mentioned post and appointed teacher in the *Rashidiya* School in Jerusalem. He published anti-Jewish articles in *Suriya al-Junubiya* (see Chapter Four). For his activities in the anti-Jewish riots of February 1920 in Jerusalem, he was sentenced *in absentia* to ten years' imprisonment and fled to Transjordan. After being amnestied by High Commissioner Sir Herbert Samuel, he returned to Jerusalem (1921) and immediately became Mufti.

 * "The Arab Executive Committee," the spokesman for, and highest authority of, the Arab nationalist movement in Palestine, was elected by the third Arab Congress in Palestine (Haifa, December 1920), with Mussa Kazim Pasha al-Hussaini (1852–1934) as its first president. In spite of constant friction between the Hussainis—who controlled the Supreme Moslem Council and the Arab Executive Committee—and the opposition, led by the Nashashibis—who controlled the Jerusalem Municipality—the Arab Executive Committee continued to be acknowledged as representative of all sections of the Arab movement until it was disbanded in 1934–1935.

thereby fortifying his position as leader of the Arab and Moslem world. It was only in 1937, after the assassination of Mr. Andrews, the British district commissioner in Galilee, that Haj Amin was dismissed from the post of president of the Moslem Council. He then fled Palestine and continued from abroad to wage his war against Jews (Lebanon, Syria, and Nazi Germany during World War II).

Authoritative evidence concerning the role played by British authorities in the evolution of Arab-Jewish relations is to be found in the Palestine diary of Colonel (later Brigadier) P. H. Kish (1888–1943), who was head of the political department and chairman of the Zionist Executive in Palestine from January 1923, to August 1931. Colonel Kish, a British officer with a brilliant war record, was obviously free from the slightest tinge of anti-British feeling. When told by Riad as-Sulh (the prominent Lebanese leader of the Arab nationalist movement and several times Prime Minister of Lebanon, until his assassination in 1951) that on the basis of his observations and impressions "the Government is not sincere . . . they do not wish to see a rapprochement between Jews and Arabs." Colonel Kish noted in his diary (April 3, 1923): "I cannot believe this to be the case, but there is no doubt that the Goverment has acted, and is acting, as if it were true."

According to the testimony of Raghib Bey Nashashibi (*Ibid.*, February 21, 1923), "in matters relating to the participation of the Arabs [in the legislative council then planned], the High Commissioner is guided by the advice of Richmond, who makes all cooperation with the Jews impossible." Of this same Ernest Richmond,* Colonel Kish reports in his diary (February 21, 1923) that "Jews and moderate Arabs considered Richmond as identified with the policy of the Mufti." Yet Richmond was assistant chief secretary, in charge of the political department between 1920 and 1924.

In this connection, Kalvarisky's letter of August 3, 1923, to the political department of the Zionist Executive in London is of interest. Kalvarisky, who was one of the ten unofficial members appointed by Sir Herbert Samuel in October 1921 to the advisory council, noted the British authorities' painstaking search for Arab members for the council, to replace those who refused to take part in 1921. (See page 172): "The government continues to show special sympathy to people outstanding in their opposition to us, all of whom belong to the Moslem-Christian Association. Anybody with the slightest predisposition toward us is considered disqualified."[2]

Thus the impressions of Riad As-Sulh, Raghib Nashashibi, and many other Arab leaders, were not without foundation. In those first years of British

---

* An authority on Moslem architecture and director of antiquities in Egypt before the war. Although he was strongly and vociferously opposed to the Balfour Declaration, Sir Herbert Samuel appointed him as his principal political advisor in order to demonstrate his objectivity.

rule in Palestine, when Arab-Jewish relations clamored for benevolent official guidance, not only did senior officials in the British administration encourage Arabs to oppose the Jews, but they actively intervened in order to foil and frustrate Arab-Jewish negotiations.

Sabotage of Arab-Jewish Negotiations

In 1922, basic negotiations were embarked upon (in Cairo, Geneva, and London) between representatives of the Arab nationalist movement and the World Zionist Organization. On the Arab side, the negotiators were Sheik Rasheed Rida, President of the Central Committee of the Syrian Unity Party and veteran Arab leader, Sheik Kamil, Riad As-Sulh, and Emile Ghoury, then foreign editor of the most important Egyptian newspaper, *Al-Ahram*. On the Jewish side, the participants were Dr. Eder, then head of the political department of the Zionist Executive in Palestine; Baron Felix de Menashe, a leader of Egyptian Jewry; and Mr. Asher Sapir, a man with extensive connections among the leaders of the Arab nationalist movement since Turkish days (see Chapters Three and Four), whom Dr. Chaim Weizmann had authorized to take part in the negotiations.

Report No. 1 of the minutes of those negotiations states:

On March 18, 1922, at 5 p.m., two delegations met in Cairo—one representing the Zionist Organization, and the other the Executive Committee of the Congress of Parties of the Federation of Arab states—to exchange views and reach an understanding that would enable both sides to work shoulder to shoulder for the benefit of Mesopotamia, Syria, Palestine, and the other Arab countries, on the basis of equality of rights and interests.

In convening this meeting both parties were permeated by a common desire to initiate a new era of peace and tranquility and to put an end to the contention and misunderstanding dividing them, which, should they continue, are likely to adversely affect our interests, both public and private, and delay the realization of the just aspirations of both parties.

Both parties having recognized this necessity, each of them declares that it recognizes its fellow as a force with which it is very desirable and useful to arrive at complete understanding.

The Arab delegation declares that the Arab countries, after hundreds of years of corrupt, ruinous, and destructive rule, see no possibility of resuming their rightful place in the world without trust and cooperation between the people of those countries and representatives of a more advanced outside culture. Representatives of such a culture are, in its opinion, of two categories: 1) a well-established European nation, i.e., a colonial power, which presents a grave danger to political independence and unity in backward countries; 2) the Jewish people, whose origins are in the East and whose members have been scattered throughout the world, and from whose ideals modern civilization draws strength and courage. Taking into consideration the antiquity of the Jewish people (who are historically close to the Arabs), and the fact that Jewish settlement does not constitute a political danger, and that in settling Palestine and making it their homeland, the Jews do not occupy it for the benefit of any foreign power—the Arabs declare that in order to spur their countries on toward advanced civilization they give the Jews priority and will be happy to work together with them, so that the Jews shall be the main bearers of that outside culture of which the Arabs are in need.

In reply to this declaration, the Jewish delegates expressed their pleasure and happiness at the trust placed in them. After they, on their part, had emphasized the ancient racial affinity, they also declared that they were prepared to cooperate with the Arabs in order to open an era of work and peace, and to exert their influence toward peace and progress in the countries mentioned. On the other hand, they call the attention of the Arab delegates to the legitimate interests of the Jews in Palestine and to their aspirations within it as their national and historical homeland.

While recognizing these aspirations, the Arab delegates requested that neither the Balfour Declaration nor the treaty signed between Britain and King Hussain should serve as a basis for discussion. The agreement that would be signed by both parties did not need to be affected by either of those political documents. Arabs and Jews must sit together and deal with each other as nation with nation. They must make concessions to each other and recognize each other's rights.*

The negotiations began at a time when both Jews and Arabs had suffered setbacks. The Jews had gone through the bloody riots of 1920 and 1921 in Palestine, and the development of the Jewish national home faced disturbing obstacles. The Arabs had witnessed the dissolution of Faisal's Syrian government, the fragmentation of the area that was to have constituted the independent Arab state as envisaged by the Allies, and the subjugation of their countries by those same powers. These circumstances fostered among Arabs and Jews the growth of the idea that making common cause was likely to facilitate the achievement of their respective aims. The spirit of the negotiations was reminiscent of the conversations between the leaders of both national movements before the World War and immediately after its conclusion.

The minutes made it clear that there were two central ideas in these talks, namely: (1) full and definitive independence for the Arab countries in the Near East, and their union in a single federation; and (2) full opportunity for the Zionist movement to realize its aspirations in Palestine, through close cooperation with the Arabs of Palestine and the neighboring countries.

The March 18, 1922, minutes continue:

The work of joining the Jews and Arabs in concerted action will probably be a long process, and both parties are fully cognizant of the fact that the aim they aspire to is not

* The passages quoted are taken from the minutes recorded in longhand by the Arab secretary who attended the session in Cairo in March 1922. Copies of this evidence were produced for the Peel commission on February 7, 1936 by Mr. Asher Sapir, who participated in these negotiations. Mr. Sapir's own evidence, which was forwarded to the commission in writing, contained photostats of relevant original papers.

one that can be achieved overnight. All are agreed, however, that this work should be initiated immediately, with harmonious and methodical preparation in all aspects of life, and that all legal means of shortening the Mandatory period should be utilized.

After the Jewish delegation approved the declaration of the Arab delegation, the Jewish delegates presented their immediate demands: a) peace and quiet in Palestine; b) the immediate cessation of any acts hostile to the settlement of Jews in Palestine within the limits of the economic absorptive capacity of the country; c) the cessation of all anti-Jewish propaganda in the Arab press and within the Arab committees in Palestine and abroad. In return, the Jews would place at the service of the Arabs all the political and economic means at their disposal, as well as their instruments of propaganda. In a word—they would work faithfully shoulder to shoulder with the Arabs in order to realize the ultimate objective defined above.

. . . As to the guarantees that the Arabs were to give the Jews, the Jewish delegation was insistent in connection with the riots that there was reason to suspect might break out in Palestine during April, the holiday month, as a result of mob incitement. The Arab delegation voiced their agreement and immediately recognized that this demand was justified; and desirous of giving the Jews the first definitive proof of the sincerity and trust that it meant to show in its work together with the Jews, the Arabs noted that at the earliest opportunity their delegation would take upon itself the task of calming ruffled tempers in Palestine, so as to prevent riots. The delegation declared that it had already been decided to send one of its members to Palestine to preach peace to the Palestinian organizations in the name of the Congress. On the other hand, the Jewish delegation would have to prevent any demonstration on the part of the Jews.

Dr. Chaim Weizmann was in Italy at the time. The minutes of the first two sessions were sent to him by special carrier, and the two delegations met once more on April 2, 1922, when the messenger returned. The minutes of this session include the text of the cable received from Dr. Weizmann, President of the World Zionist Organization:

After reading the documents I most definitely approve your negotiations. We accept your proposed agreement in principle. We appoint Sokolov, Eder, Menashe, and Kalvarisky as our delegates in the combined commission that will continue the negotiations and determine the working of the agreements. If my presence is required I will come—if not, I will sign the agreement in Genoa. I prefer the latter course. Try to define the Palestine problem precisely.

The Arab delegation, [the minutes report], noted the contents of the telegram and expressed its desire to see the establishment of the combined commission so that it could begin its work at the earliest opportunity.

In the exchanges at that meeting (April 2, 1922), the following points are of special interest: the Jewish representatives asked the Arabs "whether the organization on whose behalf they spoke is in favor of His Majesty King Faisal of Iraq, and of His Majesty King Hussain I of Hejaz." The reply of the Arab representatives was that "Their Majesties King Faisal and King Hussain are two soldiers in the Arab movement. Like all Arabs, they work harmoniously with the Arab organization. When necessary, we shall be able to obtain documents to that effect from Their Majesties and/or get Their Majesties to issue a statement to the Jewish delegates and thereby give evidence of their complete agreement with our policy in this matter."

The Jewish representatives asked, "Do not the Arab delegates believe that it would be a good idea to add one or two Palestinian Arabs to the negotiations, since in any case they are the party directly concerned in questions pertaining to Palestine?"

The answer was, "No one can influence our decisions in regard to the composition of the executive committee. However, if necessary, we shall be able to put the Jews in close touch with Arab personalities in Palestine with whom the Jews would like to speak."

Question: "Do the Arab organizations include members representing the Christian Arab community?" *Reply:* "The Arab organization does not wish there to be any difference between Christian Arabs and Moslem Arabs. All are considered equal and brothers; but if the Jews so desire, we shall be able to demonstrate that the Christian element is well represented in our organization."

Question: "Are not the Arab delegates of the same opinion as the Jews in regard to a policy of amity toward the great powers, unless this friendship interferes in some way with the end goal to which both parties aspire?" *Reply:* "We have no desire whatsoever to show hostility to any of the Allied governments. We should like to add that we rely upon the friendship of the Allied governments who are likewise in favor of the realization of our national aspirations."

The Jewish delegates expressed their appreciation for this statement, which was precisely and sincerely expressed.

The minutes of the April 4, 1922 meeting, report that the special messenger who conveyed Dr. Weizmann's instructions "expressed Dr. Weizmann's great desire to witness the establishment of the combined commission, which should begin work as early as possible." The Arab delegates received this statement with satisfaction.

The messenger added that Dr. Weizmann was very pleased at the progress of the negotiations between the Jews and the Arabs and would be happy if they could reach complete agreement. His chief desire had always been to achieve an agreement with the Arabs. At the moment his work had kept him in Rome, but as soon as he had completed it he would come to Cairo to take part in the negotiations. If by any chance he could come, he would be very glad to be able to meet with the members of the Arab executive in order to ratify the agreement with his signature. If there was any need to prove his intense desire for cooperation with the Arabs, his negotiations with His Majesty King Faisal in London would testify to this.

In his reply, the president of the Arab executive expressed gratitude to Dr. Weizmann and declared that he did not doubt the sincerity of his desire to work together with the Arabs. Indeed, they were aware of the negotiations he had had with His Majesty King Faisal. The way to agreement and cooperation was now open. We must approach it with trust and sincerity. There are a number of Arabs, Moslem and Christian, who believe that the Jewish state is doomed to destruction and shall never arise. We believe and desire the opposite of this, and, as for myself, I gave expression to this opinion in my annotations on the Koran.

In his testimony before the Commission of Enquiry in 1937, A. Sapir indicated that in the spring of 1922 there was great trepidation in the Jewish community of Palestine; everyone feared riots much more serious and widespread than those of 1921. The information available to Jewish bodies confirmed this fear. "In accordance with the promise of the Arab delegation at the Cairo conference, Sheik Kamil was sent to Palestine to convince the Arabs not to permit disturbances. The result was that 1922 was one of the most peaceful and tranquil years since the British Mandate."

Negotiations were suspended at this stage. Representatives of the British government asked Dr. Weizmann to postpone the negotiations until after the Mandate had been ratified. In September of the same year, after ratification of the Mandate, negotiations were resumed in Geneva. For the Jewish side, Dr. Weizmann appointed A. Sapir and H. M. Kalvarisky. The Arab participants were Emir Habib Lutfalla, King Hussain's representative in Europe, and Shakib Arslan and Ihsan Al-Jabiri, members of the Syrian Palestinian delegation.

By agreement of both parties, a résumé of the discussions was drawn up, stating:

The discussions will serve as general underlying principles for a proposed agreement between Arabs and Jews. The discussions [held on September 7 and 8, 1922] achieved the following results:

1. Arabs and Jews consider each other a force to be reckoned with. These forces are capable of helping each other actively and successfully for the realization of their aspirations. If they work together rather than separately, it is within their power to achieve results that are very desirable to both sides.

2. In order to facilitate the negotiations of details with the purpose of reaching agreement, and in order to avoid bitterness, it would be most desirable for the Jewish organization handling the negotiations not to utilize, as a basis or premise, either the Balfour Declaration of November 2, 1917, or the Mandate as ratified by the Council of the League of Nations. On their part, the Arabs will not make use of the 1915 treaty between Great Britain and Hejaz.

3. The two parties will discuss details of the agreement based on mutual help and cooperation for the benefit to all Arab countries, i.e., Syria and Iraq, as well as Palestine.

4. Arabs and Jews will determine the text of a declaration concerning the particulars between the Jews and Palestine. This statement will be so formulated as to indicate clearly the connection between the Jews and Palestine, as well as the rights of the Arab residents of Palestine. The fundamental basis of this statement shall be complete and definite equality of all inhabitants irrespective of racial or religious differences.

5. The Jews, for their part, will help the Arabs of the above-mentioned countries

economically and politically, and with all other means at their command, to achieve, by all legal constitutional means, the realization of the ultimate aspirations of these countries.

6. The two sides must find common ground for an agreement that shall unite them for the benefit of both peoples, the Arabs and the Jews, who belong to one race and who speak almost the same language and have the same culture, i.e., Oriental culture. Both sides should aspire to the revival of the pride and glory of the ancient Semitic and Oriental civilization that has contributed so much to the world, and for the benefit of these countries, which have been neglected and despoiled for hundreds of years. Both sides should use all means at their disposal to prevent a rift between them, to prevent the failure of the negotiations. Finally, they must reach a definite and sincere agreement between the two peoples whose interests, public and private, moral and material, are intertwined.

7. Both sides must use all means at their disposal to find a way to regulate and define immigration to Palestine, or to any other Arab country, in a manner satisfactory to both sides.

8. In order to facilitate agreement and render possible its implementation the two parties intend to take the following steps immediately:

(a) A cease-fire must be declared immediately in order to put an end to the hostile anti-Jewish propaganda in Palestine. Further, the political hatred and sabotage of Jews and Arabs against each other outside of Palestine must stop at once.

(b) A mixed commission must be set up immediately. It will be composed of representatives of the Syrian-Palestine Congress, and of Palestinian Moslems and Christians, and of representatives of the Zionist organization, which, if it so desires, shall be empowered to admit other influential figures in Jewish circles. This mixed commission will work out all details of the proposed agreement in accordance with the principles outlined above.

(c) When the final agreement has been determined, in all its details, and accepted by both sides, a new mixed commission will be formed, representing both sides and charged with carrying out the agreement. The mixed commission assigned to prepare the proposed agreement will decide on the form of the second mixed commission, its composition and other details. The second mixed commission shall be called the "Executive Committee."

(d) Both parties agree that in order to make it possible for the delegations to achieve the desired results, it is imperative to keep secret all details of the negotiations and discussions between the two parties. Only the participants in the negotiations may know the details until a final agreement has been reached.

Dr. Weizmann approved the negotiations. Nonetheless, matters never reached the stage of working out practical details. Why? According to A. Sapir's evidence, the negotiations were halted after Dr. Weizmann submitted a complete report of their content and essence to the British minister in Rome.

Something similar in the evolution of relations within the Jewish-Arab-English triangle occurred some two years later. David Tidhar, then acting in Egypt for the political department of the Zionist Executive in Jerusalem, reports in his memoirs, published in 1938:

In 1924, Dr. Chaim Weizmann visited Cairo. He was anxious to take advantage of this visit for the benefit of Zionism. Consequently he asked the celebrated lawyer Leon Castro [a Jew and a Zionist] to arrange an interview for him with the Egyptian leader Saad Zaglul Pasha. Dr. Weizmann wanted to obtain a declaration in favor of Zionism from him. Mr. Castro, a personal friend of Zaglul Pasha's, had helped the Egyptian *Wafd* through propaganda in the European press. He arranged the appointment for 5 p.m., and meanwhile Dr. Weizmann went for lunch at the residence of the British High Commission. Out of loyalty to England, he mentioned at lunch that he had an appointment at 5 with Zaglul Pasha and that he intended to obtain a pro-Zionist statement from the Egyptian leader. Zaglul Pasha was then considered an enemy of England, having fought for the freedom of his people and his country, and the colonial office did not, therefore, want him to issue a pro-Zionist document. They consequently advised Dr. Weizmann to cancel the appointment. Naturally loyalty [to Britain] won. The Weizmann-Zaglul meeting did not take place.

Another Example: Transjordan and the Jews

When the British Mandate on Palestine, based on the Balfour Declaration, was ratified, the territory covered also included Transjordan to the east. The White Paper of June 1922 severed it from Palestine and closed it to Jewish immigration and settlement. Although it was forced to accept the White Paper, the Zionist Organization saw no justification for barring Transjordan to the Jews. The Thirteenth Zionist Congress (August 1923)—the first to take place after publication of the White Paper—included the following among its resolutions:

"Recognizing that eastern and western Palestine are in reality and *de facto* one unit historically, geographically, and economically, the Congress expresses its expectation that the future of Transjordan shall be determined in accordance with the legitimate demands of the Jewish people."

The population of Transjordan at that time was only about 200,000—for the most part Bedouin nomads. The country was badly in need of trained people, development, initiative, and the capital investment that it could obtain from Jewish immigration. Emir Abdullah visited London at the end of 1922, in an effort to increase the £180,000 annual grant-in-aid promised by the British government. In the course of five conversations with Dr. Weizmann and some of Dr. Weizmann's close friends, he sought to establish whether he could get Zionist support for his Emirate over all of Palestine (on both sides of the Jordan), on condition that he guarantee the implementation of the Balfour Declaration and the Jewish national home policy. Partial confirmation of this is to be found in the Emir's interview with a journalist representing the *Falastin*, shortly after returning from England. "This proposal," writes Medzini, "was greeted with approval by the leaders of the Zionist Executive in London present at the conversations with the Emir; not only Dr. Weizmann, but even the extremist Jabotinsky was prepared to support the idea of Abdullah's Emirate over Palestine." However, one of the primary conditions set by the Zionist leaders was the prior approval of Great Britain. And "just as eight months earlier," writes Medzini, "a British veto stopped the Cairo negotiations, so now, once again, an 'injunction' stopped the negotiations with Emir Abdullah."

Indeed, in subsequent years, when Transjordanian Arabs visiting the country west of Jordan saw the changes that had taken place there due to Jewish immigration and settlement they often expressed regret (see Chapter Seven) over the failure of the Jews to come to Transjordan. Characteristic of such regret, even though its main object was to encourage Palestine Arab capitalists to further the economic development of Transjordan, was an article in *Mira'at-Ash-Shark* (Mirror of the East),* on May 1, 1935:

> What do Palestinian Arabs think, when they ask Transjordanian Arabs not to sell their lands? Do they think Transjordan is inhabited by "superior beings" who can withstand the temptation? The people see how the Arabs of Palestine live in comfort, while they, residents of Transjordan, are subject to poverty and hunger. If you think Transjordanian Arabs will object to the Jews, you are mistaken. There is a limit to everything. . . . The people of Transjordan will be the first to demand the abrogation of the law forbidding foreigners to buy land in Transjordan, for they cannot exist without foreign capital.

If such views could be expressed in writing during the thirties, when Arab-Jewish tension was most acute, it is not hard to imagine what the situation was like during the twenties. Colonel Kish's diary records interesting details regarding an official visit paid on January 24, 1924, to Amman, by an official delegation from Palestine (consisting of Colonel Kish, Chief Rabbi Meir, David Yellin, M. P. Hasson, and Avinoam Yellin), which was received cordially and respectfully by King Hussain (then on a visit to his son Abdullah, the Emir of Transjordan, in Amman). After a greeting delivered by Chief Rabbi Meir, David Yellin conveyed to the King the greetings and good wishes of the Jewish community of Palestine, adding that it was the desire of the Jews to cooperate with their Arab brothers for the common good of the two peoples. Yellin recalled that the two Semitic peoples had always been united, especially in the Middle Ages, when Europe was still engulfed in darkness and the Jews and Arabs carried the banner of civilization. As a mark of respect to the Jewish religion, the King awarded the Chief Rabbi the Order of *al-Istiklal* (independence) and Colonel Kish expressed his gratitude to the King for this honor.

* This newspaper, founded in 1919 by Boulus Shehadah, a Christian Arab, sometimes served as the organ of opposition circles.

In reply to the statement of the Jewish delegation conveying the determination of the Jewish people to carry out its national revival in Palestine in friendship and cooperation with their Arab brothers, the King replied that "the Arabs will always be on the side of justice. They rose against the Turks because they wanted to defend their rights. The Arabs are willing to accept the help of the Jews to this end. He himself would never discriminate against Jews. His heart was open to the Jews, and so were the hearts of his people. He was prepared to give the Jews land without charge so long as they came in through the door and did not break down the walls. The future would bring emphatic proof of his sincerity and show that the Jews have no reason to fear the Arabs."

At a later meeting that day with Emir Abdullah, David Yellin asked the Emir to use his influence with Palestinian Arabs to dispell the misunderstanding between them and the Jews. The Emir replied that "in earlier talks with Zionist leaders, including Dr. Weizmann, he had already announced his friendly attitude, but it seemed to him that the actions of the Zionists belie their words." After a discussion of the intentions of the Jews in Palestine and the assurance of Arab rights, the Emir stated that "if only Arab rights were assured, the Arabs will welcome the Jews not only in Palestine but also in the other Arab countries."

In favoring the entry of the Jews into Transjordan, Emir Abdullah was faithfully expressing the desire of many people in the country he ruled. Although he himself was under the control of the British resident and his staff in the Emirate, he mustered the courage to state his views clearly:

Palestine is one unit. The division between Palestine and Transjordan is artificial and wasteful. We, the Arabs and the Jews, can come to terms and live together in peace in the whole country, but you will have difficulty in reaching an understanding with Palestinian Arabs. You must make an alliance with us, the Arabs of Iraq, Transjordan, and Arabia. We are poor and you are rich. Please come to Transjordan. I guarantee your safety. Together we will work for the benefit of the country.*

When the White Paper was issued on October 21, 1930, certain Moslem circles began to explore the idea of possible arbitration between the Jews and the Arabs. In a conversation with Ovadia Camhi,† a member of the Central Moslem Committee (whose chairman was the former Khedive,‡ Abbas

---

* From the Emir's statement of August 18, 1926, to Dr. Saul Mizan, the head of the Jewish unions for the League of Nations, quoted in *Zionism, the Treasure of Political Documents*, No. 390 (Hebrew).

† Camhi, who had extensive connections in the Arab world, was editor of *Menorah* and Paris correspondent of the Hebrew daily *Doar Hayom* in the early twenties. Details on these exchanges will be found in his series of articles, "Attempts at Agreement between Arabs and Jews," in *Echo of the East*, (1950), Issues 25–28.

‡ *Khedive* (from Persian, meaning "master"): The title of the ruler of Egypt, conferred by Constantinople on Ismail Pasha in 1866 under pressure of western powers, to stress

Hilmi) expressed the opinion that "the time has come to make peace between Jews and Arabs" and proposed a meeting between his committee and Jewish representatives. Camhi communicated this to Dr. Weizmann, who arranged to meet Abbas Hilmi, then in Paris. Their meeting took place on November 15, 1930. Abbas Hilmi spoke of the common origin of the Jews and Arabs and of the contribution of Judaism to Islam. He noted with regret the hatred developing between the two peoples in Palestine ("the two peoples are incited against each other"), hinted at intemperate references to the Arabs at the Zionist Congress in Zurich, but added that "there is no fundamental reason against cooperation between the two peoples." In his opinion, the proper course would be to enlist the help of Hussain's sons, Faisal (then King of Iraq) and Abdullah (Emir of Transjordan). Weizmann agreed in principle with Abbas Hilmi's approach, and recalled the significant effects of the cooperation between the two peoples in the days of the Baghdad Caliphate and in Spain. There was no reason why they should not cooperate once more, he said. Weizmann also reported to the ex-Khedive about his meetings and agreement with Faisal towards the end of the World War. Nothing insulting to the Arabs had been said at the Zurich Congress, he assured him. If Hilmi would examine what had really been said there, he would be persuaded of this. The two men agreed to meet ten days later in Cannes after Weizmann's return from London. Meanwhile Hilmi's secretary, Mahmud Azmi, was sent to Palestine. Weizmann was unable to go to Cannes, however, and sent Harry Sacher (a British Zionist, lawyer and journalist, later a member of the Zionist Executive), who was then on holiday in Cannes, as deputy for him. In the ensuing conversation no meeting of minds took place, and the aim was not furthered.

On January 18, 1931, Azmi reported to Camhi on his visit to Palestine and his conferences with Arab and Jewish leaders there. In meetings with Arab newspaper editors, the possibility of publishing a large Arab paper was discussed; the paper would urge a bi-national Palestine as part of a joint confederation with Transjordan, Iraq, and perhaps Egypt as well. He was pleased to find sympathy and willingness to participate in such a project. In Weizmann's letters, (dated January 23, 1931, from Switzerland, and February 1, 1931, from London) Camhi was asked to go to Tunis, where Abbas Hilmi was at the time, to request his help in arranging meetings with Arab personalities in Palestine, which Weizmann was intending to visit at the end of February. He also requested that Hilmi's secretary, Mahmud Azmi,

the special status of Egypt in the Ottoman Empire. Thereafter, Egypt was no longer subject to the laws of the Empire, and the Khedive was empowered to formulate his own laws and exercise some degree of political sovereignty. In December 1914, the British removed Khedive Abbas Hilmi, who was friendly to the Turks and Germans, and appointed as successor his aged uncle Hussain Kamil, with the added title of "Sultan" to emphasize the separation of Egypt from Turkey.

should then be in Palestine. Camhi went to London for discussion with Weizmann. In the course of these talks, he discerned Weizmann's intention of offering the Arab states and Palestine economic cooperation and support for their confederation, if the unhampered development of the Jewish venture in Palestine were assured. Among the items discussed was a Jewish-Arab newspaper, in which eminent persons of both nations would take part (Freud and Einstein were among the Jews mentioned), and a round table conference in London. Abbas Hilmi was asked to write a letter of recommendation to Emir Abdullah, on whom Weizmann wished to call in Amman.

Camhi left to find Abbas Hilmi, who had meanwhile gone to Algiers, and they had talks at the Saint George Hotel on February 21 and 22, 1931. Abbas Hilmi complained that Sacher had "buttoned up" during the whole meeting and "wanted only to listen without opening his mouth." For that reason, he had not met him a second time but requested Azmi to take his place ("out of respect to Dr. Weizmann"). "In a conversation of this sort what is needed is frankness and cordiality. They tell him [Hilmi] that he should abandon the attempt at Arab-Jewish *rapprochement*, for fear of Arab contempt, but he has become deeply involved in the task. Faisal and Abdullah conferred in Amman and at his request discussed the Arab-Jewish question." Abbas Hilmi promised to send Azmi to Palestine again and to ask Emir Abdullah to arrange a grand reception for Dr. Weizmann.

According to Camhi, a program agreed upon by the former Khedive and Dr. Weizmann was planned. There would be a round-table conference, and a combined committee of prominent people would be formed. An Arab daily newspaper in Palestine would foster cooperation. As Arab members of the committee, Azmi suggested Ahmad Lutfi as-Said (Rector of the Egyptian University and former minister of education), Dr. Taha Hussain (one of the spiritual giants of the contemporary Arab world), Dr. Enani (Professor of Semitic languages at the Ecole Normale Superieure in Egypt), Ahmad Zaki Pasha (see Chapter Seven), Ahmad Shauki (among the greatest Egyptian poets), Ali Abd-ul-Razak (a Moslem scholar, whose call for the separation of church and state caused a storm in Egypt in the twenties), the famous Iraqi poets Ar-Resafi and Az-Zahawi, and others.

On March 26, 1931, during a visit to Palestine, Dr. Weizmann was invited to dine with Emir Abdullah at Amman. Preparations were made to receive Dr. Weizmann and his party with all due honors. When the Syrian newspapers began to inveigh against the invitation, it was officially stated that the visit was not political in character, but rather an expression of respect to King Hussain (Abdullah's father), who was then in Transjordan, and who was a friend of Dr. Weizmann. However, a day before the appointed meeting in Amman, Mr. Mark Young, the Chief Secretary of the Palestine government, addressed the following letter to Dr. Weizmann:

Dear Dr. Weizmann,

      I have just learned that you were about to travel to Amman to see Emir Abdullah. I should like to inform you that the time is not right for this, and moreover I must add that the government cannot assume responsibility for your life during your visit to Transjordan. I should also like to point out that we shall not in the future be able to assume responsibility for your personal safety in Transjordan.[3]

Anyone familiar with the rules of hospitality in Oriental countries will appreciate how slight was the so-called "danger" facing Dr. Weizmann under these circumstances: he was to be on an official visit to Amman at the invitation of Emir Abdullah. The chief secretary's letter, which ruled out a visit to Transjordan not only at the time of writing but also at any other time "in the future," should go far to explain why any attempt at a negotiated settlement was doomed to failure.

This was true not only in the twenties. A statement of Emir Abdullah's to the correspondent of the Jewish Telegraphic Agency in March 1933 includes the following sentence: "The Jews of the whole world will find me to be a new Lord Balfour, and even more than this; Balfour gave the Jews a country that was not his; I promise a country that is mine."[4] It is no coincidence that Arabs from Transjordan who had meetings and friendly relations with Jewish public figures in Jerusalem and elsewhere during the thirties and forties were very careful not to let the British authorities find out.

The author can add a personal experience from the forties: On June 19, 1946, at the suggestion of the late Fauzi al-Hussaini, the author—then Secretary of the League for Jewish-Arab *Rapprochement* and Cooperation— met with a prominent Arab from Transjordan. The Arab reported that there was growing pressure on Transjordanian leaders to agree to the settlement of large numbers of Polish (non-Jewish) refugees in the northern Irbid-Mafrak district, along the oil pipeline from Iraq—an idea to which there was widespread opposition. Many Transjordanians believed, the man said, that if they had to accept outside settlers, it would be preferable to accept the Jews. In contrast to the Poles, the Jews were close to the Arabs in race; their capabilities had been demonstrated in Palestine; they would bring in capital, experts, and initiative, and develop the area east of the Jordan, just as they had done for the country west of the river. The Poles were strangers to the Arabs, would not bring in capital, would live on a meager British grant, would not develop the country, and could only have a bad influence. (At that time certain elements of the Polish refugee population that passed through from Teheran to Palestine had been accused of stealing, seducing women, etc.) The man proposed exchanges with Transjordan leaders on the possibility of Jewish settlement in their territory.

The suggestion was brought to the attention of the head of the Jewish Agency's Arab department, but to no avail. The British authorities, who considered settling Poles in Transjordan, did not even entertain the idea of Jewish settlement in that area, whose population would have been pleased to receive them.

Encouraging Arab Opposition to the Jews

One of the major objectives of the British Mandatory administration was to encourage the Arabs to resist the national home policy. Even the report of the Shaw Commission of Enquiry (1930) includes accusations that high government officials played a part in the anti-Jewish outbreaks of the early twenties. Nor did things improve afterward. In the 1929 riots, within a few days 135 Jews had been killed by Arabs and about 350 wounded, in Jerusalem, Hebron, Safed, and Jewish villages, before the government took measures to restore order. When, however, in 1933, the Arabs demonstrated against the British but refrained from attacking Jews in the course of the demonstration, the government managed to muster sufficient forces to put an immediate and decisive end to the disturbances.

Shortly after the 1929 riots, a British officer Gordon Kenning arrived, ostensibly "to study the situation in Palestine." This visitor made no attempt to conceal his intentions. At meetings with Arabs, he called for "a fight against coercion," and for the dispatch of an Arab delegation to London. Shortly afterward, an Arab delegation indeed left for London—for the first time in seven years—for political negotiations. A number of its members remained in London to continue their political activities. They also established in London a propaganda office headed by the veteran Pan-Arabist Emir Adil Arslan, Dr. Izzat Tannous (of Nablus, who was born in 1895, studied in Beirut and London, and then settled in Jerusalem), and Jamal al-Hussaini. Kenning, whom the late Fakhri Nashashibi considered worthy of the name Muhammad Gordon Kenning, sent a telegram to the British Prime Minister on Armistice Day stating that if the demands of the Arab leaders in Palestine were not met, it "will be impossible to maintain order and security even with military weapons." . . . After spending two weeks in Palestine, he appeared at a gathering in Cairo's National Hotel, where he described Palestine as "entirely Arab," and stated that the country's urgent need was the abolition of the Balfour Declaration.

Throughout, the government evinced an attitude of tolerance toward various Arab extremists who engaged, not only in incitement against the Jews, but also in terror and violence directed against those Arabs who aspired to understanding and cooperation between the two peoples. The Royal Commission for Palestine (the Peel Commission, 1937), testifies to this in its report (Chapter 5, paragraph fifty-five): "If one thing stands out clearly from the record of the Mandatory administration, it is the leniency with which Arab political agitation, even when carried to the point of violence and murder, has been treated."

The political tolerance toward Arab terrorism and the Mufti is all the more astounding when it is recalled that the British authorities in India had no compunction about imprisoning Mahatma Ghandi and his friends, who headed the great Indian national movement with hundreds of millions of members. Why was there such respect for the Mufti of Jerusalem and his men, responsible as they undoubtedly were for the shedding of so much blood—Jewish and Arab—in Palestine? Among the many laws passed by the Mandatory government in Palestine (mainly to limit the freedom of residents and new immigrants), there is not a single one defining nationalist incitement of any kind as criminal. There was never a prohibition against publishing newspapers, or founding organizations, aimed at deepening and widening the gulf between the two peoples. In a country where two peoples lived side by side, the censors and the government invariably showed unlimited tolerance for insulting and provocative articles written in the press of one of the peoples against the other. Yet the same censors were often excessively strict in their suppression of any attempt on the part of the other group to refute this propaganda and to bring to light the intrigues and plots of those who were sowing suspicion and fostering enmity between the two peoples.

Following the riots of 1929, an organization called "Workers' Fraternity" was established by Jewish and Arab workers who called on the workers of both peoples to help each other and fight together against the poison of national hatred. The government suppressed the group on the grounds that "there is reason to believe its members will engage in destructive activities." Another example of this approach is the censors' deletion, in an Arabic pamphlet issued by the *Hashomer Hatzair* and the Socialist League on May 1, 1942, of the following slogans: ". . . a united Jewish-Arab front to fight the danger of Nazism and Fascism abroad and the fifth column at home;" ". . . for the solidarity of the workers of both peoples in ensuring laws for the protection of the worker, his wages and working conditions;" ". . . for a political regime that will prevent the ascendency of one people over another and ensure the development of the country for the common good of both peoples;" ". . . to establish a common socialist front of workers, fellaheen, intellectuals, and all those in favor of progress among the Arabs and Jews in Palestine." From the slogan "Long live the joint solidarity of the workers of both peoples!" the words "joint" and "of both peoples" were deleted. When the author of this book protested against these deletions to the Jerusalem censor ('Ajaj Nuwaihid, of Syrian Druze origin), the cynical reply was that "In war time, you can write about war, but as to calls for Arab-Jewish peace and cooperation—the time is not ripe."*

By the late twenties, the Jewish prospects in Palestine had already begun

* The pamphlet, with the censor's deletions, is in the author's files; the conversation with the censor is recorded in a diary entry.

to exceed the bounds acceptable to the British authorities. The disturbances of August 1929 were a grim overture to this second period in the history of British rule in Palestine.

Shortly after the riots, in September 1929, the secretary of state appointed a parliamentary commission of enquiry composed of Sir Walter Shaw as chairman, and three Conservative, Liberal, and Labour members of the British House of Commons. The commission was charged with "ascertaining the reasons for the recent outbreak in Palestine and proposing steps to be taken in order to prevent such outbreaks in the future." The report of the commission (from which Henry Snell, the Labour M.P., dissented) absolved the government from responsibility for the riots and held that they were caused by the fears of the Arab population for its political and economic rights in light of the development of the Jewish national home. It hinted that, in order to avoid a recurrence of the riots, there was need to restrict Jewish immigration and limit the rights of Jews to purchase land, stating that "it would be most desirable to make basic changes in the constitution in order to gain the confidence of the Arab community and thus make the task of the Palestine authorities easier"—a reference to transferring some of the control of Palestine to an elected legislative body, in which the Arabs would have an assured majority. The commission's findings tended to aggravate the national conflict in Palestine by stressing "the danger of dispossession of the fellaheen from their land." On May 6, 1930, Sir John Hope Simpson, formerly a colonial civil servant, was appointed to head a commission sent by the British government to investigate questions of immigration, settlement, and the development of Palestine. On May 27, a new White Paper was issued that: (a) accepted in principle the Shaw Commission's findings on the basic question of Palestine policy; (b) reaffirmed the Mandatory's dual obligations toward Arabs as well as Jews; (c) promised a revision of land and immigration policy; (d) ruled that no steps toward Palestinian self-government were to be taken except in accordance with the needs defined in the Mandate; (e) stated that a detailed policy would be determined and announced after receipt of Simpson's report.

On October 21, 1930, the Simpson report was published along with the official government statement (the Passfield white paper). On the basis of an "examination"—and this from a plane that covered about 10 percent of the area under discussion—Simpson reduced the land area in the mountains suitable for cultivation by 60 percent; he reduced the cultivable land in Palestine as a whole from 12.2 million *dunams* (3,050,000 acres) to 8 million *dunams* (2 million acres), or 6.5 million *dunams* (1,625,000 acres) outside the Beersheba area. By considering all residents of agricultural regions as farmers, and by adopting a low figure (5.5 people) for the number of individuals per family, he exaggerated the number of Arab families engaged in agriculture.

By figuring the income of the Arab fellah on the basis of the lower-than-normal 1930 average, and the expenses on the basis of the higher-than-normal 1925–1926 average, and by making erroneous and arbitrary use of data arrived at by Johnson-Crosby (in a survey of 104 Arab villages with a total population of 23,473), Simpson decided that the land unit needed to support an Arab tenant farmer family was 130 *dunams* (32.5 acres), and that, according to these calculations, 29.4 percent of Arab farm families had insufficient land.*

Land ownership in the Arab community of Palestine was a serious problem, as it was in the other Arab countries. According to Johnson-Crosby's survey, 31.8 percent of the Arab farm community were tenant farmers. On the other hand, tremendous tracts of land were concentrated in the hands of prominent families: the Abd-ul-Hadis had 60,000 *dunams* (15,000 acres), the Al-Hussainis and At-Tajis 50,000 *dunams* (12,500 acres) each, the Abu-Khadras and Ash-Shawas 30,000 *dunams* (7,500 acres) each. The attempt to blame Jewish immigration for the poverty of the Arab villages was a manifestly inflammatory tactic. Even official data five years later showed that of the 1,481,000 *dunams* (370,000 acres) in Jewish hands, 350,000 *dunams* (87,500 acres) were swampland (included in the category of "uncultivable land"), and 500,000 *dunams* (125,000 acres) were lands never before cultivated. The Jewish community, which then constituted 29 percent of the total population, held only 5.5 percent of the total land area west of the Jordan (27,000,000 *dunams*, or 6,750,000 acres), and only 11 percent of the area defined as "arable." The land that had been farmed previously and then acquired for Jewish settlement constituted not more than 638,000 *dunams* (159,500 acres), or 6.3 percent of the land considered to be arable. Tenant farmers who had formerly been settled on that land received compensation and generally found new sources of livelihood from the economic opportunities that had developed in Palestine along with Jewish immigration.

According to the data assembled by M. Smilansky at the request of Andrews (see Chapter Seven) for the Peel Commission, in March, 1936, the Jews held 1,231,900 *dunams* (307,750 acres) of land they had purchased, and 161,800 *dunams* (40,450 acres) on lease from the government, a total of 1,393,700 *dunams* (348,200 acres). Out of the acreage purchased, 1,125,000 *dunams* (281,250 acres), or 91.3 percent, had been acquired from land owners (including 443,000 *dunams*, or 110,750 acres—or 39.4 percent—from persons residing

---

* The investigator had nothing to say on several essential facets of the problem such as, the percentage of landless Arab families in neighboring countries; the reasons for "landlessness" in such sparsely populated countries; the land area required to support a farm family under conditions of farm development (irrigation, efficient equipment, the use of organic and chemical fertilizer, improvement of breeds, agricultural guidance, cooperative buying and selling, adequate agricultural credit, etc.).

in Egypt and Syria), and only 106,900 *dunams* (46,725 acres) or 8.7 percent from the fellaheen.

Before the Balfour Declaration, according to Smilansky, 564,000 *dunams* (141,000 acres) had been purchased by Jews, and following the Declaration, 667,900 *dunams* (166,975 acres). But the Simpson report was the basis for the Passfield White Paper, the gist of which was that there was no unoccupied land in Palestine for the settlement of new immigrants—and if there were, the government would have to give it to landless Arabs. At all events, the Arab "need" was stressed in order to prevent the purchase of additional land by Jews. The employment of Jewish workers in jobs undertaken with Jewish Agency funds was "opposed to the provisions of the Mandate." For that reason, additional Jewish immigration would not be permitted "so long as it might deprive any Arab of the opportunity of getting work." In regard to the constitution, "His Majesty's Government has arrived at the considered opinion that the time has come to pursue without delay the solution of the important problem of initiating some measure of self-government in Palestine, for the benefit of the entire Palestinian population." It was clear, however, that there was no intention of transferring the actual control of Palestine to the elected legislative council referred to; it was enough that so long as the Arab leaders were not prepared to recognize the essential national rights and aspirations of the Jews in Palestine, the Jews would never agree to any legislative body that could be used by the Arab majority in it as an instrument for freezing the Jewish endeavor in Palestine for purely political reasons. The High Commission, in any case, was assured of the necessary powers "to ensure the ability of the Mandatory government to carry out its obligations toward the League of Nations, including also the promulgation of urgently needed laws and the maintenance of order in Palestine."

The White Paper shocked the Jewish public.* As a protest against the declared anti-Zionist policy of the government, Dr. Chaim Weizmann resigned his position as president of the Zionist Organization and head of the Jewish Agency for Palestine. Felix Warburg and Lord Melchett likewise resigned from the Jewish Agency executive, and Baron Edmond de Rothschild "expressed his complete agreement with their act." In a letter to Secretary of State Lord Passfield, Dr. Weizmann wrote that "the White Paper is striding toward abrogation of the rights and eradication of the hopes of the Jewish people in regard to the Jewish national home in Palestine," freezing the development of the national home in its current dimensions and providing no basis for cooperation between the Jewish Agency and His Majesty's Government.

This was the first schism between the Zionist leaders and the British

* In his memoirs (*Trial and Error*, p. 413), Dr. Weizmann wrote, of the same Passfield White Paper: "it was considered by all Jewish friends of the National Home, Zionist

authorities—evidence of an antagonism that was to grow as the condition of European Jews worsened under Fascist persecution and as the need for immigration became more and more pressing.

The vehement protest of Jews outside Palestine as well as within it, and the severe criticism of British government policy voiced in all parts of the world—and not least in the United Kingdom itself—somewhat startled the Cabinet in London. After some negotiation between representatives of the Jewish Agency and a ministerial committee appointed by the government,* a letter from Prime Minister Ramsay MacDonald to Dr. Chaim Weizmann was issued on February 13, 1931, "authoritatively interpreting" the Passfield White Paper of October 1930: "The obligation to facilitate Jewish immigration and make possible dense settlement of Jews on the land is still a positive obligation of the Mandate, and it can be fulfilled without jeopardizing the rights and conditions of the other parts of the Palestine population;" the landless Arabs mentioned in the White Paper are "Arabs who can be shown to have been dispossessed of their land when it passed to the Jews without receiving other land to settle or equally satisfactory work;" in contradistinction to Simpson's arbitrariness, the number of such Arabs "requires careful investigation" (and is not 29.4 percent as the investigating expert had determined with such precision).† An investigation into government land and other lands available for Jewish settlement was promised,

and non-Zionist alike, and by a host of non-Jewish well-wishers, as rendering, and intending to render, our work in Palestine impossible."

* In *Trial and Error* (p. 412), Dr. Weizmann described the tense atmosphere in the negotiations between representatives of the Jewish people and the British government: "In a very polite way I charged Passfield openly with a breach of faith. His Lordship never said a word or moved a muscle. I added one strong sentence. I said: 'One thing the Jews will never forgive, and that is having been fooled.' The Prime Minister smiled, and it also brought a broad grin on the faces of the officials. Thereupon I turned to them and said: 'I can't understand how you, as good British patriots, don't see the moral implications of promises given to Jews, and I regret to see that you seem to deal with them rather frivolously.' The grin disappeared."

† Lewis French was commissioned to make a survey of Arab "landlessness" and unemployment. After a great deal of work on the part of the Arab Executive and its assistants from among British officials, he received no more than 3,188 applications, of which 2,618 were invalidated by the government's own legal adviser, leaving only 570. The myth of dispossession that loomed so large in the Shaw commission report was thus proved to have been baseless, if the number of persons that had to be resettled over twelve years was as small as 600. The figure of 600 meant a yearly average of fifty dispossessed Arabs and was certainly insignificant compared to the many thousands of Arabs who found new sources of livelihood in the expanded markets for agricultural produce, the expanded opportunities for supplying building materials, and the increased employment in public works resulting from the larger government revenue accruing from Jewish immigration and Jewish enterprises in Palestine. When the government acquired some land on which to resettle these people, only about one hundred responded; about forty of these later left the new settlement.

and assurance was given that the prohibition of additional land purchase by Jews was not part of government policy: "The reasons for limits on absorptive capacity [in regard to new immigrants] are exclusively economic. . . . His Majesty's Government does not intend to interrupt or prohibit immigrants of any of the various categories. . . . Immigrants who can expect to obtain work, even of a temporary nature, will not be excluded from immigration for the sole reason that they are not assured of work for an unlimited period." The right of the Jewish Agency to employ Jewish labor on projects utilizing its funds was recognized. As for public and municipal jobs financed by public funds, "the demand of Jewish workers for a fair share of the work available will be taken into account, in view of Jewish contributions to government revenue." In sum: "The obligations laid upon the Mandatory Government are solemn international promises, and there is no intention at present, as there was not in the past, of disregarding them."

Despite the retraction of the Passfield white paper implicit in the MacDonald letter, the Passfield policy of more or less "scuttling" the Balfour Declaration obligations continued to guide His Majesty's Government. Active help for the establishment of the Jewish national home no longer formed a part of British policy; any casual measure in that direction was taken only under pressure of public opinion in Britain and in the world, or when required in order to maintain a semblance of equilibrium between Arabs and Jews. It was during this period that British policy took advantage of certain "bones of contention" between Arabs and Jews for its own ends. The first of these bones of contention was the Wailing Wall incident. On the Day of Atonement, 1928, the police, on orders from the Assistant District Commissioner of Jerusalem, burst through the crowd of worshippers at the Wailing Wall and removed a cloth partition that had been placed there to separate the men from the women. The Zionist Executive tried to calm the agitated Jewish community, all the more furious because this arbitrary interference in a religious service had received the blessing of His Majesty's Government in London. The authorities claimed that they were bound to maintain the *status quo* and could not permit placing near the Wailing Wall appurtenances that had not always been there. The Wailing Wall incident provided the Arabs with grist for their propaganda that the Jews meant to desecrate Moslem holy places and gain control of them, since the Mosque of Omar is in the vicinity of the Wailing Wall. (This propaganda was considerably reinforced by a parade of Jewish Betar members to the Wall on the ninth of Ab that same year.) In accordance with a special recommendation by the Shaw commission in November 1929, the British government raised before the Permanent Mandate commission the question of appointing a special international commission "to decide on rights and claims in connection with the Wailing Wall." The committee reached Jerusalem on June 19, 1930, and spent a month in Palestine. The report of the Zionist Executive to the Seventeenth Congress mentioned its success in organizing a Jewish delegation to defend Jewish rights in regard to the Wailing Wall; the delegation included representatives of the Chief Rabbinate, the Jewish Agency, the Jewish community, and *Agudat Yisrael*. The public hearings of this international commission—the first since the beginning of the Mandate—added to Arab-Jewish tension. Indeed, everything connected with those inquiry commissions and special investigations of various kinds (the Shaw commission, the Wailing Wall commission, the Simpson and French commissions)— like the bloody riots that they came to investigate—inflamed passions, deepened the chasm between Jews and Arabs, and strengthened the British government in their assumed role of impartial judges. The land question, the composition of the legislative body (in which the deciding vote was to be the British High Commissioner's), and the vital issue of immigration—the keys to all of which were held by the Mandatory Government—all these served to kindle national enmity between the two peoples in Palestine and give a nightmare quality to their uneasy coexistence.

Restricting Jewish Immigration

As the disturbances of 1929 and the successive anti-Jewish restrictions that followed did not succeed in crushing the Zionist movement, the positive forces in the Jewish liberation movement became stronger. Jewish immigration had been severely restricted since the middle twenties,* for the government continued its restrictive policy after the MacDonald letter. At the center of the negotiations between the Jewish Agency and the British government was the Agency's complaint that "the method applied by the government in setting immigration quotas did not permit the Zionist endeavour to progress with the rapidity made possible by the economic development of the country and demanded by the straitened circumstances of the Jewish masses in the Diaspora." Nonetheless, the scope of Jewish immigration was growing. A total of 4,075 Jews reached Palestine in 1931; 9,553 in 1932;

* In 1925, Jewish immigration to Palestine reached its first high point—35,000— bringing the total Jewish population to 160,000. But an economic crisis occurred at the end of the year, and grew more severe during 1926 and 1927. In 1926, only 15,000 Jews immigrated, and more than 7,000 left the country. In 1927, 5,100 left. At the beginning of 1927, 8,500 Jews were officially listed as unemployed, and labor immigration was completely stopped. In 1928, emigration decreased (only 2,166 left), unemployment relief was discontinued, and, at the beginning of 1929, immigration of *Halutzim* (pioneers) was resumed (for the period between October 1928 and March 1929, 600 immigration certificates were issued). The government later cancelled most of the immigration certificates issued for the April–September 1930 period (before they were used) "pending the Simpson report."

30,227 in 1933, and 42,359 in 1934; in 1935, immigration achieved a new record of 61,584 registered Jewish immigrants.*

In a conversation with representatives of the Jewish Agency early in 1936, the government stated that the 1935 immigration had been too large, and that it was not desirable for such numbers to recur.† For the following year, the government approved less than a third of the quota demanded by the Agency. The immigration of relatives and "capitalists" (which were special categories) was likewise restricted. It should be recalled that in 1935, Nazi persecution of Jews was increasing and the immigration restrictions prevented the rescue of thousands of Jews from annihilation. In a letter to the government, the Jewish Agency characteristically wrote that the government's reduction of the immigration quotas inevitably "creates the impression, which we are certain the government does not wish to leave, that the economic absorptive capacity of the country has ceased to be the deciding factor in determining government policy in this matter."[5]

The government was not satisfied with cutting immigration quotas but also began to persecute Jews who were in Palestine without government permission—the so-called "illegal" Jewish immigrants. Tourists suspected of "intentions" to stay in the country were turned back from its ports. Later, tourists who had overstayed the date stamped in their permits were deported. Finally, there began a methodical "hunting of illegals" by the police (in 1934 more than 700 tourists were expelled), but this was discontinued after a number of clashes between the public and the police. The government thereafter deducted thousands of certificates from the approved quotas to cover tourists who had remained in the country. At the same time, the government itself admitted that some 10,000 to 15,000 Haurani Arabs had entered Palestine, in addition to other Arabs who came in from Transjordan and the Sinai desert.

The flow of immigration that burst open the closed doors of Palestine, partly as a result of the Nazi rise to power in Germany, brought with it an unusual amount of capital, initiative, talents, and skills. The total Jewish capital invested in Palestine between 1930 and 1937 amounted to £.P.

---

* As the number of immigration certificates issued by the British government was not commensurate either with development needs in the country or with immigration needs from the Diaspora, Jews began to circumvent the arbitrary restrictions and to come as tourists or "capitalists," after the amount of money necessary for receipt of an immigration certificate in this category had been deposited in their names; it was about this time that the first groups of "B-type immigration" or "Illegal immigration" were organized. These reached Palestine through Lebanon or Syria, or were disembarked from clandestine ships at deserted points on the Palestinian coasts. The number of such "illegal" immigrants until 1936 was estimated at 50,000.

† Almost from the first days of the Mandate, the British fixed "immigration quotas," determined by the "absorptive capacity" of the country.

51–52 million.[6] The restriction of immigration, however, gave rise to some disturbing factors in the economic sphere. Some workers abandoned agriculture for more lucrative pursuits, such as construction and industry, and there was an artificial rise in prices and wages. The changeover of workers from one job to another lowered the productivity of labor and impaired the occupational structure of the Jewish community in Palestine, thus endangering one of its basic objectives and greatest achievements—the transfer of Jews to productive work for the Zionist movement on the land and in industry. Nevertheless, the Jewish agricultural population grew from 27,000 to 60,000 during this period, and industrial exports expanded. The rapid progress of the Jewish enterprise in Palestine was unwelcome, however, both to the Arab leadership and to the British government. Meanwhile, with the Abyssinian crisis of autumn 1935, the danger of war seemed imminent. The British increased their courtship of the Arab leadership and their assurances of friendship (the preparation of the 1936 Anglo-Egyptian treaty of alliance, the French pacts with Syria and Lebanon in the same year). Transient economic difficulties (withdrawal of bank deposits when the Abyssinian war broke out, temporary stoppage of construction work, etc.) were used as a convenient pretext for further restrictions on Jewish immigration.

On December 22, 1935, the High Commissioner again brought up the question of the "legislative council," a perennial bone of contention between Jews and Arabs during the Mandate period.* At the beginning of 1936, the government announced restrictions on the acquisition of land by Jews. The Jewish Agency contended that, apart from leasing the Kabara swamps and a few sandy areas, and giving a Jewish group the concession of draining the Hulah swamps under the most onerous conditions, the government had done nothing about allocating government land for Jewish settlement in accordance with its obligations under the Mandate. Moreover, the government had passed a number of land laws that interfered with Jewish settlement and prevented the reclamation of desert land. The restrictive law now promulgated would place an additional serious obstacle in the path of Jewish settlement, in complete contradiction to the principal provisions of the Mandate.[7]

Despite the Jewish Agency's opposition to the government plan to establish a legislative council in Palestine, and regardless of criticism leveled at it in the British Parliament, the government continued its efforts in this matter. Arab leaders were invited to London for discussions with the Secretary of State. However, the increasingly severe competition between the Axis powers and

* The proposed composition under this plan was twenty-eight members, including five officials and twenty-three members of the public—eleven Moslem Arabs, seven Jews, three Christian Arabs, two businessmen. Of the twenty-three, eleven were to have been appointed, twelve elected.

Britain and France in the Middle East strengthened the Arab leaders' intransigence. They felt that the time was ripe, not for a mere compromise with Britain at the expense of the Jews, but for an all-out attack on the Jewish community in Palestine, in the hope of putting an end to its development. Afterward, with the help of the Axis, British rule could be done away with or a more satisfactory settlement could be reached.

Interesting details on the infiltration of Axis agents into Palestine during this period may be found in Moshe Smilansky's autobiography. Smilansky learned from his friend Abd-ur-Rahman at-Taji that the Italian consul had approached him and offered him a loan so that he would not sell his land to the Jews. Although he himself had rejected the consul's offer, "others of my people did accept such loans," he said.

The same Italian pursued similar tactics of subversion among Jews as well, offering help to overthrow British rule in Palestine and trying to alienate Jews in the established private *moshavot* from the "Bolshevik" labor settlements connected with the Jewish Agency. Oddly enough, there were Jews (such as the right-wing Revisionists) who lent a willing ear to the Italian overtures.

More Riots

Violent and widespread attacks on the Jewish community of Palestine broke out again in April 1936 and lasted until October. The Arab community, in general aware of the prosperity that had come to Palestine with Jewish immigration, was not too eager to participate in the attacks; acts of terror were carried out mainly by mercenaries, some Palestinian and some from neighboring countries. Among the Arab leadership, too, there was growing resistance to the policy of the Mufti and his supporters. Some of the opposition favored negotiating with Britain on the establishment of a legislative council and some favored trying to find a way toward an accord with the Jews.

The Mufti faction embarked upon a venomous campaign against any Arab who opposed the policy of the Higher Arab Committee,* which was set up

* The Arab Executive Committee, which was constituted in 1920, broke up after the death of Mussa Kazim al-Hussain (1934), the moving spirit of the body. The various Arab factions, hitherto little more than family groups, now reorganized themselves as political parties. In August 1932, the Istiklal party was formed under the leadership of Auni Abd-ul-Hadi (born in 1888, a lawyer and one of the early leaders of the Arab national movement against the Turks); in the same year, the Youth Congress was convened under the leadership of Muhammad Yakub al-Ghussain (born 1900, scion of a family of landowners in the Ramleh district); in December 1934, the National Defense Party (*Hazb al-defa al Watany*) was organized, with Ragheb Nashashibi (born 1880, an engineer, former member of Turkish Parliament, Mayor of Jerusalem 1920-1934) as its head; in March 1935, the Hussaini family also organized itself as a political party—The

at the time of the riots as the supreme authority representative of the Arab community in Palestine. The authorities did nothing to prevent the Mufti's faction from dominating the entire Arab community, and opposition leaders were ignored. This time acts of terror were rather better planned, under the command of Fauzi Kaukji, a Syrian officer trained in Germany. The main objectives were the disruption of communications and general obstruction of Jewish commerce. But the Jews had learned a lesson from the riots of 1929. Their defense was much better organized—on a country-wide basis, under the command of a general staff using partially trained forces organized regionally and nationally. The Jews suffered losses in dead and wounded, and also considerable damage to property, but the casualties among the attackers exceeded those of the defenders. The cutting off of the Arabs from the Jewish community caused economic difficulties to the Arabs, and when the British threatened military action (troops having been reinforced in Palestine), the Arab Higher Committee agreed to stop the riots and resume negotiations. Arrangements were made for an appeal by the heads of the Arab states to the Palestinian Arabs "to rely upon the good intentions of our friend Britain, who has declared that she will do justice." On October 11, 1936, the Arab Higher Committee announced that it would accept the proposal; Kaukji and the other mob leaders were allowed to leave the country, and the attacks stopped.

A New Enquiry Commission and the Partition Plan

On May 18, 1936—a month after the Arab attacks had begun—the Secretary of State informed the House of Commons that the government had decided to advise His Majesty "after order is restored to appoint a Royal commission, which without bringing into question the terms of the Mandate will investigate causes of unrest and alleged grievances of either Arabs or Jews." The commission was appointed on August 7, 1936, with Earl Peel as chairman,

Palestine Arab Party (*Al Hizb Al-Arabi Al Falastini*), but as Haj Amin al-Hussaini wished to retain his position as religious leader, the nominal leader was his satellite Jamal Hussaini (born 1894, teacher, government official, newspaperman). In June 1935, Dr. Hussain Khalidi (born 1895, chief medical officer in the Jerusalem district, Mayor of Jerusalem after 1934) set up the Reform Party (*Hizb Al-Islah*), and in October of the same year, the National Block (*al-Kutla al-Wataniya*) was founded under the leadership of Abd-ul Latif Salah (of Nablus, born 1880 to a family of large landowners in the Tul-Karem area, a lawyer and former member of the Supreme Moslem Council). At the end of April 1936, the Arab Higher Committee was constituted. Its president was Haj Amin Al-Hussaini, and its members included the heads of the six parties listed above and Ahmad Hilmi Pasha (born 1882, manager of the Arab Agricultural Bank, afterwards Bank Al-Umma), Alfred Rok (a Christian Arab from Jaffa, supporter of the Hussainis), and Yakub Faraj, (a Christian Arab from Jerusalem, supporter of the Hussainis). The secretary of the committee was Auni Abd-ul-Hadi.

under the following terms of reference: "To ascertain the underlying causes of the disturbances that broke out in Palestine in the middle of April; to inquire into the manner in which the Mandate for Palestine is being implemented in relation to the obligations of the Mandatory toward the Arabs and the Jews respectively; and to ascertain whether, upon a proper construction of the terms of the Mandate, either the Arabs or the Jews have any legitimate grievances on account of the way in which the Mandate has been, or is being, implemented; and if the commission is satisfied that any such grievances are well founded, to make recommendations for their removal and for the prevention of their recurrence."

On November 11th, the commission reached Palestine. It left in mid-January, 1937, after hearing and receiving in writing considerable evidence. Its report, officially released on July 7, 1937, is one of the most thorough documents in the political history of modern Palestine. Its major finding was that the Mandate was unworkable "since the aspirations of the Jews and Arabs are mutually contradictory." The commission proposed dividing Palestine into a Jewish state and an Arab state, apart from regions that were to be placed under British control—part for a limited period, part in perpetuity. The Royal commission's plan envisaged a Jewish state in a very small part of Palestine (about 5,000 square kilometers: eastern Galilee, the Jezreel valley, and the coastal plain from Tel Aviv to Acre), while most of the country was to be included in an Arab state. In order to "defend British interests and protect the holy places," it was proposed to retain a British Mandate for Jerusalem and its environs, with a corridor to the Jaffa coast, and also for Nazareth, Haifa, Safed, Acre, the Sea of Galilee, and the region near the Red Sea (Eilat, etc.). The two proposed states were to sign treaties with Britain, granting her supervision of both of them. The commission recommended an exchange of population between the two states, and also a system of financial support for the Arab state by the Jewish state and by the British government. The commission recommended the cessation of Jewish immigration for political reasons, and the prohibition of land purchase by Jews in the area set aside for an Arab state, and by Arabs in the area designated for the Jewish state, until the two states were established.

The British government accepted the idea of partition in principle "as the best and most likely solution" to the Palestine problem, and undertook to carry out the program. In the Jewish community and the Zionist movement, a sharp debate ensued around the idea of partitioning Palestine once again (after the severance of Transjordan in 1922) as a method of solving the Arab-Jewish problem and the political complications that had developed in Palestine. A majority in the Zionist Organization accepted the idea of partition in principle, on the premise that even if the territory of the Jewish state were diminished, it would be possible in this generation to develop within it unhindered—and coming generations would take care of the future. An influential Jewish minority in Palestine and in the Zionist movement rejected the idea of partition for various reasons: Some (like M. Ussishkin) thought the proposed plan an attempt to suffocate the Zionist venture in a Jewish ghetto in Palestine; these elements had no faith in the viability of a state within the proposed boundaries, nor in its capacity to solve the problems of immigration that were daily becoming more serious. Others (some of the Mizrachi religious Zionist faction) objected for religious reasons to renouncing any part of the Palestine that God had promised to Abraham's seed. The Revisionists objected in principle to the partition plan and considered it an attempt to hand most of Palestine over to the Arabs while in fact retaining the British Mandate over the territory set aside for the Jewish state. Other Zionist factions—particularly *Hashomer Hatzair*—opposed the idea of partition both because it restricted the area in which the Zionist ideal could be realized and because of their basic belief that the situation then current in Palestine did not permit any solution based on the assumption that Jews and Arabs could not live together. They pointed out that Palestine had already been partitioned once, when the 90,000 square kilometers of eastern Transjordan had been lopped off, leaving the 26,700 square kilometers west of the Jordan as the area for Jewish immigration and settlement. The solution of the Jewish problem in Palestine could not lie in further restriction of the areas in which the problem was to be solved. From the economic point of view, the partition of the country was likely to prejudice extensive plans for agricultural and industrial development and to require great expenditure on security. Above all, instead of solving the problem of national antagonism between Jews and Arabs, partition was likely to aggravate it—deepening the rift instead of healing it.

The Twentieth Zionist Congress (Zurich, August 1937) resolved, by a vote of 299 to 160 (a) to reject the premise of the Royal commission that the Mandate was not workable and to demand its implementation, and (b) not to accept the partition plan of the Royal commission but to empower the Executive to conduct negotiations "to clarify the specific points of the British government's proposal to found a Jewish state in Palestine."

The Arab leaders rejected partition without reservations. Riots were resumed in June 1937 and continued intermittently until the outbreak of World War II in the summer of 1939. Encouraged by Axis support, they were aimed both at the Jews and at the British. Once again, Palestine was a land of blood and destruction.

The British, now under direct Arab attack, abandoned their "neutrality" and began to cooperate with the Jewish community in restoring order. The "special night squads" commanded by the young British officer Captain Charles Orde Wingate were organized at this time. This unit, specially

P

The Peel Commission's partition plan, 1937

trained for its task, included one British and three Jewish companies. The personnel consisted of volunteer British soldiers and Jewish supernumerary police, both specially selected. The commanders were British and the N.C.O.s Jewish. The unit's operations were based on guerilla warfare tactics— surprising the aggressors in their bases and cutting off their retreat. These operations were of considerable effect in the ultimate repression of the terror and the restoration of law and order. They also served as a fine school for the para-military training of young Jews in self-defense. In January 1939, the government appointed a new "technical commission" headed by Sir John Woodhead, to examine the Peel Commission plan in detail and to recommend an actual partition plan. The commission, made up of British government officials, began its enquiry in March 1938, and presented its report at the beginning of November. It was charged with proposing a partition plan within boundaries "that will have a reasonable chance of establishing an Arab state and a Jewish one capable of maintaining themselves with sufficient security, and requiring the smallest possible minority of Arabs and their enterprises to be included in the Jewish state, and vice versa." The commission proposed two plans, which were called "Plan B" and "Plan C" (Plan A was the original proposal of the Peel commission, according to which the Jewish State was to occupy 5,000 square kilometers). Plan B offered the Jewish state a strip including eastern Galilee, the Jezreel valley, the coastal plain to Tel Aviv, and an enclave in the south that included Rishon Lezion, Nes Ziona, and Rehovot—in all, 3,300 square kilometers (less than one-sixth of the area of Israel under the 1948 armistice agreement). Central and western Galilee, and the Jerusalem enclave, were to remain under British control for an undetermined period; the rest of the land area, including Jaffa, was set aside for the Arab state.

Most of the commission, however, supported not this plan, but rather Plan C, envisaging a Jewish state stretching only from Tantura to Tel Aviv, plus the above-mentioned enclave to the south—a total of only 1,250 square kilometers. Excluded from partition were the northern regions proposed for the Jewish state by Plan B (eastern Galilee and the Jezreel valley, Haifa, and the Carmel area to Tantura), and the whole Beersheba district (i.e., the whole Negev). These were to remain the Mandated area, where Jews would be allowed to settle, albeit on sufferance, not as a right. The commission estimated that the small Jewish state it proposed would have an excess of income over expenditure of about £.P.600,000 annually, while the Arab state would have a deficit of about £.P.600,000 and the Mandated territory would also have an annual deficit of £.P.460,000; it therefore proposed a customs union of three parts of Palestine, according to which surplus income from customs duties (mostly coming from the Jews) would be equally divided among them.

The Woodhead partition plan, 1938

Dr. Weizmann (*Trial and Error*, page 386) says of the Woodhead plan that "the expected result was the allocation of such a small area that there would hardly have been standing room for all the Jews wishing to come to Palestine; development and growth would not have been possible at all. The proposals they meant to submit had one objective: that they should not be accepted."

On November 9, 1938, His Majesty's Government issued a new statement of policy based on the report of the Woodhead commission. They had reached the conclusion that any solution of the Palestine problem based on the establishment of an independent state of Jews and Arabs could not be implemented. The British government would continue to assume the responsibility for the government of all Palestine. It was their intention to convene a round-table conference with representatives of the Arabs of Palestine and neighboring countries, and representatives of the Jewish Agency, to discuss with them as soon as possible future policy and the question of immigration to Palestine. "If these talks do not produce an accord within a reasonable period of time, the government will make its own decision and announce the policy it intends to follow; in doing this, however, it will always keep in mind the international character of the Mandate it was assigned and the obligations laid upon it because of this."

In the Jewish Agency's statement, the Woodhead plan, which allocated the Jewish state less than 5 percent of western Palestine and only 1 percent of the area designated as the national home area originally intended in the Balfour Declaration, was "a parody of the obligations that the Mandatory power took upon itself in the name of the League of Nations." The Jewish Agency protested against the inclusion of neighboring Arab countries as a party to the negotiations concerning Palestine, concluding that the Jews would be able to continue the negotiations only on the basis of the Balfour Declaration and the Mandate.

On February 7, 1939, the London talks began; separate meetings were held with Arab delegates, with Jewish Agency representatives joined by Zionist and non-Zionist members of the administrative committee, with representatives of all sections of the Jewish community in Palestine, and with a number of prominent English Jews, the president of *Agudat Yisrael*, and representatives of Jewish communities in the United States, France, Belgium, Poland, and South Africa. The question of participation in the London talks was debated as a national Jewish issue by all sections of the Jewish people. The Agency Executive decided, after much hesitation, to take part in them, "since there is a feeling that it is inconceivable to allow a trial of the Jewish people to take place in its absence."[8]

Separate negotiations took place with the Jews and Arabs, since the Arab representatives had refused to sit at the same table with the Jews in the official sessions of the commission. On February 24, 1939, the government proposed a final arrangement, the purpose of which was to make Palestine an independent state, tied to Britain by a treaty "that shall adequately safeguard the commercial and strategic interests of both countries". Until the constitution of the independent state could be drawn up by a national assembly of the people, elected or nominated, as would be agreed upon, the agreement called for an interim period during which the Mandatory government would be in control. The date for the end of the interim period and the establishment of the independent state was not determined. The Mandatory government hoped "that the entire process will be finished in ten years, but this is also dependent upon the possibility of serious cooperation of the Palestinian people with the government." In any case, the conclusion determined that "the Mandatory Government cannot consider abandoning the obligation of governing Palestine unless it is sure that the accord between the various communities in Palestine is of an extent that shall permit good government." Economic absorptive capacity permitting, within the next five years immigration would increase the Jewish community to a third of the total population. This meant the immigration of 75,000 Jews within five years. After these five years, the continuation of immigration would be determined by agreement between the Arabs, the Jews, and the British authorities. This meant, in effect, the abandonment of the criterion of economic absorptive capacity, which had been considered an accepted principle since 1922, and the establishment of a new political criterion for Jewish immigration. In regard to land, the High Commissioner was given general powers for the interim period to prohibit or regulate transfer of land and to determine the areas in which land transfer would be unrestricted, regulated, or prohibited—pursuant to the recommendations of the Royal (Peel) commission and the Partition (Woodhead) commission.

The Jewish delegation decided that "it regrets it is unable to accept the proposals as a basis for agreement, and therefore has decided to disband." The Arab representatives likewise rejected the proposals.

The harvest of blood and economic ruin of the years of riots (April 1936 to August 1939), based on official data, is totalled on facing page.[9]

The direct material losses incurred by the Jews were estimated at £.P.400,000. One hundred homes, sheds, stores, and warehouses, and a large amount of lumber for construction and packing crates was partially or totally destroyed. Five herds of cattle and flocks of sheep were stolen; 40 citrus packing plants were burned or blown up; 100,000 citrus trees, 10,000 other fruit trees, 30,000 grape vines, 70,000 trees in Jewish National Fund forests, and 1,000 in Pica forests were uprooted or otherwise destroyed; barns and grain fields were burned; fifty pumping stations and one hundred electric poles were ruined; and six synagogues were blown up or set on fire. Besides these direct losses, the Jewish community suffered from indirect

CASUALTIES	KILLED		WOUNDED
*Jews**	545		
Hanged after trial	2	547	691
Arabs [by army or police]	1,369		
By Arabs†	494		
By Jews	243		
Hanged after trial	70	2,176	1,201
British			
Army and police	119		
Civilians	7	126	202
TOTAL		2,849	2,094

* During the years of the disturbances, about 500 attacks were made on Jewish settlements, especially on outlying suburban neighborhoods and small agricultural settlements, and on convoys on the roads.

† For friendliness to the Jews (*mukhtars* of villages, Arab policemen, Arabs who worked for Jews, etc.), or for taking a stand opposing the policy of the Mufti and his comrades.

injury to commerce, industry, and agriculture amounting to hundreds of thousands of pounds.

The direct material losses of the Arabs were limited to about 200 town and village houses (which had sheltered rioters), set on fire by the government, and about £.P.30,000 in collective fines levied on Arab towns and villages. Many of these payments were forcibly extracted (collective fines of £.P.2,000 were levied on Jewish settlements as well). The indirect material losses were considerable.

Public and government property damaged included ten railway stations set on fire, the Karkuk-Haifa oil pipeline cut about one hundred times, railroad tracks, cars and locomotives damaged, roads and bridges destroyed, the water pipeline to Jerusalem cut about ten times, public and government institutions (government buildings, police stations, post and customs offices, experimental stations, surveyors' and road workers' camps, etc.) attacked about one hundred times.

The international situation on the eve of the outbreak of World War II aroused in the Arab leaders the hope of attaining their political ends through a victory of the Axis powers. But the British government, ostensibly protector of the Jewish community in Palestine against the Arab assault, nevertheless did their utmost, in view of the possibility of war, to prevent the Arab leaders from joining Britain's enemies. This was to be at the expense of the vital interests and aspirations of the Jews.

A New White Paper

On May 17, 1939, the British government issued a new white paper (the third) which remained in force until the end of the British Mandate on May 15, 1948. While summing up the achievements of the Jews in Palestine since the inception of British rule as "a marvelous constructive effort, meriting the admiration of the whole world," which "should constitute a special source of pride for the Jewish people," the government in effect repeated what it had proposed during the London talks in February. After repeating those proposals in an even more obscure formulation, the government announced:

If after ten years the Mandatory Government ascertains that, contrary to its hopes, circumstances require postponing the establishment of the independent state, it will be ruled by the opinion of representatives of the Palestinian people and by the opinion of the League of Nations Council, and by the opinion of the neighbouring Arab states, before coming to a decision on such a postponement. If the Mandatory Government comes to the conclusion that a postponement cannot be avoided, it will request the participation of the above parties in the formulation of a plan for the future, in order to implement the desired objective as soon as possible.

This White Paper left the Jews with nothing, and yet it did not give the Arabs anything definite either. The Jewish Agency, on May 18, 1939, stated that:

The Jewish people views this policy as a breach of faith, a surrender to Arab terror, the delivery of Britain's friends to her enemies, the creation of a schism between the Jews and the Arabs, and the destruction of any chance for peace in Palestine. The Jewish people will not accept this policy. The new regime as announced in the white paper is solely and simply a government founded on force, bereft of any moral basis and opposed to international law, and it will not arise except by force.

On the basis of the May 1939 White Paper, new land-transfer regulations were promulgated (on February 26, 1940), according to which the country was divided into three zones: Zone A, comprising 1,384,000 *dunams* (345,000 acres) between Acre and Haifa, Tantura and Gedera, and in the Jerusalem area, in which Jews were permitted to purchase land; Zone B, comprising 17,156,000 *dunams* (4,289,000 acres)—5,370,000 *dunams* (1,342,500 acres) of them in the Negev, in which the purchase of land by Jews was definitely prohibited; Zone C, comprising 8,500,000 *dunams* (2,125,000 acres) in the Jezreel and Hulah valleys, the strip between Haifa and Tantura, some land between Gedera and Beer Tuvya, and 6,800,000 *dunams* (1,700,000 acres) in the southern Negev, where land transfer to Jews was subject to special permission of the High Commissioner. This law completed the cycle of legislation that discriminated against Jews as such in their national home.

The London talks were a turning point in the history of Jewish relations with England since 1917. Jewish progress in Palestine had obviously exceeded the rigid limits set by the British authorities. Therefore a fundamental contradiction now existed between Jewish and British interests in Palestine. For the British, "the Jewish national home was already established," and rested on solid foundations; but for the Jews, all that had been achieved in Palestine was only a beginning, a foundation for the structure that would rise, that had to rise. The moment the British government spokesmen declared that they had never pledged themselves to more than this beginning or intended more in the Balfour Declaration, it became clear that any community of interests had collapsed. The possibility of cooperation between the Zionist movement and the British government, which had opened up at the end of World War I, no longer existed. British imperial interests in the area were now in conflict with the historical compulsion of the Jewish people to rebuild its national life in Palestine. The path along which the Zionist movement could proceed together with the British Empire had now come to an end. This was a turning point in the history of Palestine.

After the White Paper of May 1939, Jewish enterprise in Palestine still went ahead, in effect outside the framework of official laws and frequently in defiance of them. The Jewish community in Palestine had meanwhile become an influential factor that could not easily be disregarded. Between 1936 and the end of 1939—the years of the disturbances—the Jewish community grew by 100,000. Not only were efforts to cut communications and starve the Jewish community unavailing, but fifty-six new settlements (the "Stockade and Watchtower kibbutzim*) were founded, most of them in areas hitherto lacking Jewish agricultural settlement. New roads were paved to the new settlements. Because Jaffa port was closed by the Arabs to Jews, the government was forced to approve the construction of Tel Aviv port. Jewish workers were employed in quarrying works, and construction no longer depended upon stone, which had been almost an Arab monopoly. The Jews also penetrated into government service, working in railroads, ports, and offices. Jewish agricultural production increased (vegetables, eggs, milk, etc., had hitherto been obtained from Arabs). Industry expanded more rapidly, increasingly able to meet independently the needs of the Jewish community of Palestine and even making some inroads in foreign markets. During the three and a half years of the disturbances, Jewish self-defense, too, was much strengthened and consolidated. Jews became a decisive element in the defense forces of the country, took their security into their own hands, and learned to rely primarily on their own strength.

When World War II broke out during the summer of 1939, twenty-five years had passed since the beginning of World War I. During this period,

* Settlements established on Jewish National Fund land without permission of the authorities and set up overnight by the settlers and special groups of helpers.

Land Regulation zones, 1940

the Jewish community of Palestine had grown from 85,000 people (only 55,000 of whom remained at the end of the war)—or 10 percent of the total population of the country—to 500,000 people—about 32 percent of the total. The amount of land held by Jews increased from 420,000 *dunams* (105,000 acres) in 1914 to 1,533,000 *dunams* (383,250 acres) in 1939. This figure includes 486,000 *dunams* (121,500 acres) belonging to the Jewish National Fund, as compared with 16,000 *dunams* (4,000 acres) twenty-five years earlier. Against a total, in 1914, of forty-four Jewish villages, with a population of 12,000, there were now 254, with a population of 153,000. Industrial production, which in 1914 had totalled £500,000, increased to £10,000,000 annually. All this progress was achieved under the shadow of grave political uncertainty and now of imminent world war. Worst of all, the Jews in the Diaspora were on the brink of a holocaust the horror of which was to be revealed only years later.

From the point of view of Arab-Jewish relations, new objective possibilities now opened up for mutual understanding and cooperation for the benefit of both peoples. The Jews no longer had anything to hope for from cooperation with the British government; their strength in Palestine, as well as the support of Diaspora Jews, now permitted them to cooperate with the Arabs, even against Britain's will. Moreover, important changes were beginning to leave their mark on the Palestinian Arab community and reduce the disparity between it and the Jews. However, the seed of division that had been sown in the course of the twenty years of British rule continued to bear fruit among both peoples, especially in their political leadership. The Jews themselves began to believe in the theory of an insurmountable antagonism between Jew and Arab in Palestine. The theory that the British had done their best to foster, and that had been rejected for so many years by most Jews, at last began to take root.

With the world once more engulfed in war, the disturbances in Palestine temporarily ceased. The war did not allow the struggle to be resumed, but swords were sharpened on both sides, and it was clear that at the end of the war arms would have to be taken up again—unless a political solution could meanwhile be found to prevent the conflict. Unfortunately, Palestinian policy continued to bear the marks of imperialistic designs on the part of the British government, of Arab social backwardness and extremist nationalism, and of short-sighted, often mistaken policy on the part of the Jewish leadership. This unfortunate constellation signified the shape of things to come after the war had ended.

References

1. Professor M. Buber, "Report", *At the Parting of Our Ways* (1939), p. 125.
2. Central Zionist Archives, Jerusalem, File L3/27–29.
3. *Doar Hayom* (Hebrew daily), April 22, 1931.
4. *Zionism: A Treasury of Political Documents*, No. 395.
5. Report on the Eighteenth Zionist Congress, September 1933.
6. A. Olizur, *National Capital and the Upbuilding of Palestine*, issued by the head office of Keren Hayessod(Jerusalem, 1939), page 246 (based on facts and figures gathered by the Jewish Agency for Palestine and the American Economic Committee for Palestine).
7. Report to the Twentieth Zionist Congress, August 1937.
8. Report to the Twenty-first Zionist Congress, August 1939.
9. M. Smilansky: *Chapters in the History of the Jewish Community* (in Palestine), Book 6, pp. 52–62 (Hebrew).

CHAPTER SIX

IS THE GAP UNBRIDGEABLE?

Most of the Zionist leaders were convinced that the real interests of the Jewish and Arab national liberation movements were compatible and complementary, and could therefore be realized harmoniously.

However, in the course of time, part of the Zionist movement—the extreme right wing, or Revisionists—came to the conclusion that "never before in history have the native inhabitants of a country agreed of their own free will that their land should be colonized by foreigners." This conception of the Arabs as inferior "natives," and the Jews as foreign "colonialists" was rejected as pernicious and misguided by the rest of the Zionist movement. The Arabs were not "natives," as the colonialists used the word; and the Zionist movement was not a colonialist campaign by "foreigners" setting out to exploit and enslave other peoples. Rather, it was and is a movement striving to revive and rebuild the ancient Jewish homeland, without any intention of harming the vital interests of the Arab people living in the country. The most authoritative Zionist spokesman stated that the land of Israel was not too small for the realization of the legitimate aspirations of both peoples: The rebirth of the one did not necessarily entail the decline of the other. On the contrary, these Zionist thinkers maintained, with the two peoples helping and strengthening each other, they could make common progress in the spheres of economics, culture, and in social and political life.

Until the beginning of British rule in Palestine, this line of thought was also shared by many of the most outstanding leaders in the Arab national movement. It was expressed in the negotiations that had been going on for years between Jewish and Arab leaders, until British intervention made their effective continuance impossible.

The Idea of Mutual Progress

The concept of mutual Jewish-Arab progress can be summarized as follows. The Arab peoples are the inheritors of a long and glorious tradition—a tradition that has as great a future potential as its past. Historical processes have stripped the Arabs of the magnificent achievements registered during the golden age of the Arab caliphates and the prosperous Arab countries that arose on their ruins. Centuries of life under a foreign yoke, and oppression, corruption, and internal dissension have taken their toll. The Arab lands of our day, once world centers of civilization, are now backward and under-developed.

Since the Arab national awakening in the nineteenth century, the Arabs have been striving once more to secure political and social conditions that would enable them fully to develop their creative potential in all spheres and to regain their rightful place in the family of nations. But this potential must be rapidly realized. The world economy of our times is an integrated one; the Middle East cannot long remain stagnant while other areas are making rapid progress and improving their economic and social life. The poverty of the Arab lands, which (apart from Egypt) support relatively small populations in large areas, will not allow the Arabs to progress as quickly and intensely as their national interests demand. Even if the large number of nomads becomes a settled population, the Arabs will not be able of their own accord to maintain and develop countries that could hold far greater populations under average conditions, and even larger populations when all the achievements of human progress are introduced into this part of the world. Thus, Belgium, with an area of only 30,500 square kilometers (slightly larger than that of Palestine west of the Jordan) supports a population of nine million, and has come to occupy an important place on the world scene precisely because its population density prompted it to develop along intensive lines. On the other hand, Iraq, which is fourteen times the size of Belgium and has considerable water resources and much fertile land, could be a second Egypt as far as population density (in the inhabited zones) is concerned. It has vast oil reserves and other natural wealth resources as well as important arteries of communication. Why, then, should it not have a large population and a reasonable standard of living? Iraq is only one example. We know that in ancient times the areas covered today by Iraq, Syria, Lebanon, Israel, and Jordan supported far greater populations than they do today, when technological and scientific progress enable countries to reach a much higher population density than in the distant past.

The high cultural level these countries attained in ancient times was the result of population pressure. Population density rose in the areas with greater natural possibilities, while the wide expanses of desert closed in around the fertile areas and prevented emigration. These factors spurred the Arabs of those times on to improve production methods and develop socio-economic and political frameworks and standards that could support the existence of a large population. The military occupations of these countries over the centuries (such as the conquests of the Tartars in the thirteenth century and the beginning of the fifteenth century) considerably reduced their population but also destroyed the basis of their agriculture. Primitive nomads invaded these lands, the irrigation network was devastated, and the entire economic structure thereby undermined. Thus began the decline of an ancient, prosperous culture. As it began to sink into decay, the encroaching sands of the desert slowly covered it over.

The Arab countries are waiting for capable and faithful partners who will help them to repair the ravages of centuries and reconstruct what has been destroyed. From the standpoint of Arab national interests, no more potentially desirable partner could be found than the kindred Jewish people, whose past cooperation yielded such glorious results. Historically speaking, a renewal of this cooperation could bring about one of the wonders of our times.

In the eyes of most Arab national leaders, the Arab countries form a single geographical and ethnic entity, which has been carved up into various units solely to serve foreign interests; these units now strive to be reunited. In historical perspective, Palestine is but a small corner in the huge Arab world, which will attain political union of some type sooner or later. Would the entry of a few million Jews into Palestine hamper the Arabs, or aid them? It is enough to peruse the statements made by different Arab representatives at all stages of the Jewish-Arab negotiations during the present century to see at once what their reply was.

The vital positive potential of Jewish-Arab cooperation could have proven stronger than the suspicion, prejudice, and hostility that poisoned relations between these two kindred peoples under the baneful influence of imperialism.

What the Arabs Gained From the Zionist Endeavor

When the national dispute between the Arabs and the Jews was nearing its peak, the Palestinian Arab press frequently claimed that "Palestine has become prosperous not because of the Jews, but because of the state of war, from which the Jews have derived more benefit than anyone else."[1]

That claim is, of course, belied by demographic facts in the years *before* World War II. Several examples will prove this unequivocally:

During a period of approximately twenty-five years *the population of Palestine* grew at a rate unprecedented in the world*. From 1870 to 1890, the period of most intensive growth, the population of the United States rose from thirty-eight million to sixty-eight million, or an increase of 58 percent in twenty years. The *total* population of Palestine grew from 649,000 in 1922 (according to the 1922 census) to 1,845,600 in 1946 (according to official government figures)—a rate of 184 percent in twenty-four years!

The Arabs questioned the correctness of the 1922 and 1946 figures in the official statistics and condemned them as arbitrary and dictated by political considerations. Jewish population figures were based on the registration of

* When we refer here to Palestine, we mean the country west of Jordan, the area in which the influence of Jewish immigration and settlement was felt in this period.

new settlers and an exact record of births and deaths. However, the over-whelming majority of the Arabs were illiterate fellaheen, and some were Bedouin nomads from whom no reliable data could be obtained. Arab *Mukhtars*, or headmen, were not a source of accurate demographic informa-tion.

In a memorandum submitted to the United Nations special committee on Palestine in 1947, Y. Trevusch[2] proved, by quoting official figures in Mandate days, that the population of Palestine in 1922 could not have exceeded 520,000 (of whom 390,000 were Moslems and 60,000 Christian Arabs), and could not therefore have reached the figure given by that year's census of 649,009 (486,177 Moslems, 83,790 Jews, 71,464 Christians and 7,616 others). The memorandum also attempted to prove that the number of Arabs in 1946 did not exceed 705,000 (including 630,000 Moslems and 75,000 Christian Arabs)—a number approximately equal to that of Jews living in Palestine at the time. (The British Mandatory authorities estimated the Jewish population at 608,000; the British Foreign Secretary, Ernest Bevin, speaking in the summer of 1947, put their number—including the so-called "illegal" immigrants who had come in over twenty-five years—at 700,000.) On the other hand, the government estimated the number of Arabs in Palestine at the end of 1946 as 1,225,000.

The truth probably lies somewhere between these extreme estimates. In any event, the main sources of the unprecedented population increase in Palestine were Jewish immigration and the growing natural increase of the Arab inhabitants as the result of their improved living conditions, the drop in the infant mortality rate (among the Moslem community, from 199 deaths per thousand live births in 1923 to 91 in 1946), and a rise in the average life expectation (increasing from 37 years in 1926, for the general population, to 49 in 1943).

According to the official statistics, the Arab population of Palestine increased by 118 percent during the twenty-four years between 1922 and 1946—a growth of almost 5 percent per annum. When, however, it is remembered that during this period some 100,000 Arabs entered the country from neighboring lands (the government's estimate of a few tens of thousands was certainly an underestimate), and even if the rates of natural increase are severely reduced (on the assumption that the official data were deliberately inflated, in order to provide a "statistical basis" for the political ban on large-scale Jewish immigration), the rate of increase is still much higher than that in any Arab country during the same period. The United Nations committee said in its report (Chapter 2, Clause 16):

The Arab population increased almost entirely because of the increase of births over deaths. In effect, the rate of increase of the Moslem Arabs in Palestine was the highest registered statistically anywhere in the world, a phenomenon attributed to a high rate of pregnancy together with a considerable decline in the infant mortality rate, the latter brought about by the improvement in living conditions and public health services.

The rapid growth of the Arab population was particularly striking in regions of close Jewish settlement and development. The Peel commission also noted in its 1937 report (Chapter 5, Clauses 31 and 37) "the general beneficient effect of Jewish immigration on Arab welfare," and added that, whereas the Arab population of Haifa increased by 86 percent, that of Jaffa by 62 percent and that of Jerusalem by 37 percent, the population in such purely Arab towns as Nablus and Hebron rose by only 7 percent, and in Gaza there was actually a drop of 2 percent.

During the period under survey *the emigration of Arabs from Palestine ceased almost entirely.* While over 103,000 peoples left Syria and Lebanon from 1920 to 1931, only 9,272 non-Jews left Palestine during the same period. In other words, the emigration from Syria and Lebanon was eleven times as great as that from Palestine, though their population was at the beginning of this period only five times as large as the Palestine Arab population.

Between 1920 and 1941, the Jews invested 115 million Palestine pounds (i.e., pounds sterling) in the country, in both public and private funds. According to reliable calculations, *the Palestinian Arabs received about £30 million from the Jews in one way or another.* Another £3 million was received by non-Palestinian Arabs (mainly Syrians and Lebanese) in return for their lands in Palestine, which were sold to the Jewish settlers. These £30 million were allocated as follows:

In return for land, Palestinian Arabs received, according to the Land Registration books	6,000,000
Agents' fees received by Arabs for handling these transactions	1,000,000
Compensation paid to sharecroppers	300,000
Organic manure bought from Arabs by Jews	500,000
In return for agricultural produce	7,500,000
Wages paid to Arabs working in Jewish agriculture	3,000,000
For building materials (stone, sand, etc.)	3,200,000
Profits of Arab traders in commerce with Jews	1,500,000
Wages paid to non-agricultural Arab workers	1,000,000
Price of industrial products	1,000,000
Rent paid by Jews to Arabs	5,000,000
TOTAL	£30,000,000

Even if these calculations erred slightly in minor details, they are reasonably accurate and can be assumed to give a correct picture of the facts.[3] Any "counter calculation" of what Jews received from Arabs in return would certainly be far below that total sum. A study of the table will show that over half the sum was paid as wages or in return for the supply of materials (farm produce, building materials, manure); this income, too, enriched Arab fellaheen and workers.

The investment of this large sum of capital had an overall stimulating influence on the Arab economy in Palestine. According to the calculation of the late Dr. Alfred Bonne, the national income of the Palestinian Arabs, which had averaged not more than £.P.10 to £.P.12 *per capita* in 1920, reached £.P.27 *per capita* in 1937, at a time when the comparable figure for Egypt was £.P.12, for Syria and for Lebanon £.P.16 and for Iraq, £.P.10.*

The area of vegetables and fruit trees cultivated by the Arabs for the Jewish consumer market increased several times over during this period. This market increased in proportion to the increase in Jewish immigration, with which the Jewish farmers could not keep pace. Arab orange groves also expanded, thanks to the millions of pounds received from the Jews in return for part of Arab land or various goods supplied to the Jewish population. *This expansion of the Arab economy created new sources of employment for thousands of Arab workers*—apart from the thousands who worked in various branches of the Jewish economy. (Until the outbreak of the 1936 riots, about 6,000 Arab workers were employed in Jewish agriculture, mainly in orange groves.) In addition, many Arabs were employed in the large international enterprises established in the wake of the rapid development following the Jewish immigration; these included the Palestine Electric Company, the oil companies, the Dead Sea Works, the port services, railways, posts, and telegraphs, etc.

We should also not overlook the influence on the Arabs of the example the Jews set in agriculture, industry, transport, and organization. The Arabs also gained from the presence of eminent scientists, doctors, engineers, agricultural experts, and other skilled professionals who arrived with the Jewish immigration.

The wages of the Arab laborer in Palestine increased considerably during the period under review and greatly exceeded the wages of workers in any of the Arab countries. While in Egypt (where wages were similar to those in all the other Arab lands except Lebanon), a wage of five piasters a day was considered high—and fellaheen often worked for two or three piasters a day—the wage of an *unskilled* Arab worker in Palestine ranged between fifteen and twenty piasters, that of *skilled* labor rising to two or three times that rate. The wages of Arab farm workers also rose considerably in those years, reaching fourteen to sixteen piasters during the busy season in the citrus belt, which was near the center of organized Jewish labor.

* For the sake of comparison: In India (1936), £.P.4; Yugoslavia (1936), £.P.19; Britain (1940), £.P.148; the United States (1940), £.P.225; and the Jews of Palestine (1936), £.P.49 *per capita*, per annum.

The indirect benefits accruing to Arabs were no less impressive. The Palestine Arabs did not pay the British Mandatory government more taxes than they had paid to the Turkish government, nor more than was paid by Arabs in neighboring countries. According to the 1936 figures (1936 was a normal year), the average government revenue per annum *per capita* was £.P.2.30 in Egypt, £.P.1.75 for every Palestinian Arab, £.P.1.50 in Iraq, £.P.1.80 in greater Syria (which then included Lebanon and the autonomous zones), and £.P.1.00 in Transjordan. Arab benefits from government expenditure were much greater in Palestine than in any other Arab land: The average government expenditure *per capita* in 1936 was £.P.2.20 in Egypt, £.P.1.70 in Syria and Lebanon, £.P.1.70 in Iraq, £.P.1.50 in Transjordan, and £.P.4.55 for the Arabs in Palestine. In Iraq, the difference between the excess of expenditure and the income from taxation was covered by the oil revenues; in Transjordan, the deficit was covered by the British treasury and the Palestine exchequer; in Palestine, it was covered by the revenue from the taxes paid by the Jewish settlers.[4]

The following official figures, representing government expenditure in mils* *per capita*, confirm this:

	EGYPT	IRAQ	TRANSJORDAN	SYRIA AND LEBANON	PALESTINIAN ARABS
Health	153	108	42	23	156
Education	283	217	(1935) 73	96	259

The increased sums spent on health in Palestine markedly improved the health of the Palestinian Arabs as compared with that of Arabs in other countries. This is underscored by the data on the increase of births over deaths per thousand of population, taken as an average between 1917 and 1937. In Egypt this was 11; in Syria and Lebanon 14; in Transjordan 9; in Iraq 9; and in Palestine (during the 1920 to 1941 period) 25! The mortality rate among Palestine Arabs as a whole dropped from 27 per thousand in 1925 to 1927 to 21 per thousand during the 1936 to 1941 period.

For the purposes of schooling, the Egyptian government spent 283 mils *per capita* annually; Iraq spent 217; Syria spent 96; Transjordan spent 73; while in Palestine the sum spent by the government for the Arab population was 259 mil. Apart from Egypt—a relatively rich and autonomous country in those days—the Arabs of Palestine were in a better position than Arabs in any other country.†

* Mil: The equivalent, in Palestine, of 0.001 of an English pound.

† These data also refer to 1938, apart from Transjordan (1935). During the war, the real value of the currency changed, and the composition of the budgets underwent changes.

Palestine Arabs also benefited from the development of a road network, always a major factor in economic progress. Over a forty-year period, the network of roads expanded from 400 kilometers—mostly consisting of narrow roads suitable only for light vehicles—to 2,000 kilometers of macadamized roads. Bridges were built in various parts of the country, including four important bridges over the Jordan, two over the Kishon, and two on the Haifa-Jaffa road. The Public Works Department spent more than twelve million Palestine pounds between 1920 and 1940; this did not include the cost of constructing the Haifa port and improving the Jaffa port, projects that were carried out by special departments.

Before World War I, there was exactly *one* car in the whole of Palestine; in 1941 there were 16,000, apart from army vehicles. In 1920, no town except Tel Aviv had piped water supplies. The Mandatory administration installed such water supplies in Tiberias, Nablus, Jenin, Beisan, Nazareth, Tulkarm, Hebron, and Jerusalem. In other localities, too, the water supply system was under municipal control.*

The government's assistance—direct and indirect—to Arab agriculture was no less substantial. Experimental stations were established, selected seeds and plant varieties distributed, and veterinary advice given. The government waived part of the taxes due from the farmers. While these measures may perhaps have been modest by international standards, they helped to improve considerably the standard of living of Palestine Arabs, as compared to that of Arabs in countries that were richer than Palestine.

All these achievements would not have been possible without the tens of million pounds brought into the country by the Jewish settlers, which flowed into the Palestine exchequer. While in the neighboring Arab lands, the authorities struggled to balance their budgets, the *credit balance* in the Palestine treasury on April 1, 1936 reached £.P.6,267,000, or more than the expenditure in the 1935 to 1936 fiscal year, which was £.P.4,236,201.

Was the Crisis Unavoidable?

Over the economic prosperity and the remarkable development brought to the country by the Jewish settlers hung the shadow of a political crisis, which grew steadily more ominous and ultimately had tragic consequences. Yet these consequences were not unavoidable.

Thirty years after the end of World War I, there were 1,850,000 inhabitants in Palestine, according to government figures. These Jews and Arabs enjoyed a much higher standard of living than the 650,000 people who had

* According to a lecture by the director of the Palestine government's Public Works Department, Captain Wilson Brown, over Jerusalem radio, as reported in the daily newspaper *Hatzofeh*, March 9, 1942.

lived in Palestine in 1918. The country attained this great change without comprehensive development planning, without cumulative experience, without adequate encouragement by the government, and during waves of bloody disturbances that blocked the country's progress. It is not difficult to imagine what the development might have been had it not been artificially arrested, and had official policy, instead, aimed at bringing the Jews and Arabs together toward effective cooperation between them.

Claims of the anti-Jewish propaganda slogans of the 1920s that "the Jews want to get control of the Dome of the Rock and other places holy to the Moslems and the Christians" were soon shown to be totally unfounded. The arguments that the fellaheen were being ousted from their land and their economic interests harmed were also rebutted by investigations of experts and committees who could hardly be suspected of a pro-Jewish bias. In its 1937 report, the Peel commission admitted (Chapter 5, paragraph thirty-four) that: "Our conclusion, then, is that, broadly speaking, the Arabs have shared to a considerable degree in the material benefits which Jewish immigration has brought to Palestine. The obligation of the Mandate in this respect has been observed. The economic position of the Arabs, regarded as a whole, has not so far been prejudiced by the establishment of the National Home" . . . [Note the British understatement "not prejudiced."]

Ten years later, in the report submitted by the Mandatory Government to the United Nations special committee on Palestine, the same basic conclusion was reaffirmed: "The material situation of the Arab community in Palestine has particularly improved during the last twenty-seven years, perhaps because of their rapid rate of natural increase. Their standard of living has increased considerably, and their ability to hold their own in a competitive world has been strengthened."

At the same time, it was impossible to deny the claim made by UNSCOP that "even if it was proved beyond a shadow of a doubt that in its economic and social life the Arab community benefited greatly from the progress of the [Jewish] national home and the Mandatory regime, it is clear, as was emphasized by the 1937 Royal commission, that these considerations play a minor role for those who direct the political life of the Arabs." (Chapter 2, Clause 100)

The Peel commission had stated, in its 1937 report (Chapter 19, Conclusions and Proposals, Paragraph two): "Although the Arabs have benefited from the development of the country owing to Jewish immigration, this had no conciliatory effect. On the contrary, improvement in the economic situation in Palestine has meant the deterioration of the political situation."

In short, the problem was a *political* one.

References

1. *Ad-Difa'*, July 20, 1943.
2. Y. Trevusch: "There is No Arab Majority in Palestine (Surprising revelations concerning the distortions in the census of the Arab population of Palestine)," material presented to the Commission of Enquiry (Hazon, Tel Aviv, 1946–1947), p. 36 (Hebrew).
3. Aharon Cohen: *Problems of Contemporary Zionist Policy*, (Hakibutz Haartzi Hashomer Hatzair, January 1943), pp. 28, 29 (Hebrew).
4. Aharon Cohen: *Letters to Friends* (Jerusalem: The League for Jewish-Arab Rapprochement and Cooperation, November 1933), pp. 21–22 (Arabic).

CHAPTER SEVEN

THE POLITICAL TEST

We have dwelt upon the role played by the British authorities in the evolution of Jewish-Arab relations in Palestine. The role of the Arab and Jewish leadership should now be reviewed. When World War I ended, Palestine west of the Jordan, which contained not much more than half a million Arabs, was not a separate political unit. British Foreign Secretary Bevin was on safe ground when he said in the House of Commons, in 1945, that "we must admit that it has been impossible to find common ground between the Jews and the Arabs since the Mandate was ratified." There is, however, evidence—some of which was quoted above—that before the British Mandatory administration of Palestine there was a good deal of common political ground between Arabs and Jews. Even the Royal commission (1937) stated in its report (Chapter 23, paragraph 5) that "there was a time when Arab statesmen were willing to concede little Palestine to the Jews, provided that the rest of Arab Asia were free."

The Arab Leaders' Stand

When the declared policy of Arab leaders in Palestine crystallized in the early twenties—inspired not a little by British officialdom—it was oversimplified, inflexible and inimical to any political *rapprochement* with the Jews. Arab leaders insisted that Palestine had been an Arab country since its conquest in the seventh century (except for an interval during the Crusades). They pointed out that it had been fundamentally Arab even during the 400 years of Turkish rule (1517–1918), and that it had actually been held by Arabs longer than by Jews, who themselves had wrested it from its former inhabitants. These claims ignored the fact that after the Jews had been forcibly removed from their homeland, they had continued to regard it as their country of origin, their hope to return home remaining unquenched throughout all the generations of their wanderings among the nations. The essence of the Arab claims, in Jewish eyes, was a quite crude disregard of the basic fact that there was not another nation in the world so badly in need of a homeland of its own as the Jews.

As against these Jewish claims, whose legal bases were the Balfour Declaration and the Mandate ratified by the League of Nations on the explicit condition that it would assist the establishment of a Jewish national home in Palestine, the Palestinian Arab leaders insisted that during World War I official promises had been given to the Arabs by the Allies (particularly in the MacMahon-Hussain correspondence of 1915–1916 and the Anglo-French declaration of 1918) that included Palestine in the area promised freedom and independence; that the Palestine Mandate negated the League of Nations' declared assurance of independence to all peoples; that the wishes of the people of Palestine were not taken into account in the selection of a Mandatory power (as required by paragraph 22, subparagraph 4, of the League of Nations charter), and anything done in Palestine under the Mandate was consequently illegal; and that the Arab countries were not members of the League of Nations when the Mandate was ratified and were therefore not bound by it.

It is only fair to admit that neither the Royal commission (1937) nor the United Nations commission (1947) was able to dispel the heavy fog of ambiguity in British policy on the paramount question of the inclusion of Palestine in the MacMahon promises to the Arabs. The United Nations commission stated in its report (Chapter 2, paragraph 167):

As to the promises and undertakings given the Arabs during World War I in order to obtain their support for the Allies, it must be remarked that there is no unequivocal agreement according to which it was possible to determine whether Palestine was included in the territory promised independence, in the correspondence between MacMahon and King Hussain. Since the question of interpretation arose, Britain has continually denied that Palestine was included in the area which had been promised independence.

The United Nations commission added that in 1939, during the days of the London talks, a committee of British and Arab members had examined the MacMahon correspondence, as well as events and documents of the subsequent period that one or the other of the parties thought might shed light on its meaning. The committee examined, among other things, the Sykes-Picot Treaty, the Balfour Declaration, the Hogarth letter, the "Declaration of Seven," General Allenby's promise to Emir Faisal, and the Anglo-French declaration of December 1918. The committee reported that the representatives of the Arabs and the representatives of the United Kingdom "could not reach agreement as to the meaning of the correspondence." However, the British representatives stated to their Arab fellow members that "Arab claims as explained in the committee as to the interpretation of the correspondence, particularly as to the meaning of the sentence 'parts of Syria extending west of the Damascus, Hamah, Homs and Aleppo districts' (the MacMahon letter of October 24, 1915) are stronger than has appeared heretofore."

United Kingdom representatives likewise advised Arab delegates that they agreed "that Palestine was included in the area claimed by the Shariff of

Mecca in his letter of July 14, 1915;" in regard to British promises, however, British representatives at that Anglo-Arab committee expressed this opinion (a marvelous example of British diplomatic language):

If Palestine was not excluded from that area at later stages of the correspondence, it may be considered included in the area in which England was about to admit Arab independence and support it; *they hold to the opinion that according to a proper explanation of the correspondence*, Palestine was not actually included in the area; but they agree that the formulation of its exclusion from the whole was less definite and unequivocal than was thought in those days.

The United Nations commission report of 1947 reflects its helplessness in the face of the ambiguity of the British documents. In Chapter 2, paragraphs 171–172, the commission states:

In regard to the Hogarth letter, the Arab representatives explained that they based their position on the paragraph in the letter sent to Hussain, King of Hejaz, in 1918, stating that the settlement of Jews in Palestine would not be permitted except insofar as it did not interfere with the political and economic freedom of the Arab population.

It should be noted that the Hogarth letter was addressed to King Hussain in January 1918, i.e., two months after the Balfour Declaration. There is a clear distinction between the Declaration, which safeguarded only the *civil* and *religious* rights of the existing non-Jewish populace, and the letter, which promised *political* freedom to the Arab population of Palestine.

Thus, in view of the contradictory promises and ambiguous policy, there was sense in the suggestion of the Arab delegates at the Arab-Jewish negotiations of 1922 in Cairo that:

Neither the Balfour Declaration nor the treaty signed between King Hussain and England shall serve as a basis for the negotiations, for the agreement to be signed by both parties [the Jews and the Arabs] need not be affected by either of these political documents. Arabs and Jews must sit and consider with each other as nation with nation. They must make concessions to each other and recognize each other's rights.*

The legal position of the Arab leaders was not too sound. If they claimed that the League of Nations charter promised independence to all peoples, the same claim for independence applied also to the Jewish people; if they claimed that they did not recognize League of Nations' decisions (since they were not members when the Mandate was confirmed), this would break down their demand for rights assured by the League charter. But of course this was not basically a legal, but rather an historical and political question—a problem of the relations between two peoples who had to live together.

The Arab leaders insisted that if the Jews were in difficult straits and it was necessary to provide a refuge for those who were obliged to emigrate, why must this refuge be Palestine—or why only Palestine? There were large

* See Chapter Five.

countries like Australia, South Africa, and the United States several of whose statesmen professed friendship for the Jews and supported their immigration to Palestine; if they were really friends of the Jews, let them open the doors of their own countries to them!

This stand ignored both the special historic connection of the Jewish people to Palestine—recognized by the representatives of fifty-two countries who approved the Mandate based on the Balfour Declaration—and the firm resolve of the Jews not to pursue their wanderings in foreign countries, but to strike roots once more in their ancient homeland.

Subsequently, when the arguments about the dispossession of Arabs resulting from Jewish immigration had been refuted; when it became apparent to all that not only had Jewish immigration not *harmed* the Arabs economically, but that it had been useful and beneficent—Arab spokesmen contended that any remedy, as was well known, might be effective if given in small doses, but not if large quantities were injected all at once.

This argument also overlooked the essence of the Jewish national movement and its objectives. The immigration of Jews to Palestine was not intended to provide remedies for anyone other than Jews, though the Jews strove to avoid the least injury to Arabs living in Palestine. The Jewish return to Palestine was in their own vital interests; the urgent necessity of Jewish immigration was dictated primarily by the growing disintegration of their position in the Diaspora. Imperative Jewish needs could not be adapted to the ideas of Arab rulers who preferred the continuation of their people's deteriorated condition so long as the future of their own position as sole rulers of the whole country was assured.

Moreover, Arab leaders periodically claimed that the absorptive capacity of Palestine had already reached a saturation point, and that any additional immigration was likely to push out the Arabs. Such was their claim in 1929, when there were only 160,000 Jews in Palestine; in 1936, when the Jewish population was 350,000; and in later periods, as the number of Jews in Palestine continued to increase.

The reasons given for Arab opposition to Jewish immigration were often contradictory. To conservative Arab elements, the Zionists were "Bolsheviks" and had a bad effect on the younger generation of Arabs; to the more progressive elements, Zionism was an imperialistic and racist movement. At some times, they opposed Zionism because it dispossessed and ruined them; and at other times, they preferred to remain poor (in other words to forego the economic benefits resulting from Jewish accomplishments in Palestine) so that Palestine should not lose its Arab character. Sometimes they claimed that there was no historic connection between the modern Jewish nation and Palestine (an Arab spokesman at the United Nations even indicated that European Jews were not Jews at all, but of

Khazar origin), and sometimes that the historic connection did not justify the restoration to them of a country that had since been settled by another nation. "What would happen if other nations started to demand the return of countries they had once inhabited?" they asked. This question skirted the simple truth that there was no other people in the world, except the Jews, that lacked the earth of a homeland beneath its feet, and no historical parallel with the Jewish determination to return to the homeland—not out of a desire to conquer others' territory, but as a prime need without the fulfilment of which the nation was doomed to destruction.

When it could no longer be denied that Jewish immigration and settlement had brought great benefits to Palestine, the Arab leaders asserted that neighboring Arab countries, too, had made progress "without the benefit of any Zionist settlement." They insisted, moreover, that whatever the Jews had contributed to Palestinian Arabs had not been given freely but against their will: "The Jews never agreed to the government's levying more taxes on the richer group [the Jews] and allocating more to the poorer [the Arabs]." "The Jews," they claimed, "brought with them great economic and cultural advantages, but they never showed any initiative or provided an example of cooperation with the Arabs, either in the economic field, or in social, cultural, or political life. Socially the Jews confined themselves to their own group, culturally they were separatists, and from a political point of view they constituted an obstacle to Palestinian Arabs in the achievement of the political independence they hoped for."

All these Arab arguments sought to achieve the total prohibition of Jewish immigration and of land transfer from Arabs to Jews, the abolition of the Mandate, and the establishment of Palestine as an independent Arab country, with a parliamentary regime and an elected government responsible to the people. This official Palestinian Arab stand, propounded by the leadership since the early 1920s, negated both the national aspirations of the Jews and the international recognition they had received. Just as Arab leaders contended that British policy supported the Jews against the Arabs, so did Jewish spokesmen attack the British government for their encouragement of the Arabs at the expense of the Jewish community. The main line of the British authorities in Palestine certainly used Arab grievances as a pretext to arrest the growth of the Jewish state, while at the same time using Jewish claims as a similar means of counteracting Arab national demands. It was the exact opposite of the truth that the British Foreign Secretary, Ernest Bevin, declared in Parliament on November 13, 1945, when he said that "His Majesty's Government have made every effort to devise some arrangements which would enable Arabs and Jews to live together in peace and to cooperate for the welfare of the country, but all such efforts have been unavailing." The good intentions of the Mandatory government were put to nought, ostensibly by the Jews and Arabs themselves. . . . The truth was that the British authorities in Palestine never considered the common interests of the Jews and the Arabs as the point of departure for their policy. Virtually none of the many British statements on Palestine issued over the years conveyed a clear and simple statement to the effect, for example, that the British government would be pleased to see an effort by the two peoples toward a settlement based on politico-national equality and the satisfaction of the needs and national aspirations of both of them. All the differences between Jews and Arabs notwithstanding, both peoples appeared convinced that British policy effectively aggravated the conflict between them. This confusing and obstructive policy was reinforced to one degree or another, often unwittingly, by the official Jewish and Arab leaders.

Principles of Official Jewish Policy toward the Arabs

The Zionist movement seemed from its inception to include two schools of thought *vis-à-vis* the reality and objectives of the Arab world in whose midst Palestine was situated. This is revealed in the attitude prevalent in the movement as a whole, and in the small Jewish community of Palestine, toward the Arab national movement, the first burgeonings of which were apparent during the period of Turkish rule. Even in the romantic, paternalistic era of the Baron's officials, before the first World War, when the first primitive encounter took place between Jewish settlers and Arab peasants living in semi-feudal conditions, there was no lack of examples of a more humane and ideologically far-sighted approach on the part of some of the Zionists. To illustrate this approach, it is sufficient to recall the comments of Ahad Ha'am on the subject (see Chapter Three); the basically anti-colonialist views of A. D. Gordon on the profound significance of the return to the East; and the constant attempts of the Labor weekly, *Hapoel Hatzair*, to stress the spiritual and moral element (rather than those of power politics) in the Zionist renaissance. It is, furthermore, no coincidence that *Hashomer*, the first Jewish self-defense organization and the forerunner of the Hagana and the Israel Defense Forces of today, developed a pattern of respectful and understanding relationship with Arab neighbors, familiarity with the Arab way of life, and the beginnings of serious thought about Jewish-Arab relations.

Hashomer was considerably influenced by the ideas of its founders, members of the socialist *Poalei Zion*. On the other hand, a colonialist ideology was evident in the *Gidonim* group—an organization of farmers' sons with a definite anti-labor tendency—which was founded in 1913 in Zichron Ya'akov, to compete with *Hashomer*. This group, which lasted for only fourteen months, tried to develop its own social and national ideology, favoring the employment of Arab workers by Jews and a general ascendancy of the Jews over the Arabs. The *Gidonim* served as a breeding ground for the secret *Nili* group, which arose during World War I, founded and led by the agronomist Aharon Aaronson, his sister Sarah and other young people of Zichron Ya'akov. *Nili* engaged in espionage among the Turks for the benefit of British headquarters in Egypt, in the hope that after victory, Palestine would be given to the Jews. Most of the Jewish community opposed *Nili*, fearing the consequences of its activities under the conditions of the war and the Turkish regime of those days. There was, therefore, a certain dualism in the Zionist approach; what could be called the Oriental position receded gradually following World War I, when the political-diplomatic center for Zionism passed from Constantinople to European capitals, and political Zionism, based on international law, appeared triumphant with the issue of the Balfour Declaration. Zionism still contained within it elements sensitive to the question of relations between the peoples, and at most stages and in most periods, leaders like Weizmann and Arlosoroff, and fairly substantial political groupings and streams of thought in the Zionist movement, could be counted among them; nevertheless, a definite change had taken place, considerably influenced by British policy and by a growing Europocentric orientation in the Zionist movement as a whole.

Most Zionist leaders were temperamentally and ideologically incapable of appreciating the full historical significance of the October revolution—its impact on the colonial world and the Arab peoples within it. An analysis of the speeches and writings of most Zionist and Jewish leaders—including Labor Zionist leaders—reveals an astonishing misunderstanding of the Arab world, of Palestine Arabs in particular, and of the context in which national movements develop. A pamphlet called *The Arab Movement* by one of the Zionist Labor leaders[1] was a case in point. The writer, who was to become the second President of the state of Israel, inveighs against "an imaginary and deceptive impression that this Arab movement is built on solid popular foundations. . . . We have managed to develop Jews with an Arab orientation,* just as we already have Jews with Polish, Ukrainian, Russian, and similar orientations" (page 3). "We must determine our attitude to these inhabitants [the Arabs] with whom we are tied by concrete interests, ties of one homeland and its common future" (page 4).

---

* This is apparently a comment on the repeated warnings of Dr. Yitshak Epstein: "The mighty of the world are founding newspapers in the East in several languages, and using various means of influencing public opinion, and we . . . far be it from us to go the way of the Gentiles, we keep quiet. We who are noisy, enthusiastic, and exciting speakers in our own corner . . . to this day do not have a single publication in Arabic on our national movement, have not assigned a single person to negotiate with the people of the country." *The Question of Questions in the Community* (Community Trustee League, Jaffa), pp. 7–8 (Hebrew).

The author, Y. Ben-Zvi, who urged objective consideration of the Arab problem, reached the conclusion that "the Arab movement appears in a fixed and definite framework as a local Palestinian problem. It is not a general Arab problem, it is not the Pan-Arab movement, but a problem of the Arabs residing in Palestine, in the special manner that became manifest mainly at the end of the World War" (page 5).

He completely misconstrued the Pan-Arab movement, writing: "The Arab-speaking tribes are not and were not one nation or one race, and they have no subjective or objective tendency to join forces." And again: "Precisely because of the expansion of the Arab language, it is not possible to speak of one Arab nation within the area where the Arab language is paramount" (page 7). The explanation was that the Arab-speaking nations were somewhat united in the past, but the connection among them was gradually being weakened. "Anyone who is slightly familiar with Arab affairs," he continued, "will be forced to admit that there is no real connection between the nationalist movement in Egypt and its parallel in the Lebanese hills, and that the interests of the Lebanese Maronites are not identical with those of the Syrian Moslems and the Damascene politicians. . . . Needless to say, there is no longer any organic connection between Syria and Mesopotamia, just as there is none between Arab Egypt and the western countries [Algeria and Morocco], despite the language and remnants of a past culture that are common to a certain extent to the countries mentioned" (page 8).

The author held that the Arab movement in Palestine did not incline toward the pan-Arab or pan-Moslem idea, but rather to a "united Syria." He made mention of Arab organizations active at that time which, in the demonstrations preceding the Jerusalem riots of Passover in 1920, had exhibited the photograph of Faisal, King of Damascus, as king of a united Syria and Palestine. Although he was writing a short time after the Weizmann-Faisal agreement of January 1919, the author maintained that the rule of Faisal over Syria "might attract some of the effendis and prominent Moslems" but in fact "Faisal's rule would mean a return to the Turkish regime in a worse version" (page 10).

Against the background of the Balfour Declaration and the first steps taken in Palestine to establish the Jewish national home under British aegis, this indifference to the disappearance of the slogan calling for Palestine's annexation to Syria is understandable (Syria was under French rule after the discontinuation of Faisal's regime); the emergence of a demand for a Palestinian national government (*hukuma wataniya*), which was more realistic, constituted a step forward and, above all, provided a point of contact with Jews and even with Zionists.

In explaining the "economic, racial and national composition of the Palestinian people," the author claimed that "there are various historic and ethnographic points of evidence indicating that this agrarian community [the vast majority of the Palestinian Arab community] originated from the early Jewish agricultural community—from the Jewish and Samaritan fellaheen— the common people, who remained tied to their land and did not go into exile." The national quality of the Palestinian Arab community, "the ostensible unity between propertied persons and workers among our neighbors" was invalidated not only by class distinctions, but also by the differences between the various national and religious groupings: Moslems (Sunites), Mutualis, Circassians, Druzes, Christians (of various denominations), Samaritans, Karaites, etc.—in all, "eleven nations, peoples, affiliations, plus other smaller sects." The overall conclusion was that:

There is no place as yet for a single Arab national movement among the inhabitants of Palestine; the movement that calls itself a national Arab movement has a reactionary social basis. There is room for various national movements within the areas these special national groups are bound by, and there is a broad scope for concerted action of all these peoples and nations within the general framework of the Palestinian home- land common to the Jews and to all the peoples and races mentioned.   [Page 34].

The Palestinian Arab movement was still in its infancy. The first (separate) convention of Arabs in Palestine (Haifa, December 1920; see Chapter Five) expressed sharp opposition to the policy of the Jewish national home. It set forth a demand for home government and a legislature elected by Arabic-speaking inhabitants who had resided in Palestine before the war, protested against the British government's recognition of the Zionist commission, and against immigration and the recognition of Hebrew as an official language. The author of the pamphlet agreed that the relations between the peoples had been neglected and wrongly evaluated, but failed to draw any conclusions from this; instead he emphasized "the common interests of the Jewish worker and the Arab worker." Instead of coming to grips with the national problem and indicating a basis for mutual understand- ing and cooperation between the national movements of the Jews and the Arabs, the belief grew that it was possible "to solve the problem" through cooperation with the ruling power. This gave rise to a covert xenophobia in the guise of various theories: that the "Arabs are not a nation," but rather a sort of conglomeration of tribes and religious sects; that their national move- ment was only an "imitation of Europe," "a foreign import." Traces of these discredited theories can still be found in current Hebrew political writing. In contradistinction to this trend, a different attitude—more profound and far- sighted—was already discernible in the Zionist movement. Politically, this was represented by Dr. C. Weizmann's efforts towards agreement with Arab leaders. Its two most brilliant advocates from an ideological point of view were the great philosopher Martin Buber (an early Zionist and associate of Herzl) and the outstanding young statesman Chaim Arlosoroff (1899–1933), who was twenty years younger than Buber and, to some extent, his disciple.

In the early days of the Zionist Organization, Buber was one of the few Zionist thinkers who warned that a national life cannot be revived solely on the basis of organizational processes and political declarations. His classic speeches (especially "Three Speeches on Judaism," of which the first was delivered in Prague, in 1909), and his essays, prompted a more correct evaluation of the real issues in Zionism. At a time when Zionists knew little of the Arab world, the problem of Arab-Jewish relations had already loomed large in Buber's thinking. In his speech on "The Spirit of the East and Judaism" in 1912, Buber already envisaged the awakening and liberation of the Oriental peoples; he saw a profound symbolic meaning in the simultaneous return of the Jewish people to its Oriental homeland, and the challenge inherent in the peaceful reassimilation of the Jews into the awakening East. The essay concludes by saying that:

> Jerusalem is still more than ever what it was in ancient times: a gateway of the nations. It is the eternal passageway between East and West. It was there that ancient Asia trained its legions when it set forth on westward conquests in the days of Nebuchadnezzar and Cyrus, there that the Europe of Alexander the Great and the Romans marched to rule the East. Through an assault from East to West, the first Jewish state crumbled and was destroyed, through an assault from West to East the second Jewish state disintegrated. Since those days, the value of Palestine for the world has grown greater and more profound. Today Jerusalem is a gateway of the people in a more precise and inclusive sense, encompassing greater danger and greater promise. The time has come to pray for the welfare of Jerusalem, the welfare of all peoples.[2]

A fierce opponent of war, Buber postulated in August 1917 that "the Zionist movement exists beyond the world of this war, and has no connection with it. It is not a party to this war nor does it wish to be; it is not a participant in the game, either openly or secretly." He insisted that the Zionist movement refrain from entangling itself in the net of political intrigues being cast over the face of the earth at that time. In March 1919, when the question of post-war political arrangements came up, he wrote:

> If at the beginning of the war it seemed to be in our power to remain outside the net of error and malice, fate, which cannot be deflected in one direction or the other, has caused us to be drawn into it; no nation caught in this tangle can get out of it by its own efforts. More than this: we could not reject our obligation to insist on our rights in Palestine from the moment it was known that its fate was to be decided; since then we have had to protect our rights assiduously and explicitly before the bodies that acquired authority in the matter. But the main thing is the use we put this right to after it is recognised. Upon this depends our ability to defend it successfully before a higher court with more justified authority than this peace conference.

Buber spoke passionately of the role the Jews were capable of and called upon to fill, "since they are at once of the East and of the West":

However, we shall stride toward this destiny not as servants of a great Europe doomed to destruction, but as allies of a young Europe, still weak but consecrated to the future, not as middle men of a degenerating civilization, but as champions of a new civilization whose creation we are party to.

Our loyalty to the League of Nations and its representatives is self-evident; and also that we have no connection with its present methods, which are imperialism decorated with the flags of humanism. We must hereby emphasize that we will refrain from any foreign policy—except for the paths and activities necessary for instituting a permanent and friendly accord with the Arabs in all areas of life, to achieve a comprehensive fraternal creation.

A year later, in April 1920, viewing the growing tension in Palestine, Buber returned to an analysis of the political reality of the Zionist movement, stating:

We who intend to serve in Palestine as mediators between Europe and Asia, must not appear before an East awakening from a dazed dream as emissaries of a West that is doomed to destruction, lest a justifiable suspicion should fall upon us as well. We were chosen to herald the renascent West. We must help our brothers in the East to lay the foundation of a life of true brotherhood, aided by an alliance with the West and their own strength. . . . It depends on us whether we appear before the awakening East as hated agents and spies or as beloved teachers and creators.

At the Twelfth Zionist Congress in Karlsbad, in September 1921, Buber again sounded the alert: "We must not give our attention only to Europe." He insisted on serious consideration of the "Arab problem." It was Martin Buber who warned the political committee of the Twelfth Congress that Palestine would not be bypassed by the historic law that two peoples living together in a common political framework will affect each other's development—the nation more advanced in national consciousness and political organization accelerating the development of the less developed. There was no escaping this law. As the Jews progressed in their work they would advance their Arab neighbors; as Jewish achievements grew, the achievements of the Arabs in their neighborhood would grow, along with their sensitivity to social and political discrimination. It was in the Jewish interest to favor the progress of their neighbors and to make them their allies, rather than to waste this opportunity and make them enemies to whom it would later be most difficult to find a peaceful path. As a basis for assuring the success of negotiations with the Arabs, Buber demanded a great settlement program and a definite economic and political platform as a basis for the negotiations. ("It seems to me that we lacked both of them," Buber later stated.)

The ideological foundations of Buber's statement at the Twelfth Congress, in the name of the *Hapoel Hatzair* (Palestine) and *Zeire Zion* (in the diaspora) factions, for many years constituted part of the official Zionist policy and the general Zionist credo. He said:

R

At this first meeting of representatives of the Jewish people after eight years of separation [since the Eleventh Congress, which had taken place in Vienna before the war], we hereby renew our declaration before the nations of the East and the West: a solid nucleus of the Jewish people has determined to return to its ancient homeland and to build a new life in it based on independent work, which will develop and be perpetuated as one of the organic elements of a new humanity. No government on earth has the power to shake this decision, which generations of our pioneers have sanctified with their lives and their deaths. Any act of violence touching us because of it will seal the declaration of our national will with a seal of blood.

He affirmed, however, that this "national will" was not directed against any other people:

Our return to Palestine through increasing immigration has no intention of harming anyone. In a just alliance with the Arab people in our common land, we desire to create a culturally and economically flourishing community, whose rise will assure each of its national components unhampered autonomous development. Our own settlement, whose sole purpose is the rescue of our people and its rejuvenation, neither aims at capitalistic exploitation of territory, nor serves any imperialistic ends; its essential quality is the creative work of free men on community land. This social character of our national ideology is the great guarantee of our assurance that a profound and constant solidarity of real interests will develop between us and Arab working people, and overcome all opposition that may result from fleeting complications. Recognizing this tie, the members of the two peoples will come to respect each other, and each will seek the other's good in private and public life. Only then will there again be a real meeting of the two peoples whose confrontation has such great historic value.

These principles were also advanced at that time by A. D. Gordon, a second *Aliyah* spiritual leader, whose ideological and moral teachings left a considerable mark on Jewish labor. (For his stand on the Jewish legion on the eve of World War I see Chapter Four.) Gordon, who was among the few in the Zionist movement to pay attention to the Arab national movement, stated at the Eleventh Zionist Congress in Vienna (1913):

And the Arabs? A great national awakening, containing a great idea and a grand spiritual quality, similar to the awakening of the children of Israel leaving Egypt or the Arabs in the days of the prophet of Islam, with great external as well as internal strength. Here the vital force is not physical (what physical force there is is meagre and insignificant), it is a voice which has a cosmic timbre and cosmic courage, and its words are heard, particularly when they contain cosmic truth. This is important for us. Truth is the basis of our world. The truth is modest, but its strength is greater than anything —liberty, equality, fraternity, which are printed on banners. It is even stronger than love. The strength of the truth is great not only in relations between man and his fellow, but also in relations among peoples.[3]

In spite of his contempt for anything smacking of politics, Gordon postulated that "We and they are natural allies: more than by internal racial unity,

we are united by external hate toward both parties." In a letter to Joseph
Aaronovitz in December 1913, he wrote: "The aggressive nations of Europe
hate both us and the Arabs. Under the pretext of protecting us or them, they
will probably use every opportunity to harm us. This external hate unites
us more than any internal links."[4]

Gordon treated the problem not as a foreign policy issue but as a domestic
issue, writing, at the end of the war:

> What are our relations to the Arabs, who are after all, whether we like it or not, our
> partners in social and political life? What do we know of them, or wish to know
> more than anti-Semites know of us? This affects us directly, certainly not less than
> matters like the International. Before us is a great vision—more than that, a great
> moment in life—the first lesson and the first direct practice in fraternal living between
> two peoples. Here again the important thing is ourselves, each and every one of us.
> If we try to be more humane, more alive, we will find the right relationship with
> people and with nations in general and the Arabs in particular.[5]

After the disturbances of May 1921, Gordon wrote to the central committee of *Hapoel Hatzair*:

> The Arabs have all the traits and attributes of a living, but not of a free, people.
> They are settled in a country, live in it, work its land, speak its national language,
> and so on. Accordingly, their claim to Palestine is that of a people living in its natural
> country, even if it is expressed in an ugly and uncivilized manner, such as by wild
> shouting or violence. Everything needed actually exists. . . . While we are deciding
> whether or not there is an Arab national movement, life goes on, the movement
> flourishes and grows, for all the conditions for its flowering and growth are present.
> It is very dangerous for us to shut our eyes to this living fact, to deceive ourselves and
> say that we are witnessing merely a middle-class effendi plot and no more. The people
> initiating the movement, its main operators and its leaders, are indeed the effendis and
> the Arab intellectuals in general, but they are not the only ones, and not the most
> important. That's the way things are in any movement, and not just in national ones.[6]

Chaim Arlosoroff, one of the brilliant younger disciples of Buber, soon
became an eloquent advocate of Buber's Zionist ideology. Arriving in
Palestine a few weeks before the riots of May 1921, only twenty-two years of
age, he took part, gun in hand, in the defense of Neve Shalom, between
Jaffa and Tel Aviv. His views on the riots and on the fundamental problems
underlying them were expressed in his article "The May Riots." While
others were attempting to evade the problem of two peoples in a common
homeland, he presented it clearly:

> We are posing the Arab question here as a political one, not, as is usual with us, as a
> social, economic, ethnographical, or moral one. We must ask: is there a political
> force in Palestine called "The Arab Movement," and if there is—how does it operate,
> in what direction does it modify the interplay of forces outside it, and what relations

should there be between it and us? Those who pose the question differently are misleading.

Others could see only the incited Arabs doing violence to the Jews, or the hostile British authorities vindicating the incited as well as the inciters; many nonetheless maintained that the "political partner" with whom negotiations should be held was not the Arabs but the British, who should be asked to suppress the anti-Jewish Arab movement. Arlosoroff warned against this oversimplified attempt to deny the existence of the Arab national movement by trying to compare it with European nationalism: "Let us not ignore this fact: there is a popular mass in Palestine caught up by the force of Arab slogans; and it doesn't matter whether we call it an Arab national movement or not."

Arlosoroff did not deny that there were outsiders who influenced Arab-Jewish relations adversely, but called for a full understanding of the Arab national movement:

An Arab movement really exists—and no matter what sort it is—it will be calamitous if we negate its importance or rely on bayonets, British or Jewish. Such support is valid for an hour, but not for decades. Anyone who refuses to embark on an ostrich-like policy and shut his eyes to reality, will realize that in our situation, in our desire to assure ourselves maximum freedom of action in building our national home, only one course is open to us: the peaceful one—and only one policy: a policy of mutual understanding. It is precisely at this time, at a time of anger and embitterment, that we must speak out in clear and reasoned words. The "strong arm" policy never attained its aim. In a place where forces of such magnitude operate, such movements and vital interests confront each other along the same path—only accord can lead to success. Of course we have wasted much valuable time, and very likely it would have been possible for us to reduce the antagonism, but even today we can reach only one conclusion: the actual conditions force Jews and Arabs in the same direction, and they therefore must have a policy of accord. The road to it will be long and hard. But all this should not prevent us from expressing our desire for this course, for it is the only possibility for us and for the Arabs. . . . In spite of mourning and bitterness in our hearts today we must start along this path and try anything likely to bring us to a policy of accord.

Arlosoroff's views did not gain general recognition among the Jewish leadership.

Y. Lufban, one of the heads of the *Hapoel Hatzair*, Arlosoroff's political group, criticized the article because it was "somewhat in dissonance with the general public reaction to the riots in the Palestine Jewish community and in Zionism." In his speech to the Karlsbad Zionist Congress in 1922, Arlosoroff said:

Our party submitted to the Twelfth Congress a resolution on Zionist policy. I hope that the stand of our leaders on this question is not merely the result of our present difficult situation, but reflects the principled stand of Zionism. The only possible course is the establishment of a *common* state in Palestine for Jews and Arabs as peoples with equal rights. Logical conclusions must be drawn from this assumption, and this the Zionist leadership has not yet done. Certain steps taken by the Executive are in direct contradiction to our stand. We cannot submit a memorandum on a Jewish legion to the British government a few weeks after the Twelfth Congress's resolution on this point, especially when its rejection by the British government was a foregone conclusion. We should have refrained from such a move. When we say that we aspire to be integrated into the bloc of Eastern nations, we must not announce to the press at the same time that with our help or mediation a European power was given a mandate over an Eastern nation, which in any case is an exaggerated estimate of our influence in the matter.

We must also reexamine our slogans. We have seen how much trouble we got into because of the words "Palestine must be Jewish as England is English," though I believe that they were misconstrued, and our true intention was to state that the Jewish nation would be able to develop freely in Palestine as the English nation does in its country. This is true also as to the slogan about a Jewish majority. We must not blast this slogan into Arab ears ten times a day while wanting to reach an accord with them.

Arlosoroff was to some extent "exceptional" in official Zionist thinking. The Zionist leaders who came from Europe were far removed in spirit and mentality from even the Jewish intelligentzia of Eastern countries, some o whom were solidly established in the Arab cultural world and could have constituted an excellent bridge between the Jewish and the Arab national movements. Men like Professor A. S. Yehuda, David Yellin, Rabbi Nahum of Egypt, and several leading Sephardi Jews in Palestine, could have contributed a great deal to the creation of a relationship of understanding and cooperation between the two peoples, but were not given the opportunity to do so. The upshot was that they resigned in an atmosphere of bitterness, and some of them even became confirmed opponents of anything connected with Zionist leadership and its policy.

If Eastern Jews reacted thus, how much more so did prominent Arabs! Arab personalities, who at one stage had lent an attentive ear to the Jewish national movement and had even begun to show sympathy for it, in the course of time retreated and changed their line. An example may be found in the case of one of Egypt's distinguished scholars, Ahmad Zaki Pasha, sometime minister of education in that country (he died in the thirties). After World War I, he became close to Zionist leaders and in 1922 wrote to Dr. Eder[7] (then head of the Zionist political department) that "the victory of the Zionist ideal is also the victory of my ideal." In those days, informed sources say, Ahmad Zaki dreamed of being professor of Arabic at the Hebrew University and on several occasions expressed the view that Palestine could not be revived without Jewish ability and capital. But after the disturbances of 1929, he changed his mind; he began to support the Palestine-Syrian Committee and the Committee for the Defense of Palestine, which operated in Egypt at that time against the Zionist movement; he began to publish articles in Egyptian papers and even published an appeal in *Al-Ahram*—the largest Egyptian newspaper, entitled "Hear, Oh Egypt and I Shall Speak"—calling on Egypt to mobilize for the defense of Palestinian Arabs. Thereafter, he was considered capricious and even earned the title of Jew-hater. But Professor A. S. Yehuda, who was a regular visitor at Ahmad Zaki's house, an Arab intellectual salon, wrote of him:

Ahmad Zaki Pasha is a cultured and enlightened man, and one of the prominent Arab scholars who favour the idea of the renaissance of the Jewish people in Palestine, and believe in the necessity of cultural cooperation between Jews and Arabs in Palestine and in the east in general. Zaki Pasha, who was always friendly and on good terms with Jews, at first welcomed the return of Israel to its land, and several times spoke to me about the need for reaching friendly understanding with the Arabs, and wished to mediate between us. But Zionist leaders did not know how to use his influence when the time was still ripe for it; this infuriated him and he gradually moved over to the other side as did other prominent Arabs who were insulted because the Zionists, they said, as Europeans, looked down on "the natives who lack education and culture."[8]

It was probably no accident that while extensive information was widely distributed by the Zionist movement in many European languages, hardly any of this information was published in Arabic.

On November 26, 1930, Mr. M. R. Achtar, editor of *Falastin*, addressed a group of Jews. His lecture (which was published in *Our Aspirations*, Volume 2, Pamphlet A) was not lacking in unjustified attacks on the Zionist movement and its work in Palestine, but one of his complaints was significant:

Another mistake that continually surprised me was that so much money and time and paper and ink were wasted on propaganda to explain Zionism to the Western nations. If only even the thousandth part of this effort were expended to clarify Zionism to the Arabs. . . . I suspect that you will not find a single leaflet in Arabic in which Zionists explain their needs, their rights, their claims—absolutely none. You yourselves know better than I the extent to which this was explained to the Americans, the English, the French. Though they must live among Arabs, the Zionists did not care whether or not the Arabs understood. They thought it more essential for someone in Vienna or in Paris to know what Zionism desired.

The truth of the matter is that from this point of view, the basic situation did not improve even in later years.

When the Zionist movement met with Arab political resistance in Palestine, which was exploited (and even aggravated) by the British government, the Zionist and Palestine Jewish community leaders were again forced to consider the problem of Arab-Jewish relations. In March 1920 the Zionist commission stated:

The people of Israel and Arab people had a common destiny in the past. We were both strong peoples, materially and spiritually, but by the sword of the oppressor we were both subjugated in the course of time to other nations. Let us now work together; let us awaken and arouse the slumbering East for our benefit, for your benefit, and for the benefit of our country.

On October 7, 1920, the first Elected Assembly of Palestine Jews declared that it:

viewed the maintenance of peace and friendship with the Arab people as an essential condition of the success of our work, leading to the realization of our national aspirations. The Jewish people and the Arab people, who are close in race, language and culture, will accelerate their own revival and that of the East through cooperation and mutual aid.

The Twelfth Zionist Congress at Karlsbad, in September 1921, passed a resolution stating:

The hostile stand of part of the Arab population of Palestine, incited by unscrupulous elements . . . cannot weaken our resolve to build the Jewish national home, nor the firm intention of the Jewish people to live a life of tranquility and mutual respect with the Arab people in Palestine, and thereby transform our common homeland into a flourishing community that will assure both peoples unhampered national development.

But such declarations were little more than pious wishes that were not translated into practical policy. It was feared that a daring policy of Arab-Jewish accord might—as has been noted concerning the 1922 negotiations—endanger the good relations between the Zionist movement and the British government. The possibilities for cooperation with Britain had not yet been exhausted, and the mass of the Jewish people still pinned their faith in cooperation with the British government. Unfortunately, this became the only plank in the Zionist political platform. Inevitably, any Arab-Jewish accord would be based on the liberation of Palestine from British rule; on the other hand, Arab hostility to Jewish aims in Palestine made it very difficult for Zionist leaders to think along these lines. Whether the Zionist leaders wanted it or not, official Jewish policy was bound to the British authorities in the hope that with their help the Jews would be able to overcome Arab opposition (which that same British government continued to encourage covertly and overtly).

Parallel to the rise of anti-Jewish forces among the Palestinian Arab community in the mid-twenties, there arose an extreme nationalist faction—the Revisionists—within the Zionist movement. Ignoring the national aspirations of the Palestinian Arabs completely, they were willing to harness the Jewish endeavor to British rule in Palestine and its environs. The Revisionists advocated "a Jewish state in Palestine on both sides of the Jordan," and the formation of a Jewish legion to guarantee the unhampered progress of the

Jewish effort in Palestine. This Revisionist ideology, distorting the original aims of the Zionist movement, represented Zionism to the Arab world as being allied to imperialism. This, in turn, strengthened the more extreme nationalist objectives among the Arabs, and thus deepened the schism between the two peoples.

The vast majority of people within the Zionist movement—including the Zionist labor movement in its entirety and most of the General Zionists (the center faction)—opposed the Revisionists' slogan. Official Zionist policy adopted the principle of non-domination of one people by another, and the unhampered development of each within an autonomous national framework based on equality between them, regardless of numerical strength. The official policy of the Zionist labor movement in those years was clearly defined by David Ben-Gurion in the fall of 1925:

There was a time when the Zionist movement completely ignored the question of the Arab community in Palestine and made its calculations as if Palestine were completely uninhabited. The time for such naïve Zionists is long past, never to return. There may still be individual Zionists, such as Jabotinsky, who, though they are aware of the existence of the Arab community in Palestine, consider it a mistake that can be corrected. . . . Responsible Zionism, especially socialist Zionism, cannot entertain such delusions. The Arab community in Palestine is an organic, inseparable part of Palestine, rooted in the country, working in it and here to stay. Zionism has not come to inherit its place or rise on its ruins. There is no need to pontificate on honesty and justice—the thing is simply not possible: the forcible dispossession of masses of people from their land is not impossible even in our day, and we have just been witness to the dispossession of hundreds of thousands of Greeks from Turkey and hundreds of thousands of Turks from Greece, but only madmen or scoundrels can ascribe a similar desire to the Jewish people in Palestine. Palestine will be for the Jewish people and the Arabs living in it. We foresee the realization of Zionism in the immigration of masses of Jews who will establish in Palestine a new economy, not instead of the existing Arab economy, but in addition to it, and who will create many new work opportunities, not in the present Arab places of work, but outside of them. They will extend the economic frontiers of Palestine so that it can absorb a large Jewish majority that will live in Palestine together with the Arab people settled in it.[9]

Two years later, Ben-Gurion added an explanation of the question of basic rights of Arabs and Jews in Palestine:

In my view of morality, we have no right to discriminate against a single Arab child, even if thereby we attain everything we desire. Our work cannot be based on depriving anyone of his rights. Of course, the Arabs should not deprive us of our rights . . . based not only on the vital need of the homeless Jewish people, but also on the fact that Palestine is not sufficiently populated and the present community is not capable of settling and working it all. The Arabs are not entitled to exclusive ownership of the whole country. In my opinion, they have the right to control their own affairs, their property, their community, their culture, and their domestic affairs, and have the right to ensure their own unhampered development. However, all those unsettled and un-farmed areas of the country, all the opportunities that have not yet been realized and that the Arabs are not likely to realize when they are in power—all those hidden possibilities that are a moral and practical basis for our settlement in Palestine—over these the Arabs have no proprietary rights, and they must not be allowed to intefere with us.[10]

A memorandum presented to the Shaw commission in December 1929 by the General Federation of Jewish Labor in Palestine stated:

The Jewish labor movement considers the Arab people an integral part of this country. It is inconceivable that Jewish settlers should uproot the population from its place or settle permanently in Palestine at their expense. Not only is this impossible from the political and economic point of view, but it also contradicts the moral principles underlying the Zionist movement. Jewish settlers who come to the country to live in it and earn their living by manual labor consider Arab laborers their brothers in the same homeland and their comrades at work, people with needs identical to theirs, whose future is their future. The realization of Zionism, therefore involves the creation of a new economy, aiming not to dispossess the Arab economy, but an addi-tion to it.

These principles meant that the Jews would come to Palestine whether the Arabs agreed or not, but that the Jews did not wish to construct their lives anew in Palestine at the expense of the Arabs' livelihood or by curtailing their rights in the country.

Principles and Practice

Having declared these principles, however, the Zionist movement never, in effect, acted on them. While Zionist leaders articulated the principles of non-domination, political equality, and accord between the two peoples, they formulated no concrete political proposals as a basis for effective negotiations. On this vital question of the relations between the two peoples in Palestine there was no considered or far-sighted Jewish policy on the type of political regime envisaged; without this, no real effort could be made to plan the *rapprochement* of the two peoples and achieve peace and cooperation between them.

The *Palestine Diary*[11] of F. H. Kish* sets forth the numerous threads con-necting one people to the other. In those days, the head of the Zionist political department and other official representatives of the Jews were

*Kish was head of the Zionist Executive for Palestine and director of the Political department in Jerusalem from 1923 to 1931. After leaving the Zionist Executive, Kish settled in Palestine. During World War II, he was chief engineer to Montgomery's army in the Western Desert. In the spring of 1943, at the age of fifty-five, he was killed when he stepped on a mine.

frequently welcomed at meetings of sheiks in the Jordan and Jezreel valleys, at parties given by mayors and prominent Arabs in Jerusalem, Haifa, Tiberias, and other cities, and at the homes of Arab leaders of the Nashashibi, Dajani, and other families; they could also meet Arab leaders in Jewish homes. There were various joint Arab-Jewish projects, such as one for the benefit of the poor and aged irrespective of religion, a joint "health week," a joint delegation to London urging the improvement of the Jaffa shore, a joint union of Jewish and Arab guides in Palestine, a joint union for journalists representing the foreign press, a joint poster against violence, a joint strike of Jewish and Arab carters in Jerusalem in protest against a tax rise. Hundreds of official and semi-official meetings took place among important Jewish and Arab representatives from all parts of Palestine and neighboring countries, in an atmosphere of good will and the desire to find a path to cooperation. But matters never reached the point of accord. British authorities sabotaged the efforts, and Zionist leaders saw this clearly (the author of *Palestine Diary* adduces considerable evidence but kept silent.) The hypocrisy of the authorities was never publicly denounced or explained to either the Jewish or the Arab masses. Colonel Kish was not suspected of anti-imperialist views, a fact that gives added interest to his factual daily entries; these present the picture of high government officials encouraging, even fostering, Arab opposition to the Jews; various attempts at cooperation between Arabs and Jews being deliberately foiled; the government openly and systematically encouraging only those groups among the Arabs hostile to Jewish activity in Palestine, and definitely combating or repressing numerous important groups striving for cooperation with the Jews; and propaganda preaching national enmity, developed with at least the tacit blessing of the Palestine government. "The time has not yet come when Jews and Arabs can work together" was the constant contention of the British authorities in justification of their obstructive policy. Why, then, did not Jewish leaders denounce them? How did it happen that no countermeasures were taken? A partial explanation of this will be found in the October 1, 1930, entry in *Palestine Diary* (after a party also attended by important Arab Leaders): "The time has come to renew discussions between us. For my part, I am definitely willing, but without a clear Arab policy in the Jewish Agency it is impossible to make much progress." When Kish left his position and the political influence of the labor element in the Zionist movement increased, the Seventeenth Zionist Congress (1931) appointed as head of the political department Chaim Arlosoroff, known for his bold ideas concerning a real policy for Jewish-Arab accord, the integration of Jewish and Arab national revival, and the establishment of the Jewish people as an independent and influential factor in the region.

However, the Congress did not establish a definitive political basis for accord, but instructed the executive to take "energetic measures in the economic, social, and political areas, to arrive at peaceful and close relations between Jews and Arabs in Palestine on the basis of the principle that the two peoples should not dominate each other—regardless of what the numerical strength of each may be." This decision provided Arlosoroff with a basis on which to fight for a progressive initiative within the Zionist Executive and the general Jewish public on the question of relations between the two peoples. But Arlosoroff, like Kish who had preceded him in the job, found himself in a position he described in his diary entry of October 4, 1931 (after taking part in an argument on the Arab policy of the Jews):

> As to the political side, we have made no progress at all in recent years! We have no policy and we don't know according to what line we should act. We are still at the stage of vague generalities, mostly very abstract. In the meantime, things are continually happening in the Arab camp. There has been a reshuffling of the parties. Arab public opinion is crystallizing.

Arlosoroff's *Jerusalem Diary* (published by the Palestine Labour Party, in 1949), gives evidence of his considerable attention to Arab affairs in and out of Palestine, and discloses the feelers he put out to various Arab groups. His personal letter of June 30, 1932, to Weizmann (quoted in the *Diary*, pages 233–342) throws light on his original and profound ideas concerning the pitfalls of Palestinian politics, and on his strong intuition of the worldwide disturbances that were approaching, as well as his courage in seeking radical and unusual solutions to pressing problems. This was graphically described later by his widow Sima Arlosoroff:

> In those days, the spring of 1932, I used to find in the morning notes he had made in his fine handwriting the night before. I knew that something unusual was going on in Chaim's mind. He was more tense and concentrated than usual. One morning I asked him: What were the notes on his desk?
>
> "I am preparing my political testament!" and then he told me of his plans for the next ten years.
>
> We spent many late hours discussing his contemplated ideological revolution, and I asked a lot of questions. I remember asking, "Assuming that we work things out with the English, what about the Arabs?" He would explain that we would not be able to carry out the program without making contact with Arab factors.[12]

The report of the Jewish Agency to the Eighteenth Zionist Congress in Prague, August 21 to September 2, 1933 (Volume 2, Part A, "Political Report," page 217) relates the Arab repercussions of Arlosoroff's appointment to the political department:

> The change of personnel at the helm of the political affairs in the Jewish Agency in Jerusalem aroused great interest among the Arabs. Arlosoroff's statement at his press conference in September 1931 was fully reported in the Arab press and elicited con-

siderable response. There was evidence of a desire on the part of various Arab groups to make contact with the political department, in order to examine the possibilities for Arab-Jewish understanding. The political department adopted a policy of welcoming any opportunity to meet, and responding to any declared wish to exchange views. Long discussions were held with representatives of various Arab functions and groups in town and country. These meetings made it possible first of all to study the situation, and enabled the political department to learn the temper of the Arab community at first hand; they also helped explain to the Arab leaders the basic Jewish position in regard to the future of Palestine. There was no lack of Arab plans for joint activity. Most of these had to be rejected because they entailed far-reaching obligations by the Jewish Agency in matters that, by their nature, must advance slowly and carefully.

The records of most of those meetings are still secret. The notes on them in *Jerusalem Diary* were carefully censored before being issued. Thus, the *Diary* makes no mention, for example, of a meeting at the King David Hotel on April 8, 1933, between representatives of Transjordan, the President of the Zionist Organization, Dr. Chaim Weizmann, and members of the Jewish Agency for Palestine and the National Council of Palestinian Jews etc.

The background to this meeting is set forth in the report to the Eighteenth Zionist Congress (pages 218–219):

During the past two years the question of Jewish settlement work in Transjordan has arisen. The reason for it can be found in the growing contrast between the difficult economic situation in Transjordan and the relative prosperity of western Palestine. Tribal leaders and public figures in Transjordan have repeatedly expressed a wish to negotiate with the Jewish bodies in Palestine, and they took active steps in this direction. . . . In the course of time, a considerable change took place in the political atmosphere in connection with the possibilities of Jewish-Arab cooperation in Transjordan. The local authorities campaigned extensively to dissuade public opinion from any support for the idea. Thus, several important delegates left the national convention in Amman in April 1932, in protest against the tabling of anti-Zionist resolution. A bill prohibiting land sales to non-citizens submitted to the Transjordanian legislative assembly by a member of the extreme nationalist faction aroused vociferous protest, and was deferred indefinitely.

The aim of the April 8 meeting was to lay a foundation for extensive co-operation and Arab-Jewish unity. Arlosoroff had intended using the accord with representatives of Transjordanian Arabs in his political efforts with Palestine Arabs. Arab participants at the meeting included Sheik Mithqal Pasha al-Faiz, Chief of the Sakhr and former member of the Transjordanian legislative council; Rashid Pasha al-Khaza'i, supreme sheik at Mount Ajlun, also a member of the legislature; Mitri Pasha Zurikat, leader of the Christian community in the Al-Karak district, member of the legislature; Shams-ud-Din Bey Sami, leader of the Circassian community and their representative in the legislature; Salim Pasha Abu al-Ajam, supreme sheik in the Belka region;

and Muhammad Abu-Khalid of Amman. Jewish participants included the president of the Zionist Organization, Dr. Chaim Weizmann, the representative of the Jewish Agency, Chaim Arlosoroff, Immanuel Newman, Dr. Hexter, and Dr. Berkson, representatives of the National Council of Palestine Jews Y. Ben-Zvi and Abraham Elmaleah, Abraham Shapiro (who had close connections with the Transjordanian sheiks) and Moshe Shertok (Sharett), Arlosoroff's secretary.

In welcoming the guests from Transjordan, C. Arlosoroff stressed his belief that the future of the country depended and would continue to depend on the joint efforts of the two peoples. Sheik Mithqal al-Faiz, who replied in the name of the Arab participants, expressed the hope that the meeting would lead to a true and lasting alliance between the two peoples. This hope was reiterated by Shams-ud-Din Sami and Rashid al-Khaza'i. . . . Salim Pasha Abu al-Ajam spoke of the need to restore the friendly relations that had existed between the two peoples in earlier generations, and of the great desire of Emir Abdullah and all Transjordanian leaders to cooperate with the Jews. Mitri Pasha Zurikat said that the leaders of the Jordanian people recognized that cooperation with the Jews can only be beneficent, and called for an end to acrimony and bitterness, and for joining hands in peace. Similar feelings were expressed by Shams-ud-Din Bey Sami, and Abraham Shapiro (who spoke Arabic). I. Newman emphasized the policy of Weizmann, who had always preached cooperation and friendly and fraternal relations between the Jews and the Arabs, and the work of Arlosoroff in the two years of his incumbency. . . . He also praised the wisdom of Emir Abdullah and his concern for his people. Abraham Elmaleh (who spoke in Arabic and himself translated into Hebrew) recalled the close ties between the two peoples in the past, mentioning prominent Jews who made valuable contributions to the Arab world in poetry, literature, science and philosophy, medicine and finance, economics and commerce, and culture. Only after the seeds of jealousy and hatred, dissension and competition had been sown, was there a deterioration in the atmosphere and the relations between the two peoples. He called for a resumption of cooperation, for the benefit of the two peoples and of humanity at large. Dr. Weizmann, who described the meeting as one of the great hours of his life, spoke of his constant hope for mutual effort with the Arabs, his meetings with Faisal at the end of World War I, the agreement between them, and on their joint efforts at the peace conference. . . . He also hinted at his suggestion to the British Prime Minister in 1930 to allow Jewish bodies to launch enterprises in Transjordan to improve its economic position —a suggestion that was not accepted. Dr. Weizmann praised Arlosoroff's initiative, which had brought about the meeting. Dr. Weizmann also spoke of the wonderful cooperation between the two peoples in the Middle Ages and called for its resumption to the common advantage and the benefit of mankind. He concluded by saying, "The work we shall now begin will be like digging a tunnel in the hills. Both sides must start tunnelling—you from one end, and we from the other, until we meet in the middle"—and he prayed that the day of meetings would not be far off. "Both peoples, Israel and Ishmael, were brothers once and will continue to be brothers in the future."

In concluding for the Arabs, Shams-ud-Din Bey Sami said, "The excavation of the tunnel that Dr. Weizmann referred to is not, in my opinion, too difficult, and with joint effort the diggers can manage to meet. But I fear that in the middle of the mountain we shall run into a steel partition that will prevent our meeting. This partition is the British government. Dr. Weizmann is charged with the burdensome task of removing this partition. If he succeeds peace will be assured and established on firm foundations."*

In the Central Zionist Archives (File S25/3510) containing the minutes of that meeting at the King David Hotel are also notes on the reactions of Palestinian Arab leaders. On April 12, 1933, the Arab Executive met at the home of Musa Kazim al-Hussaini (see Chapter Five) to discuss the King David meeting. Auni Abd-ul-Hadi said that his Istiklal party had decided publicly to discredit the Arab leaders who had met with the Jews. Jamal al-Hussaini (see Chapter Five) held that those people were not the sort against whom public opinion could be aroused; their influence in Transjordan would always be greater than that of the Palestinians. All that could be done was to prevent their being joined by others, and also to try peacefully to influence those who had already joined forces with the Jews.

Mithqal Pasha was a hard nut to crack. The Beni-Sakhr tribe would go through fire and water for him. The economic situation in Transjordan, which had impelled the tribal chieftains to do what they were doing, should be taken into account. It was decided to invoke the help of the Mufti Haj Amin al-Hussaini in getting a number of sheiks to approach the Transjordanian Bedouin tribes.

Letters were addressed to Adil al-Azma, Dr. Subhi Abu-Ghneima, Muhammad Hejazi, and Mahmud al-Cherkessy in Transjordan. Auni Abd ul-Hadi wrote to Faisal (King of Iraq): "The scion of Allah's prophet† has failed in his duty by opening the gateway of the Arabian peninsula to the Jews. Please take drastic steps." A copy of the letter was sent to Emir Adil Arslan and to Nabih Al-Azm. Auni wrote also to Fuad Hamza and Yusuf Yasin, high officials in the office of King Ibn Saud, urging them to hold up the treaty of alliance with Emir Abdullah until he broke off all relations with the

* The words are quoted from *Haboker*, September 25, 1944; memoirs by A. Elmaleh (unpublished) and documents in the Central Zionist Archives in Jerusalem.

† The Hashimites claim direct descent from the Prophet Muhammad, who was a member of the Hashim family of the Quraish tribe in Mecca.

Jews. The mufti wrote Emir Abdullah politely: "I am sure that the Arab-Jewish gathering was arranged without your knowledge and against your will. I have high hopes that you will do everything possible to put Mithqal al-Faiz back on the right track." The mufti decided to go to Amman for this purpose. The Jerusalem meeting of April 8, 1933 seemed likely to open a new chapter in Arab-Jewish relations in Palestine.

But while Arlosoroff was still deep in preparatory work, he was killed at the Tel Aviv seashore on a June night in 1933. An unknown hand murdered the promising thirty-four-year-old statesman for whom all forcast a great future in directing Zionist policy.

The direction of political activity in the Zionist movement now passed into the hands of David Ben-Gurion. Years later (at the *Histadrut* conference, April 6, 1944), Ben-Gurion summed up his abortive attempts to find some common ground with Arab leaders. His statement, like so many other Jewish Agency statements, glossed over a most important element: the question of what basis for accord was proposed by Jewish representatives. The only basis that provided any chance for reaching an agreement—political equality and parity* in government among the two peoples, and the establishment of a bi-nationalist framework—was never proposed to the Arabs; the idea was rejected by the same Seventeenth Zionist Congress that led to a reshuffle in the Zionist Executive, and forced Weizmann to resign from the presidency of the Zionist Organization after he had, in his opening speech, expressed willingness "to welcome an accord between the two racially close peoples on the basis of political parity." While the Congress was still in session, in an interview with the Jewish Telegraphic Agency Weizmann was quoted as saying:

> I believe that an accord with the Arabs is possible on the basis of parity. If Jewish and Arab representation is equal in the legislative council, it will provide a good opportunity for joint activity—I neither like nor understand the demand for a Jewish majority. A majority by itself is no guarantee of security. We can be in the majority in Palestine and even so we shall not have security. Neither is the majority necessary for Jewish cultural development. The world will interpret this demand in one way only, as if we are seeking to create a majority for ourselves in Palestine so that we can oust the Arabs. Why should we submit a demand which can only leave a provocative impression?[13]

Weizmann later claimed that he was quoted incorrectly. But in his speech to the Congress on July 1, 1931 he said: "We must and can arrange our life with them [the Arabs] on the basis of complete political equality, regardless of our relative numerical proportions now or in the future."[14]

* Political parity: A political system based on the recognition of two (or more) peoples within the state as sections of equal status and as equal factors in the legislative and executive bodies of the state, irrespective of the numerical strength of each.

When Weizmann was attacked at the Seventeenth Congress, in the famous debate on the "ultimate aim" of Zionism, and accused by the Revisionists of "withdrawal from the policy of the founder of political Zionism [Herzl]" he analyzed Herzl's policy first as defined in his book on the Jewish state, then at the 1897 Congress in Basle, and finally by Max Nordau in 1916. From these three statements of Herzl's policy, Dr. Chaim Weizmann claimed, "it is evident that the concept of a Jewish state can be found only in the book on the Jewish state; now, at the time this was written, it was not at all definite that Herzl intended Palestine to be the country where the realization of his plan was most likely. . . . Herzl's *Jewish State* appeared to view Palestine as an academic proposition and a pious wish that did not call for any special attention. It is not at all certain that he envisaged the Jewish state in Palestine. The whole tenor of his book justifies the assumption that when he wrote it he was thinking of some other country (Argentina), with Palestine as only a second best, probably added to please his Zionist friends." As to Herzl's *Altneuland*, even its author intended it "for the distant future."

In Weizmann's view, the correctness of this evaluation of Herzl's policy was borne out by subsequent political developments:

At the First Zionist Congress in 1897, when Herzl definitely joined the Zionist movement and thus accepted the idea of Palestine as the land for Jewish renaissance, the term "Jewish State" disappeared entirely from his plan; the version established by Herzl and the Zionist movement at the 1897 Basle Congress was "to establish in Palestine a refuge for the Jewish people secured by international law." The final stage of development in Herzl's policy, as he adapted to reality, was expressed by Nordau in the introduction to Paul Goodman's book *Zionism—Its Problems and Chances*, published in 1916, "that is, at the time of the first slight possibility that Palestine would become the subject of practical Zionist policy."

Weizmann quoted that statement of Nordau's verbatim, after describing it as a "very wise passage":

Zionism does not claim to return all the Jews of the world to the Holy Land of their forefathers. The return, settlement, and naturalization of all who remain devoted to Palestine with all their hearts cannot be considered. Only those who feel that they will find moral and material satisfaction in their lives and their happiness there alone will march eastward.

Zionism has no ambitions to found an independent Jewish state, be it a kingdom or republic. It has a single aim, that those who believe in it should be able to immigrate to Palestine without restriction, buy whatever land they can with their money, enjoy autonomous local government and not be hindered in their efforts to create a culture and economic prosperity. Naturally, Zionist Jews undertake to be most generously and scrupulously loyal to whatever power may rule Palestine.[15]

Thus, the principle of non-domination remained little more than a pious wish. It was not given concrete expression in the form of political proposals capable of serving as a basis for Jewish-Arab negotiations. In fact, over the years the great majority in the Zionist movement rejected the political concepts of Revisionism, but did not replace it with any positive political program.

The Political Regime of Palestine

The question of Palestine's political regime was first publicly debated at the fourth convention of the *Ahduth Haavoda*—the most important Jewish party of the day. The convention was held at Ein Harod in the spring of 1924, in accordance with a resolution taken a year earlier, at the third convention of the same party.

The political address was delivered by Shlomo Kaplansky (1884–1950), then the representative of the world office of *Poalei Zion* in London; in 1924, he was elected to the Zionist Executive in London. Summarizing the varied efforts that had been made to gain the support of the international labor movement for labor-Zionist aspirations, and analyzing the political situation in Britain (at whose helm the British Labour Party then stood), Kaplansky stated that "for years the Zionist Organization has been lacking political initiative, trailing behind political events in Palestine. For years the political negotiations in Palestine have been held between the British and the Arabs, and the role of the Jews has not been felt at all; we are either passive spectators or complain when everything is over."[16] He urged Jewish labor in Palestine and their allies in the world to "take the initiative, tell the Labour government that we are prepared to do something positive to arrive at a solution of the questions troubling us in Palestine."

"It is well known," said Kaplansky, "that the British administration in Palestine is full of reactionary and anti-Semitic elements. Not only do we Jews have cause for complaint, but even Arab circles suspect the government of double-dealing, and some among them believe that the government is purposely making use of this type of rule to stir up dissension between one people and the other."

Kaplansky noted three political possibilities:

(a) Direct control by the Mandatory government through its officials, without any consultation with the local inhabitants;

(b) the constitution of a legislative council (which was never carried out, since the Arabs boycotted it);

(c) joint Arab-Jewish self-government.

The speaker definitely rejected the first possibility on the ground that it could not survive in Palestine while self-government was developing in neighboring Arab countries. He also rejected the second possibility, because the excessive power it would give to appointed officials might make it synonymous with direct Mandatory control. The question was how to

S

advance toward a system of self-government. In preferring the last alternative, Kaplansky recommended a plan for self-government based on political parity —a parliament of elected members, and an upper house with equal representation for Jews and Arabs so that the majority might not abuse its prerogatives to the detriment of the minority.

Kaplansky did not ignore the many difficulties ahead:

> Any form of government will enable the effendis to strengthen their control over the masses, and I know how hard it is to reach an agreement with the leaders of Arab public opinion who hate us as workers and as bearers of a new culture and way of life. . . . Despite all the defects of democratic government, we should not forget that any honest nationalist movement begins with the ruling class, which initially uses its ideas to increase its strength and control. This is perhaps the only opportunity for the ruling class to wrap itself in a mantle of liberation and freedom, but such were all beginnings of national liberation. In spite of the fraud in all this, it is clear to us that a national movement is beginning in the East. We must look ahead and see to it that the effendis do not assume the guise of liberators of the Arab people. We must disclose the whole truth to the masses of the Arab people.

Kaplansky did not delude himself into thinking that the development of a concrete political program would dissolve Arab opposition to the Jewish endeavor in Palestine as if by the waving of a magic wand:

> When I speak of concrete proposals, I do not mean to say that they will immediately produce concrete results. But we must clarify for ourselves this political system; we must show that we have an opinion on the future of Palestine. . . . The British government must know not only our dissatisfaction with the existing order, but also our definite proposal. We must show British public opinion that in reply to Arab hostility, we have not only a principled stand but also a practical proposal on the form of future government. We must find a proposal that will not only be acceptable to our opponents, but also satisfy our own socialist conscience and that of the socialist movement the world over.[17]

Kaplansky's proposal found little encouragement in the conference and was attacked from all sides. The strongest opponents were B. Katznelson (1887–1944) one of the top leaders of Mapai and of labor Zionism, and David Ben-Gurion. Instead of developing a political program that would improve relations between the two peoples, the conference decided that "the main and most reliable means of strengthening friendship, peace, and mutual understanding between the Jewish people and the Arab people is, in the opinion of *Ahduth Haavoda,* the accord, alliance, and joint effort of Jewish and Arab workers in town and country." It instructed the executive committee of the party to work out ways and means to achieve the realization of a Jewish-Arab workers' alliance.

The experience of subsequent years proved that this decision was inadequate, for the Arab worker was not yet a decisive factor in the Arab national movement, and it was with this movement, not with the Arab workers, that the Zionist movement had to reach an accord. Experience proved that unless the Arab workers were shown a positive political perspective common to both peoples, there would not arise in Palestine an Arab workers' movement permeated with a spirit of brotherhood and real workers' solidarity.

The Jewish endeavor in Palestine had exerted, from its inception, a revolutionary influence on the Arab masses in Palestine and outside it, but the national conflict between the two peoples distorted and limited that positive influence. National tension not only corroded labor solidarity but also had intensified nationalist extremism. Instead of being liberated from the influence of the nationalist leadership, the Arab masses were impelled further toward them. The International Union of Railroad, Post, and Telegraph Workers, which was founded in 1919 on the initiative of Jewish workers, and to which both Jews and Arabs belonged, disintegrated. Despite the help given by the General Federation of Jewish Labor (the *Histadrut*) to the Arab workers in their initial organization moves in 1925, their "Union of Palestine Arab Workers" was under the influence of the Mufti and his men.

The Palestine Workers Alliance, set up by the General Federation of Jewish Labor, sought to draw into its ranks Arab elements with a more advanced political consciousness. But these could not be won over on the basis of economic interests alone, without an ideological-political foundation. The Alliance, therefore, had to fight an ideological battle among the Arab workers, opposing the nationalistic ideology with the ideas of brotherhood, a common homeland, a common political future, and class solidarity. This was an almost impossible task in a period of increasing politicization among the Arab masses, particularly since the organization of Jewish workers was itself also based on a nationalist platform. All that the Alliance could offer to Arab workmen at that moment was better economic conditions.

The rift deepened. The Jews never concealed their hopes for a large immigration, which would change the numerical relationship between the two peoples in Palestine. Moreover, the Jewish refusal to agree to determining the basis of the political regime of the country so long as they were a minority enabled Arab nationalist leaders to proclaim that the Jews aspired to become the majority in Palestine—to dominate and force the Arabs out. These nationalistic contentions naturally found widespread support among Arabs in Palestine as well as in the neighboring countries.

After the disturbances of 1929 and the Passfield white paper (1930), and in view of the growing political conflict, there were indications in the leadership of *Mapai**—the Israel labor party—of a trend toward the idea of binational parity. In his "Premises for the Determination of a Government in

* Jewish Palestine's (and later Israel's) largest party, established in 1930 through a merger of the *Ahdut Haavoda* and *Hapoel Hatzair* workers parties.

Palestine (in compliance with the demands of the Mandate, the aspirations of the Jewish people, and the needs of the Arabs in the country)," David Ben-Gurion stated in October 1930:[18]

> It is essential to establish just relations between Jews and Arabs, which are not dependent on the relations of majority and minority. The regime in Palestine must at all times assure both the Jews and the Arabs the possibility of unhampered development and full national independence, so as to rule out any domination by Arabs of Jews, or by Jews of Arabs. The regime must foster the rapprochement, accord, and cooperation of the Jewish people and the Arabs in Palestine.

He wished to see:

> ... Palestine as a federal state, comprising an alliance of cantons [autonomous districts], some with Jews in the majority, and some with Arabs; national autonomy of each people, with exclusive authority in matters of education, culture, and language; matters of religion: under the control of autonomous religious congregations, organised as free statutory bodies; the highest body of the state: the federal council, consisting of two houses—(a) one representing nationalities in which Jews and Arabs will have equal representation, and (b) one in which representatives of the cantons will participate in proportion to their respective populations. Any federal law and any change in the federal constitution can be enacted only with the agreement of both houses.

This was, in effect, Kaplansky's conception, which Ben-Gurion had rejected in 1924. Strong inclination toward bi-national parity was also expressed by Berl Katznelson in his address to the *Mapai* conference in 1931 on "Questions of the Political Regime of Palestine":

> As to the future form of political regime in Palestine, two points of view are current among us. One would postpone the constitution of any legislature "as long as we are not a majority in Palestine." The second would accept the legislative council that was proposed by Samuel, and again by Passfield in the 1930 white paper, or any similar substitute, so that we might not be accused of withholding self-government. The first point of view is ... obviously inadmissible—a ... morality which offers its brother what it rejects for itself; the rule of one national unit unacceptable today while we are a minority, will be valid tomorrow "when we are the majority."
>
> Mr. Greenberg of *The Jewish Chronicle* wants a Jewish state. He is bitter against any who contend that Zionism does not want to rule or dominate. That is not his idea. For two thousand years strangers ruled us, why should we not have a taste of ruling? I admit I have no such political appetite, just as I do not wish to see the realization of Zionism in the form of the new Polish state with Arabs in the position of the Jews and the Jews in the position of Poles, the ruling people. For me this would be the complete perversion of the Zionist ideal. ... Our generation has been witness to the fact that nations aspiring to freedom who threw off the yoke of subjugation rushed to place this yoke on the shoulder of others. Over the generations in which we were persecuted and exiled and slaughtered, we learned not only the pain of exile and sub-

jugation, but also contempt for tyranny. Was that only a case of sour grapes? Are we now nurturing the dream of slaves who wish to reign?

In the same address, Katznelson clarified the real meaning of the concept of a bi-national state, which had often been decried and ridiculed for partisan reasons:

Its meaning is not solely ethnographic—that is, to note the fact that two nations inhabit a certain area. States with two or more peoples in their confines are not rarities in the world, and this does not make states bi-national or tri-national, so long as one nation is the ruler in them. What is a bi-national state? One in which the two nations in it are equal in freedom and independence, in the degree of government and representative privileges, a state in which one nation does not dominate the other. The Arabs, like us, are interested in establishing democratic patterns for national life. These patterns will bring with them the satisfaction of national needs in the hands of the nation itself and within its competency, the limitation of the rights of foreign officials, internal social differentiation, and the creation of democratic national representation.

He stressed the necessity of assuring the Jewish people unhampered national freedom, and the need for international recognition of the establishment of the Jewish national home in Palestine. Katznelson concluded, "All this obliges us to seek the solution in a form of government that will prevent the domination of one people by the other, and we will find it if the legislative body is made up of two equal national groups."[19]

But these tendencies in *Mapai* to formulate a program for Arab-Jewish accord on the basis of bi-national parity were never fully worked out. According to the "Premises" of Ben-Gurion, the time for self-government on the basis of political equality between the two peoples in Palestine would come "upon our completing the construction of the Jewish national home." Even after the *Mapai* council resolutions in the spirit of Ben-Gurion's address, the party never took a definitive practical stand based on bi-national parity. Indeed, even Katznelson spoke of political equality between Jews and Arabs *when the time comes.*

That attitude was confirmed by the Seventeenth Zionist Congress, which forced Weizmann to resign, when it reiterated the equivocation about the general desire of the Zionist movement "to develop friendly relations and create amity between Jews and Arabs in Palestine based on the fundamental principle that whatever the number of the two peoples may be, no people shall dominate the other or be subject to the government of the other."* One of the weaknesses of Zionist policy has always been the subordination of foreign policy to internal party politics. At that time, the influence of the

---

* The statement of Nahum Sokolov (who was elected president of the Zionist Organization in succession to Weizmann), which was accepted as part of the new Zionist Executive's policy.

Revisionists was increasing, their nationalistic propaganda was spreading in Palestine and the Diaspora, and the Zionist labor movement was not strong enough to swim against the stream in defense of the basic values common to all its components.

Kaplansky described these developments aptly when he said later, "These buds never blossomed. The Hitler catastrophe, the disturbances of 1936–1939, the Peel commission and the partition plan, the growth of pro-Nazi ideas among the Arab leaders: All these put an end to the crystallization of positive and constructive Zionist thinking."[20]

In the spring of 1936, five years after the retirement of Colonel Kish, and three years after the direction of Zionist policy had been given to David Ben-Gurion and M. Shertok (Sharett), riots broke out again, after a few relatively peaceful years and considerable progress in Jewish immigration and settlement. The Hebrew press once more took the Zionist leadership to task for ignoring the political problem of Arab-Jewish relations, noting that "When the situation is good, we do not want to speak with the Arabs, and when it is bad, we say it is impossible to speak."

Such criticism was voiced not only by opposition circles, but also by circles responsible for the direction of Jewish policy. M. Assaf, one of the Mapai experts on Arab affairs, wrote in *Davar*, the daily paper of the *Histadrut*, on August 3, 1936:

> What have all the Zionist Executives up to now done, if not to solve, at least to ease the severity of the Arab-Jewish problem? What initiative did Zionists take in this field? And what deliberate and practical cultural, economic, or social activities were undertaken toward this aim by the higher Zionist bodies? Was a complete and inclusive program on the Arab-Jewish question ever formulated in any higher Zionist body? Not a single serious attempt (or even a desultory one) to deal with the question! In the forty years of political Zionism we have had congresses, conventions, councils, and committees on all sorts of topics and matters, all of them doubtless important, but when did a Zionist quorum ever get together to formulate a plan on the Arab-Jewish question, the importance of which is indisputable? Have they not dealt with the question hastily and without the great seriousness such a vital problem deserves? It is shocking: for dozens of years we have known that this terrible question faces us, and we have not yet devoted serious attention to it. . . . What preparations were made [by the Zionist movement] for this, where are the signs that it paid one thousandth of the attention to this problem that it did to every detail of the upbuilding of Palestine? Have we lost the ability to admit our omissions?

The idea of political parity once again came up during the 1936 disturbances in Palestine. I. Lufban, the editor of the *Mapai* organ *Hapoel Hatzair*, wrote, in August 1936:

> Zionism has repeatedly declared publicly that it aspired to a kind of government in Palestine in which there will be no domination of one people by the other, and not

only for the period when the Jews are a minority in Palestine, but also for the days when the Jews are a majority. The declaration alone, of course, is not yet binding, and it is not sufficient to allay any suspicion that may be present. But there is no doubt that the Zionist movement was always willing, and is willing now, to agree to an international guarantee that will establish the principle of non-domination as a basis for a . . . lasting Palestine constitution.

The truth was that the idea of political parity was not accepted as a basic principle by the Zionist movement even then. The sharp conflict within the various Zionist parties between those favoring parity and those opposing it was never resolved. In these circumstances, no responsible Zionist body could do more than offer the vague slogan of "non-domination."

The Rise of Fascism

The Palestine disturbances—which continued intermittently between 1936 and 1939—and the partition plan proposed by the Peel commission in 1937 had a far-reaching impact on Arab-Jewish relations. The international political situation, too, contributed to the aggravation of the national conflict. Arab leaders now aligned themselves with the Nazi-Fascist axis, which was using Arab nationalism as a convenient tool in a violent campaign against its imperialistic opponents in the Middle East. The Arab-Jewish struggle over Palestine thus became a contest between hostile foreign powers as well as between Jews and Arabs. Jewish-Arab accord, which had not been achieved even under more favorable local and international conditions, was now even more difficult to attain. On the eve of the war, the Fascist powers were able to promise the Arabs more than they could expect to obtain in negotiations with the Jews. For the same reason, the British government sought to appease the Arab leaders.

The Jewish community had withstood the campaign of Arab violence and had recorded noteworthy achievements in the fields of settlement, politics, and security, which it had not managed earlier (see Chapter Five). Unfortunately, Zionist policy did not tackle the political problem of Arab-Jewish relations with equal zest. The political report of the Executive of the Jewish Agency for Palestine, presented to the twentieth Zionist Congress in August 1937, contented itself with noting that "the tendency to compromise and make peace with the progress of the Zionist effort, which was apparent in various sectors of the Arab community during the time of the largest immigration, ceased to make headway, and the line of those opposing peace became paramount."

Zionist Policy and Arab Reaction

For a long time—and perhaps even today—it was widely believed that while Jewish leadership wanted accord with the Arabs, Arab leadership was united in extremist opposition to the Jews. Some spokesmen for official Jewish policy could not deny that one Arab leader or another seemed inclined toward agreement with the Jews, but it was generally believed that the vast majority of Palestinian Arabs supported extremist opposition and made impossible any effective accord. In Arab circles, the opposite view was widespread, there it was believed that there had been Arab attempts to find the way to understanding but that Jewish policy alone had made accord impossible. The fact that there were also Jewish groups striving consistently for Arab-Jewish cooperation had no great importance, argued the Arabs, since these were a minority and did not determine Jewish policy.

There were, of course, people on both sides looking for a way to understanding. Jewish and Arab leaders had more than once tried to bridge the gap between the two national movements. The failure of any such attempt added grist to the mill of Arab extremists and increased Jewish pessimism. This sort of chain reaction shaped the relations between the two peoples in the period under discussion.

The Status of the Two Peoples

Zionist leaders would often remark in despair, "We did what we could to achieve an accord with the Arabs, but our efforts were in vain."* But few Jews are willing to admit that similar complaints were voiced by the Arabs against the Jews. In any case, it was in the interest of Jewish policy to help and encourage Arab trends toward a compromise agreement and thus weaken extremist influences.

This was possible. There were several Arab intellectual leaders who opposed the policy of the *Mufti*. Some did so in the hope that Arab-Jewish cooperation would play an important part in the economic development of the Arab east, the Arab National revival, and the international standing of the Arab world; others did so from their realistic understanding that the Arabs did not have the power to counteract the Jewish effort in Palestine and would have, sooner or later, to come to terms with the Jews if they were to realize their own aspirations to Arab unity and independence. In view of later developments, it is important to note that various attempts to bring about negotiations between the leaders of the two peoples were actually supported by Istiklal (Independence) leaders in Palestine and in the

---

* H. M. Kalvarisky, who played an important part in the negotiations, stated, "It turned out that though we stretched out our hand in peace, we withdrew it immediately when the other party expressed a willingness to take it. This dangerous game did not help to raise us in their estimation as honest people, and their charge, that we are pursuing a two-faced policy—on the one hand pretending to seek an accord, and on the other merely biding time—is not groundless." (*At the Parting of Our Ways*, p. 35).

neighbouring countries—in other words, by the very faction in the Arab national movement that placed the unity of the Arab world at the centre of its political credo and program.

Indeed, it was easier to solve the Arab-Jewish Palestinian problem within a common framework with the neighboring Arab countries, than within the confines of the 27,000 kilometers of Palestine west of the Jordan. The fact that actual political conditions, such as foreign rule, the distribution of the various Arab countries among different outside powers, the socio-political back-wardness of the Arabs themselves, militated against the establishment at that time, of a broader political framework, made it difficult to find an immediate solution but did not invalidate it as an acceptable basis for the two peoples for a common struggle to achieve their aspirations.

It was obviously an oversimplification to contend, as did some Jews, that "the Arabs were never ready for any accord." Official Jewish bodies could not deny several impressive facts: In 1928, the year before the 1929 distur-bances, the well-known Syrian leader Ihsan al-Jabiri visited Jerusalem. A prominent Jew who had worked for many years for Arab-Jewish *rapproche-ment* launched serious political talks with him, and a party of *Istiklal* leaders—including Auni abd-ul-Hadi, Rashid al-Haj Ibrahim, and Emir Arslan. They decided that it was to the advantage of both sides to stop the dissension as soon as possible. As a first step, the Arab notables undertook—contrary to prece-dent at the six previous conferences—to exclude from the agenda of the seventh Arab conference about to convene any reference to the Balfour Declaration or any protest against it. This silence, the Arab leader said, would be understood as silent acquiescence, while overt public consent on the part of all Arab parties would come later, when the negotiations between the two parties had achieved accord.

The Arabs kept their word and there was subsequent reference to this at the Shaw commission of enquiry. The Arab spokesman who claimed that the Arabs always opposed the Balfour Declaration and protested against it "in all their conventions" was asked to explain the absence of such a protest in the resolutions of the seventh convention. The spokesman tried to explain it away by saying that "we demand the creation of a parliament, which is the same thing" (i.e., a parliament in which the Arab majority could abrogate the Declaration). That explanation was not very convincing: All the Arab con-ventions, before the seventh and after it, had without exception, not believed that demanding a parliament and protesting the Balfour Declaration were "the same thing," and invariably passed express resolutions against the Bal-four Declaration. When the Arabs later insisted that the counter-promise to continue negotiations be kept, "we had not the courage and shirked under pretexts of all kinds. I must say I was ashamed to face the Arabs after this behavior," wrote Kalvarisky later.[21]

The failure of this attempt naturally strengthened extremist influence; it was at this time, in fact, that the Mufti rose to prominence—the concomitant of this rise being the outbreak of the 1929 riots. Colonel F. H. Kish, the head of the Zionist Executive's political department in Jerusalem, pointed out at the time how much the absence of any "definite Arab policy" contributed to the failure of any chance for real negotiations. In the absence of any concrete proposals, it was natural for the Arabs to harbor the impression that the peace declarations of the Zionist congresses were only tactics aimed at dulling Arab alertness and gaining time.

After the 1929 riots, the Zionist Executive recalled H. M. Kalvarisky to the political department and instructed him to use his connections and experience to look for a way toward Arab-Jewish accord. Not long thereafter, he was to leave the work in disappointment. But in the meantime he wrote, "On August 4, 1930, at the request of the most important members of the Arab Executive a draft of an Arab-Jewish agreement was submitted to the Arab mission that had returned from London; this was done with the knowledge but not the official approval, of the Zionist Executive, and here were the seeds of the failure. The Arabs accepted the program as a basis for negotiations* and insisted on its formal confirmation by the Jewish Agency. But such confirmation was postponed until Arab patience was exhausted and the negotiations stopped. Whatever the real reason for such dilly-dallying, the facts tell a sorry tale: that from 1930 to 1931 the question of an agreement with the Arabs, based on a program all Arab parties accepted as a basis for negotiation, was under consideration; that the president of the Zionist Organization himself, Dr. Chaim Weizmann, supported it as being compatible with his plans; that the other members of the Agency Executive from 1930 to 1931 with the possible exception of one found no flaw in it, nevertheless I was obliged to terminate the negotiations."[22]

An Attempted Settlement and Its Failure

Until the publication in 1953 of Moshe Smilansky's autobiography, *Revival and Holocaust*, few knew of a significant, if abortive, landmark in the history of attempts at political accord. This occurred in the summer of 1936, a month after the outbreak of the disturbances. In *Revival and Holocaust*, Smilansky wrote

Among the Arab leaders there were also some who genuinely tried to find the road to a compromise between the two hostile peoples. They were among the friends of

* Kalvarisky held that this was not yet a detailed political program but rather a formulation of several fundamental principles as a basis for practical negotiations: both parties' recognition of each other's rights, acceptance of cooperation and mutual help, Arabs' consent to Jewish immigration to Palestine and the neighboring countries (without mentioning numbers), Palestine as a bi-national state.

Dr. Magnes and Kalvarisky, and discussed with them ways of containing the stream of evil that had swept over the people of Palestine.

"Ever since the beginning of the riots, the High Commissioner had tried to bring the two parties to negotiate at a round table conference in London. (Because of the Axis incursions against Britain, the British were not interested at the moment in the development of an armed conflict in Palestine.) To bring the two parties together, it was necessary to establish in advance basic lines of agreement between them. For this purpose, five Jewish personalities, some of whom had reached the point of close negotiations with the influential Arab leaders, got together and by common consent, a draft of an agreement was formulated. This was to have been approved by the Jewish Agency and the Higher Arab Committee before the High Commissioner declared it illegal (on October 1, 1937). The five prominent Jews were Pinhas Rutenberg (the managing director of the Palestine Electric Company), Dr. Magnes (president of the Hebrew University), Justice Gad Frumkin (of the Supreme Court), M. A. Novomeyski (the founder and manager of the Palestine Potash Company at the Dead Sea), and M. Smilanski ("Yehuda," as he called himself in his autobiography). Among the Arab leaders were the Assistant Crown Counsel Musa al-Alami, a man of wide influence in the Arab community who participated with the knowledge and assent of Emir Abdullah, of Transjordan, and several others close to the Higher Arab Committee."

In a personal note submitted to the Jewish Agency, Pinhas Rutenberg made the following suggestions:

1. Any serious attempt to find a way out of the Arab-Jewish tangle should aim not at a temporary accord with Arab leaders in Palestine but at a permanent settlement with the Arab world as a whole.

2. To achieve this the Jews must submit precise, far-reaching, and sincere proposals.

3. Economic concessions alone are now insufficient to pacify the Arab national movement. The concessions would have to be both economic and political.

4. No worthwhile practical arrangement is attainable unless it includes eastern Transjordan within the area of Jewish interests; Palestine and Transjordan must be considered a single unit.

5. The governments of Britain, Palestine, and Transjordan must be parties to any agreement between the two communities.

ECONOMIC PROPOSALS

a) The question of immigration must be considered by a tripartite Jewish-Arab-British committee. The absorptive capacity of Palestine shall be the main yardstick for deciding the annual number of Jewish immigrants permitted to enter Palestine. The number of unemployed in Palestine, to be determined every six months, shall be the criterion for the country's absorptive capacity. When determining the number of unemployed, only those people actually making their living from wages shall be taken into account. Farmers and nomads shall not be taken into account.

b) If the number of unemployed is 10 percent of the total percentage of wage earners, the situation shall be considered normal and have no effect on immigration quotas.

c) The entry of immigrants in the categories of capitalists and relatives of agricultural settlers shall not be affected by unemployment.

LAND

A joint Arab-Jewish committee of experts must survey the land held by Jews and Arabs with a view to an agreement on future purchase of land, as follows:

a) The areas in Palestine and Transjordan in which Jews are permitted to buy land should be determined, as should the extent of such purchases.

b) The minimum land area that may not be sold should be fixed, so as to avoid landless fellaheen selling their land to Jews or Arabs. The committee may specify cases in which the sale of land shall be absolutely prohibited and also permit exchange of land areas.

WORK

a) In all Jewish settlements and industrial enterprises, except those financed and directed by the Jewish national bodies (Jewish National Fund, Palestine Foundation Fund, Jewish Agency), Jews as well as Arabs must be employed. The proportion of Arab labor must be 25 percent in Palestine and 50 percent in Transjordan.

b) Every government department, public works, posts and telegraph, Palestine Railways, customs, etc., must employ Jews at least proportionately to their number in the country (now 30 percent of the total Palestinian population).

JOINT ACTIVITY IN COMMERCE AND INDUSTRY

a) Arabs must be enabled to invest in any new commercial, industrial, or transport enterprises of more than £25,000, and to take part in its management in proportion to their investment.

b) In any enterprise with a capital of £25,000, a seat on the board of directors must be offered to an Arab representative, even if the Arabs are not partners in the enterprise.

c) Where established companies decide to increase their capital, they must allow Arabs to participate and assure them representation in the management of the company in proportion to the capital they invest, and one seat on the board of directors, even if they have not participated in the investment.

d) Any commercial, industrial, or transport enterprise of £25,000 capital, save such as are financed, directly or indirectly, by Jewish public bodies, must employ up to 25 percent Arabs; at the same time, Arab enterprises shall be required to employ Jews at their offices. The government must employ Arab and Jewish officials in proportion to their number in the country.

e) Some method of joint effort must be found for both existing and prospective Arab and Jewish cooperative ventures.

f) The government must find a way to treat Palestine as a dominion for purposes of tariff preferences in all markets of the British Empire.

POLITICAL PROPOSALS

a) A legislative council, based on Arab-Jewish equality, with full powers to make laws, shall be constituted in Palestine. This equality shall not be affected in the future by changes in the population figures of the two peoples. The chairman of the council shall be a person appointed by the High Commissioner from among candidates nominated by the Arabs and the Jews.

b) Immigration, land, and employment shall be brought up to the council only after Arab and Jewish agreement on them has been reached in committees, in accordance with the above-mentioned principles.

c) The Commissioner for Palestine and Transjordan shall be appointed only after consultation with the two groups, the Jews and Arabs, and upon their approval of the candidate.

d) Palestine together with Transjordan shall be treated as a dominion, in accordance with the principle laid down by the Empire conference at its last session, i.e., they shall have the right to secede from the British Empire if the two peoples so decide.

e) The participation of Palestine and Transjordan as an independent member of an Arab union, should it be created, may be considered, but must be dealt with on the basis of the following conditions: [1] The British government alone, or in conjunction with the French government, must guarantee the security of Palestine, the preservation of its constitution, and the rights of the Jews. [2] No discrimination against the Jews of Palestine and Transjordan must be permitted in the other countries forming the union, and in all of these countries Jews residing in them must be treated like the rest of the population as regards participation in land cultivation, commerce, or industry, or at least their rights shall not be less than those other residents, according to law.

Rutenberg concluded:

Possibly the proposals for a permanent solution to the Arab-Jewish problem set out in this note embody certain dangers, but so important and exalted their purpose is, that it is worthwhile taking a risk, and we must accept them. In addition, the dangers menacing the development of the Jewish national home at present and in the future, if matters remain as they are, are much greater.

Magnes and Musa al-Alami submitted their own report proposing that an agreement be made between Jews and Arabs, which would be valid for five or ten years, after which it would be reconsidered. The agreement should be made immediately, without the intervention of the government but with its subsequent confirmation. The agreement should cover political and economic matters. The more important points were:

a) *Immigration.* [1] Arab workers shall not be permitted to enter Palestine from neighboring countries. [2] Immigration permits for Jewish workers shall be issued in accordance with the absorptive capacity of the country, and on the condition that a certain number of Arab workers shall be employed. Capitalists and relatives shall have unrestricted entry. [3] Jews shall be employed in government offices in proportion to their numbers. [4] The determination of the absorptive capacity must take into account the number of unemployed, but only those earning their livelihood from wages, and not agricultural workers or Bedouin. [5] Jewish immigration during the years of the agreement must not increase the number of Jews in Palestine to more than 40 percent of the total population.

b) *Land.* [1] The fellah may sell only three quarters of his land, but not the last quarter. He must be assisted in working the rest of his land efficiently. [2] If land worked by tenants is sold, they must be left a viable area there, or be given one elsewhere in the country, and the purchasers of the land must help them to work their land rationally.

c) *The political aspect.* [1] A legislative council should be established on the basis of equality between the two peoples, and in such a way that one people may not dominate the other. [2] The participation of the Jews and Arabs in the senior governmental posts in the country must increase; as a first step, one Jew and one Arab respectively shall be appointed directors of two important government departments; and one Arab and one Jew shall be appointed members of the executive council.

METHOD OF NEGOTIATION

The Agency Executive should empower the above-mentioned five Jews to negotiate with representatives of the Arabs, likewise unofficial, to determine definitely the policy on immigration, land, and a legislative council. Their recommendations thereon should be submitted to the Jewish Agency and the Higher Arab Committee for approval. If the two official bodies reach an agreement on the main points, they should meet to issue a statement authorised and approved by both, as follows: "The executive of the Jewish Agency and the Higher Arab Committee have decided to enter upon official negotiations, in the course of which the Higher Arab Committee will stop its strike, and the Jewish Agency will cause to be suspended the entry of immigrants above last year's quota."

Smilansky continues, "The five Jewish negotiators, after internal deliberations as well as talks with official and unofficial Arab leaders, submitted a detailed report to the Jewish Agency in which they stated":

Immediately after the beginning of the Arab strike, we learned that the riots would continue and were likely to impel the government to take measures prejudicial to Zionist aspirations. We therefore met and discussed the situation to see whether it was not possible to work out a fair program for negotiations with influential Arabs, so as to put an end to the present strike, and later perhaps to arrive at some means of achieving permanent peace between the two peoples. All of us have been in this country for some years, have had contact with a number of Arab leaders in Palestine, Transjordan, Syria, and Iraq, and have had various opportunities to establish the views of the Arabs on Jewish-Arab relations. We have all had contact with government officials, and their views are clear to us; and although we disagree on some details, we are united on the fundamental points of approach, as follows:

a) The establishment of the Jewish national home will not be assured of success if an agreement with the Arabs in Palestine is not reached.

b) Even if it were possible, despite Arab opposition, this would involve inevitable disturbances that invariably lead to loss of life and property, and would waste precious time. The advantages of carrying out the work of settlement with Arab consent are therefore incalculable.

c) Now that a new generation of Arabs is growing up in a nationalist spirit, it is harder to reach an agreement than it was ten or fifteen years ago. But we are convinced that now, too, there exists a possibility of reaching an understanding with influential Arab leaders who would be prepared to urge most of their community to come to an agreement with the Jews.

d) All Arab circles believe that at the present rate of immigration, the Jews will soon be a majority in Palestine and the Arabs a subjugated minority. We believe, therefore, that a basis for an agreement with the Arabs can be found only on the basis of a pre-determined immigration quota for a limited period.

e) In recent talks with several Arab leaders, we learned that a minimum of 30,000 immigrants a year for the next ten years (which will place the Jewish population at 800,000 in ten years, in 1946, or 40 percent of the total Palestinian population) would be considered a basis for negotiating a comprehensive agreement.

f) We believe that an agreement on immigration will lead to accord on other matters: land, labor, the civil service, and a political arrangement on the basis of equality between the two peoples.

This was the report of the five to the Jewish Agency Executive. Smilansky continues:

On the 29th of May, a month after the outbreak of the disturbances, Rutenberg and Frumkin asked the head of the Jewish Agency to arrange a meeting between "the five" and the Jewish Agency Executive. The meeting took place on June 1, attended by "the five," three members of the Executive, Ussishkin, and Berl Katznelson. The Agency members sought to delay a final decision pending further consideration. After a few days, the head of the political department advised that opinion was divided in regard to the immigration quota, and they therefore wished to consult the chairman and Weizmann in London. Although "the five" urged an early effective decision, for the situation was getting worse and worse, the reply arrived only on June 16, saying that the Agency agreed to setting immigration quotas for a limited period, but on the basis of the preceding year's quota, 62,000, and that the negotiations with the Arabs must be by the Agency department set up for this purpose, not by private individuals. The five continued their pressure, and on the twenty-fourth another meeting took place with the Agency leaders at the home of Ussishkin, who summed up as follows:

(a) The Agency Executive welcomes the offer of assistance in negotiations with Arab leaders.

(b) The proposal to fix an immigration quota for ten years is acceptable, but on the basis of the 1935 quota.

(c) The question of whether certificates already issued should be utilized should not be raised.

(d) The five can continue the negotiations with Arab leaders and maintain close contact with the Agency and exchange information with them. But they may act only on the course determined by the Agency.

The five knew that the immigration conditions would make their task difficult, especially since some of the moderate Arab leaders had left the country, but they decided in any case to try their hand, and insisted that the Agency lay down the general lines immediately. The head of the political department promised to supply the answer after consultation with the chairman of the Executive [David Ben-Gurion], who was then in England. The latter returned to Israel and left again, and there was no reply for four weeks. The whole matter—and not only this particular matter—was hushed up.

Additional information on these negotiations, provided in Justice Frumkin's autobiography (*A Judge in Jerusalem*, Dvir, 1954/5, Chapter 6), confirms Smilansky's story. Frumkin quotes the memorandum of the five to the Jewish Agency Executive, July 14, 1936, as concluding:

"The undersigned wish to express their great concern and sorrow at the stand of the Executive. Once again a last-minute opportunity to pave a path for the unhampered development of the Jewish national home has been missed."

In his covering letter to Shertok (Sharett), Frumkin requested that copies be circulated to all members of the Executive. In his reply of August 14, 1936, Sharett confirmed that copies, with his (Sharett's) comments, would be circulated to all members of the Jewish Agency Executive, and that a copy of the comments would be supplied to Judge Frumkin.

Three months later (November 4, 1936), Judge Frumkin wrote to Sharett to say that the promise had not been kept. "I am informed by two of my co-signatories," he wrote, "that at least four members of the Jewish Agency Executive have not received copies of the report."

Meanwhile, Mr. Sharett communicated directly with Musa al-Alami, without the knowledge of the five negotiators. The latter gave details of their conversation to Dr. Magnes who informed Rutenberg. Rutenberg complained that this action was detrimental to the efforts of "the five."

Sharett wrote to Dr. Magnes on August 13, 1936 to correct some inaccuracy in details. Dr. Magnes checked the details of his report again with Musa al-Alami, and after confirmation by Musa al-Alami, submitted it to Mr. Sharett on August 20, 1936.

Dr. Magnes recorded that:

Mr. Sharett called on Musa al-Alami at his office in the law courts and told him that any agreement with the Arabs must be confirmed by the Mufti and Jamal al-Hussaini, who were the only honest leaders among the Arabs. Raghib [Nashashibi] is unreliable. Alami said that he was prepared to continue the discussions, but there must be prior agreement on essential points if they were to be fruitful. He would not be able to communicate with his friends before such a provisional accord were worked out.

Shertok and Alami agreed to meet again in a few days. Shertok said he would reserve a room at the King David Hotel in the name of Dr. Bernard Joseph, who would henceforth be his spokesman.

On the appointed day, Alami found Shertok in Dr. Joseph's room at the King David. For about three-quarters of an hour there was desultory talk, after which

Shertok got down to business and gave Joseph the floor. Joseph spoke for twenty minutes, and said that Shertok was an important official person carrying heavy responsibility for any action he did or decision he made or any word he uttered, while Alami, an unofficial person, would not want to be like Dr. Magnes, a charming gentleman who carried no weight. Joseph asked whether Alami was speaking for the Mufti or some other leader. Alami said no, he was speaking for himself. Up to now he had treated all the conversations as confidential and not told anybody about them. In that case, said Joseph, Shertok would not be able to talk to Alami until he was convinced that Alami alone, or jointly with someone else, had the Mufti's authority to hold conversations with him.

Alami said he believed that it had been agreed the first day that they would first try to work out the general basis for an agreement. Alami was volunteering to be the guinea pig. He was among the most moderate in the Arab community; if it was not possible to settle a general basis for an agreement with him, there was very dim hope of success with others.

Shertok then said that without such authority it was useless to continue the talks. Alami himself, or together with someone else, must be authorized to tell him in advance, even before they began to discuss the general principles of the accord, that the Arab side was prepared to accept a reasonable agreement. He would leave it to Alami to decide whether to obtain the approval of all the Arab leaders or only a few of them. What was important to Shertok was the Mufti's authority. Alami said he could ask. Did Shertok want him to get directly in touch with the people mentioned or to wait until an opportunity arose?

Shertok said that he left that to Alami's discretion, but time was pressing. Joseph offered to call on Alami on Saturday or Sunday to get a reply. Shertok repeated what he had said in the first talk as to Joseph's authority to speak and act for Shertok. Joseph did not communicate with Alami again.

That was Dr. Magnes' record. In his covering letter to Sharett, Magnes wrote:

The impression we got was that there was not much desire on the part of the Jewish Agency Executive to continue negotiating with the Arabs, but that there was a tendency to bring about a situation where the negotiations would be broken off, not by them, but by the Arabs. For this reason, for example, they insisted that the maximum immigration quota of 62,000 serve as a basis. This was no compromise at all and would clearly not be acceptable to the Arabs. Then they communicated with Alami directly and pressed him to say he was speaking for the Mufti, which of course he could not announce officially even if the Mufti and Jamal knew the details of the talks—just as we would not say that we were speaking for Shertok and the Agency Executive though we were careful not to go further than would be acceptable to them.

Justice Frumkin comments on this important political episode:

A person viewing that period in retrospect will no doubt find that Shertok and his colleagues maintained their position wisely and with foresight. The state of Israel and our numerical preponderance in it prove the rightness of their stand. An accord

T

with the Arabs would have postponed the end; we would not have achieved what we did in the war of independence with arms and Divine guidance. But we were not prophets or sons of prophets, and although we were believers and sons of believers, and felt that liberation was not too far off, we did not expect it so soon.

I had before me only what my eyes could see—the foreseeable future. Who knows whether in the final analysis our loss would not have been our gain? The difference between 40 percent and 50 percent would not have been difficult to overcome within a few years. Under conditions of an agreement with the Arabs, World War II would have found the Jewish community in Palestine stronger by at least 100,000. We would not have reached the white-paper limit; who knows how many hundreds of thousands we would have saved from the Nazis during the war period. Again, had an accord been reached, it would have opened the gates of Transjordan to large immigration and unlimited opportunities in that extensive territory. There were certainly good intentions on all sides.

Smilansky reports on another set of negotiations he held because in his heart "he knew that nothing could be done by honest and open methods alone. Musa al-Alami was of course an upright man, and there were perhaps one or two others among them who were disinterested, but the members of the Arab Committee, not only those of the Mufti's party, would do nothing without some private advantage, and if the Arab Committee was unwilling, all the agreements in the world would not improve the situation." While his friends in the committee of five were laboring "to find a way to an accord with the best of the leaders," Smilansky believed that "an agreement of this sort could of course provide a 'paper bridge' to bring official Arab public figures closer to the desired aim, but there was need also for a 'money bridge' to change minds, as was customary in the East, and not only in the East, and even by those who could back up the authority with force."

On the advice of an Arab friend, Smilansky turned to his neighbor in Nes Ziona, Tawfik Bey al-Ghussain, whose son, Yakub al-Ghussain, was one of the ten members of the Arab Higher Committee. "Although Yakub represented nationalist youth, among whom there were honest people," Smilansky wrote, "he himself was neither pure nor innocent." Smilansky met with Tawfik Bey a number of times and spoke frankly to him, and it did not take long for the two to reach an agreement. The Bey understood matters as follows: "You have an 'innocent' who behaves altruistically, Magnes; and we have our own 'innocent' who is also altruistic, Musa al-Alami. Let the two of them work out a formula that will convince people, and we, practical people, will help them by arriving at our own acceptable 'formula.'" The Bey's "formula," settled after a number of visits to Jerusalem and discussions with several members of the Arab Higher Committee was as follows: the Jews would give £50,000; £5,000 to each of the eight members of the Arab Higher Committee, £5,000 to the Bey for his trouble, and an additional £5,000 to his son for " expenses." In return, the members of the

Higher Arab Committee would agree to the High Commissioner's proposal to stop the strike, and go to London with Jewish representatives to negotiate on the basis of the Magnes-Alami draft. The money would be held in trust or on deposit in a bank until the Arab Higher Committee kept its promises.

"Why only eight of the Arab Higher Committee members, since they are ten?" asked Smilansky. "The other two are Haj Amin and his brother-in-law Jamal. The first gets amounts of money from the Italians and Germans that the Zionists cannot match, and the second is a fool, he doesn't take money." This sort of talk was repulsive to Smilansky, but he knew that only through those dubious means was it possible to secure effective political gains. He promised a reply as early as possible. Knowing that he could not tell the truth of the story to his friends in Jerusalem—they would not find a source of money, and Magnes would reject any such negotiation with abhorrence—he decided to consult Rutenberg, who listened with great interest and agreed without hesitation to the bargain in principle. Without such tactics, so common in the East, nothing would get done; therefore, he agreed to give £25,000 from Electric Company funds for this purpose, the rest of the money to be given by the Jewish Agency. The Electric Company had already suffered losses to this amount as a result of the riots, and every additional day might cause additional damage.

But how could the money be obtained from the Agency? Here not only the money was important, but also the acceptance of the proposed agreement. Weizmann, who was again president of the Zionist Organization, was a resident of Rehovot; Yehuda [Smilansky] was a frequent visitor at his home, but he did not believe that he alone could influence him. Smilansky and Rutenberg went to Weizmann together. "Weizmann reacted favorably to the proposal, adding that such methods were used when necessary, even in larger countries, to prevent unnecessary bloodshed.... Weizmann undertook to convince the Agency but did not succeed."

"Yehuda was not surprised; he had long since reached the conclusion that the Agency leaders did not want an agreement that entailed concessions. An idea occurred to him: Could the High Commissioner be persuaded to provide the necessary sum of money? He conveyed this thought to Rutenberg, who doubted its efficacy; after all, it was not the money that was the stumbling block, but the Agency's unwillingness to negotiate. If they agreed to the principle, they would find a solution for the money.

"Smilansky disagreed with Rutenberg. If only the Arab and Jewish representatives would meet in London, it was very possible that they would come to some compromise agreement; any sacrifice was worthwhile if it could bring about such a meeting. He also believed that if the money were obtained and the Higher Arab Committee agreed to accept the proposal of the High Commissioner [Sir Arthur Wauchope] to stop the strike and send a joint mission with the Jews to London, the Agency would not be able to refuse. He therefore asked his Australian friend Andrews to tell the High Commissioner of his agreement with Tawfik Bey al-Ghussain. Andrews was happy to undertake this mission, but a day later he returned, obviously disillusioned. The High Commissioner had not accepted the proposal, though he was pleased at its initiation; he, like Rutenberg, held that the Agency's refusal proved its unwillingness to reach agreement—so why bother for nothing? Andrews added that the High Commissioner was disappointed by the Agency's attitude. It was not only Arab extremists who were preventing any chance of peace in Palestine, but also the Jews. This was the abrupt and unsuccessful end of the efforts of the five, as well as of the private initiative of Yehuda (Smilansky). . . ."

In the summer of 1937, two weeks after the issue of the Royal commission report (which was the first to suggest the partition of Palestine), Kalvarisky was asked to communicate to the Jewish Agency a proposal of the Higher Arab Committee to open Jewish-Arab negotiations to prevent partition of the country. The proposal called for an Arab-Jewish conference of seven Jews—two of them chosen by the Arabs—and seven Arabs, two of them chosen by the Jews (so as to ensure the participation of moderates as well as extremists and the successful result of the negotiations). The person submitting the proposal for the Arab Higher Committee (July 23, 1937) said, "We have despaired of the British. Whatever they do is done for their benefit, and every solution is worse than the preceding one. The time has come for us to take matters into our own hands, sit around a table, and try to find a way out of this complicated situation through joint efforts." The proposal was passed on to the highest Jewish body, which, according to Kalvarisky, "received it and gave it the full consideration it merited." However, "for various reasons those negotiations were never carried out, and in the meantime many of those interested in it were obliged to leave the country,"* At all events, "if I should be asked who contributed to the failure of this attempt, I would be lying if I said that only the Arabs were responsible for the failure."

---

* After the Royal commission report (July 7, 1937), Arab terrorist activities increased. Lewis Andrews, the Assistant District Commissioner of the Nazareth district (an Australian who was sympathetic to Jewish agricultural settlement), was killed on September 27. On October 1, 1937, the Arab Higher Committee was declared illegal, and Haj Amin al-Hussaini was dismissed from his post as president of the Supreme Moslem Council, which was disbanded. Moslem affairs, including charitable endowments (waqf) were taken over by a commission of two British Officials and an Arab unofficial member. Warrants were issued against several Arab leaders, including members of the Arab Higher Committee. Some of them were arrested and imprisoned in Palestine, five were exiled to the Seychelles Islands, and others—including the Mufti—fled Palestine and found refuge in neighboring Arab countries, from which, during the war, they went on to Iraq, Turkey, Saudi Arabia, Germany, etc.

In October, when the Arab leaders were no longer in Palestine, the Agency Executive submitted to the British government a proposal to convene a round table conference. The government's reply (October 26, 1937) was "In the present circumstances, it is not practical to convene such a conference."

In Palestine, bloodshed continued; The Woodhead commission, in January 1938, was instructed to propose boundaries for the partition; but when its report was issued on November 9, 1938, His Majesty's Government stated that no solution of the Palestine problem based on the establishment of Jewish and Arab independent states was practicable. In February 1939, the "London talks" began. After they proved ineffective, on May 17, 1939, the British government published a new White Paper, which continued in force until the end of the British Mandate on May 15, 1948.

1937—A Turning Point

The partition proposal of 1937 was a definite turning point in Jewish-Arab relations. It had far-reaching consequences. After a debate, which was among the bitterest in the Zionist movement, the Twentieth Zionist Congress (Zurich, August 1937) resolved, by a vote of 299 against 160, to authorize the Executive to negotiate with the British government on the establishment of a Jewish state in part of Palestine. The Peel commission recommended a Jewish state of some 5000 square kilometers—a hopelessly small area. Some Zionist leaders hoped that it would be possible to enlarge the area of the proposed state through negotiations with Britain,* but the proposal itself was received by a part of the Zionist leadership "with the greatest enthusiasm" (Ben-Gurion at the 1937 Zurich Congress).†

That "enthusiasm" was a measure of the loss of faith in the community of interests among Jews and Arabs, and in the possibility of foiling the restrictive British policy through a bilateral Jewish-Arab accord; it also derived from the hope that even a puny Jewish state would immediately make possible unhampered immigration and settlement. "Coming generations will take care of the future," argued its proponents.

Arab leaders, who had followed the internal Jewish struggle on partition, could read into that enthusiasm an intention to use the proposed Jewish state as a point of departure from which to transform the whole country into a Jewish state in the future. They opposed any such partition. The proposal for Arab-Jewish negotiations submitted at the end of July 1937 by the Higher Arab Committee—an attempt forced on the extremist wing of Arab leader-

---

* The Woodhead commission later recommended its reduction to only 3,300 square kilometers, or even to 1,250 (see Chapter Five).

† B. Katznelson, who had opposed partition at the 1937 Zurich Congress, warned against excessive enthusiasm (*Writings*, Vol. xii, p. 359).

ship by its more moderate elements—stressed that these negotiations were designed to prevent the partition of the country; "We shall not discuss partition at all, the Arabs will not accept it, and the whole Arab people will fight against it."

When the Arab Higher Committee was disbanded in October 1937, and those of its members who were not arrested fled to neighboring countries, they continued to direct Arab terrorism from there, with the increasingly substantial help—political, financial, and technical—of the Fascist Axis countries.

The Palestine Communist Party and the Mufti

Astonishing as it may seem in its very absurdity, it is an uncontrovertible fact that in the political campaign and acts of terror against the Jews during that period, Arab leaders, headed by the Mufti, also received moral and actual backing from the Palestine Communist Party. The Communists had a morbid hatred of anything connected with the Jewish national renaissance. At the outbreak of the 1936 riots, its central committee joined forces with the Arab "revolt administration," which seemed to it "the more progressive of the two opposing camps."

The Palestine Communist Party's (P.C.P.) support of the Arab administration founded by the Mufti was not exclusively political (as, for example, the slogans aimed against the Jewish national movement), but included concrete assistance "in the methods and means with which the Arab camp fights"—in other words, acts of terror. "By destruction of the economy of the Zionist conquerors," a P.C.P. poster said on October 17, 1936, "through acts of sabotage and guerrilla attacks, the Arab liberation movement is trying to make the continuation of Zionist colonization impossible."

A memo sent to the Comintern in September 1939 by a faction of the P.C.P. ("The Jewish Section") that opposed the official line of the party, included an admission that the Jewish members of the P.C.P. were required to help in the terrorist acts of the Arabs by throwing bombs at Jewish property, including the buildings of the Federation of Labor. The memo, which subsequently came into the hands of Jewish security forces, also revealed that when "the Jewish Section" wanted to condemn the terror against the Jews and recognize their rights to defend themselves against it, the P.C.P. opposed this. It was only in May 1939, or close to the end of the disturbances in Palestine as the outbreak of World War II drew near, that "the central committee at last recognized the fact that the leaders of the Arab revolt were working according to the directives of international Fascism." When that "Jewish Section" organized into a separate party, its first convention (August 1940) passed a resolution stating, "The convention sees in the rebellion of 1937 to 1939 one organised by Fascist agents. . . . The convention views these mistakes of the Communists as evidence of their attachment to the Hussainis, and of the liquidation of the party's independent course."

Another resolution adopted at that convention leveled against the P.C.P. the accusation that its disregard of the background of the political conflict in Palestine "prevented the party from perceiving the Fascist inroads in the colonial countries, aimed at creating points of support in the second imperialistic war" and that "this mistaken evaluation led the party to support nationalistic slogans on independence and the cessation of immigration, which in the Fascist period were exploited by it to acquire positions in the country."

The P.C.P. continued to idolize the Mufti even after the Comintern had branded him a Fascist agent. In the view of the P.C.P., the White Paper of 1939 was "one of the great achievements of the Arab liberation movement;" it was only at the convention of August 1940 that the White Paper was found to be "a tool in the hands of British imperialism to facilitate the preparation of the imperialistic war. . . . the White Paper," the resolution stated, "did not grant Palestine any progressive advances, it implied a continuation of the policy of 'divide and rule' under conditions of the eve of an imperialistic war."

After various splits and re-mergers, the central committee of that party tried to represent its pro-pogrom policy and blind submission to the leadership of Haj Amin al-Hussaini as "past mistakes of the party that were never approved by the masses of party members" and that "were, as is known, swept out of our party together with those responsible for them."*

With the dissolution of the Higher Arab Committee and the flight of its leaders abroad, the influence of the Mufti reached its peak. Palestinian Arab leaders now cast their lot exclusively with the Axis. This policy did not change even after the issue of the White Paper of May 1939, which proposed the perpetual restriction of the Jews to one-third of the total population, and would have destroyed their hopes of being once again a free and independent people in their homeland. Indeed, the early German military victories in the first two or three years of the war encouraged Arab leaders' hopes in the final triumph of their cause; now it appeared that through hitching their star to the Axis countries, they would rid themselves in one fell swoop of both the British rule and the Zionist movement. This increased Arab intransigence further stimulated the Jewish community's reassessment of its position.

* Correspondence between the central committee of the Palestine Communist Party and the *Histadrut* Executive on the nomination of candidates to the Sixth Conference of the *Histadrut*. A letter of the Palestine Communist Party's central committee dated July 29, 1944, in the *Histadrut* bulletin, August 1944, p. 4.

Nazism, with which the Palestinian Arab leaders had now thrown in their lot, was the bitterest and cruelest enemy of the Jews, whose only hope lay in the defeat of the Axis and the victory of the forces opposing it. The schism between the Jews and the Arabs, always deep, continued to deepen even more.

The Second World War

The first years of the war found the Palestinian Arabs, like those of the neighboring countries, in fluctuating moods that varied according to the ups and downs on the military and political fronts.

When the war broke out on September 1, 1939, disturbances ceased completely in Palestine. The Arab community was weary and tired of suffering. Arab terrorism, which had at first been aimed at the Jews, eventually spread to Arabs as well, as political feuds became increasingly interwoven with personal and family grudges. Fund raising for Arab political activity and acts of violence was often accompanied by extortion, kidnapping, and even murder. Where terrorism affected British interests directly, the British army imposed collective punishment on the Arab villages. Many of the wealthier Palestinian Arabs escaped to Lebanon and Egypt, Syria and Transjordan, in order to avoid the pressure of the terrorist commanders, many of whom were common folk who took advantage of their power to give the members of the upper classes a taste of their own medicine. Traditional *fasad* (personal quarrels and intrigue) was also in evidence, and such personal accounts were often "settled" by murder. After the October 1938 murder of the important opposition leader Hassan Sidky ad-Dajani* the National Defense Nashashibi Party left the Higher Arab Committee. Soon Arab "peace bands "made their appearance and were cooperating with British operations against the Arab gangs.

The first organizer of the peace bands was Fakhri Nashashibi, a police officer who for many years had worked closely with Raghib Nashashibi and acted on his behalf in political, economic and workers' affairs. Fakhri was one of the most active organizers of the April 1936 riots. After Arab opponents attacked him, he seceded from the Arab Higher Committee and began to organize the peace bands. He was murdered in Baghdad, in 1941. In a memorandum he submitted to the High Commissioner,† Fakhri complained that the terrorism sponsored by the Higher Arab Committee had received encouragement from the government and that 130 men from among the best Arab forces had been killed by the terrorists. He mentioned only the

---

* A writer and publisher, important delegate on committees, among the organizers of the 1936 riots, a follower of Raghib Nashashibi.

† This memorandum was presented to UNSCOP by the representatives of the Sephardic community, at the hearing of July 14, 1947.

notables, but the number of "ordinary Arabs" killed by Arab terrorists was much greater. According to Jewish Agency comments (March 28, 1946) on a survey submitted by the Palestine government to the Anglo-American Enquiry Commission, some 1,000 Arabs lost their lives in the Arab civil war at the end of the period of disturbances. Even according to Smilansky's figures, based on official data (see Chapter Five), the number of Arab victims of their own terrorism approached that of Jewish losses during the riots of 1936 to 1939.

As gang fought gang, internal terror poisoned the atmosphere in the Arab community and led to disintegration and depression. British tactics added fuel to the fire: While the civil administration was holding political negotiations with the leaders of the Arab rebellion and seeking ways to reach the members of the Arab Higher Committee who had fled or been exiled from Palestine, the British Army was heaping destruction on the simple folk, encouraging the peace bands, and appointing men of the opposition (especially Nashashibis) in place of Mufti adherents as heads of Arab municipalities.

Worn out by years of bitter, damaging, and inconclusive struggle and the internal strife that had accompanied it, Palestinian Arabs welcomed the end of the riots with relief. The increase in employment and economic prosperity that marked the beginning of the war, and the return of Arab-Jewish relations to their former course—which contained many elements of economic contact and even friendly intercourse* had their placating and healing effects. There was still, however, considerable Arab sympathy for the Axis powers as a stick with which to beat the hated British and French. The call for a war effort against the Axis found no response among the Arabs, while fifth columnists found fertile ground for propaganda. The radio broadcasts of the Axis, and especially the speeches of Haj Amin al-Hussaini and his friends in Germany, were listened to avidly. Here and there, anti-British leaflets were distributed, some of them inveighing against enlistment in British army units. At the beginning of the war, there were also some attempts at sabotage, and enemy broadcasts confirmed that there was a regular and effective information service from Palestine to Nazi and Fascist espionage and propaganda services. Some Arabs understood the lies and demagoguery in Axis propaganda, and the fate of the Lybian Arabs under the rule of Fascist Italians was a kind of object lesson. However, there was something stronger operating than the fear of what awaited the Arabs in case of an Axis victory—the hope of seeing the defeat of those who for decades had forced their rule on the Arab nations had overridden their most elementary rights, and trampled down

* The cessation of violence in Palestine after the war broke out strengthened the belief of many Jews and Arabs that the continuance of the interracial strife and disturbances was, at least in part, the result of British interest in having both Jews and Arabs exhaust their strength.

their national aspirations. Any possibility of defeat of the French and British armies gladdened the Arabs and raised their morale. At the same time, Palestinian Arabs showed some restraint and in general preferred to wait and see how the fortunes of war developed. Very different, of course, was the feeling of the Jews, who knew that a victory for the Axis meant the annihilation of the Jewish people.* It was abundantly clear what the lot of the Jews would be if Palestine were occupied even for a short time by the Nazi legions. The Jews considered the war against the Axis to be their war.

Despite the deep rift between Jewish leadership and the government after the May 1939 White Paper, when war broke out the Jewish Agency announced its willingness to put the entire Jewish potential at the disposal of the powers fighting Nazi Germany. The war office was asked to mobilize Jewish units in Palestine to defend that country and serve in the Middle East, and also to form units of Jews in neutral and other countries where military service was not compulsory. In a National Service Mobilization census undertaken by the Jewish Agency and the National Council of the Jewish community, 119,293 people (86,770 men and 32,523 women), aged eighteen to fifty registered for enlistment. The Jewish announced policy then was, "to fight in the war against the Axis as if there were no White Paper, and to fight the White Paper as if there were no World War." The first part of this policy was implemented. When the Axis Africa Korps advancing toward the Nile reached Al Alamein, in the hinterland of Alexandria (spring, 1942), and there was a danger that the British might retreat from Palestine for strategic reasons, a special unit—the *Palmach*—was set up within the framework of the underground defense organization of Palestinian Jewry. This unit was made up mainly of young people from the kibbutzim and the kibbutz-oriented youth movements, and it was trained in commando-type work to enable it to carry on guerrilla warfare against Axis armies, should Palestine be conquered by the enemy. In the Allied invasion of Syria (June 1941), a vital role was played by scouts and guides from the Jewish *Hagana* organization—this is where General Moshe Dayan lost an eye. Among these soldiers were members of the "Group of 43," who were first arrested by the British authorities while undergoing military training and then released to enable them to take part in the campaigns against the Axis. A boat carrying twenty-three *Hagana* members sent to sabotage the Vichy oil installations at Tripoli in Lebanon never reached its destination, and the cause of its disappearance remained veiled in secrecy.

The British authorities did not approve of the Jewish community's desire

* The Nazi leader Ley, stated in a speech: "We must now repair the record. In the Middle Ages we could have finished with this nation of usurers, we could have dug them out by the roots, and instead we let them escape to Poland. Now they are in our hands once more and will not escape. This time we must get rid of them completely."

to take part in the war as an organized group, and did their utmost to block it. Though in September 1940, they consented to the establishment of 200-man Jewish infantry units, two years passed before they agreed to concentrate them in battalions, and two more years passed before they approved the formation, in September 20, 1944, of a Jewish Brigade fighting under its own flag.* Typical of the strange British vacillation was an order of January 23, 1943, which actually prohibited any public encouragement of mobilization or its organization. Draft badges of mobilization were forbidden, and those "caught" wearing them were prosecuted. The order defined calling for individuals to join up as "provocation," for which a person could be prosecuted. A search conducted at the Jewish Agency mobilization office in Tel Aviv in April 1943, led the Agency to close all its draft offices, which were reopened only in July 1943, following negotiations in Jerusalem, Cairo, and London. The Agency was promised an opportunity for unhampered activity, but even then the January 1943 order—dubbed "the law for the protection of shirkers"—was not withdrawn.

In spite of all these British obstructions, 26,000 Jews (including 4,000 women) volunteered, a number (in proportion to the Palestine Jewish community) matching the two-and-a half million serving in England and the six-and-a half million in the United States. More than 400 Palestinian Jews were killed in the war, and 1,600 were taken prisoner by the Germans during the retreat from Greece and Crete. Geographically, Palestinian Jewish soldiers were widely scattered; they fought and served in Palestine, Egypt, the Western Desert, France, Greece, Crete, Syria, East Africa, Ethiopia, Malta, Iraq, Persia, Cyprus, North Africa, the Sudan, India, Sicily, Italy, England, Belgium, Australia, and Holland. The range of military service was most extensive: Jews participated as sappers, in transport units, as engineers, in medical services, workshops, signals corps, artillery, air force, navy, women's auxiliary corps, commando units, and as parachutists behind enemy lines. For a long time, the authorities attempted to ignore the participation of Jews in the war, concealing their presence behind the term "Palestinians;" but the national badges finally obtained for the Jewish units, and their actual war record, guaranteed the good reputation of the Jews wherever they served. Besides the members of the armed services, about 800 Jews served in the regular police and 6,000 as supernumerary police in special units charged with emergency duties: guarding the railway, air fields, military stores, etc.; 12,000 special volunteer policemen were trained for

---

* On March 3, 1945, the Jewish Brigade began to fight on the Italian front. When the enemy surrendered, the Brigade was given guard duties, first on the Italian-Austrian border, later in Belgium and Holland. Despite the request to keep the Brigade intact and transfer it to Palestine as part of the local garrison, it was disbanded on the demobilization of the Palestinian volunteers.

service in the Jewish Settlements Police Force and various defense tasks involving the use of arms.* Moreover, Palestine Jews contributed to the war effort by manufacturing military goods and medicines (the total value of military orders was thirty-six million pounds), in scientific and technical services provided especially by the Hebrew University, the Technion in Haifa, the Sieff Institute in Rehovot, and the Goldberg Institute in Tel Aviv. The Allied armies in Palestine and outside it were assisted by Jewish workers and experts in important construction and repair jobs. Jewish contractors, engineers, and skilled workers built roads, air fields, barracks, and bridges in Syria, Cyprus, and even Iraq and Bahrein, and helped enlarge the oil refineries in Abadan. In playing its part in the war against the Nazis, the Jewish community gained valuable experience in organization as well as in military tactics, in anticipation of their own war of national liberation.

As against this Jewish mobilization in the war effort, only 9,000 Arabs, including Transjordanians, Syrians, and Lebanese, joined up in Palestine; and long before the end of the war, their numbers had been halved by discharge or desertion.

Towards the End of World War II

With the turning point of the war, at the end of 1942 and the beginning of 1943, the military center of gravity passed over to Europe, and the "freeze" that had operated since the beginning of the war in the political life of the Middle Eastern countries began to thaw. The mood in Palestine after 1939 was one of an unfinished battle bound to break out anew when external political conditions permitted. After the years of Arab terror (1936 to 1939), there was new evidence of *rapprochement* and cooperation between the Jews and the Arabs. Some vital interests (in supply and manufacturing, passive defense, etc.) were common to the two peoples and entailed cooperation. Jewish and Arab orange growers again worked together in defending their interests; Arab and Jewish officials and government workers, or those engaged in army projects and foreign companies, (oil, potash, and commerce), cooperated in trade union campaigns, and there were numerous cases of good-neighborliness and friendly relations between the two peoples. The Jewish community of Palestine was now able to reap the benefit of its wise behavior during the three-and-a-half years of the disturbances, when, despite terrible provocation, it had adopted a policy of self-restraint, concentrated on self-defense, and had not permitted itself to embark upon indiscriminate vengeance and retaliation. The Arabs became aware of the fact that it was no longer possible to "uproot" the Jewish endeavor in Palestine by force, and many more Arabs began to believe that a compromise with the Jews was

* Data according to the *Report to the Twenty-second Zionist Congress*, 1947.

essential. The traditionally anti-Jewish leaders were almost all abroad, some as political exiles—prisoners of the British or under their supervision—some in Fascist Axis countries. Among Palestinian Arabs, there were new signs of an inclination toward *rapprochement* and cooperation.

Characteristic of these new winds was the renewed attempt of 1940-to 1941 to negotiate an Arab-Jewish accord. Adil Jabr, member of the Jerusalem Municipal Council and a highly educated Jerusalem Arab with many accomplishments and connections, took a bold initiative in that direction. He communicated at the suggestion of Kalvarisky with the political department of the Jewish Agency and received its consent (and support). Before leaving for Baghdad in the autumn of 1940 to make direct contacts with leading Iraqi, Syrian, and Palestinian Arabs (who were then exiled in Iraq), Jabr attended two meetings in the home of the head of the political department, Shertok (Sharett), with Kalvarisky and Mr. Eliahu Sasson (then head of the Arab section of the political department). A general exchange of opinion took place. Shertok expressed the Jewish stand, saying, "We do not suppose that any solution to the Palestine problem that is unacceptable to us can be a permanent solution; our stand on 'federation' will depend on the extent to which it ensures the realization of our basic aspirations." It was agreed that Jabr's trip would be considered private, and that if he felt it necessary to report the mood of the Jews to the Arab leaders, it would be in the guise of personal impressions.

On his return to Jerusalem, Jabr reported his impressions to Shertok and Kalvarisky. Following his talks with several Arab statesmen and leaders (of Iraq, Syria, Egypt, Transjordan, and Palestine), he now sought to advance the negotiations, and repeatedly asked for concrete Jewish proposals. After several months had passed with no response, he expressed to Kalvarisky his dismay and indignation over the sloppy and neglectful handling of this last, renewed, stage in the negotiations.

Adil Jabr had drafted the following five-point proposal, which he and Kalvarisky considered could serve as a basis for discussions with Arab leaders: [1] A federation or confederation of the Semitic peoples; [2] Autonomy for all its component states; [3] Palestine to enter the confederation as an autonomous country; [4] A bi-national Palestine based on full equality; [5] Opportunity for Jewish immigration to all countries of the federation, by agreement with the federated autonomous states. Jabr stressed that he would be able to negotiate on the basis of the above points if they were approved by the head of the political department of the Jewish Agency.

The proposal was no more than a point of departure for negotiation, and concrete details were yet to be worked out on such matters as the area of the planned federation; the extent of centralization and/or autonomy of its component political entities; the pace of realization of the full plan, etc. If matters had advanced to the stage of actual negotiations, they would no doubt have dealt with concrete questions involving Jewish immigration after the Jewish population had grown to equal the Arab (in previous talks, the Arabs had spoken of reaching this parity within eight to ten years, which implied an annual Jewish immigration of about 80,000). It was clear that current and future problems could not be fully resolved all at once; the objective at that point was to extricate the relations between the two peoples from their present impasse and safeguard both Jewish and Arab vital interests—for the Jews, unhindered immigration and settlement; for the Arabs, the beginning of political unity and independence for Palestinian Arabs.

On July 7, 1941, Sharett communicated to Kalvarisky his remarks on the proposed Arab-Jewish accord, in four short paragraphs, which included critical comments on the five points. Jabr requested some clarification. In the absence of Sharett, Kalvarisky conferred with Ben-Gurion on July 21, 1941. "I wanted to inform him of the situation," Kalvarisky wrote in his diary the following day, "and of the several trends in the Arab community, and to obtain his views. I wanted to find out for myself the reason for postponing the reply from day to day and week to week".

In the same diary, Kalvarisky noted Jabr's reactions to Sharett's remarks: "You see, Mr. Kalvarisky," Jabr had said, "Auni [Abd-ul-Hadi] was right when he told me in Egypt that as long as talk on accord is vague, the Jews would be found to be very agreeable to accord and peace, but when matters progressed to the stage of concrete proposals they will put all kinds of obstacles in your path and cause its failure."

When reporting to Ben-Gurion on his last talks with Jabr (and "in order to make it easier for him and recall the details of the matter to him"), Kalvarisky laid before him the Jabr proposals and Shertok's remarks. "Before he had had a chance to even glance at the Jabr proposal, he pushed it aside in unrestrained anger and said: 'I don't want to deal with this document at all, it's an abomination.'" When Kalvarisky rose to leave, "Ben-Gurion changed his tone. . . . There were signs of good will on his face. It looked as if he did not want us to part in an unfriendly way." According to the diary, he even promised a reply to Jabr's questions within a week. On August 19, 1941, Eliahu Sasson transmitted Sharett's reply, as follows:

(a) I reported to the Executive on the negotiations with Jabr. General objection to submitting written drafts was expressed, and I was criticized for doing so.

(b) A favourable attitude to the Federation will be conditional on a Jewish State being part of it.

(c) The C.I.D. [British Intelligence] is aware of the fact that we are in negotiation with the Arabs through him [Kalvarisky] and that written documents are being circulated.

Thus the negotiations ended. The bottleneck was Jabr's fourth proposal suggesting a bi-national Palestine, based on parity in government. Ben-Gurion's unwillingness to agree to parity (which he had ostensibly favored since 1931), and not the oft-heard complaint that "there is no one to talk to in the Arab camp," was the real obstacle on the way to accord. Nonetheless, the failure of the negotiations here described did not absolutely terminate all such attempts among the Arabs. As it became clearer that the Axis powers were losing the war, the trend became stronger. There were now several cases of *rapprochement* and reconciliation between various Jewish and Arab circles. It was again made clear that had relations been methodically and consistently nurtured, it would have been possible to work out a definitive working basis for agreement after the war. But the leadership lagged behind and looked in other political directions.

Change of Ideas in the Jewish Community

The Royal commission's partition proposal (1937), which was accepted by the majority of Jews, led to second thoughts among large sections in the Zionist movement. The prospect of an Arab-Jewish accord, which for years had been one of the declared political principles of the movement, began to give way to other ideas. Before then, only the Revisionists foresaw no chance of Jewish-Arab accord and believed it was the sword alone that would decide the fate of Palestine. For Jewish arms to prevail, they would have to consider themselves allies of the dominant power, or of some other Western country hostile to Britain if the latter did not properly understand its own interests and did not support the Jews in their conflict with the Arabs. (On the Revisionists' anti-British orientation see Chapter Five.)

Revisionist leaders bluntly declared:

We do not expect every nation to achieve sovereignty, and we are not for national self-determination under all conditions. We have an egotistical nationalist point of view. . . . In case of an East-West conflict, the people of Israel will always be on the side of the West. India and Britain? Our position on this question is what Churchill's has been from 1934 . . . in case of conflict between Eastern nativism and Western imperialism—we are for the second party."[23]

On the other hand, the great majority of the Zionist movement consistently claimed that there was no essential contradiction between the real interests and just national aspirations of the two peoples; hence their deep-seated faith in the practical possibility of establishing the relations between Jews and Arabs on a basis of mutual respect, understanding, cooperation, and reciprocal help, which would be a blessing to peoples in Palestine itself and in the entire region.

This was both a humanistic belief, founded on progressive ideas and values, and a very realistic attitude, based on the geopolitical situation of the country as a small island in the sea surrounding Arab lands.

The thinking of the Zionist movement now underwent a period of reconsideration. A large part of the Jewish community was tired of the protracted struggle. The war years had revealed the unparalleled tragedy of the Jewish people in all its horror. Millions of Jews had been murdered by the Nazis with no rescue at hand. Calls like that of a small uninfluential group in England, the Independent Labour Party, to exchange Germans and Italians held in Allied territory, for Jews—and above all for Jewish children in the ghettoes—evoked no response. Humanity seemed to have died. Hundreds of thousands of Jewish refugees hovered between life and death, trapped in countries conquered by the Axis; it seemed that it was "nobody's business" to save them, and appeals to transfer them to neutral countries or to Palestine were in vain.

Characteristic of such apathy was the reply of Lord Moyne, British Minister Resident in Cairo, to a proposal to save a million Jews from Nazi occupied countries. "What would I do with a million Jews?" he asked.*

Secret United States diplomatic documents regarding the United States policy on Palestine in 1941 (published in June 23, 1959 *Haaretz*) shed light on the efforts of British and Turkish diplomats to stop pro-Zionist activity in the United States for fear that it might "enrage the Arabs." The United States minister in Cairo demanded that United States Zionists should themselves state that the Jewish endeavor in Palestine had "not only failed in the past, but is also impossible of realization in the future." In any case, he wished the United States State Department "to abandon the national home" [of the Jews in Palestine], as "present notions about Zionists constitute a prime obstacle to the successful prosecution on the war." The acting Secretary of State meanwhile replied to the minister in Cairo that since the regions inhabited by the Arabs had interest and importance mainly for Britain, "it is natural for Britain to be first to issue political statements on those regions. If the British see a need for changing Zionist aims, they must be the first to take such steps."

In his book *Harvest in the Desert*, the American-Jewish author Maurice Samuel wrote:

In Palestine over half a million Jews waited with open arms for their tormented and homeless kin while over the Mediterranean and Black Seas unclean little cargo boats crept from port to port or tossed on the open waters waiting in vain for permission to discharge their crowded human cargoes. Hunger, thirst, disease and unspeakable living conditions reigned on those floating coffins. . . . There is a list of mass tragedies already available; incomplete though it certainly must be, it is sickeningly long.

* In the year 1944, Lord Moyne was assassinated in Egypt by members of the Jewish underground group *Lehi* (whom the British called "the Stern Gang"). The assailants were tried and sentenced by an Egyptian court, where their speeches made a strong impression on the Arab listeners and public.

It was only in 1943, under the pressure of the unending reports of the mass murder of Jews, that the British government agreed that Jewish refugees reaching Constantinople should be transferred to Palestine. But this decision, which the Jewish Agency was asked to treat as confidential and naturally did not publicize, was not even reported to the Turkish government until nine months later, thus clearly reducing its value. Only when the Jews no longer had the opportunity to escape from hostile countries did the British government deign to assign a certain immigration quota to them, while cancelling the certificates allocated to Jews outside enemy territory. A Jewish Agency memorandum to the Anglo-American Committee of Enquiry (1946) stated: (Chapter 8, paragraph 52) "There is no doubt that many of the people who are among the dead would have been alive if the gates of Palestine had been left open."

Information on the holocaust of the Jews in the Axis-conquered countries came down like a crushing deathblow upon the heads of Palestinian Jews. "If a man doesn't lose his mind these days," said the great author Rabbi Benjamin upon apprehending the news of the tragedy, "it's a sign that he has nothing to lose." In view of the stormy emotions and reactions that accompanied the revelation of the holocaust, it was very difficult to retain a clear head, to believe in the traditional values of the past when grappling with the cruel reality of the present and the dangers of the future. The British government had definitively abandoned the obligations of the Balfour Declaration and the Mandate. The Arabs maintained their bitter opposition to the Jews and part of their leadership cooperated with the Axis and looked forward to its victory. What part would the Jews play in the assembly of nations that would arise after the war? How would they be represented in it? Who would defend their vital interests and aspirations, and who would fight their battle in the international forum in which, after the war, at least a few Arab countries would be represented? How would the Jews finally emerge from the position of a minority lacking political independence even in the land of their birth and revival? How would they finally win external and internal security? It was against this background that Jewish policy began to move toward a postwar solution of the Palestine problem

Unity and Disunity in Zionist Policy

When, in 1942, the Zionist movement began to work out its plans for the future, there was no argument as to the ultimate goal but only as to ways and means. As a report written in 1943 stated:

The argument that has now been resumed on the objectives and paths of Zionist policy is in no manner an argument on the extent of Zionist realization, nor on the place of Palestine in the solution of the Jewish problem in general, nor on the contribution Palestine can make to binding the wounds of the Diaspora and easing its suffering

U

immediately after the war. We are united in our assessment of the great and terrible calamity of the Jewish Diaspora, in the appreciation that only Zionism can provide a fundamental solution to the Jewish problem. The argument is about the most effective way of realizing Zionism in our day, about the direction Zionist policy should take in order to realize the greatest possibilities for extensive and unhampered immigration and settlement. The question is: how shall we most effectively exploit our full strength; how shall we escape political isolation; which political objectives and programs are likely to open the way for the support of those who will determine the fate of the world tomorrow, and shall Zionist policy be directed in accordance with historic trends that we can already perceive—or contrary to them.[24]

When, in October to November of 1942, the Zionist Executive pondered Zionist policy during the war and after, all were united in the demand that the new world order after victory should provide a definitive solution of the problem of the Jewish people's homelessness. All Zionist parties were united in the demand that the gates of Palestine be thrown open to Jewish immigration, that the political regime in the country should be such as to enable the Jewish Agency to conduct Jewish immigration in accordance with maximum economic absorptive capacity of Palestine, and to an extent in keeping with the straits in which the Jewish diaspora would find itself at the end of the war. All agreed that the Jewish Agency must have the necessary powers to develop the country, including state domains and other waste areas, according to a development plan for the benefit of both Jewish settlement and the economy of the Arab fellah in Palestine.

There were subsidiary differences of opinion on the methods of rescue and transportation to Palestine of large numbers of immigrants when the time had come; on the place of construction and settlement in the political struggle that was going on during the war; on the manner and purpose of Jewish self-defense in countries where this was possible; on the winning of Soviet sympathy for the Jewish endeavor in Palestine, etc. But now, as always, the cardinal differences pertained to Arab policy on the question of the political course which would advance the Zionist movement towards its goals.

Would it remain faithful to its traditional path and work for a solution fair to both peoples, or would it adopt that viewpoint of "egotistic nationalism" that it had always rejected?

Would the Zionist movement continue after World War II in the exclusive sphere of influence of the West, or would it strive for maximum of independence in the international arena, with the possibility of alignment with all social and national liberation movements in the world?

These differences of opinion naturally affected the political campaign against the White Paper as well as postwar Zionist policy. The "Biltmore program,"* which was supported by most of Mapai, the Israel Labor

---

* Biltmore—the name of the New York hotel where a Zionist Conference was held

Party, the Mizrchi (religious) parties, the centrist General Zionists, and the Revisionists (extreme right-wing), set forth the demand that the British Mandatory regime be abolished and Palestine become a Jewish state. *Hashomer Hatzair* and the left *Poalei Zion*, and various other non-socialist groups believed that after the war a political regime based on political equality should be established in Palestine, in order to facilitate the unhampered realization of Zionism and advance the country toward political independence under a bi-national regime. They opposed the slogan of a Jewish state.

The opponents of the Biltmore program claimed to be faithful to the best Zionist traditions, quoting Ben-Gurion at the Seventeenth Zionist Congress (1931): "We declare before world opinion, before the workers' movement, and before the Arab world, that we shall not agree, either now or in the future, to the rule of one national group over the other. Nor do we accept the idea of a Jewish state, which would eventually mean Jewish domination of Arabs in Palestine."

In his evidence to the Royal commission (January 7, 1937) Ben-Gurion dissociated himself from the Revisionist aim, saying, "If Palestine were uninhabited we might have asked for a Jewish state, for then it would not harm anyone else. But there are other residents in Palestine, and just as we do not wish to be at the mercy of others, they too have the right not to be at the mercy of the Jews."

It was not because they denied the rights of the Jews to a state of their own that the opponents of the Biltmore program objected to it. They put forward several other reasons:[25]

(a) Although those who drafted the Biltmore program had included in it a demand to make all of Palestine a Jewish state, its opponents believed that such a demand would not be practicable after the war, and it would be necessary to partition the country again and establish a Jewish state in only part of it.

(b) The demand to make Palestine a Jewish state, even with Arabs in the majority or as a large minority, was sustained by a belief that the Arabs might well be disregarded, as the defeat of Hitler would be their defeat as well; the opponents believed that Arabs would continue to be an important factor after the defeat of the Axis and in the world as a whole growing importance would be won by forces supporting national independence and ready to support it.

(c) While the supporters of the Biltmore program claimed that their policy would lead to a solution of the Arab-Jewish problem, its opponents believed that partition would tend to aggravate the conflict.

on May 9 to 11, 1942, addressed by D. Ben-Gurion. There the slogan "Jewish Commonwealth" (a vague substitute for "Jewish state") was launched, which was later adopted by the majority of the Zionist Executive meeting in Jerusalem. It was called the "Jerusalem Program."

(d) While the Biltmore supporters considered the Arabs the enemy number one and put their trust in Britain and the United States, the opponents—and especially the socialists among them—regarded imperialism as the principal enemy of the Jewish liberation movement and demanded all-out efforts to reach an accord with the Arabs in order to overcome the common enemy of both peoples. The Biltmore program not only was seen as paving the way to partition but it also slammed the door on a Jewish-Arab agreement and expressed disillusionment with the struggle for such agreement.

Although partition was, to all intents and purposes, dead and buried by the report of the Woodhead commission favoring the sort of boundaries that even the most enthusiastic proponents could not accept, it continued to retain a semblance of political realism. To the British, it was a convenient bone of contention thrown between Jews and Arabs. Among the Arabs, an increasing number understood that the attempt to destroy the Jewish endeavor in Palestine by violence had failed, and that the idea of partition was a warning of the possible results of an extremist Arab stand. Among the Jews, there was an increasing number who now considered partition the way out of the impasse. Ben-Gurion, who had already been willing in 1937 to accept partition as a solution ("with the greatest enthusiasm"), now envisaged a better partition proposal. But those who had viewed the repartition of Palestine as a tragedy when the idea was first launched saw no reason to change their stand now. In their evaluation, no realistic observer of the Palestine scene could fail to conclude that the real and living reality of Palestine was a bi-national reality and this would not change quickly even under pressure of the enormous modifications Palestine was to undergo as a result of extensive Jewish immigration and settlement. Calculations proved that even if two million Jews immigrated in the next fifteen to twenty years, at the end of that time—say in 1960—Palestine would have about three million Jews and two million Arabs. Though the absolute numbers would be greater, the ratio of Jews to Arabs would be similar to the 1940 proportion but in reverse, and the same political problem would pertain: Neither of the two peoples would be able to rule Palestine by itself.

The British drew their own conclusions from these facts:

Manifestly the problem cannot be solved by giving either the Arabs or the Jews all they want. The answer to the question "which of them in the end will govern Palestine" must be "neither." We do not think that any fair-minded statesman would suppose now that the hope of harmony between the races has proved untenable, that Britain ought either to hand over to Arab rule 400,000 Jews, whose entry into Palestine has been for the most part facilitated by the British government and approved by the League of Nations, or that if the Jews should become a majority, a million or so Arabs should be handed over to their rule.[26]

The British government was contemplating a possible partition of the country among the two peoples ("When this will be found possible " as the Peel commission put it) meanwhile it would continue British rule. The choice offered the Arabs and Jews in Palestine became clear: partition of either the government or the country. There did not appear to be a third solution.

The position of the opponents of repartition may be summed up as follows:

Palestine had already been partitioned once, when the 90,000 square kilometers of eastern Transjordan were cut off from it, leaving an area of 26,700 square kilometers west of the Jordan for Jewish immigration and settlement. Any further contraction of the territory was unthinkable. The further partition of the country would nullify the extensive plans for agricultural and industrial development, which were conditions of prosperity and progress for Jews and Arabs alike. Partition would burden both peoples—Jews and Arabs—with heavy expenditures for defense and domestic and border security.* The precedent of partition in India was not relevant, for despite all the damage that partition had brought to India, and the grave complications that followed (some of which are still extant), the partitioned states supported populations of several millions each. The dissection of a tiny Palestine into two separate states, with enclaves like Jerusalem, which would remain outside the Jewish and the Arab states, was a different constitutional proposition. The political and economic independence of the contemplated states was viewed with doubt; there were grounds for the suspicion that they were likely to be pawns in the hands of foreign powers and hotbeds of international intrigue and nationalist incitement.

Most important were the political considerations. The opponents of partition believed that it could not lead to Jewish-Arab accord, but rather would aggravate national hostility and hatred. Since partition would not have materialized through agreement between the two peoples, each party would regard it as a purely temporary arrangement, to be adjusted to their advantage when the time was ripe. Arab-Jewish tension would increase, and the youth of both states would tend toward militarism. In Jewish eyes, the border of the Arab state would appear to be an arbitrary bar preventing the development of the whole country for the benefit of Jew and Arab alike. The Arabs would regard the frontier of the Jewish state as a foreign barrier in an Arab world, blocking their approach to an important part of the Mediterranean coast and cutting off direct contact between the northeastern Arab bloc (Syria, Lebanon, Transjordan, Iraq) and Egypt and the other Arab countries in Africa.

* According to the partition plan accepted by the United Nations in November 1947, the area of the Jewish state was 15,850 square kilometers (the Peel proposal plus the Negev), and its frontiers 1,400 kilometers long (of which 145 were sea coast). The boundary between France and Germany, for example, was about 300 kilometers long.

Every partition proposal left several hundreds of thousands of Arabs in the Jewish state.* In the political climate then prevailing it was difficult to hope that Arabs of the Jewish state would be a cooperative element. Northern Ireland, among other examples of partitioning, gave cause for grave fears.

Two tactical courses could now be traced in Zionist policy. One urged a solution that would be just to both peoples, and strove for some cooperation, however limited, as a start. The other course was forcefully represented by Ben-Gurion, in his statement against a compromise to the Zionist Executive on July 5, 1943.† He repudiated the view that "the British and Americans will accept neither the full Arab demands nor the full Jewish demands, and so we [the Jews] must propose some middle course."

"Since the middle," said Ben-Gurion, "is only a relative concept, determined by the extremities, the middle course we would propose would immediately become the maximum, and the compromise will have to be made at a new middle point, between our middle which became an end, and the end of the Arabs. If we propose a new middle, that too will become an end, and so ad infinitum."

A different point of view was expressed by Y. Hazan at the Zionist Executive on October 15, 1942:

If we are able to appear together with the other people living in Palestine, is there any doubt that it will be to the advantage of us both? It will make it easier for us to win the sympathy of the progressive and democratic forces in the world to our cause. If we do not succeed in this, we will go forward on our own. We shall not give up immigration. That is unconditional. But we will have done our utmost to emerge from this isolation. Perhaps in this way we might more easily pave a way to those socialist powers—with the Soviet Union at their center—who, we believe, will be stronger after the war than before it. . . . The great powers have not changed their spots. "Divide and rule" policies will flourish again. They will try once more to keep us and the Arabs apart . . . the only remedy lies in Arab-Jewish accord.

The other school of thought held that the Arab factor had no decisive importance in Jewish policy; the Arabs would be on the opposite side of the fence and their demands would be rejected, while the Jews would be re-

* According to the partition plan approved by the United Nations Assembly in November, 1947, the area of the Jewish state contained a population of 865,000, of whom 514,000 were Jews (close to 60 per cent) and about 351,000 of whom were Arabs, about 40,000 of them Bedouin.

† Ben-Gurion refers to an article "Toward Peace in Palestine," by J. L. Magnes, published a year before in an American anthology. The writer had urged outside, especially American, intervention for the purpose of imposing a compromise solution on both Arabs and Jews in order to break the present deadlock. This would open the way for a more constructive solution in line with future political developments—a federation of Middle Eastern countries with a bi-national (independent) Palestine as one of its units. Arab fears of Jewish domination would thus be lessened, and the numerical relationship between Jews and Arabs in Palestine would lose its former importance.

warded for their loyalty to the Allies. Declarations on "a harmony of interests between Jews and Arabs" should be replaced by recognition of an "unbridgeable contradiction". International opinion should be enlisted for maximum political ends, in disregard of those reservations that the Zionist movement had hitherto nurtured.

Two Tactics—Two Fronts

On Ben-Gurion's return from the United States in the autumn of 1942, there was considerable agitation in Zionist political circles and among Palestine Jews. Since the Biltmore program accepted at the Zionist conference in New York had been proposed by Ben-Gurion without consultation with any Palestinian Jewish body, it had yet to be ratified by the Jewish Agency and the Zionist Executive. Ben-Gurion attended various party conferences to obtain support of the program. When the Palestine Labor Party (Mapai) was asked "to concur in the Biltmore resolutions, which laid down the direction of Zionist policy in anticipation of the end of the war and the new world order," the so-called "B Section" (then a part of Mapai, later organized as the independent *Ahduth Haavoda* party) was strongly opposed to partition. The majority, however, backed Ben-Gurion's Biltmore program.

A protracted propaganda campaign by Ben-Gurion and his supporters reinforced the mistaken impression that it was Ben-Gurion who in the early forties first proposed as a realistic aim the conversion of Palestine into a Jewish state. Documentary evidence shows that this was not so. Dr. Weizmann preceded Ben-Gurion in putting forth the idea, but he had had the courage to admit that its implementation under the conditions then prevailing would mean the repartition of the country (after it had already been partitioned in 1922). After the outbreak of World War II, Weizmann returned to the idea, which underlay his negotiations with Feisal at the end of World War I, suggesting an overall political solution to the problems of the region that would satisfy Arab aspirations for national unity while ensuring political independence for the Jews in Palestine west of the Jordan, or most of its area. These ideas were first expressed publicly in his interview with *The Zionist Record* in April 1941. He stated that after the war there would probably arise an Arab federation stretching from Persia to Libya; a Jewish community, he said, could live peacefully with that federation. He expressed the same idea in his speech to American Zionist leaders in New York on July 17, 1941 (adding, "I would like western Palestine, perhaps without the Nablus-Jenin-Tul Karem triangle'), as well as in his article, "The Jewish Problem in the Coming Reconstruction," in *The New York Times* on August 13, 1941, which hinted at the possibilities of solving the Arab-Jewish problem within a federation of the neighboring Arab countries.

In adopting these ideas of Weizmann's, Ben-Gurion postulated much higher numbers than had Weizmann regarding the immigration of Jews to Palestine at the war's end. The two leaders did not always see eye to eye, and while Weizmann had spoken of a "Jewish community," possibly not in all of western Palestine, Ben-Gurion preferred the vague expression "Jewish commonwealth," and refrained from admitting that such a policy would inevitably entail the repartition of Palestine west of the Jordan.

Ben-Gurion embarked on a lightning campaign to win over the Palestinian Jewish community. If, a few months earlier, he had explained in America that the Palestinian Jewish community desired the Biltmore program and that everything depended on the support of American Jews, he now explained in Palestine that the Jews of America, or at least the Zionists among them, wanted that policy, and everything depended on the Jews of Palestine. At meetings and in the press, a crusade was waged against those who dared to recall the very truths that had long been pressed home by Zionist leaders (other than the Revisionists), including Ben-Gurion and his friends. Anybody who did not agree was castigated as destroying Zionism and denying the vision of national freedom and independence.

This sealed the fate of the research commission on the Arab-Jewish problem set up under the Twenty-first Zionist Congress (Geneva, August 16–25, 1939) resolution that stated:

The Twenty-first Congress instructs the Zionist Executive to appoint a research committee to investigate Jewish-Arab relations in political, economic, cultural, and social fields, ascertain the possibilities of cooperation between Jews and Arabs in all these, and submit its findings and proposals to the competent bodies of the Zionist movement.

The commission, appointed by the Jewish Agency Executive,* worked intermittently until August 1942, when it completed and submitted the main part of its report. The committee analyzed the relations of the two peoples, surveyed possibilities of mutual agreement on questions of government, immigration, land, and an autonomous Palestine binational state as part of a federation with neighboring Arab countries, the termination of the Mandate, and a treaty with England as a guarantee of the new regime.

Its report recalled the question often asked in Zionist debates: Where are the Arab groups that favored an accord with the Jews, and how far would they go in a possible compromise with the Jews? This same complaint was voiced by the Arabs; they, too, sought to be assured that the Zionist movement was prepared for accord, and wanted to know how far the Jews were willing to go. A positive stand and a clear Zionist political program were likely to hasten developments among the Arabs in the desired direction. The

* The chairman of the commission was S. Kaplansky, and its members were H. M. Kalvarisky, Dr. J. L. Magnes, Dr. Y. Thon, Rabbi Ouziel, D. Auster, and M. Assaf.

authors of the report had no illusions as to their programs being "good, ready, and feasible immediately or under all circumstances," but believed that it was "logical and just to the vital aspirations of both peoples and that real conditions for its realization are ripening in the political and economic development in Palestine and the Middle East in the postwar period." The advice of the Commission to the Zionist movement in the conclusion of its report was "to concern itself that when the historical situation will present itself it should not find us unprepared for action compatible with the greatness of the hour."

The commission report thus approached the Arab-Jewish problem in the traditional manner of progressive Zionism. But its spirit and political objectives were in complete contradiction to the new objectives devised by the Zionist leadership. At first, an attempt was made to hold up the report through the opposition of two members of the commission itself, on the ground that no agreement was attainable and therefore no agreement program called for. When that attempt failed and the report *was* submitted, over the signature of most of the commission members, it was pigeonholed and not presented to the Zionist Executive which was asked to confirm the Biltmore program. As for Dr. Weizmann, the report did not reach him until 1945!

The fate of the report heralded the shape of things to come. The supporters of the Biltmore program included some of the most influential elements in the Zionist movement, among them Mapai, the largest single Zionist party. They controlled organization, finance, and the diplomatic and propaganda resources of the Zionist movement, even if within Mapai there existed certain groups who for various reasons could not accept Ben-Gurion's new policy.

The opposition consisted of those Zionists who continued to strive toward an Arab-Jewish accord. An approach that had long been part of the official policy of the Zionist movement had now become the platform of the opposition alone.

The Front for Arab-Jewish Accord

Political efforts towards Jewish-Arab *rapprochement* and cooperation had been made since the late twenties by various Jewish elements. In 1926, the *Brit-Shalom* (Peace Alliance) organization was founded with its publication of *Sheifotenu* (Our Aspirations).* At the request of Henry Snell, a British

* Dr. Magnes was not a registered member, though he wielded considerable influence on its program. Other leading founder members were: Arthur Ruppin, director of the Palestine office of the World Zionist Organization from 1908 on, and until his death head of the Jewish Agency settlement department; Professor S. H. Bergman, of the

Labour M.P. and the member of the Shaw commission who dissented from its report (see Chapter Five), the organisation formulated detailed proposals, in August 1930, for a joint Jewish-Arab effort in administration, economics, education, medicine, culture, and politics. It was beyond the power of the *Brit-Shalom* itself—which was composed mainly of Jerusalem intellectuals— to carry out all or any of the proposals. But the Alliance was the first Jewish public body to prompt a public debate on Jewish-Arab relations in their political context, and to come out for a bi-national state with equal rights for both peoples, regardless of their numerical proportions. However, this Society did not have a definite political program, and in its ranks could be found both people who desired a large Jewish immigration and also—and these in the majority—members holding opposite political beliefs, to whom Arab-Jewish peace was paramount, and who were prepared to make far-reaching concessions from the Zionist point of view to attain it. Because of its vagueness on basic political questions, the Society became a target for the attacks of Revisionist and other rightist groups, and also evoked the reservations of various elements, (like *Hashomer Hatzair*) who also inclined toward political equality between the Jews and the Arabs in Palestine. Its work did not reach a wide public and many of its people began to put their faith in Mapai. When Mapai gained control of the political direction of Zionism in the early thirties, this was the end of the public activities of the *Brit-Shalom*.

A few years later, before the outbreak of disturbances in April 1936, preparations were made for the formation of another body with the same program—the *Kedma Mizracha* organization,* which was comprised of former *Brit-Shalom* members, as well as notables belong to the oldest Jewish families in Palestine, and Sephardic leaders. The new organization described itself as "a non-party association whose aims are knowledge of the East and the creation of cultural, social, and economic ties with Oriental peoples, and the proper presentation of the Jewish people's work in Palestine." In view of the controversy that had surrounded the *Brit-Shalom*, most of the founders insisted that the new organization should refrain from a detailed formulation of its intention to bring about peace between Jews and Arabs; thus, the general term "Oriental peoples" was adopted.† In common with all

Hebrew University in Jerusalem; Y. Thon, director of the Palestine Land Development Company; Joseph Luria, director of the Department of Education; the writer Rabbi Benjamin; H. M. Kalvarisky; Dr. A. Katznelson; Dr. Ernest Simon; Professor G. Shalom; Dr. G. Landauer; and others.

* After a number of preparatory parlor meetings, the founding meeting of the association was held on June 22, 1936, with about seventy leaders of the Jerusalem Jewish community participating.

† "As if Persia, India, Indo-China, or Japan interested us to the same extent as our Arab neighbors," gently mocked H. M. Kalvarisky in the stencilled report on the activities of *Kedma Mizracha* made at its Jerusalem conference on February 6, 1938.

such organizations, this one was beset with the problem of what its main activity should be: Information to the Jewish public on the importance of the Jewish-Arab problem—an area that official Zionist policy had neglected and distorted—or similar work among the Arabs? Some of its founders inclined toward coordination with official bodies; others strongly opposed it on the ground that their organization was designed to do exactly what these Zionist bodies had failed to do. The compromise accepted was that propaganda for Jewish-Arab *rapprochement*, peace, and cooperation would be done independently by the organization, while political contacts and parleys would not be undertaken without prior consultation with official Jewish bodies.

One of its first publications was, *A Collection of Articles on the Arab Question*, edited by Rabbi Benjamin,* which included contributions by writers and newspapermen of different parties on this political topic. The pamphlet appeared as the Zionist Executive was meeting in Zurich (the summer of 1936) and evoked much interest. Shortly thereafter, it issued the German pamphlet, *On the Arab Question: A Word at the Twelfth Hour*, by Rabbi Benjamin. An important plan for the publication of a major Arabic daily newspaper to serve the idea of Arab-Jewish cooperation, to be edited by a brilliant Arab journalist† who favored friendship between Arabs and Jews failed to materialize because the potential backers withdrew. "One [potential]

---

* The writer Rabbi Benjamin (pen name of Yehoshua Redler-Feldman, 1880–1957), member of the second *Aliya*, a great writer and active publicist. Following the publication, in 1907, in Brenner's *Hameorer*, of his well-known essay on Jews and Arabs, he was among the constant fighters for *rapprochement* and cooperation between Jews and Arabs, and took a leading part in all the organizations established with this objective over the years.

† Dr. Mahmud Azmi (1889–1954): In the twenties, editor of *As-Siasa* (Policy), the organ of the Constitutional-Liberal Party in Egypt. A courageous fighter for freedom of thought and against Moslem clericalism. One of the ideologists of the Pan-Arab movement and among its best publicists. First visited Palestine for his paper to cover the inauguration ceremony of the Hebrew University at Jerusalem, in April 1925. Became friendly with H. M. Kalvarisky and Dr. J. L. Magnes, met Dr. Chaim Weizmann (see Chapter Five), Arlosoroff, and other Zionist leaders. In 1937, was invited to head the law faculty in Baghdad, but declined after encountering hostile demonstrations by Fascist students (then quite influential there). In the early forties, headed the Institute of Journalism at the Egyptian University. Was persecuted by the Farouk regime for his liberal views. After the revolution, headed Egypt's delegation to the United Nations. Died in the course of a speech at the Security Council (November 5, 1954). Among his eulogizers at the United Nations was the head of the Israeli delegation, Abba Eban, who said: "I wish to include the Israeli delegation in the expressions of respect and admiration proffered in the memory of our Egyptian colleague, Dr. Mahmud Azmi, who died yesterday in such moving circumstances. In our contact with him we learned to respect his honest qualities and international idealism. He was a zealous fighter for his cause, was a brilliant opponent, and noble in behaviour. . . . The government and people of Israel respect his memory and express their deepest sympathy to his family, his colleagues and his compatriots."

source spent its money on a different similar project, a second refused because
the form and direction of the paper did not appeal to it, and the third backed
out because his participation depended on that of the first two,"* a report stated.

Lack of funds, limited participation, absence of a clearly formulated
political platform, and also the changing political winds following the Peel
commission's partition proposal in the summer of 1937—all these led to the
dissolution of *Kedma Mizracha*, although some of its founders sponsored a
more extensive project in the same direction at the end of the 1936 to 1939 riots.

In March 1939, there appeared an anthology *At the Parting of our Ways*, a
compendium of essays on Zionist policy and Arab-Jewish cooperation. Some
of its contributors addressed meetings throughout the country on the scope
of their publishing effort, and in May of the same year it was decided to
found a "League for Jewish-Arab Rapprochment and Cooperation."† In
August, a second anthology, *Our Ways*, was published. The organizing
committee of the League initiated a petition, "Thou Shalt Not Kill," which
appeared over the signatures of 240 prominent Jews, headed by Henrietta
Szold, Berl Katznelson, Professor A. H. Frankel, and S. Y. Agnon. The poster
spoke in strong terms against the terroristic trends among some Jews on the
periphery of the Jewish community (in opposition to the official policy of
"self-restraint"). They also published the pamphlet "Against Terror,"
containing articles and essays by about forty spokesmen for various Jewish
groups, and organized meetings on these subjects.

At the beginning of October 1939, some sixty political leaders, scientists,
and writers who believed in Jewish-Arab understanding met in Jerusalem at
the League's invitation. The conference passed a resolution calling for an end
to the deplorable national conflict between the two peoples, joint action in
the face of the new World War that had broken out at the end of August,
and generally for accord and cooperation between Jews and Arabs after the
war. The conference also demanded the appointment of the commission of
enquiry on the question of Arab-Jewish relations envisaged by the Twenty-
first Zionist Congress. A delegation of the conference submitted the resolution to the Jewish Agency Executive.

During 1940 and 1941, consultations were held with various organizations
and bodies to ascertain the possibility of their cooperation with the League;

---

* The report on *Kedma Mizracha* at its Jerusalem conference on February 6, 1938.
According to Kalvarisky, the three sources were: the *Histadrut*, which preferred to devote
its funds to the establishment in 1937 of an Arabic weekly, *Hakikat-ul-Amar*; the Jewish
Agency, and the Palestine Jewish Colonization Association (PICA).

† The organizing committee included H. M. Kalvarisky, Dr. Y. Thon, Rabbi Benjamin,
Dr. S. Hirsch (member of the Zionist Executive for the *Aliyah Hadasha* party founded by
German immigrants), Dr. E. Simon, and Yaakov Peterzeil (1889–1954, among the
earliest and most important left *Poalei Zion* members, the League secretary and moving
spirit until the spring of 1942).

a campaign for larger membership, and one for closer links with Arabs, were other tasks involved in a fairly substantial initial program. To this end, sub-committees were set up for political affairs (Dr. F. Rosenblith, M. Bentov, M. Bilski, P. Naphtali, Dr. N. Nir-Rafalkis); for economic affairs (Dr. I. Gelfatt, Dr. D. Weissmann, Z. Abramovitz, M. Erem, Dr. Z. Moses, M. Bader); for education and culture (Professor M. Buber, Professor S. H. Bergman, Dr. M. Brill, Dr. Braun, Mrs. H. Bart, Dr. Z. Zohar, Dr. E. Simon, Dr. S. Sambursky, Professor R. Kebner, Professor G. Shalom, Y. Shamush); for social and health work (Mrs. H. Thon, Dr. Ollendorf, Dr. Y. D. Wilhelm, Mr. H. Naaman, Dr. G. Lubinsky). A survey of the teaching of Arabic in Hebrew schools was submitted to the education department of the National Council; some of its specific recommendations were in part implemented. In the summer of 1940, it circulated to the Jewish Agency Executive and the delegates to the elected assembly a memorandum and detailed proposals on emergency work during the war. A poster was issued opposing the boycott of Arab goods and urging closer economic ties between Jews and Arabs, and joint action against war profiteering—signs of which had been appearing. In Jerusalem, there were a number of joint Arab-Jewish social gatherings (one of which was broken up by the Revisionists). For a while, a joint Arab-Jewish youth club existed in Bat Yam, near Jaffa. A number of other plans, such as the establishment of a joint committee for tenant protection in Jerusalem and detailed plans for cooperation between Jewish and Arab workers and farmers, were submitted to the *Histadrut* Executive in the summer of 1941, but no action could be taken on them. Political conditions became less and less favorable. The Palestine government did not favor joint Arab-Jewish effort, and there was a good deal of political uncertainty and fluctuation among the Arab population. Official Jewish bodies were deep in work on day-to-day war emergencies, and there was no decision as yet on political questions, although it was already possible to distinguish the germ of new political trends in the summer of 1942, when the growing sympathy for the Axis among the Arabs seemed to harbinger the improvement of the future political chances of the Jews. Indeed, it was the appearance of this political shift among the Jews that was to turn the League of Arab-Jewish Rapprochement and Cooperation into a united front that opposed the new Zionist policy as mistaken and dangerous.

In June 1942, the Kibbutz Artzi *Hashomer Hatzair* (federation of H.H. communal settlements) and the Socialist League,* which had hitherto taken

* The Socialist League was a Jewish political organization whose political ideas were identical to those of *Hashomer Hatzair* but whose members did not belong to kibbutzim. The League, which was ideologically and organizationally connected with the *Kibbutz Artzi,* and cooperated with it on all political matters, was founded in 1936; when the *Hashomer Hatzair* Workers' Party was established in 1946, the two groups merged.

a limited part in the League's work (as "observers"), now joined it. The *Hashomer Hatzair* stand on the Arab-Jewish question had always been a fundamental part of its world outlook. The political platform adopted with the establishment of the Kibbutz Artzi (the Haifa Conference, April 3, 1927) envisaged "a bi-national socialist society in Palestine and its environs," and the concentration of most of the Jewish people in Palestine and adjacent countries. *Hashomer Hatzair* advocated gradual creation of an international federation of workers, which would lead the socialist revolution in Palestine when the time came.

As against the views of another left-wing element, the left *Poalei Zion*, which at one stage had favored the abolition of the Jewish Labor Federation (*Histadrut*) and its immediate conversion to a bi-national organization, *Hashomer Hatzair* considered the establishment of a bi-national workers federation a long-range process, which would go forward along with the expansion of the Jewish working class in Palestine. This dictated the development of the Jewish Federation of Labor concurrently with joint trade unions for the workers of both peoples, and the formation of special units of Arab workers connected with the General Federation of Jewish Labor. As it crystallized in the course of time, this political concept maintained that Palestine was by nature bi-national and thus had to be a common homeland for the Jews returning to it and for the Arabs residing there. From this followed the practical and principle objections to any new partition of the country, to any suggestion of removing the Arabs from the country, and to any regime that meant the domination of one people by the other. Thus, *Hashomer Hatzair's* policy aimed at the establishment in Palestine of a bi-national regime, based on political parity that would ensure the unhampered development of each of the peoples and the non-domination of one people by the other, regardless of their numerical proportion.

The idea of a joint Jewish-Arab Federation of Labor in Palestine was first formulated about a year before the establishment of the Kibbutz Artzi *Hashomer Hatzair*. The platform of the "Kibbutz List" (various streams within the settlement movement) for the third conference of the General Federation of Jewish Labor in Palestine in 1926 included the following clauses on "ties with the Arab workers in Palestine and their organization":

In recognition of the common interests of the Jewish and Arab worker in day-to-day class struggle, and in appreciation of the general future development of the Palestine economy, the General Federation should take the following action toward a joint organization of Jewish and Arab labor:

1. A full joint organization for government and municipal employees, and for those employed in industry. (Note: The joint organization is at present local, with the exception of those trades in which conditions exist for a country-wide organization.)

2. In other trades and branches of the economy, a parallel organization of Arab labor in the General Federation of Arab labor.

3. A country-wide alliance of the General Federation of Jewish Workers, the General Federation of Arab Workers, and the combined federation. (This is conditional upon (a) free Jewish immigration; (b) the principle of an open union.)

The combined alliance will deal with all matters of common concern to Arab and Jewish labor.

As to local organization of the alliance, wherever there are parallel unions, a local council shall be established composed of representatives of the parallel organizations and the combined one.

This stand was accepted in principle by the third *Histadrut* conference (July 1926), whose resolutions specifically instructed *Histadrut* bodies to take action to form the international alliance of Jewish and Arab workers as autonomous national units. But this decision of the *Histadrut* convention was not acted upon. The resolutions of the second (general) council of Kibbutz Artzi, which met at Haifa on December 21–24, 1928 stated:

The Conference notes the lack of any direct *Histadrut* action to enforce the resolutions of the third convention on the organization of Arab workers. The conference stresses the urgent need for initial and thorough action toward the formation of the combined organization, first among employees in the service of industry, municipalities, and government service, and of international firms.

In 1930, the Kibbutz Artzi again stressed the need to carry out the plan of the combined organization of Arab and Jewish workers, including Arab workers permanently employed in Jewish agricultural settlements. The conference also called for the establishment of joint workers' committees in places where both Jews and Arabs worked, committees of Arab workers in places where the workers were exclusively Arab, and proportional representation of organized Arab workers in the Labor Exchange.

The *Hashomer Hatzair* plan was not confined to trade unions. Its conference in Haifa, on May 23–25, 1929, confirmed the basic points in Meir Yaari's address on "Our national conceptions and our stand at the (Zionist) Congress." He said that although Zionism postulated "the concentration of most of the Jewish people in Palestine and its environs" by "creating an economic base leading to political independence in Palestine," nevertheless, "we are for the complete equality of the two peoples in Palestine in the future bi-national socialist society in Palestine."

In all its subsequent conferences, and in the *Histadrut* forums, *Hashomer Hatzair* worked for class and political solidarity of the workers of the two peoples, as a basis for peace and security in Palestine and the unhampered advancement of the Zionist endeavor.

In September 1931, *Hashomer Hatzair* actively supported thirty Arab workers in Binyamina, who went on strike in defense of their rights and, showing trust in Jewish labor and their federation, asked them for help and guidance. The Arab strike committee and the Binyamina workers' council were to direct the strike jointly. It was largely thanks to the efforts of the Kibbutz Artzi representatives that the Binyamina workers' council, with the concurrence of the *Histadrut*, decided on solidarity with the striking Arab workers and was prepared to offer help, moral and material. The council stressed "that help to the strikers cannot end on the day the strike ends; the rights of the Arab workers must be defended later against retaliatory attacks by the employers." Under pressure from the orange growers, the majority of the Binyamina workers' council (the Mapai faction) retreated. The council's new decision was "that Jewish workers shall not be strikebreakers," which meant in practice that Jewish workers would not take part in the picketing, Arab workers would be left alone, and the promises given them previously by the council would not be kept. This retreat determined the outcome of the strike, which rapidly weakened. *Hashomer Hatzair*, the organ of the movement, which appeared from November 1931, brought the entire affair to the attention of workers all over the country.

During the economic boom of 1934 resulting from increased Jewish immigration, there was increased agitation among Arab workers in several agricultural settlements where both Jews and Arabs were employed: in Rehovoth, Rishon Lezion, Petah Tikva, and especially Nes Ziona. In the course of the eleven-day strike of 300 Arab workers in agriculture, building and transport, an organization of Arab workers was formed there with the help of the left *Poalei Zion*. The *Hashomer Hatzair* kibbutzim in the south helped the striking Arab workers, and the Kibbutz Artzi Executive lent the services of an Arab-speaking liaison officer for the strike. At successive meetings in cities and settlements, and in newspaper articles, members of *Hashomer Hatzair* enjoined Jewish workers to play their part in the formation of Jewish-Arab trade unions that could lead to a political alliance between them.

At the Kibbutz Artzi conference in Hedera (December 13-15, 1935) on cultural work, a special resolution was passed calling for the study of Arabic and also for the formation "of special study groups to learn the problems of the Arab community in Palestine and its environs." The nucleus of an Arab department of *Hashomer Hatzair* had been formed in 1935. *Hashomer Hatzair* kibbutzim continued to devote the most serious attention to Arab affairs in the late 1930s, and the movement's special approach to this area became one of its hallmarks. Their work included plans for the education of Arab-speaking cadres in the settlements, the fostering of good relations between the kibbutzim and local Arabs—through advising the fellaheen in modern agriculture, peaceful solution of disputes over pasture, etc.—medical help, contact with Arab schools, joint celebration of festivals, publications in Hebrew and Arabic, joint trade-union work, etc. Much of this effort was hampered by lack of suitably trained personnel in the kibbutzim as well as by the Arab riots of 1936 to 1939.

The endeavor continued in the early 1940s.* Typical of the practical approach adopted was the training program for six kibbutz members (including the author), who lived for half a year in the Arab village of Usefiyah on Mount Carmel and in Nazareth in order to learn the language and customs of the Arabs.

The Arab department of Kibbutz Artzi *Hashomer Hatzair* was formed in 1940, and cooperated with the League for Rapprochement and Cooperation, which helped in the above training project. The Kibbutz Artzi and its urban ally, the Socialist League (which was later to constitute an important part of Mapam) joined the League in June 1942. Kibbutz Artzi resolutions of April of that year reiterated that "the chief guarantee for Arab-Jewish peace is the creation of a joint common front formed by Arab and Jewish workers, in town and country." They urged that "the political program of the Zionist Organization should include a willingness to set up a bi-national regime in Palestine based on the unhampered advancement of the Zionist endeavor and on parity in government, without regard to the numerical strength of the two peoples. The Zionist Organization should also favor the federal association of Palestine with neighboring countries." So long as Arab-Jewish accord had not yet been achieved, the conference urged "vigilance over international supervision in Palestine for the fulfillment of the obligations included in the Mandate and the Balfour Declaration, and the preparation of the ground for a bi-national regime in the country."

In June 1942, the League for Arab-Jewish Rapprochement and Cooperation adopted the following platform, based on agreement between the League and the Kibbutz Artzi *Hashomer Hatzair* and the Socialist League:

(A) The League believes that the construction of Palestine as a common homeland for the Jewish people returning to it and the Arab people therein residing must be based on lasting mutual understanding and agreement between the two peoples;

(B) The principle of the return of the Jews to their historic homeland to build their independent national life in it is unequivocal, as are also the rights of the Palestine Arabs to their independent national life, and their ties with other parts of the Arab people;

(C) The League will carry on its work on the basis of its recognition of the right of the Jews to immigrate to and settle in Palestine in accordance with its maximum absorptive capacity and to an extent that shall ensure the growth of the Jewish community in Palestine toward a full and independent economic, social, cultural, and political life, in cooperation with the Arab people;

* In 1941, twenty-three kibbutzim had 481 members studying Arabic, including forty-three advanced students. These settlements had contact with 120 Arab villages.

W

(D) On the basis of the immigration principle as defined in paragraph B, agreed immigration quotas may be set for a number of years, it being understood that the League will oppose any aim to perpetuate the position of the Jewish community as a minority in Palestine;

(E) The League considers the basic principles for Arab-Jewish accord to be:

1. Acceptance of the right of the Jews to return to their historic homeland, there to build their independent national life; acceptance of the rights of Palestine Arabs to their independent national life and of their ties with other sections of the Arab people;

2. The non-domination of one people by the other, regardless of their respective numerical strength;

3. A bi-national regime in Palestine;

4. Positive attitude towards the participation of Palestine as an independent bi-national unit in a federation with neighboring countries, when the necessary conditions for this will have been prepared, and the basic rights and vital interests of the Jewish people returning to its homeland, and the basic rights and vital interests of the Arab people living in Palestine, will have been secured;

(F) The League shall undertake the following tasks:

1. Campaign within the Jewish community and the Zionist movement for a policy of rapprochement, cooperation and accord between Jews and Arabs.

2. Campaign for the formation of a corresponding Ally within the Arab community on central and local activities without, however, requiring all of them to belong personally to branches of the League.

3. Strive to improve and enhance Arab economic, social, cultural and political standards.

4. Research.

5. Training people for public work among the Arab population.

(G) The local branches of the League will be centers of activity and influence; the parties and groups composing the League will detail some of their members to work on central and local activities without, however, requiring all of them to belong personally to branches of the League.

Signed: H. M. KALVARISKY, M. BUBER, E. SIMON, S. HIRSCH, G. STERN, H. NAAMAN,
         I. PETTERSEIL*, V. SENATOR, Y. THON, RABBI BENJAMIN, MEIR YAARI,
         Y. HAZAN, AHARON COHEN, A. LICHTINGER.

* with the exception of paragraph D.

With the adoption of this platform, the foundations of the League were reset, a clear programmatic basis was created, and the public behind it was considerably broadened.

In August of that year, a conference of about one hundred participants met in Jerusalem to deliberate on the establishment of the *Ihud* (Unity) association, and to launch its periodical *Current Problems*. Dr. J. L. Magnes*

* J. L. Magnes (1877–1948): Born in California, ordained as a rabbi at twenty-three, two years later graduated from the University of Heidelberg. Was secretary of the Zionist Organization of America between 1905 and 1908. In 1909, founded the Bureau of Jewish Education, which had a considerable effect on the development of Jewish

was elected president, and its other leaders were Henrietta Szold, Professor M. Buber, H. M. Kalvarisky, Moshe Smilansky, and Judge Valero. *Ihud* adopted the platform of the League for Rapprochement and Cooperation, and associated itself fully with it.

At the outset of the League's work, various groups besides the left *Poalei Zion* Party, the *Hashomer Hatzair*, the Socialist League, and the *Ihud* organization remained formally unaffiliated with it but supported its work. Gradually a united front was forming, whose scope was not to be belittled. But this development took place simultaneously with the crystallization of the new Zionist policy as expressed in the Biltmore program, against which the League had to struggle.

The "Bentov Book"

Characteristic of the spirit of the times was the vilification of a document known as the "Bentov Book." It was named for the chairman of the public committee appointed by the League and *Hashomer Hatzair* to submit to the Jewish Agency committee of enquiry headed by S. Kaplansky (the committee that the Twenty-first Zionist Congress at Geneva in August 1939 had decided to set up) proposals for the regulation of the political and constitutional relations between Jews and Arabs in Palestine. The public committee, consisting of M. Bentov, Dr. M. Bielsky, P. Naphtali, F. Rosenblitt, and Dr. N. Nir-Rafalkis, began work in February 1940. In June 1941, it completed the first part of its report, which was printed at the office of the Jewish Agency political department; and on September 18, 1941, the first volume of the report was submitted to the chairman of the Agency committee and was circulated to a number of Zionist and Jewish leaders.[27]

The introduction to the report stipulated that in regard to the sections of the survey dealing directly with the responsibilities of the Jewish Agency Executive, committee member F. Rosenblueth (then one of the leaders of the *Aliyah Hadasha* party, later Minister of Justice Pinhas Rosen) "although he agreed with the general trend of the analysis in Part One, as a former member of the Agency must refrain from any criticism directly touching on the Agency Executive." A second committee member, P. Naphtali (Mapai leader, also a member of the Israeli Cabinet at a later date) held that "the

education in the United States. Between 1910 and 1922 was president of the United New York Jewish community. Was one of the founders of the Joint Distribution Committee in World War I. In 1916, toured Europe with a committee to provide help for Jewish war victims. Visited Palestine in 1907 and 1912, and settled there in 1922, devoting his efforts to the establishment of the Hebrew University, over which he presided until his death. Throughout his life, was one of the first to call for a policy of peace and accord with the Arabs, and to labor for the cause.

basic directives of the committee, to formulate a plan for the regulation of
future Arab-Jewish relations, should not comprise a discussion of the shortcomings of the policy followed hitherto, referred to in our critical survey,
and [that he] wishes it to be understood that his signature to the report does
not extend to Part One" (Pages 1–37 of the report, an analysis of future
Arab-Jewish relations).

The report did not presume to be the definitive pronouncement on the
subject. Its preface stated clearly that it was but a first draft of the committee's
findings, for "it was necessary to leave many details for further consideration," and "there is no doubt that before the final draft of our proposals
many useful changes will be made, in the wake of forthcoming criticism."
The committee did not intend at this stage to complete its work, but solely to
report on four sets of problems: [a] fair plans for an ultimate solution that
could serve as a basis for a Jewish-Arab accord; [b] transitional stages,
between the current period and the early stages of the ultimate solution;
[c] the prospects for the acceptance of the proposed plans by Jews and
Arabs; [d] intermediate political moves by the Zionist movement and the
Palestine Jewish community, pending an accord with the Arabs.

Thus, the committee intended to continue its work upon receipt of the
comments of those to whom the first volume was submitted for perusal.
Some of those who discussed it with the chairman commended the study
without necessarily subscribing to all its findings; some wrote encouraging
letters to the committee. Others pointed to dangers in some parts of the
report, while commending other sections. All these showed a responsible
approach commensurate with the importance of the subject. Not so Ben-
Gurion, chairman of the Jewish Agency Executive. Although his copy of the
report specifically stated, "This draft is a top-secret document, not to be
mentioned publicly or distributed privately without authority," on Ben-
Gurion's return from the United States in 1942, a violent campaign was
launched against "Bentov's Book," with the object of discrediting the
idea of a bi-national state as the solution to Arab-Jewish conflict, and attacking any who favored a Jewish-Arab accord. It was not until a year and a half
after the beginning of the slander campaign against him—at the *Histadrut*
conference in March 1944—that the chairman of the committee, M. Bentov,
was given the opportunity to reply publicly to criticisms of his colleagues and
himself. This was also the first occasion that the public was given precise
information on the report that had been attacked so violently. This venomous campaign, the poisoning of the atmosphere that came with it, and the
tense inter-party relations that resulted—all these factors made it impossible
for the committee to continue its study, as it had intended. If this was the
object of the slander campaign against the "Bentov Book," it must be admitted that it was achieved.

Arab Political Development, 1942–45

Palestinian Arabs gradually resumed political work at the end of 1942 and the beginning of 1943. The changing fortunes of the war appeared to convince them of the ultimate defeat of the Axis; it was necessary to seek again a solution to political problems, with Britain continuing as a decisive factor in the region. The British, too, began to think of postwar problems. They sought to set up a group of Arab states, not strong enough to expel them from the Middle East, but fit to be used as a stick to beat and counteract both American competition and Soviet penetration. Just as they sought allies among the ruling classes of neighboring Arab states, so did they seek support among Palestinian Arab leaders.

The party structure of the Palestine Arab community was very different from what it had been five years earlier, when the Higher Arab Committee was dissolved. The Palestine Arab Party (founded by the Hussainis) was without a leader; Haj Amin al-Hussaini was in Berlin collaborating with Hitler against Britain and her allies; several of its other leaders had been interned by the British or were living as political exiles in other countries. In Palestine, the Hussaini party had only third- or fourth-class leaders, who could not follow a policy at variance with that of the real leaders and yet had no hope of taking over.

The Nashashibi leaders had been disappointed by earlier British moves against them, and showed no inclination to embark upon a new political campaign. In these circumstances, the initiative in renewed political activity among the Arabs of Palestine passed to the Istiklal leaders who returned to the country (Auni Abd-ul-Hadi, Rashid Haj Ibrahim, Subhi Khadra, and others). In the absence of the traditional leaders, these could pose as being "above party," calling for a new Arab image, unity, and the formation of a new Arab representation under their leadership. For this purpose, *ad hoc* slogans were proclaimed to educated Arabs and young adults, many of whom began to have leftist tendencies. At the end of 1945, the Arab National Fund* resumed work as part of an attempt to usurp influence and leadership authority among the Arabs. But the Istiklal leaders failed in all such efforts. No new

---

* Since the early thirties, there had been talk in the Arab community of setting up an instrument to handle the "rescue" of Arab lands about to be sold to Jews and their transformation into *waqf*. In 1932, the *Sanduk-ul-Uma Al 'Arabia* (Fund of the Arab Nation), a corporation with a capital of 10,000 Palestine pounds, was incorporated, with the Supreme Moslem Council as largest shareholder. The Fund led an uneasy and not too active existence for a few years until, in 1943, it was revived. By the middle of 1946, its income was £150,000, and it owned 15,000 *dunams* (3,750 acres) of land. Its head was Ahmaed Hilmi Pasha (1883–1963), of the Istiklal party—a financier, founder and director of the Bank of the Arab Nation, and a member of the Higher Arab Committee. He was exiled to the Seychelles islands in 1937 and returned to Palestine in 1939.

Arab leadership developed, for there was no concrete program to support it. The previous Arab policy had proved sterile, incapable of achieving its aim. The Arab community was confused, and no new policy appeared on the horizon.

A New Negotiation Attempt

Against this background, great importance attaches to the negotiation attempt made in the summer of 1943 by a group of influential Arabs. Through the League for Rapprochement and Cooperation, a proposal was submitted to the Jewish Agency for the negotiation of an accord on the following basic terms: (a) parity in government (legislative and executive bodies); (b) Jewish immigration until numerical equality were reached (about 700,000 immigrants, according to Arab calculations); (c) participation of a bi-national Palestine in a federation with the neighboring countries; (d) effective co-operation between the two peoples in economics, politics, society, and culture. Those were the main foundations, while a host of other matters still required clarification.

The most significant of these points was immigration. The League representatives said they would not submit to the Jewish Agency any program that froze the number of Jews in Palestine for political reasons. The Arabs refused to diverge from numerical equality (after numerical equality was achieved, the continuation of Jewish immigration would be allowed only to make up the difference in natural increase). They were prepared for joint effort in regard to Jewish immigration to the neighboring countries, according to quotas to be agreed upon. Even considering the difference in numbers between the two peoples in Palestine at that time, the difference in natural increase during the period of the realization of agreement, and the number of immigrants settling in neighboring countries close to Palestine—all this would add up to about a million Jewish immigrants. As to the subsequent continuation of immigration, some Arabs were inclined to agree that this should be regulated by legislation based on the principle of economic absorptive capacity. But most did not agree to such a condition; they claimed that such stipulation might breed distrust, and it should not be considered before Arab mistrust and fear of the Jews had been removed. In preliminary talks, the League representatives broached the possibility of a provision that would represent neither a repudiation on principle by the Jews nor a definite pledge on the part of the Arabs (on the question of future immigration after numerical equality between Jews and Arabs was reached), but a compromise formula that would express "the common hope of both sides that, since mutual fear and distrust shall have been removed, and the value of cooperation proven in practice, it will be possible to continue working together in a manner that will secure to both parties what is most important to each." The phrase "what is most important to each" was of course the substance of the compromise, without which there could be no hope of a peaceful solution. The objective was a peaceful solution that would make possible a large Jewish immigration, within a short time, and with the agreement of the Arabs. The Arabs did not say that this proposal was beyond the scope of their discussion, though it was clear that hard work was yet to be done to achieve agreement.

The Arabs wanted the negotiations to be secret and informal, through the League for Rapprochement at least during the early stages. They were prepared to bring to the final stages an Arab delegation that the Jewish Agency would consider authoritative and adequate. The Arabs wanted each side to pledge not to accept the proposal of any third party, even if it proved to be more convenient than that which had been agreed to with the second party.

Submitting these proposals to the Jewish Agency on June 21, 1943, the League representatives (H. M. Kalvarisky and the writer) stressed that if the Jewish Agency approved the proposals as a point of departure for serious negotiations, it would be necessary to clarify certain points with the Arabs, but that there was no point in meeting with them without a clear stand on the basic principles of the proposal. They quoted the Arab negotiators as hinting that after the different attempts at negotiation with the Jews, they were approaching this new attempt with a considerable measure of scepticism, but with a willingness arising out of their conviction that this was their last chance to solve the problem peacefully.

After an exchange of questions and answers, Shertok summed up as follows: He appreciated the proposal as indicating a great change in the situation, in that an important Arab group had come a long way. The Jewish Agency, however, was being asked to agree to an overall proposal before various details had been settled; such agreement would mean abandoning other plans and demands. Despite the secrecy, the fact of the negotiations would be known even if the negotiations ended unsuccessfully. The proposals would have to be laid before the Executive (which was to meet a few days later), especially because they conflicted with the Jewish Agency policy. A reply would be sent after the Executive meeting.

It would take too long to tell the sorry tale of the way the Jewish Agency foiled this last attempt. For reasons of politics, the Jewish Agency chairman, Ben-Gurion, virtually sabotaged the proposal by breaking the secrecy pledge and referring the proposal to the political department making the affair into the subject of an amusing story at a large Party meeting. The Arabs later complained that the Jewish Agency was making unfair use of the negotiations by telling the British that "the Arabs themselves are offering us half, and you only have to add the rest."* This happened shortly after the

---

* All details on these negotiations and the causes of their failure are confirmed in authoritative official memoranda in the author's files.

confirmation of the Biltmore-Jerusalem program by the Zionist Executive. Embarking upon negotiations might have made it necessary to choose one of two courses: (a) to advance toward an agreement, but not in accordance with the Biltmore program, or (b) to acquiesce with the Biltmore policy and abandon all attempts toward an alternative policy. The impression was that the political department sought to avoid being involved in negotiations, and provided itself with an "alibi"—just as it had in the 1936 negotiations—to show that it was not through its fault that the parleys had broken down. Now, as on other occasions, consideration of domestic politics appeared dominant. Advocacy of negotiations was ridiculed, even vilified. The Arab negotiators could not fail to note the indifference and even hostility with which the attempt had been received by official Jewish leaders and by the Jewish community. They could draw their own conclusions from this. Perhaps a different approach on the part of the Jews could have helped to develop new leadership for Palestinian Arabs (before the return of the Hussainis and their cohorts to the country) and open a new chapter in the relations of the two peoples.

The negotiation attempt of the summer of 1943 was a warning to the Hussainis and the "traditional" Arab leaders. The failure of the attempt was their success and strengthened their position. In 1944, the Palestine Arab Party (founded by the Hussainis) resumed activity and tried hard to regain its prewar standing in the Arab community. The post of president was left vacant for Jamal Hussaini (until 1944 he was interned by the British in Rhodesia, then released but not allowed to return to Palestine until 1946). The two young and uninfluential parties—the National Bloc, headed by Abd-ul-Latif Salah of Nablus, and the Youth Congress, headed by Yakub Ghussain—also renewed their activity.

The die was not yet cast. There were now young Arab economists, scholars, lawyers, and newspapermen who could not find their place in the old parties. In 1945, an attempt was made to organize the People's Party headed by Musa al-Alami.* Arab leftist circles set up the League for National Liberation (which, at the end of 1948, after the establishment of Israel, joined with the Jewish communists in the Israel Communist Party) and the Union of Arab Intellectuals, which published the bi-weekly, *Al-Ghad* (The Morrow).

* Musa al-Alami: Born in 1897 in Jerusalem; a graduate of Cambridge University; was a member of a prominent Arab Palestinian family, which, it is believed, came to Palestine from the Maghreb in the seventeenth century. In 1931, was appointed Arab Private Secretary to the High Commissioner, and later a senior assistant to the Attorney General. Resigned during the disturbances; was one of the Mufti's close advisers, and joined him in Syria at the end of the riots. In 1938 to 1939, worked in London preparing the Arab case for the round table conference at which he appeared as Haj Amin's personal representative. Thereafter, resided in Iraq until the Rashid Ali al-Kilani rebellion, when he returned to Palestine (at the end of 1941).

Among Palestinian Arabs, as among those in the neighboring Arab countries, there was a general awakening. In the cities and important villages, clubs and groups were established and periodicals began to appear, such as the leftist *Al-Ittihad* (Unity) and *Al-Ghad*. There was increased trade union activity: To the established Society of Palestinian Arab Workers (founded in 1925 and following Hussaini policy and discipline) was added, in August 1945, the leftist-led Congress of Arab Workers, which was a symptom of the radicalization that had evolved during the war years.*

The rise of new, more radical and progressive elements among the Arabs should have rendered easier the efforts towards Jewish-Arab *rapprochement*. These circles, most of them composed of young people, were more alert to the realities of Palestine and its problems and were free of the rigidity of "traditional leadership." The support of the socialist world for the just demands of the Jews in Palestine (as seen in the 1945 preparatory and founding conventions of the World Federation of Trade Unions, in London and Paris) had a considerable effect on the thinking of these Arab groups. The tactical error of the Arab left† was their belief that "first of all we must first become strong, so as to contribute something to the struggle." Their strength in fact, depended on their courage to explore new horizons of understanding, accord, and cooperation between Jews and Arabs, and on their appeal to the Arab people to give them the power to carry out a new policy. In the absence of such political courage, their public statements were weak and mumbling and could not draw the people to them. Hence, they were destined to trail behind the Mufti and his friends.

When Arab political activity was resumed in 1943, there was a feeling among Arabs that in the preceding eight to ten years, the Jews had become a decisive force in Palestine, and that the Palestinian Arabs were too weak to withstand the Jewish community and the Zionist movement without the help of the Arab world outside Palestine. As it became clear that British policy aimed at the consolidation of the Arab East into a force that would stand with Britain and through which the problems of the area, including Palestine, would be solved, Arab control of matters pertaining to Palestine passed to the Arab League, which, after preparatory work in 1944 was officially founded in March 1945.

The League's "Alexandria Protocol"‡ included a Palestine resolution, which stated:

* The nucleus of the congress was the Association of Arab Unions, founded in Haifa in 1942, and headed by the people who later founded the League for National Liberation and the *Ittihad* weekly.

† The greatest weakness of the opposition within Jewish public opinion, especially of the leftist part of it, was at this time the absence of a parallel Arab partner with a frank and courageous policy.

‡ These were the resolutions of the preparatory committee (for the establishment of the

The [preparatory] committee is of the opinion that Palestine is an important unit among the Arab countries and that the rights of Arabs [in Palestine] cannot be infringed without prejudice to the peace and stability of the Arab world. The committee believes that Britain's undertakings to stop Jewish immigration, protect Arab lands, and bring Palestine to independence are among the permanent rights of the Arabs; the acceleration of its realization will be a step toward the desired aim and toward peace and security. The committee declares its support of the interest of Palestinian Arabs by action for the realization of their lawful aspirations and the defense of their just rights.

The committee declares its grief, which is not less than that of others, at the tragedy and suffering caused the Jews of Europe by a number of European dictatorships; but the problem of those European Jews is not to be confounded with Zionism, for there is no greater wrong or abuse than to redress the injustice to European Jews by another wrong, done to the Arabs of Palestine.

Not only the political struggle of Palestinian Arabs against the Jews, but also their domestic affairs, began to be directed more and more by leaders of the Arab national movement in neighboring countries. We have seen that in earlier stages there were some among them with a broader vision of the Arab movement as a whole, inclined to explore a constructive solution of the Palestine problem, and expressing a willingness to work to that end (as witnessed by the Faisal-Weizmann agreement and the 1922 and 1928 attempts to negotiate). In 1938, an important Arab leader, who held a prominent political post in Syria, stated to a representative of the Jewish Agency (according to an internal document of the Jewish Agency):

I recognize the right of the Jews to be parties to any discussion on Palestine. I told this to my friends, as well as to Palestine Arab leaders. Last year I said to them: the Axis will not bring the Arabs freedom; instead of the Zionist problem in Palestine they will have greater troubles—the immigration of masses of Italians to Palestine, Syria, Iraq, and Egypt, which in a short time will change the Arab character of the Middle East. The Jews can play an important role in the postwar development and advancement of the Arab countries, without in any way endangering their independence. The Arabs themselves are too weak to exploit the resources and possibilities latent in their countries; without economic and social advancement their independence will be deferred, and they will not take their rightful place in the world. . . . I am fully occupied with my country's interests, but I am prepared to devote myself to a positive solution of the Palestine problem, and I believe I can help to solve it, thanks to my connections with Ibn-Saud, Nuri Pasha Said, Nahas Pasha, and the other Arab leaders and rulers, including Palestine Arab leaders.

He repeated the same opinion even more strongly in 1942.

Arab League), which met at Alexandria between September 25, and October 7, 1944, and worked out the protocol, which was signed by representatives of Egypt, Iraq, Syria, Lebanon, and Transjordan (Saudi Arabia and Yemen subscribed to the League's charter when it was founded on March 22, 1945).

At the beginning of November 1943, Mustafa Nahas, Wafd leader and then prime minister of Egypt, expressed his view that Palestinian Arabs should make an effort to reach an understanding with the Jews. According to an JTA Cairo dispatch, Nahas stated that "the Arab world must admit and recognize the presence of the Jews in Palestine as a permanent factor, and in all plans for the future this factor must be taken into account, and some way or other to cooperate must be found." A week later, the words of the Egyptian Prime Minister were confirmed by the Jaffa *Falastin*. Its news editor, Issa al-Issa, wrote: "Nahas considers the recognition of the Jews a precondition to Jewish understanding for a solution of the Palestine problem and holds that the Jews should be a party to a conference of Arab nations."

The Revisionist *Hamashkif*, and other Jewish newspapers, sought to explain that the Egyptian leader's statement meant that he was prepared to recognize the present Jewish community in Palestine and its status under the 1939 White Paper. Such a conclusion was wrong and unreasonable; for the Arab states actually recognized the White Paper while the Jews opposed it bitterly, and there would obviously have been no point in a statement on the recognition of the White Paper made through the medium of the Jewish Telegraphic Agency. Informed Arab and Jewish sources interpreted Nahas's statement as a hint to the Jews to negotiate for the solution of the Palestine problem in a way that would meet the interests of both parties. Official Jewish bodies did not react to it officially or unofficially, for the very reasons that brought to nought the proposals submitted to the Jewish Agency by the representatives of the League for Rapprochement and Cooperation in June of the same year.

The need for a competent representation of the Palestinian Arabs was particularly acute in the autumn of 1944, when the Arabs were asked to send their representatives to the preparatory committee in Alexandria. The Hussaini party, which re-formed in 1944, opposed any representation that was not led by "traditional leaders." When Riad as-Sulh passed through Haifa on his way to Egypt, a delegation of Palestinian Arab leaders met with him to request action that would lead to the return of Jamal al-Hussaini and Rafik at-Tamimi, "for only they can represent Palestinian Arabs." He replied, "Suppose they were dead—what would you do then? Well, do that now," adding, "Your extremism will harm you, just as the extremism of the Jews will harm them eventually. You must find some common ground with the Jews, just as I did with the Christians in Lebanon and Nahas is doing with the Copts in Egypt. I spoke to Nahas, and he is of the same opinion."

Riad as-Sulh, a founder of the Arab League, saw the Palestine problem in the broader perspective of the Arab movement as a whole. The strength of the Hussainis and their various opponents was at that time more or less equal. All efforts to organize a mission to Alexandria that would represent the various currents of Arab opinion failed. It was only at the last moment, through the intervention of a former member of the Higher Arab Committee, Dr. Hussain al-Khalidi, that it was agreed to send Mussa al-Alami to Alexandria as the single non-party delegate acceptable to all. For a time, Alami became the principal leader and representative of Palestinian Arabs. On Arab League instructions, and with its funds, he established, in 1945, propaganda offices in Jerusalem, Washington, and London. He himself selected their directors and senior staff, most of whom were young intellectuals (who were accused of pro-British tendencies) without definitive party affiliations, although they were generally sympathetic to the policy of the Mufti.*

This period between the Alexandria Conference of Autumn 1944 and the founding of the Arab League in the spring of 1945 was a turning point in the political development of the Arabs in relation to the solution of the Palestine problem. What followed was definite deterioration toward a major war between the Arabs and the Jews in Palestine.

Opportunities During the War Years

After everything that had happened in Palestine, in the world Jewish community, and in international affairs between 1939 and the end of World War II, political initiative and the balance of power passed more and more to the Jews. At the same time, there took place a basic change in the approach of the great mass of Palestinian Jews to the problem of the country's political future. In the middle thirties, almost all sections of the Jewish population believed that it was essential to reach an accord with the Arabs. The Committee of Five, which had made a bold attempt to find a peaceful way out of the impasse, was not castigated for this by official bodies. But their efforts had proved abortive. During World War II, there was a change in the attitude of the Jews, or at least in the majority of them and their official leaders. Now the head of the Jewish Agency political department could be heard to strike a new note: "Accord is desirable, and important, but not indispensable, and it is impossible."† A few years later, any talk of working for an accord with the Arabs was represented by Jewish leaders as harmful and "diverting the people's thinking from the way to achieve their goals." Now the people were

* The propaganda offices, which were officially considered the political instruments of the Palestinian Arabs, were actually financed by the Arab countries. With the assistance of the diplomatic staffs of those countries, of Arab immigrants in America, and of British "Friends of the Arabs," they engaged in newspaper propaganda (especially in Britain and the United States), in organizing meetings, in directing British and American support for the Arab cause, and generally in the publication of propaganda material.

† M. Shertok's lecture in Jerusalem. See *In the Emergency*, a collection of articles regarding the problems of Zionist policy and Jewish-Arab cooperation (Jerusalem, September 1940), page 5 (Hebrew).

called upon to gear themselves for a "difficult period of non-accord"—to prepare for confrontation, political and even physical.

Unsuccessful Efforts

In order to understand these historical developments—which are important in order to deal with the future as well as to analyze the past—we must ask whether Arab-Jewish accord was indeed impossible. This decisive question is, of course, highly debatable. Our survey of the progress of Jewish-Arab relations across a broad historical spectrum obliges us to try to supply as clear, documented, and comprehensive an answer as possible. This is our purpose in the various chapters of this work.

An indication of the efforts made to move the *Histadrut*—one of the most important of all the Jewish institutions—toward the sort of activity that was necessary and possible after the early years of the war, can be gained from an examination of the following letter:

June 25, 1941

To the Histadrut Executive,
Tel Aviv

DEAR COMRADES,

In these difficult days, we venture to turn to the *Histadrut* Executive on a matter that may appear at first sight to lack urgency, but that the undersigned believe to be vital and urgent, even at a time like this. The more so because political and military developments in our part of the world will probably long continue their course as in the past months, and we will have to continue our lives and our struggle, fluctuating between hope and fear. Should organized labor refrain from action on one of the important aspects of our life throughout this period?

Ever since the end of the disturbances, there has been an important change in Arab-Jewish relations. Hostility has been replaced by peaceful relations, and here and there, by instances of friendly and neighborly relations, rapprochement and cooperation in a number of different spheres. These happy manifestations were spontaneous, and underscored the need for cooperation between the two peoples. Since the end of the disturbances, we have witnessed increased contacts between various Arab and Jewish circles (municipal institutions, teachers and newspapermen, scientific conferences, youth and sport groups, etc.), even planned and comprehensive cooperation between parallel groups of equal importance. Jewish and Arab orange growers have established a joint organization and have developed close cooperation in defending the special interests of that industry; Jewish and Arab landlords, business groups, and other middle-class people have discovered a common language, and now work for their common interests. Only in the labor movement has there been hardly any change during this period, and a wall of estrangement, separation, and aloofness continues to divide Jewish and Arab workers all along the line. Many respected members of the

Histadrut cannot understand the present inactivity of the Palestine Workers Alliance, which was set up under resolutions passed by two national conferences of the *Histadrut* and as an inseparable part of the *Histadrut* constitution (chapter 17), and cannot understand why the Committee for Arab Work set up by the *Histadrut* Executive was just as inactive during this period and hardly exists.

We are living in a war, with its inevitably fluctuating fortunes. The events in Iraq, the developments in Syria and Egypt, and the situation at the front a few weeks ago had their effect on the political mood in this country. The wall between the two peoples, which had been considerably lowered since the end of the riots, seemed to have been raised once more, and the process of rapprochement between the two peoples seemed to have been stopped. But before many days had passed, the political and military changes around us once more revised—this time for the better—attitudes in Palestine. Evidence of good will and rapprochement is again manifest in daily life, and if matters continue as at present, there is cause for hoping that in spite of tension and fluctuations this period will continue to be an important juncture on the road to solidarity, cooperation, and joint organization of the masses of workers of both peoples in Palestine. The political lessons learned by the masses at the end of the riots, the abatement of the vindictive propaganda of foreign agents (in the war situation), the vital interests common to Jews and Arabs in Palestine in this very war period (passive resistance, supply, etc.), and the inclination to rapprochement and cooperation among the mass of Jews and Arabs, all combine into a most important opportunity for putting into effect new policies. . . .

Are we to miss this opportunity? Some groups, individuals, and institutions (notably the League for Jewish-Arab Rapprochement and Cooperation, in whose work members of all the main *Histadrut* trends take part) are of course doing their utmost to take advantage of the present opportunity; the *Histadrut* Executive is probably aware of what is being done here and there in this connection. But individuals and small groups alone are not equal to the task, and only public institutions with their resources can carry the full burden. Projects such as the establishment of the Alliance of Palestinian Workers; cooperation between Arab and Jewish workers to obtain cost-of-living allowances for workers employed by the large government companies; a public works program by government and municipal institutions to relieve unemployment; encouragement of producers' cooperatives among Arab workers in town and country; far-sighted and planned efforts to settle the problems of marketing the products of Arab and Jewish workers; provision of medical help for neighboring Arab settlements; agricultural and veterinary instruction and guidance, and the development of mutual aid and cooperation between Arab and Jewish farmers; the establishment of joint centers for adults and youth in mixed residential areas, and help in establishing such centers in friendly Arab settlements; the dissemination of Arabic among Jews, and Hebrew among Arabs; extensive educational work in the economic, social, cultural and political fields—all these are waiting for the directing hand of the *Histadrut*.

The signatories of this memorandum, who attach the greatest importance to *Histadrut* intervention in the fields mentioned, and each of whom is doing his utmost to this end in his own circle, hereby request the *Histadrut* Executive to receive them as an inter-party delegation for an exchange of views on this weighty problem.

The members of the delegation, who are familiar with the intricacies of public life and activity in Palestine, are not unaware of the causes that prevent the *Histadrut* from playing its part in these affairs. They believe, however, that there is a consensus as to the many opportunities for extensive *Histadrut* intervention on the Arab front.

Yours sincerely,

E. BAUER—Kibbutz *Hazorea* (*Hashomer Hatzair*)
DR. Y. THON—Jerusalem (Mapai delegate to the National Council)
L. TARNOPOLER—Tel Aviv (left *Poalei Zion*)
I. ITZHAKI—Tel Aviv (left *Poalei Zion*)
A. COHEN—Shaar Haamakim (*Hashomer Hatzair*)
A. LICHTINGER—Jerusalem (the Socialist League)
H. NAAMAN—Jerusalem (Mapai)
MOSHE EREM—Jerusalem (left *Poalei Zion*)
Y. PETERSEIL—Jerusalem (left *Poalei Zion*)
H. RUBIN—Tel Aviv (the Socialist League)

After waiting in vain for an answer for nearly two months, a reminder was sent to the *Histadrut*. In a letter dated August 28, 1941, David Remez agreed to a discussion "within the next few weeks," and requested practical proposals on the Arab activity of the *Histadrut*. These were submitted by Aharon Cohen on September 7, 1941, and read as follows:

Assumption: The work must be carried on continuously, according to a consistent plan, regardless of any fluctuations in the attitude of the Jewish community resulting from current or anticipated changes in the country.

1. The Organizational Structure of the Work.

A) A department for Arab activity shall be set up by the *Histadrut* Executive for the training of community workers, for fostering contacts with Arab workers, organizing a Palestine workers alliance, directing joint activities, publicity, and the supply of information on all such *Histadrut* activities.

B) Regional activity centers shall be set up in four or five places(Jordan and Hulah valleys, the Bet Shean area, Haifa, Hedera, Tel Aviv, and Jerusalem), under the supervision and guidance of the department.

C) Local committees for Arab work shall be constituted by the workers' councils in mixed settlements or mixed employment centers, and by settlement blocs.

D) A seminar on the Arab question (the Palestinian Arab community, economics, society, culture, public life, politics, mutual relations with the Jewish community) shall be held by the department to train and instruct the staff directly engaged in such work.

E) The *Histadrut* Executive shall provide the staff and the necessary funds for this work:

2. Initial Area of Work.

A) Establishment of branches of the Palestine workers alliance, support of groups of Arab workers friendly to the *Histadrut*, activity among Arabs employed on temporary jobs together with Jewish workers.

B) Organization of joint activity by Arab and Jewish workers to obtain increased cost-of-living allowances in government departments, municipalities, and large international firms.

c) Provision of medical services (at a nominal fee) for Arabs in their settlements. The construction of clinics for this purpose in some areas. Facilities for doctors' visits, information on hygiene, preventive medicine, child care, etc. (A special committee including sick-fund directors will work out a plan for these medical facilities.)

d) A campaign to obtain contracts for public works carried out by the government and municipalities, for the benefit of the unemployed.

e) Planned long-range efforts to solve the problem of marketing Arab produce. As a first step—regulation of the sale of certain Arab produce at specific seasons in our markets. (A special committee, including Tnuva executives, shall formulate a detailed plan for this important service.)

f) Expert agricultural instruction in various farm branches. Veterinary service. Arabic supplement to the *Histadrut's* agricultural journal *Ha'sadeh*. Organization of model Arab villages. Joint representations to government, joint irrigation projects, roads, sewers, public water supply, etc. Encouragement of cooperation among Jewish and Arab farmers, development by the Rehovot Experimental Farm of plan for the fellaheen economy. (A committee formed by the agricultural center and the agricultural organizations will work out a plan.)

g) Establishment of joint community centers for adults and young people in mixed population centers. Help in establishing community centers in friendly neighboring Arab settlements. Joint playgrounds for children.

h) Cooperation in sports. Joint jamborees, youth days, friendly competitions. (A committee in which *Hapoel* will take part is to work out plans.)

i) Joint activity among youth. Fostering contact between teachers and schools of both peoples. (A committee made up of youth organization leaders and teachers' associations will work out the program.)

j) Instruction of Hebrew to Arab workers and fellaheen, and of Arabic to Jewish workers. Discussion with the educational center of the status of Arabic instruction in our schools.

k) Publicity and information (pamphlets, periodicals, posters, *Hakikat-ul-Amr*).

l) Launching loan funds to free Arab workers and fellaheen from the burden of usury. (A committee in which youth group leaders and teachers will take part is to determine the program.)

m) Establishment of a *Hakikat-ul-Amr* editorial board, measures to increase its circulation.

n) Encouragement of cooperative credit, producers', etc. societies among Arab workers. A special department in the cooperative center of the *Histadrut* to deal with this problem.

o) A committee to investigate the agrarian problem in Palestine and develop the agrarian program of the Palestine workers' movement. (Development, intensification, extension of Jewish settlement, improvement of the Arab economy.)

p) A regular column in *Davar* on "In the Arab World—in Palestine and Adjacent Countries."

The above are proposals intended for direct action by the *Histadrut*, its organizations and institutions. But the standing of the *Histadrut* in the Jewish community obliges it to contribute to the work of rapprochement and cooperation also through channels that are not directly connected with the *Histadrut* and its institutions. The department for Arab activity to be established by the *Histadrut* will have to act through the proper channels to carry out general joint ventures, by guiding workers' representatives in general institutions in the following directions:

1. Establishment of a Jewish-Arab banking institution to encourage and finance joint ventures.

2. Establishment of a joint Jewish-Arab school to train government officers.

3. Establishment of a special association or chamber of Arab and Jewish journalists.

4. Joint chambers of commerce.

5. Increased cooperation between Jews and Arabs in governmental advisory bodies.

6. The enlistment of Arab students and professors in the Hebrew University.

7. Use of radio programs to encourage cooperation and friendship.

This correspondence was submitted to the members of the *Histadrut* council for consideration at its meeting of May 19, 1942, with the following comment:

Those who submit these proposals see no need to add anything to the above documents, except to note that the *Histadrut* Executive's promise included in its letter of August 28, 1941, has not been kept to this day, and the signatories of the memorandum are still waiting for the statement that was promised "within the next few weeks" eight months ago.

Having adopted the Biltmore program, the Zionist leadership cut short the possibility of negotiations with the Arabs; it could not enter upon such negotiations except on the basis of demanding all of Palestine for the Jews, while respecting the minority rights of the Arabs (who, at that time constituted two-thirds of the Palestinian population). No Arab was willing to discuss a settlement on this basis. Under the circumstances, the League for Jewish-Arab Rapprochement and Cooperation could have played an important role in the cultivation of contacts and in preparing the ground for negotiations between the two peoples.

When the League was reorganized and its program confirmed in June 1942, its leaders decided to study possibilities of cooperation between the League and the political department of the Jewish Agency. At a meeting between the Secretary of the League (the author) and M. Shertok (Sharett) on June 23, 1942, the approved platform of the League was submitted, and it was stressed that this established the League on a solid political foundation and made it an influential public body with clear objectives. The head of the political department was asked to explain how he envisaged future relations. It was decided that closer exchanges on various matters would at least help to prevent avoidable incidents.

The reply of the political department, after several weeks, was that they

x

were not prepared to support even the desirable operations of the League, as such support might impart moral encouragement to the League,* and they had no wish to lend such encouragement. This position was all the more perturbing because considerable sums of money were contributed month after month to the so-called "Mobilization staff" of the Revisionists. (A. Zisling stated "definitely that the monies allocated and expended by the mobilization fund for purposes of mobilization were used for the other needs of the Revisionist machinery. None denied this allegation—not the Revisionists, not Shertok, not the mobilization center.") What was denied to those favoring Jewish-Arab cooperation was therefore permitted to its most violent opponents. The League for Rapprochement and Cooperation thus had no alternative but to seek ways to achieve its objectives without the blessing of the Jewish Agency, or its help.

As we have seen, public opinion was not encouraging. Although the League remained virtually the only link between the Jewish and Arab communities, it was subjected to constant attack. The very attempt to "reawaken" the question of the possibilities of contact with political leaders in the Arab world was condemned as a crime. Thus, the question was raised at the Zionist Council meeting of November 1942. The Executive was asked "to take steps" with respect to the forthcoming visit of the League's president and secretary (H. M. Kalvarisky and the author) to Syria and Lebanon (in September of that year) to make contact there with Arab public figures, in order to study the situation and examine the possibilities of action in the line of the League's objectives and program.† There were also angry reactions in the press. In the end, the question was deferred by the Executive, which refrained from clarifying the matter further.

* All quotations are from the *Bulletin to Members* published by the League for Jewish-Arab Rapprochement and Cooperation (Jerusalem, December 20, 1942) and then circulated to the Jewish Agency.

† Talks were held with several public figures in Lebanon, including members of the Nakash family (Nakash was president of the Christian community), Riad as-Sulh and Sami as-Sulh (leading Moslems, Lebanese Prime Ministers in postwar years), the Omar brothers, Muhammad and Ali Salameh (Moslems active in the national bloc); with Syrian leaders including Jamil Mardam (at various times Syrian Prime Minister) and Hashim Al-Atasi, President of the Republic; with Dr. Hussain al-Khalidi (former mayor of Jerusalem and member of the Palestine Arab Higher Committee, who after three years of exile on the Seychelles islands was released and permitted to settle in Lebanon); and with the heads of the Jewish communities in Beirut and Damascus. There were meetings also between the author and members of various leftist circles: Among these were the leaders of the League to Fight Nazism and Fascism in Syria and Lebanon, the editors of the bi-weekly *At-Tarik*, trade union leaders, and the editors of *Saut-ush-Shaab* (the news paper of the Communist party of Syria and Lebanon). Contact with these groups was particularly important because of the meetings between the Soviet delegation (to a convention of the League for Soviet Friendship in Palestine in August of that year) and anti-Fascist Arab groups in Palestine.

The following are some excerpts from the report to the League prepared by its representatives on their return from neighboring countries:

Discussions with civilian leaders were held in order to seek their views on the Palestine problem against the background of the general Arab movement fighting for the independence and unity of the Arab countries; to explain our approach to the Jewish-Arab problem and its solution; and to examine possibilities for negotiating an Jewish-Arab accord that should have effect after the war.

Discussions were held with leftists on the true character of Zionism, the achievements of the Jewish endeavor in Palestine, ideological clarifications of the Jewish problem and its solution under capitalist as well as socialist regimes, and the possibilities of cooperation between the various socialist groups in the Middle East, etc.

The report contained the following general impressions:

A) Intellectual circles evince admiration for the Jewish venture in Palestine; they both exaggerate the political influence of the Jews, and fear its political power, which they consider an obstacle in the way of the Arabs' struggle for their political interests;

B) There is great distrust of the higher Jewish bodies. The absence of any positive declared policy by Zionist leaders, irresponsible statements by this or that Jewish leader, the attacks in the Jewish press on any attempt to reach accord, the clamor about Jewish military strength, and the political implications of the appeals for mobilization —all these continue to increase this distrust.

C) These circles know what the political department has been saying to the Lebanon Christians on the federation; what was said by some Zionist representative to several British or French officials about the leaders of the national bloc, their ability and their weaknesses, etc. Even if we assume—and this is reasonable—that these things are told to them first-hand, it is astonishing that they are familiar with the smallest details on talks and exchanges that are usually considered top secret.

D) It is not always possible to refute the charges of these people against Jewish leadership. As viewed from their angle, the political activity of official Jewish bodies often arouses astonishment because of its inconsistency, short-sightedness, and absence of planning.

E) Deep distrust of official Jewish policy is almost general among all those with whom we spoke. It is doubtful whether efforts to mitigate the distrust and mollify them were completely successful. On the other hand, they listened with great interest to the purposes and development of the movement forming round the League, though it was invariably stressed that at this stage this was only a movement representing a minority fighting for a course that was not yet adopted by most of Jewish public opinion.

F) There is no willingness to discuss a plan that includes a Jewish state, but most of those with whom we spoke were prepared to discuss a solution of the Arab-Jewish problem on the basis of the League's platform. Its principles for Jewish-Arab accord were found by a number of the most important of these leaders to be a "serious, fair, and honest plan, which has a chance, though much work remains to be done to prepare the conditions for its realization."

G) The general impression is that despite the importance of the position taken by the main leaders of the general Arab movement, no real progress can be made toward the solution of the Palestine problem without the participation of Arab leaders from Palestine itself. However, a number of the prominent leaders with whom we spoke expressed their willingness to influence the Palestinians in favor of our program when they come (as they surely will) to ask their advice.

H) At the beginning of the talks, the Syrians and Lebanese took the general position that any negotiation should wait till the outcome of the war was clear, though it was evident from the conversation that they assumed the defeat of the Axis. However, in the course of the conversations there developed a common evaluation that the preparation of conditions for the proper solution of the Arab-Jewish question should not await the end of the war, and should proceed now.

I) As to Palestinian Arab representation in the negotiations, the feeling is that there are enough competent Arab representatives in Palestine to take part in the negotiations. Of the Mufti and his assistants now in Axis territory, a prominent person said: "These need no longer be taken into account, unless—God forbid—the Axis wins."

The general impression was that if serious political efforts were made, on the basis of a plan likely to be accepted by both sides, it would be possible to obtain substantial results. This is by no means an easy task, but it has a chance. However, this impression is subject to doubt if we remember how and on the basis of which ideas and plans political activity of the Jews is being carried on today.

Important contacts were made with leftists. It was agreed that two of them would visit Palestine for a few weeks to study the problem at first-hand. Agreement was also reached on a number of technical arrangements (exchange of periodicals and other material), and on the examination of proposals such as a joint Arab socialist publishing venture for all socialist groups in the East; joint consultations on trade union questions; education of youth, etc., which may have considerable importance in fostering contacts with socialist and progressive Arab circles in Palestine itself.*

The meetings in Syria and Lebanon—like those with Arab statesmen from Egypt, Iraq, and Transjordan on other occasions during that period—were encouraging and positive. The fruits of one year of such activity were the June 1943 proposals of the Arab group mentioned. Despite the ignominious end of the proposals, contact was maintained with various Arab groups from whom it seemed possible to obtain general support for the League plan, albeit not immediately. Along with a comprehensive information campaign among the Jewish public,† oral and written information in Arabic was disseminated;‡ it was effective, and encouraged those Arab groups whose work

* From the League for Rapprochement and Cooperation, *Bulletin*, October, 1942.

† The boycott of the League activities, almost universal in the Hebrew press, was broken by the appearance, on June 30, 1943, of *Mishmar* (organ of *Hashomer Hatzair* and the Socialist League), which advocated *rapprochement* and accord between Jews and Arabs and reported in this spirit on developments in the Arab world.

‡ Noteworthy Arab publications of these days included a general pamphlet on the League for Jewish-Arab Rapprochement and Cooperation—its history, members, objectives, and activities between 1939 and 1941; a collection of documents containing the proposal for an Arab-Jewish accord, worked out in 1930 by H. M. Kalvarisky; the

among their people paralleled the League's work among the Jews. These Arab circles included out-and-out political leaders, groups of workers and fellaheen with whom members of the left *Poalei Zion* Party and of *Hashomer Hatzair* had developed relations, influential fellaheen from the Nablus region,* and Arab intellectuals from various districts of Palestine who wanted to establish an independent Arab political organization with a progressive program, that would include Arab-Jewish accord and cooperation.

In discussions in the Arab department of the *Histadrut* (which was activated in 1943), members of *Hashomer Hatzair* and left *Poalei Zion* insisted that the *Histadrut* should not confine its work to the less enlightened sections of the Arab people, but should seek possibilities of cooperation with more sophisticated Arab groups and with circles of intellectuals active in the national movement of their people.

Members of Mapai expressed grave doubts as to whether educated Arabs could be found who would be willing to cooperate with the *Histadrut*, which was known as a Zionist organization. On the other hand, *Hashomer Hatzair* and left *Poalei Zion* members contended that there were serious Arab groups that could be induced to cooperate with a political program based on the interests and aspirations of both peoples. The head of the *Histadrut* Arab department, S. Solomon, said that if this was corroborated by a suitable Arab spokesman, they would be prepared to support cooperation. The author undertook to have Solomon meet the chief spokesman of the Arab group mentioned. The conversation took place (23.11.43) and was recorded at Solomon's home. A. Agassi, the department secretary, also took part in the conversation. Asked whether he would be prepared to speak to his friends and to the Arab public on the need for Arab-Jewish cooperation, the Arab intellectual answered:

Obviously, the widespread view among the Arabs is that the Jews are the Arabs' mortal enemies and their intention is to drive the Arabs out of Palestine. That is their

program of the League for Rapprochement and Cooperation of June 1942, and "Letter to Friends," by Aharon Cohen, dealing with the progress of Palestine in the last twenty years, the economic absorptive capacity of Palestine (1943), the Jewish problem and the Palestine question (1945). The League's publications were sent to several hundred Arabs and to Arabic newspapers in Palestine and other Arab countries.

* Some of the villages in the region still showed signs of the work done there in 1930 with the help of Kalvarisky (who was then the head of the special bureau of the Zionist Executive and the National Committee). One of the Arab Bureau documents, dated March 1930, gives details on "a delegation from one of the important villages near Nablus, and another from Nablus notables, pleading joint Arab-Jewish action to defend common interests against the common enemy. . . ." Activity in the Nablus area, begun after the 1929 riots, for the establishment of a national agricultural party, ceased on the restoration of quiet, and was not resumed. In April 1942, the author and Mr. Kalvarisky conferred with leading social workers in Nablus, and visited various villages in the neighborhood in order to renew old ties.

general "political education," the source of which is the propaganda of the Mufti party and others; whoever reads the press (*Falastin* and *Ad-Difaʿ*) must reach a similar conclusion. . . . The short-term aim should be the establishment of a party that will appear among the Arab community as a progressive organization, stressing progressive slogans for improving the social and economic situation of the Arab masses. Naturally, a central element in the program must clearly be the problem of relations between Arabs and Jews and I would like to discuss this problem frankly, in a limited circle that I wish to see organized, until a basis is worked out for a clearer and more open stand.

My position on this issue is that we must establish the principle of non-domination of one people by the other. If this is agreed, I do not object to immigration. In general I mean to address intellectual and middle-class circles, since we have no organized working class similar to yours that can act as the mainstay of the progressive public. For that reason, it seems to me that we must turn to the educated people who have accepted the presence of the Jews as an incontrovertible fact, and teach them the conclusions that must be drawn from the fact. I am acquainted with a group of people in all cities of Palestine who think as I do, and I believe I will be able to organize them for this purpose. . . . I am prepared to undertake this task. Lengthy consideration has led me to the definite conclusion that this work must be undertaken, and that now is the time for it: [A] The Allied victories led many Arab intellectuals to reexamine their general political beliefs, including those on Arab-Jewish relations. Certain groups in the Arab community are beginning to recognize the Jewish community as an established fact. That fact cannot be changed and must be taken into account, and a permanent arrangement with it achieved. [B] The long paralyzed Arab political parties are now trying to reestablish themselves. This is the time to fill the vacuum, for if we do not fill it, others will come and do so. [C] The Communist party was hard hit, but it is still a party with a great power of attraction, because there is widespread admiration among the youth for the Soviet Union, and this mixes them up. Although there are some who can make the distinction, an Arab socialist . . . is usually a Communist. . . . We should found an Arab socialist party that would prompt changes in domestic Arab affairs and would gradually lead to a reorientation on the issue of Arab-Jewish relations.

To Mr. A. Agassi's undiplomatic question, "Would a man known as an active Communist who made anti-Zionist speeches at public meetings, especially at workers' meetings, wish to cooperate with Jews and found a party based on such cooperation?" the reply was: "I was a Communist for the simple reason that most of us were—for us the Soviet Union was the model of socialism. But in time I learned that Palestinian Communists are misguided; one of the main reasons for my leaving them is the want of understanding of the Zionist question, and the refusal to reach agreement with the Jews."

Other things said by the Arab guest are included in a memorandum recorded by the author, and their accuracy was confirmed also by S. Solomon:

The first problem is the development of a cadre of progressive Arabs who will themselves guide the Arab masses, especially the workers, in the desired direction. This leadership group must know what it wants. The stated program should be concise: action to raise the general position (cultural, economic, and social) of the Arab masses in Palestine, and especially the workers; striving for Arab unity; democratization of public life; striving for a solution of the national conflict in Palestine on the basis of political equality and cooperation. He thought, however, that the new organization must gain strength before embarking on an open struggle. A progressive Arab force honestly striving to improve the standard of the Arab people, especially Arab labor, is bound to realize that cooperation with the Jews is an essential precondition. He admitted that Jewish immigration, were it not for its explosive political nature, was to the interest of the Arabs. A way must be found to remove the sting. In the program of the League for Rapprochement and Cooperation, with which he was quite familiar, he saw an acceptable path to a solution.

He did cooperate with the Communists at one time, though he was never wholehearted about it. But that is how political experience is gained. As to Zionism and the Arab-Jewish problem, even when he spoke and wrote against Zionism, he always stressed that it was against reactionary Zionism, and nobody will deny that there is Zionism of this sort and that its intentions are reactionary.

The *Histadrut* Arab department people said that precisely because this conversation had made such a great impression on them, it would be necessary to include responsible leaders in the talks. A second meeting was set up, but it was continually postponed by the *Histadrut* people and never took place. Mapai members later claimed that this was because the Arab would-be collaborator "rejected the demand that he appear publicly from the early stages of cooperation." But it would not be baseless conjecture to say that they had difficulty in crediting the idea of the existence of an independent Arab organization desiring to cooperate on the basis of equality around the political program of the League for Rapprochement and Cooperation. On the other hand, the Arabs represented by this gentleman had no faith in Mapai members and considered the *Hashomer Hatzair* liaison a guarantee of success. The attempt ended with no results.

The work of bridging the gap between Jews and Arabs had necessarily to be done under difficult external political conditions. It should be noted that the League always worked with unbelievably meagre funds. In 1947, a calculation showed that the League did not even possess 0.05 percent of the parallel funds of the political department of the Jewish Agency. A small grant to the League in the second year of its activities, from sympathizers in the United States of America, was discontinued after the intervention of an official Zionist emissary, according to Manya Shochat. (*Report to the League Secretariat*, February 6, 1942.)

Direct contact with various Arab individuals and groups in Palestine and the neighboring countries continued even under these precarious political and financial conditions. Special attention was paid to the contacts with leaders in the neighboring countries; members of the League visited Syria, Lebanon, Transjordan, and Egypt, had exploratory meetings and talks there, and also met with Syrian and Iraqi leaders who visited Palestine. In spite of the difficulties of the war, written material was distributed to these people in their own countries.

A letter from the League headquarters,* sent through secret channels to Weizmann in London, concluded by saying: "You will wish to know that there are now prominent Arabs not only prepared to cooperate in a political effort against the White Paper, if we evince willingness to agree to a political program that takes into account the interests and wishes of both parties, but also to acknowledge that partition is not the only solution, and that there is another alternative that assures large immigration and settlement in all of Palestine under conditions of peace and accord with the Arab world."

This estimate was valid throughout all of 1944, and was still quite well-founded at the beginning of 1945.

When Weizmann was in Palestine, during February of 1945, he invited the representatives of the League for Rapprochement and Cooperation, the leadership of the *Ihud* organization, and S. Kaplansky, chairman of the Committee of Enquiry on Arab-Jewish relations, to a conference. Two meetings were held: the first at Rehovot (February 2, 1945), in which the participants were H. M. Kalvarisky, Dr. S. Hirsch, Z. Abramovitz, and the author (representing the League), Dr. J. L. Magnes, Professor M. Buber, and Moshe Smilansky (of *Ihud*), and S. Kaplansky, Jewish Agency representative E. Kaplan, and E. Epstein (later Eilat). Also present were Professor A. Volcani (the host) and Mr. Linton, secretary of the London Zionist Executive. The second, on February 13, 1945, was held in Jerusalem, and was attended by H. M. Kalvarisky, Dr. Magnes, Professor Buber, the author, and, for the Jewish Agency, M. Shertok and E. Kaplan. E. Sasson and Leo Cohen of the political department of the Jewish Agency were also present.

Weizmann was informed about the work of the League and that of the Committee of Enquiry headed by Mr. Kaplansky, and about the negative stand of the political department in regard to preliminary attempts to formulate an alternative Zionist policy. League spokesmen explained that the declared Zionist policy in operation since 1942 could not bring about peace, and meant unceasing war. The new course destroyed the last vestiges of Arab trust in the desire of the Jews to live peacefully with them.

Weizmann's sincere hope for accord and peace with the Arabs had been well known since his agreement with Faisal. It was suggested that perhaps the new policy would not have the expected results after all; the national interest called for an alternative program. All who came to the meeting placed

* Dated March 2, 1944, and signed by H. M. Kalvarisky, Dr. S. Hirsch, and Aharon Cohen.

themselves and their energies at the disposal of the president. All they asked was that unofficial contact with Arab leaders be considered worthy of encouragement. In spite of bitter past experience with the political department, these contacts were so fateful that no one could retreat because of difficulties, for it appeared that direct negotiations were still practicable.

Weizmann was told of a talk held a few days earlier with a most important Arab leader. The Arab had spoken carefully and diplomatically, but it was clear that he had been charged with preparing the conditions for a meeting in Egypt with Weizmann and only with Weizmann—and with no other representatives of the Jewish Agency, in whom the Arabs had no faith. When one of the Palestinians objected to the meeting, he was asked, "What makes you better than Faisal?" The Arab leader replied in the affirmative to the question of whether he thought the basis of the negotiations would be similar to the proposals of the summer of 1943. Asked "What about the question of immigration after we reach numerical equality between Jews and Arabs?" he replied, "This is a serious problem," but he thought that the Arabs would be prepared to go half way if there were a parallel willingness on the part of the Jews.

" 'What impels the Arabs to seek a way?' many wondered. They had recently overcome a major internal obstacle and reached an agreement with Saudi Arabia in favor of a *League of Arab People*. There was reason to believe that Saudi Arabia would not oppose a quadruple federation (of Syria, Lebanon, Palestine, and Transjordan), since Egypt guaranteed that Iraq would not join the federation without Saudi Arabia's consent. A congress of Arab nations was about to convene. (The founding convention of the Arab League convened in March 1945.) The Palestine question was a thorn in their side. Without Palestine, no plan for the federation could be implemented. Neither could they leave the Palestinian Arabs without at least the same measure of independence that the other Arab states had already attained. They also had two choices—partition, or a compromise that would maintain the integrity of the country.

" 'Is there still time to act?' a number of people asked. The feeling was widespread that the hour of decision was actually upon us; but there was reason to believe that among the various possibilities we were accustomed to consider—a Jewish state in all of Palestine, the partition of the country, the perpetuation of the White Paper, the amendment of the White Paper, the outbreak of violence, etc.—the most likely was perhaps the possibility that the present equivocal situation would continue for a considerable time. The war was still going on; but even if it ended that did not mean that all the knotty problems would be solved immediately. Our own problem did not weigh on others as it did on us.

"There was still time to act. It was essential that agreement be preceded by an armistice, by the creation of an atmosphere of good will, by a recognition by both sides that it was essential to find a common path, and by faith in the possibility of an agreement. It was essential to put an end to the attitude of decision by force, to the rivalry *vis-à-vis* the outside world between the two parties, which defeated both of them.

"And there was one more problem, which though delicate, could not be avoided. The universal custom is that if one wants to change a policy one sees to it that this is expressed also by people who represent the desired policy rather than the prevailing one. Our situation was well known and could not be ignored. But if there should really be a desire to change, it would be necessary to change at least the political staff, to make action possible for people who not only had a different attitude to the matter, and faith in the new way, but who also, and this was very important, enjoyed at least a minimum of the Arabs' faith. This would be evidence of good will on our part, as well as for the good of the matter itself.

"Yes, there were two possibilities for action: coming to the opposing side with a specific program—and there was danger in this—or working through investigating and sounding out what the second party was prepared to propose. There was no doubt that the second method was preferable for a start, but were we only at the point of departure? Hadn't we lived through twenty-five years of investigating and sounding out? The Arabs said we have talked and talked in a general way—what did we actually propose? The Arabs had a feeling that conversations were being held with them in order to obtain concessions from them and then use the concessions against them. ... Most sincere Arabs—and we may assume that there are such—had the impression that the Jewish Agency did not have the intention, the constant objective, of reaching an accord with them. It was very difficult to fight this judgment. And if this is so, if we, the participants in this discussion, did not exist—we would have to be brought into being."

A very authoritative participant noted that the idea of an alternative was not new to him, nor did he think that it was unfamiliar to the Executive, for with all the insistence on the Biltmore program there was no assurance that it would be implemented. The Executive was taking into account the possibility that whatever happened, the Biltmore program would not be accepted in its entirety. Was it not necessary, then, it was asked, to prepare something for such a contingency, something serious that could be presented to the people and the whole world? The question was toward what end all the effort was to be invested. The official policy led to an abyss, to a blank wall, the alternative policy also required great efforts and time, but with it there was hope of getting out of the impasse.

The above are only a few excerpts from a full record of the two meetings, which cannot as yet be fully divulged. Despite the League's criticism of the political department and its counter complaints, the conference was marked by frankness and mutual respect. But the meetings were inconclusive. Shertok summed up by saying, "After everything that has been said, I find it difficult to reply to all the proposals put forth."

There were some, however, who believed that these meetings were not entirely a waste of time because of their importance in influencing the universally respected Weizmann. The record of this meeting concludes with a summary of Weizmann's remarks:

It is not easy for an organization like the Jewish Agency, to accept the accusation that there were important opportunities missed, but he thanked A. Cohen for giving an exhaustive answer to his question in a few words. If they [the political departments of the Jewish Agency] agreed to give the League the opportunity proposed here, he would say to the assembled people: "You are honest people who understand the significance of these affairs. Do you believe that it is possible to come to an agreement with the Arabs on equality?" He had not discussed the matter earlier with Shertok, but if the Arabs seriously agreed to parity, he would consider it very important for Zionism, and would feel that it would be worthwhile to rack our brains and think the matter through to the end in order to reach an agreement.*

After this last fruitless attempt, any chance for accord on the Arab-Jewish problem during the period was blocked. The proposed meeting between Weizmann and Arab leaders in Egypt did not take place. In March 1945, the Arab League was founded. Its constitution included an "appendix on Palestine," which stated:

Since the end of the last war, Palestine has been liberated from Ottoman rule, as are the other Arab countries separated from the Ottoman Empire. Palestine became independent and does not belong to any other country. Under the Lausanne treaty the peoples were to be given self government. Although Palestine was not allowed such self-government, the League of Nations recognized its independence in 1919 without determining its future regime. From the legal point of view, there is no doubt of its international existence and independence, just as there is no doubt of the independence of the other Arab countries. If for reasons beyond its control this independence could not achieve external expression, this does not prevent the participation of Palestine in the activities of the [Arab] League Council.

Therefore, the signatory countries of the Arab League Charter believe that in view of the special circumstances of Palestine, and pending its definitive independence, the League Council should appoint a representative of Palestine Arabs to take part in its activities.

* Information on the talks with Professor Weizmann derives from notes now in the Weizmann archives at Rehovot, confirmed by all the participants except those representing the Jewish Agency. When Mr. Sharett was asked to confirm the statements in the record of the Jewish Agency representatives, he replied that he "did not consider that those talks could be reported in any way." (Letter of May 11, 1945, from Z. Sherf to the author).

The British, who wielded at that time considerable influence on the Arab League, continued to pose as "defenders of the underdog" and to strive for increased Arab League intervention in Palestine affairs. They wished to convert this intervention into one of the unifying elements of the League, in view of the various conflicts among the Arab countries themselves. Ever since representatives of Arab countries had taken part in the London conference on Palestine in 1939, British statesmen ostensibly consulted Arab statesmen on all Palestine affairs and sought their agreement to all British moves and measures on the political fortunes of the country. With the founding of the Arab League, Arab political initiative regarding the Palestine question passed to the League Council, while Palestinian Arabs themselves became merely an auxiliary factor.

During 1945, Musa al-Alami continued to be almost the only representative recognized by the Arabs of Palestine and the Arab League. In August 1945, he published a plan for the establishment of "the constructive venture."* The basic idea was that the transfer of land to Jews should be prevented, not by purchasing the lands for sale ("The Arabs did not have the means to save all the lands in danger"), but by eliminating the reasons for its sale which were, primarily, the backwardness of the Arab villages and the low standard of living of the fellaheen. If the Arab fellah's standard of living could be raised, if his economic conditions, agricultural skill, health, cultural and social life improved, he would not sell his land. The declared aim of the new company established by Alami, with Hussaini support, was to undertake development projects by giving loans, establishing model farms, providing professional guidance for farmers, and setting up schools and clinics in the villages. The only condition for such grants was a promise by the village to prevent the transfer of its land to the Jews. According to Alami's calculations, about £30,000 was required to improve the condition of the average Palestinian Arab village, so that £1,000,000 would suffice to "save" about thirty villages a year.

The "constructive venture" evoked much controversy in the Arab community. Alami was accused of endangering the existing National Fund by publicizing unrealistic plans. The National Fund continued to decline even more, and the Arab countries offered no effective help to the floundering organizations. The regulation of the relations between the National Fund and the "constructive venture" became an important task in the program of the Arab League, whose political guidance was accepted by all Palestine Arabs.

* There were many who believed that this was, in effect, an attempt to destroy the Fund of the Nation, founded by the *Al-Istiklal* people, when the fund failed to raise any substantial amounts among Palestinian Arabs and it became necessary to solicit funds from neighboring countries. In June 1945, the Hussaini party officially announced its opposition to the Fund and forbade its members to support it.

The appointment of Alami as the representative of Palestine Arabs in the Arab League did not solve the problem of political leadership for Palestinian Arabs. The Arab League Council, which convened in November 1945, asked the chairman of that session, the Syrian statesman Jamil Mardam to mediate among the Palestinian Arab leaders, with a view to bringing about their agreement on a single representative body that could make peace between the National Fund and the "Constructive venture" ("so that it will be possible to decide on the League's practical help in saving Palestinian lands"), and to determining the direction of propaganda offices, etc. The mission headed by Jamil Mardam came to Palestine, succeeded in setting up a common control committee for the two rival enterprises, found a compromise formula for the propaganda offices (which actually remained under Alami's supervision), and, most important—set up a new Higher Arab Committee, whose composition had been a cause of violent controversy since 1943. In this atmosphere of national fronts organized for battle, the Hussainis got what they wanted: A new Higher Arab Committee was set up in Palestine, and they were promised that the president of their party, Jamal Hussaini, then under British internment in Rhodesia, would be released and returned to Palestine and that the presidency of the new Higher Arab Committee of twelve members* would be reserved for Haj Amin al-Hussaini.

It quickly became apparent, however, that the establishment of the new Arab Higher Committee did not solve the problem of full and competent representation of the Arabs of Palestine. The committee set up after such arduous efforts consisted, substantially, of old time prewar politicians, and included no representation of the young forces that had since appeared in public life: the non-party young intellectuals, leftist groups with their political, cultural and trade organizations, and other factions. These did not recognize the new Higher Committee and demanded a supreme representative body based on democratic elections. This challenge to the authority of the new Higher Committee again led to a crisis in Arab public life. A number of the Committee members (Nashashibi, Khaldi, Salah, Hilmi, Alami) had reservations about it, some of which they aired publicly. Thus, the effective enterprises of the Palestinian Arabs—the National Fund, the "Constructive Venture," and the propaganda offices—were actually withdrawn from the supervision of the Higher Committee. Lacking both the power to do anything and public backing, the Committee became the center of increasingly sharp conflicts and debates.

* Five Hussaini men: Tawfik Salih al-Hussaini, Jamal al-Hussaini's substitute till his return to Palestine; Rafik at-Tamimi, Kamil Dajani, Emile Gouri, and Yusif Sahyoun; five heads of other parties: Raghib Nashashibi, Auni Abd-ul-Hadi, Dr. Hussain al Khalidi, Abd-ul-Latif Salah, Yakub al-Gussain, and two "neutrals": Ahmad Hilmi (sympathetic to the *Al Istiklal* party), and Musa al-Alami (sympathetic to the Hussainis).

At the beginning of 1946, Jamal Hussaini returned to Palestine and took up the position that had been reserved for him at the head of Palestinian Arab leadership. He tried to strengthen the authority of the Higher Committee by increasing its membership to twenty-nine: ten from the five non-Hussaini parties, seven from the Hussaini party, and twelve from other groups not included in the above (the non-party intellectuals, the propaganda office people, workers' organizations, leftist political groups). When the twelve "neutral" members turned out to be Hussaini sympathizers, confusion resumed. Representatives of the five opposition parties advised that they did not recognize the committee proposed by Jamal al-Hussaini and set up their own committee, called "The Higher Arab Front."

At this point, the League once more intervened. Palestinian Arab leaders were invited to attend its conference in London, in June 1946. The League's Secretary, Azam Pasha, heard their complaints, and when he failed to get them to compromise, the League Council decided to establish a Higher Arab Committee in Palestine composed of five members: Haj Amin al-Hussaini, president (the post was left unfilled pending his return), Jamal al-Hussaini, acting president; Dr. Hussain al-Khalidi, secretary, Ahmad Hilmi and Emile Gouri, members. The direction of the propaganda offices was wrested from Musa al-Alami, while the inclusion of Ahmad Hilmi in the new small committee was meant to make peace between the Hussainis and the National Fund (founded by Istiklal). The League Council's decision irritated the groups who remained unrepresented in the new supreme body, in which the Hussainis—this time with the assistance of the League—had totally defeated their various opponents. But in view of the decisive role played by the Arab League in the Arab struggle for Palestine, all the discontented elements swallowed this bitter pill.

With the guidance of the Arab League, and in view of the change that had taken place in the relative strength of the forces in Palestine, the representatives of the Palestinian Arabs desisted from any more threats of terror and extremist slogans. They now presumed to don the mantle of democracy and generally resorted to the use of a more civilized political language. Having failed to overcome the Jews in direct conflict in Palestine, they now set out to wage a victorious political battle in the international forum.

References

1. Y. Ben-Zvi, *The Arab Movement* (Jaffa: Avoda Publishers, 1920–1921), p. 39 (Hebrew).
2. Martin Buber, *Mission and Destiny* (Jerusalem: Zionist Library, 1959), p. 69 (Hebrew).

3. A. D. Gordon, "Work and Nation", *The Congress* (Zionist Library, 1952), p. 203 (Hebrew).

4. *Ibid.*, "Letters and Notes," p. 52.

5. *Ibid.*, "Work and Nation," pp. 242, 245.

6. *Ibid.*, "Letters and Notes," p. 40.

7. Letter dated August 22, 1922 (French), the Central Zionist Archives, Jerusalem, File S30/2493.

8. A. S. Yehuda, *The World* (Hebrew), (London, June 27, 1924), Vol. XXVI, p. 517.

9. Ben-Gurion, *Cuntres*, organ of the *Ahduth Haavoda* Party, No. 237, autumn, 1926.

10. Ben-Gurion, Sept. 1928, Quoted in *We and Our Neighbors*, Digest published by Davar (Tel Aviv, 1931), pp. 150–151.

11. F. H. Kish, *Palestine Diary* (Victor Gollancz, London, 1938).

12. Chaim Arlosoroff, *Selected Writings and Biographical Sketch* (Zionist Library and Am Oved, on the twenty-fifth anniversary of his death), p. 40 (Hebrew).

13. *Ha'olam* (The World), July 14, 1931, Vol. XXVII, p. 541 (Hebrew).

14. *Ibid.*, July 7, 1931, p. 515.

15. Chaim Weizmann, *Speeches* Vol. III (Mitzpeh, 1936–1937), p. 622 (Hebrew).

16. *Report of the Fourth Convention of Ahduth Haavoda* (Tel Aviv, 1925–1926), pp. 17–18.

17. *Ibid.*, pp. 21–22.

18. *Hapoel Hatzair*, No. 22, 1931.

19. B. Katznelson, *On Questions of the Political Regime of Palestine*, Vol. IV, pp. 150–167 (Hebrew).

20. Shlomo Kaplansky, "Thoughts on Sovereignty, Autonomy, and Federation," December 1941, from a selection of his works, *Vision and Realization* (Sifriat Hapoalim, 1950), p. 349 (Hebrew).

21. H. M. Kalvarisky, in the anthology *At the Parting of Our Ways* (Jerusalem, 1939), p. 34 (Hebrew).

22. *Ibid.*, "Programs and Speeches," p. 34.

23. A. Achimeir, *Hamashkif* (August 28, 1942).

24. Aharon Cohen, *Problems of Contemporary Zionist Policy* (Hakibbutz Haartzi, Hashomer Hatzair, January 1943), p. 6.

25. Speeches by Y. Hazan and M. Yaari at the Zionist Executive, October–November 1942, in *Against the Stream* (Hakibbutz Haartzi, *Hashomer Hatzair*, January, 1943).

26. *Report of the Royal Commission on Palestine*, July 1937, Part 3, par. 19.

27. *Report of the Commission on the Question of the Constitutional Development of Palestine*, July 1941, Vol. I (Jerusalem).

CHAPTER EIGHT

THE END OF AN ERA

In 1943, the British Cabinet set up a ministerial subcommittee on the Palestine problem. Its members were Colonial Secretary A. Stanley, Lord Cranborne, L. Amery, and H. Morrison (chairman). It submitted its report at the end of December of that year. Some of its members favored cantonization (the division of the country into semi-autonomous regions) and some, partition; in view of such basic differences of opinion, the problem remained "open," and His Majesty's Government continued to enforce the policy of the 1939 White Paper.

On May 8, 1945, when World War II ended in Europe, the problem of the political future of Palestine became all the more urgent because of the pressing need to find a constructive solution for the plight of the D.P.s (displaced persons). Several hundred thousand Jewish refugees, who had survived the Nazi holocaust and were now looking to Palestine, were denied permission to enter because of the 1939 White Paper policy.

Ever since the end of the European war, Palestinian Jews had been feeling increasingly bitter over the continuance of British restrictions on immigration. The mass of the Jewish people had been led to believe that the defeat of the Axis would be the defeat of the Arabs as well, while the Jews would be rewarded for their loyalty to the Allies in the war against Hitler. Now the end of the war had come. The Arab League emerged, with British encouragement; and the founding convention of the United Nations in San Francisco (April 1945) was attended by delegations from Arab countries who associated themselves with the demand of Palestinian Arab leaders for the enforcement of the White Paper policy (which they had rejected in 1939 as inadequate to their aspirations). While for the Jews, the matter was incomparably urgent, the Arabs could now afford to be patient, confident that the British government would enforce a policy that would finally stifle the Jewish endeavor in Palestine.

The Labour Government Maintains the Restrictive Policy

Zionists throughout the war cherished the hope that at the end of the war, the "friendly" Labour Party would come to power in Britain. At the end of July 1945, elections were held in Britain and the Labour Party won a majority; but British policy in Palestine showed not the slightest change.

"No one could have imagined," the Executive report to the Zionist Congress later stated, "that the party that used to attack the White Paper and demand that the gates of Palestine be opened to Jewish immigration would immediately upon coming to power adopt the old restrictive policy." Faith in the Labour government was completely shaken, to be replaced by despair and disillusionment, and doubts about the legal authority of the government.*

Bartley Crum related (in *Behind the Silken Curtain*, Simon and Schuster, New York, 1947, p. 51) that when the Anglo-American Enquiry Commission asked the Labour M.P., Mr. Thomas Reid, how they were to understand the Labour government's disavowal of its party's earlier resolutions on the Palestine question, "Reid was forthright. His party's pledges on Palestine had been highly overplayed, he told us. They were 'hurried through' the Labour Party conferences. There was practically no discussion of them. He added, smiling, 'I think the average member who attended these conferences had about as much knowledge of the Palestine problem as I have of the moon. These resolutions were put forward and accepted because nobody objected, as far as I can remember.'"

Yet ever since the Labour Party had resolved, at its Southport conference in 1939, that it "confirms the stand of its parliamentary delegation against the government declaration on its policy in Palestine," it had never stopped stressing that the difficulties in Palestine were the result of a malicious policy deliberately designed to create hostility; that obligations to the Jews were not subject to revision, and that the Jewish venture in Palestine did not harm the Arab masses, but rather benefited them. This position was confirmed at the party conferences in 1942, 1943, 1944, and 1945; that was how these Labour leaders had always spoken. When they came to power as ministers, however, these same Labour leaders adopted a policy of delay and evasion. The new Prime Minister, Mr. Attlee, stated in reply to a question in the House of Commons concerning Palestine that "at this time he had no comment to make on the matter," and that he "preferred not to make an announcement before he had a chance to study the situation." Hundreds of thousands of Jews who had survived the Nazi slaughter meanwhile languished in European refugee camps.

To the number of victims of the white paper policy during the war years were now added those of the post-war years. In May 1945 the Jewish Agency asked for 100,000 immigration certificates to meet the most urgent needs of the surviving European refugees. But it became clear in Jewish Agency talks with British authorities that the latter intended to enforce the White Paper and authorize only 1,500 to 2,000 immigrants a month. This was not

* "No one could have imagined" was merely a manner of speaking. There were many who had warned the Zionist leadership against false hopes based on disregard of British imperial interests and traditional policy in the Middle East.

Y

contrary to the White Paper, since the 75,000 total was not a definite ceiling. The political injunction that the number of Palestine Jews should not exceed one-third of the total Palestine population made it possible to permit a trickle of immigration to make up the difference in rates of natural increase between Jews and Arabs. This difference was estimated at about 30,000 a year, and it was therefore possible to authorize the immigration of some 20,000 Jews annually. The Jewish Agency could not accept this ridiculous quota. On September 25, 1945, a Jewish Agency spokesman in Jerusalem stated that the 1939 White Paper had been issued by the British government on their own responsibility, while the Permanent Mandates commission of the League of Nations had unanimously ruled that "the policy formulated in the White Paper is not in accordance with the commission's construction of the Palestine Mandate agreed to by the Mandatory power and the Council of the League of Nations." A special convention of the Jewish community, called in Jerusalem on September 27, expressed its horror at the astounding report on the British government's intention of basing its Palestine policy on the 1939 White Paper. Addressing "a pressing request to His Majesty's Government, to the British people and to the world to prevent this tragedy, to cancel the White Paper without delay, and open the door of Palestine wide to Jewish mass immigration," the convention declared that:

The Jewish community will oppose the White Paper regime with all its strength, and will not surrender to its restrictions. Jewish immigrants will enter Palestine in all circumstances and by every road; the Jewish people throughout the world will extend a brotherly hand to them. The Jewish community will open the gates of Palestine to their homeless brothers; the will to redemption of our people will destroy the restrictions of the White Paper, and the Jewish people will renew its independent national existence in its land.

The significance of this statement soon became clear.

Between August 1945 and the establishment of the state of Israel in May 1948, sixty-five "illegal" immigrant ships, carrying 69,878 persons, arrived from European shores. In August 1946, the authorities began to intern these "illegal" immigrants in Cyprus camps. All told, about 50,000 people were detained in the camps, and 28,000 were still there when the state of Israel opened its gates to them in the first months of its existence.

United States Intervention

Since the early 1940s, the United States had been keenly following developments in the Middle East and in Palestine. An authoritative source who visited the United States consulate in Jerusalem in the summer of 1942, reported that an investigation of the Jewish-Arab question and Anglo-Jewish relations had been undertaken by order of the State Department. A Jewish economist was asked if the Jewish community were against the British administration. He answered, unwillingly, that in general it was. Then he was asked if it was possible to say that in general the Jewish community in Palestine was anti-British. He replied in the negative. The American asserted that his information failed to confirm this. It is impossible to understand the Jews, he said. On the one hand, they have a war against the Axis in coopera- tion with the British; on the other hand, they can have no fondness for the British in view of the policy announced in 1939. The Jews were, therefore. hanging in mid-air with nothing to support them.*

The profound disillusionment of the Jewish community as the war ended provided a convenient background for American diplomacy, which at that time was already openly attempting to oust the British from the region. There were also domestic developments in the United States that had their impact on American foreign policy. Harry Truman succeeded President Roosevelt, who died on April 12, 1945 (before the surrender of Germany). Truman lacked the great prestige of his illustrious predecessor in office so that he and his advisors were sensitive to the feelings of millions of Jewish voters, whose views on the Jewish struggle in Palestine were not in doubt.

Earl G. Harrison was sent by President Truman to investigate the problem of refugees in Europe. He described in grim terms the plight of the masses of displaced Jews. The President then wrote, in September 1945, to the British Prime Minister in support of the recommendation of his representative that the limitations of the 1939 White Paper be modified "so as to allow the immigration of 100,000 displaced persons," since immigration to Palestine was "the essence of the problem," and the rapid immigration of a large number of Jews who could not be returned to their countries of origin was obviously the principal solution.

In the new international conditions at the end of World War II, with the growing struggles for liberation of colonial and semi-colonial nations, and the growing international influence of the anti-imperialist forces supporting these struggles, the British government needed American help. The consti- tution of the Arab League was, however, designed to protect British policy against excessive American influence in the Middle East. One of the means of attracting the Arab elite to Britain's side was a Palestine solution that would appeal to Arab leadership, based on the 1939 White Paper. The British sought American support for that policy.

At the beginning of 1945, on his return from the Yalta conference (the meeting of Roosevelt, Churchill, and Stalin to decide on matters of war and subsequent peace arrangements), President Roosevelt had explored the pos- sibilities of mediation between the Arabs and Jews; to this end he had con-

* Diary entries, June 19, 1942.

ferred with King Ibn-Saud, who had close oil connections with the United States. British diplomats saw to it that the President's impression of that meeting should conform to their political designs. King Saud willingly accepted British explanations that his position would largely determine the ultimate stand of the President on the Palestine problem. Roosevelt's impressions accorded with British plans. In the few remaining months of his life, he took no further steps in the matter.

President Truman's appeal for immigration certificates for the Jewish D.P.s was not at all welcome to the British foreign office; it was likely to add political weight to the Jewish Agency's claims, and undermine British plans. The British Foreign Secretary, Mr. Ernest Bevin (1884–1951), shrewdly announced the dispatch of a new Anglo-American Committee of Enquiry made up of people with no previous contact with the Palestine problem (six from each country). According to the American B. Crum, Bevin promised that if the commission's conclusions were unanimous, the British government would carry out its recommendations. The British Foreign Secretary thereby hoped that the "twelve beginners" of the commission (most of whom were expected to be loyal to British and American political interests in the Middle East) would approve British policy, frustrate Jewish political power in the struggle, and constitute a "moral" basis for deciding the issue by force.

A New Declaration of the Old Line

On November 13, 1945, Bevin made another evasive and hypocritical statement on Palestine in the House of Commons. His Majesty's Government was doing its utmost to relieve the plight of Jewish refugees, but was unable to accept the view that the Jews should be forced to leave Europe and not be allowed to live freely in these countries and contribute their ability and talents to the rehabilitation and prosperity of Europe. "While Palestine may make its contribution," Bevin said, "it does not by itself provide sufficient opportunity for grappling with the whole problem. . . . His Majesty's Government did not spare any effort to arrive at an arrangement that would permit Arabs and Jews to live together in peace and cooperation for the benefit of the country as a whole, but the best will of His Majesty's Government was put to nought," . . . ostensibly by the Jews and Arabs themselves. Once again, the British Foreign Secretary belabored that "dual undertaking [included in the Mandate] to facilitate the immigration and dense settlement on the land of the Jews, and at the same time ensure that the rights and status of the rest of the population are not prejudiced." The main point in the statement was that "His Majesty's Government has decided to invite the government of the United States to cooperate with it in establishing a joint Anglo-American Committee of

Enquiry, under a rotating chairmanship, to examine the question of European Jewry and to make a further review of the Palestine problems in the light of that examination." The Foreign Secretary was pleased to inform the House that the United States government have accepted this invitation.

After six years of expectation, Bevin's statement was a heavy blow to Palestinian and Diaspora Jews, whose patience had already been sorely tried. Its intentions were obvious: To treat the Jewish problem and the Palestine problem as separate issues, to blur the historical background, to confine a world-wide problem within the bounds of the European-Jewish refugee problem. Even so, a solution was to be sought in the further dispersion of the Jews, their assimilation among other peoples, and their destruction as a nation. Be that as it may, for the Jews there was no choice, and it was necessary once again to appear before a new commission.

A New Commission of Enquiry

On December 10, the composition of the new commission was announced, and it was requested to submit its findings 120 days after the beginning of the investigations. On January 5, 1946, it held preliminary sessions in Washington, then in London; subsequently it toured Germany, Poland, Czechoslovakia, Austria, Italy, and Greece, and also received reports on the Jews of Rumania and Hungary. On February 28, the commission flew to Cairo; after taking evidence there, it arrived in Jerusalem on March 6, and opened by hearing testimony from Jewish and Arab spokesmen. Subcommittees also visited the capitals of Syria, Lebanon, Iraq, Saudi Arabia, and Transjordan. On March 28, it left Palestine, and on April 20, completed its report in Lausanne.

The commission found itself helpless in confronting two such violently opposed political stands. Each side defended its own claims ardently while completely ignoring the other's, and each side propounded the identical view: "Let them leave us alone, both of us, on our own, and the problem will be solved by a test of strength." The commission's report reflected its confusion, for rather than stating what the political future of Palestine should be, it stated what it should not be: "Palestine will be neither a Jewish state nor an Arab state." According to the commission's directives, "Palestine should after all be a state that protects the rights and interests of Moslems, Jews, and Christians together, and grants all its inhabitants self-government to the fullest extent."

The commission began its report with the admission that "the information on countries besides Palestine did not provide the hope of any real help in finding a home for the Jews who want or are forced to leave Europe." At the same time, "Palestine alone cannot fill the immigration needs of the

Jewish victims of Nazi persecution. The whole world is responsible for them and for the resettlement of all the displaced persons." The commission viewed the problem of the displaced Jews of Europe—some 500,000, according to their estimate—as part of the general problem of "displaced persons, regardless of religion or nationality, whose connections with their former communities were irrevocably severed." It recommended that the governments of Britain and the United States, in cooperation with other countries, "find a new home immediately for all the displaced persons," and that until that new home was found, they "ensure the immediate enforcement of those provisions of the United Nations Charter requiring the respect and protection of the rights of man and the basic freedoms for all, regardless of racial, sexual, linguistic, or religious differences. . . . We have come to the conclusion," the recommendations summed up, "that the enmity between the Jews and the Arabs, and especially the resolve of both parties to achieve sovereignty by violence if necessary, makes it almost certain that any attempt made now, or for some time in the future, to establish an independent Palestinian state or states will bring about civil war, which is likely to endanger the peace of the world." Therefore, the commission recommended that "until this enmity is eradicated, the Palestine government shall continue as heretofore according to the Mandate, pending the arrangement of a trustee agreement supervised by the United Nations Organization."

The first recommendation of the commission was "immediately to approve 100,000 immigration certificates for Jews who were victims of the Nazis." These certificates were "to be issued so far as possible in 1946," to speed up the actual immigration, which would then progress "as fast as conditions permitted." The report also recommended repeal of the restrictions in the 1940 land regulations, while ensuring the protection of small farm owners and tenants and the protection of holy places—making clear to both Jews and Arabs that any attempt to obstruct the endorsement of the report would be vigorously suppressed. "The Jewish Agency must immediately resume cooperating with the Mandatory administration to suppress terrorism and illegal immigration and to maintain law and order throughout the country, which is essential for all, including the new immigrants."

The shortcomings of the report were obvious: It left the fate of Palestine, and the relations between the two peoples, more or less to the arbitrary will of an administration that sought to perpetuate the rift between them; it indicated no constructive way to solve the national conflict; it injected the factor of religion as an additional complicating factor (no longer a conflict between Jews and Arabs alone, but "the interests of Moslems, Jews, and Christians"); it abounded in ambiguities and reservations, whose overall effect was to give the British administration a free hand. However, the unanimous recommendation of the commission for the immediate issue of

100,000 immigration certificates, like the other recommendations that meant the virtual abrogation of the 1939 white paper, definitely vitiated hope for American support for the British Palestine policy. Subsequent disclosures by some of the commission members (R. Crossman, Bartley Crum, and Mr. MacDonald, the latter the first United States Ambassador to Israel) revealed that the written evidence of the *Hashomer Hatzair* Workers' Party[1] was of considerable assistance to the commission, and had had an effect on its conclusions. In view of the dead-end created by the one-sided demands of each of the parties, the memorandum pointed a way out of the impasse by suggesting an accord between Jews and Arabs on the basis of a regime of political equality and cooperation—if the problems of Palestine were solved in a way that would permit the Jews immigration and settlement, and at the same time would not prejudice the true vital interests and just aspirations of Palestinian Arabs for political independence and political ties with their brother Arabs in neighboring countries.

This was noted also in the Jewish Agency memorandum to the special United Nations commission in September 1947 (page 54 of the English version): "The official Zionist program was against the bi-national conception, but it seems that this idea made a certain impression on the Anglo-American Enquiry commission, and its judicial proposals for the ultimate solution of the Palestine problem—although they lack clarity and detail—seem to intend an arrangement of that kind."

The American members of the commission wished to prove to the Jews of the United States their willingness to come to the aid of the Jewish survivors in Europe and to try to repeal the 1939 White Paper; at the same time, they did not want to appear to the Arabs as supporting all the Jewish representations. The British members of the commission, so anxious for cooperation with the Americans, thus found themselves called upon to meet some of the American political intentions. That explains the unanimity of the report, which recommended the immediate repeal of the White Paper, and the opening of Palestine to a large immigration of Jewish refugees, but contained no long-range recommendations as to the ultimate political future of the country.

The commission's report was the first political blow to the British Palestine policy. Bevin's hopes of earning the support of the United States for this policy were dashed. This paved the way to the complete defeat of the British government on the Palestine question when it later reached the international forum in the United Nations General Assembly.

The day after the report was published, even before the public had had the chance to react to it, British Prime Minister Attlee announced that the Palestine government (i.e., the British government) could not authorize the hundred thousand Jewish immigrants "unless the private armies in Pales-

tine were disbanded and their arms confiscated," and that the British government would want to know to what extent the United States government
was prepared to share any financial and military responsibility that might be
entailed in the enforcement of the report of the Anglo-American committee.

The demand that the Jewish community should lay down its arms was
nothing but a provocation by which the British Government intended to
evade its promise to carry out the recommendations of the Anglo American
Commission. The government well knew that the Jewish community was
unable to do so as long as the Arab leaders continued their threats and the
administration maintained its restrictive immigration and settlement policy.

A declaration of the Jewish resistance movement in Palestine expressed
willingness to keep law and order if 100,000 certificates were issued, but
would not agree to disarmament, since "these arms are needed to defend
Jewish life and property." Thus, the Prime Minister's statement meant, in
effect, continued refusal to carry out the practical emergency recommendation of the committee of inquiry. President Truman expressed his satisfaction
with the commission's recommendation to issue the 100,000 immigration
certificates and mentioned the rest of the commission's recommendations,
noting that by them "the commission in effect proposed the nullification of
the 1939 White Paper, including the existing restrictions on immigration and
land purchase, in order to assist in the growth of the Jewish National Home."

President Truman's announcement (July 2, 1946) that the United States
government was prepared to finance and to make the technical arrangements
for the transfer of 100,000 Jewish refugees to Palestine again angered the
British government.

A New Abortive Scheme. The Morrison-Grady Plan

The British and United States governments, patrons of the joint enquiry
commission, began consultations. Each of the two governments appointed
a special commission for this purpose. At the head of the British commission
was Herbert Morrison (Lord Privy Seal and Minister without portfolio).
Heading the American team sent to London for this purpose (consisting of
personal envoys of the Secretaries of State, Treasury, and Defense, and with
them, fourteen military and economic advisors) was the United States Ambassador to Britain, Henry Grady. Out of negotiations between these two new
commissions was born a new abortive scheme, known in the political history
of Palestine as the Morrison-Grady Plan.

According to this plan (which was submitted by Morrison to Parliament
on July 30, 1946), Palestine was to be divided into four "cantons," one
Jewish, one Arab, a Jerusalem district, and a Negev district. The Jewish
region was to include eastern Galilee, the Valley of Jezreel, and the coastal

strip from Haifa to Tel Aviv (excluding Jaffa)—a total of 17 percent of the land area of Palestine west of Jordan, and its most populous region. The Arabs were assigned 40 percent of the country; the remaining districts, intended for direct British control, comprised 43 percent. The frontiers of the Jewish and Arab cantons had no particular importance, for defense, customs, excise, and transport—as well as foreign affairs, police, and the judiciary— were to have been administered by the central government under a British High Commissioner. Separate legislatures were to be set up in the Arab and Jewish areas, but their decisions, even on matters within their all too limited scope, would be subject to approval by the British High Commissioner, who could appoint "cantonal governments" (from among the members of the cantonal legislature), and had the right to intervene, if he saw fit, in the internal affairs of the "independent" regions. In the Jewish zone, where not much unoccupied land remained, the 1940 land restrictions were to be abolished, while the continuation of immigration (to this zone) was assured within the limits of "economic absorptive capacity, with the approval of the High Commissioner." From the economic point of view, the Morrison-Grady plan was based on the assumption that "the governments represented in the Arab League are considering the possibilities of economic development in their countries" and that the United States had to be prepared to "grant extensive development loans through a suitable administration for the development of the Middle East region, including Palestine." From the political point of view, the plan paved "a way to peaceful progress and constitutional development toward federal unity or partition."

This plan, which intended to leave the government in the hands of the British while allowing the United States an economic foothold, meant the end of any extensive immigration, both because of the minimal area provided for the absorption of immigrants and because of continued British control of the rate of immigration. It provided for the closure of western Galilee and the Negev to Jewish settlement; the removal of Jewish Jerusalem from the area of Jewish "self-government;" the denial to Jews (and to Arabs) of access to the resources of the Dead Sea—all this to be offset by some dubious "self-government" in 17 percent of the area of Palestine. In return for Jewish acceptance of this plan, His Majesty's Government was prepared to agree to the immigration of 100,000 refugees to the area within one year.

If the cantonization plan was worthless to the Jews, it was equally worthless to the Arabs, who viewed it as a preparation for the partition that they vehemently opposed. The Morrison-Grady plan was therefore flatly rejected by both peoples. President Truman, who then recalled the Grady commission to Washington, announced, upon consultation with the American members of the joint Anglo-American enquiry commission in October 1946, that he could not support their plan. The question remained open as before.

Basic Contradictions Between Jews and Britain

The British refusal to issue the 100,000 immigration certificates recommended by the Anglo-American commission marked the termination of Jewish diplomatic and political representations. Arab threats of more violence in the event of the acceptance of the commission's recommendations could no longer deflect the now strong *Yishuv* from their determination to force a showdown.

Palestinian Arabs resumed their campaign in 1944 and 1945; the work of para-military training was likewise resumed, in sports clubs, among Boy Scouts, and in para-military organizations of older people. At the beginning of 1946, there were sixty-five Arab sports clubs united in a country-wide association, and several sports sections in general Arab clubs or associated with them.

The Arab Boy Scout movement (affiliated with the Baden-Powell Scouts) had developed originally at government schools, where the teachers were leaders, and then spread to private schools and clubs, especially Christian ones. According to a government report to the Anglo-American commission, at the beginning of 1946, 1,900 Boy Scouts and Girl Guides belonged to the International Baden-Powell Association. Since 1945, there had also been a country-wide organization of Arab nationalist scout units, which seceded from the international Boy Scout organization. Its branches were active in all the Arab cities of Palestine and in some of the villages. Their activities included physical education, close-order drill, field training, and secret training with light weapons.

At the end of 1945, several para-military organizations were established: The *al-Najada* (The Redeemers), centered in Jaffa, with an estimated membership of 3,000, aimed at "unifying Arab youth, closing their ranks, arousing national feeling in them, and educating them to discipline and sacrifice." Although it was established through Hussaini inspiration, it began to demonstrate excessive independence, and the Hussaini party decided to revive its youth organization, *Al-Futuwa* (Youth), which developed primarily in the Jerusalem region.

These organizations were not strong compared to Jewish security forces. The Jewish community was now strong enough to ensure safe immigration and settlement without the help of British forces. There was a tendency among the Arab League leaders then cooperating with British officials to content themselves with sharp protests and to accept *de facto* the immigration of 100,000 Jewish refugees without a full-scale war in Palestine. But the British government reaffirmed its refusal to retreat from the white paper policy, for fear of total collapse of British policy. Between the vital and immediate needs of the Jews and British interests in Palestine and the Middle

East, there now developed a full-fledged and fundamental contradiction that could no longer be mitigated. Indications of this had been apparent since the 1939 White Paper (see Chapter Five), though the outbreak of the war in 1939 had the effect of suppressing it for the duration. When the war ended, the crisis was revealed in all its severity.

The British policy of delay, could be accepted as temporarily satisfactory by the Arab leaders who comforted themselves with the thought that time would dull the sharpness of the European Jewish refugee problem, and make obsolete a powerful instrument for breaking down those gates of Palestine which had been locked to Jewish immigration since the days of Munich. But for the Jews there was no time to lose and it was a life-and-death struggle.

In contrast to former periods of Jewish self-restraint, the political developments in Palestine since 1945 were increasingly bringing into the open the real strength of the Jewish community which had grown during the war and could no longer be held back. The weight of this armed strength was to put an end to the power of the British authorities to decide unilaterally on Palestine affairs. For decades British policy had sown the seeds of the failure which was now immanent and at last the time had come for them to reap the whirlwind.

The character of the struggle; its political goal; ways and means, to what extent the use of arms should be linked to the concrete aims of Jewish immigration, settlement and self-defence, political and moral restrictions; tactical and strategic considerations, the organizational-political direction— all these were subjects of bitter differences of opinion within the Jewish community itself. But for all such differences, the Jewish people of Palestine were united in their determination as events rushed them towards the unavoidable war against the British policy of strangulation, a war to halt the progress of everything for which the Zionist movement and the Jewish community stood.

We shall not attempt a detailed account of Jewish retaliation or British counteractions as recorded in all histories of the period. What follows is merely a summing up of events.

On June 29, 1946, the British authorities embarked upon an extensive campaign of repression. On orders from the General Officer Commanding British forces in the Middle East, troops occupied the Jewish Agency building in Jerusalem and arrested four members of its Executive and David Remez, Chairman of the National Council of Palestine Jews; they were then interned in the Latrun camp. A warrant was issued for the arrest of David Ben-Gurion, Chairman of the Executive of the Jewish Agency, who was then abroad. There were searches in the Jewish Agency offices and important Jewish institutions in other places, accompanied by acts of unrestrained destruction. In the course of searches made in more than thirty settlements, nearly 3,000 people were arrested and imprisoned for months in the detention camps of Latrun, Atlit, and Rafiah. A number of people were killed during the searches, and many were wounded. A curfew was imposed on extensive areas of the country. Only in kibbutz *Yagur*, where it is believed that an informer was involved, was any considerable quantity of arms or ammunition found. All these measures were described by the authorities as "the first stage," a description whose obvious intent was to intimidate the *Yishuv*. On July 30, Tel Aviv was cut off from the rest of the country, a curfew was imposed on it, and residents were warned that curfew violaters were liable to be shot. Twenty thousand armed soldiers equipped with armored cars and tanks spent four days searching the city's houses and checking the identities of its 102,000 adult residents. Of 787 people arrested, 30 were found to be "suspect."*

The Jewish Agency buildings in Jerusalem were vacated by the British on July 10; members of its Executive and the chairman of the National Council were released on November 5, after having spent 130 days in the Latrun detention camp. Meanwhile, a special conference of all Jewish public bodies had resolved to follow a policy of non-cooperation. The first steps were that all the Jews representing the community on government committees would cease to take part in them; and that the National Council, the municipalities, the Jewish local authorities, and the committees of local communities would "undertake to allocate immediately £100,000 for the immigration of Jews to their country, disregarding the 1939 White Paper restrictions, which have no legal validity."

The aggravated repressive measures led, of course, to increased Jewish resistance. Curfews in many districts, raids on large and small settlements, searches, death sentences, arbitrary emergency regulations, barbed-wire fortifications around government buildings, and the proclamation of "military zones" all over the country—all these increased the tension and gave the country the appearance of a country at a bitter and desparate war.

Arab Reaction

The British authorities attempted to divert the prevailing tension from the Jewish-British to the Jewish-Arab plane. This was the obvious intention of the boycott declared at the end of 1945 by the Arab League against

---

* This punitive measure against Tel Aviv was taken after the explosion at the King David Hotel in Jerusalem, which housed both the Palestine Government Secretariat and Middle East Military Headquarters. A time bomb laid by the *Irgun Zvai Leumi* exploded at noon on July 22, 1946. Although a warning had been issued half an hour before, the building was not evacuated, and there were ninety victims, among whom were senior government officials, clerks, and visitors—British, Jews, and Arabs.

"Zionist products" of the Jews in Palestine—a measure that was in complete contradiction to the logic of Jewish-Arab economic relations and the economic interests of the Arabs themselves, and that was one of the methods of poisoning the atmosphere and aggravating the relations between the two peoples. Unfounded rumours from both sides also caused unnecessary anxiety in various parts of the country.

Arab reaction to government measures against the Jewish community was not uniform. The Arab press urged the government "to go all the way," to disband the Jewish Agency and deport its leaders. After "the first stage," the Communist *Al-Ittihad* wrote that the main purpose of the anti-Jewish measures was to serve as a precedent for the subsequent repression of the Arab nationalist movement. It was surprising to hear everywhere—among Arab intellectuals, storekeepers, workers, and fellaheen—the sentence, "Now it is your turn." It contained elements of pleasure at another's misfortune but was often accompanied by the recognition that decrees imposed on one people today would apply to the other tomorrow.

But there were also evidences of genuine friendship on the part of Arabs toward Jews. Aba Hushi, then secretary of the Haifa Workers' Council, reported to the *Histadrut* Executive meeting on November 6, 1946: "Eleven Arab villages sent delegations to offer me refuge in their villages, and gestures of friendships on the part of city Arabs, both workers and non-workers, are countless. An ardently nationalistic Arab offered me sanctuary in his home, adding that he would send his only son to my home for the period I would be in his." D. Remez, Chairman of the National Council and one of the Latrun internees, stressed the humane attitude of the Arab policemen and the Arab prisoners who were brought to the camp to clean up saying that, ". . . the remarkable simple humanity of the Arab policemen and prisoners—a very human attitude—cheered us all."[2]

In this period, as in others, the Palestinian reality had two faces: The officially proclaimed reality, and the one beneath the surface. No sooner did Jamal al-Husseini and Auni Abd-ul-Hadi "prove" to the Anglo-American Committee the existence of an "unbridgeable gap" between the Arabs and Jews than a lengthy strike of 35,000 government workers—Arabs and Jews—broke out, achieving its objectives only because of their united stand. Thousands of Arab and Jewish workers and officials marched with banners proclaiming, "In Unity is Our Strength." Equal solidarity was demonstrated in a subsequent strike of 1,500 Arab and Jewish workers at the Iraq Oil Company in Haifa. In the very days when Arab leaders were threatening war "if one more Jew is admitted to Palestine" in Haifa, and many Jews were openly resisting British police and military measures against "illegal" immigrant ships, there were numerous cases where Jews in danger who retreated into Arab houses were received there with understanding and sympathy.* While Arab leaders were pouring fire and brimstone on every new Jewish settlement, the Arab fellaheen of the neighborhood would welcome their new neighbors cordially and take part in the celebrations to which they were invited by the Jewish settlers. Despite anti-Jewish propaganda, good relations developed between the new Jewish settlements in the Negev and their Arab neighbors. The simple Arab, even when drawn by the widespread anti-Jewish slogan ("to defend the south against Jewish infiltration"), was pleased to have in his neighborhood a Jewish settlement that provided hope for a proper water supply, regular transportation, medical service, and similar amenities. When some Jewish settlements in the Negev were cut off by floods, the neighborhood sheiks came bearing sacks of flour and rice and eggs and offering the services of their camels, refusing to accept payment for such help.

There were no "diplomatic relations" between the official leadership of the two peoples, but there certainly prevailed neighborly relations between Jews and Arabs in everyday life. Meetings between Jews and Arabs would take place in secret.† After British repressive measures in Jewish settlements, Arab neighbors paid condolence visits, in several places, they came to apologize for various irresponsible acts committed in Jewish vineyards during the army searches and even produced the offenders. During the siege on isolated Jewish points in the Negev, Arab neighbors guarded the fields and the agricultural machinery left in areas far from the farmyard, and they even sent food and gifts to the besieged kibbutz members. Many an Arab neighbor solicitously enquired after the welfare of wives and children of Jewish friends in detention camps and brought candy and money. Indeed, even some of the soldiers of Glubb Pasha's "Arab Legion"—who were not generally trained in excessive sympathy for Jews—evinced genuine friendliness for Jews by warning them in good time of impending searches or conveying information to the families of internees, etc. A nationalist Hebrew newspaper reported, during the siege of Tel Aviv, that "many Jews can tell heartening episodes of Arabs living outside the besieged area, who more than once 'smuggled' Jews from Tel Aviv to Jaffa and back for no material benefit." Arabs used to bring food to their besieged Jewish friends and pass it through the barbed wire to the displeasure of the British guards.[3] This was another aspect of Palestinian reality.

* This belies the official assertion that the "illegal" immigration was a cause of "tension between the Jewish and Arab communities," an assertion used to justify the repression by the British Navy of "illegal" Jewish immigration.

† Characteristic of the spirit of the times was the participation of Arab guests in the dedication ceremony of a new school in Kfar Ata. Their spokesman made an enthusiastic speech on peace and understanding between the two peoples, but the Arabs requested that no pictures be taken and that they should remain unnamed, for fear of Arab revenge, as well as to avoid any propagandistic utilization of the event by Jewish authorities.

Arab-Jewish Political Cooperation: A Daring Attempt

This stormy period not only included many colorful incidents that were the other side of Palestinian reality, but it was also marked by one of the most daring attempts made by Arabs to cooperate with Jewish political groups in order to extricate Palestine from its impasse through joint efforts.

On November 11, 1946, an agreement on cooperation and mutual help was signed by an Arab association called *Falastin Al-Jadida* (New Palestine) and the League for Jewish-Arab Rapprochement and Cooperation. The agreement read as follows:

> The management of the *Falastin Al-Jadida* union, after having become acquainted with the platform of the League for Rapprochement and Cooperation formulated in June 1942, and after having ascertained the objectives and the activities of the League, hereby expresses its willingness to support the League's activities and assist it to succeed to the best of its ability.
>
> The League for Rapprochement and Cooperation has taken note of the objectives of the *Falastin Al-Jadida* union and its intention to advocate its program to Arabs verbally, as well as through its organ *Al-Akha* (Brotherhood), to maintain the integrity of Palestine and seek a solution for its political problem through an Arab-Jewish accord based on the following principles: complete cooperation between the two peoples in all fields; political equality between them in Palestine toward the independence of the country; Jewish immigration according to the country's economic absorptive capacity, and the future alliance of independent Palestine with the neighboring countries. The League hereby expresses its willingness to support the program of *Falastin Al-Jadida* and assist it to the best of its ability.
>
> In proof of our sincere will for cooperation and mutual help this memorandum—formulated and signed in identical texts in Arabic and Hebrew—is hereby signed.

Jerusalem, November 11, 1946.

For the League for Rapprochement and
   Cooperation

H. M. KALVARISKY
Z. BAR-NIV
AHARON COHEN
ERNST SIMON
GABRIEL STERN

For *Falastin Al-Jadida*

FAUZI AL-HUSSAINI
and four other signatures.*

The founder and leader of *Falastin Al-Jadida* was the late Fauzi al-Hussaini.† On July 22, 1946, he explained his group's position at a public meeting in Haifa:

* As these other signatories are now in neighboring countries, their names are deleted in concern for their safety.

† Fauzi Darwish Al-Hussaini (a cousin of the Mufti Haj Amin): Born 1898. Active for many years in the Arab national movement. Formerly took part in anti-Jewish disturbances. Was for a time interned in a British concentration camp. Later came to

There is a path to understanding and accord between the two peoples, however numerous the obstacles in the way. Accord is essential for the development of the country and the liberation of the two peoples. The conditions for accord are the principle of non-domination of one people by the other, and the establishment of a bi-national state on the basis of political equality and full economic, social, and cultural cooperation between the two peoples. Immigration is a political issue, and within a comprehensive accord it should not be difficult to solve this problem on the basis of the economic absorptive capacity of the country. The accord between the two peoples must have international sanction through the United Nations Organization, and it must assure the Arabs that an independent bi-national Palestine will join an alliance with the neighboring Arab countries.*

On another occasion, in the course of a large Arab-Jewish meeting at the home of Kalvarisky in August 1946, Fauzi al-Hussaini said:

The efforts made by Mr. Kalvarisky for decades, till he reached a stage where 20 to 30 per cent of the Jewish community support his aims, are well known. No serious action in this direction has yet been taken in the Arab community. The hour is late, and we must hurry. My friends and I know that we too will have great difficulty, the more so since political conditions have changed for the worse. While many more Arabs are politically minded, the popularity of extremism has grown. The Arab party [of Jamal al-Husseini and the mufti] is strong, materially rather than morally, and is supported by the government. Those of the Arab people who do not wish to be led astray by this party have no one to help them. Jamal goes from town to town and village to village winning supporters, as there is no one to seek another way, and thus flout his influence.

Since we are late, we must act quickly and energetically. We must work in all possible circles. We must immediately set up a club in Jerusalem, enroll members, begin publishing a journal, arrange propaganda visits to other cities. . . . Experience has shown that the official policy of both sides [the Jewish and the Arab] brings only harm and suffering to both. Jews and Arabs were once friendly and cooperative. There are Jews and Arabs of the earlier generation who were nursed by one mother. I myself for years went along with my cousin Jamal al-Husseini. I and others like me made Jamal a leader, took part in various political activities with him. I took part in the 1929 riots, but in the course of the years I came to know that there is no sense in this way. Imperialistic policy is playing with both of us, Arabs and Jews alike, and we have no choice but to unite and work hand in hand for the benefit of us both.

One of the Jews attending the meeting asked the Arabs present whether they had thought of the measures that would be taken against them in the Arab community. What would they do if their club were attacked or their

believe that the only way to realize Arab aspirations was through accord with the Jews, the solution of the Palestine problem through political equality of the two peoples, and complete cooperation for the realization of the just national aspirations of both.

* These words, quoted in *Mishmar* of July 25, 1946, were published in the Arab supplement and known to many Arabs. Fauzi al-Hussaini expressed these ideas publicly on many occasions and propagandized them as much as he could.

journal could not be printed? Fauzi replied: "We thought of all this before. There will certainly be opposition, and we may even be attacked, but if we have organizational, political, and moral help, especially if we are able to show concrete and useful cooperation with the Jews, other Arabs will follow us, for many of those following Jamal do so only because they have no alternative."*

Fauzi and his friends got to work, enlisting supporters, teachers, officials, businessmen, students, journalists, and laborers, Moslems as well as Christians. There were many Arabs holding such views, and these found ,in Fauzi a determined and courageous leader. He applied himself devotedly to the manifold tasks ahead—the finding of club premises and the arrangements for publication of a newspaper. He was undeterred by warnings and threats. To one warning by Jamal al-Hussaini he replied bravely, "History will judge which of our ways was right." But the Arab leadership was not willing to leave it to history, and Fauzi paid with his life for his daring and courage. On November 23, 1946, he was murdered by "unknown persons." Some time before his death, he had applied for, but had not received, a license to bear arms. Several members of the Higher Arab Committee were issued such licenses.

In the Arab community, there was an initial attempt to conceal traces of the murder. The day after the assassination, the Hussaini paper *Al Wahda* reported that "Fauzi Darvish was killed in Tur village." They tried to hide the last name until it was disclosed by other Arab papers. Then they tried to cover up the political background of the murder by spreading a rumor that Fauzi had been murdered because of "land deals" or for "family reasons." Only after the news agencies and the B.B.C. had announced that the murdered man had been an active proponent of Arab-Jewish understanding did the Arab Information Agency also admit that there was a political background to the murder. ("The murdered man is alleged to have belonged to a movement for Jewish-Arab rapprochement.")

The significance of this murder went well beyond the fate of the victim. Many people saw the attack as a warning to all opposition elements in the Arab community who dared to express strong views against the official Arab leadership and denied the authority of the revived Arab Higher Committee. The Arabs waited to see government and Jewish reactions. The reaction was, indeed, instructive.

Official investigation did not uncover a thing. It followed the routine procedure in ordinary criminal cases and meticulously avoided any reference

* Quoted from the minutes of the meeting and read by the author at a public lecture (Tel Aviv, December 24, 1946), "Why was Fauzi al-Hussaini Murdered?" which was published in the January 3, 1947 issue of *Mishmar* and distributed by the *Hashomer Hatzair* Workers Party.

z

to politics. No one really believed, however, that the Palestine police knew less about the murder than the man in the street.

The Egyptian weekly *Akhbar-ul-Yaum* published an interview some time after the murder with Jamal al-Hussaini, the Acting Director of the Higher Arab Committee. When asked his opinion of his cousin's murder, Jamal al-Hussaini answered. "My cousin tripped up, and got his just desserts." The indifference of the government to this murder and other cases of political murder, the "neutral" and "non-interventionist" policy it adopted, had one clear and simple meaning: The blood of Arab friends of understanding and accord with Jews, the blood of opponents of the Hussaini leadership, was expendable. Jamal al-Hussaini openly declared that he was responsible for what he called "actions against traitors"—and he was recognized by the government as the legitimate representative of the Palestinian Arabs. The British authorities saw how the leaders of the Arab community suppressed any spark of peace overtures and aspirations for accord with the Jews. They saw and kept silent. This position of the government encouraged the extremist nationalists and warned off those who thought differently.

Much of the Jewish press was indifferent to the incident, with the exception of *Mishmar*, which (subject to British censorship) gave the affair the attention it deserved; Moshe Smilansky in *Haaretz*; *Amudim*, the organ of the *Aliyah Hadasha* Party, and *Baayot*, the organ of the *Ihud* group. *Davar* contented itself with a few lines saying that "recently there have been many murders among the Arabs." On the other hand, *Hakikat-ul-Amr*, the *Histadrut* Arab newspaper quoted verbatim the *Mishmar* article, "Ideas Cannot Be Murdered." It seemed that there was no fear of telling the Arab readers of the *Histadrut* paper what had really happened in this affair; no fear that this might cast doubt on the political stand of those Jews who claimed that there were no Arabs who would agree to understanding and cooperation between the two peoples, nor was there any chance of finding such people. The December 22, 1946 *Davar* published an article by its correspondent at the Zionist Congress in Basel (Bracha Habas) on the statement of I. Hazan, the *Hashomer Hatzair* spokesman at the Congress. The story "of an Arab, a Zionist sympathizer, killed in Jerusalem because he believed in Arab-Jewish accord and wanted immigration, aroused laughter and hilarity. Someone from the Revisionist ranks commented, 'Well, this one Arab was killed and now there's nobody left.'"

In general, the approach of the Hebrew press to this episode often left much to be desired; for example, *Davar* evaded publication of the League for Rapprochement and Cooperation's reply to the anti-Zionist declaration of Bevin in November 1945. *Ha'olam*, the official organ of the World Zionist Organization, did publish the reply, though with hostile comment.

The oft-repeated Jewish question, "Is there at least one Arab who agrees with our program?" had been answered. But Fauzi was not alone. The work for brotherhood that led to his murder was not done in a day. It could not have been done at all, were it not for the single-minded dedication of certain sections of the Jewish community who in spite of everything remained faithful to the idea of Jewish-Arab brotherhood and cooperation. But even the affair of *Falastin al-Jadida*, like others previously noted, was only a hint of what could have been done, and what might have been achieved, if that stand had been taken by the entire Jewish community and Zionist movement in all their strength, rather than by minority opposition groups with limited possibilities and meager resources.*

To the International Forum

In July and August of 1946, when some of the Zionist Executive leaders were detained at Latrun, the free members from Jerusalem, the United States, and London met in Paris, led by Ben-Gurion. Following the rejection of the Morrison-Grady plan, it was necessary to determine the direction the political struggle would take.

The situation was gloomy. After 6 million Jews had been slaughtered by the Nazis, the European refugees were now the most important reserve for immigration, but these could not enter "legally". The British government presumably sought visas to British dominions for some of these refugees; Brazil was prepared to accept some of them, and even the United States was willing to admit 100,000. The international position of the Jews was not promising. There were at that time five Arab states in the United Nations (Egypt, Syria, Lebanon, Saudi Arabia, Iraq), and the Jewish people had no representation at all. The smaller countries who used to support the Jewish political case in the Mandates commission of the League of Nations had lost much of their influence in prewar years. From day to day, it became clearer that agreement with the British government was not feasible. Hopes now hinged on Washington. To move the United States government to take any political action, a political plan that would gain its attention was needed. What had been said more than once in Zionist debates was now clear to all:

* The newsletter distributed to members of the League for Rapprochement and Cooperation of April 5, 1946 gives a long list of planned measures that the League had to abandon for lack of funds, including a press office to explain events and guide public opinion (Jewish and Arab); an information campaign directed toward Jews abroad; an Arab-Jewish publishing firm; agricultural cooperation with a group of fellaheen in the Nablus area; various plans for Jewish-Arab economic cooperation, and the encouragement of several cooperatives. The same newsletter stated: "Experience has shown that financial resources without proper direction are not very promising, just as proper direction alone, without adequate means cannot ensure any notable success." (On the means available to the League see Chapter Seven.)

The Biltmore program (all of Palestine as a Jewish state immediately) could not be presented as a concrete proposal.

Dr. Nahum Goldman, a prominent Jewish leader (later to become President of the World Zionist Organization), who arrived from the United States for consultations after his exchanges with officials in Washington and delegations to the United Nations, undertook the thankless task of eschewing all propaganda and producing a clear statement of Zionist policy that could have some significance in an international campaign.

"The Biltmore program," he wrote, "is not a practical one at the moment because we have no Jewish majority [in Palestine], and cannot wait to obtain the state until we have one." Dr. Goldman held out the hope of American support for certain Jewish demands only if the Zionist executive resolved that, "We are prepared to accept partition. We have rejected the consideration of this question for years. We were afraid of internal difference of opinion. We were afraid to play our cards and take a stand. I have always warned that the time would come when we should have to make a decision without prior notice. This time has come. Unless we are ready to tell the President that we are prepared to accept a Jewish state in a reasonable part of Palestine, there will be no sense in going to Washington."*

The Executive finally concluded that it was prepared "to consider the proposal of establishing a viable Jewish state in a suitable part of Palestine." This meant in effect the "Peel plan plus the Negev." Goldman returned to Washington equipped with that resolution.

This was the first specific statement made by the Zionist leadership—since the start of the great internal debate on Zionist political objectives in preparation for the end of the war—of its intention to accept the partition of Palestine and the establishment of a Jewish state in part of it. While continuing to demand the 100,000 certificates recommended by the Anglo-American commission, the Zionist Executive now stressed that these immigrants would enter the territory of the contemplated Jewish state and demanded that all immigration affairs be transferred to Jewish bodies that would have complete self-government in it.

Dr. Goldman received from the President of the United States the assurance that he supported the plan and had advised the British government accordingly.

His Majesty's Government was, however, anxious to convene another round table conference in London with representatives of the Arab countries, the Palestinian Arabs, and the Jews. Its aim was to "prove" that everything possible had been done to find an acceptable solution and that since one had

* Dr. N. Goldman's documents on his political activity during 1945 and 1946. See "En Route to the State: How United States Support for Partition was Obtained," *Haaretz*, April 4, 1958.

not been found, they were now free to adopt such policy and measures as they saw fit. Since the British government refused to accept as a basis for the negotiations the Zionist plan of August 1946, the Jewish Agency refused to take part in the proposed conference. The Higher Arab Committee also refused to participate in it, and it never took place.

In December 1946, the Twenty-second Zionist Congress—the first postwar World Zionist Congress—met in Basle, representing some two million organized Zionists. The Congress reaffirmed the declared Zionist policy calling for the whole of Palestine as a Jewish state, but it defeated by a large majority a motion forbidding the Zionist Executive to conduct negotiations toward the establishment of a Jewish state in part of Palestine.

In January 1947, talks between Zionist representatives and the British government began. D. Horowitz (later to become Governor of the Bank of Israel), who took part in the talks as representative of the Jewish Agency, reported:*

The proposals submitted to the Zionist movement—"the 1947 Bevin plan," as M. Sharett called it—were: continued British rule in Palestine as a trustee government confirmed by the United Nations for another five years, with the object of preparing the country for independence as a unitary state. During this period, legislative and executive authority was to remain in the hands of the British High Commissioner, while certain limited rights of self-government were to be given in independently administered districts, Jewish or Arab, according to the majority of inhabitants in each district, without any intention of assuring either people self-government in any specific territorially continuous zone. It was proposed that an advisory council be set up by the High Commissioner, consisting of representatives of the district administration, and an executive council, consisting of British and Palestinian members. As for immigration, it was proposed that 4,000 certificates a month be issued in two years, i.e., 96,000 new immigrants in 1947-1948. The Anglo-American committee had

_____

* D. Horowitz, *In the Service of a State in the Making* (Shocken, Jerusalem, Tel Aviv, 1951(2)), p. 164 (Hebrew):

"The Jewish position was defined chiefly by Ben-Gurion. It was expressed in three negative assumptions and three alternative positive proposals. The negative assumptions were: (1) resistance to any prohibition or limitation of the settlement or entry of Jews in Palestine or any of its parts. If these rights are abrogated, in any part of the country, this must be compensated for by the establishment of real Jewish self-rule in the other parts of the country; (2) resistance to any artificial limitation of immigration based on criteria other than the economic absorptive capacity of Palestine; (3) resistance to any attempt aimed at turning the Jews into a minority in an Arab state.

The positive proposals were: (1) making all of Palestine a Jewish state; (2) if this is impossible—whatever the reason—the complete abrogation of current British policy and implementation of the Mandate as stated, according to the pre-1937 lines—before artificial limitations were placed on immigration and especially before the 'white paper'; (3) if the [British] government proposes the establishment of a viable Jewish state in a suitable area of Palestine, Jewish representatives will be prepared to consider the proposal."

recommended 100,000 immigration certificates immediately, and even according to the Morrison-Grady plan, this number of Jews was to have been brought in between July 1946 and June 1947. For the last three years of the trusteeship, the British foreign office proposed that the High Commissioner should decide, after consultation with the advisory council; and if the High Commissioner and the council disagree, a court appointed by the United Nations would decide. After four years of the transitional period, an elected constituent assembly would adopt the constitution of the united independent state. On the passage of such constitution, the High Commissioner would form the government upon consultation of the advisory council; if no agreement was reached in the council, the matter would be referred to the United Nations Trusteeship Council for its "advice as to future procedure."

On February 13, the Jewish Agency replied to the British foreign office proposals. Rejecting them completely, the Agency again expressed its willingness to negotiate a compromise that would assure a Jewish state in part of Palestine so as to permit the Jews control of immigration and development in that part of the country and representation in the United Nations. The Jewish state in part of Palestine, declared the Jewish Agency in its note would be based on guarantees of full equality for all its citizens and on guarantees that would safeguard the religious, cultural, and linguistic needs of all communities.

The Jewish Agency note of reply to the British government was the last official document in the thirty-year history of political relations between the the Jewish national movement and the British government.

On February 18, the British Foreign Secretary stated in the House of Commons that since negotiations with the Arabs and the Jews had been inconclusive, and since His Majesty's Government felt unable to deliver the country to one of the two disputants or to divide it between them, they had decided to refer the issue to the United Nations Organization. The government would explain that, as the Mandate contained contradictory provisions, it was not enforceable. His Majesty's Government would make no recommendation of its own, but it would ask the United Nations to recommend a solution. The statement said nothing of any British intention to abdicate the government of Palestine, nor of any undertaking to carry out the United Nations recommendations.

What did the British government intend by this statement? D. Horowitz, has reported (*In the Service of A State in the Making*) his conversation with Mr. Harold Bailey, Bevin's advisor on Palestine at the foreign office. That conversation took place after the negotiations between Jewish Agency representatives and the British government had reached an impasse. D. Horowitz quotes Bailey as saying:

Why did you agree so easily to the idea of submitting the Palestine problem to the U.N.? Look at the U.N. Charter and at the list of countries belonging to it. In order to obtain a favorable decision, you will need two-thirds of the votes of those countries, and you will be able to obtain it only if the Eastern bloc and the U.S. unite and support both the decision itself and the same formulation. Nothing like that ever happened, it cannot possibly happen, and will never happen.

M. Sharett (in *At the Gate of the Nations*, page 61) reported on a similar "very private and friendly" conversation he had at that time with a member of the British Cabinet. The Minister wished to prove, relates Sharett, that no good would come to the Jews from submitting the Palestine affair to the United Nations Assembly and implied that the Jews would be better off to give up any such idea and compromise with Britain.

"The United Nations Organization," he claimed, "was a divided, conflict-ridden body which was not capable of a considered decision on so complex an issue. America and Russia were at daggers drawn, the Jews and Arabs were divided by a chasm. The probability was that the Asian countries would identify themselves with the Arabs. A few countries might be on the side of the Jews, but most would be confused by the issue. In the circumstances there was no chance at all of a favorable solution. Chaos would prevail and the situation in Palestine would go from bad to worse." British designs were clear: First, hints that they would withdraw from Palestine, and leave the Jews alone facing the entire Arab world, might shock the Jews and make them accept the Procrustean bed thus prepared for them. As for the United Nations, it would be incapable of finding a solution to the complex problem, which would thereupon be returned to Britain. In the event the British government would be free of any moral inhibitions, and embark on a relentless campaign to break Jewish resistance and bring the Jewish people to its knees. There were at that time 100,000 British troops in Palestine to do the job.

This calculation was, however, oversimplified. The Jewish representatives could not possibly accept the British "compromise," and there was no escape from resort to the United Nations Organization. In any case only one way was open before them now: to remove the question from the closed circle of imperialist policy and to raise it as an *international* question in the highest world forum, the United Nations.

This course held a great surprise for the British foreign office, and perhaps the greatest surprise came from the socialist camp. Just as the exaggerated optimism that the Zionist leadership placed in British and American "friend-ship" was belied, so was its skepticism as to the ultimate political orientation of the Eastern "bloc" toward Jewish national aspirations.

Those who had judged that help from these forces for the historic interests of the Jews was inconceivable were in for a shock.

The U.S.S.R. and the Palestine Issue

Since the early years of the war, the Soviet Union had been paying attention to the Middle East and its problems, including Palestine and the Jewish endeavor. Soviet leaders and the people of the U.S.S.R. were not indifferent to the sympathy of the mass of Jews for the life-and-death struggle of the great socialist state against Nazi Germany. On October 2, 1941, the *Histadrut* Executive announced an emergency campaign to acquire medical supplies for the Red Army. A few weeks later, £10,000 was remitted to London, and the *Histadrut* representative there, B. Locker, presented Soviet Ambassador Maisky with instruments purchased with the proceeds from that campaign. At the end of October of that same year, "A Public Committee to Help the Soviet Union in its War Against Fascism" was constituted in Palestine. Many Jews rallied to it, and it led to the formation of a special organization for this purpose. In May 1942—at the most critical stage of the war—a special conference, presided over by S. Kaplansky, was held and resulted in the establishment of the "V-League to Help the Soviet Union." All the parties in the *Histadrut* joined and these were thousands of members in dozens of branches.

Its first national convention at the end of August 1942, in which some 250 delegates took part, was an event of great importance in the life of the Jewish community and was attended by two representatives of the Ankara Soviet Embassy, Michailov and Petrenko. These two Soviet emissaries were deeply impressed by their meetings with various Jewish groups and also with a Bethlehem group of anti-Fascist Arabs. They were also impressed by their visits to various settlements (Ramat Rahel, the Dead Sea Works, Maabarot, Nahalal, Merhavia, 'Ain Harod, Afikim, Degania, Ashdot, Kfar Giladi), and to *Histadrut* institutions, Sick Fund headquarters, etc. "A friend in need is a friend indeed," said S. S. Michailov at the League convention in Jerusalem and added, "The help Palestine Jews offered to the peoples of the U.S.S.R., who are fighting the Fascist enemy, will strengthen the ties of friendship between Jewish Palestine and the peoples of the Soviet Union. We appreciate your help, for which you have created the V-League, and we will not forget it."[4]

The League to Help the Soviet Union had a double purpose: to organize the help of the Jews of Palestine for the Soviet Union in its fight against Fascism, and to try to bring about the understanding and support of the Soviet Union for the national and social aspirations of the Jewish people in Palestine. The moral and political significance of the League's work went far beyond the effective value of medical and other relief sent to the embattled Red Army. The work of the League contributed to *rapprochement* between Palestine Jews and the Soviet Union.

It also provided opportunities for direct talk with Soviet spokesmen on the problems of the Jews and Palestine. In a conversation with a member of the V-League delegation which, in April 1943, brought to Teheran three ambulances and field operating-rooms and miscellaneous medical equipment

—a gift of Palestine Jews to the Red Army—an important Soviet representative admitted that until then they had not known much about Palestine affairs, nor taken an interest in them: "Twenty years ago," said the representative, "a box was labelled 'Zionism is reactionary,' and it has never been opened since then." What had been created in Palestine, the endeavor made there, the effect of this venture on adjacent countries, the ideological differentiation within the Zionist movement itself, all these had been unknown to the Russians, he went on, they had been busy with their own affairs, not with the Palestine issue, but it seemed to him that from then on a new era might begin.*

The visits of various Soviet representatives to Palestine and those of V-League delegations in Teheran (April 1943, December 1943, and November 1944) created opportunities for friendly contact. Soviet representatives in Teheran expressed to the Palestinian Jewish delegation their warm appreciation of the help given the Red Army by the Jews of Palestine. At an official reception for the Palestinian delegation in November 1944, Dr. Baroyan the Soviet representative in Teheran, said:

The help given us by the Jewish organization of Palestine is particularly touching. No one knows as well as the peoples of the Soviet Union the suffering and torment caused this people [the Jews] by Fascism, the enemy of mankind. We know how earnestly the Jewish people desire the destruction of this medieval ideology, and therefore how sincere is its help to the Red Army.

One burst of fire in an average section of the front consumes ten carloads of metal. For a single front to operate properly, it needs thousands of carloads of supplies, equipment, fuel, etc. in a single day but we know that these gifts embody not metal alone, but also the stuff of Jewish hearts.

At the beginning of October 1943, A. Maisky, Deputy Foreign Minister of the U.S.S.R., visited Jerusalem. The government advised the Jewish Agency that he wished to see Jewish settlements, but that "his time is very limited— one afternoon until dark." Jewish Agency representatives David Ben-Gurion and A. Kaplan, and *Histadrut* representative Golda Meirson (later Meir) conferred with him. In their company, Maisky and his wife visited the kibbutzim of Kiryat Anavim and Ma'aleh Hahamisha and had the opportunity to discuss the problems of Jewish settlement in Palestine. They also visited the Jewish quarters of Jerusalem. "It was obvious," said Golda Meirson, "that his visit was no mere courtesy visit to the Jewish Agency after his meetings in London with David Ben-Gurion, M. Shertok and B. Locker, but that he really wanted to know whether it was possible to do something in this country, so that when the time came, when they would have to express an opinion on the

* See Aharon Cohen, *With Ambulances to Teheran* (104 pages) (Sifriat Hapoalim, 1943) p. 64 (Hebrew).

Jewish problem and on Palestine, he would have first-hand knowledge. We had the feeling that this visit was of great value."[5]

Indirect confirmation of Maisky's impressions, on his short visit to Palestine, is contained in a book by Bartley Crum, who, in the spring of 1946, spoke in London with the Soviet statesman Dmitri Manuilsky, former head of the Comintern and one of Lenin's close associates. Crum had known him from the United Nations San Francisco conference; now he wanted to hear something from him about Palestine. "Manuilsky," reports Crum, "was very cautious. He said that Ivan Maisky, the former Russian Ambassador to London, had visited Palestine in 1943 and submitted to the Kremlin a report full of admiration at the wonderful progressive achievements of the Jews in Palestine. He, Manuilsky, had seen the sufferings of the Jews in his own town, Kiev. He knew well what they had undergone, and was proud of the fact that anti-Semitism was not tolerated in Russia." According to Crum, Manuilsky said that by not demanding that the Soviet Union participate in the United Nations enquiry commission on Palestine, the United States government had made the situation more difficult, since the nonparticipation of the Soviet Union could cause delays. "He said he would do everything in his power to help, both in connection with Palestine, and with opening the gates of Soviet Russia to those Jews who wanted to find refuge there and build their lives anew."

"I asked him," writes Crum, "whether Moscow still believed that the Zionists were tools of British imperialism. Manuilsky smiled again: 'They are not tools of British imperialism, Mr. Crum, but Dr. Weizmann and his group are such great believers in British honesty, that Russia sometimes believes that they are unknowing tools of British imperialism.'

"'The real difficulty you encounter in negotiating with Mr. Bevin,' he said, 'is that he handles the foreign affairs of England as if he were trying to win an election in his union and as if the leaders of all the other countries were only rival leaders in an election campaign. I suspect that he believes that the U.S.S.R. too is only a dissident splinter of the Transport Workers Union, and therefore he might fight it as he would fight a rebellious faction. Since there are only two first-class powers in the world today, the United States and Russia, Mr. Bevin makes things difficult for all of us by acting as if he represented a first-class power."[6]

The many efforts to win the understanding and support of the Soviet Union were based on the conviction of large segments of the Zionist movement that the struggle of the Soviet Union for socialism and peace and that of the Jewish people aspiring to a national and social revival in its homeland, were not contradictory and would eventually converge.

In a conversation with a senior Soviet representative in Teheran, in November 1944, the author was told that in one of the party debates in Moscow

Malenkov, then one of the party chiefs, had stressed that "the Soviet Union will have to heal the wounds of the long-suffering Jewish people."

The growing gap between the Zionist movement and British policy; the widening chasm between Jewish interests and that policy since 1939 and especially during World War II: the terrible holocaust that overcame European Jewry of those days, the obviously progressive character of the Jewish endeavor in Palestine against the background of what was taking place in the region as a whole during the war years; the British political manipulations with the more reactionary Arab elements against Jewish national interests—all these were bound to have their effect on the Soviet Union's stand *vis-à-vis* Palestine, and the Jewish people's rights in the land.

The first indication of this was the position of the Soviet delegation at the first London Congress of Trade Unions in February 1945. This international convention, in which fifty million workers from all over the world were represented, passed, on February 17, 1945, the following special resolution on the Jews and Palestine:

> This convention is of the opinion that after the war a basic remedy must be found through international action to repair the evil done to the Jewish people. Protecting the Jews from oppression and discrimination, in any country, must be the obligation of the new international authority. The Jewish people must be given the opportunity to continue building up Palestine as their national home—an endeavour whose beginnings were crowned with success through immigration, agricultural settlement, and industrial development—while securing the just interests of all the population in it, and equal rights and opportunities for all.

A representative of the Soviet delegation stated that he was in favor of this dual policy on the Jewish question—equal rights for Jews in all countries, and the establishment of a national home for all the Jews who wished to immigrate to Palestine.* This was the first time since the October revolution that any official Soviet representative had expressed support for the policy of the Jewish national home in Palestine. The Soviet attitude did not, of course, mean complete identification with Zionist policy but only a realistic appreciation of the Jewish effort in Palestine and a willingness to help in its continuation for all such Jews as wished to immigrate to Palestine and build their national home there. The position of the Soviet delegation, though not

---

* The proceedings of the London conference appeared in extenso in the March 1945 issue of *Bahistadrut* (pp. 13–19). The *Histadrut* representative, B. Locker, proposed a Palestine resolution along the lines of the Biltmore program, but the committee refused to accept it even as a basis for amendment. It was agreed not to insist on a resolution of the kind Locker had suggested, but to formulate one on a Jewish national home in Palestine —a proposal that was finally accepted by the standing committee and later by the convention. (It was opposed only by the delegates of Palestinian Arabs, Gambia, Nigeria and India.)

expressed in debate or in plenary session, was well known to all the delegates and had a decisive effect on the outcome of the vote.

On September 25, 1945, the founding convention of the new Trade Union International met in Paris. It was attended by some 3,000 delegates representing some sixty million workers.

On October 9, its Executive passed unanimously the following resolutions:

In the wake of an urgent note from the Jewish Labor Federation in Palestine,

1. the secretariat confirms the decision of the London convention to the effect that the Jewish people must be enabled to continue the upbuilding of Palestine as their national home through immigration, agricultural settlement, and industrial development, while safeguarding the interests of all the inhabitants of the country, their equal rights and opportunities.

2. the secretariat of the International's Executive calls upon the British government to adopt a policy that will assure the upbuilding of Palestine as a Jewish national home.

3. the Executive urges the need for mutual understanding and unity between Arab and Jewish workers in Palestine.

At a press conference in Paris, at about the time the secretariat of the International's Executive was meeting, Vassili Kuzentsov, the chief Soviet representative on the new Executive, stated that "the general and political resolutions adopted at the world convention of trade unions in London (including the Palestine one) are very good and will commit the new international organization of workers."[7]

The new international situation at the end of World War II brought the U.S.S.R. yet closer to the Jewish endeavor in Palestine. After the war, the Soviet Union had supported the efforts of Arab countries to achieve their complete independence. Soviet representatives at the United Nations supported Syria and Lebanon in their pleas for the evacuation of any alien forces from their soil, and they unreservedly supported Egypt's demand for the withdrawal of the British army from the Suez Canal zone. When the Egyptian demand to evacuate British forces from the Nile valley (including the Sudan) and from the canal zone became more insistent and the February 1946 demonstrations seemed to portend things to come, rumors arose that the British planned to leave Egypt and establish Palestine as a rear base for the canal. This could be avoided only by expelling the British from Palestine and giving the country political independence. Furthermore, a careful examination of the Palestine question indicated that it could not be solved if Jewish aspirations were ignored.

Experience of History

Stalin's thesis against the Zionist movement (in *Marxism and the National Question*, 1913) was based on the premise that the Jews were not a nation.

Purporting to analyze the Jewish question in the light of the Marxist scientific conception of the national question ("A nation is a human society which results from historical development, united by a solid community of language, territory, cultural and economic life") Stalin asked, "For instance, what kind of nation are the Jews, composed of Georgians, Dagestanis, Russians, Americans and others, who do not understand each other, live in different parts of the world, will never see each other, will never stand together either in peace or in war?" He replied to his own question, "No! Not for 'paper' nations such as these is social democracy evolving its national program. It can take into account only real nations which influence and move and consequently must be taken into account."[8]

How was it possible to recognize the national liberation movement of a non-existent nation? These two assumptions—the denial of the Jewish nation's existence, and the consequent denial of Zionism (defined by Stalin as "a reactionary-nationalist political faction")—formed the basis of the anti-Zionist ideology built up throughout the years by the Communist movement, not without the significant help of assimilationist Communist Jews.

Decades have passed since Stalin's pronouncement. Historical experience proved:

1. Although Jews were forced to live "in different parts of the world," they never ceased to be a people, nor lost the hope of returning to their homeland to resume their normal national life there.

2. Although "they did not understand each other" (spoke different languages), the unity of their common historical destiny had brought Jews from various countries together in the furnaces of Maidanek and Treblinka; when an emergency befell the Soviet Union, the Jews of the U.S.S.R. ("Georgians, Dagestanis, Russians and others") did not refrain from requesting help from their brother Jews in America, England, Palestine, and other countries. (See the proclamations of the Jewish Anti-Fascist Committee in Moscow during World War II.)

3. Millions of Jews had contributed to the rebuilding of the Jewish homeland in Palestine. At the first postwar Zionist Congress in Basle, December 1946, some 2 million Zionists (about 5 million, with their dependents) were represented, out of a total of 12 million Jews in the world—after a third of them had been destroyed in World War II. Did the national movement of any other nation so scattered ever include a larger percentage on the road to national liberation?

4. The experience of history has shown that in peace as in war "the Jews stand together" no less and no differently from other nations: The progressive elements find their way to the progressive forces in the international arena, while the reactionary elements find their way to the forces that suit

them. In the war against the Nazis, one of whose declared aims was the annihilation of the Jewish people, virtually the entire Jewish people joined the anti-Fascist front. As the war ended, the ideological-political battle raged once more among sections of the Jewish people, as it raged among other peoples still living under capitalist regimes. The fact that some of the French people sought peace while others were in favor of war does not make the French less of a nation.

5. The struggle of the Jewish masses for the right to return to Palestine and reestablish their national life there, and their brave fight against British policy, were the best proof that the Jews were not, and never had been, "a paper nation," but were rather a "real nation," within the Marxist understanding of the term.

When the combined problem of Palestine and the Jewish people came up for discussion at the United Nations, the U.S.S.R. continued to pursue the basic principles of Soviet foreign policy—namely the freedom and right of self-determination of all peoples, the national and social liberation of subject peoples, peace and international security. This was a great hour for the Jewish people. But with all the historical significance of the support given by the revolutionary world to the cause of Jewish national rights, those who believed that this heralded a complete revision in Soviet basic ideology vis-à-vis the Jewish problem were destined to be disappointed (see also Chapter Ten).

The Palestine Question at the United Nations

On April 2, the British government asked the United Nations Secretary-General to place the problem of Palestine on the agenda of the next session. The British government recommended an early special session of the Assembly to set up a commission to study the problem.

The special meeting of the United Nations Assembly opened at Flushing Meadow, near Lake Success, on April 28, and closed on May 15. At their request, the Jewish Agency and the Higher Arab Committee were invited to appear before the commission (which included one representative of each country's delegation). This was the first time that the Palestine problem had been taken out of the narrow context of the Arab-Jewish-British triangle and laid before a broad international forum.

On May 14, one day before the special meeting of the Assembly was to close, Soviet representative Andrei Gromyko made an important political speech that may be said to have opened a new chapter in the history of Palestine and the Jewish people.

Gromyko spoke of the complete bankruptcy of the Mandatory administration, which had deteriorated into an arbitrary regime hated by both the peoples in the country. Drawing on the report of the Anglo-American committee for an example, he quoted its conclusions:

Even from a budgetary point of view, Palestine has become a sort of semi-military and police state. . . . When we consider the problem of Palestine, we cannot fail to take cognizance of another important side of this question. It is well known that the deepest feelings of a large part of the Jewish people are connected with Palestine and the question of its future regime. . . . In the last world war the Jewish people suffered unparalleled tortures and torments. I do not exaggerate when I say that these tortures and torments are indescribable. Dry figures cannot possibly express the magnitude of the tragedy of the Jewish people or the losses caused by the Fascist conquerors. In the areas that Hitlerites controlled, Jews suffered almost complete physical annihilation. The number of Jews killed by the Fascist hangmen has been estimated at about six million. In western Europe at the war's end, only a million and a half Jews survived. But these figures, though they give an idea of the losses of the Jewish people, cannot express the grave plight of many thousands of Jews after the war. Many of the Jews left in Europe after the war are stateless, bereft of home and liveli-hood. Hundreds of thousands of Jews are wandering through various European countries, seeking subsistence and refuge. A large percent are in Displaced Persons camps where they continue to live lives of suffering and want.

The United Nations Organization cannot regard with equanimity such a state of affairs, which is incompatible with the lofty principles of its charter, principles meant to protect the rights of man irrespective of race, opinion, religion, or sex. The time has come to give these people help, not in words, but in deeds. It is essential to show concern for the vital and urgent needs of the people whom such tortures overtook as a result of the war caused by Hitler's Germany. This is the obligation of the United Nations.

Past experience, especially in World War II, has shown that no nation in western Europe was able to extend the required help to the Jewish people in defending its rights and its physical survival against the violent deeds of the Hitlerites and their allies. This is a grave fact. But unfortunately it is impossible not to admit its truth. It explains the aspiration of the Jews to create their own state. It will be unjust if we ignore this aspiration and deny the Jewish people the right to realize it.

Reviewing the various plans for the future status of Palestine and the solution of the Jewish problem there, Gromyko said:

The incontrovertible fact must be noted that the population of Palestine is composed of two peoples, Arabs and Jews, each of whom has historic roots in Palestine. Palestine has become the homeland of these two peoples, and each of them has a respected place in its economy and cultural life. The historical past as well as contemporary conditions do not justify a one-sided solution of the Palestine problem either through the estab-lishment of an independent Arab state that does not take into account the legal rights of the Jewish people, or through the establishment of an independent Jewish state that ignores the legal rights of the Arab community. These two extreme courses cannot provide a just solution of this complex problem, for they are not likely to settle the relations between Jews and Arabs—and that is the most important task. A just solution to the problem can be found only on condition that we take into account the rightful interests of both peoples. These considerations lead the Soviet delegation to conclude that the rightful interests of the Jewish and the Arab peoples in Palestine will be properly protected only by the establishment of an independent, democratic and bi-unitary Arab-Jewish state.

Contemporary history provides examples not only of racial and religious discrimination, which unfortunately prevail in a number of countries, but also of cooperation and peaceful existence between various nations living within the territory of a united country. As cooperation evolves, it is likely to provide each nation with the unlimited opportunity of investing its labor and showing its abilities within the framework of a single state and for the common good of the population as a whole.

Such a solution to the problem of Palestine's future can serve as a healthy basis for joint existence through peace and joint Arab and Jewish endeavor in the interest of both people for the benefit of the population of Palestine and the peace and security of the Middle East. Should, however, it transpire that such a solution prove unworkable because of the deteriorated relations between the Jews and the Arabs, it will be necessary to examine a second solution, which, like the first, has gained currency in Palestine, namely, the partition of the country into two independent autonomous states, a Jewish one and an Arab one. I repeat that such a solution to the Palestine problem is justifiable only if it transpires that the relations between the Jewish community and the Arab community are so bad, that they can no longer be improved or assure peaceful co-existence.

Gromyko demanded a thorough United Nations investigation of the problem "in order to bring up at the next regular session of the Assembly well-founded and thought-out proposals likely to help the United Nations Organization attain a just solution of this problem, a solution commensurate with the interests of both the peoples in Palestine, the United Nations Organization, and the maintenance of international peace and security."*

The Soviet representative's speech was a blow to those who had hoped that the United Nations would be unable to untangle the Palestinian knot. The unusual, daring, and frank position adopted by the Soviet Union in this preliminary debate in the United Nations Assembly confused all the calculations of the British foreign office. The special session of the Assembly closed with the selection of a "Special commission on Palestine," composed of representatives of eleven nations: Two from the British Commonwealth (Australia, Canada) two from western Europe (Holland, Sweden), two from eastern Europe (Yugoslavia, Czechoslovakia), two from Asia (India, Persia), and three from Latin America (Uruguay, Guatemala, Peru). September 1947 was the deadline for the submission of the commission's report and recommendation.

* The speeches by Gromyko and other Soviet representatives at the U.N. are translated from the Russian in the collection "The U.S.S.R. and the Rise of Israel" (Hebrew), published for the League for Israel-Soviet Friendship by M. Neumann, distributed by Sifriat Hapoalim, 1950.

The Special United Nations Commission on Palestine

The United Nations commission arrived in Palestine in June 1947 and began to tour the country and take evidence.

The Mandatory administration showed no abatement in its enforcement of increasingly severe anti-Jewish measures and in the sowing of national dissension; although there were tens of thousands of British soldiers in Palestine, the administration often detailed troops of the Transjordan Arab Legion (stationed in Palestine) to pursue illegal immigrants or besiege Jewish settlements. It was the Arab firemen of Haifa who were ordered to use jets of water against the Jewish illegal immigrants who refused to move from the shaky boats in which they had reached Palestine to the ships of the British Navy sent to chase them away from Palestine; teachers in Arab government schools who had become friendly with Jews from neighboring settlements were deported to distant places; with indirect and even direct British help, the Hussaini party was once again placed in control of the Arabs. Jamal al-Hussaini returned to Palestine, and even the former mufti, Haj Amin al-Hussaini—who since the end of the war had been interned somewhere in France—reappeared in the Middle East. Senior British officers like Sir Edward Spears (called "the Arab oil friend" by Arab leftists), and General Clayton, the head of British Intelligence, openly encouraged Arab opposition to the Jews, directed (through Arab League channels) the Arab boycott against Jewish goods and services, and helped Haj Amin again to become the unchallenged leader of Palestine Arabs. These anti-Jewish measures aimed to force the Jews to surrender in dread of the possibility of remaining alone in Palestine to face the Arabs. There were, of course, in some Jewish circles, people who still thought along these lines. As to the Arabs, senior government officials posed some intriguing questions to Arab leaders in connection with the United Nations investigations. They asked, for instance, (a) What would the Arab stand be if Britain were asked to leave Palestine, and the Jews then brought immigrant ships to Palestine? (b) How did the Arabs intend to defend themselves after the departure of the British if the Jews turned the murderous arms now aimed at Britain at the Arabs?

Since the Jewish community had grown and gained strength, it became difficult to claim that British rule was needed in Palestine in order to protect the Jews from the Arabs. A new pretext was prepared for the perpetuation of British rule in Palestine—the protection of the Arabs from "the murderous weapons of the Jews."

This was the background against which the United Nations commission opened its investigation. The Arab Higher Committee decided to boycott the commission and have no contact with it on the ground that the case of the Palestinian Arabs was clear and should not be the subject of a new investigation. The United nations, they said, should abolish the Mandate and grant independence to Palestine as it was, without regard to the problem of the Jewish refugees or the Jewish people. The Higher Arab Committee's decision to boycott the United Nation commission of enquiry (but not the Anglo-American committee, before which it did appear) and the general hostility demonstrated by Arab leaders to the commission during its visit at various places in Palestine—in contrast to the sympathy and hope with which it was received in Jewish settlements—could not fail to give the impression that the Jews were imbued with the sense of right and were prepared to plead their case before any unbiased tribunal, while the Arabs felt unsure of the justice of their case, and were afraid to bow to the judgment of the nations.

In contrast to the offensive Arab attitude, Jewish bodies gave the commission their full and respectful attention. The Jewish Agency detailed two highly qualified representatives (D. Horowitz and A. Eban) to serve as liaison officers and escort the commission on its tours, to provide it with information and help to organize the appearances of witnesses before it, and generally to prepare all documentary evidence to be submitted to the commission in writing.

The government submitted to the commission a memorandum summarizing its administration of Palestine during the Mandatory period. It repeated the contention as to the "double obligations" (to the Jews and Arabs) contained in the Balfour Declaration and the Mandate, and described the difficulties in the implementation of the Mandate. It placed the major responsibility for the complex situation in Palestine on the shoulders of the Jewish Agency, which, it said, had "exceeded its authority and is operating a state within a state." The government also referred to the "inequality that the Jews bring to Palestine," since in the Arab community "there is nothing comparable to the mighty political organization, the economic firms, the workers' organization, and the financial resources of the Jews".

The official stand of the Jews was presented to the commission by representatives of the Jewish Agency: On political affairs, David Ben-Gurion, M. Shertok, (Sharett), and Rabbi I. L. Fishman (Maimon); on economic affairs, D. Horowitz, Dr. F. Bernstein, and Eliezer Kaplan. Representatives of various political bodies also appeared before the commission: Among these were Y. Ben-Zvi, Dr. M. Eliash, and Dr. A. Katznelson for the National Council; Zalman Rubashov (Shazar), Pinhas Lubianiker (Lavon) and Levi Shkolnik (Eshkol) for the *Histadrut*-General Federation of Labor; Chief Rabbis Herzog and Uziel; Rachel Katznelson and Rebecca Sieff of the Council of Jewish Women's Organizations, and a delegation of Sephardic Jews consisting of Rabbi Uziel, E. Elyachar, and the lawyer Sasson. Professor Chaim Weizmann, who at that time held no official position (having resigned from the presidency of the Zionist Organization at the Twenty-second Congress), appeared before the commission as a "private individual."*

The Jewish Agency's official course was to urge the immediate repeal of the 1939 white paper, the end of Britain's Mandate on Palestine, and its establishment as a Jewish state. Nevertheless, members of the commission were given to understand in private conversations that if the establishment of a Jewish state "in a suitable part of Palestine" were proposed, such a proposal would not encounter difficulties as far as the Jews were concerned. Only Chaim Weizmann actually spoke of partition before the commission, hinting that a possible boundary might be "the Peel plan improved by the addition of the Negev."

The Jewish Agency Executive forbade the separate appearance of delegations of parties belonging to the World Zionist Organization, and no spokesmen of the *Hashomer Hatzair* or the *Ahdut Haavoda* parties, which opposed partition, appeared before the commission.†

On the other hand, several delegations of public bodies not subject to Zionist Organization discipline appeared before the commission and pleaded for political solutions that differed from the official Jewish course. A delegation from the Palestine Communist Party (S. Mikunis, Dr. V. Erlich, and M. Wilner) demanded the immediate end of the Mandate and evacuation of British forces from Palestine, assuming that it would not be difficult thereafter for the Jews and Arabs to reach agreement on the basis of political equality between the two peoples, within the framework of a unitary or federal state.‡ The *Ihud* delegation (Dr. J. L. Magnes and Dr. M. Reiner) proposed a direct trusteeship of the United Nations on Palestine, as a transitional stage between the British Mandate and independence, and also proposed Jewish immigration for a specified period until numerical equality was achieved between Jews and Arabs. "The Communist Union"§ proposed the termination of the Mandate, the evacuation of the British Army from Palestine, a united independent country on the basis of equality between the two peoples, and Jewish immigration, in accordance with the country's

* The evidence of official Jewish bodies to the commission will be found in *The Jewish Plan for Palestine* (Jerusalem, 1947), pp. 560.

† The *Hashomer Hatzair* conference, which met at the end of June, protested against the Agency Executive's decision that forbade the parties to appear before the commission, but by a vote of 55 to 27, it decided that under the circumstances it would not appear before the commission.

‡ The Arab Communists, then organized in a separate group (The League for National Liberation) decided, after some hesitation, not to appear before the commission and to boycott it out of solidarity with the Arab Higher Committee.

§ A faction that left the Palestine Communist Party because of its stand on the Zionist question, and reorganized later as the "Hebrew Communists;" in the end, most of its members joined the United Workers Party (Mapam) founded at the beginning of 1948.

economic absorptive capacity and without jeopardizing the rights of the present inhabitants of the country. An *Agudat Yisrael* delegation (Rabbis Y. M. Levin, A. A. Klein, and M. Glickman-Porush) demanded the repeal of the white paper—with no mention of the Mandate—the facilitation of immigration, and help for development. The representative of "The Committee of the Ashkenazi Congregation," Rabbi Dushinsky, demanded a status for his committee equal to that of the officially recognized Jewish community of Palestine.

Representatives of non-Arab Christian congregations (Dr. Stewart, the Bishop of the Anglican Church, and Rev. Clark-Kerr of the Scottish Church) insisted that the Christian sects be adequately represented in whatever regime was established in Palestine; Dr. Stewart further requested that development projects be banned from Galilee, as they were likely to disfigure its traditional holy character.*

An interesting episode occurred in connection with the evidence of the League for Jewish-Arab Rapprochement and Cooperation. The usual procedure was to submit to the commission in advance a précis of the evidence to be presented. When the League material—consisting of a general introduction by the Chairman, Dr. E. Simon, and a more detailed presentation by the Secretary, Mr. Aharon Cohen—was submitted to the commission, the government liaison officer sought to prevent a hearing of this testimony at a public hearing of the committee. When the time came for the League Secretary to speak, the Chairman of the commission suggested that he confine himself to written evidence, in which case "the address would be included in the stenographic record of the session." But a number of the commission members, particularly those of Yugoslavia and Guatemala, disagreed with the Chairman and insisted that there be no digression from the usual procedure, namely oral evidence given at a public hearing. After a short intermission for consultation, the League secretary was allowed to give the usual oral evidence. It included, a comprehensive and impartial analysis of British policy in Palestine, the Arab leaders' harmful stand and the policy of official Zionist leadership.

The statement of the League Secretary concluded:

We believe that the situation is not as hopeless as it may appear to an outsider. The extremism fostered here in the course of the years has become popular because of the mistaken assumption that this extremism would benefit those who follow it. But it

* Dr. Stewart claimed that he had been asked to present also the views of "a certain group of independent religious Jews" (He had in mind the fanatical *Neturei-Karta* and other groups of extremely orthodox Jews, who seceded from the officially recognized Jewish community, Knesset Israel. "They claim", said Dr. Stewart, "that they have 25,000 people and could have 50,000 if they were allowed to organize." In the same breath, Dr. Stewart went on to plead for concessions for Christian converts.

is becoming clearer to increasingly large groups that this way leads only to the brink of disaster. If it is shown that striving for accord and cooperation holds out real prospects, that an attempt to bridge the temporary conflict of interests is more promising, the feeling among both peoples will change fundamentally. From this point of view, the right decision by the U.N., and the assurance of its implementation, will have a very great influence.

If Palestine is guided with all possible speed toward becoming a bi-national state, in which both nations are equal in their national status and in the administration of the country without regard to their numerical proportion, [such a solution, with international political constitutional guarantees] would be able to remove the mutual fear of domination of one people by the other, the status and basic interests of each would be secured and protected, a new chapter in the trouble-torn history of this country would be opened, and its prosperity would be a beacon for the entire East. Help for this must and can come from all lovers of peace and progress in the international arena.*

The full cooperation of the Jewish community in Palestine naturally made a great impression on the commission. From the Arab Community, there was not even evidence from those whom the committee knew were opposed to the policy of the Arab Higher Committee. Above all, it could not fail to be impressed by the decisive fact that even if there were different conceptions on the political solution, *all* Palestinian Jews disapproved of British policy and demanded the repeal of the White Paper and the opening of Palestine to Jewish immigrants—that in this struggle the Jewish Agency could rely on the whole community. On their many tours in the country, the members of the commission could see the constructive work of the Jews from Galilee to the Negev, and the dynamic spirit inspiring it. Their secret meetings with Hagana commanders gave them an appreciation of the effective, disciplined strength behind the political struggle of the community. They also had secret meetings with leaders of I.Z.L., the dissident military organization of the right wing Revisionist Party.

During the commission's investigation, the campaign against the White Paper policy continued unabated. Five new Jewish settlements were set up (Eyal, on the east shore of Lake Hulah, Ha'ogen and Herev Le'et in Emek Hafer, Saad and Sdeh Akiva in the Negev), and six illegal immigrant ships arrived with some 9,000 people. A day before the commission left the country, it witnessed one of the most stunning chapters in the dramatic tale of illegal immigration—the arrival, on July 19, of the immigrant ship *Exodus 1947*, the largest ever, with some 4,550 on board. A British cruiser had intercepted it on the high seas (in defiance of international law) and opened fire on it, killing three immigrants. Judge Sandstrom, the Swedish chairman of the commission, Mr. Simic of Yugoslavia, and Dr. Granados of Guatemala

* A full record of the evidence of the League for Rapprochement and Cooperation appeared in *Mishmar*, July 16, 1947.

watched in Haifa the disgusting spectacle of immigrants being forcibly transferred to three British warships and cruelly deported from Palestine. While the commission was preparing its report in Geneva, they continued to receive information on the sequel to that tragedy. On July 20, the three victims were buried in Haifa; the entire Jewish community staged a protest strike, and there were countless mass meetings against these murders. That same night, the Hagana sappers blew up a fortified British radar station on Mount Carmel. One of the Jewish attackers was killed by British fire, and his funeral at Ekron was the occasion for further country-wide demonstrations. On July 23, the Hagana blew up *H.M.S. Empire Lifeguard*, which had taken part in the deportation of the *Exodus* immigrants. It was learned, meanwhile, that the immigrants had not been interned in Cyprus but had been returned to Europe, as an object lesson to other displaced Jews. An attempt was made to disembark the immigrants in a small French port, but they resisted, and the French authorities refused to compel them. The deportation ships then passed Gibraltar on their way to Hamburg (then in the British zone of occupation), where the passengers were disembarked amid further scenes of horror. Some time later, they set out for Palestine in other illegal immigrant ships and were interned in Cyprus.

With the departure of the commission from Palestine, Jewish-British relations worsened. On July 29, the British hanged three members of I.Z.L. in Acre prison. The next day, two British sergeants, who had been kidnapped on July 12 and held hostage, were found hanged in a wood near Netanya. On August 5, the Revisionist Youth Organization was proclaimed illegal, and, "as part of the security forces' war against terrorism," as the official communique read, dozens of Jews were arrested, including the mayors of Tel Aviv, Netanya, and Ramat Gan, who were ordered to help the authorities in their actions against I.Z.L. Despite the opposition of the great majority of Palestinian Jews to indiscriminate Jewish terrorism and the activities and methods of the dissidents,* the British were not able to stir up dissension within the community. There was a general protest strike on August 7, and a representative conference in Tel Aviv demanded the release of the mayors, the return of the deported immigrants, and an end to strong-arm policy.

---

* In view of British policy in Palestine, it was natural for any act of vengeance against the British to earn the sympathy of Jews. In its life-or-death battle, however, the Jewish community could not possibly approve independent anti-British action by those who refused to submit to the discipline of the organized majority and its institutions. Acts of retaliation with no moral or political reservations (harming the British only because they were British and not in the course of defending immigration operations, settlement, or stocks of defensive weapons) could provide the British authorities with a pretext for total suppression in Palestine and for an anti-Zionist atrocity campaign throughout the world; the Zionist movement was eager to win world opinion, restrain British actions in Palestine, and put an end to their oppression of Jewish endeavor in the country.

The Arab leaders resumed their campaign of violence. The signal was given after years of a kind of undeclared truce between Jews and Arabs: A number of armed Arabs burst into an isolated café in northern Tel Aviv (Gan Hawaii), killing four Jews and wounding seven. For a week there were attacks against Jews, especially on the Tel Aviv-Jaffa border. The Hagana defeated the attackers and the attacks ceased. Arab leadership knew that the Palestinian Arabs had no wish to enter a war with the Jewish community, as their forces were not then strong enough to counter Jewish resistance; consequently, they avoided a decisive showdown.

The Arab leaders continued, nevertheless, to hold the Arab public in a vise of political terror. An attempt made in August and September 1947 to found an Arab workers' party free of Arab Higher Committee control ended in the murder on September 12, 1947, of Sami Taha, the longtime (since 1935) leader of the Palestine Union of Arab Workers. His successor, Dr. Omar Khalil, issued a letter pledging loyalty to the Arab Higher Committee. Against the background of these events, the United Nations Commission met in Geneva to prepare its report.

The United Nations Commission and Representatives of the Arab States

Because it had been boycotted by the Arab Higher Committee, the commission heard no Arab evidence in Palestine. Its members were familiar with the Arab case, however, from their study of several documents presented to them on their way to Palestine and during their stay in it. The Indian member of the commission, Sir Abdur-Rahman, had received material from the Arabs (and most of his questions to the Jewish witnesses had been based on it). Nevertheless, the members of the commission decided to stop in Beirut, on their way from Palestine to Switzerland, to hear the representatives of Arab countries.

Generally speaking, these Arab representatives reaffirmed the rigid policy of the Arab League and the Higher Arab Committee. Camille Chamoun, then Lebanon's chief delegate to the United Nations (and President of Lebanon after September 1952), was the principal Arab spokesman before the commission. He said that the Arabs would never accept the partition of Palestine, and the most he was prepared to assure the Jews was a guarantee for minority rights. As to immigration, "the Arabs will never accept more Jews," he said. To a question on the status of the "illegal" Jewish immigrants and all the other Jews who had not received Palestinian citizenship, Hamid Franjiya, the foreign minister of Lebanon, replied:

All the Jews who entered Palestine after the Balfour Declaration—since November 1917—must be considered illegal immigrants. But as the Mandatory administration granted Palestinian citizenship to some of them, these are *de facto* citizens. The Jews who entered Palestine illegally would be subject to the regulations applying to illegal immigrants and deported from Palestine. The status of those who entered Palestine according to the immigration laws in force, but did not apply for Palestinian citizenship, would be decided by the independent government [with an Arab majority] to be set up in Palestine. All immigrants complying with the naturalization conditions will be treated as citizens, the others as aliens.

He held that the number of such Jews in Palestine thus liable to deportation or at the mercy of the Palestine government (he hoped the government of the mufti) was about 400,000.

The chairman, Judge Sandstrom, read an excerpt from an Arab memorandum stating that if a Jewish state were established by force, the Arabs would likewise reply with force, and asked, "Will you consider a state set up by the United Nations as one established by force?"

"None of the Arabs replied clearly or to the point," relates Granados. "They said that the United Nations would not come to a decision like that, the United Nations would not succumb to the mistake made by the League of Nations when it supported the Mandate."

Sandstrom then asked, "You say that the United Nations will not make such a decision; but if such a decision is nevertheless made, in spite of your hopes, will you then also be of the opinion that the Jewish state was established by force? Will you reply also by force?"

"In our opinion," answered Fuad Hamza, the Saudi spokesman, "this is a hypothetical question. We prefer not to say anything unless such a decision is made. We have undertaken to obey the United Nations Charter. We cannot diverge from the framework of the Charter. If the United Nations itself diverges from the framework, the very fact of the Jewish state's existence will leave us no choice in making our decision."

Lisitzky, the Czechoslovak member of the commission, noted the complaint that contradictory promises had been given Arabs and Jews by the Allies and said that it was essential to find a compromise solution. "I have listened to your demands," he said, "and it seems to me that in your view the compromise is: We want our demands met completely, the rest can be divided among those left."

The Iraqi representative, Dr. Fadil Jammali, indirectly confirmed Lisitzky's words: "We have not come to the United Nations" said Al-Jammali, "to ask for a compromise between justice and injustice, we want just solutions and just solutions are not always based on compromise. . . ."

Sandstrom continued to seek some point of agreement. Listing all the possible solutions he turned to the Arab delegates, asking, "Gentlemen, why do you ignore these solutions? Do you believe that they all have the same number of faults?" But the chairman's efforts were useless.

"In their replies," writes Granados "the Arabs reiterated their stand. The establishment of a Jewish state in all of Palestine or part of it was simply not acceptable, nor even anything that might be called a Jewish bridgehead in Palestine. They want Palestine to be an Arab state, the Jews to be a minority in it. The whole question of immigration would be determined by the Arab government of this Arab State. This and this only do they believe to be the single democratic solution."

Some of the commission members met with a group of Lebanese opposition leaders. These, mostly Maronites, questioned the right of the Lebanese government to speak for the Lebanese people, asserting that the government was a tool of the Arab League. Expressing the opinion that "neither Palestine nor Lebanon were part of the Arab world and they should not be forced to belong to it," these leaders stressed that "the Maronite Archbishop, Monsignor Mubarak, was an enthusiastic supporter of an alliance between a Lebanese Christian state and a Jewish state. Unfortunately he is not here; at the moment he is at the Vatican." (Ignatius Mubarak was later demoted in the priestly hierarchy because of his stand, whereupon he retired. He died in May 1957, at the age of eighty-three.)

In the commission's meetings with representatives of the Arab states, Transjordan was not represented and they were not invited with the explanation that this was because the country was not a member of the U.N. At the conclusion of the Beirut meeting, the commission was told that the President of Lebanon had received a telegram from the King of Transjordan stating that "he was unable to come to Beirut because he was awaiting the visit of the commission or of some of its members in Amman. Transjordan will take, as it always has, the same stand taken by the other Arab countries on the Palestine problem." The chairman of the commission and some of its members and staff left for Amman.

The members were received by King Abdullah. "They found the King to be a short man, but quite at ease, majestic looking and handsome, who spoke only Arabic in very musical cadences and never stopped smiling," reported Granados. Abdullah "evaded all questions in regard to the type of solution he wanted in Palestine, saying that there were many such solutions, but it was necessary to adopt one solution and force its acceptance vigorously and unhesitatingly. . . . Whatever the solution, he said, the incontrovertible rights of the Arabs must be protected. It would be very difficult for the Arabs to agree to a Jewish state even in part of Palestine."

Asked whether partition would cause disturbances in the Middle East, he replied smilingly, "There are plenty of troubles already in the Middle East. If all countries treated the Jews fairly, there would be no Jewish problem and no Palestine problem." Abdullah insisted on the need for a speedy solution and expressed his belief that there would be no more enquiry commissions and that this commission would find the final solution. To a question regarding the immigration of Jews to Palestine, Abdullah replied that "there are enough Jews in Palestine."

The Transjordanian Prime Minister read a document in English explaining Transjordan's position on the Palestine question, " and it did indeed accord with the stand of the other Arab countries. In an unofficial conversation, however, the Prime Minister told the commission members: 'The Jews should be permitted to remain a minority group with equal rights to those of the Arabs. More Jews should not be permitted to enter Palestine. The Jews now in Palestine, legally or illegally, should be granted citizenship in the Arab state.' When he was told that it could be inferred from the statements made in Beirut by the representatives of the Arab countries that if the United Nations decided on the establishment of a Jewish state they would consider it a state established by force and resist it by force, the Prime Minister seemed downcast and said: 'That is a very serious statement, for if the Arab representatives really mean what they say, this is a declaration of war against the United Nations. I can tell you that Transjordan will not take such an extreme stand.'" And the discussions stopped on this important note.*

A subcommittee of the commission which visited the D.P. camps in Europe, presented a gloomy report.

The Commission's Report

We have seen that while the Arabs and the British belittled the work of the commission and did little to influence its conclusions, the Jews treated it as a tribunal whose decision would in great part determine the fate of the political struggle for the future of Palestine. This is why they made considerable efforts to convince the commission of the justice of their case. These efforts continued in Geneva, where the commission worked on the preparation of their report.

Finally, after long internal deliberations, on August 31, the appointed time, the report was signed and published. Some of the conclusions were unanimous: The Mandate must be terminated soon, and Palestine must be granted independence after a short period of transition in which it would be subject to the tutelage of a United Nations authority; any political regime established in Palestine after independence must be democratic and assure minority rights, and its constitution must include the basic principles of the United Nations Charter; all extraterritorial rights in Palestine of citizens of

* Details of the meetings in Beirut and Amman are according to Granados, *Birth of Israel* (New York: Simon and Schuster).

foreign states should be cancelled.* The commission also unanimously called for the cessation of all violence in Palestine.

On the question of the stages of independence and the formation of the new regime, the commission was divided. Seven members (representatives of Uruguay, Guatemala, Peru, Holland, Sweden, Czechoslovakia, and Canada) proposed the partition of the country into two states: one Arab and one Jewish, each sovereign and independent, but economically linked to each other. Three commission members (representing Persia, India, and Yugoslavia) proposed the establishment of an independent federated Palestinian state containing a Jewish district and an Arab one, each with an independent administration. The majority proposed that the independence of the two states should begin in two years, the minority stipulated three years. The economic unity of the two states, according to the majority proposal, was to cover customs, communications, and development; while in the minority proposal, the central federal government was to control defense, foreign affairs, immigration, currency, communications, copyrights and patents, etc.

The eleventh member, from Australia, declined to support either of the proposals, claiming that both recommendations should be submitted to the plenary session of the United Nations "which would itself decide."

The commission's majority and minority proposals differed also in the boundaries they stipulated for the two states. The majority proposed that each of the states should consist of three areas; the Jewish state was to include eastern Galilee and most of the Jezreel valley, the central coastal plain (from just south of Acre to just north of Ashdod), and the Negev. The Arab state was to include western Galilee, the mountainous area in the center of Palestine, and the southern part of the coastal plain. According to this plan, the connection between the various sectors of each state would be through contact points, which were to be exclusively for purposes of passage—one southeast from Affula and another northeast from Majdal near Gaza. The majority also proposed that Jerusalem and its near environs be an international enclave (within the Arab state) directly controlled by the United Nations. The governor appointed would not be a native of Palestine and he would command a police force, likewise not native. The economic unity was to encompass Jerusalem as well. Sixty-two percent of the area of the country (excluding Jerusalem) was to be allotted to the Jewish state, and 38 percent to the Arab one.

According to the minority proposal, Jerusalem, the capital of the federal union, was to be included in the Arab zone, except for its Jewish districts,

---

* On the ratification of the Palestine Mandate, the capitulations system of Turkish times (for which, see Chapter Three) was cancelled for "so long as the Mandate shall apply." Now that the Mandate was to be terminated, it was proposed to abolish the capitulations definitely.

which would be established as a separate municipality. The minority also recommended adding to the Arab zone most of the Negev and the city of Jaffa (as an enclave in the Jewish district). In the minority proposal, the legislature of the federal state was to have two houses—a lower one with proportional representation and a higher one in which each people would have equal representation. The question of immigration was to be dealt with by a committee of three, consisting of a Jew, an Arab, and a United Nations representative, who would have the casting vote; in the transition period before independence, this three-man committee was to determine the extent of immigration authorized on the basis of economic absorptive capacity.

The Zionist Executive and the Commission Report

Between August 25 and September 2 1947, the Zionist Executive met in Zurich to discuss its official stand in relation to the report. By a vote of fifty-one to sixteen, the Executive resolved to accept the majority recommendations of the commission as a basis for representing the Zionist case to the United Nations General Assembly. A joint proposal of *Hashomer Hatzair* and *Ahdut Haavoda-Poalei Zion*, which aimed at assuring Jewish interests while maintaining the territorial integrity of Palestine, without abandoning efforts for Jewish-Arab cooperation, received ten votes.* A Revisionist proposal calling on the Zionist Executive "to continue its efforts for the immediate establishment of a Jewish state in the historic boundaries of an undivided and unreduced Palestine" received six votes. The meeting ended with the appointment of a special seventeen-man all-party committee, with deputies consisting of representatives of the parties in the Zionist congress to advise the Executive in matters pertaining to the debate on the Palestine question in the United Nations. It was decided that "no member of the committee may negotiate with any member of the United Nations Assembly or with the representatives of any government."

Meeting with the Arab League Secretary

The plenary session of the United Nations Assembly was scheduled to open on September 16. Jewish Agency representatives D. Horowitz and A. Eban meanwhile set out to explore the possibilities for an agreement with the Arabs based on the United Nations commission's report. British newspaper-

* The *Hashomer Hatzair* and *Ahdut Haavoda-Poalei Zion* factions expressed in a joint statement their opposition to the Agency leadership for (1) taking the initiative for partition contrary to the decision of the Zionist Congress, (2) failing to seek a path toward Arab-Jewish accord in an unpartitioned Palestine, (3) failing to draw the proper political conclusions from the stand of Soviet and popular democratic representatives at the United Nations in the debate on Palestine.

man Jon Kimche arranged for them to meet in London with Azam Pasha, the Secretary General of the Arab League.

These Jewish spokesmen told the Arab League secretary,* "The Jews are an existing fact in the Middle East. Sooner or later the Arabs will have to accept the fact and take it into account. The Arabs will not be able to rout or destroy over half a million people. The Jews desire accord with the Arabs with all their heart and are prepared to make sacrifices for it."

To prove that they were serious, they took the opportunity to propose a concrete plan based on: (1) An agreement on the relations between the proposed Jewish state and the Arab League that would clearly determine the rights and obligations of each state which would be clearly defined, (2) a security agreement with effective guarantees by the Jews and by the United Nations in order to dissipate Arab fears of Jewish expansion; (3) an economic agreement to provide a coordinated development of the Middle East for the benefit of the Arab masses.

Azam Pasha's reply was negative:

> The Arab world is not at all in a compromising mood. The proposed plan may be logical, but the fate of nations is not decided by rational reasoning. Nations never give up. You will achieve nothing with talk of compromise or peace. You may perhaps achieve something by force of your arms. We will try to rout you. I am not sure we will succeed, but we will try. We succeeded in expelling the Crusaders, but lost Spain and Persia, and may lose Palestine. But it is too late for a peaceable solution.

To the Jews' comment that the United Nations report created the possibility of a reasonable compromise and why should an attempt not be made to reach agreement on the basis of the United Nations report, Azam Pasha replied:

> Such an agreement is possible only on our terms. The Arab world considers you invaders, and is prepared to fight you. Conflicting interests of this kind between peoples cannot usually be settled except through war. . . . The forces that move peoples are beyond our control. There may have been in the past a chance for an understanding—but this is no longer possible. You speak of the Middle East. For us there is no such concept; for us there is only the concept of the Arab world. Nationalism is the great force that moves us. We do not need economic development. For us there is only one test, the test of strength. If I were a Zionist leader, perhaps I would behave as you do. You have no choice. In any case, the problem is likely to be solved only by force of arms.

"Despite the courteous and cordial personal atmosphere in which the conversation took place," writes D. Horowitz in his memoirs, "we all felt the full historical importance of this dramatic meeting. With it the last attempt

---

* All details on this meeting from *In the Service of a State in the Making*, by D. Horowitz, pp. 255–258 (Hebrew).

to bridge the gap expired. The last illusion that a solution might be achieved through peace and accord was destroyed."*

The Struggle in the United Nations Assembly

On September 16, the United Nations Assembly met at Lake Success, New York. To speed up the consideration of the report, the United Nations Secretariat proposed, and its proposal was accepted, that an *ad hoc* committee be appointed, parallel to the political committee of the Assembly and similar to it in composition (one representative from each national delegation to the Assembly), and of equal status. The parallel committee began its work on September 25. The next day, British Colonial Secretary Mr. Creech Jones stated that as his government was not prepared to undertake the military enforcement of a solution that was acceptable neither to the Jews nor the Arabs, they had decided to relinquish the Mandate and to leave the country.

The commission chairman, Judge Sandstrom, who submitted the report, stressed the impossibility of finding a solution to the problem that would be acceptable to both sides. After that, Jewish and Arab representatives were invited to appear.

Jamal al Hussaini, who appeared for the Higher Arab Committee, welcomed the British government's decision to relinquish the Mandate on Palestine and remove its forces and expressed the hope that they would not reverse that decision "under Jewish pressure." He characterized British policy as "most evil," stating that the Mandate favored the Jews to the detriment of the Arabs and that the Zionists and the British had formed an alliance to destroy Arab national life in Palestine. The United States also came under attack for authorizing fund-raising campaigns "for the purpose of breaking the laws of Palestine, disturbing the peace, in contrast to the efforts made by the United States government to keep the peace in another country."†

Without paying too much attention to the United Nations commission report, the Arab spokesman maintained that this report—both its majority conclusions and its minority ones—could not serve as a basis for discussion on the situation in Palestine. He said that the Arabs would resist with all means at their command any partition of the country and any plan granting privileges or special status to "any minority whatsoever." "The only just, practical and democratic plan" for the solution of the Palestine problem, as proposed by the Arab representative, contained four points: (1) All of Pales-

* The report of D. Horowitz (*In the Service of a State in the Making*, p. 239) says that the account of the Jewish Agency representatives on their meeting with Azam Pasha made a deep impression on members of several delegations. "We were free to utilize the story in various meetings," he writes, "for we had agreed only not to publish it, and Azam Pasha himself submitted a detailed report of this conversation at the Arab League convention in Bludan."   † Greece.

tine should become an Arab state based on democratic foundations; (2) the Arab state would respect the human rights and basic freedoms and equality of the individual according to law; (3) the Arab state would safeguard the legal rights and interests of all minorities; (4) freedom of religion would be respected, and access given to the holy places.

Declaring that the Arabs were not anti-Semites, Jamal al-Hussaini accused the Jews of "attempting to conquer by force of arms a state which is not theirs by right of birth," and announced that the Arabs would vehemently oppose immigration of any kind. "The Jews should seek a homeland in Birobidzhan, in Siberia or in Uganda," while elections should be held in Palestine for a constituent assembly to work out the constitution of an independent Arab state to arise at the earliest opportunity and take over the government from the Mandatory power.

The Jewish case was represented to the *ad hoc* committee by Dr. A. H. Silver, speaking for the Jewish Agency. He expressed willingness to accept the majority recommendations of the enquiry commission—the partition of Palestine into two independent states, joined by an economic union but subject to further consideration of the constitution and the territorial provisions of the plan. The proposed partition, said Dr. Silver, seriously prejudiced the rights of the Jewish people and demanded the greatest sacrifice, since the Balfour Declaration and the Mandate envisaged the whole of Palestine as a Jewish state. But the Jews were willing to accept that sacrifice because it made possible the immediate creation of a Jewish state. The speaker opposed the exclusion of western Galilee from the proposed Jewish state and noted that this area had been included by the Peel commission (1937) in its plan for a Jewish state; and he opposed the exclusion of Jerusalem from the Jewish state, not only because its new section had developed into a modern city of 90,000 Jews, but also because Jerusalem was of unequalled importance in Jewish daily life and in the religious and national tradition of the Jews.

Silver took the British government to task for its unwillingness to accept the solution recommended by the United Nations commission while offering no alternative. No solution, he suggested, would be realized without the use of force: "Why is it that Britain shows no hesitation in using its 100,000 soldiers to force upon Palestine a policy that was never approved by an international body?"

Silver stressed that though economic union between the two proposed states meant a large Jewish subsidy for the Arab state, the Jewish Agency was prepared to undertake this as one of the burdens likely to make possible a way out of the impasse. The Jewish state, declared the spokesman, would safeguard the rights of the Arabs within its borders, and would pursue good neighborliness with the Palestinian Arab state as well as with the other Arab states in the Middle East.

He urged that the transition period from the Mandate to independence be as short as possible ("two years are much more than are desirable or required"), and that any military or police force required during this transition period in order to guard law and order should include those Palestinians prepared to serve with the United Nations in the event of the British forces not undertaking this in the transition period.

He went on:

The Jewish Agency assumes that the transference of sovereignty and administrative functions to the two peoples will begin immediately, and not at the end of the transition period; the Jewish Agency also expresses its hope that the change to a new status in the two independent states will be carried out with a minimum of conflict. Immediately after the determination and demarcation of the boundaries, and the establishment of the states by the U.N., all will have to respect their territorial integrity and sovereign rights, and defend them, like other peoples, in accordance with the principles of the United Nations Charter. . . . We are being asked to sacrifice a great deal in order to obtain what has long been our right. With heavy hearts, we are prepared to make the sacrifice demanded, but we shall go no further.

We offer the Arabs peace and friendship, sincerely and without reservation. If we are met with the same spirit, all of us will enjoy the blessings of wealth and plenty. If not, we shall be forced to do what any people in those circumstances does: defend our rights to the end. The Jewish people is not impressed by empty threats. If the British army leaves Palestine, the Jews of the country are prepared to provide immediately the forces required for the maintenance of security.

After the positions of the Arabs and the Jews had been presented, a general debate ensued in the special committee. The representatives of Arab states, who supported the Palestinian Arab delegate's position, did not feel obliged to analyze the report of the United Nations commission but repeated the routine claims against Jews and Zionists; their statements were mainly threats that the Arab and Moslem world would rise up in case the proposal for the establishment of a Jewish state in part of Palestine were accepted. They were supported in a more restrained vein by the representatives of a number of Moslem countries (Afghanistan, Pakistan, Persia). More moderate still was the support of the delegate from India (with a large Moslem population, most of whom had opposed the partition of India itself); she called for making Palestine an independent Arab state with home rule for Jewish districts.

The most effective spokesman for the Arab case was Muhammad Zafrullah Khan, a brilliant Pakistani jurist of international standing, who stressed five points:

1. *Legal objection.* The Balfour Declaration and the British Mandate have no legal validity, since Britain could not give what does not belong to her. The Mandate in its letter, as well as in its spirit, was contrary to the United Nations Charter, which is based on the principle of self-determination.

What the Mandate promised the Jews they have already obtained: a refuge for some of their people in Palestine. The United Nations has no authority to make decisions on territorial arrangements. Decisions of this kind would not be in accordance with international law and the natural rights of peoples, which the United Nations charter recognizes. Such disputes should be referred to the World Court.

2. *Historical objection.* The Jews of our times are not the descendants of ancient Israel (one Arab spokesman said that they were direct descendants of the Khazars, a people of Tartar race living in the lower Volga and near the Caspian Sea, whose king and leaders in fact embraced the Jewish faith in the eighth century A.D.); in any case they have been in Palestine for only a short time, while the Arabs lived there for all of the last 1,300 years. Where will we get to if we begin to turn the wheels of history back everywhere? The Arabs of Palestine are part of the now reawakened Arab world. On the other hand, the newly arrived Zionists were not rooted in the land, and had no prospects of survival. In Arab eyes they are foreign invaders who endanger Arab rights and aspirations for freedom and unity.

3. *Formal "democratic" objection.* Every nation has the right to decide the fate of the country it inhabits. Palestine has a clear Arab majority, and by democratic principles the people of a country should be left to decide their fate, with no outside interference.

4. *Political objections.* The solution proposed by the enquiry commission is not workable. The proposed boundaries are absurd, and the political structure proposed is artificial and must collapse. As the Arabs strongly oppose the proposed solution, an attempt to carry it out will lead to military conflict endangering the peace of the East and the world, and will also prejudice the safety of Jewish communities in Eastern countries.

5. *Economic objections.* The proposed Arab state is not viable from the economic point of view, and it is not possible to force it to be dependent on the support of a state whose establishment the Arabs oppose so strongly.

Representatives of a number of delegations (Salvador, China, Argentina, Cuba) opposed the commission's recommendations and made several proposals for an interim period so as to allow more time for finding a solution that would be acceptable to both sides. There was, however, substantial support in the *ad hoc* committee for the majority recommendations of the enquiry commission. Most representatives (Sweden, Panama, Haiti, Peru, and even Canada, New Zealand, and South Africa) merely registered their support, but a few made impassioned speeches in favor of the Jews—among these were Fabrigat of Uruguay and Granados of Guatemala, members of the United Nations enquiry commission who had been deeply impressed by both the Jewish endeavor in Palestine and the suffering of the Jewish refugees in the European D.P. camps.

BI

For some time, the *ad hoc* committee was in suspense as to the definitive stand of the Socialist bloc countries. The Jewish delegation was aware that a clear change had taken place in the Soviet attitude toward the problem of the Jewish people and the contact between this and the Palestine problem. The Yugoslavs had tried at a meeting of Eastern delegations to win Soviet support for the minority recommendation of a federal solution. But Mr. Vishinsky, then one of the principal makers of Soviet policy, reminded the Yugoslavs that they were ignoring the most important Jewish problem. "During World War II," he said, "the Hitlerites attacked the Jewish people, and exterminated millions of them. A sea of Jewish blood was shed; their sufferings, which have been terrible for many generations, have now reached their peak, and they have the right to a refuge and independent political life."9 This was, however, said at a private meeting of the Socialist bloc, and public opinion and the press continued to note that while the Czechoslovak representative on the United Nations enquiry commission supported the recommendations of the majority, the Yugoslav member supported those of the minority. The rift that was then developing between Yugoslavia and the rest of the Socialist countries was not yet widely known, and Jewish Agency circles feared that the Yugoslav position might be indicative of that of the U.S.S.R. and her allies.10

The mystery did not last long. On October 8, the Polish and Czechoslovak representatives on the *ad hoc* committee made their position clear, expressing full support for the majority recommendations. The Polish representative condemned the British "divide and rule" policy in Palestine, and particularly the British treatment of Jewish refugees. He rejected the Arab demand for the domination of the whole country and expressed the hope that the economic union between the Jewish and Arab states recommended by the enquiry commission majority would gradually lead to the reunification of the country, possibly in the form of a bi-national democratic state.

Several days later, Soviet delegate S. Tsarapkin made his statement. Like A. Gromyko at the special United Nations spring session of that year, he described the sufferings of the Jews in the war, explained the motives behind Jewish aspirations for a state of their own, and repeated that "it would be a sin to deny the Jewish people the right to its own homeland."

Tsarapkin said:

The problem of establishing a Jewish state is timely and urgent, and no matter what attempts are made to complicate the problem and drown it in a sea of historical argumentation and events of hundreds and thousands of years ago, its solution cannot be evaded. The Jewish people, like others, has the right to its own destiny, its security and its existence, without being exposed to the mercy of one state or another. It is in our power to help the Jewish people if we work in accordance with the principles of the U.N. Charter, which assures all peoples the right of self-determination and independence.

Noting that the United Nations commission of enquiry had "done great and useful work, the results of which will assist in finding the most suitable solution for the Palestine problem," Tsarapkin called for Palestine's independence at the earliest possible time. While acknowledging the advantages in the enquiry commission's minority recommendations ("advantages arising out of the idea of establishing a single Arab-Jewish state in Palestine"), he noted that it must be borne in mind that the relations between the Jews and Arabs had reached such a state of tension that no solution acceptable to both was possible, and the minority recommendations were therefore unworkable. Approving the majority plan of the enquiry commission, he said that "from the point of view of the Soviet government, the economic unity of Palestine will not only meet the needs of the overall economy of the country, but will be a means to bring the two peoples in Palestine together, and thus prepare the ground for closer political ties in the future."

In connection with the majority plan of the commission of enquiry to divide Palestine into a series of separate regions joined only by narrow corridors, the Soviet spokesman noted that perhaps because of lack of time the commission found no solution for the border problems of the two states and called for "a detailed alignment of the borders in order to remove as many as possible of the present disadvantages." In the course of the discussions in the committees of the Assembly the Soviet delegation also opposed the reduction of the proposed Jewish state, and the exclusion of the Negev from its territory (as suggested by the United States representative). The modifications of the contemplated partition plan proposed by the Soviet delegation toward better territorial continuity were largely favorable to the Jewish case.

The assumption that because of their traditional objections to the Zionist movement or their unwillingness to arouse the enmity of representatives of the Arab or other Moslem states the Soviet Union and her allies would not back up the Jews proved false. When the Socialist bloc took its stand in favor of the demands of the Jews, the United States could no longer sit on the fence and allow the Soviet Union the opportunity to appear before the world (exclusive of the Arabs) as the chief fighter for justice and defender of the Jewish people's rights, thus earning the gratitude of Jews everywhere.

H. Johnson, the head of the United States delegation, likewise announced his support of the recommendations made by the majority in the commission of enquiry.* Pointing out the urgency of the problem in view of the continuing violence in Palestine, and noting the report of the commission of

---

* "The instruction he [Johnson] received," writes S. Horowitz, "directed him to give reserved and verbal support to partition, without any special activity and without applying any pressure" (on countries subject to United States influence).

enquiry and the British government's announcement, the American representative asked the Assembly to recommend a decision on the problem during
the current session. He also spoke of the need for "making certain changes
and improvements in the majority plan in order to implement more exactly
the principles upon which this plan is based." At various stages, Johnson suggested appending Jaffa to the Arab state and removing Safed from the
Jewish state. However, the bitterest controversy was over the Negev. "Here
the American position was aggressive and stubborn," writes Horowitz. "The
State Department instruction to the United States delegation was to fight
energetically for the severance of the Negev, or at least most of it—including
Eilat—from the Jewish state."

The Negev was a desolate area with very few Bedouin inhabitants, and its
development was absolutely vital for the Jews. The Americans argued that
"the area allotted to the Jews should not be much greater than that allotted
to the Arabs" and that "the aim should be to divide Palestine into half," but
the real issue was that the British did not want anything separating their bases
in the Suez Canal Zone from those in Transjordan. Furthermore, they considered the Negev an alternative base if they were forced to evacuate the
Canal Zone.[11] When the *ad hoc* committee had accepted the majority plan in
principle, said Johnson, it would be necessary to set up a subcommittee to
work out the details to be recommended to the Assembly. He indicated the
need for establishing an international volunteer army to implement the
Assembly's decisions, warned the Arab countries against the use of force, and
called for stopping the acts of violence in Palestine.

Arab and Jewish spokesmen were then called upon to make their final
statements. Jamal al-Hussaini repeated the usual Arab complaints and threats
against Jews and Zionism. A direct and detailed reply to the Arab case was
given by M. Shertok (Sharett), head of the Jewish Agency political department. He called on Britain to participate in the implementation of the United
Nations decisions. The Jewish community of Palestine had taken measures
for their own defense, and his people were steadfast in their determination.
"I pray that there will be no conflict, but we are prepared for it."

An impressive speech, on the broad historical aspects of the problem, was
delivered by Dr. Weizmann. He expressed his hope that the Jewish state would
serve as a laboratory whose experiments would be equally beneficial to its
neighbors. When Jewish independence is realized, he declared, "the traditional friendship between the Jews and the British will once more come to
the fore, and the present tension will disappear like a nightmare." Of the
Soviet statement, Weizmann said: "I was profoundly moved at hearing the
Soviet delegation describe the Jewish tragedy with such passionate and able
rhetoric and put such stress on the results of Jewish homelessness. The Soviet
declaration showed enlightened understanding of our deepest historical

feelings. It diagnosed our illness as the lack of a national home, and pre-scribed a national home of our own as the only remedy."

The Arab spokesmen, by taking such an inflexible stand in the debate, absolved themselves in advance from the need to fight for favourable results in the assembly debate; they contented themselves with general attacks "for the record" and threats tending to disparage the highest international forum. On the other hand the Jewish representatives not only made their case effectively but also left no stone unturned in their efforts to assure the help and the unity of those who were with them and to overcome obstacles likely to be put up by opponents in complex diplomatic efforts to convert opposi-tion into irresolution and irresolution into support.

When the enquiry commission report was submitted to the United Nations Assembly and it became apparent there that the partition solution proposed by the majority was now the only way to resolve the conflict and was the last chance to defeat Bevin's plans of destroying Zionism, the internal debate in the Zionist movement stopped. There was no longer any point in dwelling on the past, and everyone felt it an obligation to make his contribution to the fateful United Nations debate, pregnant as it was with opportunity and with danger. The *Hashomer Hatzair* Party instructed its representatives in the United States and Europe to lend their full support to the diplomatic and informational effort being waged to ensure a favorable majority vote in the Assembly.

The published records of the debate in the United Nations Assembly and its committees, and the behind-the-scenes diplomacy that took place, are important both in themselves and for an understanding of current inter-national developments. Although the major powers are still very influential, they are no longer the only decisive factor. In international decisions like that on the Palestine issue, smaller countries, and even very small ones, have considerable importance; the votes of Luxembourg, Haiti and Liberia carried no less (quantitative) weight than those of the United States, the Soviet Union, or China.

At least two-thirds of the votes were required for a valid Assembly resolution on the proposed plan. The vote of each nation was vital. A relatively small number of the member nations—the Arab states, some of the other Moslem countries, and perhaps one or two more—definitely opposed it. Another group, likewise small in number and consisting mainly of the Socialist bloc and the Scandinavian countries, appeared certain to vote in the affirmative. But arduous diplomatic efforts had to be made to win the sup-port of the remaining countries whose votes were to count in the decision.

Thus, for example, the Yugoslav delegates often expressed sympathy for the Jewish case and, while proposing the solution of a single federal state, they were confident that Jews would dominate the joint state thanks to their cultural, economic, and social supremacy. But Yugoslavia had a large Moslem community (in Bosnia and Herzogovina), which was likely to be sensitive to the position of the Arabs and the Moslem states supporting them. Moreover, Yugoslavia was herself a country of many peoples organized on a federal basis and could not possibly recommend a solution to the Palestine problem basically opposed to her own federal system.

The Dutch delegate, too, was sympathetic to the Jewish problem and the solution sought for it in Palestine. From their experience in their own country (over 10 million inhabitants in an area of about 34,000 square kilometers), the Dutch understood that the "economic absorptive capacity" of any country was a flexible concept. But they had to reckon with the many millions of their (colonial) Moslem subjects in Indonesia, and found themselves more or less constrained to support the British course.

The French were attracted by a solution that would dislodge the British from Palestine, since the latter had helped to push France out of Syria and Lebanon. The partition solution would indeed lead to the evacuation of the British, but it was opposed by the Arabs—and there were many millions of Arabs living in the Maghreb countries then under French control. As a great power, France could not be responsible for the failure of the United Nations to find a solution to the Palestine question; but any solution unacceptable to the Arabs would only add to the numerous French difficulties in the Maghreb. France was thus in a delicate position: While she could not forget the old score she had to settle with the British, she also had to coordinate her policy with that of her Western allies.

She believed indeed that a Jewish state in Palestine would be a natural ally of the Maronites in Lebanon (who were then France's last support in the region); but she could not ignore the strong influence of the Catholic elements, who were not too fond of the idea of Jewish sovereignty in Palestine. These conflicting considerations explain the hesitancy and vacillation of the French stand.

The Turkish representative told the Jews that they need have no doubts as to his country's sympathy (the Turks, too, had their old accounts to settle with the Arabs), but this sympathy could not be expressed in the voting because of the importance Turkey attached to her relations with the Arab countries.

Many of the Latin Americans, who at that time represented almost a third of United Nations member-states, sympathized with the pioneer endeavor of the Jews in Palestine and wished to help the Jewish people, but they were under the strong influence of the Vatican (to whom the rebirth of a Jewish State in the Holy Land did not appeal) as well as, in some cases, British diplomatic briefings and could not ignore the large and substantial Arab populations within their territories. The equivocal policy of the United

States* stood out in contrast to the good will of people like Fabrigat and Granados, whose membership in the United Nations commission of enquiry had made them familiar with Palestine and the related Jewish refugee problem, and who were prepared to labor mightily to see justice done.

Not much hope was placed in Asian delegates, who were alien to the Jewish people, and were in the throes of internal competition for leadership of the Asian Bloc (Chang Kai Shek's China and India) as well as having a natural tendency to support the Arab members of the Asian family of nations.

The Assembly included several leading statesmen (e.g., Herbert Evatt, the Australian Foreign Minister, who was chairman of the *ad hoc* committee on the Palestine Affair; Lester Pearson, head of the Canadian delegation to the United Nations, and Trygve Lie, the United Nations Secretary General) who considered the Palestine problem a test of whether the international body could find real and just solutions to complex international problems.

As to the great powers—Britain opposed any definitive solution. The United States was hunting with the hounds and running with the hares. In public, there were diplomatic declarations of friendship without commitments to act; behind the scenes, excessive indifference and attempts to foul the Jews' steps, accompanied by blatant tendencies to further British aims— to the extent that this would not be likely to provide any political or moral advantage to the U.S.S.R. or her allies in the international arena. The position of the Socialist bloc thus largely determined the United States position. Fortunately for the Jewish case, the Socialist bloc's stand was firm.

On October 22, after a long procedural debate† the *ad hoc* committee decided to set up three sub-committees: one to prepare a detailed partition plan according to the principles recommended by the enquiry commission and to make recommendations on the administration of the country during the transition period; a second to report on the proposals of the Arab representatives, who were questioning United Nations authority to force a partition solution on Palestine and were insisting on the proclamation of all of Palestine as an Arab state; and a third to find a way toward Arab-Jewish compromise within the Assembly.

The Soviet delegation sought to oppose a third subcommittee on the ground that the chairman might himself undertake negotiations for a compromise between the two sides. When, however, the chairman (Dr. Herbert Evatt of Australia) announced that he intended to set up a committee of only

* In the cautious wording of official Jewish representatives, "America supported its own proposal half-heartedly, and was hesitant, inclined to compromise, and beset with doubts." (Horowitz, *In the Service of a State in the Making*, pp. 278–279).

† The Egyptian representative demanded "asking the opinion of experts in jurisprudence and international law" (the World Court) as to whether the United Nations was at all competent to recommend a solution to a problem that involved territorial change. There was some support for the motion.

three members—consisting of a chairman (himself), a vice-chairman (the delegate of Siam) and the proposer (the representative of Salvador)—even the Soviet representative voted for it, and that motion too was passed. The obstructive Arab stand prevented the submitting of any report by the second committee.

The second subcommittee was composed of representatives of the six Arab states in the United Nations (Egypt, Iraq, Syria, Lebanon, Saudi Arabia, Yemen) and those of Pakistan, Afghanistan, Persia, and Colombia (the latter resigned a few days later). Its very composition was a political move; not a single great power agreed to take part in it, and it remained a "purely Arab and Moslem" committee. It did not have much work to do. Arab delegates easily had the better of their more moderate and discreet ally, Zafrulla Khan of Pakistan. They dealt with two major questions—that of the possible continued residence in Palestine of Jews who had come after the Balfour Declaration, and the matter of minority rights for the Jews—and also presented a detailed program for an Arab state in all of Palestine, with a Jewish minority.

The first of the *ad hoc* subcommittees was the most decisive body in its treatment of the Palestine question. It repudiated the policy of the Arab delegates. Its task to work out the details of the partition plan was all the more practicable in that all its members were favorable to the partition solution: These included Uruguay, South Africa, Guatemala, Venezuela, Poland, and Czechoslovakia, and the two leading powers—the United States and the U.S.S.R.—both of whom had voted against a subcommittee to report on the proposals of the Arab delegates. Waverers and "neutrals" (including France) were not included in it. Ksaveri Prushinsky of Poland was made chairman.* The subcommittee examined every detail of the partition plan. Jewish Agency representatives and experts were permitted to offer help through their knowledge of the country, its economy, and inhabitants.

The main issues were the question of boundaries,† the enforcement of partition, and the economic ties between the two proposed states. Some of the committee members were inclined to compensate the Arabs, and others sought to reduce the Arab minority in the Jewish state. In contrast to the wavering or cautious stand of some members, representatives of the delegates

* Ksaveri Prushinsky: An aristocrat, gifted writer and poet, who turned to the left and supported the new regime in Poland. According to M. Sharett's testimony, Prushinsky invested great energy and was deeply involved personally in the Jewish cause. D. Horowitz notes that Prushinsky "presided over the committee with a genuine wish to bring about the establishment of the Jewish state."

† The preliminary work in preparation for the debate on this question was assigned to a special small committee composed of Prushinsky, Fabrigat, and Dr. Paul Mohan of Sweden. The Jewish Agency placed at their disposal M. Sharett, D. Horowitz, and Z. Liff (an expert on topography and maps).

of the Soviet Union, Canada, Uruguay, and Guatemala supported the claims of the Jewish representatives almost without reservation. The tenor of the relations between representatives of the Jews and those of the Soviet Union is described by D. Horowitz:

They addressed themselves to examining our problem with characteristic thoroughness. Their questions touched on every detail, every part of the broad spectrum of the problem. They showed interest in questions of Jerusalem and the borders, in the implementation, in the economic alliance, in our administrative ability and military strength. Their constant questions were friendly and polite, and at the same time penetrating and clear. . . . They preferred to indicate their own answers in deeds— in their stubborn fight for our cause in every stage and aspect of the United Nations deliberations.

Our contact with Soviet representatives remained close during the entire campaign at Lake Success. We would meet between sessions to consult and coordinate our tactics. Only rarely was some shadow cast on these relations. Several times we were forced to retreat from one position or another for fear that a victory would cost us the support of a number of countries. The Russians thought our flexibility was a sign of opportunism and weakness, while we illuminated our stand by explaining our special needs. In time the Russians also showed some flexibility and this ensured the successful conclusion of the whole Lake Success affair. On the other hand, the Russians asked us to let them know in advance when we intended to compromise, since sometimes a situation developed in which they would protect a position that we had long abandoned or were about to abandon. We promised to do so and kept our promise. The consistent support of Tsarapkin and Shtein for our cause, their clear and decisive logic, played a telling part and left their mark on the whole Lake Success affair.

It was not easy to achieve practical cooperation between the United States and the U.S.S.R. When the British hopes of making use of one or another of the two chief powers to achieve its aim were dashed, they tried to operate in two directions at once: (a) They exerted pressure on the great powers who were striving to prepare a solution of the Palestine problem without paying attention to the British stand, and (b) they sought to prevent any effective cooperation between the United States and the U.S.S.R. by confronting them with presumably formidable technical difficulties, such as the question of how the partition would be realized. It was clear that the best plan in the world would be worthless if it were not workable.

Nor could Arab threats be totally ignored. The well-equipped armies of Arab countries, which had armored vehicles, airplanes, and artillery such as the Jews did not possess, might not invade Palestine, but infiltration of armed Arabs from neighboring countries would be a constant threat. This would be the moral responsibility of the United Nations, and many members were consequently hesitant. American hopes that the British would agree to an orderly transfer of authority in Palestine to the two provisional governments, along with the gradual evacuation of their forces, were not fulfilled. Entrusting the enforcement of partition to the Security Council might well be construed as providing "a Soviet foothold in the Middle East," a move that could not be acceptable to the Americans. They opposed this on the ground that the composition of the Security Council at that time was not favorable to the implementation of partition. Of the eleven members of the Security Council, four (Britain, Syria, Colombia, and China) opposed partition, and two (France and Belgium) did not support it. Alternatively, the continuation of British rule during the transition period—in other words, postponing the end of the Mandate—was not acceptable to Soviet representatives.

This problem was dealt with by a subcommittee of four consisting of Messrs. Johnson of the United States, Tsarapkin of the U.S.S.R., Pearson of Canada, and Dr. Granados of Guatemala. Their deliberations were off the record. The Jewish Agency representative was asked for his views on an international army for enforcement. His answer was that such a force in Palestine during the period of enforcement was important and desirable, but its formation or otherwise did not depend on the Jews, who could not say whether or not it was possible. Should it prove to be impossible, the Jews were willing to assume the responsibility, for enforcement with their own forces, but they hoped to receive help in equipment and material. When it appeared that the whole partition plan might collapse on this point, the Russian delegate agreed that the British Mandate might continue for a while. At a later stage, the Soviet delegates helped remove yet another obstacle: They agreed that the supervision of the international zone of Jerusalem (as stipulated in the partition plan) might be handled by the United Nations Trusteeship Council, of which the U.S.S.R. was not then a member.

D. Horowitz gives a graphic account of these last stages:

In our contacts with the two great powers we adopted one general policy: behaving with complete frankness. We told the Americans about our meetings with the Russians, and the Russians about our meetings with the Americans, without omitting or concealing anything. Since we had no physical strength to aid us in case of complications, we had to retain our moral force. Even if we had wanted to, we were not in a position to fabricate intrigues and play the game of secret diplomacy, as if we were a great power. Both to the Russians and to the Americans we stressed that our only consideration was the Jewish cause. We did not wear false colors and we advised both powers that we were asking for everybody's help and that we would welcome such help no matter where it came from. This stand earned the admiration of both sides. The Americans would often say to us: "Perhaps you will discuss this with your Russian friends." And, vice versa, the Russians would encourage us and say: "For this it would be worthwhile getting the support of your American friends."

Harold Beiley, Bevin's adviser on Palestine, persisted in calling upon Arab delegates "to unite, to forget all their differences in view of the dangers, and to fight relentlessly for their cause." The head of the British delegation,

Sir Alexander Cadogan, made no secret of the British intentions. He stated frankly at the special session of the *ad hoc* committee on November 13 that if partition were decided, Britain would have no share in its implementation, in the establishment of a new administration, or in the organization of a militia, and would evacuate its forces by August 1, 1948. This fact, "in no way means that we will continue to maintain a civil administration in Palestine during the transition period." At the same time, he said, "The British government will retain adequate control in zones where the British Army will be stationed, to assure it security and orderly existence.

Cadogan's replies to some of the questions of committee members also revealed British intentions not to arrange the evacuation in a way that would enable United Nations bodies and the Arab and Jewish provisional governments to replace the British administration in an orderly fashion, but rather to create in Palestine political, security, and administrative confusion that might invalidate the United Nations Assembly's decision and permit the Arabs from Palestine and the neighboring countries to destroy the Jews and gain control of the country.

When the subcommittee on partition had completed its work, partition was put to a vote in the *ad hoc* committee as a whole and approved by a vote of 25 to 13. This was sufficient to refer the *ad hoc* committee's recommendation to the Assembly, where it would require a two-thirds majority to be passed. At that time, there were fifty-seven member-nations in the United Nations.

The Assembly met on November 26, 1947, at Flushing Meadow, halfway between Lake Success and New York, in a solemn and tense atmosphere under the chairmanship of Dr. Aranha of Brazil. It heard further statements and speeches for and against partition. There was a majority for the Jewish state, but a two-thirds majority was still uncertain.

An impressive speech in favor of the partition proposal was made in the Assembly on November 26 by A. Gromyko of the Soviet Union, who again explained his government's support of the proposed solution and denied the contention that the U.S.S.R. ignored Arab rights:

The Soviet Union does not, as is known, have any direct interest in Palestine, material or otherwise. It is interested in the Palestine problem as a member of the United Nations Organization and as a great power who, with other great powers, bears responsibility for the maintenance of peace.

The special session of the Assembly [in the spring of 1947] appointed a Commission to study the Palestine problem, with a view to arriving at the best solution. When this Commission completed its work, we were pleased to note that its proposal—or rather the proposal of the majority of the Commission—confirmed one of the two possibilities indicated by the Soviet delegation at that special session. I refer to two independent democratic countries—a Jewish one and an Arab one.

It is now clear that not only the special Commission, but also the great majority of the delegations in the Assembly, in other words—of member-nations of the U.N. have come to the conclusions of the Soviet delegation, upon exhaustive study of the Palestine issue.

This can be explained only by the fact that any other possibility of solving the Palestine problem seemed unrealistic and impractical. I refer also to the possibility of establishing a single Arab-Jewish independent state with equal rights for Jews and Arabs. A study of the Palestine problem, including the experience gained through the work of the special Commission, has indicated that the Jews and the Arabs in Palestine do not want to and are unable to live under one rule. The logical conclusion of this is that if the two peoples residing in Palestine—each with deep historic roots in the country—cannot live together within the same framework, the only thing left to do is to set up, instead of one state, two states—an Arab and a Jewish one. The Soviet delegation believes that there is no other possibility.

Those who oppose the partition of Palestine into two independent democratic countries contend that such a decision aims at injuring the Arab population in Palestine and the Arab countries. The Soviet delegation cannot agree with this point of view. The partition proposal is not aimed against the Arabs. This decision is not meant to cause injustice to either of the two principal peoples of Palestine. On the contrary, in the view of the Soviet delegation, it intends to benefit the basic national interests of the two peoples, in the interest of both the Arab people and the Jewish people.

Representatives of the Arab states represent the partition of Palestine as an historical injustice. But this point of view cannot be justified, if only for the reason that the Jewish people has been connected with Palestine for a lengthy historical period. Nor is it possible to ignore the postwar condition of the Jewish people. The Soviet delegation already dwelt on this in its statements at the special session. But it is not superfluous to recall again that the Jews suffered more than any other people from the effects of the war waged by Hitlerite Germany. You also know very well that in Western Europe there was not a single country able adequately to protect the interests of the Jewish people in the face of the lawlessness and tyranny of Hitler's men.

Stressing that "the Mandatory system is bankrupt," and that the government of Great Britain had declared to the United Nations Organization that it could not bear the responsibility of carrying out in Palestine the necessary steps arising out of the solution that the United Nations Assembly would decide on, Gromyko called upon the Assembly to approve the plan submitted by the committee and entrust the enforcement of it to the Security Council:

"The Soviet government," he concluded, "unlike some other delegations, has adopted a clear and open stand from the first moment, and continues to adhere consistently to that course. It is not engaged in maneuvers or voting tactics—with which the Assembly has unfortunately been afflicted, even in connection with the consideration of the Palestine problem."

Horowitz relates that the members of the Jewish delegation gathered in a corner of the corridor for consultation, with gloomy faces and downcast eyes. The speeches went on relentlessly, and the session ended without coming to a vote. November 27 was Thanksgiving Day, and there was no meeting. When the Assembly met on Friday, November 28, the French delegate, Ambassador Parodi, moved a further delay of twenty-four hours, so that the two sides might come to terms. His proposal was accepted.*

The postponement of the final Assembly vote at the suggestion of France gave the Jews and their supporters more time to enlist the necessary support for the majority. "The phone was in constant use," one of the participants in the campaign relates, "cables flew to all parts of the world. People were pulled out of their beds at midnight and sent on various and sundry missions. There was not a single influential Jew, Zionist or not, who refused to extend a helping hand at all times. Each one put his weight, great or small, on the scale, in a desperate effort to tip it in our direction." At zero hour, on orders from the President of the United States, the State Department joined the diplomatic efforts that finally ensured the requisite majority.

When the Assembly met again on the evening of Saturday, November 29, the chairman, Dr. Aranha, announced that if no compromise had been reached, the Assembly would vote.

One after the other, Arab delegates repeated their delaying tactics. The Lebanese delegate, Camille Chamoun, said that contrary to their previous stand, the Arab states were now prepared to consider the plan for a solution on a federal basis, similar to the minority recommendations of the enquiry commission. Other Arab delegates favored a renewed debate on the problem —in other words, a delay of several weeks or months. The United States and U.S.S.R. called for an immediate vote. Gromyko said that there was no sense in even a twenty-four-hour postponement such as had been suggested by France: "How could a change be expected within twenty-four hours in regard to a problem that has been under discussion for twenty-five years?" he asked. The Arab delegates would change nothing by their statements, he maintained. They spoke of federation, but that proposal had been originally discussed without the Arabs agreeing to consider it at all. A return to the proposal now would mean that the United Nations would go back to the situation of six months ago. After the special session of the Assembly in the spring of 1947, all possibilities had been considered. As a result of extensive deliberations, the *ad hoc* committee had accepted the decision by a majority vote. Was all this to be begun all over again? Such action would prove the failure of the efforts in regard to Palestine. The United Nations undertook to solve this problem and it must carry the matter to its

---

* The French representative had abstained during the vote in the *ad hoc* committee. Although there was no hope of a compromise, France wished to demonstrate to the Arab world that before giving its support to the partition plan, it had done what it could to avoid a solution that the Arabs opposed. In view of the delicate fluctuations in voting trends in the Assembly, this French course could easily have upset the balance and seriously endangered the Jewish case.

The U.N. partition plan, 1947

conclusion. The Soviet delegation held that the matter must be submitted to an immediate vote, and the Soviet delegation would vote "yes."

The chairman then announced that the vote on the partition proposal would be the first priority; after that, if necessary, there would be a vote on the remaining proposals.

The vote was by name. The name of each country was called, and the head of its delegation said simply "Yes," "No," or "Abstains." Only once was the calm disturbed: When the French delegate replied "Yes," the Jewish spectators overflowing the balcony burst forth in wild cheering, and the chairman reprimanded those who had caused the interruption.

Thereafter, the only sounds heard in the hall were "Yes," "No," and "Abstains." The results of the voting were thirty-three in favor of the partition plan, thirteen against, ten abstentions. The two-thirds majority had been achieved. Those in favor included Australia, Belgium, Belorussia, Bolivia, Brazil, Canada, Costa Rica, Czechoslovakia, Denmark, the Dominican Republic, Ecuador, France, Guatemala, Haiti, Iceland, Liberia, Luxembourg, the Netherlands, New Zealand, Nicaragua, Norway, Panama, Paraguay, Peru, the Philippines, Poland, South Africa, the Soviet Union, Sweden, the Ukraine, the United States, Uruguay, Venezuela. Those opposed were Afghanistan, Cuba, Egypt, Greece, India, Iraq, Lebanon, Pakistan, Persia, Saudi Arabia, Syria, Turkey, Yemen. Those abstaining were Abyssinia, Argentina, Britain, Chile, China, Columbia, Honduras, Mexico, Salvador, Yugoslavia. One nation (Siam) was absent when the vote was taken; following a political coup d'etat in that country, a new government had been established that terminated the mission of its delegates to the United Nations.

After the vote, the chairman proposed an implementation committee, to which were elected delegates from Bolivia, Czechoslovakia, Denmark, Panama, and the Philippines. The motion of the Swedish delegates to vote a sum of two million dollars from United Nations funds to cover the work of that committee was also passed. The struggle in the United Nations General Assembly was over.

References

1. "Bi-National Solution for Palestine," Memorandum of the *Hashomer Hatzair* Workers' Party of Palestine (March 1946), prepared by a committee headed by M. Bentov.
2. *Davar*, November 7–8, 1946.
3. "Information and Impressions on the Reaction of the Arab Public," published by the League for Arab-Jewish Rapprochement and Cooperation, (Jerusalem, August 20, 1946) (Hebrew).

4. *Palestinian Jewry to the Soviet Peoples* (V-League Collection, 1943), p. 70 (Russian).

5. *Bulletin, Histadrut* Keymen (October 1943), p. 11 (Hebrew).

6. B. Crum, *Behind the Silken Curtain*, Simon and Schuster, New York, 1947.

7. *Mishmar*, October 4, 1945.

8. Joseph Stalin, *Marxism and the National Question* (1913), Chapter 1, "The Nation."

9. Horowitz, *In the Service of a State in the Making* (Shocken, Jerusalem, Tel Aviv 1951(2)), p. 276 (Hebrew).

10. *Ibid.*

11. *Ibid.*, pp. 278–279.

CHAPTER NINE

THROUGH BLOOD AND SUFFERING

The decision of the United Nations Assembly on November 29, 1947, was not the end of the struggle but only the end of an important phase of it. There can be no doubt that the vote had represented a moral and political victory for the Jews. Bevin's plan had been to let the Jews and their supporters defeat the enquiry commission's minority recommendations, while he and his supporters would defeat the majority recommendations returning the situation to what it had been before submission of the problem to the United Nations. This plan failed. For the third time, the British government failed to obtain international approval for its 1939 White Paper policy. The first occasion was when the Mandates Commission of the League of Nations ruled that the restriction of the Jewish endeavor in Palestine was contrary to the aims of the Mandate; its second defeat came with the report of the Anglo-American commission; and finally, Britain failed for the third time on submitting the problem to the United Nations, which recommended that since British rule in Palestine had been a severe moral and political failure, Britain must evacuate Palestine without delay. That recommendation was based on the majority recommendation of UNSCOP and was supported by thirty-three member states who voted for it, including the Soviet Union, the United States, and France, as well as four British Dominions—Australia, Canada, New Zealand, and South Africa.

The Assembly decision awakened in the Jewish people much latent national strength. The Jews were now recognized as a sovereign nation possessing international status—a situation that opened the way for new political, economic, and security possibilities.

It was an historic decision for the mass of the Jewish people. "At the moment," wrote D. Horowitz, "no one wanted to set his mind to the future. The wells of exhilaration burst forth and came to the surface. In the great hall and the corridors, the members of the delegation, friends, and newspapermen, gathered along with crowds of celebrating Jews. Jewish New York cheered and rejoiced on its greatest holiday. We spent the evening with Weizmann, who looked majestic, a living symbol of our dreams and ideals. We didn't close an eye the whole night through. We were full of feelings of deep satisfaction and anticipation of the future."[1] There was of course deepest gratification among Palestine Jews where the news of the United Nations decision aroused fantastic popular joy. When the radio announced, "33 in favor, 13 against, 10 abstaining," thousands in the cities and villages of Palestine burst forth into the streets, in cheering and acclamation such as the Jewish community in Palestine had never experienced before.

The United Nations partition plan was, however, a difficult one. The Jewish state was allocated 15,850 square kilometers out of the total of 27,000 west of the Jordan, and over 9,500 of them were in the Negev desert. The planned area of the state was divided into three blocs, connected only by narrow corridors. Jewish Jerusalem was outside the boundaries of the state and connected to it by a road that passed through territory almost entirely within the Arab state. The boundaries of the state were of a total length of 1,400 kilometers (of which 145 were seacoast). The population of 865,000 in the planned Jewish state at the end of 1947 included 515,000 Jews and 350,000 Arabs. About 92,000 of the Arabs lived in four urban settlements (Haifa, Safed, Tiberias, and Bet Shean), 40,000 of them were Bedouins (mostly in the Negev), and about 218,000 (70.4 percent) lived in 233 villages and held the vast majority of the agricultural land in the area of the Jewish state.

The Jewish state was supposed to provide financial support for the Arab state in the other part of Palestine. This economic union—with all the promise it held for the reunification of the country and the establishment of cooperation between the two peoples—in the meantime was likely to be a burden on the young state's economy and plans for development. Nevertheless, in the situation then current in Palestine, the Jews accepted the partition as a binding international ruling, and no responsible Jewish leader could think of reversing it in any way through the use of force.

What was the significance of the partition for the Arab world? It meant that of a total of 11,500,000 square kilometers occupied by the Arab states, 16,000 had been allotted to the Jewish state. Of the 50 to 60 million Arabs, 350,000—slightly less than one half percent—would have to live as a minority in a Jewish state (itself surrounded by Arab states), whose vital political and economic interests were to live in peace with its neighbors. This, in itself, would oblige it to grant the Arab minority living within its borders a status and rights which few minorities in capitalist countries ever enjoyed or hoped to enjoy.

Yet the Arab leaders did not accept the decision. The historic decision of the United Nations Assembly was reported in *Al-Wahda*, the newspaper of the Hussainis under a page-wide headline saying "What was written in black at Lake Success will be erased in red in Palestine." The words of the Arab League secretary—"For us there is only one test, the test of strength . . . we will try to destroy you" (see Chapter Eight)—began to be felt the day after the Assembly decision.

In his speech in Philadelphia on December 2, Chaim Weizmann said, "Bombs and threats from the neighboring countries will not frighten us; we stretch our hand out to the Arabs in peace, and suggest that they think hard before they reject it." But the Arab leaders (and their supporters abroad) pressed on to war.

Britain Sabotages the United Nations Decision

Five months passed from the time of the United Nations Assembly's decision on a Jewish state to the establishment of the state of Israel.

At the time of the decision, it was already clear that Britain would try to sabotage its implementation. The British government and its allies in the American State Department had hoped that the Arab leaders would succeed in *de facto* nullification of the United Nations decision. "I do not yet believe that I have failed in regard to Palestine, the affair is not over," said Bevin in Parliament on February 10, 1948. The British forces, which were still officially responsible for the security of Palestine, took positions of "neutrality" between the attacked and the attackers. The British encouraged Arab terrorist aggression by searching Jews for arms (e.g., disarming the defenders of the Hayotsek factory near Mikveh Israel on February 29, and abandoning them to an Arab mob, which murdered them), and blocking the road to Hagana forces in Jerusalem and other places when they hurried to help settlements and quarters under attack or siege. Quite often, the British abandoned their so-called "neutrality" by actively encouraging the conflagration: "The main panic in Haifa," said Elias Kussa, the Haifa Arab leader, "was created by the British. They would approach neighborhoods in armored cars under cover of night, shoot a few rounds toward the emplacements, and thus incite the Arabs and Jews to fire at each other's neighborhoods."[2]

The British authorities refused to cooperate with the United Nations implementation commission; this commission, composed of representatives of five of the smaller countries that had voted for partition, had to carry out the decisions of the Assembly with forces that were exclusively moral. It was a commission of "five lonely pilgrims," according to the sad description of its chairman, Dr. Karl Lisitsky of Czechoslovakia. On January 3, the British delegate to the United Nations, Sir Alexander Cadogan, stated in reply to the commission's questions that, (a) His Majesty's Government would not favor the arrival of the commission in Palestine earlier than two weeks before the end of the Mandate; (b) it would not put at the disposal of the commission any civil personnel or police, or give any help toward the demarcation of the borders between the two states; (c) until the termination of the Mandate (May 15) His Majesty's Government would not recognize the authority of any provisional government councils, Jewish or Arab, and would not allow the establishment of local militia of either state; Britain would thereafter have nothing to do with Palestinian affairs and would content herself with ensuring the safety of her army and lines of communication until the evacuation was completed on August 1; (d) the United Nations Assembly decision that Britain was to vacate one of the ports on February 1 for the purpose of Jewish immigration would not be complied with—not on February 1, and not on any date before the end of the Mandate. The British Foreign Secretary had already announced earlier that the continued arrival of Jewish "illegal" immigrants would be deemed a provocation, but the immigrant ships continued to arrive.

The implementation commission could only advise the United Nations Security Council on February 2 1948 that Britain was unwilling to cooperate with it. The commission requested the provision of an international military force to ensure the maintenance of order in Palestine during the period of transition, but that request was refused by the Security Council (a British veto was likely in the event it had granted the request). On March 10, a "pioneer group" of the implementation commission (including a Norwegian military expert) reached Jerusalem but was not permitted to do anything. Its request that the Trusteeship Council of the United Nations formulate a constitution for the "Jerusalem Corpus Separatum," as well as the draft statute it proposed to this end, remained, in effect, unheeded.

Chaos, British-Made

As the battles between Arabs and Jews increased, the British began to create in Palestine economic, administrative, and military chaos. Despite the earlier promise of Colonial Secretary Creech Jones (in reply to a Parliamentary question) that Britain would be responsible for Palestinian currency till the end of the Mandate, the government announced, on February 22, that Palestine was no longer in the sterling area, in other words, the British treasury renounced its responsibility for the value of the Palestine pound. At the same time, the "sterling surplus reserves" that Britain owed Palestine (more than £100,000,000) were frozen, precisely when there was a need to stock up on commodities that the Jews, in any case, were not likely to obtain from neighboring countries.

The operations of the British civil service were stopped in the most anarchical manner, without any attempt at geographical or temporal order. Government files that should normally have been transferred to the succeeding authorities were destroyed (a few documents were photographed and a few transferred to Britain). In the middle of April, various postal services began to shut down as well.

The manner in which the army was evacuated likewise fanned the conflict between the Jews and Arabs and increased the confusion. In most cases, the evacuated bases were not handed over to the Jews or Arabs (depending on the location of the camp on the partition map) but were abandoned suddenly, thus becoming a field of battle for armed Jewish and Arab forces.* Under the patently false pretext of "neutrality," the British refused to permit the armed escort of Jewish transport convoys, whose path Arab efforts aimed at blocking. The British broadcasting station in Cyprus (Radio Middle East) surpassed all Moslem Brothers in Egypt called on the Egyptian broadcasting station to take an example from it! By leaving British forces in certain areas until the final stages of the conflict, the authorities prevented the establishment of Jewish self-rule in those areas.

The United States, which on November 29 had voted to grant Jews and Arabs independence in Palestine, quickly changed its tone. The United States "embargo" on the export of arms "to any Middle Eastern country"—at a time when Britain continued pouring arms into Egypt, Transjordan, and Iraq, and even announced this publicly—was tantamount to an embargo against the Jews. United States authorities knew how meager were the "illegal" arms held by the Jews in the face of the regular armies of the Arab countries; nevertheless, when American Jews tried to help by sending some arms to the Jews of Palestine, they were arrested and brought to trial.

This was the background against which the first battles between Jews and Arabs were fought.

The Jewish Community Defends Itself

The Mufti Haj Amin al-Hussaini wanted an immediate full-scale attack on the Jewish community, but the leaders of the Arab states believed that outside military intervention was impossible so long as the British and their army were in Palestine. Meanwhile, the Higher Arab Committee decided to take action with their own forces. Although there was no Arab enthusiasm for a new war, they rapidly organized intermittent attacks on rural Jewish settlements, on the outskirts of mixed cities, and on the roads. This strategy was intended to "raise morale" in the Palestinian Arab community and to force the neighboring Arab states to come to its aid.†

The day after the United Nations Assembly vote, an attack was made on a Jewish passenger bus *en route* to Jerusalem, the first step in a general assault

* A typical example was the large Tel Litvinsky camp. Armed Arabs were allowed to enter the camp and dig in before the British evacuated it; Jewish forces then captured it in battle. The British took a step of prime tactical importance when they surrendered to the Arabs the Iraq Suweidan police fort, commanding the whole of the Negev and the roads from west to east and from the north to the Negev. The Arabs immediately stationed forces there. Jewish combatants could capture what was called the "monster on the hill" only after eight attempts and after suffering grave losses.

† According to the information of Jewish security authorities, from 1946 to 1948 the Arab Higher Committee received no more than about £600,000 in all.

on Jewish communications. On December 2, the Jewish commercial center of Jerusalem was set on fire. According to eye-witness reports, the arsonists obtained gasoline from British police cars (the Arab leftist newspaper *Al-Ittihad*, which reported this, was closed down for a while by the authorities). This was the start of a series of attacks on Jewish sections of the large towns (such as the Hatikva quarter near Tel Aviv, and Ramat Rahel in Jerusalem) and on remote agricultural settlements: Kfar Szold, Kfar Uriya, the Etzion bloc. On January 15–16, 1948, an entire company of thirty-five, most of them Hebrew University students who had rushed to defend the Etzion bloc, was wiped out in a fight to the finish. On January 20, Kibbutz Yehiam in western Galilee was fiercely attacked. A pickup truck scouting the Mikve-Israel-Jerusalem road was attacked near Yazur and its seven special police-guard occupants killed (January 21). From December to January, nearly 400 Jews were killed by Arab bullets, and many others were wounded. But attacks on Jewish settlements were repelled, and Jewish communications—one of the main targets of Arab assault—were not cut off. At this stage, the relations between the two peoples in the country had not yet been entirely severed; and here and there efforts were made to stop the situation from deteriorating still further, and to prevent wholesale bloodshed. As disturbances ensued as a result of the November 29 United Nations decision, the Jewish leadership in Palestine called on the Arab public not to follow those leading them to ruin. A proclamation in Arabic issued on December 4, 1947 said:

To our Arab neighbors:
   The Jewish *Hagana* organization appeals to you for peace and calm, but at the same time we also warn you. For two days peace has been disturbed by groups of incited Arabs shooting and killing and setting fire to various places. We know that the Arab community as a whole does not desire the abandonment of law and order, but apparently the influence of provocateurs has grown. We have restrained ourselves up to now, because we want peace, neighborly relations, and to work quietly, and because we are interested in the good of the country. We appeal to you for peace but we give you fair warning: if bloodshed continues, we shall be forced to take severe measures against those responsible for disturbing the peace. Pay attention to our appeal for peace, pay attention to our warning.

The Hagana

   Characteristic of this period was the tacit agreement between the Jewish Medical Association and the Arab Medical Association, which published separate statements—differing in wording but similar in content—on January 5, 1948. In order to understand the conditions under which this agreement was achieved, it is necessary to examine the verbatim texts of the two statements:

Proclamation of the Hebrew Medical Association:
   The announcement of the National Council of the Jewish Community on Decem-

ber 30, 1947, described attacks made on medical workers as "inexcusable sins against the law of immunity of medical workers who extend help to all sick and wounded regardless of religion or race."

The Palestine Jewish Medical Association repeatedly proclaims the sanctity of the international principle that is to be maintained under all conditions and circumstances —the immunity of medical services, including hospitals, clinics, ambulances, and any other means of transport serving medical workers or the sick or wounded.

All these workers—doctors, nurses, and others—will bear the symbol of their calling: A Red Star, a Red Cross, or a Red Crescent. These signs will also be displayed by medical institutions, ambulances, and other transports of the services and their workers, and they are not to be used except for this purpose.

> The Jewish Medical Association
> DR. Z. AVIGDORI, *Chairman*
> DR. S. SHERESHEVSKY, *Secretary*

Proclamation of the Arab Medical Association:

Further to the proclamation of the Arab Higher Committee published in the press and broadcast by Radio Jerusalem, the Arab Medical Association of Palestine hereby appeals to the Arab people in this proclamation, in the hopes that they will confirm their respect and appreciation for medical people and all those who help them to discharge their important duties, such as nurses and first-aiders. They are not to be interfered with in the execution of their humane duties, nor harmed or hurt in any way. They are all, regardless of religion, faith, or nationality, agents of mercy and servants of humanity, without discrimination or difference in nationality, faith or color.

We also request respect for the immunity of hospitals, health institutions, ambulances, and doctors' vehicles bearing the symbol of service—the Red Crescent, Cross, or Star. All of them are likewise servants of humanity, their work is holy, and they are therefore to be respected, and any harm to them avoided. We call on doctors and their helpers to pay special attention to making their association with the health services clear. They must conspicuously display the Red Crescent, Cross, or Star on their person, buildings, or cars. We pray and hope that they will not take advantages that are in any way contradictory to their loyalty to humane duties.

We are sure that you will behave according to this proclamation, and God direct your hearts.

> The Arab Medical Association
> DR. TAWFIK CANAAN

The *Hagana*, which at first only returned fire, later embarked on counter-attacks such as ambushes, infiltrations, and retaliatory actions. Arab houses serving as headquarters and arms stores for Arab gangs were blown up. The number of Arabs killed in these months was much larger than that of Jewish victims. Panic set in among the Arabs. Those of means in the mixed cities (especially Haifa) began to leave for quieter Arab parts in Palestine itself, or fled to Lebanon, Transjordan, and Syria. The Arab press began to publish appeals saying "Don't panic!" The *Shaab* daily wrote: "We have not succeeded in getting organized and overcoming anarchy."

The first half of February was marked by *Hagana* counterattacks throughout the country. Six bridges near Palestine's northern border were blown up. Tirat Zvi in the Bet Shean valley was attacked, and repulsed the attack, after which the Jews made a retaliatory raid on Beth Shean (February 17). More minor clashes took place in other parts of the country.

At the beginning of March, the war on the roads reached its height. On March 4, sixteen members of a Jewish defense force returning from an operation in the Jerusalem hills were attacked at Atarot and killed. On the twelfth, seven Jewish defenders fell in battle at Gilboa. On the fourteenth, *Hagana* forces blew up the main street of Faluja in the south, breaking their way through to Kibbutz Gat. Jewish convoys battled their way from March 10 to 26 to the Negev settlements. An Arab convoy carrying arms to Haifa was destroyed near Kiryat Motzkin on March 17. A Jewish convoy to Hartur was attacked on March 18. A large convoy returning from the Etzion bloc to Jerusalem on March 27 to 28 was attacked near Nebi-Daniel by a big group of Arabs, was extricated by the intervention of the British Army, but lost its vehicles and arms. A convoy that left Nahariya for Yehiam was attacked and destroyed, its forty-two escorts killed, and the Jewish settlements of western Galilee cut off on March 28. A convoy headed for Jerusalem was attacked near Hulda on March 31 and seventeen of its people killed in battle.

The Arab attacks were not coordinated. The Arab Higher Committee was in actual command of only the Jerusalem-Hebron-Ramalla area and some of the Jaffa-Ramle area. In other parts of the country, various other Arab factions operated, some of them under the guidance of anti-Arab Higher Committee groups, who received support from units of the Jordanian "Arab Legion" commanded by the British. The "Legion" units were stationed west of the Jordan as part of the British garrison in Palestine. Some of them were directly involved in murderous assaults on Jews (such as the murder of fourteen Jews by Legion soldiers near Ben-Shemen on December 14, and the Legion attack on a passenger vehicle on the Neve Shaanan road on December 27). Some Legion soldiers served as escorts for bands of armed Arabs who infiltrated from the neighboring countries. Legion units were stationed near Jewish settlements as a direct threat to their existence.* The oft-repeated demands of the Jewish Agency to remove the Legion units from Palestine

---

* A detachment of the Arab Legion was stationed on the hill across from the Jalami bridge, about 1.5 kilometers from Shaar Haamakim. The writer, who had personal contact with one of the detachment's officers (the son of a Transjordan friend) knew that the range of the unit's mortars was set for his kibbutz, as well as for kibbutz Yagur and nearby Kfar Hassidim.

were not complied with. It was only on April 16 that Sir Alexander Cadogan stated to the Security Council (and Bevin confirmed that statement in Parliament on April 28) that the Legion units would be evacuated from Palestine. Indeed, a week or two before May 15, they were removed from the Jewish zones only to be concentrated in the hills near Jerusalem and the Jericho valley while Arab armies were presumably beginning their invasion.

As it became apparent that the armed strength of the Palestinian Arabs was not equal to that of the Jews, the infiltration of armed Arab forces from neighboring countries increased. Under the supervision of the military committee of the Arab League, an Arab "Rescue Army" (*Jaish-ul-Inkadh*) was still further, and to prevent wholesale bloodshed. As disturbances ensued as organized on Syrian soil and commanded by Fauzi al-Kaukji (see Chapter Five) under the overall supervision of Taha al-Hashimi, a former C. in C. of the Iraqi Army. This unit, which was hastily trained at the Katanah camp in Syria, numbered 5,000 men, including 1,000 Palestinians who were then returned to their country.

Information from an Arab source obtained by the author at that time presented a revealing picture of the motley composition of the "Rescue Army" brought to fight the Jews in Palestine and prevent the implementation of the United Nations decision: Its members were various backward elements from Syria and Iraq; ignorant, unemployed, and plunder-seeking adventurers; members of Fascist and reactionary organizations such as that of Anton Saada in Syria and Lebanon, "Young Egypt," and "The Moslem Brotherhood;" Circassians from the Caucasus, who had deserted to the Nazis during the war, been captured and "educated" by them, and now wished to settle in Transjordan with British approval, and Moslem Yugoslavs held in Italian prison camps who, instead of returning to their liberated homeland, preferred to sail British ships to the shores of Lebanon. This mixed, unsavoury band included a few Poles from Anders' army, some German SS men who had miraculously disappeared from Egyptian prison camps, as well as some Spanish Falangists. In their activities in Palestine, this "Liberation Army" also had the help of some British adventurers and the perpetrators of the explosion in the Palestine Post building and the blowing up of Ben-Yehuda street in Jerusalem (the British drove explosive-loaded cars into the street on February 22. About fifty people were killed and hundreds wounded).

The Rescue Army infiltrated into Palestine but the British authorities pretended not to notice. Great Britain, whose navy could discern a miserable illegal immigrant boat plying its way under cover of darkness to the shores of Palestine, was unable to perceive the long convoys of "Rescue Army" trucks and camps, which openly crossed the borders of Palestine in the light of day.

The Rescue Army commanded by Kaukji was not the only source of Arab strength from abroad. There were foreign Arabs operating under the command of Abd-ul-Kadir al-Hussaini (related to the Mufti Haj Amin) in the Jerusalem and Judean hills area, and under Hassan Salameh (who was active in the disturbances of 1936 to 1939, spent World War II in Germany, and parachuted into Palestine in 1944 from a German plane), in the Jaffa-Ramle area. The end of March and beginning of April also saw the appearance in the south (near Gaza) of Egyptian fighting forces from the ranks of the fanatical Moslem Brothers.

The Rescue Army units and groups of other foreign Arabs attacked Jewish settlements including Kfar Szold, Yehiam, Tirat Zvi, Kfar Darom. Some of them held positions in Arab border neighborhoods of the mixed cities, from which they sniped at—and even tried to invade—Jewish streets and quarters. However, even in this phase, which lasted until the beginning of April, though the Jews suffered many and costly losses,* the Arab forces were routed. The Jewish forces were vastly superior in military ability; and in contrast to the adventurer-mercenaries of the Arab Rescue Army, the Jews were defending their home and the hope of their lives.

The Jews Take the Initiative

At the beginning of April, the initiative passed to the Jewish combatants. The turning point came with the opening of the road to Jerusalem, which had been cut off and besieged. For this operation, arms and men were concentrated from all fronts. The severe shortage in arms was mitigated one night toward the end of March when a four-engined plane landed at one of the concealed air fields of the *Hagana* with the first shipment of arms from Czechoslovakia. Shortly thereafter, a ship arrived carrying several thousand rifles and several hundred medium machine guns. "Operation Nahshon" began at dawn on April 3, and after ten days of heavy fighting against large Arab forces controlling the commanding heights, the corridor connecting Jewish Jerusalem with the Jewish settlements of the coastal plain was taken. Abd-ul-Kadir al-Hussiani, commander of the Arab forces in Jerusalem and the Judean hills, was killed in one of these battles in the Kastel sector on April 8.

* According to Israeli military sources, about 1,200 Jews, more than half of them non-combatants, were killed in the disturbances up to the beginning of April. Among soldiers, an average of two a day died in December, while in March the average went up to ten a day.

On April 13, in the Sheik Jarrah quarter of Jerusalem, a convoy of cars with medical personnel was attacked on its way to Mount Scopus and dozens of doctors, nurses, and other employees of the Hadassa Hospital and Hebrew University were killed. Various Jewish settlements in all parts of the country were shelled. From April 4 to 12, Kibbutz Mishmar Haemek courageously withstood the attack of two infantry battalions of the Kaukji army, which used cannon and mortars. The bravery of the kibbutz, and the reinforcements that came to its aid, defeated the attackers, whose aim was to capture the Haifa road. Following battles in the neighboring Arab villages, some of which changed hands several times, the area was completely cleared of the aggressors. On April 10, Kfar Hadarom near Gaza repulsed the attack of Moslem Brotherhood volunteers who had arrived from Egypt. Between April 13 and 16, Kibbutz Ramat Yohanan repulsed the heavy attack of a Druze unit of the Rescue Army. These battles during the first half of April hastened the implementation of the *Hagana* operational plan to control the entire territory of the Jewish state as defined by the U.N. decision and secure its borders against a possible invasion of regular Arab armies when the British Mandate ended. The premature evacuation of the British Army from some regions forced *Hagana* headquarters to begin the operational plan before the date originally set, even before the more than 30,000 infantry and shock troops for the operation had been fully alerted.

Battles initiated by *Hagana* forces led to the capture of Tiberias on April 18, and Haifa on April 22. A Jewish attack on the Nebi-Yosha police station in upper Galilee failed on April 20, and twenty-two Jews fell in combat. On the other hand, the police stations of Gesher and Zemah were taken between April 27 and 29 in battles with the Jordanian Legion. Fighting was not over in the Jerusalem area. Two enormous convoys had reached the city on April 15, but the road was once more blocked after an attack on a Jewish convoy near Dir-Ayub on April 20. On April 21, Jewish fighters captured the Abu Gosh police station, an important fortress on the road to Jerusalem, not far from the city. That same day, convoys to Jerusalem were attacked near Saris, and there were battles on the outskirts of the city itself. The next day, Ramat Rahel was again attacked. A Jewish attack on Nebi Samuel failed and there were heavy losses. The Sheik Jarrah quarter of Jerusalem, which had been taken by Jewish forces on April 25 and 26, was evacuated under pressure by the British forces. On the thirtieth of the month, the Katamon quarter of Jerusalem was captured by the *Hagana*.

The first half of May continued to be marked by Jewish military initiative. On May 1, Yazur and Salameh were taken, and an Arab attack on Ramot Naftali in the Galilee was repulsed. On May 4 and 5, the Etzion bloc was attacked by the Arab Legion, and Jewish forces gained control of the area between the Sea of Galilee and Lake Hulah; Arab Sejera was captured on

May 6. Between May 1 and 12, while defending Galilean Jewish settlements that had been attacked (Dan, Dafna, Maayan Baruch, Kfar Szold, Ramot Naftali), Jewish forces won control of eastern Galilee, captured Safed, and assumed control of lower Galilee and the Bet Shean valley (the city of Bet Shean fell to the *Hagana* on May 12). In the course of battles which lasted for ten days (from May 4 to 15), Jewish forces took charge of the region from Rehovot to south of Beersheba, capturing Arab villages that were blocking traffic in the Negev. On May 13, Jaffa surrendered. The attack mounted there by "IZL" was checked by the British garrison: the *Hagana* forces surrounded the city and forced it to surrender. Operation Ben-Ami was begun on May 14 to lift the siege on the settlements of western Galilee and liberate the coastal plain in the north. Throughout that period, the campaign in the Jerusalem corridor continued, the road blocked and cleared alternately by the fighters of both sides, and fierce battles taking place for the settlements and the hilltops on that long front. Kfar Hadarom repeatedly repulsed the attacks of the Moslem Brothers on May 10 and 11.

During this period, from Operation Nahshon, April 3 to May 14, Jewish casualties totaled 753 fighting men and over 500 non-combatants. This military campaign brought about the disintegration of the Palestinian Arab community, at all events as a military factor in the fight. Then came the third phase of the war—the invasion of Palestine by the regular armies of the Arab League countries, which began with the end of the British Mandate and the proclamation of the state of Israel (May 14, 1948). At this stage, we must return to the political front.

United States Retreat from the November 29 Decision

When, in view of the outbreak of fighting in Palestine, the Soviet delegate requested the Security Council on December 9 to examine the possibility of facilitating a speedy implementation of the Assembly decision, the United States delegate announced that it was not the duty of the Security Council "to enforce partition." This statement was all the more significant in that a Security Council resolution could only be valid if at least seven of its eleven members voted for it and none of the five great powers who were permanent members voted against it.

At the beginning of February 1948, the Palestine problem came before the Security Council in a debate on the first report submitted by the "implementation commission" (see this Chapter). The Syrian representative, who was then a member of the Security Council, again expressed the opposition of the Arabs to the November 29 resolution; and the Colombian delegate (who had earlier voted against partition and served on the subcommittee to work out the Arab proposal) moved that the Assembly meet again to repeal its resolution, which had proved to be "unenforceable."

Since in its February session the Security Council did not accept the motion to repeal the November 29 resolution, the American delegate, Austin, with the support of France and China, made a new proposal, which was essentially as follows: Since partition could not be carried out peaceably, the "implementation commission" should stop working, a new session of the United Nations Assembly should be convened, and the Security Council should recommend a "temporary trusteeship regime" for Palestine "in order to maintain peace and give the Jews and Arabs an additional opportunity to come to an agreement."

The Jewish Agency representative, Dr. A. H. Silver, expressed his astonishment at such a drastic turn in United States policy from its vote in the Assembly on November 29. He announced that the Jewish people could not retreat, and he asserted that if the implementation commission was not capable of performing its task, the Jews would do so to the best of their ability. The Soviet delegate supported the Jewish stand. Knowing that the Soviet delegate could veto the Council decision, Austin did not insist on his motion being put to a vote. No objections were made by the Soviet delegate, and it was decided to call a special session of the United Nations Assembly.

The special session opened on April 16. It transpired in the political committee that the United States delegation had indeed retreated from the November 29 vote and now proposed an international trusteeship for Palestine, such as the one the November 29 decision had stipulated for Jerusalem—a governor appointed by the United Nations Trusteeship Council, along with a legislative council and international police force. The proposal did not fix the duration of the international trusteeship regime, and made no mention of regulating the problem of Jewish immigration. The proposal aimed at "a temporary solution—until the Jews and Arabs in Palestine reach an accord between themselves."

Will the United Nations Decision be Revoked?

The new American proposal was received with considerable opposition. Needless to say, the Jewish representatives opposed with all their power a proposal which, at almost the last moment, wished to turn the clock back. On April 22, Dr. Silver had bitter things to say about a new "Munich" in regard to Palestine. On the twenty-seventh, M. Shertok (Sharett) reported to the political committee on the situation in Palestine the disintegration of the British administration, and the abandonment of the Jewish community, which was compelled to defend itself, organize its self-defence and government in order to fill the vacuum which had been formed.

Sharett explained that the clock could not be turned back; he advised the political committee of the danger of invasion by extra-Palestinian Arab armies and appealed to the United Nations to meet its commitments to the Jews, who were merely carrying out its decision.*

Representatives of New Zealand, Sweden, and Brazil spoke against the new American proposal. Arab representatives, who rejoiced at the United States admission that partition had failed, nevertheless rejected international trusteeship. At most, they were prepared to accept it as a preliminary to the establishment of Palestine as an Arab state. The British also objected, above all because of their innate opposition to American succession to the "British presence" in Palestine under the pretext of international trusteeship.

The most determined and consistent defense of the Assembly regulation came from the Soviet delegation. The Soviet stand was represented in the speeches of A. Gromyko (April 20), V. Tarasenko (April 22), A. S. Faniushkin and L. A. Kaminsky (April 23), V. Tarasenko (April 30), S. K. Tsarapkin (May 3), and A. Gromyko (May 4)—all defending the Assembly resolution of November 29. The Soviet delegates exposed in great detail the British government's acts of sabotage ("Great Britain's subversive role") and "the strange political game of the United States." Gromyko mentioned in his April 20 speech in the political committee that in the Security Council debate on December 9, it had already been clear "that the U.S. does not want to implement the decision it voted for in the Assembly, and that it is initiating some new maneuver in the Palestine problem." In his April 22 speech to the political committee, V. Tarasenko recalled a statement of Bartley Crum, (a member of the Anglo-American commission in Palestine) in his book, *Behind the Silken Curtain* that in the very days when a promise was made to the United States Jews in connection with Palestine, the State Department was assuring Arab states that it would do nothing to change the *status quo* in Palestine without prior consultation with them.†

---

* In his address to Mapai on May 11, 1948, analyzing the United States government's retreat from the November 29 United Nations decision, M. Sharett listed a number of causes and reasons: Forces antagonistic to the United States government's support of the Assembly decision continued to undermine it even after it was passed; "a lapse in the alertness of the White House;" the end of the United States delegation's activity when the session ended, and the resumption of State Department control; the military weakness of the Palestinian Jewish community at the beginning of the fight, which disappointed its supporters and strengthened its opponents; and the "rise of the Communists to power in Czechoslovakia in February 1948." (*At the Gate of the Nations*, pp. 230 (Hebrew).)

† In his book [pp. 36/37], Crum relates that when the commission was leaving the United States for London, he was handed a file marked "Contents of file of confidential communications on Palestine supplied by Division of Near Eastern affairs for use of Anglo-American Committee of Inquiry". It dealt with seventeen items—despatches, cables, correspondence, memoranda of conversations. This was a résumé of the State Department secret file on Palestine, the existence of which apparently not even President Truman had known. According to this file, since September 15, 1938, each time a

The Soviet delegates analyzed the United States proposal for an international trusteeship for Palestine paragraph by paragraph, proving that the proposals were basically invalid, since they conflicted with the right of nations to self-determination, and that "the imperialist interests of the U.S. and Britain diverge from the basic interests of the Jewish people and the Arab people."

In his April 20 speech in the political committee, Gromyko pointed out that the implementation commission, which was to take practical steps to guide the Security Council in setting up the Jewish and Arab states, had not been permitted to perform its task:

After the Assembly made the decision, the Security Council should have taken the proper steps, especially because certain states, instead of helping to implement the decision, began to put obstacles in the way of its enforcement. Has the Security Council taken any steps of this kind? No, it has not, and thus not only did not facilitate the implementation of the partition plan under the supervision of the Palestine committee, but on the contrary, made the implementation more difficult and jeopardized the realization of this important decision taken by the United Nations. The reason for this is that other countries, headed by the United States, had already set out on the road leading up to the revocation of a decision already approved.

Ever since the Assembly passed the resolution on Palestine, not only has the United States government not demonstrated any concern for the implementation of the decision, but during this period has prepared, instead of the approved decision, a new plan of its own, publicly announced on March 19.

One of the basic claims usually made in defense of this strange and astonishing political game of the United States in regard to the Palestine question is that the partition decision cannot be peaceably enforced. However, this claim is not at all convincing and there is nothing to back it up. A claim that it is impossible to implement a decision taken might be worthy of attention if the Security Council had taken any real steps to implement it and not succeeded. The Council was incapable of taking any decision at all to facilitate the implementation of the partition plan because of the stand adopted by the United States, Great Britain and several other countries that followed their lead. The Council took almost no action; this fact is known to the whole world.

The decision was not implemented, not because it is bad, but because several

promise was made to American Jewry regarding Palestine, the State Department promptly sent messages to the Arab rulers discounting it and reassuring them, in effect, that regardless of what was promised publicly to the Jews, nothing would be done to change the situation in Palestine. This file confirmed the charges of double-dealing that had been hurled at both the United States and Great Britain.

It was a sorry and bitter record for an American to read.

"I said, 'I think I ought to book passage home as soon as we arrive in Southampton. I don't see that there is any purpose in going on with our work.'"

"Sir John [The British chairman of the committee of Inquiry, Sir John Singleton] said dryly, 'It appears that Great Britain is not the only power who promises the same thing to two different groups.'"

countries, on whose cooperation the United Nations had relied, refrained from implementing it. Among these countries is first of all the United States.

Certain countries are ignoring the legal rights of the Palestinian peoples, just as they are ignoring the general interest of the United Nations in keeping the peace. They are trying to cover up plans based on the political, economic, and military-strategic considerations of one or two powers. These powers hope to manipulate the failure of any aspiration of the peoples of Palestine, and especially the Jewish people, for an independent existence. It is obvious that this decision of the United States government was dictated by oil needs and the military-strategic interests of the United States, behind which are certain very influential circles in the United States who are trying to turn Palestine into a military-strategic base for themselves, and from the economic point of view, into a half American colony.

Speaking of Britain's activities in sabotaging the partition plan, Gromyko said:

The British government is trying in vain to justify the acts of the British authorities in Palestine. Great Britain's behaviour is so blatant that this defense is not likely to deceive anybody. The bloody events now taking place in Palestine are in great part the result of British behaviour since the Assembly decision, dictated by the desire to sabotage the decision. British behaviour likewise encouraged all those groups in the Middle East who also set themselves the goal of cancelling the decision since they felt that their actions would incur no penalty.

G. Granados, who had been a member of the United Nations enquiry commission, tells (in *How the State of Israel was Born*, pp. 279–289) of a cocktail party and supper that Senator Austin held on April 26 for the chief delegates of twenty Latin American countries in an attempt to convince them to support the new American plan for a trusteeship on Palestine. "'I wish,' said Austin, 'to use this opportunity when our good friends from this continent are gathered together . . . to assure you that my government wants to do what it can to solve the Palestine problem. We submitted a trusteeship proposal, and we sincerely believe that trusteeship is the only way. The U.S. government is acting with the best intentions. It is prepared to carry out what is imposed upon it as regards a trusteeship for Palestine.'"

"When he had finished," writes Granados, "there was a dead silence. All of us now knew that the object of the party was to gain votes; to convince us of the necessity of a trusteeship for Palestine, and urge as many of us as possible to get our countries to support the United States proposal."

Granados emphasized at the party that both the Jews and Arabs were opposed to a trusteeship government; that the question at the moment was not "How much strength is needed to implement the partition?" but rather "How much strength is needed to sabotage it?" and that nothing could be done about a trusteeship unless 150,000 soldiers were sent to Palestine. He expressed the hope that he was speaking for his friends as well in saying that "it would be very difficult to obtain soldiers from any Latin American country for this purpose."

"On the 15th of May," said Granados "we shall stand before a new position and we shall be obliged to meet it realistically and courageously." When Granados finished, Senator Austin looked at him and said: "I think our friend Mr. Granados has a negative and extreme outlook. We have no right to sit and do nothing while people are killing each other in Palestine. I cannot accept the claim that trusteeship is not implementable. I still hope Britain will keep her forces in Palestine and use them in order to press the trusteeship with the help of the U.S.A. and all those nations which will be ready to help."

On April 27th, Gromyko again spoke vigorously in the political committee, putting the record straight with the utmost clarity: "Only if the General Assembly will resolve by a two-thirds majority to abrogate the decision on the partition of Palestine, will it be possible to discuss a different suggestion."

Discussions in the political committee of the Assembly went on endlessly. Simultaneously, in bitter battles in Palestine, Jewish forces gained control of the areas allotted to the Jewish state according to the United Nations. The "implementation commission" was unable to do anything, and in the meantime the date (April 1) on which the provisional government councils of the two states were to take over had already lapsed.* A joint convention, in the middle of April, of the Jewish Agency administration and the *Vaad Leumi* confirmed the establishment of a provisional "people's council" of thirty-seven members, representing all sections of the Jewish people of Palestine, and the formation of a "people's administration" of thirteen members as the executive body. The establishment of these bodies reflected the overriding urgency to set up an effective successor government. It was rightly held that only such a government would translate into reality the United Nations decision of November 29.

In the May 4 session of the United Nations Assembly, Mr. Gromyko stated:

The United Nations Assembly must recognize the fact that while the powers are still seeking substitutes for the original decision, it is in the meantime being carried out in practice, as is indicated by the information of the representative of the United Nations Secretariat, by the Jewish Agency, and by the news in the press of America and the other countries. While the United Nations Assembly is still engaged in discussion, the Jewish state is turning into a real and existing fact, despite the efforts of a number of United Nations members to strew obstacles in its path. If a number of

---

* According to the Assembly decision, April 1 was the date on which the implementation commission of the United Nations was to appoint the provisional government council of each state, "after consultation with the democratic parties and public organizations."

United Nations members had not interfered with the process of partition, the obstacles at present would be fewer, and the sufferings of the Arabs and Jews less.

The creation of these facts in Palestine made the abrogation of the U.N. decision more difficult and protected the legal basis for the proclamation of Israel's establishment as a state the day the Mandate ended.

Continued Sabotage Attempts

During the time that remained before the end of the Mandate on May 15, the United States State Department tried ceaselessly to prevent the proclamation of the establishment of the Jewish state. When it began to appear impossible that such a resolution could be passed in the United Nations Assembly or Security Council—because of the sharp opposition of the Socialist bloc—the State Department initiated direct pressure (as well as indirect, through certain American Jewish groups) on the Jewish Agency to agree to some "temporary solution" and not comply with the Assembly decision. It also tried to obtain a similar agreement from the Arab leaders for an "interim arrangement;" this eventually took the form of a proposal for a "temporary armistice government," which was actually to be the "arrangement" for an unlimited period of time.

The essential points of this temporary armistice regime, which the Americans did everything to impose on Palestine in the dying moments of the Mandatory regime, were described by M. Sharett in his previously mentioned book. They included:

[A] The cessation of all military activity; [B] prevention of the entry of any force that were armed or meant for fighting; [C] prevention of the import of arms; [D] the deportation or imprisonment of anyone found responsible for violence (foreign Arabs deported, local Jews or Arabs imprisoned); [E] existing administrations, Arab or Jewish, to operate as "temporary armistice regimes" in the areas they control; [F] no sovereign states to be proclaimed in Palestine or any part of it, and no requests for international recognition to be submitted; [G] establishment of a United Nations armistice commission to oversee the relations and cooperation between Jews and Arabs; [H] supervision by the armistice commission of freedom of movement in Palestine; [I] all displaced persons to be returned to their places of residence; [J] the existing laws [i.e., the Mandatory laws] to remain valid unless the United Nations armistice commission decides otherwise; [K] the armistice commission to control immigration; [L] guarantees of the inviolability of the holy places and free access to them.

Four thousand immigration certificates a month were promised, but this was not put in writing in order, the explanation went, to ensure the Arabs' agreement to the entire arrangement.

In a letter of April 29 to American Secretary of State George Marshall, the Jewish Agency stated its objections to those proposals. The main reasons

were that the plan meant the postponement of immediate independence and
made the chances of attaining it in the future very doubtful; that since the
effective implementation of the armistice required the presence of considerable
military force, it appeared that the intention was to keep the British Army in
Palestine as an army of occupation and control, and that the armistice plan
involved inequality of Jews and Arabs regarding the acquisition of arms and
military training. Since the administration suggested would apply only to the
Palestine area, the Arab states would be free to purchase arms and prepare for
a future attack, and the Palestinian Arabs would be able to train in neighboring countries—opportunities that the Jews would not have.

In talks between Jewish and United States representatives, the former "expressed their refusal to discuss any plan that made immigration subject to
foreign rule in the future as well, and astonishment was expressed at the
absence of any link between the [new] proposal and the November 29
decision."

In the course of this war of nerves, a meeting took place in Washington on
May 8—just a week before the end of the Mandate and the proclamation of
the state of Israel—between Secretary of State George Marshall, his assistant
Robert Lovett, and Jewish Agency representatives M. Shertok and E. A.
Epstein (Eilat). On May 12, M. Shertok reported on this conversation at a
meeting of the "People's Administration" in Tel Aviv:

> Our latest contacts with the State Department people were accompanied by threats
> on their part. The most serious ones were not stated to us, but reached us circuitously.
> Two things that sounded like threats were told us directly: First of all, if we did not
> accept their armistice plan—which was actually a plan for a political arrangement—
> they would go to the Security Council and ensure a majority for declaring the situa-
> tion in Palestine as detrimental to world peace. Then, if we did not accept the ruling,
> or if the Arabs disobeyed the Security Council, the Council would impose sanctions
> against the recalcitrant party and we would eventually be forced to accept the same
> armistice plan that they were proposing in advance. Secondly, we were told bluntly:
> if you go your own way, you will not have any claim to our help in case of invasion
> (as if they had helped up to then!); if you want to fight, fight to your heart's content
> but don't come to us later!

In the same conversation, which lasted one and a half hours, M. Sharett
tried to clarify "whether we could adjust our position to theirs [the Americans'] without jeopardizing basic Jewish interests." He posed "one penetrating and fundamental question: What did the United States government
want? Where was it heading? If it honestly and sincerely wanted a Jewish
state and was prepared to help in its establishment, but foresaw difficulties and
was trying to find a way to remove them, that was one thing. But if it was
not at all clear that the United States government wanted a Jewish state; or
if it was clear that it did not want one and that its proposal was only meant

to postpone the proclamation of the state in order to entirely preclude such a possibility, that was a completely different matter, and there was no hope of obtaining our consent to it. There was no positive reply forthcoming to this formulation of the question." In the face of this hard-hearted indifference of a Great Power over the fate of a small people which had suffered so much, Mr. Sharett continued:

We are standing on the threshold of realizing the hope of hundreds and hundreds of years, standing before the completion of an endeavor to which three generations have bent their efforts. We feel that it is just ahead of us—we need only to stretch forth our hands and take it. This is a unique opportunity in the history of a people. We shall be condemned by Jewish history if we agree to any postponement without having the assurance that the state will arise after the postponement. The United States government did not help us establish the state—it aided us only by voting in the Assembly; we appreciate this very much and will never forget it. But our war in Palestine we have fought on our own without help. When we asked for arms, they were not given to us; we asked for military guidance and this was not given either; we did not get even steel plates for armoring buses—there is a letter signed by the Secretary of State himself saying that it is not possible to let us have steel plates because the embargo applies to them as well. We have achieved what we have with our own power. At this point there is no question of obtaining help from the United States. There is only the question of avoiding hindrance. The United States now comes to hinder the establishment of the Jewish state through its plan.

M. Sharett even tried to help his American companions "get out of the mess":

It seems to us that [the United States] has another way open. It can tell the Arabs: We made an effort to retreat from the November 29 decision, but we were not successful. The United Nations does not accept the idea. In the meantime, a new situation has been created, through no fault of ours. We haven't raised a finger to help them even when we were requested to help but we cannot ignore reality and have no choice but to return to the former decision, which in any case is being realized. . . .

The pace at which authority is being transferred in Palestine is increasing daily, from the point of view of area and of duties. Any leadership which would try to stem this impulse would be swept out of the picture. We are asked to postpone independence with our own hands. We are asked to agree to a temporary regime called "temporary armistice regime"—a thing of which there is no trace in the Assembly decision. This means that we are being asked to dissociate ourselves from that decision. In regard to immigration, we are being asked to agree to the current situation—to agree that on May 15 and thereafter the control of immigration will not be in our hands but once more in the hands of a foreign authority. Furthermore, we are asked to agree that all existing laws shall remain valid. All the preparations we have made to take over the government are cancelled, legislation will not be in our authority. How can we agree to all this?

The United States government representatives were not moved by these words. Lovett, Marshall's assistant, said, "You apparently assume with excessive confidence that the Arab Legion will not harm you, and that you will be able to reach an agreement with Abdullah. An invasion will begin, and you will be in great trouble. Don't come to us then with complaints!"

At the end of the conversation, Marshall turned to the Jewish representative and said:

Everything you have said is engraved in my memory. I understand very well the importance of these reasons. It is not my job to tell you what to do. But as a military man, I should like to say to you: Don't rely on your military advisers. They are now intoxicated with success after the recent victories. What will happen if there is a lengthy invasion? Are you taking into account how it will weaken you? I had such an experience in China, when I was sent there to mediate between the two sides. At that time one of the sides (Chiang Kai Shek) had had an easy victory and therefore refused to compromise. And what happened? Now they have been fighting for two years, and have already lost Manchuria. If it turns out that you were right, and you can establish the Jewish state, I will be happy. But it is a very great responsibility.

The Proclamation of Independence

Indeed, there was now no retreating from the path to the longed-for independence and sovereignty. The danger of postponing the proclamation of independence was greater than the danger in proclaiming it.

The People's Administration, which heard M. Sharett's report on May 12, decided unanimously to proclaim independence on May 14, 1948. The text of the proclamation was confirmed on May 13. The next day at four o'clock in the afternoon, David Ben-Gurion—moments before the head of the People's Administration and now the Israeli government's first Prime Minister—read the Declaration of Independence, signed by all the members of the People's Council.

The Declaration had this to say on Arab-Jewish relations:

The state of Israel will be open to Jewish immigration and the ingathering of exiles. It will devote itself to developing the Land for the good of all its inhabitants.

It will rest upon foundations of liberty, justice and peace as envisioned by the Prophets of Israel. It will maintain complete equality of social and political rights for all its citizens, without distinction of creed, race or sex. It will guarantee freedom of religion and conscience, of language, education and culture. It will safeguard the Holy Places of all religions. It will be loyal to the principles of the United Nations Charter.

The state of Israel will be prepared to cooperate with the organs and representatives of the United Nations in carrying out the General Assembly resolution of 29 November 1947, and will work for the establishment of the economic union of the whole Land of Israel.

We appeal to the United Nations to assist the Jewish people in the building of their State, and to admit the State of Israel into the family of nations.

Even amidst the violent attacks launched against us for months past, we call upon the sons of the Arab people dwelling in Israel to keep the peace and to play their part in building the State on the basis of full and equal citizenship and due representation in all its institutions, provisional and permanent.

We extend the hand of peace and good-neighborliness to all the States around us and to their peoples, and we call upon them to cooperate in mutual helpfulness with the independent Jewish nation in its Land. The State of Israel is prepared to make its contribution in a concerted effort for the advancement of the entire Middle East.

The people's council became the provisional state council and the people's administration became the provisional government of the state of Israel. At midnight, the Mandatory regime came to an end, and in the early morning hours, the regular armies of the Arab states began to invade Palestine.

As the establishment of the independent state of Israel was being proclaimed in Tel Aviv, the political committee of the United Nations Assembly was still deliberating. The Israeli proclamation of independence put an end to the discussion on the trusteeship plan proposed by the Americans. The political committee adopted a resolution calling for the appointment of a United Nations mediator who was to try to work out the possibilities of a peaceful solution to the Palestine problem under the present circumstances. The political department also passed on to the Assembly plenum a plan for temporary international control over Jerusalem. The Assembly immediately approved the mediation proposal, but the proposal on temporary international control of Jerusalem did not receive the required two-thirds vote and was defeated. When the appointment of a mediator was accepted, the Assembly decided to put an end to the activities of the implementation commission, expressing its thanks to "the five lonely pilgrims" for their loyal service.

The Birth of the State of Israel: Confronting the Regular Arab Armies

If the Arab leaders had accepted the United Nations Assembly's decision, they would have saved their people untold tragedy and suffering. The United Nations decision was not based on any assumption that Arabs would be displaced from the area of the Jewish state. The Arabs could safely have stayed within its boundaries. "The Arabs are here," said M. Sharett to the United Nations commission in Jerusalem on July 16, 1947, "and nobody in his senses will try to uproot them." The economic union between the Jewish and Arab states that the United Nations Assembly had decided to establish in Palestine could have provided a bridge for the reintegration of Palestine into a common homeland for the two peoples.

The Arab leaders encouraged by the British and also by the United States stand refused to accept the judgment of the United Nations and chose war instead. The Jews were left no choice but to mobilize for a defensive battle. As the Mandate came to an end on May 15, 1948, the Jews held most of the area that the United Nations Assembly had allotted to the Jewish state. Even at that stage, the way was still open for the Arabs to accept the partition of Palestine on the basis of the United Nations decision. However, the heads of the Higher Arab Committee and the leaders of the Arab states blindly followed the assurances of some British agents that the "Zionist bands," lacking any heavy equipment, would be unable to hold out against the regular Arab armies for more than two weeks at most (and some "experts" considered even this an exaggerated estimate).

The Arab leaders showed once again their inability to overcome the weaknesses which had dogged them before, including a reckless disregard of realities and a stubborn adherence to a course that was neither vital to the Arab national good, nor practicable; unfounded exaggeration in their estimate of their strength, and underestimation of the opposition's strength and a superficial and one-sided evaluation of international conditions that stressed only the aspects unfavorable to the Jews and ignored the possibilities in their favor. When the political committee of the Arab League decided (on April 12) that the regular Arab armies would invade Palestine on the day the Mandate ended—"a temporary invasion, with no intention of occupation, and after the liberation of Palestine the invading forces will be evacuated and it will be handed over to its lawful inhabitants to choose whatever regime they desire"—they obviously saw only one side of the picture. They were counting on the Arab armies' great advantage in heavy equipment (tanks, cannon, planes, armored vehicles) that the Jews did not then have, on the alliance between Egypt, Transjordan, Iraq, and Britain, and the American embargo against the shipment of arms and strategic materials to the Jews, and on the considerable numerical advantage of the Arabs over the "Zionist bands," which they promised to "throw into the sea" (the population of the Arab League countries at that time outnumbered the Jews of Palestine about 55 to 1). These were the facts that supplied the basis for the extravagant statements of Abd er-Rahman Azam, the Arab League secretary, who on May 15, 1948, announced at a press conference recorded by the B.B.C. that "this war [in Palestine] will be a war of annihilation, and the slaughter taking place will be remembered like the Mongol invasion and the Crusades."

The next few months were to prove that the calculations of the Arab leaders and their spokesmen and supporters overseas were mistaken. When the war began, the Jews could not remain long on the defensive. Self-defense dictated that they must go over to the offensive, beat the invaders in battle, and drive them away from the boundaries of the young state of Israel. When the conflict in Palestine became a full-scale war, with the intervention of foreign regular armies and involving the political and strategic interests of certain world powers, it was no longer the exclusive affair of the Arabs and the Jews. Paralleling the help that the Arabs received from the Western powers—directly (from Britain), and indirectly (from the United States)—was help coming to the Jews from another direction. The Palestine war became part of the international political scene, in which the Western powers were no longer the only deciding factors. War has its own laws and he who declares war is not entitled to think only of the death, destruction and casualties in life and property which will be the lot of the other side. There was no lack of indications that the war would be a cruel one. This was shown in the incidents that preceded the Arab armies' invasion of Palestine—acts of cruelty and massacres committed by Arabs against Jews, the Dair-Yassin affair,* and the slaughter of Jews by Arabs in the Etzion bloc†—to the cries of "Dair-Yassin!" according to Israel defense sources.

Nevertheless, the Arab leaders did not flinch from these horrors. They decided on "a radical solution" of the problem. On the morning of May 15, 1948, the armies of the Arab League countries began to invade the borders of Israel: Egyptian forces moved in from the south, Arab Legionnaires and Iraqi forces from the east, Syrian forces from the northeast, and Lebanese forces from the north. The Arab kings, who were known to be amenable to British influence, organized this general Arab onslaught. The most immediate problems confronting the Jewish command were how to hold back the Arab armies, block their way, and prevent them from occupying areas of Jewish settlement that were likely to be destroyed in even a temporary occupation; and how to hold out in the face of enemy advantage in equipment until the Jewish fighting forces, who had just emerged from the under-

---

* On April 9, members of the two "dissident" military organizations, I.Z.L. and *Lehi*, killed more than 200 people in the Arab village of Dair-Yassin near Jerusalem. They wounded some 200 others and took some prisoners, whom they paraded in a degrading fashion through the streets of Jewish Jerusalem. The great majority of the Jewish community condemned the act as a disgrace and a "defilement" of the defensive weapons of the Jewish war of independence.

† The Etzion bloc (Kfar Etzion, Masuot Yitzhak, Ein Tsurim, and Revadim) was for months cut off from the rest of the Jewish community. Only a few convoys were able to break their way through to them. The only contact with them was through airplanes, for which runways were prepared within the bloc. At the beginning of May, the Arabs began to storm the bloc with the help of Arab Legion armored cars. On May 12, the Legion attack on the bloc began. The reply of British headquarters to the Jewish Agency protest was that the Legion was no longer under British orders. The bloc surrendered after a fierce two-day battle with tanks and armored cars, in which many of the defenders were killed. Surviving defenders were taken prisoner by the Legion, while the badly wounded were brought to Jerusalem by the Red Cross.

The invasion of Palestine by the Arab armies, 1948

ground, had received military equipment with which they could return the aggressors' fire and push them back.

On May 15, the Iraqi and Syrian armies appeared in the Jordan valley, there was a battle with the Lebanese forces in Malkia, and the Egyptian Army unsuccessfully attacked Kfar Hadarom and Nirim; Beerot Yitzhak in the south was heavily shelled, and Tel Aviv was bombed by Egyptian planes. Neve Yitzhak and Atarot near Jerusalem were evacuated by the Jews. Between May 16 and May 19, Jewish forces raided bridges and military camps across the Lebanese and Syrian borders. By blowing up the Litani bridge on the Lebanese border and the Banias bridge on the Syrian border, as well as a large concentration of Syrian arms and ammunition in the customs house opposite the Bnot Yaakov bridge, the Israeli forces disrupted the invaders' northern offensive. The Israeli Army captured the Nebi-Yosha fortress in upper Galilee (on May 17) and at dawn on May 18, the city of Acre was taken, opening the road to western Galilee. On the same day, the Syrian Army seized Zemah in the Jordan valley, the Arab Legion entered the Shaar Hagai area, Shaar Hagolan and Masada in the Jordan valley fell, and Hartuv was vacated. In the city of Jerusalem, Jewish forces seized key positions as the British left on May 15; among strategic areas taken were sections of the German colony, the Allenby Barracks, the railroad station area, the Russian compound, the Notre Dame convent near the Old City wall, the Sheik Jarrah quarter, the Italian Hospital. On May 19, the Israeli Army captured Mount Zion, the Old City wall was breached, and a temporary corridor was pushed through to the besieged Jewish quarter within the walls. Sheik Jarrah fell to the Arabs. Communications between Jerusalem and the coast were cut off. The same day, the Jews evacuated kibbutz Bet Haarava and the potash works at the north end of the Dead Sea. On May 20, the Syrian Army's attack on the two Deganias was repulsed and its retreat from the Jordan valley began. On that same day, Jewish forces captured Sarafand. The Arab Legion still held Naharayim,* which it had overpowered on May 14.

On May 21, the Egyptian Army began its bitter attack on Negba, which lasted until May 27, when it was forced to retreat (for the Negba battles, see page 435). On May 22, the enemy left the battlefield near Gesher in the Jordan valley. The Israeli Army took Kfar Kabri near Nahariya, the extended siege of Yehiam was relieved, and the liberation of western Galilee com-

---

* On the eve of the war, the British-owned Electric Corporation negotiated with King Abdullah an agreement whereby he would take over the plant (located in Transjordan territory, and a source of income for it) and its workers. The workers and engineers, whose families had already been evacuated, were to give up their arms and work under the King's protection. On May 14, after setting unacceptable conditions, the Legion took over the plant, as well as the arms that had not yet been removed, and took thirty of its workers prisoner. The next day the plant was blown up and its equipment destroyed.

pleted. The next day, Israeli forces took the Rosh Hanikra police station on the Lebanese border. On May 24, Bet Eshel near Beersheba was attacked, Yad Mordechai fell after a five-day Egyptian attack, while Zemah, Shaar Hagolan, and Masada were retaken by Israeli troops. A cruel battle raging around isolated Ramat Rahel ended with the rout of the Arab forces, on May 25; the Israeli forces' first attack on the Legion positions in Latrun on May 27 and 28 was repulsed, but with the capture of Bet Sussin and Bet Jiz, contact was made with Israeli fighters in the Jerusalem corridor. The important Julis camp and the Bir-Asluj police station were taken by Jewish forces. On May 28, after an extended siege, the Jewish quarter of the Old City of Jerusalem surrendered to the Arabs.

The situation of the Jews in the Old City had been getting steadily worse since the fall of 1947, when there were 1,800 Jews (with a large percentage of children and old people) battling 22,000 Arabs within the walls. Some of the Jewish population escaped outside the walls during the battle, while the Arab population within was swelled by the stream of refugees flowing to it from the new city. The British prevented the transfer of reinforcements in men and material to the starved and besieged Jewish quarter. A local industry manufacturing Molotov cocktails and primitive hand grenades and mines was started. Some extra arms and ammunition were acquired from Arabs or the British. Several attempts made by Jewish forces outside the walled town to form a permanent bridge to the quarter ended in failure. The pressure of Arab forces increased, and at noon of May 28, the quarter surrendered to the Arab Legion. According to the terms of the surrender, the Jewish fighters were taken prisoner, serious casualties and non-combatants were passed through to the Jewish lines, and their weapons were surrendered to the Legion, which assumed the responsibility for the safety of the Jewish residents until their transfer to the Jewish lines outside the walls. The same day (May 28) Geulim fell but was retaken by Jewish forces. In battles in the Jenin region, Israeli forces took the villages of Zer'in, Nuris, al-Mazar, Megiddo, and Lejun. The next day, Israel recaptured Malkia in upper Galilee, while in the south, Egyptian forces reached the Ashdod region and were stopped short.

The battles lasted until June 11, when the first cease-fire was proclaimed. The invaders still retained the initiative, while the defenders sought chiefly to contain the invasion. Fortified "porcupine settlements" in various parts of the country, strengthened to some extent by outside fighters, disrupted the advance of the Arab forces and gave the defenders time to set up strong points to block enemy progress toward their principal goals—the main centers of the state of Israel. Because they were interested in advancing rapidly, the invaders left the "porcupine settlements" behind them; at a later stage these served as key points from which to assault and repel the invaders.

On the Jerusalem front on June 1, the first convoy of jeeps reached the city through the specially improvised "Burma road," built in a superhuman effort to bring arms, ammunition, and basic supplies to Jewish Jerusalem under siege. On June 2 to 3, the Israeli attack on the Egyptian column at Ashdod failed. Negba repulsed a new Egyptian attack on June 2, and Jewish forces closed on Jenin on June 3. Egyptian ships approaching Tel Aviv were driven off on June 4. The Jewish forces at Jenin were obliged to retreat. On June 6, Malkia in Galilee was again taken by the Arabs since, after Israel forces had taken Rosh Hanikra, it blocked the only road between Lebanon and central Galilee. Syrian forces attacked Mishmar Hayarden, Israeli forces captured Yavneh in the south and the large village of Kakun in the Sharon plain. On June 7, Nitzanim in the south fell to the Egyptian Army. The Israeli attack on Lubiya village in lower Galilee failed on June 9, and on that same day, the third unsuccessful Israeli attack on the Jordan Legion positions at Latrun was mounted. On June 10, the Syrians defeated Mishmar Hayarden —the only settlement in the north that the Syrian Army managed to take, despite continual assaults on many eastern Galilee settlements, generally with planes, tanks, and armored vehicles. On the same day, Ein Gev and Ramot Naftali repulsed enemy attacks, and Gezer (between Latrun and Naan) fell to the Legion, but was recaptured by the Israel Defense Force a few hours later. On June 11, the day the first cease-fire began, important events took place in the south: Israeli forces occupied Julis and Yassur in the south and Bir-Asluj in the Negev, their assault on the Iraq-Suweidan police station failed, the Egyptians captured the Iraq-Suweidan crossroads and blocked the road to the Negev, while Israeli forces dug in on the heights north and south of the crossroads (the "Hill 113," Kaukabah, and Huleikat heights).

The Fruits of Valor

The resistance of the Israelis in face of the regular armies of five Arab states was a crucial test for the young state. In the first days of the invasion, the defenders had only light weapons. Israel did not even possess a single field gun. To combat the tank and armored brigades of Egypt, Syria, Jordan, and Iraq, Israel had only a few dozen homemade armored vehicles and two Cromwell tanks; to confront the invading squadrons of fighter planes and bombers, Israel had only slow, light "primus" planes and a few transports, which, in the absence of air protection, were forced to hide as best they could in daylight and operate exclusively at night; there were few anti-tank guns. It was imperative to check the invading forces until the arrival of the heavy equipment on order.

Typical of the conditions under which Israel fought in those critical days was the reply given by the Chief of Operations at H.Q. to a delegation of old-timers from the Degania kibbutzim who, on May 20, came to ask for reinforcements in men and heavy equipment. "Let the Arabs [who were attacking with tanks and armored cars followed by infantry] get to within twenty to thirty meters of the gate, and then fight hand to hand with their tanks. There is no choice. It is of course a very dangerous method, but it is the only way," the officer told them. When the Syrian armored and tank assault on Degania-A began on the morning of May 20, the defenders did not succeed in stopping it with the light weapons on hand. As the tanks and armored cars entered the farmyard and the trenches around it, they were hit with Molotov cocktails and Piat shells; when their crews jumped out, they were cut down by the defenders' fire. The Arabs' spirits fell and they began to retreat. In attacking nearby Degania-B, they did not dare to come closer than 400 meters from the settlement fence. When the infantry made an attempt to go ahead of the tanks in order to approach defense positions, they were repulsed by rifle and machine-gun fire. Two 65 millimeter short-range field guns (the first in Israel, unloaded just a few days earlier in Tel Aviv port) had reached the Jordan valley that very day and were decisive in the eight-hour battle.

Syrian forces retreated eastward in a panic, leaving the defenders considerable amounts of ammunition, two tanks, and one armored car. Battles such as these, in which tanks were fought with Molotov cocktails and hand grenades thrown at close quarters into the apertures, were familiar to more than one settlement in those fateful days. The courageous resistance of the defenders prevailed against the attackers' advantage in equipment. On May 15, the first five field guns reached Tel Aviv port. A week later, another ship brought additional guns and 120 millimeter mortars. A third ship on May 28 carried 75 millimeter field guns, whose range equalled those of the Arab Army guns; heavy machine guns, light and medium guns, as well as several thousand more Czech rifles, arrived. A few days later, fighter planes also began to arrive (the first were Messerschmidts), Israel's skies stopped being undefended, and enemy planes were engaged in battle.

With the arrival of heavy equipment, human reinforcements also started coming, expressing the solidarity of Diaspora Jewry with the renascent state of Israel. *Mahal* (Overseas Volunteers), 2,500 strong, arrived, and included Jews from France and England (500 from each), the United States, South Africa, Canada, Latin America, the Scandinavian countries, and others— most of them experienced military men (especially in the Air-Force, Navy, Artillery, Engineer Corps, etc.). *Gahal* (Overseas Draftees) included some North Africans and displaced persons from Germany, but the majority were from Eastern European countries and had had experience in partisan units and in the armies fighting Nazism there.

The Israeli forces were reorganized amidst critical battles. On May 31, an order of the day was issued officially setting up the Israel Defense Forces (I.D.F.) on land, sea, and in the air. Compulsory military service was announced in the state.

The Political Battle Resumed

As the guns roared in Palestine, a significant political development took place abroad: President Truman recognized the state of Israel. "When President Truman learned of the proclamation of Israel's independence," wrote United Nations delegate Granados, "he decided immediately to bring his full authority to bear upon the State Department," for "in this way [the United States government] would again acquire in the eyes of the progressive nations interested in the existence of the United Nations some of the prestige that it had lost by wavering between conflicting tendencies. Furthermore, if it recognized it [the state of Israel] the United States and not the Soviet Union would be the country leading the peoples of the world. ... When the President made his decision, wheels began to turn. The Israeli representative in Washington was advised to write a letter requesting recognition; he wrote, and the recognition was granted."[3] The United States was the first government to recognize the "temporary government as a *de facto* government of the state of Israel." *De jure* recognition by the United States followed only in January 1949.

When the Foreign Minister of Israel's provisional government asked the Soviet Foreign Minister for recognition, the Soviet Union immediately granted the state of Israel full *de jure* recognition without reservations.

Israel gradually secured the friendly support of some United Nations delegates, while the Arab leadership had the support of others. The decisive influence, however, was that of the two main powers in the United Nations—the United States and the Soviet Union.

On May 14, Count Bernadotte of Sweden was appointed by the United Nations as mediator. His assignments were to bring about a cease-fire in Palestine and to supervise it, and to find a basis for peace between the opposing sides. From May 15 on, the Security Council had been discussing the cessation of the fighting in Palestine. The Western powers failed to take concrete steps to restrain the attackers. Thereupon, the Soviet representatives brought the Council up to date on the situation in Palestine, established that Britain was a party in the war, and demanded effective decisions for the cease-fire. The Council appointed a cease-fire commission with vague powers, and failed to adopt the following draft resolution moved by the Soviet Union and the Ukraine: "The Security Council orders the governments of the countries involved in the current conflict in Palestine to ensure the cessation of military activities within thirty-six hours after the approval of this proposal by the Security Council." In opposition to this motion was the British motion whose principal provisions were: appealing for a cease-fire and prohibiting the import of arms or soldiers. The amendment proposed by Gromyko to emphasize the fact that it was the Arab states who had refused to comply with the Security Council's May 22 decision [which generally called for an end to military action] was supported only by the Soviet Union and the Ukraine, though two days earlier the American representative had "reprimanded" the Arab states for invading Palestine.

A Four-Week Cease-Fire

It was only after progress in the Palestine battles had refuted the promises of the British experts to the Arabs that "they would finish the job in two weeks at the most" that the Security Council adopted a resolution on a four-week cease-fire. A United States amendment providing that the prohibition of the entrance of draft-age men to Palestine during the cease-fire should apply to the Arab countries was described by Gromyko as an empty gesture that did not change the clearly anti-Jewish character of the motion. The amendment, proposed by Austin, that the embargo on shipment of war material apply also to the Arab League countries likewise elicited Gromyko's criticism, to the effect that this prohibition was actually aimed exclusively at the Jews, since the Arabs had managed to accumulate a large reserve of military equipment and supplies earlier. These amendments were passed without Soviet support. Only the paragraph on the protection of the holy places in Jerusalem was unanimously passed.

The cease-fire began at 10 a.m. on June 11. Between the invasion and the first cease-fire—twenty-seven days of battle—about 1,200 Jews were killed, 876 of them combatants.

An Israeli military survey stated:

The front quieted down, and the soldiers of both sides came out of the posts and bunkers. Where the positions were close, they even met and talked to each other. The Egyptians were curious to meet the "Zionist gangs," about whom so much had been told and with whom they had been fighting for almost a month. In Kfar Darom, the Arabs of Dair-ul-Balah wanted to hold a *sulha* (conciliation with a roasted sheep and coffee). The resistance of the place had filled their hearts with admiration and fear.*

* Kfar Darom, a small isolated Jewish settlement in the Gaza strip, was heavily attacked, first on April 10 by Egyptian irregulars, members of the fanatic "Moslem Brothers." After the decision on invasion by the regular Arab armies, Egyptian headquarters took them over and turned them into a regular unit, commanded by an army officer. From May 11 on, the settlement was almost completely surrounded, while tanks and infantry attempted to capture it. The besieged settlers allowed these to come very close, then fought back and repulsed them. The Egyptians suffered heavy losses in shelling and bombarding the little settlement, but it did not surrender. After brave and

For the Jews there had been failures, of course, and many losses; it had been necessary to retreat in some places, some attacks were unsuccessful, and a few settlements fell to the aggressors. But the defenders could be proud of their overall achievement. All the Arab armies' attempts at penetration had been stopped. Despite their enormous advantage in operational reserves, artillery, armor, and air power, the invaders' main goal had not been attained: the state of Israel had not been destroyed, and its army had not been routed. The twenty-seven Jewish settlements in the Negev held out (excluding two that had been temporarily evacuated). Two combat battalions sent to the Negev as reinforcements gave the invaders a great deal of trouble and inflicted casualties and damage. Jewish Jerusalem held out although the Jordan Legion had done its best to conquer it before the beginning of the cease-fire, shelling all parts of the city heavily, while fierce battles raged at all intersections on the road to it from the coast. Bitter experience indicated that with added reserves and training, and especially with the additional equipment whose arrival was hoped for, the young state would be able to withstand the forces invading it from all sides.

The United Nations Mediator and his Objections

The four weeks that had elapsed since the beginning of the invasion had demanded a superhuman effort on the part of the defenders. The cease-fire, originally calculated for a two-week period, enabled the Arab armies to renew their stocks of ammunition and fuel, but it also gave the Israeli Army the opportunity to build up strength, reinforce its combat units, and replace its dead and wounded. The commanders had an opportunity to exchange opinions on the lessons of the four weeks of fighting and to draw conclusions.

In accordance with the cease-fire regulations, United Nations observers and Arab Legion officers checked the convoys travelling the main road to Jerusalem, to prevent the increase of stocks. But the "Burma Road" was not subject to such supervision. The rapid improvement of this road made it possible to increase the supply of ammunition and food in the city. A proposal to evacuate children from Jerusalem was rejected, and measures were taken to prevent the residents from leaving. The weeks of the cease-fire were utilized also to raise the organizational and training level of the army, to raise the fighting morale of the entire community, and to increase the quantity of war production in Israel (which was not subject to restriction).

As the cease-fire began, the United Nations mediator, Count Bernadotte, began to explore the possibilities for the successful discharge of his second

prolonged resistance, it was decided to evacuate the settlement on the eve of the "Ten-Day Battles."

task: the finding of a basis for permanent peace. The trial suggestions he presented to the two parties for consideration meant essentially that he did not consider himself bound by the November 29, 1947, decision of the United Nations Assembly, and that he was proposing a solution of his own even if both sides were asked to make their own suggestions. While recognizing the fact of Israel's existence, he supported the Arab demands in several key questions: these called for the inclusion of the Negev ("in whole or in part") in the Arab state ("in return for the inclusion of Western Galilee, in whole or in part, in the Jewish zone"); the inclusion of the city of Jerusalem and all its environs in the Arab state, with municipal autonomy being assured for the Jewish community, and special arrangements made for safeguarding the holy places; "a reconsideration of the status of Jaffa;" the creation of a free airport zone at Lydda and a guarantee that all persons who were displaced as a result of the events in Palestine will be able to return and repossess their property." The mediator's "ideas" included an attempt to limit Israel's sovereignty with respect to immigration. Count Bernadotte suggested that when the accord had been operating for two years, either side would have the right to propose that the joint council of the Jewish state and the Arab state (which, according to the mediator's suggestion, was to include "the entire original area of the British Mandate on Palestine, excluding the state of Israel" i.e., Transjordan as well) should discuss the immigration policy of the other state; if the joint council did not reach an agreement, the question would be referred to the United Nations Council on Economic and Social Affairs. The mediator added verbally that the intention was a council on a parity basis, and that the United Nations Social and Economic Council would consider the immigration question in the light of the economic absorptive capacity of the country, the mediation to be binding on both sides.

These "ideas," which postulated an obvious surrender of vital national interests by Israel, were, of course, rejected by her provisional government. The mediator's efforts to prolong the cease-fire consequently failed. The Arab leaders, too, declared their inability to extend the cease-fire. On July 8, the mediator ordered the United Nations observers to leave their posts, and on July 9, fighting was resumed.

The "Ten-Day" War and the Second Truce

The fighting that broke out anew proved that the Israeli Army was stronger, better organized, and better equipped than it had been at the start of the invasion on May 15. In the ten days following the first cease-fire, Israeli forces managed to consolidate their strategic positions with substantial resultant improvement of their territorial, security, and military status.

EI

The Israeli attack now concentrated on one front, while holding the enemy down on the others. By the use on the central front of a classic pincer movement Lydda and Ramle were captured, together with all their surrounding Arab villages (July 11 and 12); the topographical advantages of the Arab Legion in the Sharon plain were nullified, and its pressure diminished on the coastal plain in Israeli hands. The Israeli corridor to Jerusalem was considerably widened. Areas of lower Galilee controlled by the Kaukji forces were liberated in the east (the Sejera region), the west (the Shfaram area), and the south-central part (including the city of Nazareth, which came under Israeli control on July 16). In Galilee, the only territory still retained by the invaders was the mountainous northern tip near the Lebanon border. These battles enlarged the Israeli area of control by about 1,000 square kilometers and improved its strategic position in that part of the country. Tens of thousands of new Arab refugees, who had been displaced from their homes because of the fighting, made their way to areas under Arab control, where they were a burden on the Arab authorities and interfered with their military operations.

There was fierce fighting in eastern Galilee, with both sides using artillery and air power. Israeli forces attempted to push back the Syrians from the bridgehead they had captured at Mishmar Hayarden, while the Syrians were attempting further penetration through the Machanayim-Rosh Pina area, in order to cut off upper Galilee from the rest of Israel. This battle ended in a stand-off, and when the second cease-fire was proclaimed, both armies were at their previous positions.

Under pressure by the Iraqi Army in the Jenin area, Israeli units were forced to retreat on July 10 from the positions they had previously held in an open valley (the Dotan valley), three to four kilometers from the town, to a more convenient line (the Mazar Zer'in line) on the Gilboa ridge. The fierce Iraqi assaults on this line were repulsed, and it remained the boundary when the second cease-fire was proclaimed, and also when the armistice was finally declared.

Furious battles raged also in the Jerusalem area, as both sides tried to reach new positions before the second cease-fire. Despite the strenuous efforts of both armies, the front line within the city itself did not change. Israeli forces took a considerable area west of the city (Ein Karem, Malcha, etc.), but an additional attempt on July 16 and 17 to break into the Old City failed.

There was heavy fighting in the Negev, where Israeli forces had lost key positions to the Egyptians on the eve of the first cease-fire. Great importance was attached to the Ashkelon-Bet Jubrin crossroads in the Hebron hills and the road between Ashdod and Beersheba (the Huleikat-Julis crossroads near kibbutz Negba, and the road to Gedera, which connected the north of Israel to the Negev). In this area, heavy fighting took place during the "Ten Days," with commanding heights passing to and fro.

The night before the resumption of fighting on July 8, Kfar Darom was evacuated. Despite a brave resistance during months of siege and lack of communications, there was no further possibility of holding it. The Egyptians began a heavy mortar attack on the settlement and then assaulted it with tanks and infantry, only to find it empty.

After several days of heavy attack, in which the dominant heights in the neighborhood changed hands several times, the Egyptians began their great assault on kibbutz Negba (July 12). In this operation they used three infantry battalions—an armored battalion, a field artillery battalion, A.T. gun units, mortars, and bombers. After a bombardment by guns and mortars and bombing from the air, which began at dawn, the Egyptian armored corps tried to enter the settlement at 11 a.m. Fifty meters from the outside fence, the attacking wave was stopped and the defenders' fire forced the Egyptians to retreat in order to reorganize. In the afternoon the attackers returned to the offensive and reached the inner fence, but after very heavy fighting the Egyptians retreated in the evening with an estimated 200 casualties against 5 dead and 6 wounded on the Jewish side.

An Egyptian officer taken prisoner a few days later described the astonishment that Negba's resistance aroused at Egyptian headquarters: "How did Negba hold out? There were 150 defenders in the settlement. We rained 4,000 shells down on you. According to our calculations, 50 percent [of the defenders] should have been hurt, and 25 percent should have been taking care of the wounded."

The kibbutz newsletter of July 13, the day after the battle, replied to the question, "The fire was terrific. . . . We were surrounded on all sides by an enemy fully armed and equipped. Tanks, infantry, planes, and dozens of guns. . . . They lacked the one thing that we possessed—a dauntless spirit, and recognition of what the battle was about, and the knowledge that with our bodies we were blocking the enemy's progress northwards."

Another epic struggle was conducted in kibbutz Yad Mordechai, which had been named after Mordechai Anilewitz, the young leader of *Hashomer Hatzair* in Warsaw who fell commanding the Warsaw ghetto revolt (1943). A report said:

The attack on Yad Mordechai began with the usual softening-up by guns. After three hours of attack, a pillbox 400 meters south of the kibbutz was destroyed. The defenders were forced to retreat, and the Egyptians occupied it. They then tried to take advantage of their success to break through into the kibbutz, but were repulsed in hand-to-hand fighting. The attack was resumed on May 20. Four assaults were repulsed that same day. The casualties were already great—eighteen dead and twenty wounded. The remaining defenders cried out for reinforcements in men, arms, and ammunition. That night a company from Brigade 2 reached us, but the bombardment grew worse in the next two days. . . .

Yad Mordechai fell, but this victory cost the enemy great losses and five vital fighting days, which were of incalculable importance to us. These five days made it possible to set up a line of defense north of Ashdod and concentrate forces for defensive operations.*

As the initiative in the northern Negev passed to the Israelis, they embarked upon an operation whose purpose was to cut off the Majdal-Bet Jubrin road and open the way to the southern Negev. Despite partial successes, this aim was not achieved; when the second cease-fire began, late on July 18, the Egyptians again returned to the commanding heights (in the Kartiya area) and nullified Israeli advances in battle. The road to the Negev remained blocked.

A few days after the cease-fire began, armed Arab resistance in the "little triangle" near Haifa was destroyed. They had blocked the coastal road and forced Tel Aviv-Haifa traffic to detour around Mount Carmel and use the Wadi-l-Milh road. Although the cease-fire restricted military activity, the operation was in the nature of a police action against local residents who refused to recognize the state's sovereign authority. For the villages were within Israel territory according to the United Nations decision and under actual I.D.F. control. The three villages were conquered.

In this phase of the war, from the beginning of the first cease-fire to the second, 1,150 Jews were killed, 838 of them combatants.

During the "Ten Days," the young and ill-equipped Israeli Navy (its first ships were former immigrant boats with some armament added) asserted itself for the first time. The Lebanese city of Tyre was shelled on the morning of July 18, and escort service was provided for immigrant ships as they neared the shores of Israel. The Air Force, too, began to bomb the enemy on his own ground: On their way to Israel, three Flying Fortresses (acquired in the West) bombed Farouk's palace in Cairo and military camps in Rafah and El-Arish; two bombing raids were carried out in Damascene skies, and dozens of sorties were made over enemy concentrations in Palestine itself.

There was a great improvement in Israeli military equipment. Light weapons were received from Czechoslovakia (a single shipment contained 10,000 rifles and more than 3,000 machine guns). The "air lift" between Czechoslovakia and Israel brought fighter planes, heavy machine guns, and many other kinds of arms and ammunition.† The material acquired in Western Europe—especially France—included tanks, field guns, communications equipment, and various vehicles. These substantial arms orders were wholly

---

* For a description of the resistance of Yad Mordechai, see *The Hand of Mordechai*, by M. Larkin, London, Victor Gollancz, 1968.

† An Israeli military survey stated that "this air lift played a vital role in the war of independence." It began on May 20, a few days after the start of the invasion, and continued until August 10.

financed by Jewish communities in all parts of the world, especially by the Jews of the United States.

Despite the negative political stand of the French government, French personalities—sometimes in secret, sometimes with the government's knowledge—provided Israel with very important military equipment. The 65 millimeter guns that played such a vital part in the battle for the Jordan valley and were the I.D.F.'s main artillery prior to the first cease-fire, were sent from France, even before May 15, as illegal arms to Mandatory Palestine. Some of the first tanks came from France. It must be noted that the "air lift" from Czechoslovakia also had enjoyed the assistance of French friends of Israel; the first planes had nowhere to land on their way to Israel, but subsequently the intervention of a prominent Frenchman made it possible for them to land at a Corsican airfield.

The Security Council Deliberates

In view of the resumption of fighting at the end of the first ceasefire, the Security Council was again called upon to discuss the Palestine issue. Its chairman, D. Manuilsky of the Ukraine, invited both "the representative of the state of Israel" and the Arab Higher Committee representative, Jamal Hussaini, to take their seats. The Arab representative stated that he would not take part in the deliberations and left the meeting. Sir Alexander Cadogan, the delegate of the United Kingdom, took exception to the Council chairman's wording, and stated that his government "was retaining complete freedom of action on this matter." De la Tournelle, the French representative, also stated that his government was "reserving complete freedom of action." Because his government "had not recognized the state of Israel," he believed that the invitation to the representative of that government, as it had been worded, would make an already complex issue even more complicated.

Faris al Khour, the Syrian representative and a member of the Security Council, claimed that "the Security Council had never recognized the state of Israel," and expressed the hope that the Council chairman would address the representative mentioned as the representative of the Jewish Agency.

A lively debate ensued, focusing primarily on the question of the propriety of the chairman's move in inviting the Israel representative to confer on an equal basis with the Arab Palestinian representative, as one representing an officially recognized state. The chairman put the question of his procedure to a vote, and it was approved by the Council, with only five votes against it (Belgium, the United Kingdom, Syria, China, and Canada).*

* Corresponding to the position taken by the Soviet representatives on the wording of the invitation to Israel's representatives, A. Y. Bogomolov and D. Manulisky objected, in the political committee of the Assembly on October 23, 1948, to having the Palestinian

On July 15, the Security Council ordered (whereas the May 29 decision on the first cease-fire had said, "the Council demands") the cessation of fire and stoppage of all military activity in Palestine within three days. This was the first time that the Security Council had referred specifically to "the provisional government of Israel" rather than to "the Jewish authorities." It was also the first time that the Security Council had definitely established Arab responsibility for the war; it defined the situation in Palestine as "jeopardizing peace, according to Article 39 of the Charter," and threatened sanctions against the party defying the order.

As a result of the ten days of fighting the Arab representatives now agreed to the cease-fire, which began on July 18. This time the Council ordered a "cease-fire until a peace agreement is reached; and not merely a temporary truce."

Fighting in Galilee and the Negev

Thereafter, there was no regular fighting on all fronts, although battle developed here and there before the armistice agreements were signed.

Three months after the second cease-fire, fighting broke out again in the Negev. The Egyptians disobeyed the United Nations observers' conditions and refused to allow the passage of convoys to the Negev, which was still separated from the rest of Israel by an Egyptian roadblock (along the Ashkelon-Faluja highway). Apart from the difficulties of communication (by air) with the cut-off Jewish settlements it was imperative to foil any design to cut the Negev off from the rest of the country. On October 15, following notification by United Nations headquarters, a convoy of vehicles left for the Negev.

When it reached the positions near the Arab road block, it was attacked by the Egyptians. The United Nations representative present gave the Israelis permission to counterattack. In a vigorous and imaginative campaign, Israeli forces thereupon captured key positions and ensured direct communication with the Negev (Operation Yoav). Some Egyptian invading units were destroyed, and one of its brigades remained surrounded in the "Faluja pocket."* After a fierce five-hour battle, Beersheba, the Negev capital, was

Arab representatives invited as coming from "the all-Palestine government." Soviet delegates held tenaciously to the view that the November 29 decision called for the establishment of two states in Palestine, a Jewish one and an Arab one, within well-defined borders; while "The Palestinian State" mentioned in the application extended meant the area of Palestine before the end of the Mandate, not according to the boundaries set by the United Nations. For this reason, the Soviet representatives insisted that the Arab Higher Committee and not "The All-Palestine Government" be invited to attend the debate.

* Among the officers there was one Gamal Abd-ul-Nasser.

occupied on October 21. The encircled Egyptian forces were forced to evacuate the coastal strip between Ashdod and Bet Hanun near Gaza. The Israeli Army captured Majdal and Yad Mordechai. Egyptian forces now remained only in the Gaza-Rafah strip, along the desert road between Oja and Bir-Asluj, and in the Faluja pocket.

In the eastern mountain zone on the edge of Mount Hebron, Israeli forces took several areas that considerably widened the Jerusalem corridor (including a section of the railway from Nahal Sorek to Jerusalem) to Bet Jubrin in the south and Kfar Husan (10 kilometers from Bethlehem) in the east. These localities later served as the armistice line in this sector.

A week after the cease-fire again operated in the Negev, fighting was resumed in Galilee, where Fauzi Kaukji's troops still held an extensive enclave in the northern part of central Galilee. The Arab commander refused to acknowledge the United Nations cease-fire order and continued to attack Jewish settlements in the area. On October 29, Israeli forces began "Operation Hiram" to clear all Galilee of the invaders. Within sixty hours, the operation was completed. The so-called Arab "rescue army" managed to survive by escaping to Lebanon, leaving behind considerable spoils in vehicles and supplies. While pursuing the fugitives, Israeli forces entered Lebanese territory and captured 14 villages most of them parallel to the border.

In accordance with the Security Council decision of October 19, the cease-fire in the Negev began to operate once more on October 22. But Egyptian violations led to local clashes.* Although this cease-fire was now set for an unlimited period, it could not long endure while the armies were ranged against each other.

Count Bernadotte's Report and the United Nations Assembly

Israel's proposal to open peace negotiations, which was forwarded to the Arab countries on August 6 through the United Nations mediator, received no reply. Simultaneously with the military operations, the political campaign continued unabated. Following negotiation feelers extended to both parties, Count Bernadotte, the United Nations mediator, forwarded his report to the United Nations Secretary General on September 16. In substance he reaffirmed the "ideas" that he had put forward in June. The next day, as he crossed Jewish Jerusalem on his way to Government House in no-man's land, Count Bernadotte was assassinated by members of *Lehi* (Stern group).† His companion, Colonel Andre Serot of France, was also killed. The efforts of

---

* One of these operations was the occupation of the Iraq Suweidan police fort (near Negba), which Israeli forces had tried unsuccessfully to take many times. The "monster fortress" was captured on November 9, 1948.

† This organization (like the I.Z.L.) continued to exist in Jerusalem even after the provisional government's order of May 26 forbidding the existence of any armed force

the acting mediator, Dr. Ralph Bunche, to bring the parties to negotiate, were abortive. Despite the Security Council's appeals and the military defeats they suffered in the periodic resumption of fighting, the Arab states refused to embark upon armistice negotiations.

After his death, the mediator's report continued for a while to serve those from whom he had received his political inspiration. The Palestine question was again on the agenda when the annual session of the U.N. Assembly opened in Paris in September, this time to consider Count Bernadotte's report, which was unfavourable to Israel. It was supported by the British and U.S. delegations, who sought to secure the necessary two thirds majority for the adoption of a resolution different from that of 29th November, 1947 for the final settlement of the Palestine issue.

But Israel's victories on the battlefield blunted several of its recommendations. Galilee and Jaffa were no longer subjects for discussion. A compromise was suggested on the Arab refugee question—compensation for the abandoned property of those who did not want to return to Israel. But the report failed to lay down a policy for ultimate peace, and merely recommended that the cease-fire be replaced by an armistice. This meant that both sides would continue to maintain their armies, and also agree to demilitarized zones subject to U.N. supervision. For the invading Arab forces, this could import no surrender of territory, but for Israel it meant retreating from territory won at considerable sacrifice.

Moreover, international supervision over part of the country meant a virtual revival of that "trusteeship" which the U.S. had tried to force upon Palestine at the special session of the U.N. Assembly in the spring of that year. The provision on the removal of military forces and their demobilization was no less dangerous. It envisaged the return of Arab forces from Palestinian territory to neighboring countries there to establish a base for a further offensive on Israel, while the demobilization of the Israel army meant abandoning the State to those bent on its destruction. Instead of setting up an independent Arab state in the parts of Palestine outside Israel, the report proposed attaching these to the Kingdom of Jordan. In view of trends towards union between this country and Iraq, this would mean making Iraq Israel's neighbor within the actual boundaries of Palestine west of the Jordan. On the Jerusalem question, though the Jews had formerly accepted the U.N. decision, there was no foundation for transferring to Arab rule the Jewish city of Jerusalem which had paid a high price in blood and suffering

aside from the Israeli Army. Until then, Jewish Jerusalem had not been officially defined as part of Israel but was governed by a military governor. After the murder of the mediator and his escort, which complicated Israel's relations with the United Nations, the government ordered the dissolution of the "dissidents" in Jerusalem as well. About 200 members of *Lehi*, including the leaders and commanders of the organization, were arrested for its freedom. Internationalization was no longer practicable, in view of the U.N.'s inability to defend the city. Since Israel forces had defended Jewish Jerusalem and even succeeded in connecting it with the main body of the state by means of a wide corridor, there was no sense in refusing to declare Jerusalem, the eternal capital of the Jewish people, an inseparable part of Israel.

As regards the Arab refugees, there was nothing in the report to relieve the pressure on Israel. The armistice—merely technically and juridically another form of cease-fire—did not mean peace, but only another stage in the war between Israel and the Arab states, a war that had not yet ended. Israel was the victim not only of a "hot war" but also of a diplomatic and propaganda war of which the mediators' suggestions looked like one part and whose object was to rob the young state of what it held. The demand for the return of the refugees—accompanied in Arab circles by talk of a "second round" and the annihilation of Israel—was a material part of that political campaign. The Israeli government was unlikely to find support in the United Nations for its claim that the question of Arab refugees from Israeli territory—like the question of the Jews in Arab countries and the responsibility of each of the parties concerned for the war itself and its consequences should and could be dealt with only in the course of peace talks and the adjustment of future relations between Israel and its neighbors.

The principal danger threatening Israel concerned the future of the Negev, which Britain, openly and directly, and the United States, covertly and indirectly, were making continual efforts to detach from Israel. In that struggle Israel could at the time be certain of the support only of the Socialist-bloc representatives.

Ever since the first cease-fire, Soviet representatives had been making unavailing demands for the inclusion of military observers from the Socialist bloc in the United Nations Truce Supervision Organization, which was then "wholly Western." Nevertheless, Socialist-bloc support for Israel was effective. Thus, Jacob Malik on July 27 rejected Britain's demand to force "the Jewish authorities to release five British officials of the Jerusalem Electric Company" who were suspected of espionage. "This is an internal matter within the competence of the provisional government of Israel," claimed the Soviet representative. "We know from the press and from official sources that many British citizens bore arms and fought against Israel's army, not only as simple soldiers, but also as officers directing military operations, such as the infamous case of Glubb Pasha [the British commander of the Arab Legion]. Let us assume for a moment that tomorrow Glubb Pasha is taken prisoner by the Israeli Army: Will the Security Council be required to investigate the matter?"

At another session of the Security Council on August 2, Malik and Chairman Manuilsky opposed coming to a hasty decision on displaced persons and refugees before the Council had obtained sufficient and reliable information "on the situation of displaced persons of Jewish and Arab nationality in various parts of the world."

Support by the Socialist Bloc

When the mediator's report came up for debate at the United Nations Assembly in Paris, Socialist-bloc representatives rallied again to the support of Israel.

On October 19, the Security Council ruled that "Operation Yoav" had been a severe violation of the cease-fire. This time, the Council appointed a special subcommittee to report on the result of the battles. On November 4, it adopted the recommendation of that subcommittee that Israel should return to the pre-"Operation Yoav" cease-fire lines—in other words, that the Negev should again come under *de facto* Egyptian control—and be cut off from the state of Israel. Israel's representative in the Security Council, Abba Eban, argued that the Egyptian forces that had been expelled from the northern Negev were an invading army, while Israel's occupation of the Negev had been based on the United Nations Assembly decision. The Security Council's order that Israel should retreat to the previous cease-fire line would mean that the United Nations was approving the Egyptian invasion, which was in direct opposition to the Assembly decision.

Eban did not fail to indicate the connection between the Security Council's demand that Israel retreat from its Negev positions and the political plan discussed in the Assembly about cutting the Negev off from Israel, in contradiction to the November 29 decision. In the end, the Security Council appealed to both parties in Palestine to "work immediately for an agreement—whether through direct negotiations or through the acting mediator—to enforce an armistice in all parts of the country." Israel's agreement to this decision mitigated the severity of the criticism leveled at her for refusing to comply with the November 4 decision, which, of course, was enthusiastically accepted by Arab representatives.

Throughout the combined campaign against Israel in the Security Council and in the political committee of the Assembly (in which the mediator's report was considered), the Socialist-bloc representatives consistently supported Israel, calling on the Security Council not to content itself with a cease-fire or armistice but to help the parties achieve permanent peace in Palestine.

Soviet spokesman Malik noted in the November 1948 debate that "an armed cease-fire of unlimited duration involving the maintenance of large military units and tremendous expenditures is senseless and harmful to both the Arabs and the Jews." Tsarapkin asked, "Can the stubbornness and excessive vigor of the British government in its aspiration to force the United Nations to accept the mediator's proposals be explained by the desire to prevent the establishment of an independent Arab state in Palestine and instead to permit the British stooge Abdulla to annex, not only those parts of Palestine that should be included in the Arab state, but also the Negev, which belongs to the Jewish state?"

On November 24, 1948, Kisiliev launched a bitter attack on British policy, which aimed at "the annihilation of the Jewish state through the armies of the Arab countries." He also accused the United States of "trying to come to an agreement with Britain at the expense of the Jews." Both the United States and Britain, he said, "must take into account the existence of a Jewish state, whose rights have been confirmed, and which has been recognized *de jure* or *de facto* by eighteen governments. Like many states before it, Israel was born out of an armed struggle for freedom and independence. . . . The Soviet Union has always supported Arab aspirations, but today the Arabs are not fighting for their independence, but rather for Anglo-American oil interests aspiring to maintain a colonial regime in Palestine. Only by executing the November 29 decision can bloodshed be prevented and peace returned to the Middle East."

On behalf of the Soviet Union, Vishinsky summed up the attempts of the United States and British governments to sabotage the November 29 decision, described British attempts to control Palestine through Abdulla, and laid bare the coordinated manoeuvers of the United States and Britain in their attempts to turn the mediator and the mediation commission into a tool for the implementation of their trusteeship plans. Comparing British policy, which refrained from recommending friendship between the Jews and Arabs, with Soviet advocacy of peace and cooperation between them, Vishinsky called for the removal of foreign armies from Palestine, the cessation of the war, and the implementation of United Nations decisions for the benefit of the two peoples in Palestine and the prestige of the United Nations in the eyes of the entire world.

The Palestine Conciliation Commission (P.C.C.)

The Assembly ended its consideration of the mediator's report by passing with a vote of thirty-five to fifteen, the Anglo-American proposal for the constitution of a conciliation commission to consist of three United Nations members, who would take over some of the duties hitherto assigned to the mediator and "take immediate action to establish contact between the parties themselves, and between them and the commission, at the earliest possible date."* The commission was directed to prepare for the next Assembly "its

* The conciliation commission was later composed of representatives of the United

detailed proposals on a permanent international regime for the Jerusalem area and its environs" and also "its recommendations on the holy places in the rest of Palestine." The approved proposal also stated that "refugees who wish to return to their homes and live at peace with their neighbors are to be allowed to do so at the earliest practicable date," and that "compensation will be paid by the responsible authorities and governments, in accordance with the dictates of justice and international law, for the property of those who will prefer not to return, and for damage done to that property."

The resolution made no mention of the mediator's recommendations regarding the detachment of the Negev from the state of Israel and the transfer of Palestine's Arab areas to Transjordan.

Israel's request to be admitted to membership in the United Nations was not accepted at that plenary session. The French delegate, Parodi, noted, "it should not be forgotten that the Arabs oppose the state of Israel and that its boundaries have not yet been fixed." United Kingdom representative Cadogan demanded that the question of Israel's membership in the United Nations be indefinitely postponed. The United States delegate, Jessup, rejected the British demand and supported Israel's application. Soviet representative Malik declared that the recognition of Israel's right to be a member of the United Nations arose from the very essence of the partition decision. The Argentinian representative also expressed his government's opinion that the admission of Israel to the United Nations would greatly facilitate the solution of the Palestine problem. In the end, there were only five supporters (the United States, the Soviet Union, Argentina, the Ukraine, and Colombia). The Security Council minimum for adopting a favorable decision was seven votes.

Israel-Egypt Confrontation in the Negev

The United Nations Assembly session ended on December 12. Despite the demands of the United Nations Security Council and Assembly to begin negotiations on an armistice, the Arab states did not comply. Egypt continued to oppose the extension of Israel's *de facto* control over the southern Negev, in accordance with the November 29 decision. It was clear that unless Egypt, the largest and most important of the Arab states, were prepared to sign an armistice agreement with Israel, no other Arab country would dare to do so.

States, France, and Turkey. The British and Colombian representatives proposed adherence to the mediator's report, while the Socialist-bloc representatives insisted that it should try to implement the Assembly's November 29 decision (as proposed by Dr. Lange of Poland). The Socialist-bloc proposal was defeated by a vote of twenty-four to thirteen. Various motions to combine the Socialist-bloc proposal with the one offered by Britain and Colombia were also defeated (one by a vote of twenty-three to twenty-three, another by a vote of twenty-five to twenty-two).

When General Reilly, the chief of the United Nations Truce Supervision Organization, advised the Israeli government that the Egyptians were refusing to enter into armistice negotiations so long as the Israeli Army did not retreat to the pre-October 15 cease-fire line, the Israeli government decided to present the Egyptian government with the choice of armistice or a war in which Israel would aim at the definitive ejection of the Egyptian Army from the southern Negev, and the army's annihilation. Israel warned that the Egyptians would no longer be allowed to hold territory that was not theirs, while simultaneously enjoying the immunity of a cease-fire.

At noon on December 22, the Israeli Army launched "Operation Horeb." This began with a ground and air bombardment of Egyptian positions along the Rafah-Gaza line and Gaza.* The attack was mounted only in order to divert Egyptian attention from the Israeli alignment along the Beersheba-Aslug-al-Auja-al-Hafir (Nitzanim) road. Some Israeli units captured some key heights of Bir at-Tamila and al-Masharafa, and others advanced along the ancient road of Wadi-l-Abiad (White River) to the Auja-Rafah road. Auja was cut off and captured on December 27 and the Auja-Aslug road was thus cleared of Egyptian forces. On December 29, an Israeli armored column advanced into Egyptian territory, capturing Abu-Agila and the El-Arish airfield near the Mediterranean coast. A wedge was now driven between Egyptian forces in the Gaza area and their homeland; its enlargement would place the invading Egyptians in danger of encirclement.

The Egyptian government's efforts to get the other Arab states to join in were unsuccessful, but suddenly help for Egypt came from another direction; Britain intervened, though she had not been requested to do so by the Egyptians. On the basis of the 1936 Anglo-Egyptian treaty—which the Egyptians had long been fighting to cancel—His Majesty's Government stated that it felt called upon to help Egypt; it addressed to Israel an ultimatum to retreat immediately from Egyptian territory. Britain at that time, had no diplomatic relations with Israel, and her ultimatum was sent through the United States government. The President of the United States supported the British demand, attaching his "request" to the British ultimatum. Israeli forces were ordered to retreat from Egyptian territory before the morning of January 2, and they did so.

The Israeli Army was about to begin its attack on Rafah, at the Mandatory border between Palestine and Egypt, and the G.H.Q. of Egyptian forces. The capture of Rafah would seal the ring round the Egyptian forces in the Gaza

---

* According to Israeli military sources, between December 22 and January 7, the Israeli Air Force took part in 243 sorties, in which 226 tons of bombs were dropped on enemy objectives. The increased capacity of the Air Force is easily noted from the fact that while, in "Operation Yoav," the number of sorties was almost the same, the bombs dropped totalled only 151 tons.

strip and force them to surrender or to be destroyed. The Rafah attack began on January 4. Unexpectedly fierce Egyptian counterattacks and sandstorms in the combat zone disrupted the operation, which lasted till the evening of January 6 and was inconclusive. The same day, Egypt intimated that if Israel stopped its operation, she would be prepared to enter upon armistice negotiations. The Security Council, which eight days earlier had ordered a cease-fire, now increased its pressure on the Israeli government to desist from any military action, and on January 7, 1949, at 2 p.m. Israel accepted the order and the cease-fire began on the appointed date.*

Armistice Agreements

The Egyptian Army was saved, at the price of Egypt's agreement to open armistice negotiations with Israel. Though nothing of this nature was acknowledged overtly, the agreement was tantamount to an admission on the part of Egypt (with a population of about 19 million) that she had lost her war against the young state of Israel (with a population of less than three-quarters of a million). The Israeli-Egyptian negotiations initiated at Rhodes on January 12, with the participation of the United Nations acting mediator, ended on February 24 with the signing of an armistice agreement. Under the terms of the agreement, Israel allowed the forces bottled up in the Faluja pocket to return safely to their country. Egypt acknowledged Israel's ownership of the entire Negev, except for the Gaza strip.† The Auja-al-Hafir

* A few hours before the armistice, an incident took place that might have involved Israel in a war with Britain. Five British fighters from the Suez Canal Zone, which were circling above the battlefield to see whether Israeli forces were retreating from Egypt as they had been ordered to do, were shot down near Nirim by Israeli fighter planes and anti-aircraft artillery. Only then was it discovered that they were British Air Force planes. His Majesty's Government addressed strong demands for explanations and compensation to Israel and despatched British reinforcements to the Aqaba garrison. The President of the United States dissociated himself from the complaint of the British foreign office, and in Britain itself, Bevin came in for sharp criticism for unjustifiably endangering the lives of British pilots.

† The Gaza strip, ranging from Khan Yunis in the north to Rafah in the south, is 40 kilometers long and an average of 8 kilometers wide (maximum width, 14 kilometers, at Khan Yunis; minimum width, 5.5 kilometers at Deir-al-Balah), with an area of 340 square kilometers. The 1958 population of the strip was 300,000, including 12,000 Bedouins, some of whom were semi-nomadic; 215,000 were refugees. Except for 2,500 Christians, the population is wholly Moslem.

Half of the area is beach sand. Annual precipitation is 300 millimeters. Irrigation is done from wells, with motor- or animal-driven pumps. Cultivated land totals 150,000 dunams, on approximately 100,000 of which are grain crops, on 22,000 of which are vegetables (half of them irrigated), and on 12,000 of which are fruit trees (citrus, dates, almonds, guavas, sycamore figs). The 8,000 dunams of groves yield about half a million citrus cases, half of them for export. The Bedouins make their living chiefly from raising sheep and camels. About 1,000 are employed in fishing, and 500 in boat building,

(Nitzanim) area was demilitarized and made a headquarters of the mixed armistice commission.

Simultaneously with the armistice negotiations with Egypt, talks on similar agreements were opened with Lebanon and the Kingdom of Jordan. The agreement with Jordan encountered initial difficulties because of Jordanian insistence that the southern Negev, including Eilat, was theirs. To remove that obstacle, Israeli forces advanced on March 5 to Eilat, and on March 10 the Israeli flag was hoisted on the shores of the Red Sea.

Another Israeli unit, headed for Sodom on March 8, sailed north to Ein-Gedi, and the next morning occupied it and the promontory above it.

After these Negev operations had been completed, armistice agreements were concluded with Lebanon, Jordan, and Syria. The agreement with Lebanon was signed at Rosh Hanikra on March 23, 1949. Israel was holding fourteen Lebanese villages that had been occupied by her forces when they pursued the Kaukji army fleeing from Galilee ("Operation Hiram"). Israel demanded that in return for being allowed to evacuate these Lebanese villages, the Syrians should withdraw from the sector they had captured in the Mishmar Hayarden region. Israelis justified their demand by pointing to the fact that Syria and Lebanon had operated jointly against Israel, with Lebanese territory even providing the Syrians with a base of operations. This proposal was rejected by the United Nations mediator; Israel had to relinquish the Lebanese villages with no compensation under the armistice agreement, and the boundary remained as it was under the British Mandate.

The armistice agreement between Israel and the Kingdom of Jordan was signed at Rhodes on April 3, 1949. (It was officially signed at Rhodes, but the actual negotiations proceeded in the Shunah Palace in Transjordan with King Abdullah himself.) The cease-fire line in Jerusalem was agreed on as the border; in the Dead Sea-Eilat area, the Mandatory frontier was retained; Israel agreed that Jordanian forces would replace the Iraqis stationed between the

net making, and fish salting. Crafts include carpentry, pottery making, the manufacture of soap, weaving and dying, tanning, and art work. The strip also has a number of flour mills, with a daily capacity of five tons. The exports in 1957 to 1958 totalled about half a million Egyptian pounds. Half of the export was citrus, the rest almonds, castor beans, carpets, watermelon. Except for the citrus crop, the exports all went to Egypt. Imports were sugar, flour, rice, textiles, medicines, wood and iron, machinery and spare parts. The strip has 1,000 stores, of which 700 are in the city of Gaza, and 450 are members of the Chamber of Commerce. The deficit in the trade balance (about a million Egyptian pounds a year) is covered by the UNRRA, Egypt, and private philanthropic organizations (such as the Quakers). Until 1955, the customs borders between the strip and Egypt were strictly guarded, but since then there have been no restrictions on import and export between them.

Of the 65,000 schoolchildren at this time, 45,000 were in the schools of the United Nations Welfare and Employment agencies. The medical services employed thirty-five doctors (one for every 8,850 people).

Yarmuk and Rosh-Haayin (the Iraqis decided to withdraw their troops from Palestine without signing an armistice agreement with Israel). In return for Israel's acceptance of this arrangement (which meant the extension of Abdullah's rule in the western and southern foothills of the Hebron mountains),* Jordan ceded to Israel the Wadi-Ara strip, sections along the Hedera-Afula road, and several villages in the Sharon plain and the Jerusalem area. There was also agreement concerning free movement on roads vital to both parties (including the Bethlehem road for the Arabs, and the Latrun-Jerusalem road for the Jews); agreement on the resumption of work in the Jewish cultural and medical institutions on Mount Scopus, and free access to them from Jewish Jerusalem; on free access to the holy places and the use of the cemetery on the Mount of Olives; on the Latrun pumping station; on the supply of electricity from Jewish Jerusalem to the Old City held by Jordan; and on the operation of the railway to Jerusalem. None but the last provision took effect.

When the agreement with the Kingdom of Jordan was reported to the Knesset the next day, it evoked considerable opposition from both the left and right, because the Knesset had not been consulted before signing; because the agreement implied recognition by Israel of the Hashemite Kingdom of Jordan and its control of areas west of the Jordan, before this had been done by any international agency (neither the conciliation commission, nor any Arab state, nor even Great Britain, had formally gone quite so far), and because the agreement meant that Bevin had returned to Palestine by the back door.

The critics' consensus was that the agreement was not a purely "military accord," as Ben-Gurion presented it, but a far-reaching political act. Reasons and attitudes varied widely. The left opposition, Mapam, stressed that the agreement perpetuated the country's partition, precluded an alliance between Israel and an independent democratic Arab state that might lead to the reunification of Palestine, and extended Anglo-American imperialism into part of Palestine—since Abdullah's was no more than a vassal state. The right-wing Herut party contended that by acknowledging the presence of the Hashemite Kingdom of Jordan on both sides of the Jordan, "the Israeli government had relinquished to the satellite-king an enormous area of the western part of the homeland, and actually ceded it not to him but to his British masters." Even the moderate General Zionist representative in the Knesset wondered "whether this did not mean renouncing all possibilities of an independent Arab state in that part of Palestine," while "from the point of view of our

* Under a secret agreement between the Israeli government and King Abdullah, the king was to have been enabled to annex to his territory the areas west of the Jordan that were to have been included in the Palestine Arab state, upon a peace treaty between Israel and Transjordan.

national and political future it is very important that an independent Arab state should be established." Tewfik Toubi, the Communist member, noted that the agreement in effect recognized the rule of a British colony over that part of the country in which an independent state was to have risen. The policy of making an alliance with a Jordanian vassal instead of helping to establish an independent Arab state in Palestine was the "crowning glory" of the policy consistently adopted by Ben-Gurion to prevent the establishment of an independent Arab state in Palestine. After a stormy debate in the Knesset, the opposition motions were defeated, and the government statement was confirmed.

Israeli and Jordanian forces proceeded to occupy their respective new positions under the agreement. The only effective benefit to Israel was that the Wadi-Ara road was opened to Israeli traffic and the Israeli railway could now serve Jerusalem.

After three and a half months of difficult negotiations, an Israeli-Syrian armistice agreement was signed in a tent in no-man's land near Mahanayim on July 20, 1949. At first, the Syrians had refused to give up the area they had taken in Mishmar Hayarden; later they agreed to retreat to the Jordan, but not to the Mandatory border, which was further east. In the end, both sides accepted the compromise proposed by the United Nations mediator, whereby the area the Syrians held would be demilitarized, as would be Dardara and Ein Gev, two Israeli settlements east of the Hulah and the Sea of Tiberias (the Syrians claimed that if they were not demilitarized, the two settlements might serve as bridgeheads from which the Israelis could threaten their security). The civil administration and manner of supervision by United Nations observers in these demilitarized zones was agreed upon after further negotiations.

With the conclusion of the Israeli-Syrian armistice agreement, Israel's war of independence was formally terminated.

In the last phase of the war (from the beginning of the second cease-fire on July 18, 1948, until the armistice agreements were signed), 2,123 Israeli soldiers were killed in combat. In all, the war lasted about twenty months; between November 29 and May 15 it was more or less continuous, while from the invasion of the Arab armies to the signing of the armistice, there were about sixty-one actual days of fighting. Israeli casualties totaled 6,000 dead, including 4,074 soldiers, and many wounded. The cost of the war to Israel—other than damage to property and indirect expenditure—was about $500 million.

The Egyptian Minister of War confirmed in June 1950 that the Egyptian casualties in the 1948/49 War were 5,731, of whom 1,500 were killed, including 137 officers. The War cost £35,000,000 over and above regular security budgets. Casualties of other Arab States are not known. Iraq spent about £13,000,000, more than half of all Government expenditure in 1948/49. To cover this deficit, social service costs were reduced and indirect taxes increased.

The State of Israel in the United Nations

On March 3, 1949, the Security Council again considered Israel's application to be admitted to the United Nations. By a majority of nine, the Council decided on March 5 to recommend to the Assembly that Israel be accepted as a member. Only Egypt voted against the recommendation, while Great Britain abstained.

On May 11, the United Nations General Assembly decided that since Israel was a peace-loving country, accepting the obligations contained in the United Nations Charter and willing and able to carry them out, she should be admitted to membership in the United Nations Organization.

This decision was passed by a vote of thirty-seven to twelve, with nine abstentions. Those voting against admission were the six Arab states (Egypt, Iraq, Syria, Lebanon, Saudi Arabia, and Yemen), and Afghanistan, Burma, India, Ethiopia, Pakistan, and Persia. Those who abstained were the United Kingdom, Belgium, Brazil, Denmark, Greece, San Salvador, Siam, Sweden, and Turkey.

After the chairman had announced the results of the vote, the head of the Israeli delegation, M. Sharett, was invited to make his maiden speech in the Assembly. The Arab delegations left the hall in protest. The flag of Israel was at last raised among those of the United Nations.

The "Miracle" and Its Explanation

The establishment of the state of Israel in the face of such fierce opposition by most Arabs in and out of Palestine, as well as by the British government and that of the United States of America at a critical period, is one of the wonders of political life in our times. Some simply call it a miracle. But "miracles" do not happen in our day and age if they have no substantive objective foundation. The elucidation of these historical foundations is not without relevance for an understanding of the relations between Israel and the Arab world in the present and in the future. What, then, were the sources of the "miracle"? How can it be explained?

A. Social and historical factors

Does the victory of the outnumbered Jews fighting with light arms against tanks, and the defeat of the Arabs in the 1948 to 1949 battles mean that the Arabs are "generally" an inferior people and the Jews superior? Fighting

The armistice lines, 1949

ability is not in itself a national characteristic; this can be illustrated by comparing the French record in two world wars in which they were once victorious and once defeated. The French debacle of 1940 does not signify that they were cowards. In 1917, the same Russian soldiers who had deserted the front in protest against a pointless war, returned a few months later and though they were now hungry and barefooted, they fought bravely and successfully against the forces of intervention whose purpose was to destroy the young Soviet state.

The Arabs of Palestine remembered the bloody riots of earlier years. The solution to the Palestine problem arrived at by the United Nations seemed to many of them a peaceful way out of the impasse. The war waged by the Arab leaders was not a defensive but an aggressive war, which did not arouse much enthusiasm or create any psychological ability to attack. The Jews were, however, fighting in the realization that they were defending their very lives.

As David Ben-Gurion said at a Mapai conference in February 1948, "This war was declared without asking the Arab people in whose name it is being waged. Moreover, most of the Arab people in Palestine are now refusing to take part in it, despite the increasing pressure on them."[4]

The military victories of the Jews in the first phase of the war were the outcome, in no small part, of the Palestinian Arab masses' nonparticipation in the war. This explains why, although the number of Arabs in Palestine was double that of the Jews, the Arab leaders had to import fighters from abroad, and it was these foreign elements—and not Palestinian Arabs—who were the mainstay of the war. But even in the neighboring countries, up to the invasion only a few thousand Arabs volunteered. The statements of Ahmad Sharabati, the Syrian minister of war, on "70,000 fighters to save Palestine" notwithstanding, Kaukji's army (the "Rescue Army") never numbered more than 5,000 to 6,000 men. Quite apart from "quality," the forces at the disposal of the Jews were numerically greater than those available to the Arabs at that stage.

Not only did the majority of the Arabs in Palestine refuse to participate in the war, as David Ben-Gurion correctly stated, but even before Jewish fighting power had increased, there were many Arab settlements that closed their doors to anti-Jewish mischief by Arab provocateurs. There were many instances of Arabs who, by "diplomatic means," and sometimes even by armed resistance, prevented the conversion of their settlements into bases for attacks on neighboring Jewish settlements.* Those segments of the rural and

* For example, the Arab village of Zubaidat, on the ridge overlooking kibbutz Shaar Haamakim and the Haifa-Nazareth road, was for a long time subjected to pressure to shelter a unit of the "Rescue Army" that sought to attack the Jewish settlements and communications in the neighborhood. The village elders explained to the instigators that

urban Arab population that showed willingness to cooperate with Arab fighting forces (chiefly from a belief in their speedy victory) were not at all prepared for any considerable or continued resistance, especially when victory ceased to appear quite so sure. Furthermore, while the Jewish public presented a solid front in its defensive war, there were considerable elements among the Arabs, especially in the Arab intelligentsia (the League for National Liberation, some parts of the Palestine Arab Workers Union, groups in contact with *Hashomer Hatzair* and left *Poalei Zion* and others) that stood aside and did not help in the war. After the November 29 vote and the Soviet Union's support of the partition solution, some of these groups even opposed the war overtly, revealing its underlying motives, stating that these were opposed to the true interests of the Arabs, and calling for the cessation of the war and the implementation of the United Nations decision.*

B. *Military ability*

The members of the Jewish defense force came from an advanced and progressive society, with the consequent advantage over the educationally and technically backward Arab soldiers, who were part of a more retarded social system. The necessity for the Jews to defend their very existence and their endeavor in Palestine over years before the war—this is what converted tens of thousands of absolutely peace-loving Jews into experienced soldiers, ready to join battle whenever called upon to do so. The experience with the British taught the Jews that even in "good times" the fate of the Jewish

they could not become involved in a war against their Jewish neighbors, for they got water from their pipes, and used their roads, workshops, and medical facilities. When pressure on them increased, they reported the development to their Jewish neighbors, and helped the *Hagana* capture the site before "the foreigners" could do so. The village residents then left until things quieted down. When Israeli military units later wished to blow up the village ("for security reasons"), the neighboring Jewish settlements interfered and prevented the action. After the war, the villagers were allowed to come back to their houses.

* At a later stage (the summer of 1948), leaflets of the Arab Communist parties were dropped on the Egyptian, Iraqi, and Jordanian zones of occupation in Palestine; these leaflets stated that the Palestinian Arabs had not asked for Arab League intervention and urged that the soldiers of the other Arab nations return to their countries and turn their guns on the warmongers and their cohorts. The leaflets also called for a joint Arab-Jewish war "to liberate the country from imperialism and its satellites, and build a new Palestine in cooperation with the Jewish people."

Despite nationalist terrorism and the presence of the Egyptian forces, a leftist underground led by Communists operated in the Hebron area during the summer of 1948. When the Israeli Army captured Abu-Agila from the Egyptians on December 29, 1948, they found in a concentration camp there a large group of prisoners from the Arab leftist circles of the Old City of Jerusalem and Jaffa, who had been caught in Gaza and Majdal. Because they supported the United Nations decision and opposed the Arab League war against Israel, they had been accused of "national treason."

community and its achievements cannot be placed in the hands of the rulers of Great Britain. The development of the Jewish defensive strength, further-more, became an inseparable part of Jewish life in Palestine. When World War II came, thousands of Palestinian Jews took part in the fight against Nazi Germany as recruits in the (Jewish) supernumerary police, in preparation (together with the British Army) for a possible temporary occupation of Palestine by the Axis in 1942 to 1943; later they fought in the Jewish brigade, and in the illegal *Hagana*, *Palmach*, etc. All these organizations provided soldiers and trained officers for medium and low tactical command. Many Jews arriving in Palestine after the war had had military schooling in the armies, and partisan groups had fought the Nazis in Eastern Europe. All these brought with them important military know-how. The extensive operations involved in settlement, illegal immigration, and forging Jewish defensive strength during the period of struggle against the edicts of the White Paper were also a training ground for the Jews. Here they gained experience in planning and implementation, and expertise in matters of military technique and administration. The technical schools in Palestine (such as the Hebrew Technion) made their contribution to the training of military specialists in the departments involving technical knowledge (mines, communications, etc.). Towards the end of the war, Jewish volunteers from abroad also made their impact felt.

In the sixty years of its existence the Zionist movement had created and maintained a great variety of economic, financial, and administrative enter-prises under public control. These included cooperative projects, transport companies, building projects (*Solel Boneh*), health services (the *Histadrut* Sick Fund, *Hadassah*), and above all, a network of rural settlements scattered all over the country. All these gave the Jews important advantages and served as the chief bases for the "miracle" of the war of independence. The Arabs had nothing comparable to such backing. Moreover, the Arab combatants, suffered from weak organization, poor general education and technical knowledge, inadequate training, and inefficient command. These weaknesses in the period before the invasion by regular Arab armies may be summed up as follows:

1. Multiple uncoordinated military frameworks resulting from internal political divisions, differed in structure and organization and were without a single operational command.

2. The High Arab military commanders were for the most part political adventurers, not trained military leaders.

3. Syrian and Iraqi officers at tactical command levels had received their military training in the British and French armies (a few also in the German Army), but found themselves unable to apply their military lessons to the type of units under their command.

4. there were hardly any lower tactical commands (such as squad and company commanders); because of the inability of supporting units to execute missions entrusted to them, even well planned actions failed.

5. Arab offensive strategy was improvised, not planned. Even their most successful actions were fortuitous, and whatever gains won were never properly exploited.

6. even as there was no real operational planning, so, too, tactical operations were basically faulty; they attempted to utilize for regular military operations soldiers who were at best fit only for guerrilla warfare.

Yet the geographical-military situation was decidedly in the Arabs' favor, as were the restraints placed on the strategic, operational, and tactical initiative of the Jewish forces, the quantity and quality of the Arab arms—vastly superior to those of the Jews—their large manpower reserves, and the extensive British aid given them at that stage in the war.

This summary omits one important aspect of the problem during the early stages of the fighting: the technical basis for the production and repair of arms and supply of ammunition. On March 23, 1948, General Ismail Safuat, the commander-in-chief of the Arab forces fighting in Palestine reported to the Arab League's Palestine committee:

> The Jews have set up many and varied workshops and factories in which they are manufacturing armored cars, tanks, ammunition for light weapons, mortars, and spare parts for all kinds of arms. They also have many garages for the repair of vehicles, and workshops for the repair of arms. The equipment in these plants is complete, and they are run by engineers and skilled workmen. In contrast, we have nothing at all of this sort, not even a little plant to repair arms. In order to ensure the necessary repairs, we must have recourse to Syrian army installations. This naturally causes many difficulties, such as the transport of arms from Palestine to Damascus for repair, and much consequent waste of time.*

When the invasion of regular armies began there was primarily a quantitative change in the situation. But qualitatively nothing very much changed: Their armies continued to be armies of oppressed and downtrodden soldiers unwilling to sacrifice their lives for their masters and for a cause not their own. The educational and technical standard of the "regular" Arab soldiers was no different from that of the semi-regular "Rescue Army" soldiers, or from that of the early irregular Arab forces. Gamal Abd-ul-Nasser reports in his memoirs that he asked an Egyptian soldier in a Palestinian battlefield whether he knew where he was, and was told, "in the training grounds in Egypt." Whereas such soldiers were not uncommon in the Arab armies, it is doubtful whether even a few like them could be found in the Jewish forces.

* From an official report by an Iraqi Parliamentary commission on the Palestinian War. On September 4, 1949, the commission submitted its report—a document of 54 pages with 184 pages of appendix—to the speaker of the Iraq Parliament.

Thus the social composition of the Arab army, the class distinction between the soldiers and their officers, the relations between the commanders and their men, inadequate military training, inferior discipline, poor military intelligence,* the neglect of the wounded and maimed, intrigues among the army chiefs themselves, the detachment of the army from its rear, the absolute dependence on foreign countries for the supply of all arms and ammunition—these undermined the efficacy of the regular Arab armies.

Political circumstances imposed further limitations on the Arabs. The Jews fought as one people, led by a single supreme political and military command and supported by the Jewish community (which identified so completely with the war that the division between front and rear was virtually obliterated) and by world Jewry prepared to offer every assistance; the Arabs, on the other hand, were fighting as a conflict-ridden coalition of states, each of which had its own political aspirations and plans aimed simultaneously at the enemy (Israel) and against a partner in the coalition (Egypt-Jordan; Iraq-Syria). This political situation prevented the establishment of a single or joint command and a single or joint operational and tactical plan.†

* In an article published in the Egyptian *Rose Al Yousuf*, General Nagib stated, "We knew nothing about the Jews. We knew everything about foreign armies, except for the army of the Jews and those of our Arab allies."

† According to Jon and David Kimche (in their book, *On Both Sides of the Hill* (London, 1960), p. 162), the number of soldiers in the invading armies was as follows (on May 15, 1948):

Egypt	10,000
Arab Legion	4,500
Syria	3,000
Iraq	3,000
Lebanon	3,000 (including the 2,000 Rescue Army men under Kaukji's command)

The authors give the following estimates of Israeli and Arab combatants on the main fronts as of May 15:

	ISRAELIS	ARAB TROOPS
South	5,000	5,000 Egyptians
Far South and Hebron	1,500	4,000 Egyptians
Jerusalem and the corridor	4,500	4,000 Arab Legion
		1,000 Egyptians
Central Front (Tel Aviv-Natanya)	3,000	3,000 Iraqis
North	5,000	3,000 Syrians
		1,000 Lebanese
		2,000 Rescue Army
	19,000	23,000

According to the same source, the number of active *Hagana* members on the day of invasion was 35,000, including all auxiliary services. (The figure given by the *Hagana* chief, Y. Galili, was 28,760, excluding the various auxiliary services.) Combat troops numbered about 25,000.

Since each Arab army operated separately (sometimes even enjoying the defeat suffered by some other Arab army), the Arabs had no opportunity of deploying their troops according to the considerations of general interest—moving troops from section to section and building up decisive concentrations of strength in ground or air operations. After the first cease-fire, the Israeli Army was able to confront and defeat each Arab separately, the rest keeping out of the fight.

Individual Arab armies were incapable of fully exploiting the military equipment at their disposal and were hampered by the inadequate training of their soldiers (especially in the type of warfare prevailing—night fighting and modern guerrilla warfare), by weak command at all levels, and by conservative tactics much inferior to the daring and dynamic approach of the Israeli Army.

In the Arab war summaries and analyses by experts, there is an understandable inclination to justify their failures by stressing their disadvantages. However, without minimizing the significance of Arab handicaps, it behoves us to mention one more factor that tipped the scales of the war, a factor of prime importance: the fighting spirit, the enthusiasm and boundless willingness to sacrifice, shown by the Jewish soldier. Such acts of courage, bravery, and devotion as the Jews showed in this war are rare in modern warfare, and it was this that told in the final reckoning.

C. The stability of the rear

In contrast to the unity and strong organization of the Jewish community in Palestine, the Arab rear began to crumble with astonishing speed even in the first stages of the war.

A few months of armed struggle in Palestine were sufficient to upset the Arab economy. In the last years of British rule, about a quarter of the Arab population had earned its living in government and army installations. The thousands of Arabs who were discharged from these jobs had lost their livelihood. The stream of capital from the Jewish sector likewise stopped. With the flight of the prosperous Arabs (and they were the first to leave), the consumer demand remaining after Jewish markets had been closed to Arab products became even more restricted. Employment and general economic activity ground to a halt. The "volunteers" who had come from neighboring countries to fight in Palestine had been promised spoils from Jewish property "after victory;" unable to obtain the promised Jewish property, many members of these foreign bands reached out for the possessions of the Palestinian Arabs. "The Arab and foreign volunteers who came to Haifa to fight for an Arab victory," wrote Elias Kussa, the Haifa Arab leader, "were a great disappointment to its residents: They behaved arrogantly, treated the local population with contempt, and indulged in acts of robbery and plunder. All complaints to the 'public committee' in Damascus that had sent these volunteers were in vain."

Clearly this increased the desperation—and the flight of many of the veterans in Haifa continued in an unabated stream. During the panicky flight from Jaffa, there was wild looting by Syrian and Iraqi troops. In Jerusalem organized gangs (mainly from Hebron) carried out robberies in the city. In the Arab areas of Jerusalem there were not a few cases of shop-breaking and robbing of stores by Syrians and Iraqis. From rural districts as well, there were reports of banditry and robbery.

What were the reasons for the panicky flight of the Arabs?

One reason for their flight was the feeling that the balance of power in Palestine had changed radically, and that the Jewish community of the 1948 war was no longer that of 1936. In his evidence to the Anglo-American commission in 1946, Jamal al-Hussaini could still boast, "Leave us alone with the Jews and the problem will be solved with fists." Nevertheless, in June 1946, the Arab League conference in Bludan passed the famous "secret" resolution on the intervention of the Arab League countries in Palestine. In any case, at the time of the November 1947 United Nations vote, Arab leaders were already planning the assistance of the neighboring Arab countries and were no longer relying on the "fists" of Jamal al-Hussaini's supporters in Palestine. Despite the Arab League's declaration that "if no international military forces are sent to Palestine [to implement the partition plan], there will be no military intervention on the part of the Arab countries either," the Kaukji "Rescue Army" was mostly composed of non-Palestinians. It became quickly apparent that this army, too, was not capable of "rescue," and hopes now were pinned on an invasion by the regular armies of neighboring countries on the termination of the Mandate.

The Palestinian Arabs were well aware of the real internal Arab situation— the inefficiency of a corrupt leadership, the organizational helplessness, the paucity of funds, the ineptness of nationalist phraseology and propaganda, the total uselessness of an immature press. They were also aware of the conflicts and disagreements within Arab ruling circles in the neighboring countries and their impact on any military campaign. The Jews' full military preparedness added to Arab feelings of depression. The first serious clashes between the Arabs and Jews, the defeats suffered by the "Rescue Army" shortly after its arrival in Palestine, the repulse of the attacks on Yehiam (January 20) and Tirat Zvi (February 16), the Jewish success in Jerusalem (April 3–15), the failure of the heavy assaults on Mishmar Haemek (April 4–12) and Ramat Yohanan (April 13–16), the *Hagana* occupation of Tiberias (April 18) and Haifa (April 22) and of contiguous areas of eastern Galilee, the Jordan valley, the Bet Shean valley, and the south—all these disappointments convinced the Arabs that the Jews were winning, and impelled them to flee.

Not only the progressive, politically-minded Arabs avoided participating in these events this time and were basically opposed to them, seeing the U.N. decision of November 29th as opening up the hope of removing the complex and wearisome Palestine problem out of the dead end in which it was situated; the simple Arab saw no purpose in this new bloodshed, in which in any case, they could not convince the Jews. Europe was saying that the English want a new Punjab in Palestine. For some time the Arab Higher Committee continued its hackneyed propaganda, albeit with meagre success. The Arab masses remained unconvinced. Their plan was firstly to start with acts of terror primarily in the main centres, by 'professional' terrorists, which would create a blood feud between the Jews and the Arabs and rouse among the Arabs a feeling of self-defense driving them to war.

Inflated propaganda describing "splendid Arab victories" (even after recurrent defeats) was meant to stimulate a warlike attitude. But most of these efforts were ineffective. The great majority of local Palestinian Arabs watched from the sidelines as passive observers. Those who sought to incite war in Palestine realized that it was imperative to bring in fighters from abroad.

A rift developed between the foreign "Rescue Army" and the Arabs of Palestine. The "rescuers" extended their control to the "triangle" and other Arab regions. While the expiring British administration appeared to acknowledge this domination, Palestinian Arabs themselves viewed the foreign "rescuers" with mixed feelings. Conflicts between local Arabs and the "Rescue Army" on matters of housing and supply, and even authority, were common occurrences. Arab books on the Palestine war,* cite interesting facts that indicate the refusal of the "Rescue Army" to help the Palestinian forces when they were in a critical situation. They not only refused to help them, but local fighters often had to expel "rescuers" who stole, confiscated, and looted Arab arms and property. There are stories of rape, violence, and murder committed against the local Arab population. According to Muhammad Nimr Al-Khatib, the Arabs of Jaffa began to fear the "Rescue Army" more than they feared the Jews. There were little more than crocodile tears shed among Palestinian Arabs over the successive defeats of the "rescuers" by the Jewish forces. In their heart of hearts, many Palestinian Arabs hoped that such defeats would shorten the duration of the war and the suffering it caused.

"The Arabs were scared to death at the idea that the Jews might do to them only half of what their people would have done to the Jews if the situation were reversed," was the explanation given by a British sergeant to an

* E.g., *Karithat Falastin* (the Holocaust of Palestine) (Baghdad, 1949), *Min Athar an-Nakba* (After the Catastrophe), by Muhammad Nimr Al-Khatib (Damascus, 1957), etc.

American newspaperman on the day that Jaffa fell to the *Hagana*. This is a telling remark on the psychological aspects of the problem. An educated Haifa Arab expressed the same viewpoint in a somewhat different manner: "The Arabs thought that they were a backward, wild, and uncivilized people capable of anything, while the Jews were a civilized people who could control their emotions; the Dair Yassin horror [see note on page 424] made them begin to think that it was not so. As the Jews appeared to emerge victorious from the battlefield, the flight began."

The panic that overtook the Arabs was largely caused by the Arab Higher Committee itself. But the Arab Higher Committee propaganda was not content with terrorism and threatened military invasion by Arab forces from the neighboring countries, declaring, "In a very short time, the armies of our Arab sister countries will overrun Palestine, attacking from the land, the sea, and the air, and they will 'settle accounts' with the Jews." Arab propagandists could not envisage the possibility of "Arabs under Jewish rule." They frightened the Arabs into believing that "when the invasion came, they were likely to be hostages in Jewish hands, when they [the Jews] began to get what was coming to them." For masses of Arabs, whose great desire was not to get mixed up in this hopeless war, even the bullets and bombs of the Arab forces did not appeal to them. Threatening propaganda, like the horror-propaganda of the Arab Higher Committee, was not likely to make them stay in their own places. The general assumption was that a great blood-bath was approaching and the sooner one could get away, the better. Thus the propaganda of the Arab Higher Committee inevitably prompted massive panicky flight. Already in the early months of the struggle, Arabs had begun leaving the mixed cities to take up residence with relatives and friends in the purely Arab towns (such as Nazareth, Jenin, Acre, Tul-Karm) or in the country relatively far away from the centre of the struggle. People of means who could leave for one of the neighboring countries preferred to wait there "till the storm subsides." At the end of January—two months after the beginning of hostilities in Palestine—the number of Palestinian Arabs who had moved to neighboring countries was estimated at about 30,000 to 40,000. Before the *Hagana* took control of Haifa (on April 22), less than one half of its Arab residents remained in the city. "People believed that they were going to their relatives' homes for a few days or weeks, at most, and that the Arab armies were coming to rescue their country and return them to their motherland."*

The "low morale" of the Arab population as a whole was also a significant factor. The Jews were grimly determined to win or perish, but the Arabs could not possibly presume or acknowledge that they, too, were fighting with their "backs to the wall."

* Taki-Ad-Din An-Nabhani, *Inkadh Falastin* (The Rescue of Palestine) (Damascus, January, 1950).

Mass hysteria is contagious. "One family in the street leaves and all the women begin to pester their men to leave also," an Arab explained to his Jewish friend who wondered at the flight. "In the end, you also follow suit."

The Jew asked his Arab friend if the flight were carried out in accordance with instructions of the Arab Higher Committee. "In this case," came the reply, "the Arab Committee is being falsely accused. But people don't ask. They just run away, with no instructions and no order. Our women are hysterical, they have no character, and they're not prepared to endanger themselves; the men, for the most part, are not looking for a fight and do not want to leave the women and children alone. They are afraid of a second edition of Dair Yassin, even though everything indicates that the Jews behave well. Our people are even more afraid of the outbreak of a bloody battle when the armies of the Arab countries come back and retake Haifa."[5]

At a later stage, the Arab leaders tried to change their tactics and prevent the flight of the Arab population. Now they called for "fighting the fifth columnists and rumor-mongers that are causing the flight of the Arab population;" but their influence did not prevail in the face of the growing tension that spread outside the borders of the Jewish state and the areas of military activity and reached its climax as May 15 approached. On May 10, Radio Jerusalem broadcast (in Arabic) orders issued by Arab commanders and the "National committee" to stop the massive Arab flight from Jerusalem and its vicinity, Azam Pasha, the Arab League secretary, King Abdullah, and the various "national committees" appealed to the Arabs not to leave their homes. The Ramallah commander threatened to confiscate the property and blow up the houses of those who left without permission. The national committee in Ramle set up sentries on the city borders to prevent a mass exodus. Exit permits were given only to those few wealthy residents who made a payment to the committee. To the complaint that most of the members of the Arab Higher Committee and the local "national committees" had gone, it was replied that they had left on national business and would return.

At one point, the Lebanese government decided to close its frontiers to all Palestinians except for women, children, and old people. One of the Haifa national committee members complained that, while this was a very good decision, the government should also expel the rich Arabs who had fled Israel when the disturbances broke out and were now living a life of luxury and preaching nationalism. The chairman of the Haifa national committee, Rashid Haj Ibrahim, protested against the distinction between rich and poor when "the real distinction was between those with a conscience and those without." The leftist representative on the committee replied that simple impecunious folk did not run off to Sofar (a charming, expensive Lebanese summer resort) even when their conscience was not very good, while rich people frequently found reasons to justify their trips—sometimes even national reasons (a reference to some of the members of the Haifa national committee who had been "temporarily" in Lebanon for months, and whose return the committee had demanded in vain).

Don Peretz, an American lecturer in Middle Eastern history, provided the following description of the Arab domestic conditions contributing to the development of the refugee problem:

In the Arab community there was no quasi-government and few elected administrators. As a result there was little experience or training in self-rule. There was only a national sentiment, voiced through various Arab political parties which were grouped around personalities or families, rather than based on issues or tangible political and administrative organs. Nearly all functions of government in Arab areas were under the direct control and administration of British mandatory officials. Early in the Palestine fighting, the leaders of national sentiment left the country. When the British administration departed some weeks later, there was no organized Arab body to manage the services of government essential for communal organization. With the breakdown of all functions of government necessary to maintain law, order and well-being—water, electricity, posts, police, education, health, sanitation, and the like—Arab morale collapsed. The community became easy prey to rumour and exaggerated atrocity stories. The psychological preparation for mass flight was complete. The hysteria fed upon the growing number of Jewish military victories. With most Arab leaders then outside the country, British officials no longer in evidence, and the disappearance of the Arab press, there remained no authoritative voice to inspire confidence among the Arab masses and to check their flight. As might be expected in such circumstances, the flight gathered momentum until it carried away nearly the whole of the Palestine Arab community.[6]

Against the background described above, the "good advice" of the "neutral" British added fuel to the flames: "The British commander in Tiberias, Colonel Anderson, repeatedly told the Arabs that he would not be able to protect them from the Jews, and that they would share the fate of the Arabs of Dair Yassin. By persuasion and threats, the Army succeeded in getting the Arabs to leave the city. The evacuation took some days and was carried out under the supervision of the [British] Army and with its active help."[7]

On the day Haifa was taken by the Jews, some Haifa Arabs related, while the Jews were calming the Arabs and promising them that they would be able to stay in the city and live there in peace once the gangs were chased out, the English were sowing panic among the Arabs and advising them to "flee to the port, where the British Army could protect them from slaughter by the Jews." Later, with unparalleled speed, they provided transportation for the removal of 15,000 people from the Haifa area. Upon the advice of the British, a *Hagana* man reported, the Arabs evacuated Balad ash-Sheik, Hauasa, and Arab Yajur (April 23), against the advice of *Hagana* people, who urged them to stay where they were after relinquishing their arms and disbanding the gangs.

In an open letter to the *Jerusalem Post* (February 6, 1949), the lawyer Elias Kussa, a Haifa Arab leader, revealed the hypocrisy of Bevin in trying to brush off all responsibility for the flight of the Arabs and blame it all on the Jews:

Although the Israel military forces destroyed certain Arab villages and carried out wholesale transportation of the occupants, yet the primary responsibility for the panicky flight of the Arabs is the British Government's. Whether intended or not, there can be no doubt that the mischief originated from the conduct of the British, and not from the attitude of the Israel Government.

There is ample evidence for this statement. The sequence of occurrences showed that the British Government had no intention or desire to enforce law and order and that the Palestine administration was labouring to create an atmosphere permeated with fear and alarm. . . . They allowed a large force of armed Arabs to infiltrate into the country and roam about with impunity. Palestine was virtually converted into two antagonistic armed camps under the eyes and nose of the Mandatory Power. Huge quantities of arms and ammunition were openly smuggled in and recruiting and drilling of combatants became commonplace events. The Authorities tacitly encouraged the inhabitants to carry fire-arms, and to set up barricades and fortifications in towns, villages and settlements. . . .

The idea that the Arabs should quit their homes was advanced, sponsored and propagated by the British. The Government of Palestine granted its officers three months pay in advance and facilitated the departure on leave of Arab officers to adjacent territories. British Companies such as the Iraq Petroleum and Steel Brothers & Co. unnecessarily transferred a large part of their offices and the majority of their Arab employees to the Lebanon. And generally, the attitude of the responsible British authorities was such as to infuse in the minds and hearts of the Arab population a feeling of consternation and the belief that their departure was a logical necessity or, at least, a prudent precaution.

Thirdly, it was the British and not the Jews who first put into effect the dislodgement and deportation of the Arab population. When conditions in Tiberias, where the friendly relations between Arabs and Jews formed a bright illustration of the possibility of cooperation, became acute, the British authorities forcibly transported the Arab inhabitants en masse to Transjordan . . . they compelled the Arabs to abandon their homes and belongings and seek refuge in the contingent Arab territory.

. . . had it not been for the transport facilities spontaneously and gratuitously offered to the Arabs, for the free advice and encouragement to quit made by British responsible and irresponsible officers . . . the plight from which the Arabs now suffer would have been avoided.

When history comes to be written in an atmosphere of sobermindedness, the Arabs will realise that the much-trumpeted anglo-Arab traditional friendship was a curse and not a blessing to them, at any rate as far as Palestine is concerned. . . .

What were the motives of the British—and certain Arab leaders—in encouraging the flight of the Arabs?

Their intentions were to justify the belief that Jewish rule, even in part of Palestine, was tantamount to a death or deportation sentence for Palestine Arabs, and to win the cooperation of the Palestinian Arab masses in the struggle by creating a mass of Arabs for whom the war was not a political question but one of home and livelihood—of existence itself. As zero hour (May 15) drew near, neighboring countries that previously had opened their gates to all the refugees forbade the entry of men between the ages of eighteen and fifty, and even began to plan the return of refugees of these age-groups as soldiers. The assumption was that if the war continued, Palestinian Arabs would fight better than Syrian draftees from among the unemployed of Hamat and Homs. ("They told us we must rescue Palestinian Arabs, but we see that they are in better shape than we are in Syria,") said one soldier in the Rescue Army.* Thousands of Arabs, whom the Mufti and his friends had not succeeded in hitching to their war wagon, were to be dragged behind it from lack of choice.

Through the appearance of masses of refugees in the neighboring countries, they hoped to give an impetus to mobilization. Apparently this goal was achieved; the appearance of Palestinian refugees aroused strong reactions in the neighboring countries: thousands of students demonstrated in Beirut, mass demonstrations took place in Damascus and other towns in Syria and Lebanon as well as in Egypt and Iraq. But this was obviously a miscalculation, for the presence of refugees intensified defeatism and frustration. "If Palestinian Arabs themselves don't defend their country, what is the point in our shedding our blood for them?" was a question posed by people in neighboring lands who saw that many of the refugees were men of military age. The refugees were also a heavy burden on the communities among whom they dispersed, and weakened materially any further preparedness for the war effort, since people who should have been preparing for war, were busy looking after refugees, their housing, feeding and elementary needs, and preventing complications between the refugees and the local population.

In describing the development of the refugee problem, there is another factor which, if it was not decisive, should not be disregarded: the policy adopted in certain places by the Jewish armed forces.

Current Arab writing on the Arab defeat minces no words in criticizing Palestinian Arab leaders. Among the chief targets for criticism and accusation were the absence from Palestine and the flight of most of the leaders in the most critical days; inadequate leadership and inefficient direction of Arab public affairs; selfishness; want of preparedness; disregard of danger warnings; suppression of the truth; unfounded optimism and vainglorious bragging about imaginary victories; grave political blunders, and—above all—

* From an internal Arab report on the morale in the Rescue Army.

the inability to take advantage of the international political situation and the favorable bargaining position the Arabs enjoyed.

These grave charges against individual Palestinian Arab leaders might perhaps be slightly mitigated when it is remembered that the main guilt for the defeat should be attributed to the governments of the Arab States which boasted and threatened, made vain promises to the Palestine Arabs, went back on these promises and when this was revealed—brought about a decline in war morale among the Arabs, which can be seen as the main cause of the defeat. These countries suffered just as much from corruption, decay, and inefficiency. The Syrian Minister of War, Ahmad ash-Sharabati, the commander-in-chief, and high officers were publicly accused of misappropriation of funds. Fuad Mardam, a relative of the Syrian Prime Minister, was brought to trial for embezzlement of government funds and the diversion to Israel of arms shipments intended for Syria. There were also revelations of corruption in Egypt, as well as in the other Arab countries whose armies were sent to introduce order in Palestine. "What is happening now in Palestine," Gamal Abd-ul-Nasser's memoirs, *The Philosophy of the Revolution* (Chapter I), state, "is only a miniature copy of what is happening in Egypt. They besieged our country and they razed it to the ground. It was fooled and pushed into a war it was not prepared for. Fortune-seeking, luxury-loving intriguers played with it and abandoned it in the midst of the battle with no weapons on hand. Officers of independent mind became increasingly skeptical as to the justification for the questionable task they were being asked to carry out far from their homeland while their own countries were suffering from oppressive and backward regimes. "We fought in Palestine, but our dreams turned to Egypt," Nasser wrote. "Our missiles were aimed at the enemy in the trenches over the way, but our hearts turned toward our distant country, which was then the prey of its plunderers."

Abd-ul-Nasser, recalling the days when he sat in the trenches of Faluja, and the thoughts he had had then, wrote:

I often said to myself, here we are sitting encircled in these underground holes; how did they push us into this war by deceit when we were not ready? Our leadership is in the hands of fortune hunters, intriguers, and money-grubbers. . . . In Palestine, cells of free officers met in the trenches and positions to learn and study. It was in Palestine that Salah Salim and Lakaria Muhyi-d-Din [among the leaders of the Egyptian revolution], the latter serving as Egypt's Minister of the Interior and Prime Minister in the nineteen sixties came to me after breaking through the siege lines into Faluja. We sat there in our besieged positions, not knowing what the outcome would be, but our conversation dwelt only upon our country, which it was our soldiers' duty to defend.

One day, Kamal-ud-Din Hussain was sitting near me in Palestine, looking distracted, with nervous, darting eyes. "Do you know what Ahmed Abd-ul-Aziz said to me before he was killed?" he said.

"What did he say?" I asked.

He replied with a sob in his voice and a deep look in his eyes, "He said to me, 'Listen, Kamal, the biggest battlefield is in Egypt.'"

The tragedy of the Palestinian Arabs was that in the early stages of the struggle, both political and military, they had already despaired of their own traditional leaders and their policies but had not yet managed to establish a new leadership and forge a way to a new policy that would be more realistic, daring, and far-sighted. The rulers of the Arab states to whom they turned turned out to be a broken reed, and Palestine Arabs remained, in effect, leaderless and without direction. At this stage the war overtook them—against the real interests and desires of most of the Arab population of Palestine. (This is the opinion also of Ben-Gurion, as noted elsewhere in this chapter.)

An understanding of the background of the 1948 Palestinian war and its consequences is a prerequisite if we are to draw the proper conclusions about the relations of the two peoples in the period ahead.

References

1. D. Horowitz, *In the Service of a State in the Making* (Shocken, Jerusalem, Tel Aviv, 1951(2)), pp. 316–317 (Hebrew).
2. Haviv Knaan, *As the British Left* (Gadish, 1957–1958), p. 137 (Hebrew).
3. Georg Garcia-Granados, *Birth of Israel* (Jerusalem: Ahiasaaf Publishing, 1951), pp. 290–294 (Hebrew edition).
4. *Davar*, February 9, 1948.
5. *Haboker*, May 7, 1948.
6. Don Peretz, *Israel and the Palestinian Arabs* (The Middle East Institute, Washington, 1958), p. 7.
7. *Haaretz*, May 9, 1948.
8. Gamal Abdul Nasser, Egypt's Liberation (The Philosophy of the Revolution), Public Affairs Press, Washington, D.C. 1955, p. 22.

CHAPTER TEN

SINCE THE ESTABLISHMENT OF THE STATE OF ISRAEL

Many changes took place in Palestine (Israel) during 1948 to 1949, the years of the fighting. As the political circumstances changed the problem of relations between the two peoples altered greatly in its *form*. Fundamentally, however, the situation remained dangerous in the extreme for both parties. Upon its adequate solution still depended, on the one hand, the peace and security of the state of Israel—its possibilities of unhindered development and its status in the region and on the international scene; and on the other, the Arabs' prospects for preventing the Arab-Israel dispute from acting as a factor impeding progress in their national and social affairs and endangering their advance toward a brighter future.

Even at this stage, a solution to the problem still depended upon a great intellectual and political effort, which neither of the two sides was prepared to make. The armistice agreements which, according to their text and the logic behind them, were to have served as a transitory stage to peace—and indeed could have done so—did not act as a point of departure for efforts to bridge the abyss that so widely separated the two peoples. In the absence of any feeling of urgency concerning this most vital of all issues, both sides resigned themselves to the armistice regime upon which they had agreed in 1949 and, psychologically, both regarded it as a "temporary" substitute for peace. Thus, twenty years passed. The struggle did not abate, and both sides continued to pay its full price.

Losses in Human Lives and in Property

The director of the Israeli Foreign Ministry reported some time ago[1] that, from the time of the armistice up to the Sinai war (October, 1956), there had been 11,650 "incidents," in the course of which Israeli servicemen and civilians had been killed or wounded by Arab attackers. Military casualties between the War of Independence and the Sinai campaign numbered 1,176; in the Sinai war, 193; from the Sinai war until the Six-day War, 893; in the Six-day War, 744 killed and 2,586 wounded; from the end of the Six-day War until the end of 1968, 194 killed (including those who went down with the Israel Navy destroyer *Eilat*, which was sunk by the Egyptians opposite the

Sinai coast on October 21, 1967.)* These figures do not include civilian victims of border clashes and of the killings perpetrated by murderers and saboteurs infiltrating across the border; nor do they include all the wounded and invalided. The total number of invalids from Israel's defense forces (since the War of Independence and including the struggles that preceded it) exceeds 15,000.[2] It is no comfort to Israelis to learn that the number of Arab victims who fell in "incidents" and retaliatory acts by Israel in the Sinai war, the Six-Day War and subsequently is far in excess of the Israeli total. According to data of the Israeli Defense Ministry taken from Arab sources, Arab losses in the Six-day War totaled 12,250 killed and 2,800 wounded (the number of wounded does not include those of Egypt); from the time of the Six-day War until the end of June 1968, 755 killed (including members of the *Fatah* organization and civilians in the places where the actions took place), and 626 wounded.

But there were not only losses of life. The arming and training of the Defense forces, and the financing of the campaigns they have conducted since 1948, have cost the state of Israel enormous sums in foreign currency, apart from the costs in local currency and lost work days. Annual appropriations of the Israeli Defense Ministry, which during 1949–1950 did not exceed £24 million (at the time the exchange rate was I £1 = £1 or $2.8), reached a sum of I £240 million for the year 1959/1960 (from July 1, 1955, the rate was I £1.8 = $1) and in 1962–1963, (when the nominal value was I £3 = $1) reached the sum of I £410 million per annum. During 1965–1966 however, defense appropriations soared to I £850 million, and in the budget for the 1968–1969 fiscal year, the Defense Ministry estimates were I £2.2 milliard, or almost one-third of the government's entire budget, and three times the amount of its budget for development. Israel's defense expenditures, which have been growing steadily over the years, are not only relatively high for the size of the state, but as a burden they exceed even the weight of the defense appropriations of large states with substantial international commitments. The average defense expenditures for the ten years 1955–1965, as a percentage of resources, was 1.2 percent in Austria, 5.5 percent in France, 6.5 percent in England; 9.4 percent in the United States; and 10 percent in Israel.

The Finance Minister declared in the Knesset on May 6, 1968, that defense appropriations had increased fourfold over the previous five years.

According to official data, Israel's "security consumption" for the years 1950–1966 accounted, on an average, for one-half of total public consumption, and approximately 11 percent of total resources. Military technology

* According to the data given by a spokesman for the Defense Ministry at a press conference on April 28, 1968 (published in the newspapers of April 29, 1968), and the report of the Defense Minister Moshe Dayan, at the Central Committee of the Labor Party, *Davar,* June 28, 1968.

is advancing at a rapid pace, and, alongside it, military expenditures. In recent years, the proportion of defense expenditure out of total resources has risen, reaching 12–13 percent.[3]

A document reprinted by the Tunisian weekly *Jeune Afrique* on December 17, 1967, stated that the military budgets of five Arab states for the years 1949–1967 amounted to the following totals (in thousands of dollars): Egypt, 4,782,152; Syria, 1,026,159; Iraq, 1,849,057; Jordan, 675,498; Lebanon, 298,803. Total: 8,631,669 (8.63 milliard dollars).

These figures were collected from the Defense budgets published by these countries. However, the sums actually spent on military purposes are certainly in excess of the published figures. Yet this is not only a matter of direct military expenditure. The Arab boycott, for example, which forced Israel to buy from afar goods and raw materials available at close hand—transporting them by roundabout routes—and the necessity of constantly keeping a substantial supply of foodstuffs and raw materials in stock, have cost Israel very considerable sums. In the first decade of her existence alone, Israel incurred a loss of $100 million because she was obliged to import the petroleum needed from the Western hemisphere instead of receiving it via the Kirkuk-Haifa pipeline or from the Persian Gulf.[4]

The Arabs' economic losses—apart from the costs of arming and training their military forces and financing their wars against Israel in the period under review—were also far from small. Because of the stoppage in the flow of petroleum through the Kirkuk-Haifa pipeline, Iraq incurred a loss of over $400 million from the spring of 1948 until April 1958 alone.* The Arab countries—Syria, Jordan, and Egypt in particular—lost the Israeli market, which could have absorbed the various kinds of agricultural products and raw materials that Israel now imports from distant countries. Lebanon was deprived of the Israeli tourist trade which, even before 1948, had constituted a considerable source of revenue. It is not idle talk to say that enormous projects of almost inestimable value could have been undertaken for the benefit of *both* peoples if the resources and the efforts spent on war over the past twenty years had been devoted to developmental needs; nor is it mere theorizing to point out what might have been achieved if common resources and forces had been pooled for the development of this region, which has such tremendous economic potential, largely left untapped because of the prevailing political situation.

The International Background—"The Cold War"

When the armistice agreements were signed in 1949, the world was already

* The reason put forward by the Iraqi government in its statement at the end of April 1958 to explain why it was stopping payment of its share of the Arab League budget.

facing the beginnings of the "Cold War" between the two major blocs in the international arena. This situation constituted the principal factor in the background to relations between Israel and the Arab world in the period under review.

With the signing, in April 1949, of the NATO (North Atlantic Treaty Organization) Pact, which later also included Turkey and Greece, the Western powers began to plan the setting up of a political-military bloc in the Middle East. On May 25, 1950, official approval was given for this plan in a declaration issued in the United States, Britain, and France, which stated that they would assume responsibility toward the Arab states and Israel "in order to safeguard their internal security and for their legitimate defense," and in order to enable them "to fulfil the task assigned to them [i.e., to the Arab states and Israel] in the defense of the entire region." Pressure was brought to bear upon the major Arab states to participate in successive plans, which at various times took the form of an "Eastern bloc" (Arabic-Turkish bloc); a "Middle East Defense Pact"; and a "Mediterranean Command". Behind all these plans was the intention to secure the Middle East countries within the global disposition of the "West." From the viewpoint of the states themselves, this idea made their newly won independence virtually meaningless and placed its future existence in a doubtful light. The pressure exerted on the Arab states yielded no results. At the end of 1951, the London *Times* pointed out that "The Arab states can be but little relied upon," since "they do not believe there is any kind of danger from Russia and feel no need to be defended." When it became evident that the Western powers were not in a position to impose their schemes on the Arab states, there began to be talk of fortifying "the Northern section" of the Middle East. This plan eventually materialized in the form of the "Baghdad Pact" (February 24, 1955), a military pact between Turkey and Iraq, and later also joined by Britain (April 5, 1955), Pakistan (September 23, 1955), and Iran (October 11, 1955). This substitute for the previous scheme of a "Middle East Command" was intended to serve as a connecting link between the North Atlantic Pact and its counterpart in South-east Asia.* But the only Arab state included under the "Baghdad Pact" was Iraq, with the others carefully avoiding any such affiliation with one of the camps in the international arena against the other; they regarded it as none of their business.

Such was the international situation faced by the young state of Israel, after having just signed truce agreements with the neighboring Arab states which, under the inspiration and with the assistance of Bevin in London, had attacked her on the very day of her birth. To further the historical and most vital

---

* The Southeast Asian Collective Defense Treaty (SEATO), which was signed at Manila (September 8, 1954) by representatives of the United States, Britain, France, Australia, New Zealand, Pakistan, the Phillipines, and Thailand.

contemporary interests of the new state (and of the Jewish people dispersed throughout countries belonging to *both* world blocs) a policy of strict non-alignment and neutrality between the two blocs was called for. Such indeed was the declared policy of the first government of Israel, which came into power with the Declaration of the state of Israel, on May 14, 1948.

However, just as the camp under Soviet leadership was striving to rally every possible support for opponents of the Western military pacts, the Western powers too, set out to muster every ounce of support for their side—and any refusal to join in with their schemes was interpreted as "taking an unfriendly position." If the Arab states had come to terms with Israel—if they were not threatening night and day that "the day of vengeance would come," that a "second round" was imminent, and that they would "throw Israel into the sea"—it may be assumed that, jointly, the two nations could have ensured the neutrality of the region and its non-involvement in the struggle between the major powers. However, the military encirclement and economic blockade imposed on Israel by her Arab neighbors confronted her with a difficult ordeal. Those same Western powers that had previously (see Chapter Nine) attempted to prevent the establishment of the state of Israel, or to cut down its territory and sovereignty, were trying—now that the state had become an accomplished fact—to derive every possible benefit from it, using it as a threat against those Arab states that refused to put their eggs in the basket of the Western alignment.

However, there were circles in the Arab countries that understood the motives behind these pressures and that opposed the aggressive anti-Israeli policies which, they realized, were driving that country directly into the embrace of the Arabs' real enemies. In the hope that a progressive and democratic Israel could help bring about the liberation and advancement of the Arab peoples, these circles called upon the Arab states to cooperate with Israel so that the conflict between them should not be exploited by outside factors to the detriment of the peoples of the Middle East (see Chapter Nine). In Israel, the leftist Socialist-Zionist forces fought for a domestic and foreign Israeli policy that would support and strengthen the forces of peace in the Arab world. But in both Israel and the Arab countries, outside influences were still very strong and continued to be the decisive factor in the formulation of policies. The progressive forces in the Arab countries were at that time far from constituting a majority and they were for the most part persecuted by the authorities. In Israel, elections to the Constituent Assembly were held in February 1949, and on March 10, David Ben-Gurion formed a new government in which the left-wing party, Mapam* (the United Workers Party), was not represented, although it had played a major role in the war of

* Mapam (the United Workers Party) was formed in January 1948 through a merger of the *Hashomer Hatzair* Workers' Party with the *Ahdut Haavoda-Poalei Zion Smol*

independence and in the political struggle for the establishment of the state
and its defense. Now it was forced into opposition. On March 17, the Knesset
(the Israeli Parliament)—with the majority of the coalition (Mapai, the National Religious, and Progressive parties) and with the support of the right
(the *Herut* Revisionist party and the General Zionists)—approved the
"American Credits Act," which authorized the Finance Minister to accept
a $100,000,000 loan from the United States. The terms of the loan included
a clause obliging the government of Israel to supply full information on the
economic affairs of the country to the Export-Import Bank in Washington
and to departments of the United States government or its agencies. Though
advocating a positive attitude toward foreign loans granted without strings
of economic and political subjugation, Mapam opposed these terms of the
loan contract and demanded a Knesset debate on all the terms of the loan.
The Knesset majority, however, rejected the Mapam demand.

This change in the composition of the Israeli government facilitated the
efforts of those foreign powers concerned to fan the Israeli-Arab conflict and
to involve the peoples of the region in enormous expenditures on armaments,
thus increasing their need for loans and grants on potentially subjugating
terms. The increased provision of military equipment from the Western
powers to the Arab states, and the assistance given in training their armies to
make them capable "of fulfilling the function assigned to them in the defense
of the entire region," according to the "Tripartite Declaration" of 1950,
encouraged revanchist trends among the Arab leadership. At the same time,
the constant threat of a "second round," and the need to be prepared for
every eventuality, sapped the strength of the young state of Israel, whose
government sought refuge with those very elements who were themselves
among the forces fanning the dangers that threatened her.

The Struggle to Break the Vicious Circle

In the early fifties, the struggle to break this vicious circle was still being
conducted.

At the conference of the Israeli Peace Council in March 1950, the President
of the council, Knesset member Meir Yaari (leader of Mapam), pointed out
that Israel had become a part of the Cold War front and that there were

movement. In elections to the first Knesset (1949), this united party won nineteen (out
of one hundred and twenty) parliamentary seats.

Because of ideological and organizational differences, two small groups broke away
from Mapam in 1953, one moving over to the Israel Communist party and the other
moving to the right and joining Mapai. In 1954, there was a major split in Mapam, with
the section that had previously belonged to *Hashomer Hatzair* retaining the name
Mapam, and the other party reassuming the name *Ahdut Haavoda-Poalei Zion*. In 1968,
the latter party merged with Mapai.

forces who wanted to force her to buy her peace and security at the price of subjugation to aims that did not actually concern her; he stressed that it was more important to continue to strive for fraternity between the Jewish people returning to its homeland and the Arab people already living there "until the siege surrounding us is broken down, and we shall see the way out."[5]

This feeling was shared by considerable sections of the Israeli public. Across the lines, there was a responding echo: In the journal *Saut-ul-Uma* (organ of the left wing of the Wafd party, the major party in Egypt at the time), the veteran liberal writer Salama Mussa called for "an end to the cold war between Israel and the Arab states," and he urged both sides "to wind up the war by honorable means."[6] In an article published a year later, this distinguished writer criticized the increase in Egypt's military budget to the detriment of education, social welfare, health, and municipal service expenditures—all because of the war with Israel. His article concluded with a call to the Egyptian leadership "not to be influenced by blind emotions but to act out of wisdom instead of being pulled along by the currents. Make peace with Israel and reduce the [military] budget to E£3–4 million per annum! Lead the people instead of being victims of declarations![7]

In the Arab countries, just as in Israel, there were individuals who saw clearly what was happening. For instance, in a discussion held in Egypt on the question of its status on the international scene, Hafez Ramadan, leader of the National Party, maintained that Britain was deliberately fanning the dispute between the Arabs and Israel in order to safeguard her own power in the region, and that it was with inspiration from Britain that the Arab states had launched their war against Israel.[8]

Fikri Abaza, editor of the popular weekly *al-Mussawar*, revealed that "American friends" had warned the Egyptian government against "the dangers that threatened Egypt from Israel's schemes." These American "peace lovers," though not anxious that there should be an outbreak of "hot" war between the Arab states and Israel, were even less interested in the ending of the arms race between them. At the conclusion of a meeting of American diplomats held in Cairo, the chairman, Jefferson Capry, declared that there was no truth to the rumor that the United States had made its economic support of the "backward peoples" of the Middle East (under the famous "Clause 4") conditional upon the ending of the "miniature cold war" prevailing in the region. "There is no such condition," the United States Ambassador stated.[9]

The policy of "neither war nor peace," which was being encouraged by the ruling circles in the United States and Britain in the period under review, forced both Israel and her Arab neighbors to live under constant tension, constantly ready to do battle. When the Jordanian kingdom indicated a desire to reach some agreement with Israel, Moshe Sharett revealed later, the subsequent negotiations were "not in accordance with the advice of the British but, on the contrary, mainly against their advice."[10] Concerning the lengthy discussions carried on between Israeli representatives and King Abdullah, which concluded with the formulation of a draft agreement which was the cause of the King's assassination on July 20, 1950, in Jerusalem's Al-Aksa mosque) Eliahu Eilat had some more specific things to say: "Kirkbride was the King's [i.e., Abdullah's] right-hand man until the day of his death, and we may say without exaggeration that he played a pretty negative role in the negotiations held at the time with the ruler of Transjordan."*

The secret agreement signed on February 25, 1950 by representatives of Israel and by King Abdullah and his advisers was a nonaggression pact that was supposed to remain in force for five years and was intended as an interim pact prior to a peace treaty. The armistice lines, with some minor adjustments, were to have remained in force without being regarded as final. The opposition of the Arab League to Abdullah's desire for peace with Israel, and the King's assassination on account of this reflected the attitude prevalent at the time in the leading Arab circles. However, this was not the only trend. Persons representing various circles in Egypt came out boldly for a settlement between the Arabs and Israel; representatives of the intelligentsia as well as the national bourgeoisie and even court circles desired such an accord. Similar views were expressed in the illegal organs of the left and were also advocated by certain circles in Iraq, in Jordan, and elsewhere.

In September 1951, a regional council of the World Peace Movement was convened in Rome with the participation of the Arab countries, Israel, and Iran. The encounter, for the first time since the war of 1948–1949, between the Israeli delegation (consisting of M. Dorman, Emil Habibi, M.P., and this writer) and the Arab delegations was quite uneasy at first. Even these circles in Arab countries had not yet become accustomed to pronouncing the name of the state of Israel in the same breath as with those of Egypt, Syria, Lebanon, and Iraq, and the Arab representatives at first refused to sit with representatives of the Israeli Peace Movement. However, after contacts from days gone by were recalled, the ice was broken. This was the first time since 1948—and, unfortunately the last time in such a manner—that Arab and Jewish delegates held joint discussions on the problems of the region and on how to achieve peace. All the resolutions of that meeting were unanimously endorsed, an effort being made "to understand one another"

---

* E. Eilat: A veteran Orientalist, closely involved in matters of Israeli foreign policy (former Israeli Ambassador to the United States and Britain) and Israel's relations with the Arab world; Sir Alec Kirkbride (born 1897) was one of T. E. Lawrence's assistants in guiding the Arab rebellion against Turkey during the first World War, and was for thirty years—holding titles varying with the circumstances—the British representative in Transjordan.

and to avoid "treading on each other's toes." Formulae were sought that would satisfy all those concerned. Shortly after this meeting, the late Secretary of the Egyptian Peace Committee, Yussuf Hilmi wrote:

Imperialism scares the Arabs with the Israeli danger and Israel with the Arab danger. We are told that Israel is preparing for a "second round," while the Israelis are told that the Arabs are planning a "second round," and in this way they increase arms supplies to both at one and the same time.[11]

However, it was not the circles calling for peace who determined policy on either side.

With its eyes on the Western bloc, the Ben-Gurion government abandoned its links with the socialist bloc, which had contributed so much to the establishment of the state of Israel. At the start of April 1950, the United Press reported from sources close to the State Department that "Israel had notified the United States that she had stopped purchasing arms from Czechoslovakia and was concerned to achieve 'standardization' of her military equipment, based on products of United States manufacture."[12] In May 1950, the majority of the *Histadrut's* Executive Committee resolved to break away from the World Federation of Trade Unions, which adhered to the platform adopted at its founding conference in Paris in 1945. At a later stage, the *Histadrut* joined the rival break-away Federation, the pro-Western International Confederation of Free Trade Unions. At the end of June 1950, civil war broke out in Korea and the United States Air Force immediately intervened; before long, military intervention was organized under the United Nations banner by Western bloc nations including Britain, where the Labour Party was now in office. The Israeli government also came out in support of the United Nations intervention, even though, in consideration of Israel's security situation, it was agreed that she need send no troops to Korea, but only orange juice and medical supplies.

In the Vice of the Great Power Struggle

Isolated entirely from her neighbors and subjected to the constant threat of a "second round," Israel increasingly threw in her lot with those powers against whom, at the time, the Arabs were fighting for their independence. As the support for neutrality, and the opposition of the Arab states to involvement in the global strategic schemes of the Western powers grew, the latter exploited the Israel-Arab dispute as a factor that might help to implement those schemes. The possibility of achieving an equilibrium between her own armaments and those supplied to her Arab neighbours was witheld from Israel,* the idea being that surrounded as she was by hostile states, she

* "The British government maintained that, in evaluating Israel's military power

must then have recourse to the protection of the Western powers, and thus would be likely to serve as a convenient prop for them should the Arab states stand firm in their refusal to join the Western disposition in the Middle East. Accordingly, though it was clear that the state of Israel should continue to exist and not be wiped off the map of the Middle East, it was equally clear that there would be no peace between Israel and her Arab neighbors, but only an unstable truce. This policy, by its very nature, was likely to intensify the hostility between the Arab world and Israel.

As the Soviet influence increased in the Middle East and the foreign ministries of the United States and Britain sought ways to "block Soviet penetration," they tried to strengthen the position of the West in the Arab world at the price of part of Israel's territory. With Israel isolated and the Western powers supplying large quantities of armaments to her enemies, while refusing to make similar sales to her, United States Secretary of State John Foster Dulles said on August 26, 1955,—even *before* the Czech-Egyptian arms deal had been signed—that the United States would be prepared to guarantee Israel's boundaries "only after a mutual Israeli-Arab agreement is reached that would turn the armistice lines into permanent boundaries." Dulles hinted that Israel must give up part of her territory. After the Czech-Egyptian arms deal was concluded Anthony Eden, the British Foreign Secretary, made his famous Guildhall speech of November 9, 1955, in which he suggested a solution to the Arab-Israel dispute through "a compromise between the United Nations partition resolution of 1947 and Israel's present boundaries." The implication of these words required no interpretation, particularly since Eden had previously explained to the House of Commons (January 24, 1955) that the Tripartite Declaration of 1950 provided no guarantees of the existing boundaries. This also remained the position of the United States, which held that "the borders of Israel have yet to be finally determined."*

The signing of the Baghdad Pact in February 1955 spelled the failure of the Soviet Union's efforts to bring about the demilitarization of the Middle East region so as to prevent the establishment there of military bases that would constitute a menace to the principal sources of petroleum upon which Soviet industry and agriculture depended. The Soviet response was to launch a diplomatic counter-offensive in the region. The Arab countries now became one of the principal arenas for the inter-bloc struggle. Relations between Israel and the Arab world, which so far had largely been a function of the struggle between the Arab national movement and the Western

---

against that of the Arab states, other factors beside armaments should be taken into consideration—leadership capacities and mental alertness, and the quality of the fighting troops, for example." (Walter Eitan, *Israel among the Nations*, p. 132 (Hebrew).

* Dulles' speech, as reported in *Haaretz*, March 10, 1958.

powers, began to be increasingly influenced by the struggle between the two camps.

Arab Policy

It was already clear in 1948, and became increasingly evident in the light of the experience of the ensuing years, that the Arab leadership had made one of the gravest errors in Arab policy of recent generations over the Palestine issue. They had committed a fatal blunder in launching an armed attack against a young state that had come into being in accordance with an international verdict of the highest order.

Their military debacle in Palestine was a severe blow to the Arab leaders' vulnerable sense of honor, and they could not muster the strength to overcome it. Only a few days after the signing of the Armistice agreement between Syria and Israel, one of the major Damascus newspapers wrote, "Whatever may be said about it [i.e., the armistice], it is a stigma in the history of the Arabs, a stigma that will remain so long as that abominable state that is called Israel remains in existence, in the very heart of the Arab world, in the most precious and sacred place to the Arab countries and to Islam."13

Even though there were some among the Arab public who tended to conclude from the debacle in Palestine that Arab society was in dire need of far-reaching social reforms,* the official tone of Arab public opinion was one of uncompromising hostility toward Israel, which was always presented as the Arabs' first and foremost foe. The sources of this hostility were constantly replenished. The leitmotif of press and radio was to call for a total boycott of Israel and for preparations for the "second round," in which "the desecrated Arab honor would be avenged," and the "thirst for vengeance would be assuaged."

The Arab public was continually told that "the Arabs will never cease to regard Israel as a hostile country. The Jews are our enemies irrespective of the degree of appeasement they may display toward us and of how peace-seeking their intentions may be. We do not pause for a single moment in our preparations for the day of vengeance."14

Talk of this kind, which expressed helpless and unfathomable anger at the failure of the attempt to destroy the state of Israel at the hour of its birth, did not abate in the ensuing years. Not only professional propagandists of the press and radio, but also statesmen and heads of state, expressed themselves in such terms. King Saud, for example, declared: "The Arab nations must be prepared to sacrifice up to 10 million out of their 50 million human beings,

* Such were the views expressed in the pamphlet by Professor Costantin Zoreik (a lecturer in Arabic history at the American University in Beirut), *Ma'na an-Nakbah* (The Significance of the Catastrophe), published even before the signing of the armistice agreements.

if necessary, in order to wipe out Israel. . . . It must be uprooted like a cancer."[15]

When the news of the Czech-Egyptian arms deal became known in the autumn of 1955, Camille Chamoun then the President of Lebanon, declared:

> The Egyptian revolution was the beginning of the end for Israel. Israel will not be wiped out other than by military states prepared to raze her to the ground. Today Egypt is the major military state, and I believe that it is capable of destroying Israel with its own forces alone. It is my hope that, before long, all the Arab states will be prepared—in the organizational and military sense—to the same extent as Egypt. We shall then be able to say openly and with certainty that Israel has come to its inevitable end—and not only to the beginning of the end.[16]

Faris al-Khouri, who held office several times as Syria's Prime Minister, Foreign Minister, and Ambassador to the United Nations, declared that "Syria, Iraq and Egypt must agree among themselves upon a united plan that will enable them to bring about the annihilation of Israel."[17]

These are but a few examples; it would be possible to fill entire pages quoting their like. After the first disaster that befell the Arabs of Palestine, came a second, perhaps even more severe, catastrophe, which affected the entire Arab world. The formulators of Arab policy seemed to fall victim to their own propaganda. At the helm of the Arab states whose armies fought in Palestine, were shaky and unstable governments worried about their own hold on power. These unstable, inefficient, and thoroughly corrupt regimes sought to save themselves by high-sounding declarations of "Arab patriotism." Each Arab ruler tried to outdo his rivals in his saber-rattling against Israel, while pouncing on any sign of "softness" on the part of those rivals, in order to besmirch their reputation and denounce them before Arab public opinion. Opposition spokesmen tried to outdo the ruling circles in proving that, as far as Israel and Arab-Jewish peace were concerned, they were even more belligerent and aggressive in their approach. These same "patriots"failed to understand that their hostile attitude toward Israel, with all its consequences, was the very thing most sought after by the foreign elements from whose yoke the Arab world was attempting to liberate itself.

Abortive Internal Struggle

The conflicts between the separate Arab states constituted an impassable obstacle in the way of finding any *modus vivendi* with Israel. This is why, for example, the Lausanne conference, which convened on April 27, 1949, ended in September without having achieved any practical result.

In theory, the Lausanne conference was to have fulfilled the function assigned to it under the United Nations Assembly resolution of December 11, 1948—that is, "to take the necessary steps to help the governments and the authorities concerned to achieve the final settlement of all the outstanding problems between them." It should be noted that, while the Security Council had adopted plain language in describing as its specific aim the achievement of a "viable peace" between the Arab states and Israel, the Assembly preferred ("out of consideration for the feelings of the Arabs") to adopt the above formula, vaguer in form, though clear and unambiguous in content. Acting mediator Dr. Ralph Bunche, in leading up to the armistice agreements, made every effort to bring about direct and separate negotiations between the state of Israel and each of the neighboring Arab states (the Arab representatives made no protest against this). The conciliation commission—whether because of some "technical mistake" or out of some consideration aimed at winning over the Arab delegates and increasing the strength of their position in the bargaining with Israel—diverged from the path laid down by Dr. Bunche. Immediately after establishing its headquarters in Jerusalem at the end of January 1949, the commission left for Beirut "for consultations with representatives of the Arab states;" in other words, for purposes of the negotiations with Israel, the commission turned the Arab states into a single unit. This was a fatal mistake. When representatives of the Arab states appeared as a single unit before the commission, all of them virtually had their hands tied. Not a single one of the representatives of the four Arab states (Egypt, Syria, Lebanon, and Jordan) that participated in the negotiations dared, in the presence of others, to display the slightest inclination to reach any kind of settlement that might have been described as a retreat from the extremist slogans of the official Arab propaganda.

The joint statement of the Arab delegations at Lausanne to the effect that they would not sit at the same table or in the same room as Israeli representatives, and their refusal to recognize Israel as a party to the negotiations, clearly indicated a retreat from the position held when negotiations on the armistice agreements were being conducted. During the five months of the Lausanne conference, representatives of the Arab states did not meet the Israeli representatives on an official basis even once. Contacts did, however, take place secretly, in Lausanne and elsewhere, between Israeli and Arab delegates— the latter always being sure that none of their colleagues had an inkling that such meetings had in fact occurred. Above all, they were afraid that members of the conciliation commission might hear of these meetings, for this would show up as ludicrous their refusal to meet Israeli representatives on an official basis.[18]

The Israeli delegation made several good-will gestures: It expressed Israel's readiness to allow members of certain families who had been cut off from their relatives during the war to return to the country; it agreed to pay compensation for abandoned Arab lands that had been cultivated prior to the hostilities; it declared itself willing to discuss the release of Arab refugee accounts frozen in Israeli banks, as well as securities and precious possessions held for safekeeping in the safes of those banks. Finally, the Israeli delegation announced the government's willingness to repatriate to Israel up to 100,000 Arab refugees as a contribution to the solution of the problem.

The Arab delegations, lacking the power to rise above their intramural conflicts, adopted a deliberate delaying tactic.* Although they did sign the "Protocol of May 12, 1949," containing a recognition in principle of the partition of Palestine on the basis of the United Nations resolution, they did not have the courage to go any further toward solving the practical problems created by the partition and the establishment of the state of Israel. Among the main reasons for this was their lack of agreement among themselves concerning the future of those regions of Palestine outside the borders laid down in the United Nations resolution of 1947 for the Jewish state. The Kingdom of Jordan, for instance, demanded the annexation of the "west bank" to its own territory. This in itself would put to nought any negotiations over the establishment of an Arab state in their part of Palestine; Egypt violently objected. Differences also arose over the fate of the Gaza strip and those parts of Galilee which, under the United Nations resolution, were to come under the Arab state in Palestine. Syria and Lebanon demanded these parts of Galilee for themselves, arguing that they had been "linked to us under the Ottoman rule." Egypt demanded the southern Negev for herself, maintaining that this was to "protect her security" and to allow for overland links with the Arab states beyond Palestine.

Egypt attempted to turn the Gaza strip into the Palestinian Arabs' political center so as to be able to use it as a pawn in its bargaining with Israel and with the Western powers. In particular, Cairo was anxious to prevent the strip from being annexed to Abdullah's Kingdom. Through the Arab League, the Egyptian statement aspired to the establishment of a "Palestinian government" with its seat in Gaza. A "constituent assembly" was convened in Gaza on October 1, 1948, and to it were invited members of the Supreme Arab Committee, members of delegations that had in the past fulfilled political missions, mayors and heads of local authorities, the executives of the political parties and other public organizations of the Palestinian Arabs, heads of the Arabs' religious communities and of the Bedouin tribes, etc. However, from among all those invited, only about one hundred persons came to Gaza. Nevertheless, in order that it should correspond to the Arab League resolution not to recognize the state of Israel, this government was named "The All-Palestine government" (*Hukumat 'umum Falastin*). The Egyptian Premier, Mahmud Fahmi an-Nukrashi, promised this government of Gaza Egyptian aid to the tune of E £5 million for the establishment of its administration. He

* The definition is that of the Foreign Minister of Lebanon (*Al-Ahram*, November 5, 1949).

also offered support for the organization of a Palestinian army, to be equipped and trained by Egypt toward the "redemption of Palestine," and called for transfer of the Arab areas of Palestine to the rule of the newly established government. He concluded by promising that the armies of the Arab states would stay in those areas only "as allies in the victory over Zionism," that recognition would be obtained for this "government" from the Arab League states, that it would have diplomatic representations in the Arab countries, and that every effort would be made to obtain its recognition by the United Nations.

Shortly after its establishment, as the fighting broke out in the Negev, this "government" moved to Egypt. Amman had stated from the outset that it did not recognize it. One after another its "ministers" departed, some of them becoming members of the Jordanian cabinet (Auni Abd-ul-Hadi, Dr. Khaldi). After the annexation of the "west bank" by the Jordanian government in the spring of 1950, only the "Prime Minister" and his secretary remained, and they continued to issue declarations to the press and to send cables reflecting the instructions of those who gave them their backing.

Just as the Arab states had failed to reach agreement over the question of the territories designated for the Arab state in Palestine, they could not agree over the fate of Jerusalem. Israel was absolutely opposed to the internationalization of the entire city, suggesting that international rule be confined to the holy sites alone. The most enthusiastic supporters of internationalization were the Vatican, and the Latin American governments under Vatican influence. The Soviet Union, which at first supported this move, later withdrew its support, notifying the United Nations Secretary-General on April 17, 1950, that, "in view of the opposition of both the Jewish and Arab inhabitants of Jerusalem," it was withdrawing its support for internationalization of the city.

And the Arab States? Egypt, Syria, and Lebanon wanted this status to be enacted for the entire city, in accordance with the original United Nations Assembly resolution of November 29, 1949. The Jordanian Kingdom, however, which was in control of the Old City, unambiguously disassociated itself from this demand; Iraq, which at first attached greater importance to unity of the Arab front than to the special links between Baghdad and Amman (the links of the Hashemite crowns) and supported the demand for internationalization, later took the following ambiguous position: "Jerusalem should be under Arab rule; but, failing this, a full and inclusive international regime should be established in the city."*

In view of Abdullah's inclination to reach a peaceful settlement with Israel, the Arab League Council, on April 1, 1950, with the participation of the Jordanian delegate, decided unanimously that no member state would be

* Fadl Al-Jamali, before the political committee of the Assembly.

HI

permitted to conduct negotiations with Israel separately, or to sign a separate peace treaty or any other agreement—whether political, military, or economic —with her. The council also decided (April 13, 1950) that the League's political committee would be authorized to decide, with a majority of four, whether a violation of this resolution had occurred. If such a violation was found to have taken place, the state responsible was to be regarded as having broken away from the League. The following measures would then be taken against it: (1) Severing of diplomatic and consular relations; (2) sealing off of the common borders, and the cessation of economic, commercial, and monetary relations; (3) prevention of all monetary or commercial contacts— whether direct or indirect—with its subjects.

The major obstacle encountered in the negotiations occurred over the issue of the Arab refugees. The Arab delegates were not inclined to take notice of Israel's declared willingness to repatriate 100,000 refugees, claiming that so long as the refugee problem in its entirety was not solved in accordance with the Assembly resolution of December 11, 1948,* there could be no negotiations for peace. They demanded the return of the refugees to Israel, without giving any guarantees that they were prepared to abandon their declared policy of eternal hostility toward Israel and their preparations for a "second round" against her. The Israeli delegates, for their part, while expressing a willingness to discuss the refugee problem, maintained that it could be solved only within the framework of a general agreement and they, too, referred this back to the same United Nations Assembly resolution concerning "the final settlement of all the outstanding problems still under dispute between the governments and the authorities concerned."

It was over this point that the Lausanne conference reached a deadlock. Relations between the Arab states and Israel remained in a condition of "neither war nor peace."

The Arabs now awaited the fourth session of the United Nations assembly, scheduled to open in September 1949. Their reasoning was as follows: In view of the refugees' suffering, the conciliation commission might be able to impose far-reaching concessions on Israel in accordance with the Arabs' demands, without the Arabs being placed in a position in which they would be obliged to recognize Israel and to make peace with her. If she did not submit, Israel would be shown up as heartless and inhuman, refusing to obey the United Nations, and thus responsible for the failure of the world organization.

---

* "The Assembly resolves that those refugees who wish to return to their country of origin and to live in peace with their neighbors should be enabled to return at the earliest possible date. Those who will choose not to return should be paid compensation for their property, in accordance with the precepts of international law and justice, through the governments of the competent authorities."

This position of the Arab representatives was also given expression in the negative attitude shown to the delegation of the Arab refugees themselves— the fifth Arab mission—which came to Lausanne a few days after the opening of the conference. The Arab delegations took a poor view of this newcomer and would have nothing to do with it. They contended that the Arab cause— and that of the Palestinian-Arab refugees, as an integral part of it—was adequately represented and defended by the delegations of Egypt, Syria, Lebanon, and Jordan. Having earlier given the refugees the advice to leave the territory under Israeli rule "until after the storm was all over," the Arab delegations now displayed only anger, contempt, and even hostility towards their unfortunate compatriots. Thus, the Palestinian Arabs ceased to be masters of their own fate, becoming instead a pawn in the intra-Arab political game.

If the interests of the refugees had really been the guiding motive of the Arab statesmen, they would have understood that it was inconceivable to demand the repatriation of the refugees while maintaining belligerent propaganda against Israel and arming in preparation for a "second round." Yet while they demanded of Israel a humanitarian attitude toward the refugees, they hardened their own hearts toward them. The sharpening of swords against Israel in no way helped to hasten the healing of the wounds. Israel's declaration that she would be prepared to take back 100,000 refugees was rejected hastily, without any serious consideration being given to whether Israel might be ready to go further in this direction. Every idea concerning the rehabilitation of a section of the refugees in the neighboring country was rejected outright. The impression was created that the Arab states were less interested in the repatriation of the refugees and the rehabilitation of their lives than in the political advantage that could be derived from their remaining in their tragic situation, as a thorn in the flesh of Israel and a card for bargaining with her and the major powers. The Arab policy that emerged eventually over the refugee question sought to preserve the validity of the United Nations Assembly resolution of December 11, 1948, on this issue; to prevent any solution of the problem, either whole or partial, by any other means, and to obtain foreign aid for the minimal subsistence of the refugees, without such aid leading to their rehabilitation outside the boundaries of Israel. This aim was achieved with the United Nations Assembly resolution of December 8, 1949, concerning the formation of UNRRA—the United Nations Relief and Rehabilitation Administration—and with the Assembly's regular annual resolutions on the continuation of UNRRA activities. The Agency spent $30 *per capita* annually on support for the refugees, its budget being covered by contributions from various countries concerned, more than half from the United States.

Boycott and Embargo of Israel

The signing of the armistice agreements did not lead to the formation of any official relations, either diplomatic or economic, between the Arab states and Israel. The borders remained closed. Contact over local matters of vital mutual concern was maintained through the mixed armistice commissions and sometimes through the Red Cross. Israelis were banned from the Arab states, even if invited as delegates to international conferences of the United Nations or similar bodies. For this reason the regional commission of the World Health Organization, which was due to be held in Alexandria in September 1949, was transferred to Geneva, while Israeli representatives were banned from attending the conference of the Food and Agriculture Organization, which was held in Beirut. When the Israeli delegates complained of this before the fourth session of the United Nations Assembly (1949–1950), the representatives of the Arab states warded off the charges by maintaining that the ban had been imposed for reasons of security and that any outside interference over matters of this nature was equivalent to intervention in their internal affairs. On account of the Arab states' refusal to sit together with Israel in the World Health Organization's regional commission for the Middle East (in which Israel participated until 1951), the activities of this commission came to a standstill until a "solution" was found in 1954, in which the Middle East commission of the W.H.O. was divided into two subcommissions which acted separately, Israel in one subcommission and the Arabs in another.

At the twelfth session of the Arab League Council, held in the spring of 1950, a comprehensive plan was formulated for imposing a boycott and a land and maritime blockade against Israel. An entire administrative organization was set up for this purpose, with headquarters in Damascus and branches in the Arab states. "Black lists" of vessels that called in at Israeli ports were drawn up to prevent the loading and supplying of such ships at Arab ports (but the shipping companies found a way out of this by assigning certain vessels to call on Israeli harbors only). Holders of passports bearing Israeli visas were refused entry to the Arab states (but travelers got out of this by obtaining two passports—one for Israel, and the other for the Arab countries). Constant pressure was exerted on foreign firms to close their branches in Israel, failing which they would be boycotted by the Arab countries. Some firms did submit to this pressure over the years. All the Arab states that gained their independence after 1948 (Libya, Sudan, Morocco, Tunisia, Kuwait, Algeria, and the People's Republic of Southern Yemen) were brought into the pact of the Arab boycott of Israel, which also included cessation of postal, telephone, and telegraphic communications. Petroleum companies operating in the Arab countries were warned not to supply oil to Israel (and indeed undertook to abide by this). Israel then had no choice but to purchase her oil supplies from distant countries. In 1959, the Arab League made intense—though unsuccessful—efforts to prevent Israel's acceptance into GATT (General Agreement of Tariffs and Trade). The Arab states also adopted a policy of objecting to Israel's participation in various international agencies that called for the implementation of multilateral agreements on a variety of issues, such as the regional activities of the International Food and Agriculture Organization, activities of the service for combating locusts, telecommunication agreements, and the activities of the International Postal Association.

The Problem of Israeli Shipping in the Suez Canal

Following an Israeli complaint against Egypt for imposing restrictions on the passage of ships through the Suez Canal, this topic was for the first time discussed by the Security Council at the end of July 1951. The Arab League's political commission, which convened while the Security Council deliberations were being held, resolved unanimously that Egypt's stand on this matter "was not the concern of Egypt alone but of all the Arab states." Referring to the words of Dr. Bunche and General Riley (head of the United Nations observers at that time), Israeli delegate Abba Eban maintained that the Egyptian blockade was a violation of the letter and the spirit of the armistice agreements and was, furthermore, a contravention of the 1888 Treaty of Constantinople and of the Law of Nations rulings concerning freedom of navigation. The Egyptian delegate, Mahmud Fawzi, maintained for his part that the armistice agreements, though marking a *pause* in the acts of belligerency, did not bring to an end the existing state of war between the parties, which could be ended only by a peace treaty. There would be no peace treaty, the Egyptian delegate maintained, so long as Israel did not implement the United Nations Assembly resolutions concerning the repatriation of the refugees and the payment of compensation to those who preferred not to return. In sealing off the Canal to Israeli shipping and cargoes destined for Israel, Egypt was using the rights of a "belligerent party," he maintained.

After lengthy deliberations, accompanied by mediation attempts by various sides, the Security Council resolved on September 1, 1951, by a majority of eight (with the abstention of the Soviet Union, India, and Nationalist China), as follows:

a) Since the armistice agreements between Israel and the neighboring Arab countries included the undertaking to avoid further acts of hostility between the parties and were intended to restore a viable peace in Palestine; b) and since the armistice regime was of a permanent nature, no party had any justification for maintaining that it was a bel-

ligerent party at the present time, or that it was entitled to use the right to reconnais-
sance, search or seizure (of a cargo) for the legal purpose of self-defense; c) any such
practice would be in contravention of the purposes of a settlement by peaceful means
between the parties concerned and of achieving a lasting peace in Palestine, as determined in the armistice agreement, and would be a contravention of the rights of
those peoples to freedom of navigation on the seas and freedom of commerce between
them; d) the Security Council calls on Egypt to resign its restrictions on the passage
of commercial vessels and their cargoes via the Suez Canal, whatever their destination
might be, and to refrain from all interference with the movement of ships, apart from
measures necessary for the safety of the ships themselves in the Canal, and to preserve
the existing international agreements.

Despite this outspoken resolution of the Security Council, Egypt did not,
on the whole, alter either its position or its practice in this respect, and the
blockade imposed on Israeli shipping in the Suez Canal was for seven years
extended by Egypt to Israel's maritime outlet to the Red Sea via the gulf of
Eilat. This blockade was not lifted until the settlements reached in the wake
of the Sinai campaign, in autumn 1956.

The Arab states also attempted to undermine Israel's aviation communications. The ban on flights of aircraft to and from Israel over the territory of
the Arab states meant that the development of air routes between Israel and
Asia would be held up. Many airlines moved their transit stops from Lydda,
to Beirut or Cairo. Israel was, for years, cut off from the Asian countries
along maritime as well as aviation routes. Only in 1956 did *Air France* launch
its Lydda-Teheran route via Turkey (in order to circumvent Arab territories)
—a route which, though more expensive, made it possible to introduce direct
flights from Lydda to India, and from there to Far Eastern destinations.

Total Political Boycott

In accordance with the resolution of the Arab League Council of September
1952, Israel's participation in international organizations such as the United
Nations, UNESCO, the World Health Organization and the Food and Agriculture Organization constituted no grounds for preventing the participation
of the Arabs in these bodies, but they refused to join any *regional* international organizations or participate in any regional meetings to which
Israel was invited. This political boycott was demonstrated over the years in
innumerable incidents. The Arabs even went so far as to refuse to send their
teams to international sports events in which Israeli teams participated.

Because of the Arabs' threat to boycott the Bandung Conference of Asian
and African states convened for April 1955, Israel was not invited to attend,
in contravention of the principles of universal representation and equality
of status upon which the conference was convened. Though no Israeli
delegation was present, Israel was angrily condemned, and resolutions were

passed affecting her future. A similar line was naturally adopted when the Conference of Asian and African peoples convened in Cairo at the end of 1957, in Accra in April 1958, and at many similar meetings held subsequently. The Arab governments did all in their power to prevent the convening of international meetings in Israel, exerting pressure on various states to refrain from according recognition to Israel and from forming diplomatic and other ties with her. At every international conference and in every international institution at which Arab representatives appeared, the Arabs' indictment of Israel became an inseparable part of the general picture of international relations, in the period under review.

Armed Incursions in Order to Undermine Israel's Internal Security

Alongside the perpetual Arab efforts to choke Israel economically and to place a political embargo around her, a campaign of "infiltration" was launched against her, which ranged from attempts to take back some of the abandoned property to acts of robbery (sometimes ending in murder as a result of clashes with those who tried to ward off the marauders); finally this took the form of armed incursions for purposes of sabotage and deliberate acts of murder intended to make life in Israel—and particularly in the border settlements—unbearable.

In conditions of extended borders, largely passing through barren regions, it was not difficult to carry out acts of sabotage or to murder civilians engaged in their work or innocent passers-by. The Arab press, and speeches made from the highest-ranking platforms in the neighboring countries, created an atmosphere conducive to this form of action. The contention that the authorities of Israel's neighboring countries lacked the power to prevent such actions is not only incompatible with any sovereign regime but is also belied by the fact that whenever and wherever the ruling circles really wished to prevent armed infiltration into Israel for purposes of sabotage and murder, they did manage to prevent it. In fact, however, they sought to gain advantage from the ineffectiveness of the mixed armistice commissions, whose only function was to listen to complaints, investigate the charges, determine who was to blame, and denounce that side accordingly. Applications to the Security Council on more than one occasion led to the matter being referred back to the armistice commission—a vicious circle that certainly led to no solution.

In 1955, Egypt and Syria launched a planned "miniature war" against Israel, organizing the *Fedayeen* units for this purpose. At first, these groups engaged in acts of espionage, robbery, and sabotage, but later they also committed acts of murder in Israeli territory. Most of those mobilized into these units came from among the ranks of the refugees. They were paid a monthly salary of E £3–5, (but this did not replace the ration card with the UNRRA, which was still at their disposal). A special command was placed in charge of this "minor war," its activities being coordinated through military attachés in the Arab capitals. When he visited the Gaza strip in April 1956, Gamal Abd-ul Nasser told the *Fedayeen*: "You will be the core of the Palestinian army."[19] At that time, the Gaza strip was being referred to as a "springboard for the restoration of Palestine to its rightful owners."

The activities of the "minor war," which were toned down at the end of the fifties, were once more intensified during the sixties. At the beginning of 1965, an organization called *Al Fatah* began to function. Its tasks included mine-laying on roads and in buildings, the blowing up of water pipes and of bridges, the placing of anti-vehicle mines in fields, explosives in pumping stations and stores and even on a football field, the murder of civilians at their work or in their sleep, and sudden attacks on workers in the vicinity of the borders. All these acts of terrorism became regular features of Israeli life. Machine-gun and mortar fire was frequently turned on peaceful border settlements, which even suffered shelling from tanks, and were frequently subjected to artillery bombardment; attacks against units patrolling the borders, infiltration of commando units from the neighboring countries to carry out acts of sabotage and murder, and an innumerable variety of similar hostile acts, became a part of the pattern of life in Israel over long periods.

"Cold War"

The Arab leaders refused to engage in direct negotiations without prior conditions with Israel on a settlement of the problems that had remained under dispute since the war of 1948–1949. They refused to accord recognition to Israel, to turn over a new leaf and replace past disputes by a policy of good-will and sincere cooperation for the benefit of both sides. All these refusals could only be interpreted as expressions of the Arab hope to uproot Israel and destroy her at some future date. Since this hoped-for day could not be seen on the horizon, the Arabs launched their "cold war" against Israel in the meantime. The Arabic press and radio unflaggingly kept up their bombardment of hostility against Israel, describing her as a kind of monster-state that flagrantly violated international law and was entirely geared to scheming against her neighbors, undermining their interests, and hoping to build up her own strength from their ruin. The belligerent anti-Israeli declarations of official Arab statesmen—prime ministers, foreign ministers, presidents of parliament, and United Nations ambassadors—would also be sufficient to fill many long pages. Not only adults but schoolchildren, too, were served this unsavory verbal diet. The Foreign Minister of the UAR, Kamal-ud-Din Hussian, on one occasion published a statement that was read out to the pupils at all educational institutions of the UAR; designed to stimulate feelings of revenge against Israel, it concluded with the assurance that the "day of Hittin" was near[20] (referring to the battle of Hittin, near Tiberias, where Salah-ud-Din had defeated the Crusader Army on July 4, 1187). Textbooks in the countries bordering on Israel are full of "educational" material of this sort.

The essence of all this propaganda of hatred and belligerence against Israel was that the day of vengeance would come and that *they*, the Arab leaders, would decide on the time and the place for the "final" attack on Israel. Their constantly repeated threats and incessant acts of provocation deprived the leaders of the Arab states of any moral right to complain against Israel. As for Israel, believing that it was involved in a life-and-death struggle, it took measures that every now and then appeared (whether justifiably or not) to its leaders as likely to save it from impending destruction.

Nor did this course of events change when the veteran Arab leaders, who had originally involved their peoples in the war, were replaced by new Arab statesmen with a more modern mentality, who knew how to achieve important political advancements for their countries, thus increasing the self-respect of their peoples and heightening the respect with which they were regarded by others. These new leaders, brought to the helm by new historical circumstances, were not responsible for the emergence of the complex Palestinian situation; however, they could have taken action to unravel this tricky problem. But both their wisdom and their political courage appeared to be paralyzed when it came to the problem of regulating relations with Israel. Even those statesmen who dared to tackle this heritage of the past —thus showing that they were capable of understanding historical circumstances and present realities in their correct perspective—conducted a policy of ignoring realities when it came to handling *this* issue.

Every now and then, new plans were put forward. Some of these were most "original," such as that offered by Ahmad Shukairi, when he was Saudi Arabian delegate to the United Nations, which proposed "to outlaw Zionism, to expropriate Zionist funds, and to set up an agency on behalf of the United Nations that would help in the repatriation of the Jews of Israel to their former countries."[21] Another "original" plan was launched in 1965 to divert part of the waters of the river Jordan headlands, so as to prevent their flowing along the river bed through which they had flowed ever since the six days of the Creation.* The Arabs were prepared to invest vast sums

---

* The waters of the upper Jordan, amounting to approximately 500 million m³ annually, constitute about one-third of Israel's water potential (including the subterranean water that can be pumped for use). About half that quantity of the Jordan's water comes from sources inside Syrian and Lebanese territory. The water potential of these two countries is almost 40 milliard m³ per annum, and three-quarters of this amount is not utilized at all.

which could be of no benefit to themselves in order to damage Israel, to curb her progress, and embitter her life.

Israeli Policy

Israel fought with distinction in the war into which she had been forced on the day of her birth. However, to succeed in war does not mean to win peace and quiet. Experience soon proved that it is more difficult to win the confidence and good-will of neighboring peoples than to overcome them by force of arms.

To defeat the invading armies was a pre-condition for the existence of the state of Israel. But once this condition had been fulfilled, it was necessary to exert a vast effort of understanding and courage in order to win the peace. Did Israel do this?

Undoubtedly, this was no easy task. For one thing, two very different national movements were lined up against each other, one born in a relatively developed industrial capitalist society as a result of discrimination against the Jews, the other originating in a backward pre-capitalist society. Moreover, Israel is objectively connected, to a large extent, with that "Western world" which, as a result of historical circumstances, is not trusted by the Arabs, and against which, in the period under review, they struggled increasingly. Decades of foreign rule in Palestine had left behind a sad inheritance of estrangement, lack of mutual understanding, and national hatred, and now the power plays and Cold War politics of the major powers rendered peace efforts between the two peoples even more difficult. Nevertheless, when an Israeli sets out impartially to analyze Jewish-Arab relationships during this period, he will be making his work too easy if he points only to the role of other factors in this complex and avoids the need for self-criticism. That this is a difficult proposition does not release him from making the effort, but rather obliges him to make it.

The capacity for self-criticism is the secret of Israel's strength in many fields. Was it put into effect in this area? This is very much a matter of opinion.

The Necessity of Self-defense and Peace Initiatives

As long as there is no peace between Israel and her neighbors, the strengthening of her self-defense force was, and is, a vital obligation. However, this obligation must not come in place of a policy designed to abolish the need for it.

After the establishment of the state of Israel, as before it, a debate was being waged in Israel between two basic approaches to the problem of Jewish-Arab relations. One side saw peace and cooperation between the two peoples as a primary aim, in the light of which the whole of Israeli policy, internal and external, must be directed. This approach is founded on the assumption that even if peace is absolutely essential both to the Jews and to the Arabs, it will not come of itself. Proponents of this approach maintain that the state of Israel herself must be the first to work for it because she is vitally interested in peace; because it is the Jews who are returning to this area after thousands of years of dispersion, while the Arabs have been living here for many hundreds of years; because it was Israel who won in the 1948–1949 war and can therefore show more generosity, particularly in matters of prestige and in psychological efforts to heal the wounds; and because Israel is a more dynamic and unified state, whose political leadership enjoys an historical continuity, and greater maneuverability and financial resources than the Arab governments. Greater ability involves greater responsibility.

The other approach found practical expression in the policy of David Ben-Gurion and his associates. In spite of declarations about the desire for peace and the striving for it, the stand was that since peace cannot be achieved without paying a certain price (in territorial arrangements, the absorption of a certain number of refugees, and the payment of compensation to others, etc.), peace cannot be the immediate purpose of Israeli policy, and the needs of peace cannot be considered as the primary factor in its shaping. The uncompromising stand of the Arab political leadership toward Israel fostered this trend in Israeli policy, and assisted in guaranteeing it decisive influence in Israeli public opinion.

In Israel's tenth anniversary year, the director of her foreign office wrote, "Israel has proved that ten years of unbroken Arab hostility could not overcome her, and she can hold out against it for generations if need be."[22] Shortly before he became Foreign Minister, Abba Eban in an address to the Zionist Congress in Jerusalem, January 5, 1965, said, "Peace is our genuine aspiration, but it is not a condition of our existence. There is a possibility that we will not achieve it without proving that we can exist without it." Indeed, for the last two decades Israel has proved her ability "to live without it," nevertheless, she has still not won peace.

Those responsible for Israel's policy have more than once been accused by important sections of the Israeli public (including parties participating in the government coalition) of impotence in formulating and initiating a clear, well planned, active, and daring peace policy, with appropriate operative tools in keeping with the trend of historical development in the area and in the world—a policy which, if peace is not immediately realizable, would at least bring it nearer.

Tests of Israeli Policy

With the British withdrawal and the establishment of the state of Israel, new possibilities emerged for improved relations between the peoples of the country—a matter of vital interest for the young state, just as it was a debt of honor for the ancient Jewish people, whose historical inheritance is steeped in the values of human morality and social progress. In this connection, two political tests stood before Israel, one involving the state's attitude toward the Arab minority within its borders and toward the Palestinian Arab people in general, most of whom had been made into a refugee people; the second involving Israel's position *vis-à-vis* the great Arab world surrounding her. The first question was whether Israel would know how to make of the Arabs within its borders a bridge of peace with the Palestinian Arab people and with the whole Arab world. How did Israel fare in this test?

The bloody war with which the establishment of Israel was associated left a bitter psychological aftermath, and among many Jews produced a change of ideological values. About a year and a half after the signing of the armistice agreements, a writer in *Hador* (January 19, 1950), an official Mapai organ, stated that "the remaining in Israel of most of the Arabs must be seen only as a question of time." But a year later (January 19, 1951), one could read in the same paper the conclusion of its Arab-affairs writer that the pressures by means of which it was intended to make the Arabs so despair of life in Israel that they would prefer to leave did not achieve their purpose. Arab voices occasionally calling for an exodus from Israel aroused no response, except the strongest possible expressions of reservation and condemnation. The Arabs who stayed in Israel harbored no illusions as to what was in store for them outside the country. Information on the fate of the refugees in Arab countries was clear and unequivocal. The Arabs who had not left during the fighting or soon after it preferred, therefore, to suffer in their homes, rather than to be transformed into refugees. The real "achievement" of the pressure mentioned was to damage the image of Israel in the eyes of the Arabs in Israel and in the neighboring lands, and to provide ammunition for Israel's enemies.

There were, of course, circles in Israel that rose up against the line adopted toward the Israeli Arabs. For example, in the beginning of March 1950, the Mapam faction in the Knesset demanded to place on the agenda the position of the Arab minority in Israel. The Mapam spokesman said that the constant harassment of Arab citizens proved that their mistreatment was not a matter of isolated cases of discrimination, deprivation, and persecution, but the manifestation of an overall policy in contradiction to the Israeli government's own obligations. But the majority in the Knesset rejected this claim, with the government spokesman arguing that "this is not a question of a contradiction of principles but between principles accepted by all of us, and a complex reality that all of us are pondering." At the end of the state's first decade, even though thousands had left Israel willingly or by force, the Arab population numbered nearly 220,000, about 11 percent of the total population. With the outbreak of the war of June 1967, the Arab population in the state numbered about 320,000, about 12 percent.

After the troubles facing Israeli Arabs in the first years, changes for the better began to make themselves felt. This was the result of the fact that there existed in Israel, along with different types of discrimination (national, communal, or social), the freedom to fight against them, as guaranteed by law. Various public forces, which never despaired of the struggle to make the political reality compatible with the declared principles of the state, utilized this freedom.

The economic situation of the Arab community began gradually to improve, especially for owners of large farms, the skilled workers, and those employed in state and public institutions. The network of schools for Arab children was considerably enlarged, and some of the Arab villages were able to enjoy a degree of medical service. In the late nineteen-fifties, things began to move in the direction of developing Arab agricultural production; Arabs began to utilize the facilities of modern hospitals; thousands began to benefit from national insurance, from trade union membership, and from the *Histadrut's* mutual aid funds. Yet as against all the indications of progress, "the Arabs say: we are in a ghetto, you are using toward us the methods of your persecutors from the days of your dispersion."[23]

It was hard for the Arabs in Israel to become accustomed to being a minority in the state, but it was not easy, either, for the Jews to learn to be a majority, responsible for the state and for everything done within it.

Military Government

At the end of the first decade and even later, nearly 85 percent of Israeli Arabs lived under military government. Within its bounds, the laws of the state did not in fact apply, and in their place was the rule of the military governor and his henchmen.* Arabs were tried in military courts for offenses for which Jews would be tried in civilian courts. The military governor was authorized to prevent anyone from entering certain areas, to place people under police supervision, to exile them from their permanent residence, to impose administrative arrests, and to clamp down a curfew on whole towns or villages. Anyone leaving a town or village within the bounds of military government needed a special permit, which determined for how long he was entitled to

* The legal basis for the military government was contained in the emergency regulations enacted by the British regime in Palestine in 1945 for the purpose of suppressing the Jewish community's movement of insurrection. At that time, these same regulations were severely condemned by the leaders of the entire Jewish public, and first and foremost by those same members of the judiciary who were later to become ministers of justice in the state of Israel.

stay in his place of destination and by which route he would travel, without stopping at interim points. Offenses against these restrictions were punished by fine, by arrest, or by both. This situation was eased only in July 1959. The supervision of matters vital to those living within the borders of the military government (such as employment, supplies, marketing, credit, taxation, representation, etc.) was in practice handed over to various Arab "notables," who, in return for supporting the actions of the military governor's representative, received benefits for themselves and their associates.

Important segments of Jewish public opinion in Israel rejected the Arab population being ruled by military government and saw it as an intolerable stain on the face of Israeli democracy. Time and again it was pointed out that this regime fulfilled no special purpose in guarding the security of the state against external enemies, or in blocking the way to infiltrators bent on espionage, sabotage, robbery, or murder. The needs of security were and are met by the Army, the border police, the police, and the intelligence services. On the other hand, from the point of view of the integration of the Arabs as full citizens in the state of Israel, the military government was a negative factor that could only anger them and poison Jewish-Arab relations. Since 1957–1958, this became, with different nuances, the position of all the parties in the Knesset, apart from Mapai (or, to be exact, the majority in Mapai).

The refusal of Mapai, the main party in power, to give up this position of strength was the result of its general conception of the status of the Israeli Arabs, and because the party secured for itself in this way both the majority of Arab votes for the Knesset elections and the possibility of exerting pressure on Arab electors supporting contending parties.*

In addition to parties and circles that had always stood for a reorientation of Jewish policy in Arab affairs, new political circles were organized in which the struggle for a new orientation at home and abroad was the main platform. An important contribution to this campaign, for example, was made by a group that brought out, in September 1958, a *Hebrew Manifesto*, the programmatic platform of the Semitic Action group, who had published for many years the controversial paper *Etgar* (Challenge), edited by the former commander of the dissident military group *Lehi* (see Chapter Nine), Nathan Yellin-More. Their unofficial organ was the popular illustrated weekly *Haolam Hazeh* (This World), edited by Uri Avneri and Shalom Cohen. In the Knesset elections of 1965, a new list called *Haolam Hazeh—Koach Hadash* (New Force) received nearly 15,000 votes and sent Uri Avneri to the Knesset.

---

* In elections to the second Knesset (1951), Mapai and its affiliated Arab lists won 66.9 percent of the votes of Arab electors; and in elections to the third Knesset (1955), it won 64 percent of votes in Arab localities, almost twice the percentage it won among the Jewish public. Similar results were obtained in subsequent elections.

The struggle to change the policy determining Jewish-Arab relationships was voiced in the press, in the Knesset, in public meetings, and also in demonstrative acts by individuals; all of this aroused expressions of identification and solidarity with the need for change by many people.* Under the pressure of public opinion, concessions by the military government were gradually introduced, especially concerning travel permits. The question of necessity for a military government was again raised in the Knesset from time to time, and in February 1963, its continued existence was "redeemed" by only one vote (57 to 56)—this after Arab members connected with Mapai had been compelled to vote against the interests of their own people.

Concessions were widened after the resignation of David Ben-Gurion and the appointment to the Premiership and the Ministry of Defense of Levi Eshkol (June 1963). On December 1, 1966, the special machinery of the military government was abolished and its functions transferred to the police (which set up special departments for this purpose), with a few hundred people who were on a special list remaining under its supervision. However, the actual military government regulations remained in force. Even though the military government has hardly been felt recently in daily life, the public struggle to abolish this instrument, which makes possible the demotion of Arabs to the status of second-class citizens, is not yet over. Even when it is eventually abolished (along with the legal basis on which it was founded), the military government will have left behind it an inheritance whose effects will not be quickly eliminated.

Property

Since 1948, the question of Arab property the owners of which are outside the borders of Israel has been left in abeyance. Its fate is pending peace agreements and compensation arrangements, and there is also a balancing account of property that Jews in Arab countries left behind or had taken away from them. According to government of Israel statistics,[24] the custodian of abandoned property received rural assets in 350 abandoned and semi-abandoned Arab villages. Their total area amounted to three and a quarter million

---

* A widespread response was aroused, for example, by the one-man demonstration staged in 1964, by the student Uri Davies, who openly defied the law in protest against the seizure of Arab lands for the purpose of establishing the new town of Carmiel, in Galilee; by the famous flights of "peace pilot" Abie Nathan to Egypt, which, since they gave expression to the profound yearning for peace of the general public in Israel, were met with mass demonstrations of identification and support. (For violation of the laws of aviation and emigration, Abie Nathan was finally sentenced to a fine or forty days imprisonment; he chose the latter); the "Sabbath Convoys" of opponents of the military rule from all circles of the public who, in violation of the law that forbade free entry, brought hundreds of Jews who had no permits to Arab villages closed off by the military rule.

dunams (a *dunam* is a tenth of a hectare), including about 80,000 *dunams* of citrus groves and about 200,000 *dunams* of other orchards.

The urban assets operated by the administrative machinery established for this purpose included 25,416 buildings, in which there were 57,497 apartments and 10,727 businesses and workshops. However, the ownership of property by Arabs within the state of Israel was also harmed not a little because of the "Law of Abandoned Property" (March 1950) which, in addition to its very wide enforcement enabled the authorities to expropriate Arab property (when one of the partners to it was in the category of "present-absentees" or when one of the heirs was outside the borders of Israel, etc.), and to take it away from its owners according to various emergency decrees or by different types of pressure, not always entirely legal.

The "Law of Abandoned Property" was also imposed upon the assets of the *Waqf*, which included many plots and buildings in town and a number of agricultural lands that are the property of the Moslem community remaining in Israel (even though most of its members remained outside the borders of the state). Not until 1965 did the Knesset amend the law so that a part of the assets of the *Waqf* can be handed over to a trustee committee appointed for this purpose from among the Moslem community to meet relief and religious needs among the poor, scholarships for school children, and vocational training. (The government had formerly used a part of the income of the *Waqf* for similar work in the Arab community.)

The problem of displaced Arabs within the state has also not been wholly solved. These are villagers who had left their homes during the fighting and found temporary shelter in a neighboring village, or were compelled by the military authorities to leave their village, sometimes after being given a specific promise that they would be permitted to return after the fighting.

Citizenship

From the point of view of the law, the Arab citizens are equal to all citizens of the state; they participate in parliamentary elections and enjoy many rights of a democratic state. However, no such statement can obscure the fact that the Arab minority in Israel lives in conditions of painful national discrimination. The inferior status of the Arabic language in the state and the fact that any Jew arriving in Israel can receive citizenship automatically, whereas an Arab born in Israel and living there all his life is asked to prove his right to it with documents and witnesses—these and other examples cannot but be reflected in the feelings of the Arab in Israel.

Achievements and Disparity

The stormy economic development of the state and the need for working hands caused the failure of the travel-permit system and brought tens of thousands of Arabs to work in the Jewish economy. As an essentially democratic state, Israel could not carry on for very long with a policy negating the right of the Arab community within it to employment, to educational institutions, health services, etc.

It was impossible that the Arabs of Israel should remain entirely outside the influence of the dynamic development through which the state passed in its first twenty years. The country underwent a sweeping and multifaceted advancement, the like of which it is probably hard to find in other countries in our times. The population expanded threefold. Skills, talents, and a creative urge were brought in from all parts of the world. In the seventeen years from 1950 to 1967, $9.3 milliard were channelled into this little country.* It was mainly the Jews of the world, proud of the Jewish state, who provided Israel with financial help the like of which no other developing country received. This is "Israel's oil." Whereas, because of the ruling regime in the principal Arab oil-producing lands, the "Arab oil" mainly enriches a handful of rulers and their relatives from among the "aristocracy,"† in the Israeli set up the great majority of public funds is invested for the benefit of the people and of the public sector of the economy; and private investment also assists in the development of the economy and the raising of living standards. The capital imported, the creative capacity, and the strong desire of the Jews to strike roots in the land brought to the state of Israel most impressive technological, economic, and social achievements,‡ which can be seen in the following figures on page 498.

Similar achievements could be quoted in many other areas of Israeli life. Nor can there be any doubt that the Arab community in Israel registered

* According to the official statistics published in Israel, in March 1968, by the Economic Planning Authority at the Prime Minister's office, during the period 1950–1967, Israel received monetary aid from abroad ("capital import," according to the official terminology) to the tune of $9.3 milliard, of which $5,000 million were grants and gifts; $3,050 million loans, and $1,200 million as investments. The figures include close to $2 milliard as restitution and personal compensation payments from Germany; and $320 million in the form of grants from the United States government, mainly in the first years after the founding of the state. Of this sum, $1,900 million have been repaid, $845 million have been deposited as foreign currency reserves of special emergency funds, and $6.5 milliard have been spent on goods and services, apart from those that Israel has sold abroad (the surplus of imports over exports). In the emergency year of 1967 (the year of the six-day war), the foreign aid received by Israel amounted to $800–1000 million, half a milliard dollars of which constituted gifts (as against $300 million in 1966).

† During the decade 1956–1966 alone, Kuwait, Saudi Arabia, Iraq, Bahrein, Abu Dhabi, Qatar, and Libya netted an oil revenue totalling $13 milliard (not including Algeria). Their annual income from oil has in recent years exceeded $2.5 milliard, and it is still on the increase.

‡ The data are based on the *Statistical Yearbooks* for Israel.

II

	1948–1949	1966–1967
Total population of the state	873,000	2,700,000
Agriculture: total cultivated area (*dunams*)	1,650,000	4,625,000
Tractors in agriculture	681	12,120
Water consumption for agriculture (millions of cubic meters)	275	1,399
Industry: total employed	17,500	185,000
Electrical production (millions of kilowatts)	350	4,461
Value of exports (millions of dollars)	28.5	503
Exports as percentage of imports	11.3	53.8

Housing: In the years 1949–1966, 634,000 housing units were constructed in Israel (417,000 by public bodies; 217,000 by private contractors), plus many public buildings of all types.

	1948–1949	1966–1967
Education: total educational institutions	1,342	25,181
total pupils	140,817	757,220
students in academic institutions	1,635	25,541
Health: total hospital beds	6,426	19,418
hospital beds per 1,000 of population	5.55	7.31

considerable gains in general living standards, real income, food and housing, education and health services, insurance and social services, progress and status of women.* Yet their progress was far from reaching the rate of development in the state as a whole. In the absence of a special effort to diminish the disparity between the two national entities, in some areas it is even increasing.

Sources of Livelihood

Against the background of the Jewish-Arab problem, special significance is often attached to the fact that the Arabs, who constitute a national minority in Israel, are, as a whole, the most backward segment of the country's population. Their standard of living and conditions of production, in spite of having improved considerably, have nevertheless remained much lower than those of the Jewish community.

The percentage of Arabs working in agriculture is four times larger than

* Laws designed to strengthen the status of women in the family (the banning of polygamy, restriction of marriage under the age of seventeen); the national insurance law assuring a grant to women who give birth in hospital; unrestricted participation in all local and national elections; the appearance for the first time of Arab women as representatives in public institutions; their growing role in education, social work, health services, and in industry and administration; the increasing percentage of Arab girls at school, etc.

the proportion of Jews so occupied, and the percentage of Arabs employed in service industries is only a fourth of the percentage of Jews in these occupations. There is also a lower proportion of Arabs in the higher-income brackets (industrialists, businessmen, large-estate owners, financiers, urban real-estate dealers, etc.) and among the high-salaried workers (managers, professionals, technicians, civil service officials).

Arab Agriculture: The main source of livelihood for Israeli Arabs is still farming. Although excellent markets for their produce have become available and the level of production has risen, the land basis has been narrowed down considerably. The Arabs of Israel lost most of their land (60 percent–70 percent), and especially the better lands, which had been in their possession before 1948. The Arab population works about 20 percent of all the cultivated lands in the country, but only 2 percent of the irrigated area. The value of the produce per *dunam* is about four times less than the average for Jewish agriculture.

In spite of the prominent position of the Arab village in the country's agricultural production, it has remained outside the agricultural development programs, and the gap between Arab and Jewish farming is steadily increasing. The first "Five Year Plan" for the development of the Arab village (1962–1963 to 1966–1967), led to the investment of I£80 million in Arab rural development (I£52 million coming from the government and the rest from the farmers, banks, and other private sources). This was not sufficient to do more than partially make up for the previous fifteen years of comparative neglect in terms of supplying essential services to the Arab villages such as access roads, drinking water, farmyard water, electricity, school classrooms, clinics, etc. The plan hardly dealt with the development of production and sources of livelihood in rural areas. Even after the completion of the program, there were still access roads only to *most* of the Arab villages (105), though drinking water and farmyard water reached *almost* all of them. In the twenty years of the state, thirty-two Arab villages were connected to the electricity network; upward of two-thirds of the Arab villages in the country—containing 45 percent of the Arab population—have not yet received electricity (there is practically no Jewish settlement without electricity). With all the positive elements in this program, it turned out to be "too late and too little." This was clearly expressed by the Arab member of Mapam in the Knesset, Yusuf Hamis: "The declared aim of the program is to equalize the standard of living in the Arab sector with that of the Jewish sector, but this cannot be done by budgets that are not more than one percent of the general development budget of the state."[25] Indeed, the main tasks of the state in this area still lie ahead.

Wage-labor: The narrowing of the land base of the Arab village, and its arrested growth, compelled many Arabs to look for work outside the village.

The Arab wage-laborer works mainly at the harder and the less remunerative tasks with the exception of highly skilled workers—such as those employed in large enterprises, working for municipalities, or for the government—most Arab workers are discriminated against insofar as wages and social benefits are concerned. They lose much time and money in long journeys to work. Often they wander from job to job and from place to place. A good many of them have still to live close to their place of work, in abominable conditions without sanitary arrangements, without a proper social life, and cut off from home for long periods. Employment opportunities for the Arab worker are not what they should be, especially for young men and women. The situation of the Arab youth is especially severe. Most of them work for almost half the wages of young Jews of the same age, putting in more hours, with practically no social benefits.

For many years, the Arab workers struggled, together with Jewish left-wing forces, for the right to work and for membership in the *Histadrut* (General Federation of Labor). More than once an Arab was removed from a job that he had succeeded in "grabbing," and the reason given was that he was not organized in a trade union; but those whose responsibility it was to organize him refused to do so. The protracted struggle to open the *Histadrut* to the Arab workers was concluded with the decision taken in February 1959 to receive the Arab workers as members in the federation, with full privileges (in November 1952, it had been decided in principle to receive the Arab worker in the trade union and in all the mutual aid institutions). On July 1, 1967, the number of Arabs in the *Histadrut* stood at 42,000 (of whom 17,000 were wives of members), which was about 4.5 percent of the toal *Histadrut* membership.

Municipal Institutions: During the first six years of the state (until 1954), the inhabitants in the military government zones were not permitted to elect local councils, even though those institutions could impose taxes for the maintenance of necessary services, such as education, health, and welfare which the government claimed was up to the inhabitants to provide for themselves. In February 1967, about a third of the Arab population still lived in places without any municipal status whatever.[26] In the Jewish sector, less than half of one percent were in this category. The development budget available to the Arab local councils in the fiscal year 1965–1966 was only 2 percent of the local development budgets in the country (I£6 million as against I£300 million).

Education: In the last years of the British Mandate, only one-third of Arab children were attending school either in government or private schools. Most of them never completed elementary school. In many Arab villages, there was no school at all. In some, the schools went up to grade 4 or 5 only. Girls constituted less than one quarter of the pupils.

In the year 1966–1967, there were 77.5 thousand Arab pupils in school (of which 20 percent were private schools). This was nearly 85 percent of the entire Arab population of school age (education is compulsory for ages six to thirteen). No Arab country has such a high percentage of its children at school (the Jewish population of Israel has 95 percent). But, whereas in the kindergartens and elementary schools, the proportion of Arab children to the total number in the country was about 1 to 10,* the proportion in secondary schools was 1 to 15, in teacher's institutes 1 to 57, in various higher institutions of learning almost 1 to 100,† and in trade schools 1 to 135.

What should be pointed out as an important achievement is the increase in the proportion of *girls* among the elementary school pupils—from 18.6 per 100 in the year 1948–1949 to 41.2 percent in the year 1966–1967. But even in this year, out of a total of 26,331 Arab girls in government schools, there were only 385 studying in secondary schools.‡

Severe criticism has been leveled at the content of the Arab education. For example, educator Aliza Levenberg has said: "The curriculum is dry, little is taught of national Arab values and of the place of the Arab people in the world."[27] Until fairly recently, the question was asked more than once, "Why do Arab pupils in Israel have to be examined in Bible and to study history in the Jewish spirit?"

The position of the Arabs in all that was connected with the study of trades and management skills is reflected in some of the census statistics of 1961. (see page 502.)

As in other awakening nations, the Arab intellectuals in Israel are, on the whole, permeated with a sense of national consciousness, responding to the pulse of the nationalist movement in the Arab world and feeling themselves a part of it. More than any other section of the Arab population, this group is sensitive to national discrimination. Having grown up in Israel, generally since the establishment of the state, members of these circles are especially hurt by the small role that the Arab Israeli community plays in the fields of

* As already mentioned, the Arabs in that year constituted about 12 percent of the country's total population; however, because of their demographic structure, the proportion of Arabs in the younger age groups was higher than that in the Jewish community. At the end of 1967, children under the age of fifteen constituted 51.6 percent of the total Arab population in the state, while the same age group constituted only 31.6 percent of the Jewish population.

† In the institutions of higher learning, there were, in the year 1966–1967, 112 Jewish students per 10,000 Jewish population, while the Arabs had somewhat less than 10 for every 10,000 persons. (In 1963, there were in Egypt 50 university students for every 10,000, in Syria, 60, in Lebanon, 74. The proportion is continuing to rise in these countries.)

‡ Data from the *Israel Government Yearbook*, 1967–1968.

§ From a speech by Jusuf Hamis, contained in a pamphlet published in Arabic by Mapam, April, 1959.

Occupation	Total No. in Israel	No. of Arabs thus occupied
Engineers, architects, technicians	12,055	200
Doctors	5,390	45
Nurses and midwives	10,905	375
Scientists and social researchers*	5,375	80
Teachers	34,130	1,960
Judges and advocates†	2,755	55
Artists and writers	5,095	145
Managers of public and government institutions‡	9,015	160
Managers in commercial establishments, banks and transport companies	6,225	15

* There was not a single Arab lecturer in institutes of higher learning.
† Of 152 judges in all the courts in the year 1966, there was only one Arab judge.
‡ Out of some 2,000 high officials only five were Arabs.

literary creation and the arts, and by the fact that most of the institutions and social organizations in the country are barred to them, for all practical purposes. They are sensitive to such things as the inferior position of the Arab language in the state, the disrespect sometimes expressed toward Arab culture and history, and to a disparaging attitude toward the achievements of the modern Arab world.

Arab intellectuals could have been activated in modernizing the Arab-Israel community and making it more progressive; in developing the Arab schools, in efforts to eliminate adult illiteracy,* and in publication of Arab newspapers and literature. Israel should have, and could have, been a center of free and progressive Arab creativity. But in contrast to the twenty-four daily papers of all kinds (some of them in foreign languages, for the benefit of new immigrants who do not as yet read Hebrew), that the Jews put out in Israel, there is not a single daily paper of the Arabs themselves. The daily government paper printed in Arabic by Jews *for* the Arabs finally closed down in the twentieth year of the state. In its stead, there is to appear another daily paper in which Arab writers and editors will participate. Of course, it is hardly possible to remedy the situation without the adoption by Jewish intellectual circles of a positive, principled attitude toward the struggle for national and social liberation in the Arab world and to its growing desire for

* The population census of May 1961 showed that only 48.3 percent of the Arab population aged fourteen and over were literate (as compared with 88 percent of the Jews, 70 percent of whom knew how to read and write in Hebrew). The percentage is different for men (68 percent) and for women (28.5 percent) and varies between the different communities. Moslems: Men, 60.7 percent; Women, 14.4 percent; Christians: Men, 86.6 percent; Women, 66.1 percent; Druzes: Men, 72.9 percent; Women, 26.8 percent.

independence, though it must of course be understood that this does not mean that one can ignore the limitations of the Arab nationalist movement and its mistakes, or that one can give *a priori* consent to all that takes place in the Arab countries. The relations between Israel and the Arab world in general, and the policy of the Israeli government, do not help the Arab intellectuals in Israel to carry out their potential function of building a bridge of peace between the two peoples.

Health: In the matter of health, there is no doubt that the Arabs of Israel have made considerable headway. The infant mortality rate in the first year of life went down from ninety-six per thousand live births in the year 1947, to 39.4 in the year 1966. (Jews had twenty-two.) The percentage of births in hospitals rose from 4 percent of all births of Arabs before the establishment of the state, to 80 percent in 1967 (in the Jewish population, almost 100 per cent of all births are in hospitals). Recently, immunization against infantile paralysis embraced all the children in the country, Jews and Arabs alike, and an attempt was made to provide all infants and young children with immunity against rheumatic fever, partly by use of mobile teams. The medical supervision in schools has helped to eliminate or reduce diseases that formerly troubled many Arabs. The Ministry of Health has set up health stations, community centers and mother-and-infant clinics and stations in Arab villages. The Arab members of the *Histadrut* receive medical aid at its Kupat Holim clinics.

However, as in other realms, the achievements in improving the health of the Arab population do not keep up with those of the state as a whole, and as time passes, the gap becomes more obvious and more painful. Even in June 1966, almost half of the Arab villages did not have a doctor and were almost entirely without medical services.

Housing and Sanitation: There is a large gap between the conditions of Jewish housing and sanitation and those of the Arabs within the state. While nearly 100 per cent of Jewish families (according to the 1961 census) lived in houses with running water, electricity, kitchen, and sanitation, more than 40 percent of the Arab families (apart from the Bedouins) lived in houses without such amenities. "Part of the buildings in the Arab villages are slum dwellings built of clay, or are structures without light, air, or sanitation. In Nazareth and in mixed cities like Haifa, Acre, Lydda, Ramle, and Jaffa, theirs are the poor living quarters in the older sections."[28] The housing programs for the Arab sector of the population have not even answered the needs of natural increase, which require an additional 2,000–2,500 units annually, not to speak of the need to eliminate some of the older, run-down living quarters described above, and without taking into consideration the problem of housing some 30,000 Bedouins.

The larger Arab villages, each with several thousand inhabitants, are increasingly becoming townships composed of wage-laborers who are compelled to seek a livelihood further afield. They are, in fact, urban settlements; but in terms of housing, sanitation, roads, lighting, services, and public institutions, they remain in the category of backward villages.

As for the state of crowding in the homes, the census of 1961 indicates the following conditions:

	Jews (%)	Arabs (%)
In Urban Centers		
Less than 2 souls per room	62	30
From 2 to 4 souls per room	31	38
4 and more souls per room	7	32
In Rural Centers		
Less than 2 souls per room	51	13
2–4 souls per room	39	43
4 and more souls per room	10	44

The scope of building in the Arab sector, rather than diminishing the gap, is likely to increase it.

Among Jews, the prevailing view is that "the position of the Arabs in Israel is much better than it ever was and is better than that of their brethren of the Arab countries." This sort of thinking actually avoids the essence of the problem. It cannot be assumed that, were it not for the state of Israel, the Arabs within her borders would have remained static in terms of general development, public services, etc., over the past twenty years, the developments in neighboring countries bear witness to this.

The term "in the Arab countries" as such, is an oversimplified generalization: The levels of development and living conditions in Lebanon are different from those in Jordan, and those in the Damascus area of Syria differ from those of upper Egypt.

Above all, the Arab population of Israel—constantly hearing talk of democracy, civic equality, and so on, and seeing all this being increasingly realized in the Jewish sector—judges its own situation, not in comparison with that of its brethren in this or that Arab state, but in comparison with that of its Jewish neighbors in the same state.

Moreover, in the state of Israel, as was the case under the Mandate, it is precisely that degree of economic and social progress already achieved by the Arabs that makes them more sensitive to manifestations of discrimination, disparity, and separation. Witnessing the personal and national pride of the neighboring Jews, as individuals and as a community, only deepens that sense of discrimination that Israel's Arab citizens feel is shown toward them, as individuals and as a nation.

Furthermore, national and social liberation movements are flourishing all over the Arab world. The Arabs have finally achieved political independence. The Arab peoples are striding forward proudly. Even the real achievements in raising material standards cannot obscure the fact that the Arab community in Israel in many important spheres—such as secondary and higher education, status of its intellectuals, opportunities for its youth, industrialization, rural development, spiritual creativity, level of national, cultural, and democratic community life—lags behind, not only the standards set by their Jewish fellow citizens, but also those of the more developed Arab countries.

Even if the older Arab generation appreciates the economic progress that has been made, and enjoys the present level of social services as against those existing under Mandatory rule (or the days of the Turks), the great majority of Israeli Arabs cannot make such comparison. By the end of 1965, seventy-five out of a hundred of them had been born after the inception of the state of Israel, or were under ten years old when it was established. For them, the only criterion is the neighboring Jewish community and its living standards. So in reality, the Arab citizen generally sees, as it were, a sort of glass partition dividing him from full participation in the great possibilities unfolded by a modern state and a relatively progressive regime.

There is no getting away from the fact that in Israel there is also a problem of disparity between the established Jewish community, dating from pre-state days and most of which is of European origin, and those who came after the establishment of the state, who are mostly of Asian and African extraction. The latter, who make up about two-thirds of the Jews in Israel, are somewhere between the "Jewish average" and the Arab minority in their economic-professional and socio-cultural status. This, too, is one of Israel's gravest problems, loaded with social and political dynamite.

In this area, however, all are united in seeing the need for integration, and nearly all agree that the way toward it is to lessen the economic-social disparity. It can readily be understood how different in its gravity is the problem of a *national* minority with its own language and historical traditions, related to a group of neighboring peoples undergoing a surge of national revival.

The instinct for survival, and the knowledge that any new war is likely, first and foremost, to harm the Arab community in Israel most gravely, explains why this community cherishes the strongest aspirations for peace and seeks peaceful ways of solving the problem of Israel and the Arab world. The Israeli Arabs, aware of Israel's internal strength, know that the refugee problem can only be exacerbated by additional wars. The same applies to the whole problem of the Palestinian Arab people, the existence of which Israel has ignored for twenty years.

The loyalty of the Israeli Arabs to the state of Israel (which stood the test of critical periods like the Sinai campaign, according to the evidence of

Ben-Gurion) stems from this realistic approach. It explains their feeling of common destiny with the Jewish community despite all the acts of injustice, discrimination, and sometimes degradation, that they have experienced. It was in a sense symbolic that in the days of tension that preceded the war of June 1967, Arabs voluntarily helped in the fortification of Jewish settlements, contributed blood to the hospitals, and in some places volunteered to take the place of Jewish reservists at work.

A bold policy of fostering equality and peace could still stimulate the great potential for harmonious development latent in the state of Israel. Such a policy could turn the Arab minority into a bridge of peace between Israel and the Arab world. The policy that was adopted toward the Arab minority in the period under review did not utilize this potential which still presents a vitally important challenge to all concerned with Israel's well-being and with the building of peace between her and her neighbors.

In the Field of Foreign Policy

It would be hard to determine today exactly to what extent Israeli foreign policy was a reaction to the hostility of the Arab world—to siege, blockade, intrigue, armed infiltration, and constant threats—and to what extent it was a factor in building up and fortifying this hostility. At any rate, once this chain of cause and effect became operative, with the one strengthening and accelerating the other in a vicious circle, it became more and more difficult for either nation to break out of it. The refusal of the Arab leaders to "accept" Israel as one of the countries in the area began to bear fruit. The policy of the state of Israel, for its part, helped in this.

Ever since it crossed the Rubicon over Korea in the summer of 1950 and started to join consistently with the Western powers, the government of David Ben-Gurion unremittingly sought ways of forming a military pact with them. The hopes being incorporated into plans for a "Mediterranean Command" were dashed when these plans failed. Thoughts of an "India-Israel Axis" came to nothing when India took up a position of non-identification with either of the blocs in the international arena. For a brief moment, there flickered a hope that the vicious cycle would be broken. On the day when the agreement was signed between Egypt and Britain for the British evacuation of the Suez Canal, Abd-ul-Nasser declared, "The Egyptian position toward Israel depends on Israel's behavior toward the Arab peoples."[29]

In fact, this was a repetition of what General Muhammad Naguib had said on other occasions, namely that a prime condition for peace between the Arabs and Israel is that Israel should see herself as a state belonging to the area and not as a European bridgehead, foreign in essence to the Middle East area.[30] The Arabs evaluated the relationship of Israel to themselves in the light of its stand on the dominant question then being disputed—the integration of the area into the military plans of the Western powers. While the Arab countries took up a negative position toward the "Mediterranean Command" and toward the Baghdad Pact, which the West was increasingly building up, the press agencies announced from Ankara that "Israel is making vast efforts to strengthen her relations with Turkey and asking to be indirectly associated with this Pact."[31]

When Turkey drew back from fostering too much friendship with Israel, preferring to consolidate her relations with the Arab world (which it was intended to draw into the Baghdad Pact), Israel renewed her attempts to achieve a military pact with the United States with increased vigor. When these hopes of achieving the longed-for military guarantee from the United States were also dashed, efforts were then directed toward partnership with France, and eventually led to the Sinai-Suez campaign. The Suez war failed and it became clear—especially after the British backed out—that France was not economically or politically strong enough to change the balance of forces in the Middle East. At the beginning of 1957, there appeared the "Eisenhower Doctrine," a new attempt to integrate the Middle East into the global alignment of the Western powers, this time under the direct custody of the United States. The government of Israel hurried to "welcome" the doctrine—which roused strong opposition in the neighboring countries— and to join it officially.

"This is the first time," wrote the director of the Israeli foreign office, "that Israel has linked up, even if with only the most tenuous of ties, with the aims of American foreign policy in the Middle East."[32] This step taken by the government brought about a cabinet crisis: Mapam and *Achdut Avodah-Poalei Zion* voted against the cabinet's statement on the matter. However, because they considered that the doctrine had no chance, they saw fit not to leave the government but only to abstain from voting on the statement when it came before the Knesset on June 3, 1957. (Out of 120 members, 59 supported the government statement and 39 abstained.) After a short time, the doctrine was dead and buried.

Now Western Germany appeared on the horizon as a rising economic-military power that soon became the backbone of NATO. Israeli foreign-policy efforts were turned toward Bonn. With her help, it was hoped to incorporate Israel (like Turkey and Greece) into the North Atlantic Treaty Alliance and in this way to receive security guarantees. In January 1958, the government of Israel fell, when a leakage to the press prevented a journey by "an important personality" to West Germany for negotiations with the military leadership there over Israeli admittance to NATO. In 1959, a governmental crisis broke out in Israel over an arms deal between an Israeli company and the Bonn Army—confirmed by the ministry of defense, but not by the government. Mapam and *Ahdut Haavoda* opposed such deals with Germany. This time, Ben-Gurion, in fact, admitted that the purposes of the "deal" were to strengthen Israel-Bonn relations and to prepare the way for the integration of Israel into NATO.

However, none of these efforts yielded the hoped-for results. When the Ben-Gurion government revealed its disappointment and embarassment at not being privileged to participate in the military alignment planned for the area, it was asked to be patient. The director of the Israeli foreign ministry, Walter Eitan, reveals in his book that, as for Israel, the great powers initiating the pact said that "they would welcome hearing her views later on, when they have made progress in the organization of the command." The Turkish representative clarified the significance of these words when he said that Turkey hoped that Israel would adopt a "realistic position,"—in other words wait in a corner, at least until all the Arab countries had been won over.[33]

The day before the Baghdad Pact was signed, Mr. Abba Eban, the Israeli Ambassador in Washington, announced that he was in the middle of negotiations that he hoped would bring about the inclusion of Israel in mutual security pacts for the defense of the Middle East. This statement was confirmed by a spokesman of the Foreign Ministry in Jerusalem. Yet on the very same day, an official American spokesman declared that "it is true that the Israeli Ambassador told the United States Foreign Minister of the Israeli government's wish to join a Mediterranean defense pact" but "there has been no change in the State Department's position as regards such agreements with the state of Israel until the efforts to move the Arab States to join a pro-Western security pact will have achieved real results."[34]

The Western powers continued to show caution about including Israel as an ally in public references, lest this harm their efforts to win over the Arabs.

With the Western Powers against the Eastern Peoples

In retrospect, it is hard to prove what might have happened if Israeli foreign policy efforts had been directed towards *rapprochement* with her neighbors instead of towards profiting from the dispute between them and the Western powers.

The stand adopted by Israeli policy on the side of the West, both in the general international arena and in the struggle between the Western powers and the liberation movement of the Middle Eastern peoples, took on many and varied forms. Sometimes it was a matter of ideological identification with a point of view opposed to that of the Middle Eastern peoples. For example, in 1952, the American magazine *The Nation* conducted a symposium on the Middle East, in view of the growing national movement in the Arab East. The acting Israeli Consul Mr. D. Goetein, expressed the following view:

"Not all self-rule is progressive and not all independence is better than the colonial rule of a progressive empire. Very often, more social reforms are achieved under the rule of an imperial government than under the rule of an oligarchy such as the existing Arab oligarchies."

The same ideological viewpoint underlay the various theories widely circulated in the press, literature, radio broadcasts, and large and small "information" projects in Israel—all, in effect, designed to show that the Arabs are not a nation, but rather some conglomeration of tribes, sects, and religious communities. According to this view, the Arab national movement is an "artificial movement," a "copy of Europe," "imported from abroad," "the work of foreign agents," "the invention of the foreign office in London and Paris," or, more generally, simply a "hatred of foreigners." One can put in this same category the talk sometimes heard from Israeli representatives that most of the independent Arab states "owe their existence to the allied victory" and that "the blessing of independence fell into their mouths like ripe fruit." The prolonged, unremitting, and costly struggle of the Arab national movement hardly enters the picture in this version.

Their own prejudices, blind emotions, and mistaken political outlook prevented such Israeli commentators from seeing the reality—the worldwide and deeply significant drama of an anti-colonialist liberation movement on the swelling tide of which the Arab peoples were also advancing to the independence for which they longed. The Arab struggle for national and social liberation cannot be correctly understood without viewing the social-historical changes then taking place on a world scale, and the alignment of the forces and conditions prevailing in international affairs. However, it was precisely this sort of vision that was lacking among the Israeli leaders.

This ideological outlook was not a matter of abstract theory; rather, it served to consolidate practical policies. There was hardly a matter of controversy between the people of the area and the Western powers in which official Israeli policy did not side with the latter. This was the case in connection with the demand in the early nineteen-fifties that the British evacuate their forces from the Suez Canal area (which Israeli shipping was not allowed to use even when the British were stationed there). When the question of Tunisian independence came to the United Nations in 1952, Israel voted against (with the French and South African representatives). When the Afro-Asian bloc asked, early in 1953, to bring the problem of the French colonies in North Africa before the United Nations, Israel, along with France, voted against.

How did the Israeli foreign office justify this position? Among their many arguments, the main one was that independence for the Arab states in North Africa might harm Israel and that, moreover, Israel must strengthen her ties with France, many of whose interests in the Middle East were identical with those of Israel. In 1956, Israel sided about five times with France against the Algerian liberation fighters. Not a few Israelis smouldered at hearing on *Kol Yisrael*, the official radio station, broadcasts referring to "the Algerian terrorists." After all, less than ten years had passed since Israel had been established, in the wake of a struggle that in its essence was quite similar to that of the Algerians, and that had also been described as "terrorist" by the late Ernest Bevin and his assistants in the British foreign office.

In 1958, when one vote was lacking in the United Nations for an African victory, Israel voted with France over the Algerian question. When, after an impressive struggle by the Afro-Asian bloc, the United Nations General Assembly, by a two-thirds majority, on November 18, 1958, resolved to forbid nuclear experiments in the Sahara, Israel voted with the minority. The then Minister of Agriculture, Moshe Dayan, sent a telegram of greeting to his friend General Shall on the occasion of the French atomic explosion in Sahara.

At the beginning of 1956, before the sharpening of the Suez crisis, Arthur Lourie, Israeli representative at the United Nations, saw fit to declare, in an astonishing statement, that "Israel blocked the way to the establishment of an Arabic empire which would have spread from Morocco to the Persian Gulf. Nasser's friendship with the Soviet Union," he went on, "makes his dreams of conquest into a threat to the Western world, but Israel, well armed and equipped with tanks, airplanes, and modern artillery, will constitute a strong preventive factor against any such temptation."[35]

Whenever a dispute broke out between one of the Arab states and the Western powers, the Israeli press would warn the Western leaders against "compromising with the Arab rulers." In the spring of 1958, a grave internal struggle flared up in Lebanon over the political orientation of the country; the Mapai spokesman at the Council of the Socialist International, which was convened in the middle of June,[36] urged "the free world" to save the pro-Western rule of Camille Chamoun, who was opposed by the majority of Lebanese and eventually deposed. This was done although Chamoun had been one of the leading Arab spokesmen against the Jewish aspirations in Palestine and had expressed the hope that Israel would be destroyed (see Chapters Eight and Ten).

On July 14, 1958, an uprising in Iraq brought about the total collapse of the rule of Nouri-as-Said, King Faisal II and Prince Abd-ul-Ilah. The immediate response of Washington and London was to land American Marines in Lebanon and to airlift British parachutists to Jordan. These were said to be the first steps in the measures to be taken in Iraq itself, the focal point of the crisis. The political struggle between the peoples of the area and the Western powers reached its peak. The government of Israel did not preserve strict neutrality in this struggle. The parachutists' planes to Jordan flew over

Israeli territory without any objections by the Israeli government. News-papers like *Davar* again warned the Western powers "to show consistency," "to go to the end," "not to lose valuable time lest it be too late," etc. In the United Nations Assembly's debate on the evacuation of the Americans from Lebanon and the British from Jordan (August 20, 1958), Abba Eban supported a resolution that in fact meant delaying the evacuation, whereas the Arab states and most of the Afro-Asian countries, along with many other member-states, called for immediate evacuation.

Can Peace and Friendship be Imposed by Force?

In the years preceding the establishment of the state of Israel, whenever pos-sibilities opened up for negotiations between Jews and Arabs and the Jewish leaders drew back, the essence of their reasoning was as follows: As long as the Jews in Palestine are weak, the time is not appropriate for negotiations and agreement; once it has become clear to the Arabs that the Jews are a force who can defend themselves and can neither be overcome nor destroyed, the Arabs will look for a way to come to terms with this force.

The war of 1948–1949 undoubtedly showed the Arabs that the state of Israel was a force even stronger than the leaders of Zionist policy had them-selves foreseen. But it also proved that the above-mentioned evaluation by these same leaders in regard to the way toward achieving Jewish-Arab peace was basically mistaken: The opposition of the Arab leaders grew instead of diminishing, despite the proven strength of Israel in the test of battle.

The Arab leaders now pinned their hopes on the efficacy of the economic blockade, hoping that Israel would be unable to withstand it and would quickly collapse. Once again, the leaders of Israeli policy claimed that "the Arabs will come to terms with us only when they realize that they cannot overcome Israel through economic pressure." Four to five years after the establishment of the state of Israel, it must undoubtedly have become clear to the Arab leaders that the siege and blockade of Israel could not overcome her. Nevertheless, the opposition to Israel, far from dying down, continued to grow.

In the Arab world, whereas in past years many had scorned the Jewish-Israeli factor, people now began to *exaggerate* the dangers that the Arab states could expect from the state of Israel. Cries were heard about "arming from head to foot," putting the life of the state onto a war footing," etc.[*] It must be admitted that at this stage the Arab leaders had won an apparent victory, for they had succeded in weakening the belief among the Jewish populace that Jewish-Arab peace was attainable.

---

[*] This approach was expressed, for example, in the book *Israel—An Economic, Military, and Political Danger*, published by the Union of Chambers of Commerce, Industry and Agriculture (Beirut, 1952), p. 184.

This change in political thinking was manifested in the speeches and writings of leading Israelis. Jon Kimche, who was well versed in Israeli affairs, noted in July 1957, in the London *Jewish Observer* (as quoted by *al Hamishmar*, August 2, 1957) that from 1953 onward, "the main emphasis [in the state of Israel] was placed on the military side of the problem," and that "in the adoption of political methods a new rule was determined according to the assumption that Israel must be prepared for war and not for peace." Kimche wrote that the neo-realists advocating the new Israeli policy appeared to be exploiting a moment of opportunity but in fact tended to ignore the real problem. When these neo-realists took things over, "the foreign office was asked to surrender completely to security needs, and since Sharett did not surrender easily, he was forced to go."

Moshe Sharett, one of those who had genuinely worked for peace and mutual understanding, resigned from the government in June 1956 (about four months before the Sinai campaign), after having served without a break for twenty-three years as Foreign Minister, including the period before the establishment of the state of Israel.

The controversy between Ben-Gurion, Sharett, Dr. Nachum Goldman, (President of the World Zionist Organization) and others associated with their approach, was based, essentially on their opposing answers to one question, that is: Does the way to genuine security for Israel lie in reliance only upon military force or in a far-sighted, long-term, patient and enterprising political approach? In fact, Ben-Gurion was the victor in this argument, and his stand served as a guiding light for Israeli policy, both in its military and diplomatic operations. Nobody closely following the chain of political developments in Israel, and wishing to be faithful to the truth, can justify the claim that Ben-Gurion's policy was only a reaction to the atmosphere that was being created around Israel, rather than one of the serious factors involved in creating it.

The principal point of vulnerability in Ben-Gurion's policy was its faith that peace and friendship can be imposed by force and coercion—political and diplomatic coercion and, in certain circumstances, military coercion. Instead of patient face-to-face political confrontation with the complicated and delicate problem of Jewish-Arab relations, Israeli policy set its face toward attempts at a military solution. Instead of gradually bridging the gap between the two peoples, these attempts widened it. Instead of bringing peace nearer, they pushed it even further away. To illustrate this, we shall deal with only two of the examples that could be presented—the Gaza incident and the Sinai campaign.

Acts of Retaliation: *"the Gaza Incident"*

International public opinion was not particularly shocked at the news of small-scale Arab infiltration into Israel and the accompanying terror and murder, even though, since the 1949 armistice, tens and hundreds of un-armed Israelis had fallen victim to these activities. On the other hand, there were generally angry reactions to Israeli acts of retaliation. The position of Arab leaders who attacked these acts was, in the words of the Arab proverb, *Darabani wabaka, sabakani washtaka* (He hit me and wept—and then was the first to complain).

These reprisal operations were often the cause of bitter controversy within Israel itself. It was asked to what extent the purity of Jewish arms was pre-served, to what extent the acts of retaliation stood in proportion to the provo-cations that had caused them, how correct and effective they were in light of the purpose that they had set out to serve, and whether the timing was correct.

For example, the "Gaza incident" of February 28, 1955, in which thirty-eight Egyptian and eight Israeli soldiers were killed (apart from those killed and wounded among the civilian population of Gaza), came after various provocations by the Egyptians. Even so, there were those who did not see the Israeli action solely as a reaction to the sabotage, espionage, and murder by soldiers who came from the Gaza strip, as was claimed by the official Israeli announcement. These people saw the incident as connected with a different and extraneous matter—pressure put on Egypt at that time, because of her refusal to join the Baghdad Pact, which had been signed a few days before. It is true that the Egyptian leaders who threatened the destruc-tion of Israel had no moral right to complain when the Israeli leaders exploited Egypt's hour of political isolation to strike back at her. However, from an Israeli point of view, it is still questionable if long-term political considera-tions should have permitted the striking of such a blow precisely when, in the political circumstances of the time, it would look as if the blow were connec-ted to the pressure being exerted, for their own reasons, by foreign powers against Egypt.

Something similar happened in the "Kinneret incident" of December 12, 1955, in which an Israeli force attacked the Syrian positions on the north-east shore of the Sea of Galilee (Lake Kinneret), blowing them up and killing fifty-six Syrians, wounding nine, and taking thirty prisoner, along with a booty of arms and military equipment. The official Israeli version linked the incident with Syrian attacks on Israeli fishing vessels in the Kinneret, and there were indeed provocations of this nature before and after the incident. But fate would have it that the response was timed for exactly the moment when the Western powers were putting pressure on Syria, where a fierce internal struggle was taking place in order to determine whether she would join the Baghdad Pact or the neutralist policy of Egypt.

In any event, the Gaza incident aroused strong reactions in the countries within the immediate area and around the world. On March 29, 1955, the

KI

Security Council unanimously condemned Israel. But the principal influence of the incident was on the Egyptian leadership. In a talk with American newsmen some weeks afterward, Abd-ul-Nasser said, "Before the Gaza incident, I thought we could live side by side without trouble, but I was surprised by this attack." When he was asked if the state of Israel and its government had not expressed their desire for peace and the coexistence of the two states *before* the Gaza incident, Nasser replied, "I think that in Israel there are two different outlooks on this matter. One is for an end to the incidents, and hopes for peace and coexistence, while the other, and this is Ben-Gurion's outlook, sees the solution in force. Now, Ben-Gurion has taken his outlook from theory into practice."[37]

Before the Gaza incident, sober voices had also been heard from time to time in the neighboring countries. In a debate in the Lebanese Parliament on January 6, 1955, Kamal Junbalat, leader of the Progressive Socialist Party and later a Lebanese government minister said that no danger was threatening the Arab world from Israel: "It has been in existence for six years, and the danger seen by those preaching rearmament has not emerged."[38] Voices like this were no longer heard after the Gaza incident.

Two writers well known in Britain for their political articles—Gay Wint, of the editorial board of the liberal *Manchester Guardian* and Peter Calva-coressi, one of the scientific workers of Chatham House, the Royal Institute for International Affairs—summed up political developments in the Middle East concerning what is called in Britain the Suez campaign, and the events that had gone before it.[39] In their view, the Gaza incident was "one of the most fateful events in recent Middle Eastern history. Until then, Egypt was less active against Israel than other Arab states, there were fewer clashes between Israel and Egypt than between Israel and Syria or Jordan. Egypt maintained only small armed forces in the border area. In their attack, the Jews surprised the Egyptians, degrading as well as defeating them."

They wrote that Abd-ul-Nasser's character was still a matter of controversy; he was either a realist trying to appear as an extreme nationalist in order to consolidate his power, or an emotional man capable of harmful acts of madness. At any rate, among all the Arab leaders, he was the only one who was perhaps ready to come to some arrangement with Israel. But February 1955 brought about a turning point in his position. Ever since then, he had seen Israel as his principal enemy, and he started then to seek arms everywhere in order to strengthen his country against future attack. Since the United States, Britain, and France wanted to preserve a state of military equilibrium in the Middle East—in accordance with their declaration of 1950—and thought of using Israel against the Arab states after the latters' refusal to join the Baghdad Pact, which had just then been set up and had failed to respond to the

Egyptian request, Egypt turned to the Soviet Union and Czechoslovakia. From here, the story is known.

Since basically similar evidence was provided by others as well, among them Richard Crossman in the *Jewish Observer*, once again it was not so easy to accept the official Israeli version concerning the chain of events leading to the famous Egyptian-Czech arms deal of autumn 1955. A section of the Israeli public opposed the political path taken by the government. For example, early in May 1955, the Mapam faction in the Knesset urgently demanded a debate on the negotiations concerning Israel's involvement in military pacts. Knesset member Y. Chazan bitterly criticized Ben-Gurion's position, while another member, Yaakov Riftin, demanded that the government abandon the policy of military pacts and instead adopt "an active, dynamic policy aimed at preventing war, consolidating security, and attaining peace—a policy of independence and neutralism."[40] Though this policy was also supported by other circles in Israel, it remained that of a minority.

The Sinai-Suez Campaign

When the Suez Canal crisis broke out after the Egyptians nationalized the Canal (July 26, 1956), for two months Israel adopted a restrained stand. She declared that she was only interested in the freedom of Israeli shipping in the Canal and was not a party to the dispute between Egypt, on the one hand, and Britain and France on the other.

The year 1956 started with signs of change in Arab-Israel relations. There was no letup in the acts of murder and sabotage carried out by Arabs, who infiltrated into Israeli territory, and in Israeli retaliatory actions in border areas. But this was not the whole tale. In another place, we will tell of Dom Mintoff's story about preparations for a meeting in Malta between President Nasser and Israeli representatives. The Soviet Ambassador to the United States, Georgi Zarubin, suggested holding a round-table conference between Israel and the Arab states in order "to compromise on the differences of opinion between the two sides." He said that his government wanted "a peaceful settlement of the Israel-Arab problem," and "would be happy to make its contribution in bringing the two sides to the discussion table." He was absolutely convinced that "peace would soon be established in the Middle East."[41]

A Soviet foreign office announcement on April 17, 1956, called for a settlement by peaceful means of the Arab-Israel dispute and expressed the Soviet government's readiness to help actively in promoting such a settlement. The Arab world was not indifferent to this call. In the widely read Cairo weekly *Rose al Yousuf*, which had access to the Egyptian ruler, an interesting article appeared on April 23, 1956, written by Muhamad Amin Al'Alim. He suggested accepting the Soviet proposals in the hope of achieving positive results. As for Israeli participation in the conference, he wrote, "We cannot oppose her participation, since she is a side in the dispute, but it is our right to stand out for the representation of the Palestinian Arab people."

Habib Bourguiba, the President of Tunisia, published, in the official *L'Action*, a call to the Arab states for a round-table conference with Israel in order to settle outstanding questions. To those claiming that negotiations with Israel meant recognizing her, Bourguiba mentioned the fact that in the past it had already been agreed to negotiate with Israel on the armistice and related matters.

Diplomatic observers saw another sign of the relaxation of tension in the permission granted by Egypt and Israel to Ibrahim 'Izat, a writer on *Rose al-yousuf* to visit Israel in the second half of May 1956 and publish his impressions in the Egyptian press. "Only a few years ago," said *Haaretz*, "an act like the reception of an Egyptian journalist for interviews by the heads of the two governments was not within the realm of the possible; he would almost certainly have been thrown into jail in Israel as a spy and in Egypt as a traitor." Some saw the visit as a lowering of tension in the wake of the peace mission by the General Secretary of the United Nations to the Middle East.

In September of the same year, preparations were made in Paris for the publication of a leaflet directed to the Arab world and concerning peace talks with Israel. It was emphasized in the leaflet that its signatories were "all men and women who fought without respite against imperialism and supported the struggle for the liberation of colonial peoples; and they have the moral right and obligation to issue an urgent call for the early settlement of the differences of opinion between Israel and the Arabs in accordance with the Bandung principles. The democratic elements in the Arab world must conduct suitable propaganda for such a settlement." The signatories, who came from all over Europe, Asia, and Africa, conceived of a gathering on the lines of the successful Indo-Chinese peace conference in Geneva (1954), with the participation of representatives of both the sides involved in the dispute, the great powers and various neutralist countries.[42]

Giles Martinet, an editor of the leftist French weekly *France Observateur*, reported in his paper that leftists in Egypt were anxiously awaiting initiative from the left in Europe "in order to facilitate an arrangement with Israel." In a talk with the correspondent of *Haaretz*, Martinet said that "Israel serves as a constant issue for political discussion in Egypt." He defined the line of "the members of Nasser's entourage" as being, in effect, "Regardless of what we say in public—and we have to adopt a strong anti-Israel line, for otherwise the Iraqi demagogues will rise up against us—we certainly know what is the relation of forces between the Arabs and Israel today, and we do not want a war now." As for the Egyptian progressives, both those who had access to official circles, elements who had made up the left of the Wafd, and various other leftist groups, Communist, and non-Communist, "they think that the Nasser regime, which is founded on mystical Arab nationalism, could become complete Fascism, and in their view peace with Israel is a firm guarantee against such a development." These circles had told Martinet that "in the present political circumstances, we do not dare to come out openly for peace with Israel. It is your task to help us in this from without."

Signs of Soviet pressure on Egypt in the same direction were also in evidence. According to the information services (and this was not denied), D. Shepilov, the Soviet Foreign Minister, told his French counterpart Pineau that "the principle of freedom of shipping in the Suez Canal also includes Israeli shipping."[43]

Of special and outstanding interest in this context are the revelations that were later made by Dom Mintoff, the Maltese Labor Party leader and later Prime Minister. In January 1956, when he was Prime Minister of Malta, Mr. Mintoff told Uri Dan, the Tel Aviv correspondent of *Maariv*, in an interview at his Malta home, he had visited Egypt privately and had been warmly received by Gamal Abd-ul-Nasser. In their exchange of views on various topics, the two leaders came to the subject of Israel. Since Mintoff had invited Nasser for a holiday in Malta, he asked him, "Why should you not take this opportunity for secret talks with Israeli representatives, who will come to Malta by chance, as it were?" In their talk on this subject, it was concluded that Nasser, who was to take a holiday on a pleasure boat formerly owned by King Farouk, would visit Malta in April 1956. While still in Cairo, Mintoff approached the British Ambassador (Malta was a British Crown Colony) and told him of the pending visit by Nasser and of his agreement to a secret meeting with Israeli representatives. On his return to Malta, Mintoff was about to make contact with Israel in order to assure the arrival of suitable representatives when the British Governor suddenly called him for an urgent talk. The Governor informed him most sharply and in unmistakeable language that "he had received instructions from London that there is now no place for a visit of any type whatsoever by Nasser."

At the journalist's request, Mintoff showed him a photostat copy of a document—a top secret telegram from the British Foreign Ministry to the British Governor of Malta—saying that "it is not very desirable or convenient that Nasser should now visit Malta, and he should be told that his visit is not convenient at this period because of internal affairs which are now occupying our attention. Make sure that Mintoff's letter to Nasser will be like this. Nasser must not know of our lack of desire for him to visit Malta, and make it your business that Mintoff should understand that he is not a peacemaker."

After seeing the telegram and its formulation, Mintoff recalled, he understood that there was no alternative, and the visit, of course, did not take place.

When Mintoff met Moshe Sharett in 1958 at a conference of the Socialist International, he told Sharett of the whole affair. Afterward he sent him a photostat copy of the telegram from London. A similar photostat copy was given to Nasser when Mintoff again visited Egypt in 1959. Nasser read the telegram and smiled, Mintoff concluded.[44]

This attempt at mediation by Mintoff was preceded by several other efforts during that period when Ben-Gurion temporarily resigned from the Premiership and was replaced by Moshe Sharett. Jean and Simone Lacouture, in their book *Egypt in Transition*, (page 233) relate that "there was indirect contact between Nasser and Sharett through several intermediaries, mainly British, including the British Labour M.P.s Richard Crossman and Maurice Orbach. Nasser told the latter of his hopes and of his strong sympathy for Sharett."

In an interview with the Mapam representative in London in January 1965 (see *Hotam*, January 20, 1965), Orbach pointed to this part of the Lacoutures' book and added that "every word is true, and in fact things reached an even higher stage." What Orbach refused to bring to public attention was that as a result of his talks with Nasser, the latter asked him to formulate, along with Ali Sabri, the draft for an Egyptian-Israel agreement. (Sabri was the President's right-hand man, at different times director of his bureau, Prime Minister, etc.) Its clauses would provide for the cessation of hostile propaganda between the two sides, the opening of the Suez Canal to Israeli shipping, among other things. A Nasser-Sharett meeting was then agreed on in principle, and it remained only to fix the date. However, it was at this time that a certain action took place, carried out by a different Israeli authority, that was later to be the cause of the so-called "Lavon affair" in Israel. All contact with Egyptian representatives was then stopped.

The Sinai campaign, which started on October 29, 1956, naturally put an end to all the efforts at mediation that had already been or were about to be initiated.

It may be that no state, including states much larger and stronger than Israel was in those days, could have succeeded in holding out forever against siege, political provocation, and unceasing threats of destruction, without having resort, sooner or later, to an act of desperation that, in an hour of danger, might appear to open the way to salvation. A number of factors persuaded Ben-Gurion to think that this was an opportune moment for Israel to break out of her state of siege and to compel the Arab states to make peace by force.

These factors included the tempting offers of Paris and London "to lend a hand in crushing Nasser," the Soviet difficulties in Hungary at that time, the election campaign in the United States, and various other diplomatic and military considerations. The fact that Ben-Gurion's surprise suggestion to launch an offensive in Sinai, brought before the government two days before the opening of the campaign, was, in the event, supported by the great majority of the government of Israel, cannot change at least three facts of primary moral and political significance:

1. All the political and military preparations for the Sinai campaign were conducted by Ben-Gurion and his confidants without the confirmation, or even the knowledge, of the government.

2. The preparations for the campaign were already fully under way at the time Ben-Gurion declared in the Knesset, on October 15, 1956 (two weeks before the troops moved), that "as long as it depends on us, peace, and even a shaky peace, must be preserved, and the alternative to peace is a war whose casualties are certain and whose historical effectiveness is doubtful."

3. After the event, Ben-Gurion and his aides did not see fit to tell the people the whole truth about the campaign,* for along with the military success of the Israeli Army, the Sinai campaign caused Israel grave political damage and certainly did nothing to bring nearer an Israel-Arab peace.

The Sinai campaign did much to dissipate the political and moral credit that Israel had enjoyed all over the world. Condemnation came not only from those heads of state who could naturally be expected to oppose her, but also from her sympathizers. Thus, for example, the Foreign Minister of a friendly state like Sweden declared, on February 11, 1956, that "Israel perpetrated an act of madness, which is within the realm of catastrophe." It was Gaitskell, the British Labour leader, who issued "a warning to my many friends in Israel" at the beginning of the campaign. "Naturally," he said, "Israel must continue to live among the peoples of the area and if they will see her as an ally of imperialism, then all hope for the chance of a peace agreement between Israel and the Arabs will go." A similar view was expressed by leaders of Nenni's Socialist Party in Italy. British Labour leader Richard Crossman, another old friend of Israel, expressed the position well when he wrote in the *Daily Mirror*, on November 9, 1956, "Ben-Gurion is indeed an inspiring leader in war, but unless Israel wants to lose the peace, she needs a completely different leadership."

The primary short-term gains won by Israel in the wake of her participation in the triangular attack on Egypt included freedom of shipping in the straits of Eilat and cessation of the Fedayeen attacks from the Gaza strip, through the stationing of a United Nations force along the area and in Sinai. Yet, despite such gains, within Israel itself uneasy reflections were increasingly

* In an address to Israel Defense Force officers on March 5, 1959, Mr. Ben-Gurion said (according to the official, complete version of the speech, which was later published) that "it was the wish of the providence of history that two days after we engaged in battle on the east side of the Suez Canal, the British and French armies should also join the campaign on the west of the Canal."

voiced about the policy that had reached its most complete expression in the Sinai campaign.

Moshe Sharett, who spoke of the Sinai campaign as "Eden's adventure" made some bitter comments in his diary about "the belief that it is possible to reach peace through coercion." Sharett's fundamental evaluation of the Sinai campaign was voiced in his Knesset speech of March 6, 1957, which, in spite of its careful diplomatic language, contained severe criticism of those policies of Ben-Gurion that had led up to the campaign. "Security," said Sharett, "is the first and primary condition for the existence of the state, and this is an axiom; but narrow-minded and short-sighted concentration on security problems, along with the diversion of attention from seemingly different considerations, is likely to have direct consequences on security itself."

The conclusion to which the Sinai-Suez war pointed was that the political objectives it was intended to attain were not achieved; Egypt has not been compelled to make peace with Israel; the Suez Canal had not been opened to Israeli shipping; the weakening of Egypt's military strength proved to be no more than temporary. On the credit side was the opening of the maritime passage to Eilat, and on the debit side, the intensification of hostility to Israel throughout the Arab world and the distortion of her image among various segments of world opinion. True, for several years, relative calm prevailed along the borders, and Israel gave up its policy of acts of retaliation. In a period of eight years (1956–1964), only two large-scale military actions took place, both of them against Syria (at Tawafiq, on February 1, 1960, and at Nuqaib, on March 17, 1962). Yet despite the relative calm that lasted for a few years, peace between Israel and her neighbors was brought no nearer; on the contrary, it became even more remote.

When Ben-Gurion resigned as head of the government and the Defense Ministry, at the end of June 1963, both these posts were entrusted to Levi Eshkol. The new government attempted to abandon the policy of "activism," and there were indications of feelers being put out for a change in Israel's international status which might achieve an improvement in relations with Socialist bloc states and prepare the ground for the possibility of talks with the Arabs. The then Deputy Prime Minister Abba Eban declared that "there is a connection between the relations between Jews and Arabs within the state of Israel and our relations with the Arab states," and pointed out regretfully that the Jewish citizens of the state lacked a conscious understanding of the fact that it was the destiny of Israel to "exist in a region that is entirely Arab."[45]

In November 1963, the regulation stipulating the need for travel permits in areas under the military rule was rescinded (apart from five villages situated close to the border, with a total population of 4,000 persons). When Mr.

Eshkol visited the United States in June 1964, the moderate and conciliatory tone of the statements he addressed to the Arabs was noted, though he did not gloss over the necessity for Israel to maintain her efforts to strengthen her security setup so long as the potential danger existed.

The new line that emerged in Israel's policy after Ben-Gurion's departure also appeared to be helped along by the new winds blowing on the international political scene. Despite the anxiety naturally provoked in Israel by any report of a new supply of arms to the Arab states, and to Egypt in particular, the significance of the joint declaration issued by Khrushchev and Abd-ul-Nasser upon the conclusion of the Soviet Prime Minister's visit to Egypt in May 1964 was not lost on the Israeli public. The most important elements of the declaration seemed to be the fact that the President of Egypt had put his signature to a Soviet declaration concerning the settlement of disputes between states by peaceful means alone (without reiterating his previous reservation that this guiding principle should not apply to relations between the Arabs and Israel); the Soviet statement that the arms from the Soviet Union promised to Egypt were intended for defense purposes alone, and not for attack; the joint emphasis on the importance of creating regions free of nuclear weapons, and the inclusion of the Middle East among the regions that it was felt should necessarily be kept free of such weapons.

However, before long the skies darkened once again. The root of the evil was the Arab states' refusal to recognize the actual existence of the state of Israel. Their summit conference built up the tension with a series of new plans, including the establishment of a joint Arab command to plan "a show-down with Israel"; the formation of a "Palestine liberation army," from among the Arab refugees; planning of the diversion of the Jordan river headwaters in order to deprive Israel of the small enough quantities of water at her disposal, etc. From the beginning of 1965, *Al Fatah* groups began to appear, infiltrating Israel in order to sabotage the National Water Carrier project, to lay mines along the roads, and to sow violence and destruction wherever they could. Syrian outposts along the Golan Heights once again began to shell the Israeli settlements at the foot of the Heights.

In this newly electrified atmosphere, there was no response to the realistic and courageous stand taken by Habib Bourguiba, Tunisia's President, who in March 1965, during visits to Jordan and Lebanon, put forward once again (and this time openly, in public, for the whole world to hear) his long-held credo* on Jewish-Arab relations. He declared that the partition of Palestine

---

* In 1953, Bourguiba and his associates, the leaders of *Ad-Dustour* in Tunisia, had already expressed their willingness to exert their influence in the Arab countries toward the "restoration of good relations between the disputing cousins." Bourguiba expressed an opinion to this effect for the second time in January 1955. In August 1956, the month in which Tunisia won its political independence, he called on the Arab states

was a fact, and that all talk of "throwing the Jews into the sea" was empty
and meaningless demagoguery; that, with all the tragedy involved in the fate
of the Arab refugees, wars would not solve these problems but only complicate them still further; that the solution of the problem could be attained
through cooperation between the Arabs and the Jews, since "for centuries the
Arabs lived in peace with the Jews, and many are the links between them
since the time of their common forefathers," and that "cooperation and
understanding can serve as a strong basis for a genuine peace." Bourguiba
criticized "demagogic policies" in the Arab world and the expenditure of
energies and potential on arms purchases while there was a crying need for
development in all spheres; and he warned against the practice of taking
unilateral action without consideration for what was going on elsewhere.
Bourguiba's views won the immediate support of certain segments of the
Arab world (among them, Pierre Jumail, leader of the Maronite *Kata'ib*
party, the most influential political group in Lebanon; the Tunisian journals
Al Amal and *Jeune Afrique*, and Tawfiq Matar, one of the leading personalities
in the Arab emigrant community in South America and the honorary
Jordanian Consul in São Paolo. Bourguiba's views were also welcomed in
certain sectors of the Israeli public. The circles that directed official Israeli
policy at first received these views in stony silence, and then with evasive
murmurings and reservations, warnings to the public about "illusions of
peace that would undermine the national security effort," and, finally,
contentions that "one swallow does not make a spring," and "hasty enthusiasm could prove harmful." Fears were also expressed that "Bourguiba's
arguments might be used by those who are refusing to help strengthen Israel
in face of the Arabs' build-up of force." At the same time, the Arab spokesmen levelled the customary charges of "treason," and "stabbing the Arabs in
the back," against Bourguiba—especially after the reaction from the Israeli
side became known. In the meantime, the fruit of death and destruction
ripened once again, drawing nourishment—as is always the case—from the
soil of international relations.

The Soviet Union and the Israel-Arab Conflict

The main political change in the Middle East after the Sinai-Suez war of 1956
was the penetration there of the Soviet Union and other Socialist countries;
their influence replaced that of England and France, which had almost completely vanished, and that of the United States, whose influence was also
withdrawn to a considerable extent. In the protracted struggle between the

to hold a round-table conference with Israeli representatives in order to reach a
settlement to the problems under dispute between the two sides—a plea he made
through the official organ of his party.

huge world camps, the Arab scene became one of the principal battlefields.

The appearance of the Soviet Union as a decidedly influential factor in the Middle East could have launched a new phase in Jewish-Arab relations. Her political authority, weighty international influence, and the prestige she enjoyed in both the main Arab countries and in Israel, could have enabled the Soviet Union to take the political initiative successfully and to provide valuable help in untying the tragic knot. Did the course of events justify these hopes?

There is no denying that, until the end of the fifties, a certain degree of restraint was exercised by the Soviet policy regarding the revanchist tendencies of the Arab world toward Israel. Thus, for instance, we would do well to recall the Soviet foreign office's statement of April 17, 1956, when the Arab-Israel tension reached one of its most dangerous levels. In this statement, the Soviet Union declared its support for all the means undertaken by the United Nations to find ways to effect peace in Israel, and for the Security Council's decision in this respect (to send the General Secretary of the United Nations, the late Dag Hammarskjöld, to the Middle East to ease the tension). At the same time, the Soviet Union declared that she "called upon *both* sides to avoid any action that might increase the tension along the borders decided upon by the armistice agreements between the Arab countries and Israel." Her demand was "to bring about a stable peace settlement of the Palestine problem on a basis that was acceptable to the parties involved, and that took into consideration their legitimate national interests." The Soviet Union also expressed her "readiness to participate, together with other nations, in helping to reach a peaceful solution for those questions that have still not yet been solved."

On the basis of this stand, Soviet Foreign Minister D. Shepilov refused to identify himself with the Arab position on Palestine when he visited Egypt, Syria, and Lebanon in June 1956. In circles close to the Israel Ministry for Foreign Affairs, it was pointed out then that "the Soviets had advised the Arabs to be more realistic and reasonable, and had expressed support for the United Nations efforts to prevent war in Palestine.[46] During Abd-ul-Nasser's visit to the Soviet Union in April-May 1958, it was also pointed out that the Soviet statesmen leaned towards restraint: "Israel is an existing fact" Khrushchev made it clear to Nasser, "but we have to compel her to change her policy."[47]

Nevertheless, as the influence of the Soviet Union and other Socialist countries increased in the Middle East, they increasingly avoided their obligation to fulfill that function that it was incumbent on them to perform—that of bringing peace to the area and helping to integrate Israel, as a dynamic, progressive country, into the family of Asian and African peoples newly arrived on the stage of history.

Unfulfilled Hopes

Countries like the Soviet Union and other Socialist states could have been expected to follow in the Middle East a policy of respect for the vital interests and justified aspirations of *all* nations, large and small. But since the latter part of the fifties and the beginning of the sixties, it had become clear that the Soviet policy concerning the Arab-Israel dispute would not fulfil such hopes. In spite of its recognition, in principle, of the Jewish people's right to national independence and sovereignty, the Soviet Union's stand on Israel was on every occasion influenced (apart from the alienating effects of the policy of the Israeli government) by a blind spot from which she has not yet been able to free herself.

It is only this prejudice—whose origins lie in the period previous to the Communist movement's recognition of the Jewish people's right to nationhood—that can explain the reason for the Communist leaders, having permitted themselves to behave toward the state of Israel in a way that has no parallel or precedent in their relation with other countries even smaller and more backward than Israel. It will be sufficient to recall an instance in which the very existence of Israel as a state was questioned in a letter by Bulganin, the Soviet head of the government, to Ben-Gurion, the Israel Prime Minister, at the time of the Sinai-Suez campaign in early November of 1956. This was followed by the Soviet severing of diplomatic relations with Israel, without, however, a similar diplomatic break being made with Britain and France, whose role in the campaign was no less important than that of Israel. Again, the cutting off of diplomatic ties with Israel on account of the June 1967 war is significant, keeping in mind the fact that the relations with the United States, for example, remain untouched by the long-drawn-out war in Vietnam. There are many such examples. Instead of carrying out the role of intermediary and peacemaker, (as she did, for instance, in the India-Pakistan dispute), the Soviet Union took up an increasingly one-sided position, endeavoring to gain her political profit by fanning the flames of conflict rather than by extinguishing the fire.

The Soviet Union's vilification of Israel in her press and radio—especially in Moscow's Arab-language broadcasts—the continual condemnation of Israel and of everything about the Jewish state as a "tool of imperialism," an "instrument of the oil monopolies," an "agent of an anti-Arabic imperialist plot," and the like, was intended, it would seem, to justify the fact that, whereas, concerning all other international issues, the Soviet policy was to seek solutions by peaceful means and by direct negotiations, such was not the case in the Arab-Israel question. From her readiness, in 1956, to carry out an active role in furthering peace between Jews and Arabs, the Soviet Union now went over to a policy of allowing the dispute to gather momentum. Eventually, she took up an almost unreservedly one-sided pro-Arab position.

The fact that it was not the Soviet Union that had started the flow of arms of all kinds to the Middle East after the second World War, and that up until the middle of the fifties, and on various occasions afterwards, she had even suggested agreements to stop this arms flow to the region, does nothing to diminish the danger to peace involved in such large-scale shipment of armaments and military aid by the Socialist bloc to the Arabs, who were constantly declaring themselves at war with Israel and were blatant in their dissatisfaction with the existing situation.

Therefore, even though the leaders of the Soviet Union have made it clear more than once, even in recent years, that in theory their position in relation to Israel and the Arab world is free from any bias (which is what was claimed by A. Kosygin at the special assembly of the United Nations in the summer of 1967), the position that the Soviet Union held in the conflict was in *fact* the very opposite of what should have followed from her declared policy. If, in the course of tightening her bonds with the Middle East, the Soviet Union and her partners had made efforts to establish peace between the Arabs and Israel, they would have encouraged and strengthened progressive trends on both sides and furthered the struggle against the inevitability of war and toward finding a *modus vivendi*. They would thus have led the entire region on the way to cooperation, progress, and freedom. But the Soviet Union and her allies did not act in this manner. While recognizing in principle Israel's right to exist, they evaded the issues of her security and sovereignty.

The constant stress on Israel's actions against her neighbors took no note of the provocations that incited such action, which could not be tolerated by any sovereign country. At the same time, the Soviet Union exercised her veto at the United Nations Security Council whenever there was any possibility of rebuking or condemning Arab provocations against Israel. Such a one-sided stand has shown the Soviet policy to be increasingly that of a major power, which, out of purely selfish motives, will allow the survival of the Jewish people in Israel to be threatened, if this is what is needed to strengthen Soviet-bloc influence in the Arab world.

Such a policy has necessarily forced Israel to depend increasingly on the help of those whose interests in the area are opposed to those of the Arabs. Israel's dependence on these elements then served, in turn, as a pretext for further rounds of denunciations and threats. Instead of casting a bridge over the gulf between Israel and her neighbors, this policy merely reinforced the differences. The continual oversimplified identification of Israel with reaction and imperialism, and of the Arab countries with progress and anti-imperialism, was of itself enough to incite the hatred of the Arabs. In this manner, Arab chauvinism was vindicated, and even Tufik Tubi and Emil Habibi

(Arab Communist members of Israel's Knesset—see note, this chapter) could be considered "traitors."

This one-sided policy was accompanied by an anti-Israeli propaganda campaign that distorted all truth, claiming that Israel "from its very first days had begun to threaten her neighbors," etc. This particular distortion contradicted the words of the Soviet delegate, J. Malik, who, in the United Nations debate that accepted Israel as a member nation (March 4, 1949), said that he would vote for Israel "because it was a country that aspired towards peace." In addition, he stated that "it is not the fault of the Jews that the area held by Israel is not according to the map made up by the United Nations in their decision to partition Palestine." Further, concerning the question of the Arab refugees, which was even then a sharply debated issue, he said that "the responsibility for their condition is to be borne by those who incited war between Jews and Arabs." Who incited that war? Who started it? In the Soviet press of recent years one reads that it was the Jews who started the 1948 war. Yet it is stated quite clearly in The Large Soviet Encyclopedia (in the section on the Arab League) that "the Arab League fanned the flames of Arab-Jewish hatred in Palestine, and in May 1948 called on the Arab states to launch a war against Israel."[48] The Soviet delegate to the United Nations indicated time and again that it was the Arab countries that had attacked Israel at her very birth. (See Chapter Nine of this book.)

This unprincipled policy of the Soviet Union and her fellow Socialist states, in all that concerned the Arab-Israel conflict, was more than just a serious distortion of socialist ethics concerning relations between nations. Anyone familiar with the problems of the complex Middle East framework in which Israel-Arab relations were taking place could have foreseen the extensive damage such a policy would cause sooner or later, to Arabs as well as to Jews, and to the very possibility of peace in the region. Alongside the stubborn stand of the Arab leaders (and the shortcomings of the Israeli policy), the approach of the Soviet Union and the Socialist bloc played a considerable part in the developments that led to the six-day war. Retribution for this dangerous course came, indeed, in June 1967, when, in a few days of fighting, all the efforts and military aid invested in the Arabs (many hundreds of millions of dollars worth) went up in smoke and the development of internal forces in the Arab countries themselves was set back once again. This course of events cost the Soviet Union and the Socialist bloc (excluding Roumania) a serious loss of prestige in the progressive world, as well as in Israel itself, where even the local Communist Party could not tolerate this unsavory policy, and split.*

Bitter disappointment, rage, and protest were expressed in Israel—and

---

* In August 1965, the Israel Communist Party split, most of the Jewish members rejecting the policy of the Soviet Union in the Arab-Israel dispute, while all of the Arab members and a small part of the Jewish membership continued to represent this policy

not only in Israel—at the role played by the Soviet Union and her allies in the developments that led to the six-day war, as manifested by the huge quantity of arms and the variety of equipment produced by these Communist countries for the Arab armies. While Israel was counting its losses in dead and wounded, Soviet and Communist propaganda continued to grind out vicious falsehoods. Significant political elements within Israel, and among Jews and progressive circles all over the world who, for decades, had borne the banner of friendship for the heirs of the revolution, were shocked to the core. This shock was shared by many of the better minds and more sensitive people in the Socialist countries themselves, and it is possible that its effect will still be felt in future developments in the Communist camp.

A New Explosion

The uncompromising stand of the Arab leaders toward Israel, and their unwillingness to seek a *modus vivendi* to the drawn-out dispute, finally boomeranged. Driven by accumulated despair, the masses of Palestinian refugees afforded fertile ground for the growth of sabotage organizations, the most well known and important being the *Fatah* (initials for the name Palestine Freedom Movement). With the maiden appearance of the *Fatah* groups in Israel, at the beginning of 1965, the heads of the organizations published their plans and intentions—to carry out armed incursions and sabotage in Israeli territory in preparation for "liberation of the entire Arab land from the Zionist gangs," no matter what the sacrifice; to drag the Arab nations into war with Israel "without delay" and "to the finish." Political support for this organization came from Syria, whose rulers wanted a "popular war of freedom like that of Algeria and the Vietcong." Syria permitted the *Fatah* liberty of action within her frontiers to carry out propaganda, to conscript men, and to train them in local bases; this was permitted on the condition that the sabotage operations themselves be launched from other than Syrian territory —i.e., from Jordan, Lebanon, or the Gaza Strip—in order to prevent reprisals by Israel on Syria.

The governments of Jordan, Lebanon, and even Egypt, tried at first to prevent the "separatist operations" of the *Fatah*, claiming that they gave Israel a propaganda tool and a pretext to attack the Arab states "before the military and political conditions, internally and internationally, were ready for a decisive showdown." At the third Arab top-level conference in Casablanca in the middle of September 1965, serious differences of opinion were revealed between the leaders of Egypt and Syria concerning the diversion of

and to defend it. In the elections to the sixth Knesset in November of that year, the former group, *Maki*, received one seat, and the latter, *Rakah* (the new Communist list), got three seats. (In the fifth Knesset, the Communist Party had had five seats.)

the headwaters of the Jordan river. The Egyptians and their supporters demanded that the execution of the plan be postponed until the Arabs had the strength to defend the diversion works. (On March 17, 1965, the Israeli Army had struck the Syrian heavy equipment working on the diversion scheme and the operations were discontinued; a similar action had taken place on August 12, 1965.) A report by the Arab defense council had indicated that it would take four years to prepare for a struggle with Israel. But the forces attempting to halt the sabotage actions of the *Fatah* men were unable to withstand the pressure that fed them—the bitterness of the despairing and ill-led masses of Palestinians. Political inspiration, and apparently also professional aid and some equipment, came to the *Fatah* from Communist China, who supported the policy of the terrorist adventurers in order to upset the relations between the Soviet Union and the Arab countries.

Against such a background, the operations of sabotage and murder increased constantly. The Israeli Army responded with occasional reprisal actions over the border, but these did not stop the operations. When Israel began to warn Syria that she would have to pay dearly for encouraging and giving material aid to the *Fatah*, the Egyptian forces started to concentrate in Sinai, and the tension that had been accumulating for years finally reached the point of explosion.

The Six-Day War

On May 15, 1967—Israel's Independence Day—Egyptian military units in great numbers crossed Sinai and formed along the Israel frontier. On May 18, Gamel Abd-ul-Nasser demanded the withdrawal of the United Nations forces which, ever since the Sinai campaign in the autumn of 1956, had been guarding the Sinai and Gaza strip frontier. United Nations Secretary General U Thant complied, and on the very next day the United Nations forces moved out and ceased to be a factor in the area. On May 22, the Egyptian government declared the Strait of Tiran closed to all Israeli shipping and to all vessels sailing to Eilat. In a speech to officers in Sinai on the following day, the President of Egypt said, "The Israelis are threatening war. Let them come! We are ready for war!" On May 30, Hussain, King of Jordan, signed a defense pact with Egypt in Cairo, and on June 4, Iraq joined this pact. (An Egyptian-Syrian pact had been signed in November 1966.) Jordan agreed to the entry of Iraqi and Saudi troops into her territory. Israel was surrounded on three of its land borders by Egyptian-led military power. According to published information, this alliance of military power against Israel was supported by 600 planes (of which 450 were bombers and jet fighters), and the Egyptian Navy, which was several times the size of the Israeli Navy. The balance of power between Israel and her neighbors seemed to be unsettled, and Israel felt gravely imperilled.

With the incursion of Egyptian troops into Sinai and the closing of the Tiran straits, the Israeli government made feverish diplomatic efforts to restore the freedom of shipping in the Gulf of Eilat and to remove the threat of the foreign army on its borders. At the same time, the Israeli Army called up its reserves. The diplomatic efforts were futile. France and Britain made it clear that they did not recognize any obligation to act as had been set down in the declarations of the three powers in 1950. General de Gaulle expressed only his readiness to initiate a summit conference of the four great powers, in order to find a solution that would permit freedom of passage through the Strait of Tiran and would relax the tension in the area. But the Security Council, which gathered at the request of Denmark and Canada to discuss the problem, did not reach any practical conclusion or take any action to arrest the rush of events. Meanwhile, Nasser stated at a press conference in Cairo on May 29, that the closing of the Strait of Tiran and the removal of the United Nations forces were not the end of the chapter, and that "after restoring the situation to what it was before 1956, it would be time to restore it to what it was before 1948."

Strength of Arab armies up to June 5, 1967

On June 5, the Israeli Knesset confirmed the formation of a national coalition government by adding three representatives of the opposition to the Cabinet—two from the *Gahal* Party, M. Beigin and J. Sapir, as Ministers without Portfolio; and General Moshe Dayan of the *Rafi* party* as Minister of

* *Rafi* (Israel Worker's list) split off from Mapai, the Israel Labor Party. It was headed by David Ben-Gurion who, in June 1965, declared his intention to stand for election on a

Defense. On the morning of the same day, war broke out on the whole Egyptian-Israeli front. The Jordanian, Syrian, and Iraqi armies moved into battle against Israel. Algeria, Kuwait, and Sudan also sent token military forces to the scene of the struggle.

In three hours of lightning strikes by the Israeli Air Force, at the very start of the war, almost the entire Egyptian Air Force was put out of action or destroyed. The Air Forces of Jordan, Syria, and Iraq were also defeated and Israeli planes were in control of the skies. Within a few days after that, Israeli armored units, parachute troops, and infantry smashed the Egyptian divisions in Sinai (which had had about 1000 tanks) and occupied the whole peninsula. The Jordanian forces were also badly hit and the Israeli Army entered the west bank of the Jordan. The Israelis then took the Golan Heights from the Syrians, fighting in very difficult conditions and against strongly fortified positions.

Aside from the destruction of her Air-Force, Egypt lost most of her Army, and suffered damage to her navy. More than 10,000 Egyptian soldiers fell in battle and about 5,000 were taken prisoner. Likewise, the ground forces of Jordan and Syria suffered heavy losses, as did the Iraqi troops that had been sent into Jordan. After six days of fighting, a cease-fire was announced by the United Nations. Israeli forces were positioned along the Suez Canal and at the Strait of Tiran, along the Jordan river and on the Golan Heights. The astounding victory had cost the lives of 759 Israelis. About a billion dollars had been expended.

The six-day war removed the immediate threat to the existence of Israel, and, insofar as current security was concerned, it allowed the country to breathe freely. Almost no part of Israel (aside from a corner of the Jordan valley and the Bet Shean valley) was within range of enemy guns. The Arab world, beaten on the field of battle, was bewildered and perplexed. But Israel, in spite of its amazing victory, was far from being at rest.

A new generation of Israelis had now gone through the horrors of war and had met death face to face. Yet the basic problem of Israel's relations with the Arab world remained as painful and sharp as ever. The issues that had existed before the war remained unsolved. Some of them had even become more severe (the addition of another few hundred thousand refugees), and new problems had been added (areas and populations taken over in the course of battle), which, in the long run, were likely to prove more complicated than the old ones. After having declared for years that there "was

separate list for the sixth Knesset, and was thus separated from Mapai. In the elections at the beginning of November, 1965, *Rafi* received ten (out of 120) seats in the Knesset. The alignment of Mapai and *Ahdut Haavoda* received forty-five seats; *Gahal* (*Herut*, the extreme rightwing party and the "liberals") received twenty-six seats, the National Religious Party, eleven seats, Mapam, eight.

no return possible for the refugees," the government of Israel suddenly found itself saddled with more than a million additional Arabs, both residents and refugees of the occupied territories, over and above the 320,000 Arabs that had been in Israel before the war.*

The June war of 1967 proved once again that the Arabs were unable to destroy Israel; but they were still a long way from reconciling themselves to her existence and recognizing her as an integral part of the region. The war had also proved that, no matter how strong Israel was, it was impossible to force the Arabs to accept peace by armed might. Operationally, in the course of the June war the Israeli Army might have been able to take Amman, Damascus, and even Cairo. Yet it is universally agreed that had she done so, Israel would only have been worse off. This indicates that under certain given conditions, problems that are basically political cannot be solved by military means, but only by peaceful negotiations. And when we refer to "peace," we do not mean submission to a formal act of compulsion, but a true peace—one of reconciliation, based on sincere intentions on both sides to do away with the wretched past, to turn over a new leaf and to try to understand each other as the basis for cooperation for mutual welfare.

What the Arabs Did Not Understand

When the results of the war became evident, the press of the Arab countries and of the nations friendly to the Arabs began to speculate on the wisdom oj the Arab propaganda strategies before the war. The slogan "Annihilatio:. oj Israel," they maintained, had "harmed the Arab cause," just as it had been harmed by the gap between the slogans and the reality. Those who were responsible for Arab policy and Arab public opinion, however, would do well to delve deeper into the significance of these recent events. Rather than merely reconsidering tactics and propaganda, they should show more intellectual and political courage in getting to the roots of the matter. The Arabs paid a

* According to a census made by the Central Bureau of Statistics for the Israeli Army Staff, it was found that there were in the Golan Heights (August 10, 1967) 6,396 inhabitants; in the west bank (from September 17, 1967 to September 25, 1967), 596,637 inhabitants; in the Gaza strip (September 13, 1967), 356,261 inhabitants; in northern Sinai (September 10, 1967), 33,441. Altogether in these territories, there were 994,735 inhabitants. Another 65,857 persons were in east Jerusalem (September 27, 1967), that part of the Old City and the various Arab suburbs that were made part of the undivided city at the end of June 1967.

Of the 994,735 persons who were counted in the occupied areas (aside from east Jerusalem), there were 313,000 "who were originally from somewhere in Israel" (before the six-day war), and another 39,300 whose origins were "unknown." According to a report published by the General Secretary of the United Nations, U Thant, (August 18, 1967), the number of those who fled from the territories conquered by the Israeli army in the six-day war was 325,000 persons.

The cease-fire lines, June 1967

heavy price for failing to understand some fundamental facts that they should have grasped long ago.

1. Israel is the homeland of a people that has experienced a holocaust without precedent in history. The destruction of 6 million Jews, a third of the nation, can be compared to the destruction, proportionately, of 30 million Arabs. Hundreds of thousands of Israelis, many of them with the number of the death camps tattooed on their arms, are still keenly aware of the horrors of that time. They have already learned from experience how to relate to the advice "not to take threats of annihilation seriously." After many generations in which the bitterness of exile and oppression was their lot, this is a people privileged to savour anew the sweet taste of national freedom and human dignity. Such a nation will not give itself to slaughter. In defending their lives, their freedom, and their future, this people will stand with a strength that their enemies can hardly imagine. The Jewish people in the Diaspora, whose pride was bolstered by the establishment of the state of Israel, will also not stand idly by if the country is threatened with extinction. No matter what the position of Israel internationally, there are also in the non-Jewish world forces that will come to the aid of Israel in such an hour of danger, either out of genuine humanitarian impulses or in the hope of exploiting the Jewish-Arab war for their own purpose.

2. The essential difference between the situation of the Arabs and of the Jews is that the Arabs can afford to lose a war once or twice or three times, or more, and still continue the struggle; Israel cannot afford to lose even once, for one defeat is a total loss. Therefore, in a time of danger to the country, the whole people will rise up, to the last man and woman—old and young, secular and religious, rightists and leftists, from the east and from the west. Realizing that it is not only the state that is in peril, but that their very lives are at stake, they will fight with the utmost desperation. It is therefore impossible to destroy Israel without destroying its defenders to the last man.

The roots of the Arab leaders' second mistake lay in overestimating the patience of the Israelis in the face of continual provocation. There is no denying that in Israel, too, there are militaristically minded groups and no lack of the extreme chauvinism that is so prevalent in other countries. At the same time, it would be most unjust not to recognize that the people of Israel, as a whole, are not a warlike, but a peace-loving people. The ideal of peace, like those of freedom, justice, and human dignity, is a foundation stone of their ancient tradition and culture.

Yet no matter how peaceful they are, their capacity to endure the provocations of other nations is not infinite. No sovereign nation would have been able to tolerate the acts of sabotage and murder perpetrated on Israel's soil by trained commando fighters of other nations, glorying (sometimes exaggeratedly) in their deeds of murder and destruction. Only people of the caliber of the Jewish pioneer settlers (most of them kibbutz members), could have endured so many years of constant threat to life and limb beneath the guns of the enemy in the Jordan and the Hulah valleys and elsewhere, bringing up a whole generation of children for whom underground shelters are a natural and indispensable part of daily existence. Those who formulated their policy toward Israel on the supposition that, given the present political constellation of the world it would be possible to make her swallow all provocations without compelling her to take arms to defend herself had no notion of how far the Israelis would permit them to go, and they are rightly bewildered by the results of their fatal error.

In essence, it is quite irrelevant to know "who fired the first shot." What it is important to know is who really started the war. It was a mistake to think that Israel could see the concentration of Egyptian troops along its frontiers, the thrusting aside of the United Nations force, the closing of the Strait of Tiran and the blocking of all Israel's outlets to Asia and Africa, could watch the military pact encircling her with enemies whose intention was to "restore the situation to what it was before 1948," and to believe that she would merely look on quietly. Even those who assumed that Nasser's provocations were not intended to start a war but that he was "only" carrying out all these provoca-tive acts in the belief that Israel would reconcile herself to the new situation would have to admit that he was playing with fire. And, indeed, the end of such a dangerous game could only be the igniting of a huge and destructive conflagration that punished each party in proportion to its responsibility in creating the blaze. Those who provided political encouragement to the pro-cess that gave rise to the explosion (even if from behind the scenes they had reservations about one or another of the moves) must also bear responsibility for the results.

3. A third serious error was the miscalculation of the comparative fighting capacity of the two sides. It was wrong to measure the strength of Israel in terms of simple numbers. Israel represents the essence of an ancient people with a very special history. For almost a hundred years, a renaissance move-ment had been sifting and accumulating social-cultural values from all over the world. The pioneering spirit, which is so vital to the renewal of a people and to the reconstructing of a country, was nurtured here for generations. For decades, Israel's ability to defend herself had been forged and tempered in the knowledge that this was, and is, the only real guarantee for the continued existence of the Jews in Israel. Simple arithmetical calculations, therefore, which did not take into consideration these historical factors, were shown up in all their absurdity when tested by reality.

The war made it apparent that a plentiful supply of modern arms and equipment was not enough. The use of modern weapons on land, sea, and air, and, even more than that, the planning and logistics of modern warfare, the organization of intelligence systems and various subsidiary services—all require a high technological level which, in turn, is made possible by the civilian population's standards and habits of living. Furthermore, not only its technological development, but also the nature of the country's political and social system, is of decisive importance. This determines the individual's identification with the society, his education toward personal responsibility, habits of planning and improvisation, his capacity to get things done and to work with others, and his devotion to a task—all of which are essential and decisive elements on the battlefield. No amount of propaganda or moralizing can avoid defeat in modern warfare if the social foundations of the army, both in its preparations for battle and in the actual fighting, are such that an abyss yawns between the officers and the ordinary soldiers, if the officer is not the first to thrust forward into battle, and if his absence through death or desertion causes the whole military set up to collapse.

There is a world of difference between a war for freedom, which is by nature a guerilla war against a foreign oppressor, and a face-to-face encounter with the modern army of a developed country compelled to fight for its life. In failing to differentiate between political support for relatively progressive regimes in Arab countries and unqualified identification with their rule, the Soviet policy fell into the trap that it had set for itself. The Soviet Union lost all power of judgment concerning the facts as they were; evaluation of reality was subordinated to preconceived notions. A realistic analysis of the actual conditions must lead to the conclusion that if the previous policy is maintained, it cannot but produce similar results. Israel, in any case, had no choice. Even if the price of freedom and security had been much greater than that which she actually paid, she would have been compelled to ensure victory at any cost, in the knowledge that the alternative would be to surrender all hopes for independence—and survival itself.

Israel's Mistaken View of the Situation

By misunderstanding certain essential facts about Israel, the Arabs lost the military confrontation. Is it possible that by misunderstanding certain essential things about the Arabs, Israel will miss the opportunity to make the June 1967 war the last Israel-Arab war?

There is no doubt that Israel is in a more comfortable position now as a result of the six-day war, however cruel the price. But it should not be forgotten that the importance and value of even the most successful military operation depend on the degree to which it serves the purpose for which it was carried out. Otherwise, the whole achievement can prove a loss. Those who believe that Israel's primary political aim, aside from security and the ingathering of the exiles, was and continues to be peace and understanding with the Arab world, and integration of the Jewish state into the Middle East, will ask: Now that Israel has proven herself on the battlefield, will she prove herself to be so able on the political front?

The most prevalent attitude in Israel since the June war can be paraphrased as follows: "The Arabs wanted to wipe us out; they were defeated, and now they have to sit down with us and negotiate peace terms". This is a wrong point of view, and therefore quite useless. In spite of the Arabs' frustration, they do not feel that they have lost the struggle for good and that therefore they have no choice but to sit down face to face with the victor and accept the sentence. The most prevalent viewpoint in the Arab world is, "True, we have lost another battle, but the struggle will be continued. You have won once, twice, three times—you will perhaps win ten times—but one time you will not win, and then you will lose everything." No matter how the Israeli sees it, or how a neutral observer may see the situation, this is how it appears in the eyes of the Arabs.

In spite of the Arab losses in men, equipment, territory, and prestige, they did not give in. A people numbering one hundred million, in conditions like those of the Arab world, do not count losses in life as would a people numbering a few million only, whose families tend to have few children, and whose way of life is altogether different. The military equipment that was lost was soon replaced. The territories conquered by Israel (59,000 square kilometers in Sinai, 6,000 square kilometers in the west bank, about 1,500 square kilometers in the Golan Heights, and 340 square kilometers in the Gaza strip) are almost three-and-a-half times the size of the state of Israel; but they constitute only about one-half percent of the vast area of the Arab world. Aside from Jordan, no Arab country is incommodated by the loss of territories that the Israeli Army occupies, except for reasons of prestige. It is hard to believe that Jordan can do anything about the situation on her own in the prevailing political situation.

The vastness of the Arab lands is a strategic factor of the first order. Whoever has a place to retreat to can keep reorganizing his forces even after the most humiliating defeat. The natural resources of the Arab countries (except for Jordan) have hardly been touched. The proportion of 1 to 40 between the Arab populations and Israel will not change in the foreseeable future. The growth in Israel's population, from natural increase and from immigration, is only one-tenth the natural increase of her near neighbors. The changes taking place in the Arab countries as a result of global historic processes provide a basis for assuming that the qualitative gap between the two sides will gradually narrow, though not rapidly. Just as high quality can balance superiority in numbers, so numerical superiority—not necessarily in manpower—can, under certain conditions, constitute an advantage.

The political dissensions in the Arab world, resulting from the varying social systems, internal contrasts, and foreign orientations, should not be considered eternal. In any case, the degree of Arab solidarity in the face of the "Israeli enemy" is continually growing. The problem of prestige, too, internally as well as internationally, is not so simple a matter as the ordinary Israeli thinks. The Arabs feel themselves to be a great people, with a splendid past, with considerable political achievements in the last generation, and with a vast potential for the future. They are of the opinion that their struggle with Israel is nothing more than a small part of a much larger struggle with infinitely greater powers who stand behind Israel, powers that are, historically, on the decline. On the other hand, the forces that the Arabs represent, and to which they have allied themselves, are on the rise.

Besides the long-term perspective, the Arabs are in possession of certain definite advantages, even today. In the international scene, their weight in number of countries is four times their relative numerical weight in the world. (Arabs are 3 percent of the world population of 3.3 billion, and have fourteen states, about 12 percent of the number of nations at the United Nations.) They have a huge area at their disposal (11.5 million square kilometers which is about 1 million square kilometers more than all of Europe to the Ural Mountains). One must consider the strategic global importance of their lands, and their importance in terms of world communication lines, shipping, air and overland; their vast economic potential in agriculture and industry; and, above all, their oil resources, which (without Iran) constitute 60 percent of the known reserves in the capitalist world, and supply 60 percent of the world market. Again, as a potential market for industrial equipment and modern agricultural technique, the Arab countries show considerable promise.

All this explains why the Arab leaders do not feel it *necessary* to sit down at a table and negotiate with Israel. Under present conditions, this would only be, in their eyes, a surrender to the demands of the conqueror. Far from feeling isolated in the world, they can obtain enough support to avoid reconciliation with unpleasant realities. The tone in which Israel speaks grates on Arab ears and raises obstacles instead of making room for negotiations. For, in present circumstances, direct talks can only constitute a part of the process of conciliation, as the result of negotiations, and not as their beginning. Fruitful negotiations can be held only in a climate of mutual trust. Such trust cannot be acquired by forcing the other side to negotiate against its will or by removing from all possible discussion certain problems that are in dispute (as, for instance, the future of Jerusalem).

The Importance of the "Image" of Israel

Peace between Israel and the Arabs is to a large extent dependent on the "image" of Israel in Arab eyes. Israel's actions and omissions, as well as its declarations to the effect that, "we are a European nation that is only geographically located in the East," have made the Arabs identify Israel with those foreign factors from whose rule, directly or indirectly, they have been trying to free themselves.

One of the basic errors of Israeli policy toward the Arab world is rooted in a certain ideology adopted by most of the country's experts and advisors on Arab affairs, which holds that "the Arabs don't understand anything except the language of force; therefore we have to talk to them in a manner they will understand." To be sure, like everyone else the Arab does not belittle strength, but a demonstration of force will not arouse his respect. Justice, generosity, and open-heartedness are more impressive and are more likely to win his trust.

The function of Israeli strength was to secure the existence of the new state (as it served to safeguard the Jewish settlement in Palestine before that) until such time as the Arabs would reconcile themselves with the state and abandon the idea of eliminating it. However, at the same time, even more importance was attached to Israel as a new and dynamic factor in the region which could show with deeds and not with words that it had no intention of oppressing the Arabs, that it was ready to relate to them with respect, as equals. Israel should show understanding for the legitimate aspirations of the Arabs. Can the Arabs be expected to understand the Jews, if the Jews don't understand them? Israel has to prove that she can be an ally in the Arab struggles towards progress, and she must avoid providing apparent confirmation of the notion that she is working together with outside forces opposed to Arab interests.

Another important factor is what the Arabs call Israel's "aspirations for territorial expansion." Every Israeli move, action, or statement that reinforces this prevalent Arab notion serves to build up an "image" whose very existence diminishes the chances of peace and sows the seeds of war.

Israel went to war in June 1967 in order to remove the threat of strangulation. Her declared aim was to achieve peace and security, and not territorial conquests. The order of the day, given by Moshe Dayan, Minister of Defense, on the morning of June 5, read: "Soldiers of Israel, we have no goals of conquest. Our single purpose is to put to naught the Arab Armies' attempt to conquer our land, to break the blockade by which they shut us in, and to thrust back the aggression that threatens us." It was natural that such a victory should intoxicate the light-headed, whetting their appetite for territorial expansion. The grave perils of the period of tension before June 5, the mutual fear and distrust that the war itself only augmented, provided fertile ground for the sprouting of slogans like, "not a single inch of liberated land is to be returned," "a rare opportunity for revision of borders," "Israel established within its historical frontiers," "Israel within the frontiers promised by the Scriptures," and the like. Even circles well known for their sincere and consistent efforts for peace and Jewish-Arab understanding have not been able to resist the temptation to declare that they were for "making necessary border adjustments in order to ensure national security" (as though true security can be won by adjusting borders rather than by creating a situation in which peace is possible). The truth of the matter is that only borders that are recognized as such by both sides are secure borders; otherwise they will always be held in question and may easily lead to a new war.

A true and lasting peace must be founded on justice. Force is no alternative to justice, and a peace that is not fair and honorable is unlikely to be a lasting peace.

Another Year of Cease-Fire without Peace

Since the end of the fighting in June 1967, the situation has, in essence, returned to what it was before the war: a cease-fire without peace. Israel returned the prisoners she had taken.* The occupied territories are under army control and supervision. The bewilderment of the conquered populations has left little room for any real opposition to Israeli rule. For some time, the generally liberal and tactful attitude of the military government† led to relative quiet in the occupied areas; this served to keep alive anticipations for a political solution of the problem. Occasional armed resistance has been vigorously put down, and houses of those involved have been blown up. A number of politicians were banished to Jordan, and many were imprisoned. According to reliable sources, from October 1967, to the end of May 1968, about 1,500 men from the occupied territories, who had been jailed for various anti-Israeli activities, were released. At the beginning of August 1968, 953 persons were in jail for such activities.‡

Along the cease-fire lines, there have been quite numerous exchanges

* On June 27, 1967, 428 prisoners were returned to Jordan, and two Israeli Air Force pilots who had been shot down over an Iraqi airfield were returned to Israel; on July 17, 1967, 591 prisoners were returned to Syria, and Syria gave back to Israel one pilot whose plane had been forced down in Syria and the bodies of two pilots and of one Israeli civilian who had been kidnapped a year before and had died in a Syrian prison; on January 23, 1968, the exchange of prisoners with Egypt was completed: Israel returned 4,481 prisoners (of whom 493 were officers) and Egypt returned six frogmen and two pilots who had been captured.

† Relative freedom of movement and continuation of commerce between the east and west banks of Jordan; operation of various services (local councils, schools, medical services, employment, etc.) by local people: tours by the inhabitants of the occupied territories of Israel, and visits by sons of west bank inhabitants who were working or studying abroad, or in other Arab countries.

‡ According to the military correspondent of *Haaretz*, August 11, 1968.

of fire, and serious clashes have occurred on the Suez Canal. Israel and Egypt announced, on August 27, 1967, to the United Nations representative, General Odd Bull, that they agreed to his suggestion to avoid all movement of ships and boats in the Canal for an unspecified length of time. The Suez Canal remains closed. On October 21, 1967, Egypt sank the Israel destroyer *Eilat* off the Sinai coast (forty-seven lives were lost and fifty persons were wounded). Four days afterward, Israeli artillery fired on two oil refineries in the city of Suez, which supplied 80 percent of Egypt's fuel, and on the oil tanks and petro-chemical plant in the vicinity, and sent them all up in flames. The Jordanians have shelled the settlements in the Jordan and Bet Shean valleys and sparked artillery duels in which Israeli Air Force planes have been used to silence the source of fire. As time went on and no political solution seemed to emerge, the various Arab sabotage organizations became more active. In the spring of 1968 about a dozen of them were operating. At their conference in Cairo at the beginning of July 1968, a "higher military council" was formed, which received the declared support of the Arab governments. In this "council," as in the various sabotage organizations themselves, there was a conspicuous shifting from one political trend to another, reflecting the differences among the various Arab countries supporting them.

Israel's security forces have meanwhile improved their powers of resistance to the *Fatah* and the other sabotage groups, many of whose men fell in various armed clashes, as did soldiers of the Israeli Army. About 1,500 Arab commando-fighters have been captured and jailed. Israeli forces have crossed over to the east bank of the Jordan to deliver smashing blows on the base camps from which infiltrators set out to murder and sabotage in Israel—Karame, March 21, 1968; Irbid, June 4, 1968; as-Salt, August 2, 1968. Only a little more than one year after the official cease-fire, the country was again confronted by an increasing wave of incidents, sabotage, and reprisals; if not checked by a political solution, such occurrences could well bring on another large-scale war.

The emergency session of the United Nations Assembly that opened on June 17, 1967, decided on July 21 to end its discussions, and charged the Security Council with taking care of the situation in the Middle East. In the course of the Assembly's discussions, a Soviet proposal "to blame the aggressive actions of Israel and to obligate her to immediately and unconditionally withdraw all armed forces from the territories conquered in the June fighting and to pay compensation to the Arab countries for damages suffered in the war," was rejected. The assembly also rejected an Indian-Yugoslavian proposal, as well as one by the Latin-American countries, which, even with their milder formulation, also demanded Israeli withdrawal from the occupied areas. On the other hand, the Assembly decided, by a large majority of votes (ninety-nine votes and eighteen abstentions) to call on Israel not to change the status of Jerusalem. Even before that, the Security Council had called upon Israel (June 17, 1967) to safeguard the peace and security of the inhabitants in the areas where the fighting had taken place and to ease the return of those who had fled from these areas during the war. On July 2, the Israeli government announced that every permanent resident of the west bank who had fled to the east bank between June 5 and July 4, could come back to his home by August 10. Afterward, this date was extended to August 31. But even by then, only 14,000 had returned. Another 7,000 who had not used their permits were allowed to return afterward.

From August 29, 1967, to September 1, 1969, there took place at Khartoum, the capital of Sudan, the fourth Arab summit conference. Kuwait, Saudi Arabia, and Libya promised financial aid to Egypt to the sum of 275 million dollars (about the income of the Suez Canal in the year before the war), and promised 103 million dollars to Jordan, whose economy had been badly damaged by the war and its aftermath. As for Israel, the conference decided to keep to the "principle of not recognizing Israel, not signing a peace, and not negotiating with Israel." The government of Israel called (Oct. 17, 1967) for direct negotiations between the Arab countries and herself in order to reach a permanent peace, but in the face of the stand of the Arab countries, as expressed in the Khartoum decisions, Israel decided to "continue to fortify her position in accordance with the essential needs of her peace and development."

After drawn-out discussions and consultations, the United Nations Security Council unanimously accepted the following resolution (November 22, 1967):

The Security Council
Expressing its continuing concern with the grave situation in the Middle East,
Emphasizing the inadmissibility of the acquisition of territory by war and the need to work for a just and lasting peace in which every state in the area can live in security,
Emphasizing further that all member states in their acceptance of the Charter of the United Nations have undertaken a commitment to act in accordance with Article 2 of the Charter,
   1. Affirms that the fulfillment of the Charter principles requires the establishment of a just lasting peace in the Middle East which should include the application of both the following principles:

    (i) Withdrawal of Israeli Armed forces from territories occupied in the recent conflict;
    (ii) Termination of all claims or states of belligerency and respect for and acknowledgement of the sovereignty, territorial integrity and political independence of every state in the area and their right to live in peace with secure and recognized boundaries free from threats or acts of force;
   2. Affirms further the necessity

(a) For guaranteeing freedom of navigation through international waterways in the area;

(b) For achieving a just settlement of the refugee problem;

(c) For guaranteeing the territorial inviolability and political independence of every state in the area, through measures including the establishment of demilitarized zones;

3. Requests the Secretary General to designate a special representative to proceed to the Middle East to establish and maintain contacts with the states concerned in order to promote agreement and assist efforts to achieve a peaceful and accepted settlement in accordance with the provisions and principles in this resolution;

4. Requests the Secretary General to report to the Security Council on the progress of the efforts of the special representative as soon as possible.

United Nations Secretary General U Thant, chose Dr. Gunnar Jarring, the Swedish diplomat and his country's ambassador to the Soviet Union, to undertake this task. In the middle of December he began to make contact with the governments in the area.

The three "nos" of the Khartoum conference constituted, of course, a serious obstacle to all talks. Only at the beginning of May 1968, did the government of Egypt declare that it accepted the decision of the Security Council in its entirety and awaited Dr. Gunnar Jarring's schedule for carrying it out. (Until then, Egypt demanded withdrawal of all Israeli forces from the occupied territories as a first step in carrying out the resolution.) Ever since the Security Council's decision, the government of Israel had interpreted it as an indivisible entity in which no one section should be separated from the rest. Israel's own stand was expressed (May 20, 1968) in the statement: "The single solution for lasting peace in the region is the signing of peace treaties between Israel and the Arab countries. Peace treaties can only be achieved by direct negotiations."

Israel's Foreign Minister, Abba Eban, said in August 1968, "Israel's conception is that transition from a state of war to a state of peace obligates a written and signed contractual agreement. This must determine all the conditions of coexistence, must put an end to all manifestations of belligerence, and must fix political borders."

Two basic Problems Demanding a Solution

Any solution to the problem of Israel-Arab relations must be tested by its ability to provide at one and the same time an acceptable answer to two basic and interrelated problems:

1. Recognition by the Arabs of the state of Israel, and the integration of Israel into the political totality of the area, which is basically Arab.

2. Satisfaction of the personal and the national-political rights of the Palestinian Arabs—permanent population and refugees alike.

It is in the common interest of both peoples to thwart any possibility of extraneous elements exploiting the Arab-Jewish dispute for their own ends at the expense of the parties directly concerned. Then, and only then, can Arabs and Jews alike invest their energy in mutually beneficial cooperation instead of mutual alienation and war.

After all that has happened during the last twenty years, peace cannot come overnight. Peace needs time to take root and develop. The main thing is that a change in the right direction emerge in the relationship between the two peoples, that the seeds of peace be sown. It is imperative that a new line be drawn up on both sides; the wisdom of knowing how to dig into fortified positions must go along with the courage to push forward to the achievement of a just peace, founded on respect for the basic rights and legitimate interests of both sides.

The decision of the Security Council, which was accepted unanimously on November 22, 1967, can provide an impetus for this move forward. All concerned must accept it in its entirety and without reservations, and all must be prepared, in order to facilitate its implementation, to enter without delay into negotiations in every form that can serve this cause.

This effort must be made, not only in order to solve the new problems arising from the June 1967 war, but also in order to eliminate the bloody conflict stretching back to 1948 and beyond.

Peace cannot be won without paying a price. But all concerned should remember that even a high price will be much smaller than the combined price of regular wars (unavoidable without peace) and periods of uneasy truce between such outbreaks.

It is in the government of Israel's power to make a valuable, perhaps decisive, contribution to the breaking of the deadlock. It should give up the position adopted ever since the end of the fighting in June 1967 that "only at the negotiation table will we show our cards." While safeguarding the cease-fire lines determined by the cease-fire agreements, Israel should clearly announce to the whole world that her peace aims are no different now from those announced on the eve of the six-day war of June 1967.

If the November 1967 decision of the Security Council is to serve as an impetus, the point of departure for the elimination of the dispute must be the place where it started in the wake of the United Nations Assembly resolution twenty years before (November 29, 1947): In Palestine itself.

The state of Israel, on whose establishment the United Nations decided twenty years ago, has been established and is a fact. Now the time has come to realize the second part of the resolution as well—to establish a state for the Palestinian Arabs, the majority of whom have been converted into a people of refugees. The state of Israel must recognize the right of this Arab people to political independence, and must be prepared to the best of her ability to assist the Palestinians in the development and consolidation of their state in the areas of the country on both sides of the Jordan, outside the boundaries of the state of Israel as of June 4, 1967; nor should the possibility be overlooked of examining logical and mutually agreed upon border changes for the benefit of both sides.

The legitimate representatives of the Palestinian Arab people must participate in all peace negotiations, for there is no possibility of achieving a true and just peace without guaranteeing their interests and future. The decisive majority of the people of the Kingdom of Jordan (nearly 2,000,000) according to the June 4, 1967 borders, is the Palestinian Arab people. Apart from about 200,000–250,000 refugees in Syria and Lebanon* and the refugees in the Gaza strip, this is, in fact, the Palestine people of Mandatory Palestine in the borders that were determined when the Mandate was entrusted to Great Britain after the first World War. The population of eastern Transjordan did not amount to more than 250,000–300,000 souls even in the 1940s,† but even if the number has doubled since then from natural increase, this still means that over two-thirds of the population of the Kingdom of Jordan are Palestinians.

Mutual recognition between the two independent and sovereign states— the state of Israel and the Palestinian Arab state—within the framework of what was Mandatory Palestine, can serve as a base and a first step toward the establishment of a federal alliance between them on foundations that will be determined in free negotiations where all will strive for maximum understanding and mutual aid.‡ No outstanding problems between the two

---

* In 1949, Syria displayed some willingness to allow the refugees to settle in her territory in the extensive Al-Jazira region, which is rich in potential, and awaiting settlement and development. The Clapp commission (named after its Chairman, Gordon Clapp, Director of the Tennessee Valley Authority in the United States), in which British, French, and Turkish representatives also participated, pointed out in its report (1949) that the Al-Jazira region could (at the time) absorb 200,000 persons in agriculture alone. This was before work had begun on the large dam now being constructed in that region, on the Euphrates river. Once the dam is completed, it will make possible the irrigation by gravitation of 500,000 hectares of land (5 million *dunams*)—equivalent almost to the entire area under irrigation in all of Syria today—and will provide Syria with 2.5 milliard kilowatt-hours of electricity per annum. (In 1965, electricity generation in Syria was approximately 700 million kilowatts per hour.) The bottleneck to Syria's development programs may well prove to be the problem of manpower.

† The advocate Chaim Naaman, in his book *Abdullah Emir of Transjordan* (Hebrew, Jerusalem, 1942)—written on the basis of a visit to Transjordan and with the help of well-informed persons, including members of the emir's entourage—stated (p. 114): "So far, no population census has been conducted in Transjordan. It is believed that the population total—including Bedouins—is between 300,000 and 350,000. Others estimate the population of Transjordan at 250,000 persons, of whom 155,000 are nomad Bedouin, some 5,000 Circassians, 40,000 semi-urban inhabitants, and a further 50,000 urban residents who have come to Transjordan from across the Jordan and from Syria and other countries."

‡ A federal union of this kind could well be joined by the Republic of Lebanon and

peoples must be left out of the negotiations. None of the controversial questions is insoluble if approached with mutual good will.

The future of the Gaza strip, for example, will certainly be a topic for negotiation. If the two parties agree that it is to be a part of the Palestinian Arab state, Israel would no doubt be ready to guarantee free passage between the strip and the major territory of the Arab state; however, for the sake of territorial continuity, the parties may agree to exchange the Gaza strip (with the agreement of its inhabitants) for another area previously included in the state of Israel up to June 4, 1967; or some other way to an agreed settlement will be found. The refugees who are at present in camps in the strip would finally be rehabilitated, some in the Gaza strip itself, others in regions of Israel in the vicinity of the strip (the refugees in that area are for the most part natives of the southern part of Palestine) or any other place of their own choosing, to which they would go of their own free will after receiving the compensation due them.

The issue of Jerusalem, which is steeped in profound emotions for both the peoples, and in particular for world Jewry, could find its peaceful solution in an agreement that the city remain united in terms of municipal government and the provision of urban services (possibly with two separate subsidiary town councils—one for the Jewish and the other for the Arab district, united under a joint general municipality) with the city freely accessible to people of all nations. Politically, perhaps, a united Jerusalem might even become a triple capital—that of the Israeli state, of the Palestinian Arab state, and of the authorities of the Palestinian federation.

The connections between, and development projects common to, the Palestine Arab state and the state of Israel (a free Mediterranean port for the Arab state on the Israeli coast and free access to it; common exploitation of the Dead Sea resources; development of the nearby ports of Eilat and Aquaba; joint projects for the development of tourism; a joint solution to the problem of irrigation water—all projects vital to both states*—can give the Palestinian Arab state much more than the $50 million to $100 million per year that the Kingdom of Jordan received in recent years from foreign

in the course of time, perhaps by other Arab states. In this way, the great ideal of an Arab-Jewish union, which has long been cultivated by the finest thinkers among both peoples, could finally be realized.

* Israel is planning a sea water de-salination plant to supply approximately 120 million cubic meters of water annually at a cost of more than $200 million. The cost of implementing the Arab plan to divert about half the waters of the upper Jordan in order to withold it from Israel is estimated at $80 to 100 million. With infinitely smaller sums, it would have been possible to undertake a joint and mutually beneficial project that would supply Israel and the Palestinian Arab state with milliards of cubic meters of water from the territories of Lebanon and Syria (water that is now flowing unexploited into the sea), for the benefit of all sides concerned.

allocations, and can assist in her economic development and consolidation.

The pooling of forces and the joint mobilization of foreign assistance will facilitate large-scale development projects in agriculture, industrialization, tourism, and services. The Arab refugees will be economically and socially rehabilitated with the help of an international consortium. This will involve resettlement along with the creation of sources of livelihood for them in a Palestinian Arab state, while some will be absorbed in the state of Israel; a small number may possibly be rehabilitated in the neighboring countries (insofar as the refugees themselves would prefer this solution and the governments concerned give their agreement)—aided by compensation payments due to them* and help from international sources.

Though it has its stark humanitarian aspects, the refugee problem is basically a political question. From an economic point of view it is entirely unacceptable to maintain that a decent and fair solution to this question was, or is, beyond the combined capacity of the Arab states, the state of Israel and the Jewish people in other countries that stand by its side, together with international factors whose moral and political responsibility it is to help. But though this grave human and political problem is the biggest obstacle to peace so long as peace talks are not begun, a solution to it could well be the point of departure for a broader settlement once it is seen that a genuine willingness for agreement exists on both sides.

In the report presented by the Secretary General of the United Nations in July 1959, and in his subsequent explanation to the press, he estimated the labor force of the refugees at 380,000, a total that would be likely to grow to 500,000 by 1970. The sum estimated for creating employment for one man came to $3,300, and the sum total needed for the rehabilitation of the refugees came to $1.7 milliard. It is easy to imagine the revolutionary influence on the forces of production and on living standards that such an inflow of funds could have on the regions in which the refugees were rehabilitated. The money required for this purpose must and can be found. An end to the arms race and to related economic losses, direct or indirect, of both sides could alone pave the way to obtaining a substantial proportion of the funds required. Another part would be forthcoming if the funds that UNRRA has for so many years been expending on maintaining the refugees in the futile and wretched kind of life they have been living were diverted to constructive purposes. Israel, which has absorbed and rehabilitated over a

* In 1949, the government of Israel had already agreed to the principle of paying compensation to the refugees for the property they had left behind in the state of Israel. Following a careful survey, the United Nations conciliation commission estimated the value of these properties as $336 million (of which $280 million was immovable property and $56 million movable property (see Walter Eitan *Israel and the Nations*, p. 117). For political reasons, $200 millions allocated for this purpose by the United Nations Assembly at its fifth session were never put to use.

million Jewish refugees, has rich experience in this work, and could put it to use for the benefit of the Arab refugees.

There is no point and no hope in continuing the arguments as to who is to blame, and to what extent, for the fate of the refugees; and such discussions serve no useful purpose. Nor can the question of who actually is a refugee, or how many genuine refugees there really are, be clarified other than in practical negotiations in which all sides are represented at joint discussion.

The guidelines for such a solution to the Palestine dispute need not have it as their aim to cut off the Palestinian Arab people from the Arab world or to place a wedge between them. The Palestinians should serve as a bridge to peace and cooperation between Israel and the Arab world as a whole. Joint government enterprises undertaken by Israel and the Palestinian Arab state, and private undertakings in which both Jewish and Arab capital and man-power are involved, will develop economic ties. Joint projects together with the neighboring Arab states can undoubtedly help to heal the wounds of the past within a short time.

Agreement between the state of Israel and the state of the Palestine Arab people, and cooperation between them in their joint concern for peace and security, would be tantamount to removing a cancerous growth poisoning the lives of the two peoples. The major pretext for the national conflict would thus have been eliminated. Yet after the cancer is removed, the poison will not disappear overnight. Mutual relations will still be marred by the infection of the past, but direct and patient treatment will now have every possibility of success. Under the existing conditions, the path to achieving peace between Israel and the Arab world as a whole will be made incompar-ably easier when for the Arabs it will be a matter of reaching agreement, not with Israel, but with a Palestinian federation composed of the state of Israel and the Palestine Arab state.

The faithful implementation of the above-mentioned Security Council resolution would pave the way for the withdrawal of forces from the terri-tories occupied by the Israel Defense Forces in the war of June 1967, with assurances of the demilitarization of these territories and the establishment of a system of security guarantees based on joint inspection (to begin, perhaps, with the participation of United Nations observers) and international guarantees. The peace agreements would guarantee freedom of navigation for Israeli vessels in the gulf of Eilat and the Suez Canal, and could provide for a north-south overland route through Israel for the neighboring Arab states. The way would be opened to a fundamental solution of the Arab refugee problem, and to an end of the "conventional" arms race; to ensuring that the region be kept free of nuclear armaments; and to creating the conditions in which, instead of an arena for great power struggle, the region would become a field for peaceful competition between the developed lands, in the provision of aid for the advancement of the peoples living there.

A solution in this vein, based on reality and furthering the genuine interests of both sides, would be potentially capable of removing the threat of war that hangs like a sword of Damocles over the heads of both Jews and Arabs; giving each of the peoples concerned the possibility of living its own life and developing undisturbed within the boundaries of its own sovereign state; creating a healthy foundation for constructive cooperation among the neighboring countries, on the basis of common interests and mutual benefits and in line with the prevailing trend in various regions of the world; launching prospects for cooperation—on a federal or confederative basis—of the entire region, based on national-political sovereignty, respect for every ethnic, religious, and cultural distinction, on mutual aid and positive neutralism in the international area, on guaranteeing to each and every state the possibility of maintaining friendly relations in all spheres with any state in the world on the basis of equality and mutual benefit, and removing the entire region from the sphere of cold war intrigues and tension, turning it into a region of genuine neutrality in search of peace.

The Choice Facing the Two Sides

The choice facing the two sides is not, in fact, a new one. In the absence of a reconciliation between the Arabs and Israel, the Arabs will be incapable of coping with the grave vital problems facing them. While the world advances, they will continue in the wasteful and futile deployment of the cream of their manpower and resources away from those constructive tasks that alone can guarantee the real progress of the Arab world. Thus, the gap between the Arab countries and the advanced countries of the world will continue to widen.

The notion that the state of Israel—like the Crusaders' state, which existed for close to one hundred years and finally disappeared from the map of the region—is bound to disappear in some unforeseeable future is vain consolation indeed. The Crusaders' kingdom was the fruit of a religious-military adventure undertaken by several thousand west European Christian landlords, knights, and townspeople in the Middle Ages. They did not come to the East to build a homeland for themselves in which to find security and freedom. Apart from their eagerness to acquire wealth rapidly and their boundless cruelty, they had no reason for giving up their home countries in western Europe in exchange for any country in the Middle East. It was not their intention to revive with the sweat of their brow the arid regions of the Holy Land, or, for that matter, to do any work at all there with their own hands. The masses who did the physical work in the Crusader kingdom were the exploited native peasantry—Moslems and Christians, Arabs and others— upon whom the conquerors imposed a heavy burden of taxation, compulsory services, and tributes. The Crusader fortresses were used as the bases for robbery and pillage from which unscrupulous adventurers would set out to loot the local population and the passing caravans of Arab merchants, then dispatching the loot to their homes in far-away Europe. Isolating themselves in their own narrow, arrogant circle, the foreign conquerors remained a class apart, entirely ignorant about the local inhabitants. Their story was no more than a passing episode in the age-old history of the East.

Is it not superficial and unhistorical to draw a parallel between this episode and the return of the Jewish people to the original homeland of its forefathers? Is it indeed possible to compare the Crusaders' adventure with the historical process embodying fulfillment of a hope nurtured over generations, for the redemption and auto-emancipation of the ancient Jewish people? Blessed with a wealth of inner resources, but exposed to uncountable sufferings, the original growth and flowering of the Jews took place in this same country and the Jews never gave up hope of returning to their homeland. Without this continuous covenant between people and land, the Jewish people would have been doomed to disappear from the face of the earth at the very time that other peoples without a past rooted in history are gaining their liberty, independence, and possibilities for development.

Talk of "preparing for the final showdown with Israel" will always remain equivalent to mapping out one's coming move without anticipating the counter-tactics likely to be adopted by the other side. The state of Israel will not allow itself to be caught by surprise. Accustomed to keeping an alert watch on what is going on around it, Israel will be forced to crush potential threats to her existence. Nor will her enemies succeed in sowing destruction and murder in Israel with a view to wearing her down or paralyzing her will to live. Unilateral denunciations and threats can only serve to compel Israel to protect her most elementary rights, those of survival and independence. For Jews in particular, it is tragic indeed to be faced with the choice between the possibility of being the "Prussia of the East" or the possibility of being wiped out. Yet with all the poignancy inherent in this choice, Israel will not opt for annihilation. The influence of this decision on the spiritual, ideological, and political development of the people of Israel will be far-reaching, a long way indeed from the moral and cultural ideals that guided the Jewish national liberation movement at its outset. But not only Israel will be affected, for those who compel her to develop along these lines will not escape unscathed or unpunished.

All due attention should therefore be paid to the words of the distinguished British philosopher Lord Bertrand Russell, who, in conversation with a Mapam representative, Abd-ul-Aziz az-Zu'abi, in London, three years before the war of June 1967, stated: "Nothing is more important to the Arabs and the Jews than a frank examination of the possibilities of finding a peaceful solution to their common problems. The alternative to full cooperation between the Arabs and the Jews within the state of Israel and between the Israeli and the Arab peoples is war and destruction."[49]

Conclusion

Nations learn not from books but from the experience of life. Over the past twenty years, the Arabs and the Jews have both continued to pay the price for their attempt twenty years ago to cut with a sword the Gordian knot of their relations, instead of making a common effort to unravel it together slowly. Experience has shown how imperative it is for both people to regulate their relations with far-sighted wisdom and tolerance rather than with hatred and force. The history of mankind is replete with examples of peoples who fought each other for long periods but nevertheless finally came to terms, achieving normal relations and fruitful cooperation.

The problem of Israel and the Arab world, too, will finally reach a solution, but only on the condition that such a solution safeguards the genuine vital interests and the legitimate historical aspirations of both peoples. Far from contradicting each other, these could complement each other. It is not the implacable verdict of fate that the way out of the impasse should continue to be strewn with death, destruction, and mutual suffering. It is essential to cut short this road of pain, which is so totally devoid of fruitful purpose or historical justification. The problem cannot be solved by adopting a fatalistic approach. However vital it may be for the parties to the dispute, peace will not come of its own accord. It will certainly not draw nearer unless and until people labor and struggle to give it flesh and blood. The task of every true patriot among both peoples is to work for this noble aim. Every individual among the nations of the world who is concerned for peace and progress should help toward its achievement.

No settlement that it might perhaps be possible in one way or another to impose by force will benefit both peoples as will a peace achieved through their own common efforts for a just and honorable solution. Herein lies the hope of putting an end to the troubles of both peoples and of blazing a trail to peace and fruitful cooperation, for the benefit of Israel and the Arabs alike, and for the sake of peace and progress in the region and in the world.

References

1. Walter Eitan, *Israel Among the Nations* (1958), p. 100 (Hebrew).
2. *Jerusalem Post*, May 15, 1968.
3. *Development of the National Economy*, published by the Economic Planning Authority (the Prime Minister's office, Jerusalem, March 1968).

4. Eitan, *Israel Among the Nations*, loc. cit., p. 92.
5. *Al Hamishmar*, March 12, 1950.
6. *Ibid.*, March 24, 1950.
7. *Al Anzar*, April 8, 1951.
8. *Al-Ahram*, January 27, 1950.
9. *Al Hamishmar*, March 24, 1950.
10. Moshe Sharett, *At the Gate of the Nations* (1958), p. 398 (Hebrew).
11. *Al Hamishmar*, October 19, 1951, based on the Egyptian *Al-Katb*.
12. *Ibid.*, April 9, 1950.
13. *Al-Aiam* (Damascus), July 23, 1941.
14. Baghdad radio, June 28, 1949, quoting *The New East*, the quarterly of the Israel Oriental Society, Vol. I, p. 188.
15. Statement issued by The Society for the Prevention of a Third World War, *The New York Times*, January 4, 1954.
16. *Akhr Sa'ah* (Cairo), October 12, 1955.
17. *Al-Ahram*, September 27, 1954.
18. Eitan, *Israel Among the Nations*, loc. cit., p. 54.
19. *Al-Akhbar*, May 13, 1956.
20. *Al-Ahram*, May 15, 1958.
21. *Al Jarida*, November 22, 1957.
22. Eitan, *Israel Among the Nations*, loc. cit., p. 108.
23. M. Assaf, *Davar*, June 21, 1957.
24. *The [Israeli] Government Yearbook* (1958–1959), pp. 74–75.
25. *Al Hamishmar*, March 15, 1962.
26. "The local Authority in the Arab Settlements in Israel," a report published by the Minorities Department of the Ministry of the Interior (Jerusalem, February, 1967) p. 24.
27. *Al Hamishmar*, July 9, 1968.
28. *Israeli Government Yearbook*, 1964–1965, p. 317.
29. *Al Ahram*, October 2, 1954.
30. Erskine Childers, "Deadlock in the Holy Land," *Encounter*, October 1958.
31. *Al Hamishmar*, February 6, 1955.
32. Eitan, *Israel Among the Nations*, loc. cit., p. 143.
33. *Ibid.*, p. 130.
34. *Al Hamishmar*, February 25, 1955.
35. *Al Hamishmar*, February 19, 1956.
36. *Davar*, June 15, 1958.
37. *Al Hamishmar*, April 6, 1955.
38. *Al-Hayat*, January 7, 1955.
39. Guy Wint and Peter Calvacoressi, *Middle East Crisis* (London: Penguin Books, 1957).
40. *Al Hamishmar*, May 10, 1955.
41. *Haaretz*, February 8, 1956; April 30, 1956.
42. *Ibid.*, September 14, 1956, the report of the correspondent in Paris.
43. *Al Hamishmar*, October 19, 1956.
44. *Maariv*, May 26, 1961.

45. *Al Hamishmar*, September 25, 1964.
46. *The New East*, quarterly of the Israel Oriental Society, Vol. 7, p. 120.
47. *Haaretz*, March 13, 1958.
48. *The Large Soviet Encyclopedia*, Vol. 2, p. 595 (Russian).
49. *Al Hamishmar*, May 7, 1964.

INDEX OF PLACE NAMES

There is no one accepted way of rendering Arabic and Hebrew names in English. I have decided that it will be for the convenience of the reader that the index should follow what my indexer believes to be standard modern practice, even where this differs slightly from the spellings in the book— A. C., *April 1970*.

INDEX OF NAMES

SUBJECT INDEX